Edward Vallance is a Reader in Early Modern History at Roehampton University. After reading history at Balliol College, Oxford, he was De Velling Willis Research Fellow at the University of Sheffield. He writes a historical blog at www.edwardvallance.wordpress.com and is a regular contributor to the *New Statesman* and *BBC History Magazine*.

'*A Radical History of Britain* is an opportune volume . . . powerful . . . This is a vigorous and wide-ranging account' Robert McCrum, *Observer*

'Anyone concerned about the future of parliament, constitutional reform and politics in general will find plenty of inspiration in this accessible, often gripping history' Frank Trentmann, *Sunday Express*

'The publication of *A Radical History of Britain* could not be more timely . . . An extremely instructive and comprehensive survey' Robert Colville, *Daily Telegraph*

'A trenchant salute to the tradition of dissent and demands for social and political reform . . . This well-written and stimulating book makes a convincing case for the radical and/or rebellious tradition as part of the warp and woof of British history' A. W. Purdue.

Also by Edward Vallance

THE GLORIOUS REVOLUTION

A RADICAL HISTORY of BRITAIN

EDWARD VALLANCE

ABACUS

First published in Great Britain in 2009 by Little, Brown
This paperback edition published in 2010 by Abacus

A CIP catalogue record for this book
is available from the British Library.

ISBN 978-0-349-12026-3

Typeset in Garamond by M Rules
Printed and bound in Great Britain by
Clays Ltd, St Ives plc

Papers used by Abacus are natural, renewable and
recyclable products sourced from well-managed forests and certified
in accordance with the rules of the Forest Stewardship Council

Mixed Sources
Product group from well-managed
forests and other controlled sources
www.fsc.org Cert no. SGS-COC-004081
© 1996 Forest Stewardship Council
FSC

Abacus
An imprint of
Little, Brown Book Group
100 Victoria Embankment
London EC4Y 0DY

An Hachette UK Company
www.hachette.co.uk

www.littlebrown.co.uk

No man can have in his mind a conception of the future, for the future is not yet. But of our conceptions of the past, we make a future.

Thomas Hobbes

To Linnie, with all my love

CONTENTS

THE FIRST BRITISH RADICAL:
ALFRED THE GREAT

King or no king . . . he ought to have minded the cakes.

Denewulf's wife's words to Alfred as imagined by
H. E. Marshall in *Our Island Story* (1905)[1]

In the early months of 878, Alfred, King of the West Saxons, was in hiding in the dank and impenetrable marshland of the Somerset Levels. He had been forced to flee the royal fort at Chippenham after a surprise attack by the Viking leader Guthrum while he was enjoying the traditional festivities of Twelfth Night. The pagan Vikings obviously knew enough of the Christian calendar to exploit its festivals for military advantage. It was the lowest point in a long military struggle against the Danish invaders, which had begun in 865, six years before Alfred's accession to the throne, when Ivar the Boneless's army landed in eastern England. The Saxon kingdoms had fallen one after another: first Northumbria, then East Anglia, then Mercia; their kings either fled or were slaughtered. By the time Alfred was made king, a second Danish force, under Guthrum, had already landed and made its way deep into Alfred's Wessex lands.

Alfred now stood in danger of following the fate of the other Saxon leaders. He already appeared a king without a kingdom, and according to popular legend, was forced to live in hiding in the home of a swineherd, Denewulf. The swineherd had not told his wife their guest's true identity: she assumed that Alfred was simply a friend of her husband's and therefore a fellow commoner. The King was not, at least as far as she was concerned, a particularly welcome guest. Alfred spent most of his time brooding, gazing into the hearth and contemplating the low ebb to which his fortunes had sunk. Determined that her sullen lodger would make himself useful, the swineherd's wife set Alfred to minding the cakes that were baking over the fire, instructing him to turn them once they had gone golden on one side. Alfred promised to tend them while she busied herself with her other chores, but his mind quickly drifted back to his predicament and the threat from the Viking invaders. The flames leaping in the hearth became the burning thatch of English homes, set alight by Danish marauders, thick smoke filling the sky.

Alfred was shaken from this dark vision by the shrieks of Denewulf's wife. The smoke had not been merely in the King's mind, but was pouring from the now blackened cakes he had been set to watch. The woman scolded him for his negligence, still not realising that the house-guest was her king. But, once her husband had revealed Alfred's identity, the King did not rebuke her for her harsh words. She had shaken him from his indolent depression and reminded him that fates were changed by action, not talk. In May of 878, from his camp at Athelney, he rallied the Saxon men and routed the Danish forces at the Battle of Edington. Guthrum surrendered and along with thirty of his followers was baptised. Denewulf, meanwhile, was made a bishop.[2]

The legend of Alfred and the cakes, which originated in an eleventh-century life of St Neot, has become one of the most famous stories in English history.[3] Though Alfred remains a celebrated national historical figure, the peak of veneration for the

Anglo-Saxon king came in the late Victorian era. Charles Dickens's *A Child's History of England* described him as 'the noble king who, in his single person, possessed all the Saxon virtues . . . As it is said that his spirit still inspires some of our best English laws, so, let you and I pray that it may animate our English hearts.'[4] The words of 'Rule Britannia' were taken from a masque based on Alfred's life, in which the King was cast not just as the creator of England or even of Britain, but of the British Empire as a whole. The celebration of Alfred reached its zenith in 1901, just as the Victorian age was coming to an end. The misdated 'Alfred millenary' of that year – Alfred died in 899 – was marked by fêtes and pageants across the country. The centrepiece of the millenary was the unveiling of a new statue of Alfred in his 'capital' of Winchester. The former Liberal Prime Minister, Lord Rosebery, led the appeal for funds for the sculpture, which was designed by Hamo Thornycroft – the same team had earlier been responsible for the statue of Oliver Cromwell which was placed outside Parliament. At the unveiling, Rosebery said that the name Alfred was synonymous with 'our metropolis, our fleet, our literature, our laws, our first foreign relations, our first efforts at education' and 'our Parliament'.[5] He spoke of his pride that the millenary celebrations had developed an awareness of English history even among the young. This was news to some. Thornycroft later recalled that an electrician working in his studio had asked who the subject of his sculpture was. When he replied 'King Alfred', the man, still none the wiser, inquired 'King Alfred what?' 'Alfred the Great,' said Thornycroft. 'Well, he's a big 'un. He's got a good sized foot,' the electrician responded.[6]

The story of the cakes became so synonymous with the great Saxon king that Sellar and Yeatman in their classic satire on the history textbook *1066 and All That* could rechristen him 'Alfred the Cake'. As that work indicated, though the legend was deeply familiar, it was not all that clear what it meant. In fact, the myth, in its most celebrated retelling in Henrietta Marshall's *Our Island Story*, first published in 1905, formed part of a radical reinterpretation of British history.

Marshall followed the glowing Victorian presentation of Alfred and his reign. To her, there 'never was a better king of England'. He was 'England's Darling', 'truthful and fearless in everything'.[7] His achievements were legion:

> He collected the laws and wrote them out so that people could understand them. He did away with the laws which he thought were bad, and made others. One law he made was, that a man who had done wrong could not be punished unless twelve men agreed that he really had been wicked, and ought to be punished. This was called trial by jury, and means trial by those who have promised to do justly.[8]

Our Island Story's combination of history and myth – as well as more historically grounded incidents, its narrative included stories relating to King Arthur, Merlin and Robin Hood – proved a great success with adults and children alike. In 2005, a century after it was first published, the right-wing think-tank Civitas, with the assistance of the *Daily Telegraph*, started a campaign to provide every primary school in Britain with a reprint of the book.[9] To many commentators, including popular historians such as Antonia Fraser and Andrew Roberts, the broad chronological sweep and gripping narrative of Marshall's work appeared to be the perfect antidote to the fragmented, Nazi-obsessed history taught in British schools.[10] The campaign was an unqualified success and the book went on to become a bestseller all over again.

Though the type of grand narrative offered by Marshall was anathema to the national curriculum, the high sales of *Our Island Story* demonstrated that this was not the case with the general public. The most popular recent television treatments of our past, such as Simon Schama's *History of Britain* and David Starkey's

Monarchy, by and large followed the model of focusing almost exclusively on the actions of kings and queens. The same has held true for historical drama, with the greatest ratings success being a 'sexed-up' retelling of Henry VIII's marital affairs, *The Tudors*.

However, if Marshall's approach in *Our Island Story* proved enduringly popular, it was also, some contended, politically suspect. The reissue had been trumpeted in a right-wing newspaper on behalf of a right-wing think-tank. It also seemed to chime with calls made by Conservative politicians for a revised history curriculum that would emphasise 'British values': something which some commentators felt smacked of a return to 'drum and trumpet stories of Britain's past', focusing on glorious leaders like 'King Alfred, Lord Clive and Horatio Nelson'.[11]

Yet, as Antonia Fraser noted, far from offering a jingoistic, imperialist view of history, *Our Island Story* was, in fact, a subtly subversive text.[12] Marshall eulogised Alfred not, as some of her Victorian predecessors did, because he was the supposed founder of Britain's naval supremacy, but because 'all his life Alfred was thinking only of his people and what was best for them'.[13] He had been a great warrior, but he fought only 'to save his country and his people', not 'for the love of conquering', as other kings did.[14] For Marshall, the significance of the story of the cakes was that it showed Alfred's humility and magnanimity. Instead of taking umbrage at being upbraided by his social inferiors, he pulls himself together and sets about defeating the common foe. Denewulf is therefore rewarded, not just for providing sanctuary to the King, but also for his wife's invaluable candour. (Indeed, it is telling that in Marshall's version of the story, unlike in others, the swineherd's wife refuses to temper her scolding even once the identity of their guest has been revealed.)

Marshall's pacifist sympathies and her view of monarchs as essentially servants of the people affected her evaluation of other English kings. Richard the Lionheart, the popular hero of so many children's books, was attacked for going away to Palestine to fight rather than staying at home and looking after his kingdom: 'No doubt he thought it was a great and good thing to fight for Jerusalem, but how much better it would have been if he had tried to rule his own land peacefully, and bring happiness to his people.'[15] Robin Hood, who robbed from the rich to give to the poor, came off far better by comparison.

Marshall was particularly harsh on the Normans and William the Conqueror, whom she portrayed as little more than a usurping tyrant. Edward the Confessor, in any case, had had no right to offer the Crown to William because he 'could not give away the crown of England to any one without the consent of the people'. The English, she told her young readers, 'had always been a free people, who had a share in governing themselves'.[16] Revealing the persistent belief in the so-called 'Norman yoke', Marshall felt Norman law had reduced the Anglo-Saxon Britons from the liberty and freedom they had enjoyed under Alfred to the status of slaves.[17] This oppression, she contended, was only reversed by the barons in 1215, when they forced King John to agree to Magna Carta:

> When the barons forced John to grant the Magna Carta, they fought, not for themselves, as barons and Normans, but for the whole English people. For the first time since the Conquest, the people of England acted as one people. The Norman had disappeared. England was England again. She had conquered the Conqueror.[18]

As we shall see, belief in the 'Norman yoke' was a key feature of many radical narratives of the past.

Marshall's history was consistently more sympathetic to rebels than to rulers. She told the tale of Hereward the Wake to reassure her readers that some brave Englishmen still resisted the iron grip of Norman rule. Wat Tyler, the leader of the Peasants' Revolt of 1381, was given his habitual bad press, but the revolt itself was generally seen, to use the terminology of *1066 and All That*, as a 'good thing': 'Wat Tyler's rebellion was the beginning of freedom for the lower classes in England. Up to this time many of the labourers and workers who were free men had been treated almost as badly as slaves, but now their condition became better.'[19] Similarly, Charles I, the only British king to be executed by his people, was painted as largely deserving his fate (he was 'wicked' and 'foolish') and the regicide as an action that was necessary, if nasty.[20]

Marshall's view of British history has been characterised as conventionally Whiggish.[21] Certainly, she emphasised the familiar Whiggish theme of the 'rise of Parliament', but her books suggest a more radical political outlook than this. In her comments on the revolt of Boudicca against the Romans she wrote that 'although the Romans were clever, they sometimes did stupid things. They thought very little of their own women, and they did not understand that many of the women of Britain were as brave and as wise as the men, and quite as difficult to conquer.'[22] A further clue to her political sympathies lies in her title for the chapter on the rebellion of the Scottish Covenanters against Charles I: 'How a Woman Struck a Blow for Freedom'. Here she dwelt on the actions of the legendary (and probably mythical) Jenny Geddes,* who in 1637 hurled a stool at the Dean of St Giles Cathedral, Edinburgh, in disgust at his reading from a new 'popish' service book.

We know frustratingly little about Henrietta Marshall's life, but it is known that she remained single and that from 1901 to 1904 she was lady superintendent of the women-only Queen Margaret Hall of Residence at Glasgow University. Boudicca was a heroine who featured in many histories written by leading suffragists, and single, educated women teachers figured prominently among the

---

* David Stevenson suggests that 'Jenny Geddes' was a generic name, rather like 'Jock Sporran', designed to signify, in one person, the prominent role of women in the Covenanter movement; see Stevenson, 'Jenny Geddes', *ODNB*.

members of women's suffrage societies. It is tempting to think that Marshall, like many intelligent middle-class Victorian women, was supportive of the suffrage movement (and perhaps even, given her love of women rebels, of suffragette militancy).[23]

Those sympathetic remarks concerning Robin Hood and the Peasants' Revolt were also suggestive. Her treatment of Cromwell in *Our Island Story* was largely conventional (indeed, it could be described as Tory rather than Whig), labelling him a 'tyrant' who was 'bitterly hated'.[24] Two years after this book was published, however, Marshall produced *The Story of Oliver Cromwell*, from which quite a different picture of the Lord Protector emerged. While acknowledging that opinion on Cromwell was divided, she believed:

> If Cromwell did not quite succeed, he showed the way, and we now have much that he tried to give to the people of his time. When you grow older you will be able to see how from Cromwell's days we date our freedom in many things, our union, our command of the seas, and even the beginnings of Greater Britain. And I hope that . . . you will learn to love the large soul of this true Englishman who, under his grimness and sternness, hid a tender heart.[25]

Rather than advocating a traditional, imperialist British history, in supporting the reissue of *Our Island Story*, the *Daily Telegraph* was recommending a book with not only pacifist, but feminist and republican overtones.

There are some contextual clues to the surprising radicalism of this deceptively traditional text. It is often forgotten that, at the time of writing *Our Island Story*, Marshall was living in Melbourne, Australia. The book begins with an imagined conversation between a father and his children, prompted by a letter from 'home'. The father is asked to explain how both Australia and the little island far away can both be 'home'. *Our Island Story* was concerned not only with the development of Great Britain, but with the creation of those values that then took root in 'Greater Britain' (the colonies) as well. By the time Marshall was writing, at the turn of the twentieth century, however, the political history of Australia and Britain had diverged considerably, with Australia unquestionably overtaking the mother country in terms of the democratic rights that it accorded its citizens. Men had received the vote in most Australian states by the 1860s, and the secret ballot had been introduced, along with salaries for MPs and fixed-term parliaments. Australia could claim the first working-class representative of any legislature in the British Empire, Charles Jardine Don, elected to the Victoria Parliament in 1860. By 1902, Australian women could vote in Commonwealth elections, a full sixteen years before their British counterparts.*[26] Rather than writing a triumphalist history of British imperialism, as is sometimes supposed, Marshall arguably produced a book influenced by the more equal and free Australian society in which she then lived.

Australia's democratic society was created by men and women who had formerly been British subjects. Some of those who came to Australia had been deeply involved in radical politics in the mother country. Charles Jardine Don, for example, was a Scottish Chartist.[27] The Chartist movement in Britain had campaigned for adult male suffrage, the secret ballot, annual parliaments, salaries for MPs, the equalisation of the size of constituencies, and an end to the property qualification for those standing for election.

By the early 1850s, the movement in Britain was in steep decline. Along with the hundred or so Chartists transported to Australia for political 'crimes', many more of the movement's supporters freely chose to emigrate during that decade. They were

* Australian suffragists played a prominent part in the women's struggle for the vote in Britain too. In 1908, Adelaide-born Muriel Matters became the first woman to speak in Parliament, albeit while chained to the grille of the Ladies' Gallery in the House of Commons.

enticed there by the Chartist press, which advertised Australia as a land of freedom and plenty. As the *Northern Star* put it in 1852: 'The future Australian republic will be a refuge and a home for those of our workers in the cause of the people, whose souls shall yearn for liberty, should they ever be . . . compelled to abandon in despair the people of the British Islands, as debased wretches, hopelessly sunk in slavish degeneracy.'[28] These Chartist immigrants played a significant role in the development of democracy in Australia. The Ballarat Reform League, formed in 1854 by Victoria gold-diggers, featured former Chartists Henry T. Holyoake and J. B. Humffray among its founder members, and its aims, aside from the reform of goldmining, mirrored the Six Points of the Chartists' People's Charter. Within twelve months of the League's foundation, and the violent clash between the state authorities and the miners at the Eureka Stockade, virtually all of the points of the Charter had been achieved.[29]

Chartism brings us full circle, back to Alfred the Great. Far from being regicidal revolutionaries, many Chartists were broadly supportive of the monarchy, at least those monarchs they saw as defending the public good. For this reason, as for Henrietta Marshall, they venerated Alfred, under whom, the Chartist *Northern Liberator* said, 'the people of England . . . became rich, free and happy, and so would have continued had not Universal Suffrage been lost amid the civil dissension of the turbulent reign of the weak Henry the Sixth'. The same idyllic picture of life under Alfred's benevolent leadership was painted by the Chartist leader Feargus O'Connor. Alfred's reign was, he said, a time when 'the twenty-four hours of the day were divided into three equal portions' – like the unions, Alfred only wanted an eight-hour working day – and 'there was neither lock nor bolt on any man's door because there was no thief'.[30] Other Chartist writers applauded his legal reforms, equating the 'Code of Alfred' with the freedoms promised in the People's Charter.[31]

The historic nature of English freedoms was important even to those Chartists, such as Ernest Jones, who subsequently became influenced by the ideas of Karl Marx. As Jones told a meeting in Tower Hamlets in October 1847,

> Liberty is a tree of long growth in England. It was planted at Runnymede; it was sunned by the fires of Smithfield; it was watered by the blood of Marston Moor, and the veins of Charles; it was fanned by the prayers of the Puritan, and dewed by the tears of the Exile – and now it is beginning to bloom beneath the fostering hand of the Charter.[32]

The Chartists' adoration of a tradition of British liberty tells us much about the nature of British radicalism itself. It was not predominantly republican but could praise 'good' rulers like Alfred, as well as the righteous rebels of 1381; it emphasised the importance of recapturing lost freedoms, often located in an Anglo-Saxon Arcadia, as much as securing new rights; and most of all, it saw itself as part of a tradition of people fighting for their liberties.

It is that 'radical tradition' which this book celebrates and explores. From the Victorian era to the present day, radical writers, politicians and historians have offered an alternative view of the nation's past to the dominant narrative of kings and queens. Leading figures on the left, of such diverse talents and backgrounds as William Morris, Belfort Bax, George Orwell, E. P. Thompson, Christopher Hill and Billy Bragg, have all attempted to demonstrate a relationship between British history, national character and radicalism. In recent years, discussion of Britain's radical tradition has been revived by Gordon Brown's call for a new sense of Britishness, centred on values of tolerance, liberty and fair play: values that Brown suggests are the inheritance of the 'golden thread' that runs through British history, the struggle against tyranny and arbitrary power.[33] Britain's radical history has even been the subject of a recent popular competition, sponsored by the *Guardian* newspaper, to find Britain's most overlooked 'radical moment'.

The idea of a British radical tradition is persistent and powerful, but it carries with it several problems. The first of these relates to its Britishness. As a Scot in possession of a history Ph.D., Brown surely knows that the starting point of his 'golden thread', Magna Carta, was an English document, not a British one. Similarly, for those radicals who traced British freedoms back to an Anglo-Saxon 'ancient constitution', the question was left hanging as to how such freedoms applied to the Celtic Britons of Scotland, Ireland and Wales. Alfred the Great, as most of his Victorian hagiographers agreed, was an English hero, not a British one. Arguably, radicalism in the British Isles did not take on a clearly 'British' character until after the Napoleonic Wars, when radicals were keen to 're-brand' themselves as progressive patriots rather than Frenchified Jacobins. Of course, it would scarcely be possible to write a history of radicalism in England without mentioning non-English figures such as Thomas Hardy, the eighteenth-century Scottish founder of the London Corresponding Society, Keir Hardie or Feargus O'Connor. Even Thomas Paine, born in Thetford, Norfolk, but a citizen of the republics of France and the United States of America, might be counted, at best, one-third English. For much of this book, then, what is offered is an 'enriched' English, rather than a genuinely British, history of radicalism.

Like British radicalism, the use of the term 'radical' itself, at least in a political context, is mainly of modern vintage. When we describe something as being politically radical, we equate it with 'thorough or far-reaching political or social reform'.[34] However, etymologically, the word originates from the Latin *radix*, meaning root, and the earlier interpretation of 'radical' was, literally, of something pertaining to the root. In the Tudor and Stuart periods, the term was often used in its early modern/medieval scientific context, as in 'radical humour' or 'moisture', indicating an inherent quality that gave plants and animals their vitality. When it was used in a political context, which was rarely, it was employed to signify something fundamental or original. It was in this sense that the Parliamentarian writer Nathaniel Bacon in a seventeenth-century treatise on the origins of the English government wrote, 'I shall first glance upon the natural Constitution of the people of *England* . . . and shew the same to be radical, and not by any force or inoculation,'[35] meaning that English government was indigenous to these islands and not the product of foreign influence or conquest. Words such as 'freedom' and 'liberty' carry similar problems of shifting historical meaning. Magna Carta's conferring of rights upon 'free men', who may have amounted to only 7 per cent of the population in 1215, was considerably less generous a grant than it might have been in the seventeenth century. Equally, freedom itself carried a different sense in an era when most people were unfree, either bound to give some sort of labour or actually enslaved. Freedom was a legally conferred status, not a natural right, nor a mental or emotional state. Liberty, too, was often understood in the past less as a synonym for freedom, as in 'liberty of conscience' or 'civil liberties', and more to mean an exceptional grant or privilege gifted from the sovereign to a particular group or area, as in the liberties or privileges of a defined jurisdiction (the county palatine of Chester, for example).

Some historians have suggested that by using such terms out of their appropriate historical context (in the case of political 'radicalism', the modern era), we are imposing anachronistic modern values upon past groups and individuals – presenting, for example, the seventeenth-century Levellers as 'the first socialists' or Gerrard Winstanley's Diggers as 'the first communists'.[36] Great works by the leading British Marxist historians Christopher Hill and E. P. Thompson undoubtedly did try to trace a lineage, however subtly, from these earlier movements to modern radical parties. Thompson was attacked by his fellow Marxist, Perry Anderson, for the 'cultural nationalist' assumptions that Anderson claimed underpinned Thompson's classic, *The Making of the English Working Class*. It was a criticism that raised Thompson's ire but carried a strong ring of truth. As he proclaimed in his last book, the posthumously published intellectual biography of William Blake, *Witness against the Beast*, he was interested in 'the long and tenacious revolutionary tradition of the British commoner', 'a dogged, good-humoured, responsible tradition: yet a revolutionary tradition all the same'.[37] Christopher Hill's work also tried to delineate an English 'revolutionary tradition', stretching from the fourteenth-century English heretics, the Lollards, to the Leveller movement and beyond.[38]

In suggesting that Lollards were the predecessors of Levellers, who were in turn the forerunners of the Chartists, Thompson, Hill and others presented English and/or British radicalism as a historical continuum in which the baton of popular struggle was passed from one group to the next.[39] This, after all, was one meaning of 'tradition', either in a legal sense (the handover of material from one party to another) or in a broader sense, the transmission of methods, customs and even language from one age to another. The notion of a continuum suggested that the content of radicalism remained essentially the same, so that the Lollards' struggle was in essence the Levellers' struggle too. When radical activity appeared nonexistent, it had simply 'gone underground', only to resurface, its fundamental nature intact, in another epoch. The idea of a continuum also inferred that each group, in turn, influenced the other.

In fact, the influence of seventeenth-century radicals on their eighteenth-century counterparts was relatively minimal, for reasons which will be discussed later. The idea of a continuum of radicalism arguably confused passing similarity with actual influence. There may have been things that the Lollards and Levellers held in common – a hostility to the spiritual monopoly of the clergy being the most obvious – but there were many more differences: Lollards would have rejected or, at best, found incomprehensible the Levellers' demands for mass manhood suffrage, broad religious toleration and the effective separation of Church and state. Equally, it conflated means with ends. Levellers and Chartists may both have argued for universal (or near-universal) manhood suffrage, but they did so for different reasons. Levellers saw the vote as the means to ensure political accountability and protect the rights and liberties that were the 'birthright' of Englishmen. Chartists, on the other hand, wanted to ensure political accountability *and* secure social and economic goals, such as better housing, land reform and an end to the invidious Poor Laws.

However, contrary to the urgings of some conservative historians, the idea of a British 'radical tradition' should not be abandoned. Most of those groups usually included within it (the Levellers, Thomas Paine, the Chartists) were undoubtedly 'radical' within the context of their own time. Even if, in the case of the Levellers, theirs was a radicalism *avant la lettre*, it was radical all the same: the realisation of their political vision would have involved the fundamental transformation of the British constitution. The term 'radical' is consequently used in this book in the modern understanding of the term as meaning thorough social and political change. My 'radicals' then, to borrow a good commonsense definition from the late historian Gerald Aylmer, advocated the transformation of the existing status quo rather than merely reforming it to ameliorate its worst aspects.[40] My barometer of 'radicalism' is also relative: what the Levellers John Lilburne, William Walwyn and Richard Overton advocated – a broader franchise, governments elected by popular mandate, religious toleration and a fair and equitable legal system – was exceptional in the 1640s but would (I hope) be taken for granted in early twenty-first-century Britain.

This definition of radicalism does exclude some groups and events that have often been included in discussions of Britain's radical history. For example, the 'Glorious Revolution' of 1688–9 was often invoked by eighteenth-, nineteenth- and early twentieth-century radicals as a key moment in the history of British liberty. However, while modern historians have continued to claim that the consequences of the events of 1688–9 were revolutionary, they now largely see these changes as the unintended by-products of England's wars with France in the 1690s, rather than as the result of the conscious will of English 'patriots'. Indeed, the motivations of some of the 'revolutionaries' of 1688–9 were deeply reactionary: they wanted to preserve the spiritual monopoly of the Anglican state Church from the threat posed by James II's tolerationist policies.

In a more modern context, the founding of the welfare state has also been seen as a transformative moment in British history. Undoubtedly, this had a profound impact on the lives of millions of people. However, though far-reaching, these changes were not genuinely radical. In the first place, it is hard to describe the architects of the welfare state as radicals: they generally accepted the constitutional status quo and wanted to blunt the teeth of a rapacious capitalist system rather than do away with it altogether. Second, ideologically, the notion of a welfare state was well within the political mainstream: by the 1940s, the policies advocated by the Attlee government had become political orthodoxy and could receive broad cross-party support.

However, even though this book disputes the inclusion of some events within a history of British radicalism, it argues that the idea of a 'radical tradition' remains viable and important. As Eric Hobsbawm reminds us, even 'invented traditions' can be powerful historical forces: the appeal to the past can be a formidable spur to radical action, rather than a tool of conservative retrenchment.[41] In any case, the British 'radical tradition' was not a mere fiction: as we shall see, there *were* a number of important continuities between radical movements. Genuine connections were embellished by radical groups' habit of creating their own retrospective genealogies: they claimed, through the benefit of hindsight, affinity with past movements and individuals. Consequently, what was perceived to be included within this radical tradition varied from century to century and from one group to another. This variegated and ever-changing tradition was celebrated and remembered not only through writing or speech, but also via what the French historian Pierre Nora has called 'sites of memory': landscapes, buildings and monuments that evoke and inspire a re-engagement with the past.[42]

This persistent memory of radical activity in sources other than written histories was crucial to its survival. We should not forget that much of the history of radical movements had to be unearthed from beneath layers of negative propaganda, official censorship and violent repression. History tends to be written by the victors. In some cases, only very recently have we come to understand the full impact of radical movements, as in the case of Kett's Rebellion of 1549, now known by its far more appropriate, original label of the 'commotion time'. What this formerly secret history of radicalism reveals is surprising. Often, historians write the history of radical movements as a string of glorious failures, an account of the struggle of men and women who were ahead of their time, perpetually thwarted by the status quo and ever condemned to have their political dreams reach fruition only after their deaths. The truth is that in many instances radical movements were able to effect real changes on the government of the nation. In some instances, as in 1381 and 1549, they temporarily *were* the effective government of the nation. At other times, as in 1649, they came within a whisker of utterly transforming the English constitution. More often than not, it was because radicals were successful that they were so gravely feared by the social and political establishment, and their achievements so thoroughly denigrated.

This book, then, sets out to do two things. First, it aims to evaluate radicalism in its specific historical contexts, uncovering in many places the formerly secret history of both its successes and its failures. Second, it evaluates the enduring power of the idea of a 'radical tradition', by examining how each age has reinvented it to suit its own ends. Consequently, the book focuses predominantly on those events, groups and individuals that have loomed largest in this narrative of British dissent. For many radicals, the story began in 1215 when, according to one version of events, wicked King John was forced by his good barons to submit to the rule of law by setting his seal to Magna Carta, the founding stone of 'British' liberty.

PART ONE

A TALISMAN OF LIBERTY[1]

Magna Carta is the greatest constitutional document of all times – the foundation of the freedom of the individual against the arbitrary authority of the despot.

Lord Denning, on the 750th anniversary of Magna Carta[2]

Does Magna Carta mean nothing to you? Did she die in vain?

Tony Hancock

I

THE GREAT CHARTER

Ｋing John has long been portrayed as the ultimate 'bad king' who had to be restrained by 'good barons' – often presented, as V. H. Galbraith put it, as 'precursors of their much later descendants, the Whigs'.[1] For Sellar and Yeatman in *1066 and All That*, John was the 'first memorable wicked uncle'.[2] His contemporary reputation was even worse. Said to be slender and handsome in his youth, he had run to fat, his voracious appetite often leading him to make frequent penances for breaking the dietary restrictions commanded by the Church. Apart from his gluttony, John was also infamous for his lechery, fathering many illegitimate children. Lurid legends claimed that his second wife, Isabella of Angoulême (who was twenty years his junior), shared her husband's voracious sexual appetite, taking many lovers, some of whom John strangled to death on the marital bed. In addition, he had a well-deserved reputation for faithlessness and treachery, having joined his brother Richard in a revolt against their father Henry II (a betrayal which, it was rumoured, precipitated the old king's death) and then, in turn, fomented rebellion against Richard while his older brother, now King, was imprisoned in Germany. When he finally succeeded Richard to the English throne in 1199, he was ruthless in dealing with threats to his power, having his nephew and rival claimant to the Crown, Arthur of Brittany, murdered in Rouen prison in 1203 (some alleged the deed was done by a drunken John himself, others that Arthur's death was the result of a botched castration). As John built up his war chest for a renewed campaign against the French, he pursued his aristocratic debtors with similar vigour: the wife and son of the Irish magnate William de Briouze were deliberately starved to death in Windsor Castle for the non-payment of exorbitant royal fines. Actions of this kind served to alienate most of the English aristocracy from him, but the murder of Arthur of Brittany left only an infant, John's son Henry, as a plausible candidate for the throne. With no obvious adult claimant to lead a rebellion, the barons were forced to rely on a new device, a great charter securing the liberties of the realm, to secure support for their uprising.

Were they alive today, King John and his barons would doubtless have been surprised by the historic veneration of Magna Carta as the founding stone of British freedom. The 1215 Charter was, after all, a document forged as England stood on the brink of civil war; after a mere ten weeks, it was a political dead letter. The circumstances that brought John to agree, at least initially, to the barons' demands were catastrophic military failures and the crisis in royal finances that followed. His continental expedition, begun in 1213, had ended in disaster with defeat at the Battle of Bouvines on 27 July 1214. During three hours of intense and bloody fighting, John's staunch ally William Longsword, Earl of Salisbury, was captured. John himself had already returned to his lands in Aquitaine in a state of despondency following several unsuccessful clashes with the French King Philip.[3] The failed French war had not only justified John's childhood epithet of 'lackland' by leading to the loss of the English Crown's possessions in Normandy, but had also emptied the royal coffers. The war had raised taxation to unprecedented levels. By 1211, the Crown's total revenue had been

£145,000, six times the amount that had been collected at the beginning of the reign. Now, in the wake of military failure, noble grievances against John's rule coalesced into open and coordinated opposition, beginning with a widespread campaign of non-payment of scutage, originally a payment allowing knights to buy out of the military service that had become a general levy on the English elite. In January 1215, the King's opponents took an oath that they would stand fast together for the liberty of the Church and the realm.

That month, both sides met in London to discuss negotiating terms, although the parties came armed. At the same time, both John and the barons attempted to bring Pope Innocent III into the struggle. The Pope, though stressing that the King should listen to all reasonable grievances from his barons, had condemned all leagues and combinations against John and upheld his right to levy scutage. Both sides were preparing to use force. The King had borrowed money from the Knights Templar to pay for foreign mercenaries and took the cross as a crusader on 4 March, a move which, though deeply cynical – John had been excommunicated in 1213 for his failure to recognise Stephen Langton as Archbishop of Canterbury – led Pope Innocent to talk of those who opposed John as 'worse than saracens'. On 5 May the barons, led by Robert Fitzwalter (whose daughter, Matilda, the King had reputedly tried to seduce), formally renounced their fealty to John.

By the late spring/early summer of 1215, the tide was clearly turning in the rebels' favour. On 17 May, the City of London opened its gates to them, despite John's attempt to curry favour with them by permitting the City to elect its own mayor. London now became the rebellion's capital, predisposed to their cause by the disproportionately heavy tax burden that the City had had to carry during John's wars. In Wales, Llywelyn ab Iorwerth, Prince of Gwynedd, and the Briouzes, led by Giles, Bishop of Hereford, scored notable victories over the King's forces, even moving into England by taking Shrewsbury under their control.

Though John retained some influential supporters, including William Marshal, a powerful magnate and soldier of international repute, and Earl Warenne, Henry II's half-brother, it was obvious to him that he would need to make concessions, if only in the short term, in order to buy himself enough time to build up his military strength. June saw the exchange of peace proposals. On the 10th, John agreed to accept the articles in the barons' proposed Charter as the terms for further negotiation, though some of the northern rebels still refused to lay down their arms. Five days later, terms were settled and the King went to Runnymede meadow to confirm the final draft of the Charter. The choice of the site was probably due to its proximity to London. According to the contemporary account of Ralph of Coggeshall, both the King and the barons were followed by well-armed retinues: before the final negotiations could begin in earnest, each side had to swear upon the gospels that they would conduct themselves peacefully. The discussions continued for several days on the basis of the barons' articles, until on 19 June a 'firm peace' was agreed. Only at this point did Chancery clerks begin drafting copies of the Charter and setting the royal seal to them.

There was not, then, one dramatic moment from which the Charter emerged. It was the final product of a protracted process of negotiation. Initially, it was only known as Magna Carta because it was such a large document (sixty-three chapters, or clauses, in the 1215 version) and to distinguish it from the smaller Forest Charter issued at the same time. But the contract of the Charter of 1215 was remarkably broad-ranging too. Its main architects, the barons, had had to appeal to a wider portion of the English population in order to gain support, making it much more than a document pandering to the aristocracy. Its broadest provision lay in chapter 40 – 'to no one will we sell, to no one will we deny or delay right or justice'. The Charter's provisions as a whole constituted an indictment not only of John's reign but of his father's and brother's as well.

But though the genesis of the Charter was protracted, its immediate life as a peace settlement was very short-lived. Chapters 52
and 61 had attempted to hold John to its terms by referring all
disagreements with the King's actions in depriving anyone of
'lands, castles, liberties or his rights' to a committee of twenty-five
barons, which, with the 'commune of all the land', could in response
'distress and distrain us [meaning John] in every way they can,
namely by seizing our lands, castles and possessions'. These parts
of John's Charter are often portrayed as a constitutional watershed,
for the first time subjecting English kings to the rule of law. Yet
these clauses represented not so much a check on royal power as
the complete abnegation of it. The committee was essentially a
cabal of the King's enemies who immediately began dispossessing
John of his castles. The inclusion of these clauses made the
resumption of armed hostility inevitable. No king who valued his
title could have submitted in the long term to such a blatant
assault on his authority. By July, John had written to Innocent III
asking him to annul the Charter. The papal letters reached
England in September: they pronounced the rebels excommunicated and stated that the settlement reached in June was 'not only
shameful and base but also illegal and unjust'. The Pope finished
by declaring the Charter 'null and void of all validity for ever'.

The Pope's response emboldened John but failed to weaken the
resolve of his enemies, including Stephen Langton, who was suspended for failing to disavow the Charter. The King now laid siege
to Rochester Castle, held by the barons, hoping that its fall would
allow him to make a decisive move on London. The rebel garrison
held out for seven weeks while the barons appealed to the French
for support, offering Prince Louis the English throne in return. In
the meantime, Alexander II of Scotland had been granted
Northumberland, Cumberland and Westmorland by the barons,
and the northern rebels quickly pledged homage to the Scottish
King. By December, Wales too had come under the de facto control of the ambitious Llywelyn, with the invasion of south-west

Wales and the capture of the English strongholds at Cardigan and Carmarthen. The situation in the borders led John to divide his army in two, leaving one force to keep an eye on the rebels in London while he went north – in his own reported words, to 'run the little sandy fox-cub [Alexander] to earth'. The King's army harried the land as it went. The Chronicler Roger of Wendover reported:

> [these] limbs of the devil covered the whole country like locusts. Sword in hand, they ransacked towns, houses, cemeteries, churches, robbing everyone, sparing neither women nor children. They put the king's enemies in chains until they paid a heavy ransom. Even priests at the altar were seized, tortured and robbed. Knights and others were hung up by their feet and legs or by their hands, fingers and thumbs, salt and vinegar were thrown into their eyes; others were roasted over burning coals and then dropped into cold water.[4]

On 13 January 1216, John attacked what was then Scotland's richest town, Berwick, setting it aflame before turning his army south again to head for rebel-dominated East Anglia. By March he had captured Colchester, but though he held the upper hand militarily, he had been unable to persuade any of the significant rebel leaders to submit to his authority. Moreover, his assault on Scotland had been a strategic mistake. John had failed to capture London and his army was now forced to fight on two fronts.

Louis's forces disembarked at Sandwich in Kent on 22 May. Yet though John had mustered forces in the county so as to resist the likely invasion, he chose not to fight, but instead withdrew westwards. Louis entered London and was paid homage by the citizens and rebels on 2 June. Four days later, the French Prince left London for Winchester, but John had already fled from his temporary base, seeking refuge in Corfe Castle. By September, two-thirds of the barons had abandoned the King, as had one-third of his household knights and some of his most trusted servants. He continued his peregrinations around the country, attempting to shore up remaining loyal garrisons at Lincoln and Dover. On the night of 9 October, at Lynn in Norfolk, he suffered an attack of dysentery, brought on according to Coggeshall by his gluttonous consumption of 'raw peaches and new cider'. (An even more colourful story attributed his sickness to eating poisoned plums.[5]) The King's health declined over the next few days, and his fortunes sank even lower as part of his baggage train was lost in the waters of the Wash. His entourage struggled on to Newark, where he died on the night of 18 October.

According to his request, he was buried in Worcester Cathedral, still under his force's control.[6] Despite the sanctified setting of his burial, chroniclers were convinced that John's soul had headed straight to hell, Matthew Paris repeating a reputed comment of the time that 'Foul as it is, Hell itself is made fouler by the presence of John.' Later historians have been no more generous about the King's character. Kate Norgate's 1902 biography called him a man of 'almost superhuman wickedness', and Sir James Ramsey dubbed him 'a selfish and cruel tyrant of the worst type'.[7]

For Rudyard Kipling, the Charter stood as an impregnable bulwark against both the tyranny of power-crazed kings such as John and the anarchy of the unfettered mob.

> And still when Mob or Monarch lays
> Too rude a hand on English ways
> The whisper wakes, the shudder plays,
> Across the reeds at Runnymede.
> And Thames that knows the moods of kings,
> And crowds and priests and suchlike things,
> Rolls deep and dreadful as he brings
> Their warning down from Runnymede.

The presentation of the Charter as the bulwark of English liberties has long been identified as originating in the work of the seventeenth-century common lawyer Sir Edward Coke, whose *Institutes* (published posthumously in 1642) included extensive commentary upon Magna Carta. Coke eulogised it as 'declaratory of the principal grounds of the fundamental laws of England'.[8] He was not, though, a proto-Whig in the strict sense of being a believer in constitutional 'progress': he saw the Charter's role as to document old freedoms, not establish new rights.[9] For Coke, Magna Carta was the embodiment of the ancient and pure laws of Anglo-Saxon England, regained after their destruction by the Normans – he spoke of the 'great weightinesse and weightie greatness' of the contents of the Charter, which he believed to be 'the fountaine of all the fundamentall lawes of the realm . . . [and] a confirmation of restitution of the common law'.[10] Close attention to the matter of the Charter was vital for anyone who wished to understand English law: 'As the goldfiner will not out of the dust, threds, or shreds of gold, let passe the least crum, in respect of the excellency of the metal: so ought not the learned reader to let any passe any syllable of this law, in respect of the excellency of the matter.'[11] So influential has Coke's interpretation been that one of the most respected twentieth-century commentators on Magna Carta, W. S. MacKechnie, suggested that there were effectively two Great Charters: one conceded by John to his barons in 1215, and the other created by Sir Edward Coke in the early seventeenth century.[12] The suggestion that Coke's reading of Magna Carta was less a commentary on it than a wholesale reinvention is not new. Robert Brady, the late seventeenth-century Tory historian who challenged many of the assumptions about England's 'ancient constitution', described Coke as writing about the law 'as if it had grown up with the Trees, Herbs and Grass'.[13]

Is it pointless to talk about a separation between the myth of the Charter, created by Coke and other seventeenth-century commentators, and its substance? Given the vagueness of some of its chapters, and given the divisions among modern scholars about their meaning, it is unsurprising that a variety of interpretations has emerged. Moreover, the Charter agreed in 1215, the one that is still celebrated to this day and whose remaining copies are cherished by institutions such as the British Library, was not the one that Coke and, indeed, all legal commentators from the thirteenth century onwards were actually referring to when they spoke of Magna Carta. This was, in fact, the Charter of 1225, issued by John's son Henry III, which was confirmed at least twenty-five times and by all the kings from Henry III to Henry V, the last-known confirmation being delivered in 1416. The authoritative text for legal purposes was the *inspeximus* (a term for a faithful verbatim recitation of an existing document) of Edward I, issued in 1297. It is this text that still remains on the statute books, though, as we shall see, in a very truncated form. Although John's Charter formed the basis for the 1225 version, the latter was much reduced in size and left out the key security provisions inserted in 1215.[14]

The leading modern authority on the Charter, Sir James Holt, argues that it was the fourteenth century, not the seventeenth, that represented the decisive period for the development of the myth of Magna Carta. Significant legal additions were made to the 1225 version in the fourteenth century that considerably broadened its provisions. It was then that the concentration on the twenty-ninth chapter (which combined chapters 39–41 of the 1215 text) first emerged. Between 1331 and 1368, Parliament passed six acts that reinterpreted this clause in terms that went far beyond the intention and sense of the original Charter. It was then also that the phrase 'lawful judgement of peers' came to include trial by peers and thereby trial by jury – a process that was in only embryonic form in 1215. The phrase 'law of the land' was also given a powerful new twist and rendered as 'due process of law', including only indictments brought by a jury or by original writ and thereby limiting royal intrusions into the common-law courts.

Crucially for the later radical appropriation of the Charter, these subsequent statutes also made its terms more socially inclusive. The words 'no free man' became in the statutes of Edward III of 1331 and 1352 simply 'no man'. In 1354, in the statute that refers for the first time to 'due process of law', 'no free man' became 'no man of whatever estate or condition he may be'. As we shall see, by the time of the Peasants' Revolt of 1381, the revised Magna Carta had become an important support to a much broader idea of popular freedom.

These fourteenth-century statutes were also central to the sixteenth- and seventeenth-century interpretation of the Charter. Some Tudor chroniclers, it is true, engaged in a brief rehabilitation of King John, largely as a result of his struggles with Pope Innocent III, which seemed to presage Henry VIII's split from Rome. As late as 1611, the historian and cartographer John Speed could be found complaining of the indignities John had had to suffer at the hands of the barons in 1215: 'Thus one of the greatest soueraigns of Christendom was now become the twenty-sixth petty king in his owne Dominions . . . What marvaille if high disdain herof pierced his swelling heart and filled his minde with reuoluing thoughts, how to vnwinde himself of those seruile fetters.'[15] However, by the early seventeenth century Magna Carta was generally being invoked to protect the privileges of Parliament and the liberties of the subject from royal encroachment. The Edwardian statutes were referred to by the defending counsel in the Five Knights Case of 1627, which challenged Charles I's resort to imprisonment without charge. The civil lawyer and MP John Selden said that 'the [Edwardian] statute is not to be taken to be an explanation of that of Magna Charta, but the very words of the statute of Magna Charta'. It was to these 'six statutes' that Sir Benjamin Rudyerd was referring when he talked about Magna Carta 'walking abroad' in the wake of the Petition of Right (1628), an indictment of Charles's actions itself modelled on the example of the Charter.[16]

So, although Coke lifted English panegyric on the Charter to new levels, he was building upon a centuries-long tradition that

saw it guarantee legal due process, prohibit arbitrary imprisonment and promise equality before the law. However, in the 1620s,
the parliamentary opposition to Charles I applied the Charter not
only to the issue of imprisonment without charge, as in the Five
Knights Case where five leading gentlemen were gaoled for failing
to pay a forced loan to the King, but also to attack taxation without parliamentary consent, a line of argument that also led these
commentators to suggest that the Charter guaranteed the existence
of Parliament. Sir Henry Spelman and John Selden claimed this
from a study of chapter 14 of the Charter:

> For obtaining the common counsel of the kingdom concerning
> the assessment of aids . . . or of scutage, We will cause to be sum-
> moned, severally by Our letters, the archbishops, bishops, abbots,
> earls, and great barons; We will also cause to be summoned, gen-
> erally, by Our sheriffs and bailiffs, all those who hold lands directly
> of us, to meet on a fixed day . . . and at a fixed place.[17]

The ability of the Charter to appear all things to all men was
demonstrated by its use as a totem by a succession of radical
movements from the seventeenth century to the nineteenth. The
seventeenth-century radical group, the Levellers, were once portrayed as making a firm break from the practice of employing
political arguments based on appeals to history and legal precedent.
Figures such as the leading Leveller John Lilburne believed that
the Conquest of 1066 meant that much English law represented
an oppressive 'Norman yoke' upon the people.[18] Certainly, some
seventeenth-century radicals, including a number of Levellers, did
reject the appeal to English history, and in particular the notion of
the year 1215 as the fount of liberty.[19]

However, the actual response of the Levellers to the past was less
uniform than this and demonstrated a more complicated understanding of what the Conquest had meant for English law and
the survival of an 'ancient constitution'. The importance of the

Charter to Leveller rhetoric was particularly evident in John Lilburne's *A Copy of a Letter to a Friend* (1645), which supported the attack on Charles I's 'evil counsellors' Archbishop William Laud and Thomas Wentworth, Earl of Strafford, because they 'trod Magna Carta . . . under their feet, and indeavoured to rule by their own wills, and so set up an arbitrary government'.[20] Lilburne was an expert at turning his own struggles with the legal authorities and his stretches in prison into a grander narrative about the threat to English liberties, and to Magna Carta in particular:

> I am a freeman yea a free-born Denizen of England . . . and by virtue of being a free-man, I conceive I have as true a right to all the privileges that doe belong to a free-man, as the greatest man in England, whatsoever he be . . . and the ground and foundation of my Freedome, I build upon the Grand Charter of England.[21]

The 'Agreement of the People', debated at Putney in 1647, which constituted the Levellers' own projected settlement for a civil-war-torn England, might be seen as the group's attempt to forge their own Magna Carta, but this time between the people and Parliament rather than the King and the barons.

Magna Carta formed an important part of the Whig case against the Catholic James II during the Glorious Revolution. In his declaration of October 1688, William of Orange appealed to the Charter, stating that James's expulsion of the president and fellows of Magdalen College was 'contrary to law, and to that express provision in Magna Charta, That no man shall lose life or goods [the freehold of the university fellowships] but by the law of the land'.[22] Yet, at the beginning of the eighteenth century, it was increasingly Tories rather than Whigs who resorted to the Charter to defend a constitution that they felt was threatened by a Walpoleian oligarchy. As the court Whigs worked to ensure the passage of the Septennial Act in 1716, replacing the Triennial Act of 1694 which guaranteed regular elections, Archibald Hutcheson, lawyer and Tory MP for Hastings, complained that if the bill passed, 'May we not in the same way of reasoning, give up the Habeas Corpus act, and all the other privileges and immunities, which have been obtained to the people from the crown, from the date of Magna Charta to this very day?'[23] These Tory defences, ironically, led court Whigs into adopting many of the arguments of the Tory historian Robert Brady, who had attacked the notion of an 'ancient constitution'. The Whig *Daily Gazetteer* dismissed the editor of the Tory *Craftsmen* as 'an historical Idiot', and reminded its readers that Magna Carta, far from being a reassertion of former liberties, was 'only an Exemption of a Few great Proprietors of Land from some Hardships they lay under on Account of their conditional Tenures': it made no difference to the majority of the English people, who were 'as much Hewers of Wood and Drawers of Water, as truly vassals and Slaves after, as before this Great Charter'.[24]

The adoption of this very narrow reading of the Charter by the political establishment marked supporters of the broader, Cokeian, version with a badge of dissent. The Charter came to public prominence again in the case of John Wilkes, the populist politician, journalist and sympathiser with the American colonists (if not an English advocate of American independence, as he is sometimes portrayed). Wilkes had got into trouble with the authorities for attacks on the ministry of Lord Bute in his political weekly the *North Briton*, in particular for an attack on George Grenville, Bute's successor as Prime Minister, for 'making' George III deliver a King's Speech praising the recent peace concluding the Seven Years War with France. Wilkes, like John Lilburne, used the language of Magna Carta to turn his own individual tribulations into a larger struggle between liberty and tyranny:

> the liberty of all peers and gentlemen and what touches me more sensibly, that of all the middling and inferior set of people, who stand most in need of protection, is in my case . . . to be finally

decided upon; a question of such importance as to determine at once, whether English liberty be a reality or a shadow.[25]

Wilkes has sometimes been dismissed as a shabby populist demagogue, and his attachment to the Charter, like his attachment to the cause of 'Liberty', no more than a flag of convenience. Yet in the late eighteenth century veneration of the Charter was key to radical arguments for parliamentary reform, to which Wilkes remained committed even when he had achieved some political respectability towards the end of his life. Moreover, it was suggested in the anonymous *Historical Essay on the English Constitution* (1771) that 'a day of public thanksgiving, festivity and joy' be instituted 'as an annual and perpetual reminder of England's deliverance from tyranny in 1215'.[26] The Charter was then revived as a symbol of English – and imperial – freedom by the defenders of the American colonies. As in the early seventeenth century, it was employed as a device to protect individuals from taxation without representation. James Burgh, the Scottish educationalist and associate of 'friends of liberty' such as Richard Price, Joseph Priestley and Benjamin Franklin, declared that 'if the people of Britain are not to be taxed, but by parliament . . . does it not directly follow, that the colonists cannot, according to Magna Charta, and the bill of right, be taxed by parliament, so long as they continue unrepresented?'[27]

As some English reformers began to look for their inspiration not only across the Atlantic to North America, but also over the Channel to revolutionary France, the freedoms grounded on Magna Carta started to seem too limited. Thomas Paine, the foremost English radical writer of the revolutionary era, rejected the appeal to the past. In fact, Paine argued, the Charter was detrimental to English liberty, as 'rights are inherently in all inhabitants; but charters, by annulling those rights in the majority, leave the rest, by exclusion, in the hands of a few'.[28] Paine's rejection of an appeal to a historic constitution was a rather unusual stance among British 'friends of liberty'. Most British radicals continued to look to Magna Carta for support against the increasingly draconian measures taken by the government. Members of the London Corresponding Society attacked the legal abuses of their day on grounds of clauses 14 and 29 of the Charter:

> The various methods [the suspension of the Habeas Corpus Act] now in constant practice by which the benefits of [clause 29] are totally defeated and destroyed, might induce us to suppose, that the Great Charter has been repealed: if we did not assuredly know, that it is the fundamental basis of our constitution; which even the real representatives of the people (much less the miserable nominees of Helstone and Old Sarum [infamous 'rotten boroughs'*]) have not the right, nor . . . the power to repeal.[29]

Even in the nineteenth century, despite radicals' increasing concern with social and economic rights and the growing influence of Marxism on radical interpretations of history, the political importance attached to the Great Charter remained undiminished. Chartists did not shirk from drawing expansive claims from its text. At a huge (250,000-strong) rally on Hartshead Moor in Yorkshire in 1838, the Reverend Joseph Rayner Stephens declared, 'We stand upon our rights – we seek no change – we say give us the good old laws of England unchanged', and when he received the shout of 'Magna Charta' to his question 'What are these laws?' he replied, 'Aye, Magna Charta! The good old laws of English freedom – free meetings – freedom of speech – freedom of worship – freedom of homesteads – free and happy firesides, and no workhouses.'[30] For nineteenth-century advocates of women's suffrage such as Richard Pankhurst, husband of Emmeline, the future suffragette leader,

---

* Seats in the 'gift' of a handful of electors. The most notorious of these, Old Sarum, had a mere eleven electors in 1831, all of whom were major landowners who lived outside the borough.

Magna Carta was also a vitally important document. For Pankhurst, the fact that its provisions were held to apply equally to men and women indicated that other statutes, namely those covering the franchise, should be interpreted in the same way. Magna Carta was even cherished by English socialists. The artist, designer and revolutionary William Morris, writing in the late nineteenth century, described it as that 'great, thoroughly well-considered deed', but argued that it could be seen only as 'the Foundation of English Liberty' on the grounds that it was the 'confirmation and seal of the whole feudal system in England'.[31]

On into the twentieth century, the Charter continued to be commemorated as the quintessence of British freedoms. The 750th anniversary in 1965 saw national celebrations, including televised special services in Westminster Abbey: the Archbishop of Canterbury, Michael Ramsey, with no trace of irony, delivered a sermon before his hereditary monarch on the egalitarian lesson that the Charter delivered that 'each single man has rights because God made him in his own image with an infinite worth for all eternity'.*[32] The same year the Society for Individual Liberty, a pro-capitalist, libertarian organisation formed by Sir Ernest Benn (uncle of Tony) and the sugar baron Lord Lyle, held a 'thirteenth-century feast' in honour of the Great Charter, with food 'served by wenches from the Elizabethan Rooms'. The chairman of the Society, Sir Ian Mactaggart, a company director, stated that its aim was to 'combine the dignity of an important occasion with as much fun as possible for ordinary men and women'.[33] Entertainment was provided by 'jousting, wrestling and feats of strength' performed by members of the 'Mayfair Gymnasium and Tough Guys Stage and Film Agency', displays of Morris, sword and folk dancing, fireworks and a 'best wench' contest.[34]

*

* Ramsey's biographer reveals that he was a prelate ideally suited to his task: as an introverted boy given to a vivid fantasy life, the future archbishop wrote letters to King John in hell, telling him he was 'a very bad man'.

Magna Carta's influence has been felt far beyond the shores of the British Isles. The wording of the Great Charter, especially chapter 29, has entered into the constitutions of many other states and countries. The Virginian Declaration of Rights framed on 12 June 1776 closely follows chapter 29 in its article VIII:

> That in all capital or criminal prosecutions a man hath a right to demand the cause and nature of his accusation, to be confronted with the accusers and witnesses, to call for evidence in his favour, and to a speedy trial by an impartial jury of twelve men of his vicinage, without whose unanimous consent he cannot be found guilty; nor can he be compelled to give evidence against himself; that no man be deprived of his liberty, except by the law of the land or the judgement of his peers.

This in turn reappeared in somewhat different form as the Fifth Amendment to the Constitution of the United States. Chapter 29 of the 1225 Charter is also represented in article 21 of the Indian Constitution of 1950, in the 1960 Canadian Bill of Rights, the Pakistan Constitution of 1956 and the Malaysian Constitution of 1963.[35]

The Charter is not only venerated in the UK. A copy of it holds pride of place in the National Archives, in Washington, DC's permanent *Charters of Freedom* exhibition, preserved in a glass display case embedded in a marble plinth under a vast wooden cupola. The site at Runnymede Meadows in Surrey was secured for posterity through the efforts of the American Bar Association, the Dulverton Trust and the Pilgrim Trust. The ABA paid for the construction of a memorial to the Charter, celebrating what it calls the document's defence of 'Freedom under the law'. In recognition of the 'special relationship' between Britain and the USA, the land of Runnymede Hill, also the site of a memorial to John F. Kennedy, was gifted to the United States.[36] Thus, the making of Magna Carta could plausibly be described as a world event, and the document itself one of global importance.

But it remains a document originally thrashed out between an English king and his most powerful subjects. Following calls in January 2006 from the then Chancellor, Gordon Brown, for a British equivalent of Spanish, French, American and Australian national days, *BBC History Magazine* conducted a poll of its readers to choose a suitable date. The anniversary of 'the signing of Magna Carta', as the BBC erroneously reported it – as every schoolboy used to know, medieval charters were sealed, not signed – on 15 June 1215 (the date on which final negotiations between John and the barons began) emerged as the most popular choice, with over 27 per cent of the five thousand votes cast, beating VE Day and D-Day. As a number of commentators mentioned at the time, it was arguably a poor choice for a prospective 'British day'. And as Andrew O'Hagan noted in the *Daily Telegraph*, if it was supposed to be a British day, why not commemorate the actual moment of political union (at least between England and Scotland), the passing of the Act of Union on 16 January 1707?[37]

The quest for totems of 'British' identity raises a further problem: how far can freedoms 'gifted' (imposed) by a colonial imperial power be regarded as freedoms at all? 'Britain', from its earliest inception as a meaningful political entity – ironically, by Scottish King James VI – in 1603, was defined in imperial terms. The values of Britishness, as Linda Colley has demonstrated, came to be very closely associated with empire.[38] This raises potential difficulties for the project of constructing a 'British freedom trail', recently discussed in the *Guardian* as part of celebrating the 'British' values of 'tolerance and fair play' identified by Gordon Brown. Some of the radical moments listed in a readers' poll for that newspaper, such as the signing of the National Covenant in 1638 and the Merthyr Tydfil rising of 1831, were, in part, nationalist uprisings against English governance. Thus, much that could be defined as 'radical' activity in a British context essentially gains its force from its opposition to the existence of a British state, at least one run from Westminster.

Magna Carta presents historians tackling the development of our rights and freedoms (even those focusing only on the English context) with other problems, too. As O'Hagan has suggested, the vote for the Charter was, in part at least, a vote for some sort of 'people power' (mediated by 'benevolent' barons, of course). Yet the claims historically made on the strength of the Charter have varied a great deal. It has been invoked in support of the doctrine of 'no taxation without representation', in defence of the continued existence of parliaments themselves, in favour of universal suffrage and, in the case of some high-flown pieces of Chartist rhetoric, to legitimise the beginnings of a welfare state. What we see represented in the struggles of past people is clearly very much dependent on the context in which we write and think and argue.

What is left of our 'Magna Carta freedoms' presents a case in point. Between 1828 and 1969, thirty-three of the chapters of Henry III's Charter were repealed as part of a process to simplify, reduce and clarify the law of England. Of the remaining clauses of Magna Carta, only one has any real value.* The main reputation of Magna Carta continues to be based on clause 29, which Burke believed to be 'engraven on the hearts of Englishmen'. Sir Ivor Jennings spoke of its translation from Latin 'into the language of the back streets'.[39]

This clause has been revered from the thirteenth century to the present day. Yet it is also the case that governments from the eighteenth to the twenty-first century have met little legal resistance when they have circumvented its terms. Clause 29 has been suspended or revoked by Parliament on a number of occasions, most notably through the suspensions of Habeas Corpus in the eighteenth and nineteenth centuries (largely implemented, it should be

* Clause 37 is a general saving clause; clause 1 a general confirmation of the privileges of the English Church, which has proved largely useless in the face of parliamentary encroachment; and clause 9 relates solely to the privileges of the City of London – as ever, the City has done very well in avoiding being reformed.

noted, to suppress public agitation *for* democratic rights) and via the Defence of the Realm Acts passed during the two world wars. Unlike in the United States, judges in the United Kingdom cannot rule that such legislation is invalid when it appears to be in breach of the constitution, and the British law lords have consistently sided with successive home secretaries rather than the Charter where such clashes have occurred, as in the cases of Rex vs Halliday (1917) and Liversidge vs Anderson (1942). In the latter case, the one dissenting judge, Lord Atkins, entered a memorable and public protest at the majority decision:

> I view with apprehension the attitude of judges who on a mere question of construction [i.e. of an Act of Parliament] when face to face with claims involving the liberty of the subject show themselves more executive-minded than the executive. In this country, amid the clash of arms, the laws are not silent. They may be changed, but they speak the same language in war as in peace. It has always been one of the pillars of freedom, one of the principles of liberty for which on recent authority [Sir Winston Churchill] we are now fighting, that the judges are no respecters of persons and stand between the subject and any attempted encroachments on his liberty by the executive, alert to see that any coercive action is justified in law. In this case I have listened to arguments which might have been addressed acceptably to the Court of King's Bench in the time of Charles I. I protest, even if I do it alone, against a strained construction put on words with the effect of giving an uncontrolled power of imprisonment to the Minister.[40]

Most recently, chapter 29 has been invoked in the case of the displacement of the Chagos Islanders, ejected from their homes in the Indian Ocean to make way for an American military base on Diego Garcia in the 1960s. A note made at the time by Denis Greenhill, then a senior Foreign Office official and later Baron Greenhill of Harrow, revealed the utter contempt with which the

British government viewed the islanders: 'Unfortunately, along with the Birds go some few Tarzans or Men Fridays whose origins are obscure, and who are being hopefully wished on to Mauritius etc. When this has been done, I agree we must be very tough.'[41] By the early 1970s, most of the Chargossians had been moved to the slums of Port Louis, Mauritius.[42] The whole US/UK enterprise in the Chagos Islands was hushed up; fear of bad publicity led the UK government to give some compensation to the islanders in 1983 after private suits were threatened. Cases nonetheless continued to be lodged against the British government, but these were all essentially based on private law claims relating to trespass and false imprisonment, which were difficult to prove (it was hard to see how expulsion could be interpreted as imprisonment).

The issue was revived, however, by the revelation that, though they now lacked any homeland, the Chagossians retained dual British/Mauritian citizenship. The islanders' English lawyer, Richard Gifford, considered that if they had a right to live on the islands, that right must originate in the same right that UK citizens had to abide in the United Kingdom. That right, confirmed in the 1971 Immigration Act, originates from Magna Carta chapter 29, especially the provision that 'no freeman shall be . . . outlawed or exiled . . . but by lawful judgement of his peers or by the law of the land'. If Magna Carta could be proven to apply to the British Indian Ocean Territory (as the islands were collectively known), then the colony's 1971 Immigration Ordinance, which banned any inhabitants on the island other than military personnel, might be invalidated.

The case went to the High Court in July 2000 before Lord Justice Laws. The verdict struck down the BIOT's 1971 Immigration Ordinance but not, as some commentators asserted, on the grounds of the provisions of Magna Carta. The judge agreed that Charter liberties extended to the colonies, but these liberties confirmed only a procedure, not a right. As the 1971 Immigration Ordinance effectively amounted to 'the law of the land' in the Chagos Islands, the exile of the indigenous population was lawful under Magna Carta, which only guarantees due process. The victory was a hollow one and, as Gifford reflected, one in which human rights were barely mentioned. Return to Diego Garcia was banned in any case, the Blair government insisted, by treaty obligations with Washington. Despite a further legal victory in 2007, repeated appeals from the government have ensured that the Chagossians still cannot return their homeland.[43]

The problem, as the case of the Chagos Islanders reveals, is not, as writers on the right such as Peter Oborne have suggested, that Magna Carta liberties are under 'sustained and ruthless attack' by the British government.[44] The problem is that Magna Carta, while it may be seen as a symbol of freedom and democracy the world over, in a British legal context guarantees very little. In fact, this 'ancient constitution', so revered by conservatives, essentially hobbles those few modern concessions to civil rights, such as the Human Rights Act of 1998, that have appeared on the statute books.

Diego Garcia is the base for many of the United States' bombing sorties over Iraq and Afghanistan. Besides the arbitrary and continued displacement of British subjects, the threat of imprisonment without charge has been resurrected by Britain's current involvement in the 'War on Terror'. British subjects have been imprisoned, in conditions at which even King John might have baulked, without charge or clear prospect of a civil trial in the American camps Delta and X-Ray in Guantanamo Bay. This is despite the additional legal protection given to British subjects by the 1998 Human Rights Act. However, as the law lord Lord Hoffmann argued in *ex parte* Simms (1999), 'Parliamentary sovereignty means that Parliament can, if it chooses, legislate contrary to fundamental principles of human rights. The Human Rights Act 1998 will not detract from this power. The constraints upon its exercise by Parliament are ultimately political, not legal.' The caveats that Hoffmann introduced into this sweeping description of parliamentary legislative power are less than reassuring, given what has occurred in the cases of the Defence of the Realm Acts, the Chagos Islanders and the prisoners in Guantanamo Bay: 'The principle of legality means that Parliament must squarely confront what it is doing and accept the political cost.'[45] Yet the British government has continued with its foreign policy in the face of massive public demonstrations against the Iraq War and opinion polls indicating clear majorities opposed to military action. To use Hoffmann's moral arithmetic, it has weighed up the political costs and decided that they are not so prohibitive as to necessitate an end to the government's human rights abuses.

The power of the myth of Magna Carta, and the weakness of the letter of it, reminds us that legal enactments alone are only part of the process by which human rights are secured. Nor are the freedoms we hold preserved in aspic; nor are we on an inevitable upward trajectory of ever-broadening liberty. The struggle to gain and preserve rights and freedoms is not part of the past, to be safely sampled on a 'heritage trail' of British liberty, but a vital part of our political present and future. Thus, the political agency of the British people has been crucial to the defence and extension of our rights and freedoms. As the late Marxist historian of the Middle Ages, Rodney Hilton, reflected: 'The noticeable tendency of the English to be self-congratulatory about having given the idea of liberty to the world with Magna Carta [should] be modified in the light not merely of the exclusion from its enjoyment of the mass of the population, but of the long-term consequences of that exclusion.'[46]

As we shall see in the next chapter, it was only through the collective actions of large numbers of the English people that the freedoms claimed in the Great Charter actually came to be enjoyed.

PART TWO

WHEN ADAM DELVED AND EVE SPAN

CADE
It is to you, good people, that I speak,
Over whom, in time to come, I hope to reign;
For I am rightful heir unto the crown.

SIR HUMPHREY
And thou thyself a shearman, art thou not?

CADE
And Adam was a gardener.

William Shakespeare, *Henry VI*, part 2, Act IV, Scene 1

THE PEASANTS' REVOLT

The late Marc Bloch, one of the greatest historians of medieval Europe, suggested that the nature of the seigneurial regime made peasant revolts as natural and endemic as are 'strikes to large-scale capitalism'.[1] Yet, though we can find some evidence of revolts against manorial authority before the fourteenth century (and some sources testifying to their successes), there is a complete absence of large-scale popular rebellions before the 1300s.[2] Around the mid-fourteenth century, something happened across Europe that transformed lower-level struggles between landowners and those who worked the land into mass revolt. The previous silence in the historical record, as far as the voice of the ordinary people was concerned, was replaced by a deafening roar.

Not without reason has the fourteenth century been dubbed 'the worst century ever'.[3] For those who were effectively subsistence farmers or landless wage labourers − much of the population − these were hard times indeed. Between 1315 and 1317, violent climate change inflicted such heavy damage on crops that food production fell well short of the demands of the growing population. In the Worcestershire manor of Halesowen, the number of adult males fell by 15 per cent between 1315 and 1321 after a period of 40 per cent growth during 1271–1311. The chronicler Thomas Walsingham claimed that the poor were reduced to eating the remains of diseased animals in an attempt to survive. Aside from the severe fluctuations in weather, between 1319 and 1321, outbreaks of murrain disease killed 25–50 per cent of sheep flocks, while rinderpest broke out among draft animals, making the tillage of land in some areas impossible. Combined with the long-term population boom that had occurred over the late thirteenth century, these natural disasters served to inflate both food prices and land rents. The economic and environmental crisis widened the gap between richer and poorer village families: the poor would starve to death while their wealthier neighbours took the opportunity to extend into their vacated tenancies.

The iniquities of late medieval England's economic system were compounded by the inbuilt inequality in taxation. Medieval and early modern governments had only one major drain on their revenues beyond the upkeep of the royal household: the cost of war. The disaster of Bannockburn in 1314 led Edward II to levy two heavy subsidies in 1315 and 1316, tax burdens that fell harder upon the poorer members of society – in that these subsidies were assessed on moveable goods alone and exempted landed income. At mid-century, war, drought, flood and famine had further strengthened the power of the landholders and further impoverished those at the bottom of the social scale.

This situation was transformed by a human catastrophe unrivalled before or since. The arrival of the Black Death in 1348 in southern England led to a 47–8 per cent decrease in the country's population. Some towns were completely wiped out: in the Oxfordshire village of Cuxham, all twelve villeins, or serfs, alive at the beginning of 1349 were dead by the end of the year. Henry Knighton, the cellarer of Leicester Abbey, described the Black Death's passing over southern England as a dark and deadly shadow: 'the dreadful pestilence made its way along the coast by

Southampton and reached Bristol, where almost the whole strength of the town perished, as it were surprised by sudden death'.

Agricultural production in some areas came to a complete halt through a combination of lack of labour and – as a result of population loss – lack of demand. Knighton recorded that while the human population was struck down by the Black Death, a similar epidemic raged through England's livestock: 'In the same year there was a great plague among sheep everywhere in the kingdom, so that in one place more than 5,000 sheep died in a single pasture; and they rotted so much that neither bird nor beast would touch them.'[4] This depopulation, according to Knighton, left many towns and villages desolate: 'and there were no houses left in them, all who had lived therein being dead; and it seemed likely that many such hamlets would never again be inhabited'. The sudden massive drop in population effectively wiped out England's surplus manpower: 'In the following winter there was such a shortage of servants for all sorts of labour as it was believed had never been before. For the sheep and cattle strayed in all directions without herdsmen, and all things were left with no one to care for them.'[5]

The crisis of the mid-fourteenth century led to popular revolt, first in France, with the Jacquerie rising in 1358. In England, peasants seem to have been quick to realise the potential of the changed economic circumstances and the sudden shortage of labour brought on by the Black Death. The men of Rudheath in Cheshire threatened to quit the manor unless their rent was rebated by a third. Aghast, Knighton recorded the rapid escalation in wage demands that his own house faced: 'In the . . . autumn [of 1350] no one could get a reaper for less than 8d with food, a mower for less than 12d with food.'[6]

England's landholders responded by attempting to turn the clock back to before 1348, via the device of a medieval wages policy enshrined in the Statute of Labourers. Occasioned, it said, by the 'malice of servants, which were idle and not willing to serve after the pestilence', the Statute required labourers to accept pay at pre-Black

Death levels or suffer imprisonment. It also attempted to restrict their movement, demanding they remain in town and ordering an end to per diem pay, insisting that they serve 'a whole year . . . not by the day'.[7] The Statute of Labourers is often presented as a law honoured more in the breach than in the letter, a legal instrument that simply could not counter the changed demographic reality of late fourteenth-century England. However, the Crown's determination to enforce the law should not be doubted. In the 1350s, 671 justices were employed to see it put into effect. Responsibility for its implementation quickly became subsumed into local power structures, handled by local justices of the peace, who were invariably the leading landholders in the county. This presented an opportunity for rank exploitation of the law by the landed classes. Lionel Bradenham, the largest landholder in the Essex village of Langenhoe, extorted unjust fines from his tenants with the assistance of an armed gang until the town of Colchester successfully petitioned for his dismissal as Justice of the Peace in 1362.

The Statute was not the only means by which the ruling classes in England attempted to weaken the leverage of the peasants. Higher wages posed a threat not just to the pockets of landowners, but also to their social prestige and security. So-called sumptuary laws were passed that attempted to regulate the dress of the lower orders, for fear that a better-off yeomanry and peasantry would attempt to ape the appearance of their superiors, leading to the blurring of the relatively rigid lines of social demarcation. A statute of Edward III's reign dictated the clothing appropriate for each class of society – yeomen and craftsmen were not to wear any clothes worth more than 'forty shillings for the whole cloth' and were forbidden to wear furs or precious jewels – and attempted to regulate the diet of the lower orders. Servants were not to eat meat or fish more than once a day, and the rest of their meals were to consist of milk, cheese, butter and bread.[8] The eating of vast amounts of stolen meat during popular rebellions was probably as much a symbolic defiance of societal constraints as a way of feeding empty rebel bellies.[9]

Aside from regulating dress and diet, the landholding classes in medieval England strove to control every aspect of the natural environment. Enclosures hemmed off common land. Later, fen drainage schemes would dry out the reedbeds that had provided fishing, fuel (in the form of peat) and building materials for the poor. The creation of private ponds and lakes, well stocked with fish, reflected the nobility's desire to enclose water as well as earth. Harsh gaming laws guarded against the threat to noble estates posed by poaching. The poor's lack of any other access to meat or fish meant, nonetheless, that the theft of game continued, and occasionally on an impressive scale. In 1356, in just one night, the Earl of Arundel lost more than a hundred swans from his ponds at Arundel Castle.[10] As we shall see, during popular rebellions, the mass slaughter of game animals was sometimes employed as a symbolic warning to the upper classes.

After 1348, the possibilities for physical as well social mobility were also severely curtailed by new laws. Aside from the provisions already enacted through the Statute of Labourers, an act of 1360 instituted further punishments for labourers who left their service to go to another town or county. 'Masterless men' – labourers who roamed the country looking for work, unbound to any particular lord – were targeted the following year. These men were seen as a particular threat, living, as they did, outside of the control of the manorial system and beyond the accepted norms of patriarchal society, which extended in theory from the macrocosm of the nation to the microcosm of the family. The 1361 Justices of the Peace Act gave JPs the power

to inquire of all those that have been pillors and robbers in the parts beyond the sea, and be now come again, and go wandering, and will not labor as they were wont in times past: and to take and arrest all those that they may find by indictment, or by suspicion, and to put them in prison; and to take of all them that be not of good fame, where they shall be found, sufficient surety and mainprise of their good behavior towards the king and his people, and the other duly to punish.[11]

Though these laws had a powerful cumulative effect in fostering discontent, they did not themselves provoke mass revolt. The final trigger to England's first major popular rebellion was Edward III's costly war with France, which necessitated new financial levies. The first of three 'Poll Taxes' was levied in 1377. Although initially successful, the Poll Tax soon became a much hated and evaded financial instrument. Opposition culminated with the third tax of 1380, which differed from both its predecessors in the massive increase in the amount to be collected, £160,000, and in the rate, 12d on every man and woman over fifteen, which was triple that imposed in 1377. The move did not meet with the unanimous approval of those at the political centre. One key dissenter from the policy at court, Thomas Brantingham, Bishop of Exeter, resigned the treasurership of England. In 1326 his predecessor in both offices, Walter Stapledon, had been lynched by a London mob that held him responsible for the financial policies of Edward II. Perhaps Brantingham did not wish to see history repeat itself.

Initially, the public responded with evasion, not resistance. There are forewarnings here of what would happen the next time a British government attempted to impose a Poll Tax. To avoid paying Thatcher's tax, massive numbers disappeared from the electoral roll – 130,000 in London alone between 1989 and 1990. Similarly, in 1380, more than a third of those who had been registered for the tax in 1377 seemed to have disappeared from the rolls by 1380, with Essex seeing a massive decline of 36 per cent.* Aware of the problem, new commissioners were sent out on 16 March 1381 to track down the missing taxpayers. The two key figures behind this drive were the Chancellor, Archbishop Sudbury, and

---

* The concealment was largely achieved by failing to register unmarried women and widows within households.

the new Treasurer, Sir Robert Hales, both of whom would become particular objects of the rebels' fury.[12]

Grievances produced by the burden of taxation dovetailed with a period of political weakness at the top, caused by the death of Edward III in 1377. The King's heir, Edward the Black Prince, had died in France the previous year, leaving the throne in the hands of a child-monarch, Richard II, Edward III's grandson. The shadow of war and the dynastic uncertainty provoked by the King's death led to fears – especially following the military humiliations of 1377–80 – of Franco-Castilian raids, or even a full-scale invasion. The Crown was clearly concerned about the circulation of these rumours, as well as hostile rhymes and slanders concerning the architects of the Poll Tax. In 1379, Parliament passed a statute 'For punishment of devisers of false news and reporters of horrible and false lies concerning prelates, dukes, earls, barons, and other nobles and great men of the realm, whereof great peril and mischief might come to all the realm and quick subversion and destruction of the said realm if due remedy be not provided'.

Revolt began in earnest in Brentwood, Essex, on 30 May with the arrival of a royal commission to assess evasion of the third Poll Tax, led by John Bampton, MP and JP for the county. The towns of Fobbing, Corringham and Stanford-le-Hope refused to cooperate further with the effort to collect the tax. Serjeants-at-arms attempted to arrest the representatives from the resisting settlements, but were driven out of Brentwood. Fearing for his life, Bampton fled to London. The success of the townspeople of Fobbing, Corringham and Stanford in sending the royal commission packing quickly led to a larger rising in Essex, with one chronicle stating that fifty thousand men had risen by 2 June. However, the numbers of rebels who marched on London, according to the research of historian Andrew Prescott, were much smaller than those given by contemporary chronicles – perhaps a few thousand. Nevertheless, their numbers were swelled considerably by Londoners themselves.

Thomas Walsingham described the initial resistance as the work of 'the rustics, whom we call "nativi" or "bondsmen", together with other country-dwellers living in Essex [who] sought to better themselves by force and hoped to subject all things to their own stupidity'.[13] But John Geoffrey, indicted later as a leading agitator of the Essex rebels, held the title of bailiff and was a literate local administrator. Overall, of 954 rebels whose names survive, the occupations of 283 were recorded. Of these, only five were unfree tenants. Most striking was the preponderance of Essex men who had served in the offices of village government, people like John Geoffrey. The rebels included fifteen tax collectors, the same number of village constables, and three bailiffs, illustrating the way in which the Statute of Labourers had eroded the power of village elites, hitherto trusted to regulate much of the daily life in their communities.[14]

According to Walsingham, news of the Essex rebels' deeds

passed rapidly through the counties of Sussex, Hertford, Cambridge, Suffolk and Norfolk; and all the people expected great happenings. They wished to have everything themselves and would pursue their enterprise (however audaciously) wherever it should lead – many hoping for a better future but others fearing that all would end to the ruin of the kingdom.[15]

Walsingham presented the rising as an elemental force, like a fire coursing through a field of stubble, the mass of the people naively caught up in its wake, following its path more in hope than in expectation. However, if the older claims of G. M. Trevelyan that Wat Tyler, John Ball and Jack Straw headed up a mass peasant organisation called 'the Great Society' are most likely an error created by a mistranslation – 'Great Society' is less plausible than the more literal translation of 'big gang' – it is clear that the speed and breadth of the rising were the result of considerable organisation. This is suggested not only by the number of counties in which risings took place, but also by the rebellion's timing. We can find many references to peasant risings beyond East Anglia and the Home Counties. An attack was reported on Peterborough Abbey on 17 June, an assault was reputedly made by tenants on the priory at Dunstable, Bedfordshire; and there were village disturbances in Buckinghamshire and rumours of trouble in Leicestershire. The prior of Worcester Cathedral reported rebellion on his estates in the first week of July; news of disturbances came from Warwickshire around the same time, while on Wirral, the tenants of the Abbot of St Werburgh in Chester were in revolt against their lord as late as 29 July.[16]

The risings began at the time of the major church feasts of Whitsun, Trinity and Corpus Christi. These were not only religious festivals, but occasions for summer games, processions and revels. The feasts also coincided with courts of leet (manorial courts) and 'law days' in the hundreds (larger administrative units), and with royal justices' visitations of the counties to hold assizes. The rebels had chosen a moment representing the confluence of religion, festivity and legal authority. The lawful congregation of people for these events (including the legitimate carrying of arms by peasants for the biannual 'view of arms') was not just a good cover for seditious meetings; it also gave the rebels the opportunity to appropriate the existing apparatus for mass organisation and rallying. This included the use of the 'hue and cry' and the ringing of church bells to summon support, thus recalling the words of the leading rebel John Ball in letters attributed to him by the chroniclers Knighton and Walsingham.

> John Ball greeteth you all
> And doth to understand he hath rung your bell,
> Now with might and right, will and skill,
> God speed every dell.[17]

In Kent, the spark to rebellion was the disputed status of one Robert Belling, then living in Gravesend. Belling was claimed as a serf by Sir Simon Burley, who sent two serjeants-at-arms to secure his arrest sometime before 5 June. The bailiffs of Gravesend refused to surrender Belling, but hoped to negotiate some form of cash redemption that would enable him to buy out Burley's claims. However, Sir Simon's demand for at least £300 in silver was far beyond Belling's means: he was arrested and imprisoned in Rochester Castle. A large group of Kentishmen gathered on 5 June at Dartford. They then marched on Maidstone, where it was said they murdered a prosperous townsman, before proceeding to Rochester, which they reached the next day. The constable of the castle, Sir John Newton, wisely surrendered Belling to the rebels. Newton himself then joined their ranks. (According to the chronicler Froissart, this was the condition for his life being spared.)

It is here, at the fall of Rochester Castle, that Wat Tyler's name is first mentioned. As with most of our medieval and early modern rebel captains, we know precious little for certain about him. It is not even clear from where he originated. The late fourteenth-century Anonimalle Chronicle is emphatic in claiming that his hometown was Maidstone, while jurors who sat on later inquisitions stated that he came from Colchester in Essex. His most recent biographer accepts Froissart's judgement that Tyler was from Maidstone, 'a tiler of houses, an ungracious patron'.[18] Whatever his origins, there is evidence that he was also identified as the key leader by rebels outside of London and Kent. William Grindecobbe, rebel leader in St Albans, requested that Tyler send a force of twenty thousand men to kill the Abbot and monks in return for the unquestioned leadership of the town.

By early June, Tyler was certainly the leading figure among the Kentish rebels. They marched on Canterbury, reaching the cathedral on 10 June during the celebration of high mass, and demanded that the monks elect one of their number to replace Simon Sudbury, 'for he who is now the Archbishop is a traitor who will be beheaded for his iniquity'. Although the Mayor and burgesses of Canterbury wisely declared their loyalty to 'King

Richard and the loyal commons of England', 'traitors' were nonetheless identified among the Canterbury townsmen and were summarily executed by the rebels. But the violence meted out was not indiscriminate. The rebels targeted those who had close connections to the court and the royal council: Thomas Haseldene, who was controller of the household of John of Gaunt, the King's uncle; and Thomas Orgrave, Under-Treasurer of England. They also seemed to know where the tax records were stored. Tyler forced William Septvans, Sheriff of Kent and a leading player in the Poll Tax enforcement commission of May 1381, to hand over his court rolls at the manor of Milton. They were then burnt. Other members of the gentry had their homes ransacked. Sir Nicholas Heryng lost 2 oxen, 27 sheep and 482 wool hides, together with goods and chattels worth £24, from his estates on Sheppey.

It was probably around 11 June that Tyler's men freed John Ball from the royal prison at Maidstone. We know more about Ball than about any of the other rebel leaders as a result of his clerical career, which saw him clash repeatedly with the authorities from the mid-1360s onwards. Ball himself suggested that he had been a chantry priest at York before moving to Colchester. His preaching had attracted royal displeasure long before the Peasants' Revolt. A warrant issued by Edward III in February 1364 withdrew the King's protection from him as a result of reports that he was wandering from place to place, preaching doctrine contrary to that of the established Church. Six months later, the then Bishop Sudbury ordered Ball's arrest as an obdurate excommunicate. In 1366, Ball was ordered to appear before the Archbishop for re-offending; in April 1381, he was excommunicated again and imprisoned for radical preaching.[19]

The late fourteenth century saw the emergence of a persistent English heretical tradition, a branch of medieval Christianity that stressed a return to a simpler faith purged of its worldly trappings. Lollardy, as this heresy was called by its opponents – the name probably originated from the medieval Dutch *lollaerd*, meaning mumbler or mutterer – centred on the ultimate authority of the Scripture in the vernacular, as opposed to Latin. Lollards also denied the priestly sacramental powers – anyone could baptise or hear confession – attacked the veneration of images, denied the efficacy of pilgrimages to the relics of saints, and disputed the carnal presence of Christ's body in the Sacrament. There was an implicit egalitarianism to elements of Lollardy: the 'democratisation' of faith by making the Bible accessible in English; the diminution of the role of the priest as an intermediary between God and man; and, most powerfully, the attack on luxury and wealth.[20]

Thomas Walsingham, the chronicler, suggested that Ball was influenced by the heretical ideas of John Wycliffe. This is unlikely. At this point the Lollard movement remained centred on Wycliffe's Oxford, but Wycliffe himself was no social radical. He viewed the possibility that his theological arguments might be used to legitimise rebellion with the same repugnance that Martin Luther would later exhibit after the German Peasants' War of 1525. Of course, Wycliffe, like Luther, could never control the interpretation of his ideas by others, especially at a popular level. But in contrast with later English revolts, like that led by Jack Cade in 1450, there is no evidence that Lollard ideas directly influenced the rebels of 1381.

Nonetheless, if the Peasants' Revolt had an ideologue, it was John Ball. We have only snippets of Ball's thought, culled from reports of sermons and letters, but what remains indicates a preacher who harnessed orthodox phraseology and eschatology to revolutionary ends. Ball's most famous utterance, 'When Adam delved and Eve span, who was then the gentleman?', was a religious commonplace in the fourteenth century. However, according to Froissart, Ball turned this conventional statement on Christian humility into a radical call for social equality: 'He tried to prove . . . that from the beginning all men were created equal by nature and that servitude had been introduced by the unjust and evil oppression of men against the will of God.'[21] Other rhymes and sayings, attributed to Ball by Walsingham, see him hinting elusively at an apocalyptic, divinely ordained come-uppance for the greedy, covetous and lecherous: for instance, 'Now pride is prized and covetousness thought wise, and lechery had no shame, and gluttony no blame. Envy reigns with treason, and sloth is high in season. God make the reckoning, for now is the time. Amen.'[22]

Ball's use of an alias, 'John Trewman', and letters of his addressed to 'Jack Carter' and other rebel captains remind us of some of the difficulties in properly identifying the leaders of popular rebellion. Both in the fourteenth century and later (with 'Captain Swing' and 'Ned Lud'), rebels used pseudonyms to cover their real identities in the event that their revolt failed. This raises problems when deciding whether a pseudonym was one specific individual's or whether it became part of a general nomenclature behind which a variety of people could hide. This is the case with 'Jack Straw'. Jack or John Straw first appears in Walsingham's narrative, administering oaths to the rebels. He is then superseded in the narrative by Tyler, only to reappear again after Tyler's death. His precise identity is further clouded by the chronicler Henry Knighton's description of the meeting between Richard II and the rebels at Smithfield on 15 June 1381: the King 'was approached by their leader, Wat Tyler, who had now changed his name to Jack Straw'. Knighton's comment, and the way in which Straw appears only episodically in Walsingham's account, led some historians to claim that they were one and the same person. Though Walsingham and Froissart were clear that Straw and Tyler were separate individuals, we have little other evidence about Straw.

By 12 June the Essex rebels had reached Dartford, though their numbers were probably far fewer than the sixty thousand given by some chronicles. On their way, they overtook the King's mother – 'Princess Joan' – who had broken off her pilgrimage to the shrines of Kent after receiving news of the insurrection and was hurrying back to London. The rebels indulged in some ribald humour at the royal party's expense, but otherwise left them unharmed. That same day, a deputation of London aldermen together with Bishop Brinton of Rochester met the Kentish rebels, now encamped at Blackheath, and urged them to disperse, but without success. Tyler's men continued towards the capital.

The royal messengers' diplomatic failure was now clear and it was decided that the young King Richard had to make a personal appearance to prevent the rebels from advancing any further into London. He travelled to Greenwich, the chosen location, by barge – a safety precaution that allowed him to leave the Tower from a water gate. As a further security measure, rather than venturing on to the riverbank the King remained on the barge. At this meeting, the rebels handed over a list of figures to be executed as traitors. The King, unsurprisingly, refused to surrender them. In response, the rebels called for a personal interview with him. In an obvious attempt to stall until a suitable force could be raised to suppress them, Richard and his ministers asked for a postponement until 17 June, when another meeting would take place at Windsor Castle.

The Kentish rebels did not heed Richard's demand for a halt to their advance. By the morning of Thursday 13 June they had reached Southwark, where they came face to face with buildings closely identified with John of Gaunt and Archbishop Sudbury, chief architects of the hated Poll Tax. What followed, described in lengthy detail by several of the chroniclers, was a carnivalesque orgy of violence and devastation, meted out against both property and persons. Though the loss of life inflicted by the rebels was severe, and the destruction of goods and houses so serious that some buildings were completely demolished, this was not indiscriminate carnage. The individuals who suffered the terrible violence of the rebel host were identified either with those 'traitors' denounced in front of the King a day earlier or with 'outsider' groups who were seen to threaten the moral fabric of society and

the prosperity of native-born inhabitants. The rebels also displayed
their own sense of justice, breaking into the Marshalsea Prison and
releasing 'all the men held there for debt or felonies, and then they
knocked down a handsome place of John [Richard] Imworth,
lately marshal of the Marshalsea, and keeper of the prisoners there,
and all the buildings of the jurors and quest mongers around the
Marshalsea were torn down that night'. As we shall see, attacks on
lawyers were a feature of many popular revolts. They were seen as
the accessories of rapacious lords, enforcing laws heavily skewed
in favour of the wealthy.

The actions of the rebels in Southwark also show that the aim
of their violence was to annihilate the property of 'traitors', not to
appropriate it. Although looting did take place, their behaviour,
even as reported by hostile commentators, demonstrates both that
the violence was highly organised and that it symbolised the transformation of society that they sought to effect. The Anonimalle
Chronicle reported that at one manor the rebels

> set fire to most of its abandoned contents, including books,
> clothes, linen: stove in wine barrels and drained them, pouring
> what wine was left on to the floor; banged together and smashed
> all the kitchenware; and all the while accompanied this behaviour,
> as if in self-congratulation of some praise-worthy feat, with shouts
> of 'A revel! A revel!'[23]

As the Kentish men were reducing parts of Southwark to rubble
and ashes, the Essex rebels, encamped at Smithfield, launched a
ferocious attack on the buildings owned by the Knights of St John,
whose prior was another leading figure in the imposition of the
Poll Tax: Sir Robert Hales, Treasurer of England. The Westminster
Chronicle recorded that at the priory the rebels killed 'everybody
who offered opposition, burned down the entire structure, going
on to consign to destruction in the ravening flames the manor of
Highbury'.[24] The Essex men then launched an assault on the

Temple, a target both because it symbolised the power of the legal establishment and because its buildings were owned by the Order of St John. They took it apart with methodical precision: locked chests of documents were broken open in the Temple Church; rolls and books of the law students were collected from their individual cupboards and burnt in Fleet Street; even the roof tiles were stripped off.

Most commented-upon was the assault on the Savoy, the London residence of the Duke of Lancaster, which had come into John of Gaunt's possession in 1360. Walsingham described the palace as it was before the Great Revolt as finer than any other in the kingdom. Gaunt took great pride in it, with its orchard and fishponds that extended from the rear of the building down to the banks of the Thames. He had the good luck to be out of London when the rebels arrived at his residence: they would almost certainly have killed him. But he was less fortunate in that during his absence the Savoy was being used as a store for all his spare furniture and fixtures. As Henry Knighton recorded, these possessions were considerable: 'no prince in Christendom had a finer wardrobe and scarcely any could even match it. For . . . there were such quantities of vessels and silver plate, without counting the parcel-gilt and solid gold, that five carts would hardly suffice to carry them.'

Fine as these objects were, they were almost all obliterated in June 1381. Breaking into the Savoy, the rebels

came into the palace and, coming into the wardrobe, took all the torches that they could find and set alight all the very valuable cloths and coverlets and beds, and all the valuable headboards, of which one, emblazoned with heraldic shields, was said to be worth a thousand marks, and all the napery and other goods that they could find, they carried them to the hall and torched them.

As it had been at the Temple, the violence was systematic. Rather than risk their being recovered and returned to their rightful owner, gold and silver vessels and other precious objects were smashed with axes before being thrown into the sewers or into the Thames itself. Knighton recorded mournfully that the rebels 'tore the golden cloths and silk hangings to pieces and crushed them underfoot; they ground up jewels and other rings inlaid with precious stones in small mortars, so they could never be used again'. Some of the violence directed at Gaunt's possessions was clearly a substitute for attacking Gaunt himself.

> In order not to pass by any opportunity of shaming the Duke completely, they seized one of his most precious vestments, which we call a 'jakke', and placed it on a lance to be used as a target for their arrows. And since they were unable to damage it sufficiently with their arrows, they took it down and tore it apart with their axes and swords.[25]

The discipline exerted over the rebels at the Savoy by their leaders was considerable. Two chroniclers state that those who were caught trying to loot any of Gaunt's possessions were killed, though two of them, John Foxgone and Roger Plomer, were later indicted for stealing from the palace. Further evidence that not all of the rebels were able to resist the lure of the Duke's possessions comes from Knighton, who claimed that thirty men were buried alive in the ducal wine cellar:

> Some of the rebels entered the wine cellar at the Savoy, and several drank so much sweet wine that they were incapable of leaving. They sang, joked and amused themselves in a tipsy fashion until the door was blocked by fire and stones. And so they died, for even if they had been sober they would have found themselves deprived of any exit. For the following seven days the trapped men were heard shouting and lamenting the enormity of their wickedness by the many people who visited the spot; but no one helped or consoled them in their trouble. And so

those drunken men who came to consume wine perished in wine – to the number (so it was later said) of thirty-two or thereabouts.[26]

It was also alleged that another group of rebels blew themselves up when they mistook barrels of gunpowder for more of the Duke's valuables and cast them on to a bonfire. The damage done to the Savoy was severe: after 1381, when John of Gaunt needed to be in London he stayed at properties rented from the Bishop of Ely and the Abbot of Westminster, using what remained of his own palace essentially as a warehouse.

The following morning, 14 June, the crowd moved on from the Savoy towards Westminster, where they burnt the house of Sir John Butterwick, Under-Sheriff of Middlesex, then broke open the gaol at Westminster and freed its inmates. The murderous inclinations of some of the rebels now became more evident. Both within and outside London, men of the law were targets for their violence. Sir John Cavendish, Chief Justice of the King's Bench, Chancellor of the University of Cambridge and a pillar of East Anglian society, was apprehended in Suffolk and beheaded; Justice Edmund Walsingham was killed in Cambridge; while at Cheapside, a law student named Richard Legett was dragged from the high altar of St Martin's Church and beheaded. The rebels turned their anger against foreign merchants and traders too, especially Flemish weavers who were resented for their success and the commercial privileges they enjoyed. On the same day that they burnt Butterwick's house, they began massacring London's Flemish inhabitants, beheading thirty-five in the street near the Church of St Martin in Vintry.

While violence and destruction raged south and east of the city, the King took refuge in the Tower, along with Archbishop Sudbury and Treasurer Hales, his two half-brothers Thomas and John Holland, his half-sister Joan Holland, Duchess of Brittany, and his cousin Henry, Earl of Derby. The perimeter defences of the Tower of London were then much greater than those that remain today, but the manpower available to the defenders in June 1381 was limited. Chroniclers claimed that it was defended by a force of several hundred, but it is more likely, given other demands on military resources at this time, that it was a skeleton garrison complemented by the few knights who were personally attending Richard. Certainly, if they had any confidence in defending the Tower, the King's entourage did not show it. Walsingham recorded that Richard's armed attendants 'appeared more like the dead than the living; for all their memory of past and glorious military deeds had been extinguished'. By the night of 13 June, the King could have looked from the turrets of the Tower to see its walls surrounded by his rebellious subjects and, in the distance, flames burning in Southwark, Fleet Street and Clerkenwell from the bonfires made from the possessions of some of his most wealthy and powerful subjects.

However furious the mayhem he witnessed, Richard's saving grace was that it was not directed at him. Those royal ministers, bishops and peers of the realm identified as traitors all had great reason to fear the rebels' reprisals, but this was where accountability stopped. The rebellion was not regicidal in its intent. Nonetheless, Richard's decision to leave the safety of the Tower on the morning of 14 June represented a considerable risk, given what was happening elsewhere. But it was to be the act that saved his government and signalled the beginning of the end of the revolt in London.

Richard met the rebels at Mile End, where they demanded the surrender of 'traitors' for punishment, a general amnesty for their own actions, and a wholesale emancipation from all forms of serfdom and labour service. The King appeared as conciliatory as it was possible for him to be, and charters were endorsed with the Great Seal of England, proclaiming the perpetual freedom from serfdom of the people of the counties represented at Mile End. These royal charters led to the disintegration of the rebel host, as men from some of the counties began to withdraw from London, feeling, mistakenly, that their grievances had been well redressed and their new freedoms guaranteed under the royal seal. This was the case with the bulk of the men from Essex and Hertfordshire. The Kentishmen, however, remained, which may explain the prominence of Wat Tyler in later accounts – a leader who emerged by default rather than one chosen by general acclamation.

Though we are uncertain of the precise chronology, it seems that some of the rebels broke into the Tower shortly after the meeting at Mile End. The fullest account comes from Thomas Walsingham, who was safely ensconced in the scriptorium of St Albans when he wrote in his chronicle that those 'who had formerly belonged to the most lowly condition of serf, went in and out [of the Tower] like lords; and swineherds set themselves above soldiers although not knights but rustics'.[27] The rebels, Walsingham continued, entered 'the chamber of the King and of his mother with their filthy sticks; and, undeterred by any of the soldiers, [began] to stroke and lay their uncouth and sordid hands on the beards of several most noble knights . . . and sat on the King's bed while joking, and several asked the King's mother to kiss them'.[28] As they entered, Archbishop Sudbury attempted to escape from the Tower through a water gate, only to be foiled by the vigilance of a woman who noticed him fleeing. Captured, he was beheaded, but only, according to Walsingham, after eight blows from the executioner's axe:

> He was first struck severely but not fatally in the neck. He put his hand to the wound and said: 'Ah! Ah! This is the hand of God.' As he did not move his hand . . . the second blow cut off the top of his fingers as well as severing part of his arteries. But the archbishop still did not die, and only on the eighth blow, wretchedly wounded in the neck and on the head, did he complete . . . his martyrdom.[29]

Sir Robert Hales, John Legge, the serjeant-at-law who had attempted to indict the Canterbury rebels, the ducal surgeon Fr William Appleton, and Richard Somenour of Stepney, a tax collector from Middlesex, were also dispatched by beheading at the same spot as Sudbury on Tower Hill. In one more imitation of the ordinary processes of medieval justice, the severed heads of the 'traitors' were affixed to poles and displayed atop London Bridge. Archbishop Sudbury's took pride of place, decorated by the rebels with a scarlet cap nailed through the prelate's skull. (Although Sudbury's torso was eventually buried with an inscription on his tomb celebrating his 'martydom', his head was not reunited with his body but taken back to Sudbury, Suffolk, where it remains to this day, mummified in the crypt of the Church of St Gregory.*)

The executions of royal servants on Tower Hill did not halt the continuing negotiations between the King and his rebellious subjects. A second meeting between Richard and the rebels took place at Smithfield on the morning of Saturday 15 June. Richard was clearly worried that the meeting might not be a peaceful one or foresaw that it would end in bloodshed. At three o'clock the previous afternoon he had prepared for his parley by praying at Westminster Abbey, at the shrine of his patron saint, Edward; while there, he was reported to have confessed his sins. When the rebels arrived at the abbey they found Richard Imworth, the notorious keeper of the Marshalsea Prison, 'a tormentor without pity'. Desperately, Imworth wrapped his arms around the pillars of the Confessor's shrine: the rebels prised him away, then sent him to the executioner's block at Cheapside.

The demands issued by the rebels on 15 June are more obscure in their meaning than those presented the day before. According to Henry Knighton's account, they called for the 'law of Winchester' to be upheld. This was possibly a reference to the 1285

---

* The Archbishop had directed the construction of this church and founded a college of canons there in 1365.

statute that provided common arms for the defence of communities and gave towns and villages responsibility for policing and for apprehending criminals. Interpreted in the broadest sense, this was a call for local self-government and regional autonomy. It is also possible that the reference to the 'law of Winchester' revealed a belief among the rebels in a repository of Anglo-Saxon laws that protected popular rights and freedoms.[30]

The new demands were certainly more radical than those that had been presented on the 14th. They called for the abolition of lordship and the division of property between all men, including the wholesale disendowment of the Church's wealth, later to become a common Lollard demand. Ecclesiastical estates, like those of the lords, were to be held in common. The Church hierarchy was to be abolished, with only one bishop and one 'prelate' to remain. Again, though, this radical levelling stopped at the person and dignity of the King, whose lordship, prerogative and estates were to remain untouched. As rebellions in other counties developed, it is possible that what was being envisaged here was a federation of 'county-kingdoms', each under the leadership of a rebel 'captain', with Kent already reserved for Wat Tyler. Taken together, the demands demonstrate the broad understanding of freedom employed by the rebels of 1381.

At Smithfield, the King and his men arrayed themselves on the east side by St Bartholomew's Priory, while Tyler's men kept to the west. What followed remains the most famous incident of the Peasants' Revolt. Caroline Barron has aptly likened the scene of Tyler's death to the assassination of President Kennedy in the sense that no effective reconstruction can be created because there are so many conflicting accounts. With the exception of Froissart, who claimed that Tyler had a plan to seize the King and, upon a secret gesture to his rebel followers, massacre the royal attendants, all of the medieval chroniclers give Richard II the initiative for seeking a face-to-face encounter. The Anonimalle Chronicle stated that Tyler was summoned by the Mayor in the name of 'Wat Tyler of

Maidstone'. He came to the King with a proud bearing, it continued, mounted on a little horse in full view of the commons, and dismounted carrying a dagger in his hand, which he had taken from another man; then he took the King by the hand and, on half-bended knee, shook him firmly and for a long time by the arm, saying to him, 'Brother, be of good comfort and joyful, for in the next fortnight you will have forty thousand more of the commons than you have at the moment, and we shall be good companions.'

The King seemed confused by Tyler's behaviour: 'Why will you not go back to your own country [county]?' he asked. Tyler responded angrily that neither he nor his companions would depart until they had their charter as they wanted it. He warned the lords of the kingdom that they would regret it if they did not concede to the rebels what they had demanded, namely, that there should be no law 'but the law of Winchester'. To this, Richard reportedly gave the ambiguous answer that Tyler 'could have all that he [Richard] could grant fairly'.

All the chroniclers agreed that the subsequent descent into violence was a result of Tyler's conduct. The rebel leader's behaviour was portrayed as uncouth and provocative: 'The said Wat Tyler demanded a jug of water for rinsing out his mouth because of the great heat that he felt, and then he proceeded to rinse out his mouth in a gross and disgusting way in front of the King and then he demanded a jug of ale, which he downed in a great mouthful.' In Knighton's account, Tyler's behaviour was not only disgusting but deeply threatening: 'He stood close the King, speaking for the others, and carrying an unsheathed knife, of the kind people called a dagger, which he tossed from hand to hand as a child might play with it, and looked as though he might suddenly seize the opportunity to stab the King if he should refuse their requests.'[31]

Having received the King's broad if ambiguous promise to comply with his demands, Tyler was about to ride back to his men when one of the royal valets reportedly insulted him, calling him 'the single greatest thief and robber in all of Kent'. Tyler ordered the valet to approach him, but he refused. Tyler then demanded one of his attendants behead the valet. At this point Mayor Walworth reputedly intervened to reason with Tyler, but instead the rebel leader rushed towards the King and Walworth. Armed attendants came to Richard's side to protect him, while either the King or Walworth ordered them to arrest Tyler, causing him to strike out at the Mayor with his dagger. The chronicles differ as to what followed. Some claim Tyler missed Walworth; others that he struck him, but that the Mayor was saved by wearing armour concealed under his clothes. Walworth then retaliated, striking Tyler, though the mortal blows were landed not by the Mayor but by a royal esquire, Ralph Standish, who ran Tyler through repeatedly with his sword. Tyler nonetheless struggled back on to his horse and managed to ride a few paces back to his own supporters before collapsing.

The rebels then took him to St Bartholomew's Hospital, but Tyler was quickly seized by Walworth's men, who dragged him back to Smithfield, where he was beheaded. By this point, given the severity of his earlier injuries, he may well already have been dead. His severed head was put on a pole and paraded in front of the remaining rebels. The scene at Smithfield could have descended into a deeper bloodbath, but Richard succeeded in convincing most of the other rebels to meet him at Clerkenwell Fields to the north, thus drawing them away from the City and allowing Walworth's men and other loyalists the opportunity to regain control of it.

Many narratives of the Peasants' Revolt found in school textbooks end at this point, but this was not a rebellion that simply dissolved after its most famous leader was beheaded. Indeed, elsewhere in the country, rebellions had not yet reached their peak by the time that Tyler had been killed. Many of these county risings were only tenuously connected to the immediate trigger of revolt in Essex and Kent, the Poll Tax of 1381. The revolt at St Albans in Hertfordshire was the result of a long-standing conflict between the Abbey and the townspeople, who wished to throw off their status as villeins of the Abbot's manor. The dispute was revived in 1381, late on Corpus Christi Day, as news of the revolt in London reached the town. By the next morning, the St Albans men had resolved to march on the City in order to secure their liberty as burgesses. Their demands were similar to those issued by the men of Kent, though they also claimed the 'right to pasture cattle, to hunt and to fish, and also to erect hand-mills for the grinding of their own corn'. The St Albans men also apparently sought sanction for their actions from Wat Tyler – an indication of his status among rebels outside his native Kent.

As in London, there were ritualistic elements to the violence in St Albans. One of the rebels' demands had been the right to 'free warren', that is, to take rabbits that had roamed on to their land. After Richard II had conceded their charter, they marked their new liberty by attaching a live rabbit to the pillory in St Albans town, a gesture that also repudiated the Abbot's judicial authority. As in London, the gaol was broken open and the occupants released on condition that they swore to be loyal to the town and community. There are echoes, too, of the demands of 15 June, with their obscure reference to the 'law of Winchester' in the St Albans rebels' claims based on charters issued by Offa, founder of the Abbey, once again demonstrating a belief in a body of English law that protected popular rights and freedoms.

At some point on 16/17 June, Richard's order countermanding his earlier charter concessions reached St Albans. This counter-charter protected the Abbey and its buildings and threatened dire punishment to any who challenged it. For the moment, however, this act of retrenchment was a dead letter. Some time on the 16th, Abbot de la Mare buckled to popular pressure and recognised St Albans as a borough and the townsmen as burgesses. On the 17th, this was followed by the Abbot's confirmation of the grant of general manumission made by Richard II to the men of Hertfordshire. The townsmen also extorted a bond of £1000 to keep faith with the agreement, and a quitclaim of all rights the Abbot had previously claimed from the townsmen. To commemorate their victory over the Abbey, the townspeople walked its newly defined boundaries, celebrating with toasts of beer at points along the way. News of the St Albans rebels' success spread to the surrounding areas of Barnet, Rickmansworth, Redburn and Watford, which then pressed for their own charters, granted on 17 and 18 June. Abbot de la Mare had caved in, well aware that military aid was unlikely to reach him in time. It would not be until 29 June that a force of fifty men-at-arms plus a large body of archers reached St Albans under the command of Sir Walter Lee.

In Suffolk, further risings were led by John Wrawe, a former priest from the Sudbury area. On 12 June, he led a group of Essex men to the border with Suffolk and proclaimed that he had come to redress the grievances of all men. The next day, Wrawe's followers attacked the manor of Overhall, owned by Sir Richard Lyons, a hated financier. Wrawe's men entered Bury St Edmunds on 14 June and the next day the prior of the Abbey, John Cambridge, was captured and beheaded, his skull fixed to a pike and carried back to Bury. The prime target of the Suffolk rebels was Sir John Cavendish, a substantial landowner in East Anglia who had his principal residence in Bury. Cavendish attempted to escape but was too well known to get far, and the rebels overtook him at Lakenheath where a woman named Katherine Gamen reputedly prevented him from escaping on to the river by pushing off a waiting boat. Cavendish was beheaded on the riverbank at the hands of one Matthew Miller.

The Suffolk rebels displayed a ghoulish sense of humour, first making the head of Cavendish appear to confess its sins to Prior John Cambridge, then making the two exchange kisses. Cavendish and Cambridge were joined on the pillory by the head of John

Lakenheath, a monk who had been responsible for managing the Abbey's lordship over the town and its outlying tenants. Like the rebels of St Albans, their Bury confreres believed in ancient, pre-Conquest charters, this time those of Cnut, which guaranteed their civic freedoms. Thomas Walsingham claimed that, as with Archbishop Sudbury, it took eight blows of the executioner's axe to decapitate Lakenheath.[32] At Ipswich there were further assaults, here led by John Battisford, a parson, and Thomas Sampson, a tenant farmer, which saw the houses of the Archdeacon of Suffolk and John Cobat, a Poll Tax collector, attacked and looted. It has been suggested that the severity of rebel actions in Suffolk was a result of greater social tensions than elsewhere, as increasingly prosperous tenants tried to escape their villein status. Overall, the Suffolk risings appear to have been the most violent of all those outside of London, and also involved the highest-status individuals: the rebels here included two knights, Roger Bacon and Thomas Cornerd.

Higher-status individuals can be found joining local risings in other parts of East Anglia too. In Cambridgeshire, leading citizens as well as poorer townsfolk joined in an assault on the university's jurisdiction over the town. The rising in Norfolk overall was probably deliberately instigated by Wrawe's men in a bid to spread the Suffolk insurrection to the neighbouring counties, but the rising in north Norfolk occurred independently of any action elsewhere. Led by Geoffrey Litster, a dyer from Felmingham, the north Norfolk rebels met on Mousehold Heath just outside Norwich on 16 June in order to prepare for a march on the city. Once inside, they proceeded to attack individuals and buildings associated with government and the law. Again, the rebels co-opted to their own cause the traditional sites for the execution of justice. The JP Reginald Eccles was captured and butchered with knives at the town pillory. Litster established himself as 'king of the Commons', reputedly presiding over his own court at Thorpe Market and banqueting in the hall of Norwich Castle.

According to Walsingham, Litster forced local nobles to wait upon him: 'As lord Stephen de Hales was an honourable knight, Littestere chose him to cut up and taste his food before he ate it himself; and he gave the rest of the knights other duties.'[33]

The Norfolk rising was not extinguished by royal commission but through the personal efforts of Henry Despenser, the 'warrior' Bishop of Norwich. Thomas Walsingham, who as Prior of Wymondham had direct experience of Despenser's administration, was underwhelmed by his diocesan, describing the man as immature, unlearned and arrogant. At times of crisis, however, Despenser's bullish personality and his evident courage and loyalty to the monarchy outweighed his deficiencies as a bishop. Again according to Walsingham, Despenser initially had with him only eight men-at-arms and a few archers. However, like many late medieval English bishops, he was more aristocratic hardman than mild-mannered man of the cloth. At Icklingham he met Sir William Morley and Sir John Brewes who, along with some of the rebels, had been dispatched by Litster to take his messages to the King. Despenser had their rebel escorts decapitated and displayed their heads at Newmarket. From 25 to 26 June, Despenser's retinue, strengthened further by local loyalists, engaged with Litster's men at North Walsham. The rebels had blocked the road to that town by excavating a ditch and constructing barricades from doors, gates and fences. But these barriers were no match for a marauding prelate, as Walsingham breathlessly reported:

> Without delay the warrior bishop, ready to fight in open battle and indignant at the audacity of the ruffians, ordered his trumpeters and buglers to sound. He himself seized a lance in his right hand, sharply spurred his horse and threw himself on the rebels with such force and courage that he reached the ditch like a whirlwind and more quickly than the arrows of his men. There was no work for the archers as a hand-to-hand battle began straight away.

The warlike priest, like a wild boar gnashing its teeth, spared neither himself nor his enemies. He chose to fight where the danger
was greatest, stabbing one man, knocking down another and
wounding a third. Nor did he cease his violent struggles until the
whole crowd which fell on him when he reached the ditch were
ready to fly.[34]

The ferocity of Despenser's charge broke the rebel lines. Shortly
afterwards, Litster was captured and summarily sentenced to be
hanged, drawn and quartered. Walsingham reported that the
Bishop, having heard Litster's confession and given him absolution
for his sins, accompanied him to the gallows, 'thereby performing
despite his victory a work of mercy and piety. He held up the
rebel's head to prevent it knocking on the ground while he was
being dragged to the place of his hanging.'[35]

By mid-June, the Crown itself was ready to take punitive action
against the remaining rebels. On the 17th, an expedition of twelve
horsemen and twenty-five archers was sent from London to Kent
under the leadership of the King's half-brother Thomas Holland,
Earl of Kent, and Sir Thomas Trivet. On 20 June, the Earl of
Suffolk together with five hundred men-at-arms entered Suffolk to
suppress the risings there. On the 28th, Essex rebels making a last
stand at Billericay were massacred by the Duke of Buckingham's
men. By the end of the month, Richard's regime felt confident
enough to renege publicly on the promises that it had given the
rebels at Mile End. On the 30th, the Crown issued orders com-
manding villeins to submit to those same conditions that they had
fought so hard to throw off during the rising. The King himself
took a keen personal interest in the prosecution of former rebels,
setting out on 1 July from London to Chelmsford, where he stayed
for seven days, overseeing the royal commission. It inflicted thirty-
one capital sentences, twelve of whose recipients were subjected to
the additional penalty of being dragged to the gallows. It is here
that Richard reputedly said, 'Rustics you were and rustics you are

still; you will remain in bondage, not as before but incomparably harsher.'

Richard confirmed these words on 2 July, when all of the charters of manumission he had granted were formally rescinded and cancelled. On 10 July, John Wrawe, captured towards the end of June, was brought to trial before the sheriffs of London. He turned King's evidence, naming twenty-four of his accomplices. Even this didn't save him. He was sentenced to be hanged, drawn and quartered the following year. John Ball was tried at the Moot Hall, Bury St Edmunds, on 14 July, and similarly sentenced to be hanged, drawn and quartered. The execution was carried out the following day and his remains were sent to the four corners of the kingdom. The other rebels in Bury had to wait until 13 October to be sentenced. The Cornishman Sir Robert Tresilian, described even by the sympathetic chronicler as 'cunning like a serpent', had manipulated the trial juries to ensure the conviction of thirty-six rebels, sixteen of whom were dragged to the gallows and hanged.

The aftermath of the Great Revolt established a pattern for those medieval and early modern rebellions that followed. After the risings were put down by force (usually followed by immediate summary executions), royal justice imposed the severest penalties of law – hanging, drawing and quartering – upon those identified as ringleaders. Their quartered bodies were parcelled out around the realm to serve as grisly reminders of the penalties for treason. Royal propaganda would follow the judicial and military repression of revolt, in the form of hostile chronicles and sermons on the duty of obedience. The legal machinery for dealing with discontented peasantry was also tightened, as in the case of the Statute of Cambridge of 1388, which strengthened the existing Statute of Labourers and established most of the foundations for later Tudor Poor Law, including for the first time making the distinction between 'sturdy' (able-bodied) beggars capable of work and 'impotent' beggars, incapacitated by old age or illness.

As a result, historians have often claimed that the main consequences of rebellion in the medieval and early modern periods were negative, leading to a retrenchment of noble power, wealth and privilege as England's often factious upper classes briefly unified in the face of the threat from below. Yet, however much Richard II may have wished, vindictively, that in the wake of the Great Revolt his subjects would be returned to an incomparably harsher form of human bondage, this was not to be the case. Though laws such as the Statute of Cambridge again attempted to restrict the freedom of movement of workers, and a further statute of 1389 gave JPs the power to set pay rates, Richard's monarchy could not return England to the way it had been before the Black Death. As the historian Gerald Harriss has eloquently put it, 'political society had always lived in fear of social revolution, and in 1381 it peered into the abyss and took heed'.[36] Wages rose steadily, by the end of the fourteenth century reaching a historic high, and the conditions of villeinage were increasingly relaxed.

If this were not the immediate act of manumission that Tyler had demanded, it was emancipation all the same. More and more labourers were released from servile obligations and instead held their land through the payment of fixed rent and a moderate entry fine. Living conditions also improved: labourers' rations at harvest time now included as much as a pound of meat a day. Exotic items such as deep-sea fish, cod and herring found their way into the peasant diet. Life expectancy rose to an average of thirty-five by 1450: an appallingly low figure by modern standards but much better than that for industrial workers in mid-nineteenth-century British cities (Liverpool, for example.) Some yeoman families, such as the Pastons of Norfolk, did so well out of the changes of the late fourteenth century that they moved from being 'good pleyn husbondmen' permanently into the gentry class. The bitter invective of the boy-king Richard, often invoked to show the futility of popular insurrection, was, in fact, so much spitting in the wind.

It was not simply that both Richard and the rebellious peasants were wrestling, albeit from opposite directions, with insurmountable environmental, social and economic forces. The events of 1381 made England's rulers aware for the first time that the established order, and not just its personnel, might be overturned through the actions of the common people. The memory of the revolt etched itself into all aspects of life. For example, a land grant of 1382 from Mettingham Castle in Suffolk described how the lease would be affected if there were another rising of the commons. The threat from the collective power of the peasantry was implicit in many laws passed after 1381. Some, such as an anti-poaching statute of 1389, suggested that the people were already gathering to rise once more. It complained not only that 'when good Christian people be at church hearing divine service' servants and labourers were often out engaging in illicit hunting, but also that 'sometimes under such colour they make their assemblies, conferences, and conspiracies for to rise and disobey their allegiance'.[37] Elite literature, as in the anonymous poem 'God Save the King and Keep the Crown', increasingly recognised the important political, as well as economic, role that the commons had to play:

> The leste lygge-man with body and rent
> He is parcel of the Crown.[38]

Popular rebellion remained more than a mere phantom threat, despite the fierce repression that had followed the Peasants' Revolt. The affluent and self-confident yeoman classes in particular were growing in political assertiveness. As the memory of 1381 continued to resonate, new rebel captains would emerge in the fifteenth century, some directly challenging royal authority.

JACK CADE'S REBELLION

On 10 March 1431, an elderly Essex priest and lapsed heretic, Thomas Bagley, was burnt alive at St Paul's Cross in front of thousands of Londoners, while the Archbishop of Canterbury rammed home the message of the gruesome spectacle with a dire public warning of the punishments for heresy. But this attempt to terrorise the people failed. That spring, a public pamphleteering campaign began, flagrantly promoting heretical and subversive opinions. Some of this propaganda smacked of social revolution, with its plans not only to disendow Church lands but also to do away with the King, lords and ecclesiastical hierarchy, and, it was alleged, redistribute the titles among the commons. Rebel 'bills' (anonymous broadsheets often posted on walls and doors or simply scattered in the streets) issued as late as May 1431 called for the replacement of bishops and peers with men from the lower ranks: a London weaver, John Cok, would be made Duke of Gloucester and Lord of Westminster, while another citizen, Ralph Bukberd, was to be installed as head of the Carmelite friars of London.[1] The Crown was deeply concerned about the impact that the rebels' bills were having on the population and issued a proclamation on 13 May against 'bille casters and keppers' and against those who read the bills aloud to spread the message to the illiterate majority.[2]

The billing campaign, which originated in Abingdon, Oxfordshire, was probably instigated by a weaver and bailiff called William Perkins, who operated like previous rebels under an assumed name – 'Jack Sharp of Wigmoreland'. (Perkins's *nom de guerre* struck resonances not just with 'Jack Straw' but also, through 'Sharp', with the territorial base of the Mortimer clan, inherited by Richard, Duke of York.) Perkins was accompanied by John Russell, a man with a record of criminal and heretical activities stretching back fifteen years. The rebels planned to make an energetic assault on Salisbury Cathedral, raze its buildings to the ground and carry off its goods and relics.

On 15 May, the Lollard rebels marched on Abingdon to attack the Abbey from the neighbouring village of East Hendred. Two days later, Perkins's followers made their presence known in the village of Frome, then in east Somerset. There, a dyer from the town and other Lollards distributed subversive religious literature, again exhorting others to rise up and attack religious houses. According to one chronicler, the rebels at Abingdon said that they would have three priests' heads for a penny. The ringleaders of the revolt were finally captured on 19 May, condemned to death before Duke Humfrey (a.k.a. the Duke of Gloucester, and Henry VI's Lieutenant and Keeper of England) and beheaded. Perkins's head was set on London Bridge as a sober warning to the Lollard contingent that the authorities well knew existed in London, while his quartered body parts went to two other main centres of trouble, Oxford and Abingdon. Russell was captured two months later and hanged as a common thief. Elsewhere in the country, other Lollard sympathisers, including several women, were rounded up and summarily executed.[3]

The failure of the 1431 rising and its swift and brutal repression by Duke Humfrey did not stem the flow of Lollard activity. A commission of 1440 uncovered a well-established local Lollard network centred on Odiham, Crondall and Farnham (then all in Hampshire). Meanwhile, at Selhurst in Sussex, the parish priest was found in possession of the four Gospels in English and was allegedly teaching the 'pestiferous opinions of John Wycliff'. In Kent, on the flat coastal marshes north of Rochester where Sir John Oldcastle's fortified manor house, Colling Castle, stood as a landmark to a seditious Lollard past, an active Lollard tradition persisted: there are references to a possible Lollard rising there in 1438. In addition, Lollards forced to make public abjuration of their beliefs in 1431 could be found in the 1440s being made to do penance once again for their heretical opinions. More importantly, names of those required to recant their beliefs in the 1430s reappear in the lists of those seeking pardon after Jack Cade's revolt in 1450.[4]

The government's concern about the ongoing popular discontent towards its regime led to a greater scrutiny of the gossip and rumour circulating in towns and villages. The 1440s witnessed a rise in the number of people charged with seditious speech. A constant theme of the comments reported was Henry VI's unfitness to rule. The King was spoken of as a fool, a simpleton, a child. Some claimed that he had murdered his uncle the Duke of Gloucester in 1447, that he was losing all the Crown's wealth, that he was grasping, that he was no soldier – and, perhaps most importantly, that it was the Duke of Suffolk and the Bishop of Salisbury who really held power. It was certainly true that during the mid-fifteenth century England experienced a crisis in political leadership. By the late 1440s, power had fallen into the hands of an unscrupulous court party headed by the Duke of Suffolk, William de la Pole and a few others, notably the Bishops of Salisbury and Chichester. Their supremacy at court was secured in 1447 when the King's great-uncle, Cardinal Beaufort, died. This clique was supported by a group of aristocratic thugs gathering around James Fiennes, Lord Saye and Sele, that included the Cornishman John Trevilian. The unpopularity of this group was reflected in vernacular rhyme:

> The Cornysshe Chowgh [Trevilian] offt with his trayne
> Hath made oure Egulle [Henry] blynde.

Suffolk's adherents extended their influence over the South East in a rapacious and often violent manner. In 1447, John Trevilian forcibly expelled three esquires, William Wangford, William Ludlowe and Stephen Wymbyssh, from the manor and castle of Stone in Kent, two miles east of Dartford and not far downriver from London. He held the manor for at least three years from its rightful owners. James Fiennes also used violence to extend his family's influence in Kent and Sussex. Allegedly, in 1447 he and Stephen Slegge, Sheriff of Kent from 1448 to 1449, ruthlessly expelled a man from his 250 acres in Elmley on the marsh flats of the Isle of Sheppey and forcibly kept this land right up until July 1450.

The grasping Slegge was as notorious as his master Fiennes for his activities when Sheriff. In 1449, the Exchequer sued him for a debt of £4078 10s 5d in unpaid revenues. That same year, with Robert Est, a gentleman from Maidstone, and a gang of some two hundred men he broke into the close of Edward Neville, Lord Abergavenny, at Singlewell, two miles south of Gravesend. They looted his granary and assaulted his servants. Men such as Est went unpunished thanks to the influence of Saye and one William Isle as magistrates. Politically, too, Saye's circle held a monopoly, completely dominating the elections for county Members of Parliament in the 1440s, strongly indicating that they were rigged.

By the 1440s, the counties of both Norfolk and Suffolk were in the grip of adherents of the Duke of Suffolk, who instituted a similar regime of extortion, violence and rough justice to that meted out by the creatures of Fiennes in Kent. The main villains in East Anglia were Thomas Tuddenham, John Heydon and John Ulveston. As in Kent, Suffolk's adherents dominated county politics. The notorious

Tuddenham of Oxburgh acted as MP for Suffolk in 1431 and, from then on, for Norfolk in three parliaments during the 1430s and again in 1442 and 1443–4. Heydon was MP for Norfolk from 1445 to 1446, and Ulveston was MP for Yarmouth in 1447 and 1449–50.

The three rustled sheep, forged judicial records, helped destroy a watermill in Norwich and colluded in the appropriation of the city tolls by the Prior of Holy Trinity. Heydon was the most violent of Suffolk's gang: on at least four occasions during the 1440s, his heavies prevented coroners from investigating various deaths. The most infamous example of his methods came in January 1449. Heydon and Lord Moleyns, Bishop of Chichester, backed by a large gang comprising several hundred armed men, incited the attack and seizure of John Paston's manor at Gresham in Norfolk. Heydon's men smashed gates and doors, rifled through Paston's possessions and, with the manor taken, combed the countryside, pursuing his friends, tenants and servants in and out of houses and barns, ruthlessly stabbing at sheaves and straw after their quarry. Poor tenants of the manor were intimidated into making false complaints in the hundred courts against these associates of Paston, who naturally did not appear in public to defend themselves in court. Nor could they even obtain copies of the complaints so as to answer them by law, because the keeper of the court was also in league with Moleyns and Tuddenham. The machinery of law and order had been completely appropriated by Suffolk's cronies, who exploited it to perform a perverse charade of justice to cover their own nefarious activities.

The crisis for Henry VI's government came in 1449–50, as military failures, Crown insolvency and consequent high taxation provided the catalysts for major popular rebellion. The Hundred Years War, begun in 1337, was coming to its denouement. The breakdown of peace between England and France in 1449 left the King with insufficient funds to raise an expeditionary force. Parliament refused to grant the necessary money, in part because those around the King were not trusted to make proper use of the tax revenue. The outbreak of hostilities further impoverished the Crown: an embargo on exports caused England's cloth trade to collapse. Suffolk was widely believed (probably correctly) to have been orchestrating the end of the truce with the French behind the scenes, through the seizure of Fougères by the English mercenary François de Surienne in a mistaken bid to regain public credit after his role in the cession of Maine to the French in 1445. By the autumn of 1449, Henry VI's government was close to collapse. The King's debts and charges were said to be running at £320,000. On 17 September, Bishop Lumley resigned his office as Treasurer, with a balance in the Treasury of a mere £480 5s 3d, to be replaced by Lord Saye and Sele. On 11 October, the French took Gavray; by 16 October the French King Charles VII was at the gates of Rouen to confront the Earl of Somerset's army. After a short and, as some saw it, token engagement, Somerset was persuaded by the Archbishop and citizens to negotiate with the French: on 29 October, the capital of Lancastrian France surrendered without a siege.

When Parliament was recalled, Suffolk came under attack as a result of a failed assassination attempt upon Ralph, Lord Cromwell, perpetrated by William Tailboys, a strongman in the pay of Suffolk and Viscount Beaumont. Cromwell survived the attempt and campaigned to have Suffolk impeached by the Commons. Further bad news for the Duke came with the murder of Bishop Moleyns, who had been sent down to Portsmouth to take wages to the force awaiting shipment to Normandy. Here, he was accused of withholding the money from the troops. On 9 January 1450, a mob of furious soldiers and sailors dragged Moleyns out of his lodgings to a field where, despite his protests that it was Suffolk who was the embezzler (evidence that was later used in Suffolk's trial), the Bishop was brutally beaten to death.

As discontent with the conduct of Suffolk's faction at court spilled into open violence against his associates, the first signs of a popular uprising against these courtiers emerged. Thomas Cheyne, brother of the Lollard gentleman and rebel Sir John, led a demonstration

that revived the idea, used in 1381, of petitioning the King by provoking the south-eastern counties into a mass demonstration
converging on London. Cheyne's rebels gathered somewhere
between Sandwich and Dover on Saturday 24 January, with a list of
royal councillors that they wanted to see beheaded, including
William Aiscough, Bishop of Salisbury, William, Duke of Suffolk,
James, Lord Saye, and the Abbot of Gloucester. They organised
themselves into a military-style array and appointed captains under
various pseudonyms – 'King of the Fairies', 'Queen of the Fairies'
and 'Robin Hood' – a trick, as we have seen, that rebels had also
employed in 1381. Thomas Cheyne himself went under the name
'the hermit Blewbeard'. On the 26th, with the number of rebels
alleged to be now in the thousands, Cheyne's men attacked St
Radegund's Abbey hospice just outside the city walls of Canterbury.
Cheyne was finally captured with the aid of the citizens of
Canterbury on Saturday 31 January, just a week after the rising
had begun. He was taken to Westminster to be judged and was
then hanged, drawn and quartered at Tyburn. His head was sent
to London Bridge and his quarters were distributed between
London, Norwich and two of the Cinque Ports; although not without some difficulty, since no one was willing, for fear of their lives,
to transport the dismembered corpse to its several destinations.

In Parliament, the campaign against the Duke of Suffolk gathered pace. On 28 January, the Commons accused him of
conspiring to surrender Wallingford Castle to Charles VII, a treasonable charge for which he was placed in the Tower the following
day. The Commons' impeachment proceedings could only be
stopped by the intervention of the King, who on 17 March ban-
ished Suffolk from his realms with effect from 1 May, imposing a
five-year exile on him. As the Duke fled the capital for his manor
of Eastthorp in Suffolk, a crowd of angry Londoners gave chase
and set upon his party. The Duke himself escaped. However,
Henry VI's intervention could not ultimately save him. On 1 May,
the vessel transporting Suffolk across the Channel was intercepted

by a ship called the *Nicholas of the Tower*. Its unknown master brought Suffolk aboard and, according to one report, subjected him to a mock trial before having him beheaded the following day in the name of 'the community of the realm'. The Duke's head was stuck on a pole and his body was flung up the high strand, washing ashore among the pebbles on Dover beach.

Suffolk's death sparked rumours that the King, in retribution, would turn the county of Kent into a wild forest. This was a period of high anxiety for those who lived in England's maritime counties. Reports of Suffolk's death had been preceded by the news of the terrible defeat of the English forces at the Battle of Formigny on 15 April, where, it was estimated, four thousand men had been killed. Rumours of imminent invasion were given substance by earlier French raids on the ports of Rye and Winchelsea and, earlier that same month, by an attack on Queensborough on the Isle of Sheppey.[5] By the second half of May, rebellion was under way. From 18 May onwards, no church court sessions were held in the diocese of Rochester because of serious insurrection in Kent. Again, it appears that popular festivity was used as cover for organising the rebels and disseminating their plans for a rising. The Rochester Fair of 18–20 May was used to communicate news and opinion from all over Kent, while other towns in the area of revolt also held fairs: Heathfield in Sussex on 15–17 June and Sevenoaks in Kent on the 29th.

These rebels were no ignorant peasants. They produced their own written manifesto, known as the 'complaint of the poor commons of Kent'. The May rebels had at least one secretary, Henry Wilkhous, a notary from Dartford. William Petur, a notary from Strood and an associate of Wilkhous who would seek a pardon after the rebellion, may well have been another. Scribes and messengers also played a part in mobilising the county through the existing system of the muster. Church bells summoned the men of the parish, and the mustered men took oaths of allegiance to one another and to their cause.

As in 1381, the rebels appropriated the machinery of local

government for their own ends. This provided them with a ready-made system of administration for organising their rising (and one which, as a result of the invasion scares of 1449–50, had recently been refurbished). More than this, though, it gave the rebellion, via the normal mustering process for the militia, the aura of legality. It also provides some evidence of a 'bottom-up' conception of political power. The constables of the hundreds in charge of summoning the militia were not appointees of the King but elected by their communities. Above all, the raising of the militia provides clear evidence that the ordinary people of England regularly owned and carried arms and armour. Hugh Latimer, Bishop of Worcester under Edward VI, recalled that his father, a yeoman farmer, had owned his own armour, which he wore while fighting Cornish rebels in 1497. In the words of the historian Montgomery Bohna, in 'twenty-first-century terms, it was as if a flak jacket, helmet and assault rifle were household items as common as the family car, and the principal natural recreations were the rifle range and assault training course'.[6] At points during the rising of 1450, this peasant militia would prove more than a match for the armed retinues of the great nobles.

By June 1450, the Kentish rebels had designated one Jack Cade as 'the Capitayne of the [h]oste'. As with many medieval and early modern rebels, our knowledge of Cade's background is sketchy at best. The government believed that his name was actually John Mortimer, possibly out of a conviction that the revolt was a product of machinations by the Duke of York, who had Mortimer connections. Various other stories circulated about Cade's origins: it was suggested that he was a physician, John Aylemere, married to a squire's daughter from Tandridge, Surrey, remembered for decking himself out in scarlet. In another tale he was a sorcerer of the black arts, capable of summoning up the Devil in animal guise; during 1449, while living in Sussex in the household of Sir Thomas Dacre, Cade was said to have murdered a pregnant woman and then fled the country. This part at least may be true. Between December 1448 and December 1449, a John Cade, yeoman, of Hurstpierpoint in mid-Sussex, did 'abjure the realm' (promise to go into exile), while the escheator for Surrey and Sussex confiscated twenty shillings from the profits of the sale of Cade's horse, gown and bed. Hurstpierpoint at this time was held by Sir Thomas Dacre, the son of Lord Dacre of the North but with links among the most prominent families of the South East. (Indeed, his son-in-law was the very Sir Richard Fiennes, future 1st Lord Dacre of the South, whose uncle was the notorious Lord Saye.)

On 8 June, Cade advanced on the western suburbs of Canterbury, with what one observer estimated to be a host of four thousand men. The rebels waited three hours in the great field that then stretched between St Michael's Harbledown and St Dunstan's, in the hope of some positive response from the city. Finally, they gave up and took the road to London. Meanwhile, groups nearer to London had already reached Middlesex. At Westminster, John Sawyer, a fruiterer and yeoman from St Mary Cray in north-west Kent, led a gang who attacked and took hostage a royal servant, Thomas Walter, until he paid a ransom of £10. The news of the rebellion had been sent up to Leicester on 6 June where Parliament was in session. The Commons was adjourned and the Duke of Buckingham and the Earls of Oxford, Devon and Arundel were commissioned by the King to proceed 'against the traitors and rebels in Kent and to punish and arrest the same'. This action came too late to nip the rising in the bud. By the 11th, Cade and his rebels were already encamped on Blackheath, a fine natural vantage point south of the river looking down at the capital, and also the place that the rebels of 1381 had chosen for their camp.

The City began to prepare for its defence: its gates were to be fortified and guarded twenty-four hours a day. The nobles' armed retainers were to be admitted only on specific errands and were not to be quartered there; and armourers were not to sell their goods outside the City. The King had in the meantime followed his nobles south and by 13 June was staying at St John's Priory in Clerkenwell. On the 15th he sent messengers over the river to Blackheath to order the Kentishmen to disband. Later the same day, the Earl of Northumberland, Lord Scales and Lord Lisle rode to the heath with an armed company, aiming to dispel the Kentishmen by force, but, seeing the size of the rebel encampment, they decided to retreat and seek reinforcements. Henry VI seems to have been tempted to ride out to them himself, like the young Richard II. Instead, though, he adopted the plan of sending out a prestigious delegation of nobles, including many with links to Kent, such as the Archbishops of Canterbury and York, the Duke of Buckingham, the Bishop of Winchester and Viscount Beaumont. Their mission: to persuade Cade to withdraw his men in return for the offer of a royal pardon.

The delegation took away with them the rebels' petition. Like the demands of 1381, it demonstrated that Cade's followers wished to be seen as 'loyal rebels', supportive of the King and wishing for the reform of the kingdom. First, their captain assured Henry of his concern for his welfare and that of his peers. He suggested that Henry take back all his demesnes so that he might reign like a 'Kyng Riall', but asked him to rid himself of all the false progeny and affinity of the Duke of Suffolk, 'the whiche ben opynly knowyn traitours'. These 'traitors' should be punished and replaced with the Dukes of York, Exeter, Buckingham and Norfolk. The petition also mentioned particular Kentish grievances: the abuse of 'summonses of the Green Wax', the burden of purveyance, the troublesome Statute of Labourers, and the activities of the 'grete extorcioners', Stephen Slegge, William Crowmer, Sheriff of Kent, plus William Isle and Robert Est.*

---

* 'Summonses of the Green Wax' were mandates authorising county officers to take fines. Purveyance was the requisitioning of goods for royal supply. The burden of purveyance fell particularly heavily on Kent.

In response, Henry marched out to meet the rebels on 18 June with a large and well-armed force, including carts of guns for firing lead and stone. But he was too late. The rebels, wisely, had already fled the heath, correctly taking his delay as a sign that he was preparing to crush them with violence. Cade's men melted into the woods of the Kentish weald. A smaller posse of royal soldiers, led by Sir Humphrey and Sir William Stafford, unwisely attempted to pursue them. The Staffords and forty of their men were killed when the rebels ambushed them near Sevenoaks, offering a clear demonstration of their potency. On that same day, 18 June, the Lords Dudley and Rivers, Sir Thomas Stanley and Thomas Daniel rode into north-west Kent with a force of two thousand men and began a three-day campaign of robbery, pillage and terrorisation. They stole horses from the Archbishop of Canterbury's park at Otford, while at Chipstead they stole silver spoons and linen sheets from one man, saffron, pepper and spice from another, and cash from both. The next day, they rampaged through Sevenoaks, and on 20 June took their mayhem to Tonbridge.

The King's campaign seemed to embolden the Kentish rebels and perhaps encouraged others in neighbouring counties to join them. In a striking development, on 19 June some of the King's own retainers and lords encamped on Blackheath were heard to suggest that Cade had a legitimate cause, and threatened to go over to the rebels' side unless something was done about Lord Saye and his circle. The King appeared to realise that he could not hope to suppress the rebellion without acting against these ministers. An order was given to Henry Holland to detain James Fiennes, Lord Saye, in the Tower, and it was proclaimed that all the named 'traitors' should be taken, wherever they might be found. Yet it was clear that the King had made this proclamation under duress. Shortly afterwards, Henry attempted to engineer Saye's escape, but Holland, as constable of the Tower, refused to release his prisoner. Following this open defiance of the royal will, Henry decided to leave London, setting out on 25 June, in spite of desperate pleas from the Lord Mayor to stay. Abandoning his wife Margaret of Anjou, Henry called first at Berkhamsted Castle in Hertfordshire and from there went on to Kenilworth in Warwickshire, the safest remaining royal castle. His capital and his queen were left to their fate.

Elsewhere in the South of England, the campaign against the 'traitors' about the King continued. On 29 June the rebels captured William Aiscough, Bishop of Salisbury, at Edington in Wiltshire, while he celebrated mass in the local church. The Bishop was deeply disliked: he was widely held responsible for the unpopular marriage of Henry to Margaret. He was dragged to a hill, hacked to death and his corpse defiled. It was probably at this time that Cade reappeared on Blackheath, accompanied, it was reported, by a 'gret Power of Men of Armes and Archiers Arraised'. Some of his men were on horseback. Sir John Falstof's servant John Payn rode out to the rebels, with instructions to obtain a copy of their articles of petition.

Payn would have been killed as a traitor the rebels viewed his master as partly responsible for the military failure in France – but for the intervention of Robert Poynings, sword-bearer and carver to Cade. The petition that Payn took away with him was, in the words of Jack Cade's foremost historian Isabel Harvey, 'couched in the language . . . of reasonable, responsible men, not rebels'.[7] The petitioners expressed their concern about the King's relationship with his commons and the manner in which this relationship had been destroyed by the circle of 'false traytours'. The King needed to come to his senses, 'ffor his lordez ern lost, his marchundize is lost, his comyns destroyed, the see is lost, frraunse [France] is lost, himself so pore that he may not [pay] for his mete or drynk; he oweth more than evur dyd kynge in Inglond'.[8] Cade was now being fêted like a noble himself. The town of Lydd on the Kent coast sent him an entire porpoise, the food of aristocrats and worth as much as a brace of swans.

When July came, Cade led his men into Southwark, where they took up lodgings in inns and hostelries and quite possibly in private houses too. Then the rebels began looting. John Payn had been abandoned in Southwark when his master fled to the Tower. Although the servant managed to prevent the rebels from burning down Falstof's house, he was unable to save his own belongings. The brigandine and the gown he was wearing were torn from his back and his chest ransacked of its valuables. As their numbers swelled, Cade struggled to keep control of his men. He had already had to have one of his under-captains, a man called Parys, executed at Blackheath for disciplinary reasons. In Southwark Cade's followers also robbed one Lawrence Hope, a yeoman from Molasshe in Kent, as well as an unidentified Southwark man from whom they took two horses worth a hundred shillings, and a bag of money.

On 3 July, having first threatened to torch the whole bridge (and the rest of the City too), Cade cut the ropes of the drawbridge on London Bridge's southern end so that it might not be drawn up again and acquired the keys of the gate that blocked his path beyond the drawbridge. Bedecked in improvised regalia of gilt spurs and a blue velvet coat furred with sable (stripped from one of the slain Staffords), a drawn sword in his hand and with another borne before him in noble fashion, he then led his men into the City, riding at the head of his army across the bridge from Southwark. Orders issued by Cade demanding discipline from his men did little good, as the rebels set about looting the house of Philip Malpas, a London alderman. Nonetheless, a semblance of justice was restored. On 4 July Cade and his followers took over the sessions of oyer and terminer – the system whereby judges were instructed to 'hear and determine' particular offences – at the Guildhall, replacing them with a commission to indict and condemn those they judged traitors and extortioners. Some of the original justices, including Thomas, Lord Scales, the Mayor Thomas Charlton and six others, remained to preside over the proceedings. Those indicted included the notorious courtiers John Say, John Trevilian and Thomas Daniel. Lord Saye was taken from the Tower to the Guildhall and, charged with various treasons, including collusion in the death of the Duke of Gloucester.

Cade waited at the Standard in the Cheap, where Saye was brought next. There he saw him not only beheaded but despoiled and publicly degraded, his naked corpse dragged by a horse through the streets. Also executed that day was William Crowmer, Saye's son-in-law. The rebels showed their keenness to restore a broader justice by also executing a man named Hawarden, a common thief and murderer who had lived for a long time in the sanctuary of St Martin le Grand.

By Sunday 5 July, Cade's men had been loose in the City for two days that had seen uncontrolled pillaging and the execution of at least five men, there and in the suburbs. Ordinary Londoners now attempted to rid themselves of the rebel scourge, planning to wait until they had returned to their Southwark lodgings for the night, then attack Cade's men guarding the bridge and bar it against their re-entry. Cade caught wind of the plan and mustered all his men, calling on them to make an armed assault on the City. Again as in 1381, he further swelled the rebel ranks by opening the Marshalsea Prison so that its inmates might assist him. An armed confrontation became inevitable as Cade's men massed on the south bank, while Londoners and royal troops from the Tower, led by Lord Scales, the veteran royal captain Matthew Gough and several aldermen, gathered on the bridge.

Fighting began around nine o'clock in the evening and did not end until daybreak. The length of the battle again demonstrated the military proficiency of the rebel host, especially given that the Londoners had access to the Tower's mighty arsenal. The latter managed to close the bridge gates but they could not keep Cade's men off its southern section. Failing to force his way across, Cade set the drawbridge section alight. As the sun rose, it must have made a dismal sight, charred and smoking, littered with dead bodies and with more corpses adrift in the water below. Matthew Gough was among the casualties. A truce of a few hours was agreed, during which time the few remaining Crown representatives negotiated with the rebels about a general withdrawal.

Large numbers of Cade's followers took up the offer, made on 6 and 7 July, of a royal pardon. It extended to all transgressions committed prior to 8 July 1450 and guaranteed that anyone holding such a pardon would go unmolested by the King's justices, escheators, sheriffs, coroners and bailiffs. Cade had been enrolled on 6 July under the name of John Mortimer, and was granted pardon at the request of the Queen – in the absence of her husband, Margaret of Anjou had played a crucial role in the negotiations. The fact that Cade was registered under another name later allowed the Crown to claim that the pardon was invalid. Cade himself showed little trust in it, setting off quickly for north Kent with a good portion of loot and a small band of supporters. He continued his rebellious activities, attempting to take Queensborough Castle near Dartford, but was unable to overcome its defenders. His supporters continued to demonstrate on Blackheath, at Rochester and near Gravesend. On 10 July a Faversham soapmaker, Robert Spenser, was one of the main figures in a demonstration of support for Cade that took place at Rochester, for which he was later hanged and quartered.

On the same day, the Exchequer sent out a writ stating that Cade was a traitor who 'laboureth now of newe to assemble the Kings people againe'. A reward of a thousand marks was put on his head, five hundred for any of his captains and ten for his followers. Cade was now on the run in earnest. Alexander Iden, the new Sheriff of Kent, was harrying his supporters westwards towards the Sussex border. On 12 July he caught up with Cade at Heathfield in Sussex, capturing and badly injuring the rebel leader. Cade did not survive the journey back to London, dying en route, probably on

13 July. His corpse was given the usual treatment reserved for traitors. His head was then displayed on a spike atop London Bridge, and the quarters of his body sent out to Blackheath, Norwich, Salisbury and Gloucester. (In Norwich, sympathisers with the rebels later stole the quarter from its position on the city gate.)[9]

The recovery of goods from Cade's men showed the scale of their plunder. On 21 July, an indenture was delivered to the Exchequer itemising the jewels and the money taken from Cade and his followers in Kent when they retreated from Southwark. Included were silver dishes and spoons, purses, girdles, a gold salver garnished with sapphires and pearls, silver pots, silver saltcellars and precious stones: in total, more than 115 items plus over a hundred pounds in ready cash. Though Iden collected his thousand marks (raised from the profits of the sale of the goods) for capturing Cade, those who had been robbed had to go to the Exchequer. There all they received was first preference in buying back their belongings at a small discount.

As in 1381, Cade's rebellion was not quelled simply by the death of its leading captain. Revolts continued to flare up after July 1450, and beyond the counties of Kent and Sussex. Depositions taken in 1453 alleged that there had been disturbances in Suffolk since March 1450. A group of Suffolk men were accused of composing ballads and rhymes claiming that the King, influenced by his evil courtiers, had sold the realm of England and its French possessions and that soon the King of France would be monarch in England. In the Norfolk town of Melton, later a centre of disturbances during Kett's rebellion of 1549, a vicar was attacked and robbed in early July. A petition from him told of how 'in the grete trobull tyme' he was assaulted at night by a large gang of parishioners, 'desciples and of the affynte [affinity] of the grete traytor John Cade', who would have beheaded him had he not fled. There were reports also of trouble in Beccles, east Suffolk, formerly an area of Lollard activity, in June 1450. Disturbances continued when, later in the summer, one of Cade's quarters was carted through Suffolk.

On 4 August in the village of Alderton, set among the flat Suffolk fields between the North Sea and the estuary of the Deben, John Squyer, the local parson and, fatally, former chaplain to the Duke of Suffolk, was murdered by his own parishioners, helped by men from the neighbouring villages of Ramsholt and Sutton.

In Kent and Sussex, other men emerged, ready to lead further risings. A smith from Faversham, William Parmynter, came forward calling himself the 'second captain of Kent'. His rising on 30 August 1450 covered a broad band of north and mid-Kent from Teynham, Faversham, Canterbury and Ospringe westwards to Marden, Sevenoaks, Otford, Hawkhurst and Appledore. Parmynter's support extended across the Weald to Mountfield in Sussex and down through Hailsham, Willingdon and Jevington to the coast at Eastbourne, where there was a further rising in September. The Eastbourne rising was instigated by a gentleman, William Howell, who again co-opted the mechanisms of the militia for the purposes of raising an insurrection.[10] Although Parmynter was eventually rounded up by a squire of the Duke of Somerset and sentenced to death, another Kent captain, an individual calling himself John Smyth, appeared soon after and evaded capture until early 1451. Apart from county risings, there was also large-scale poaching (later a feature of the 1549 rebellions). In October 1450 at Penshurst, a hundred men from Sussex and the Kentish Weald undertook a massive poaching raid on the park of Humphrey, Duke of Buckingham.

The ongoing risings in the southern counties and the evident public support for some of the rebel grievances initially forced the King to be conciliatory, even after Cade's death. On 1 August, Henry sent a commission of oyer and terminer into Kent to inquire into all miscarriages of justice, extortions, trespasses and oppressions in an attempt to address the rebels' complaints about the corrupt nature of local government.

By December 1450, however, as order was gradually restored,

Henry had clearly decided that the time to investigate the commons' grievances was over. He appointed the Duke of York to head a new commission to do justice on those rebels and traitors who had risen in Kent and Sussex since 8 July. But the commission bore only the trappings of a legal investigation. Its true purpose was punitive. The commissioners paid little regard to whether the convicted rebels had been in arms before or after the issuing of the general pardon, and hanged thirty men whom they found guilty of having risen with Cade or of having declared their disdain for the King and their preference for the Duke of York. At the end of February 1451, as Henry made his way back to London through north Kent, a host of unpunished rebels some three thousand strong awaited him on Blackheath to plead for mercy, shirtless and lying prostrate before him with cords about their necks. Though these men were pardoned, the King's judicial progress through Kent came to be known as the 'harvest of heads'.

Cade's revolt, like that of 1381, has been viewed as essentially a failure, and one whose impact was largely negative in that it provoked further royal oppression. Very few of the 'great extortioners' identified by the Kentish rebels were dealt with, and some, such as Est and Slegge, continued in the same ruthless vein as they had before 1450. It has been suggested that the main impact of the revolt was to create a base of support for the Yorkists in southern England, as a reaction to the harsh repression visited upon these counties by Henry VI and his commissioners. Cade's revolt has, in any case, traditionally been distinguished from both the Peasants' Revolt and the 'commotion time' of 1549 as a rebellion really concerned with ephemeral political matters, especially with punishing the Earl of Suffolk and his supporters.

However, as with 1381 and 1549, there is strong evidence that there was a social impetus to the rebellion as well. The 1440s were years of rising rents and falling prices. This left many people both unable to afford goods at market and unable to sell their own surplus produce to supplement incomes that had been heavily eroded by rent payments. An element of class antagonism was particularly evident in some of the later risings. In November 1450 at Hastings, would-be insurgents (including stone-roofers, a mason, a dyer, a husbandman, a tailor and a thatcher) allegedly sought the heads of certain gentry, and 'especially of those who were against Jack Cade'. Villeinage remained common in late medieval Sussex and the rejection of its burdens was one part of the rebellion of 1450. In Battle, Sussex, the customary tax levied in the autumn of 1450 upon 'aliens' (those born outside the town's jurisdiction) could not be collected until late March 1451, and even then, confiscations to take care of arrears were being challenged in the courts. There is some evidence that this resistance to paying customary fines was successful. In Chiddingly in 1458–9, existing customary tenure – with its accompanying dues and services – was replaced with a simple money rent. Elsewhere, tenants successfully negotiated their rents downward.[11]

Later risings also displayed greater political radicalism, moving on from criticising specific councillors to attacking the King directly. One indictment reported that the Sussex yeomen John and William Merford had said on 26 July 1450 that 'the Kyng was a natell fooll and wold ofte tymes hold a staff in his hands with a brid [bird] on the ende playing therewith as a fooll and that anoder kyng must be ordered to rule the land, saying that the king was no person able to rule the land'. In October of that year, John Merford was accused of saying in an alehouse that 'they wolde leve no gentilman alyve but such as thym list to have'.[12] Even the more moderate 'Complaint of the Commons of Kent' made it clear that it was not only the King's councillors who were responsible for the dire state of the kingdom. In the opening lines, its authors said that they regarded Henry as bound by and accountable to English law – if this was not the case he should not have sworn his coronation oath.

In the written petitions that Cade's followers presented to the King, they betrayed the fact that this was not a rebellion instigated by the illiterate peasantry. Even historians whose overall perspectives differ agree that the key leaders of the rebellion were not 'masterless men' but individuals who themselves shouldered considerable responsibilities at local level. The pardon roll of 1450 reveals the names of tax collectors, jurors for the hundred courts and constables. Some members of the gentry also took part in the rising – Cade's carver and sword-bearer, Robert Poynings, was the son of Lord Poynings – although they do not appear to have played a significant role in leading it. It was led by men whose own day-to-day responsibilities had given them a sense of what good government was, a government that was constituted as much by the community as by the will of a king, if not more so. The sense of community and of customary rights was further reinforced by an awareness of the legacy of the Peasants' Revolt. Just as Tyler's men had gathered at Blackheath, so had Cade's, and so would rebel armies in 1471 and 1497. Names too were reused, 'Jack Straw' emerging as a rebel leader in Kent in 1452 and again in a northern rising of 1485.[13]

The durability of this popular memory is a reminder that the largely hostile accounts of these rebellions might be understood very differently by different audiences. Just as the ballads of Robin Hood might speak of the values of chivalry to the nobility, their originally intended audience, but of a rough social justice – taking from the rich and giving to the poor – at a popular level, so the harsh portrayals of vainglorious and violent rebel captains might appeal to, rather than disgust, those they were meant to instruct in the evils of rebellion.

4

The 'Commotion Time'

The last major popular rebellion of the late medieval/early modern period occurred in 1549. 'Kett's rebellion', as the rising in East Anglia is now widely known, became an inspiration to nineteenth- and twentieth-century radicals. In the 1920s the rebel camp that its leader, Robert Kett, established at Mousehold Heath was seen as a precursor of land nationalisation schemes. For the Labour alderman Fred Henderson, the connections with 1549 were more personal: like Kett, Henderson had been imprisoned in Norwich Castle for his part in a food riot in 1885. In 1948, in the climate of buoyant socialist aspiration that followed Labour's landslide election victory, Henderson moved that a monument to Kett be erected in the city. Despite the differences between the sixteenth and twentieth centuries, Henderson said, Kett's struggle reflected the constant 'urge in the spirit of the people of this land, whatever the circumstances of their times might be, to seek for freedom and the establishment of just conditions'. The following year, a plaque dedicated to Kett was placed on the wall of Norwich Castle, in 'memory of a notable leader in the long struggle of the common people of England to escape from a servile life into the freedom of just conditions'.[1]

Robert Kett himself appears an unlikely rebel leader. Far from being of peasant stock, the Ketts were descendants of the gentry Le Chat family and Robert's wife Alice may have been the daughter of Sir Nicholas Appleyard of Bracon Ash. Robert was a tanner and his brother William a butcher, but both were substantial landowners. The Kett family had settled in Wymondham in Norfolk in 1483. Here Robert leased the manor from John Dudley, Earl of Warwick. Hostile chroniclers liked to portray Kett as the stereotypical popular demagogue: a vainglorious upstart bent on manipulating the mob for his own gain. In fact, he was a wealthy pillar of the community with much to lose by supporting the enclosure rioters. That he did so suggests not only that the politics of 1549 were very complicated, with rebels believing they were making common cause with the royal government against grasping local landowners, but also that there was a ring of truth in later romantic depictions of him. Ultimately, the Kett who emerges from recent research on the rebellion was a man of principle, who sacrificed his own material comfort, and later his life, in an attempt to secure greater freedoms for those less fortunate.

But the events of 1549 were much more than the story of one man. In the sixteenth century, the rebellion was more accurately described as the 'camping' or 'commotion time'. For, far from being an isolated insurrection that involved just East Anglia and was dependent on the leadership of one rebel captain, the 'commotion time' signified a period when the whole of southern and eastern England rose in revolt. Thanks to the work of the historians Diarmaid MacCullough, Andy Wood and Amanda Jones, we now know it was an astonishingly widespread crisis, taking in twenty-five counties as well as Devon and Cornwall – effectively all of lowland England as far north as Seamer, overlooking the Derwent Valley in the North Riding of Yorkshire, but with the important exception of London. No equivalent degree of popular disruption would be seen in England until the start of the civil war in 1642. Besides Kett's at Mousehold Heath, eighteen other rebel camps were set up, and a further nine popular petitions emerged from these camps in addition to the six from the 'western rebellion' in Devon and Cornwall and the one from the Norfolk rebels.

The catalyst to the 'commotion time' also appears to have originated outside Norfolk. In the Hertfordshire village of Northaw on 20 May 1548, a crowd devastated the rabbit warrens of the government official and lord of the manor Sir William Cavendish, blowing up burrows and killing over two thousand animals. This symbolic act of violence was a reaction to the royal commission that Cavendish had obtained to enclose the very extensive common land in the area. The protesters argued that the enclosure commission had no legal force as Edward VI was still a minor, and set up a camp on the disputed commons.

Enclosure was a massive source of political tension in late medieval and early modern England. By 1500 it has been estimated that 45 per cent of cultivable land had been enclosed. Enclosures continued apace in the sixteenth century, though now their aim was largely to help landlords increase rents (enclosed land could be rented at three times the price of unenclosed property) rather than to convert arable land to pasture. In the longer term, the social impact of enclosure was unquestionably to increase the wealth of the landowner at the expense of the wage-labourer and small tenant farmer. Socially divisive as they were, enclosures continued to be a catalyst for riot and revolt into the seventeenth century.[2] In the wake of the Northaw confrontation Edward Seymour, the King's uncle, known as Protector Somerset due to his effective control of the government during Edward's minority, established a commission to investigate illegal enclosures, under the leadership of the civil servant John Hales, a leading 'evangelical' (a zealous supporter of the Protestant Reformation).[3]

The commission failed to prevent conflict over the enclosure of common land. A year after the Northaw incident, similar disputes broke out in Wiltshire, Somerset and Bristol. Protector Somerset tried to calm the situation by issuing a conciliatory proclamation promising to redress local grievances, but it appears only to have encouraged further disturbances. On 3 July, the Lord Mayor had taken part in special watches of the City of London because of 'the rebellion in divers places of this realme'. By 5 July, Somerset was having to write a personal letter in reply to a petition articulating the demands of the commons of Essex prepared by a leader who had taken the representative name 'William Essex'. Two days later, Somerset sent a letter to 'divers unlawfull assemblies' in Oxfordshire, attempting to placate them with the offer of a royal pardon. Before Kett had even become involved in the risings, rebels in southern England and the Midlands had established camps and forced concessions from the Edwardian regime.

Though it was not the first county to rise in 1549, Norfolk did have a recent history of social revolt. The Walsingham conspiracy, thwarted in 1537, had seen Ralph Rogerson, a yeoman and lay chorister of the priory plan to seize the gentry and murder any nobles who resisted. Driven by anger at the greed of local gentlemen, it gave an early glimpse of the social forces that would drive the larger rebellion of 1549.[4] In 1548, there were complaints from the Mayor of Norwich concerning rhymes circulated touching on the 'kinge maiste [majesty]' and 'Rayling against the governme[n]t of Mr Mayor'.[5]

The 'commotion time' began in earnest in Norfolk on 20 June 1549, as people from three villages around the small town of Attleborough pulled down the hedges of a local landlord who had enclosed part of their common land. A fortnight later, from 6 to 8 July at Wymondham, while the neighbourhood gathered to put on a play, crowds again pulled down hedges in nearby villages, including those of John Flowerdew, one of the many successful lawyers among the Norfolk gentry. Flowerdew hoped to exploit the crowd's aggressive mood by persuading them to tear down the hedges of a nearby enclosure belonging to the Kett family, with whom he was engaged in a feud. The Ketts were closely associated with the local church, a former abbey that Flowerdew had demolished at the

Reformation. However, the ploy backfired: Robert Kett agreed that the common land that he had enclosed should be made common again; he would stand by the rioters, he said, until they had obtained their rights. According to the hostile chronicler Alexander Neville, secretary to Matthew Parker, the Archbishop of Canterbury, Kett said he was 'ready not only to restrain but also to subdue the Power of the Nobility: that, as they [the commons] were weary of their Misery so he hoped in a little time to make the others sorry for their Pride'. He promised to 'revenge the Losses they suffer'd in their Commons, at the expence of their cruel Oppressors', and to take care 'that the Land he had inclosed, should all be made publick, by filling up the Ditch with his own Hands'. In conclusion, 'he offer'd himself not only as a Companion, but as a Leader; not only as a Partaker of so great an Exploit, but as a General, Author and Principal: that he wou'd not only assist at, but preside over all their Counsels'.[6]

Kett decided to march on Norwich, rapidly gaining support on the way. He arrived at the city on 10 July, and found that some of the poorer citizens had already destroyed the hedge around the main close. By 12 July he had set up camp on Mousehold Heath, the same spot favoured by the Norfolk rebels in 1381. Within a few days, the rebel numbers had reputedly climbed to sixteen thousand. There were further encampments in the north-west of the county, at Castle Rising, which later moved to Downham Market, and another in mid-Norfolk, at Hingham. In Suffolk, a camp had been set up outside Ipswich and was dispensing justice to the people, while another was established near Bury St Edmunds. In Kent, the so-called 'rebellion of Commonwealth' had set up camps at Canterbury and outside Maidstone, under a leader called Latimer (once identified, mistakenly, with Bishop Hugh Latimer).[7] The site of Latimer's camp, Penenden Heath, was the spot where Wat Tyler had mustered the Kentish rebels in 1381 and where Jack Cade had raised his men seventy years later.[8]

The timing of the risings, at the beginning of July, caught the gentry off guard. Many were away in London or had followed the royal summons to court at Windsor. As in earlier rebellions, sporting events and the festive calendar were probably used as a cover for seditious meetings. The earlier, Walsingham conspiracy had been planned under the pretext of an archery tournament, while the rebels at Wymondham had used the celebration of the feast of St Thomas the Martyr to mask their activities.[9]

For over a week, Kett's rebels remained unmolested in the camp on Mousehold Heath. Kett himself was living in style, having taken over the former palace of the Earl of Surrey. From here, the rebel council, which at the time included Thomas Codd, the Mayor of Norwich, and Alderman Thomas Aldrich, issued orders, requisitioned food and recruited new followers.[10] Meanwhile, the government of Protector Somerset had been busy attempting to quell the rebellion by a combination of persuasion and force. On 21 July, a royal herald arrived offering pardon to the Norfolk rebels if they dispersed. According to contemporary accounts, Kett refused the offer on the grounds that they were not rebelling against the King and required no pardon. The herald, making a mockery of the offer of clemency, then denounced Kett as a traitor, snatching away the chance of a negotiated settlement. However, Mayor Codd, along with Alderman Aldrich, accepted the royal pardon. They, along with other Norwich gentry, now made preparations to defend the city, ordering six guns to be hauled into firing positions on the walls. The insurgents, though, had brought in their own cannon – taken from the coastal defences – and began a (largely ineffective) bombardment of the city. The following day, after the local authorities' refusal to grant a truce, the rebels attacked, armed with spears, swords and pitchforks. The chronicler Nicholas Sotherton's account provides a vivid picture of their unorthodox tactics:

So impudent were they and so desperate that of theyr vagabond boyes . . . brychles and bear arssyde came among the thicket of the

arrows and gathered them up when some of the seid arrows stuck
fast in theyr leggs and other parts and did therwith most shame-
fully turne up theyr bare tayles agenst those which did shoote,
which soe dismayd the archers that it tooke theyr hart from them.[11]

With the defenders' spirits apparently broken by this display of
bare-arsed defiance, Norwich was in the insurgents' hands by the
evening. The Mayor was seized and made to set his signature to
the warrants issued by the rebels. Leading aldermen along with
captive gentry were imprisoned in the Earl of Surrey's palace. A
royal army, led by the Earl of Northampton, arrived at the city
gates on 31 July. Though the army gained easy access to the unde-
fended city, they endured heavy rebel attacks during the night. The
next morning, the main rebel host made their assault, routed the
royal forces and killed Northampton's second-in-command, Lord
Sheffield, in the mêlée. This victory offers another reminder, even
after Cade's rebellion, of the potency of 'unprofessional' rebel
armies in this period.

According to Neville, the rebels at Mousehold Heath, 'lurking in
those wood covers, transgressed all Laws both human and divine'.[12]
His lurid account of their actions does not tally with what we
know, not only about the rebel camps in Norfolk but about those
across the country, which aimed at the restoration of good government, not its destruction. Once encamped on Mousehold Heath,
the rebels had established a governing council made up of representatives from each of the hundreds in both Norfolk and Suffolk
from which the rebel host had been drawn. A mini-parliament, it
sat under an oak tree which became known as 'the oak of reformation', and here issued warrants for food, cattle, arms and manpower
in the name of the 'King's friends and deputies'.

It is important to stress the collective nature of the decision-
making at Mousehold. There is no strong evidence from the rebel
articles of petition themselves that Kett played any particularly
prominent role in their framing. Indeed, his name was added to the

text of the articles at a later date (in the seventeenth century) simply as a means of labelling the document. Furthermore, the unnumbered articles in the original give no clear indication, either, of the rebels' order of priorities. Overall, they called for the exclusion of the gentry from the commons and from dealing in land. They appealed to the Crown to act as a fair arbiter between the lords and the commonalty and to take on some of the powers of the magisterial classes. Rents were to be fixed at the levels of 1485. The articles also hinted at the rebels' religious radicalism, calling for the clergy to adopt an educative, preaching ministry and to end their involvment in the land market. The most far-reaching of the articles seemed to combine social and religious aspirations: 'We pray that all bonde men may be made Fre[e] for god made all Fre[e] with his precious blode sheddyng.' For contemporaries such as Sir William Paget, writing to the Protector on 7 July, the evangelicals' programme had acted as the spark to social revolution just as Luther's teachings had done in Germany, unleashing the bloody chaos of the Peasants' War of 1525.[13] As we shall see, however, the extent of the Norfolk rebels' commitment to Protestantism is questionable, and the parallel with the revolutionary millenarianism of the German Anabaptists spoke more of English upper-class anxieties than of the reality of the rebels' intentions.

Throughout the 'commotion time', though anger at the greed and maladministration of the governing classes was starkly evident, it was also apparent that those involved in the rising did not see themselves as rebels. Those encamped on Mousehold Heath and elsewhere, in the language of the warrants issued under the oak of reformation, saw themselves as the King's true servants and friends who would restore good government and right injustices. Many of their leaders, including men like Kett, were individuals of substantial wealth who had experience of government themselves, albeit at a lower level than that exercised by the traditional magisterial class. John Levet, a butcher and captain of the Bury St Edmunds rebels, was a nephew of Giles Levet, a minor gentleman and one of the bailiffs of Bury. Captain Brand at Ipswich was probably Robert Brand, who held the office of chamberlain in the borough of Ipswich in the 1540s; John Harbottle was a lesser merchant of Ipswich and had been chamberlain two years before Brand.[14] Many of the petty officers who were so heavily involved in the risings saw their activities as part of their official business. The rebels' desire to maintain what they perceived to be 'right government' was so strong that those in Norfolk even issued their own commission of purveyance so as to preserve the grain already collected for the Scottish armies, despite the deep unpopularity of the levy. Beyond collecting money and supplies for the camps, the rebel administration also sought to dispense justice and right longstanding wrongs. In Suffolk, the Bury rebels put one George Swinbourne into possession of his stepchildren's property in the town and allowed him to assume custody of the children against a rival claimant. At Ipswich, two complaints to the rebel captains against leading gentry are recorded, one of which led to a detachment from the Ipswich camp been dispatched to restore the complainant to his former copyhold at Nacton, four miles away.[15]

One of the chilling lessons of 1549 for England's governing classes was, then, that large swaths of the country could be run perfectly well – arguably more equitably and efficiently – without them. The oft-repeated threat in official homilies that rebellion would lead to anarchy, terror and destruction proved hollow. However, the rebels' administration would be short-lived and their victory over the Earl of Northampton's forces a pyrrhic one. In the following weeks, insurrection in the rest of the country was gradually subdued, so that the Norwich rebels became increasingly isolated. Though Northampton had presided over a debacle at Norwich, he had succeeded in suppressing the camp at Bury St Edmunds. The camp at Thetford melted away, while the one established at King's Lynn was destroyed, apparently with great loss of life. Great Yarmouth, despite rebel incursions, remained in the hands of those loyal to the regime. Rebels at Essex and Ipswich took up the offer of a royal pardon, and dispersed.

While all this was going on, a much larger royal army of fourteen thousand men was being assembled under the leadership of the Earl of Warwick, Kett's erstwhile landlord. At Henry VIII's death in 1547, John Dudley, then Viscount L'isle, had been one of the wealthiest and most important men in the kingdom. Created Earl of Warwick in February of that year, Dudley had many years of soldiering behind him, having recorded victories against the French and Scots during Henry's reign, and was renowned for his personal courage and coolness under fire.

Warwick and his soldiers arrived at Norwich on 23 August 1549. They were preceded by a royal herald who made an offer of pardon to the rebels if they would throw down their arms. Though some reportedly responded enthusiastically, discarding their weapons and promising loyalty to the King, others viewed the offer with suspicion and contempt, none more explicitly than 'an ungracious boy [who,] putting down his breeches, shewed his bare buttockes & did a filthy act: adding thereunto more filthy words'. One of the watching royal soldiers was so revolted with this verbal and physical riposte that he shot the boy dead. Kett had to be restrained from marching across the lines to confront Warwick face to face. Negotiations had clearly failed.[16]

There followed three days of intensive door-to-door fighting in the streets of the city. At one point, on the evening of 25 August, Warwick was almost beaten, his men pleading for him to surrender. Disgusted by what the Earl saw as their cowardice, he made each of them kiss his sword in turn, demanding their loyalty to the death.[17] Warwick's resolve and, more importantly, the arrival of additional mercenaries tilted the battle the way of the royal forces. At Dussindale, the flat valley that lay south of Mousehold Heath, Warwick's cavalry broke the rebel lines and rode among Kett's men, massacring them, in the gleeful words of Neville, like 'wild beasts'. Many of those not killed in the initial slaughter were executed very shortly afterwards. The gentry of Norwich, who had proved so pusillanimous on the night of the 25th when confronted with defeat, bayed for a general slaughter once they had broken the rebel resistance. It took the intervention of Warwick himself to cool their bloodlust. Although he acknowledged the rebels' 'wickedness to be such, as deserved to be grievously punished: and with the severest judgement that might be', yet he wondered how far the gentry would go. 'Would they ever show themselves discontented and never pleased? Would they leave no place for humble petition; none for pardon and mercy?' The high-flown pleas for clemency were followed by Warwick's clincher: 'Would they be Ploughmen themselves, and harrow their owne lands?'[18]

Despite calling for restraint, Warwick nonetheless had forty-nine of the rebels hanged from the market cross.*[19] And it was estimated that in total some three hundred rebels were executed in the immediate aftermath of the Norfolk rebellion. Indeed, historians have estimated that even without further retribution, the suppression of the 1549 rebellions overall represented a demographic catastrophe for the areas involved. In Norwich, the human impact was registered in the empty market stalls left vacant because their holders were either dead or had fled the area.[20] Similar violence was meted out to the rebels outside East Anglia. In Kent, Sir Thomas Wyatt hanged several rioters. In Wiltshire in June of that same year, rioters broke up the enclosures surrounding Sir William Herbert's new park at Wilton. Herbert was a violent man who had already been arraigned for manslaughter. His response to the rioters was to 'overrun and slay them'. In the Thames Valley Lord Grey of Wilton, dispatched to deal with rebels in the Cotswolds, oversaw fourteen executions, including two priests hanged from their church steeples, before marching on to help pacify the West Country.[21]

---

* The only evidence of these summary executions comes from the dry records of the city's accounts, which itemised the nine pence spent on the removal of bodies and the thruppence it cost to repair the ladder from which the condemned were thrown.

Kett himself escaped the bloodbath at Dussindale, but was captured the next day. He and his brother William were taken to London to be tried for treason, but were returned to Norwich to be executed. William was hanged from the tower of Wymondham Abbey, while Robert was hanged in chains from the walls of Norwich Castle. According to Neville, his body, which would have been seen by the townspeople of Norwich as they traded and shopped in the marketplace, remained suspended from the castle walls until it finally rotted away in 1615.

The familiarly brutal end to this particular (and most celebrated) episode in England's 'commotion time' provided hostile chroniclers like Neville and Sotherton with the necessary moral conclusion to their tales of iniquitous popular rebellion. The fruits of revolt, according to these accounts, were always bitter, the punishments severe but just, and inescapable. Focusing on Norfolk, and on Kett's rebellion especially, allowed these writers to cast a convenient shadow over most of the encampments that sprang up during the 'commotion time'. Many of the risings in fact dissolved as a result of negotiations with the authorities that at least partially satisfied rebel demands. In the case of Sotherton, a former mayor of Norwich, this also allowed him to obscure some of the Norfolk gentry's complicity in the revolt.

The events of 1549 threatened, if they did not fully realise, a profound transformation in English politics. The 'commotion time' was inextricably linked with the programme of social reform and Protestant Reformation instigated by Somerset's protectorate. The first stirrings of revolt – ditch-filling and the destruction of hedged enclosures – were probably seen as legitimated by Somerset's enclosure commissions. The rhetoric of the 'Commonwealth' had a radical tinge at an elite as well as a popular level. If there was not an identifiable 'party' of 'Commonwealthmen' in Tudor government, it is at least true that at mid-century a number of lay and ecclesiastical figures, some very close to the centre of power, were advocating far-reaching social and religious changes. Hugh Latimer's 'sermons on the plough' linked the covetousness of greedy enclosers with the pre-Reformation Church's legacy of a non-preaching clergy who hindered 'spiritual ploughing' in the same way that the Mousehold articles linked religious and material concerns. Latimer himself joked that he was happy to be spoken of as a 'seditious fellow', as Christ himself had been 'contented to be called seditious'.[22] The authorisation of the vernacular Bible and the termination of a number of Henry VIII's heresy statutes saw England experience a level of press freedom it would not see again until the 1640s.

Some of the works that appeared at this time had deeply radical overtones. The English translation of Thomas More's *Utopia* in 1551 made significant alterations to the text that broadened the social implications of the work, seriously proscribed in More's original. *Utopia* stated that communal living and the holding of goods in common was the way of living of the 'rightest Christian companies'. However, while More had clearly identified these 'companies' only with monasticism – '*coenobia*' in the Latin marginalia of his original work – in the translation this caveat had been removed. The translator, Ralph Robinson, himself a middling-sort 'Goldsmith and citizen of London', had suggested that Utopian government was 'Godly government', implying that reformation and social transformation were two sides of the same coin. If communitarianism and the holding of goods in common were not simply the preserve of the monastic orders, then the camps established by the rebels of 1549 might equally constitute a model of 'Godly government'.[23]

Of course, Kett and his fellow rebels did not present themselves as social revolutionaries and there is no evidence that they saw themselves in these terms in private, either. Like the rebels of 1381 and 1450, those involved in the 1549 risings argued that they were the King's friends and 'true commons', not his enemies. These were not regicidal republicans. Yet in one key respect, the rebels of

1549 had a significantly different intent from that of their earlier counterparts. The rebellions of the 'commotion time' were essentially static. The rebels took control of major sites of local government but made no attempt, unlike Tyler or Cade, to launch an assault on London. This was not due to blinkered parochialism. Rather, Kett and his men believed that they were the partners and help-meets of the protectoral regime, not its enemies. Their targets were the oppressive magisterial class in their counties, not a clique of courtiers based in London. Clear evidence of this comes in the aftermath of the failure of Kett's rebellion. Hearing of the Earl of Warwick's plans to overthrow him, Somerset issued a desperate plea for support to the country at large. In response, an army of some four thousand men assembled and offered to die in defence of his cause, denouncing Warwick and his supporters as plotting the 'utter undoing of the commons'.[24] Somerset rejected the offer to lead a popular revolt and was toppled from power by Warwick in October 1549.

Unlike 1381 and, to a lesser extent, 1450, the upper classes did not rally to the Crown. Somerset's policies had alienated the majority of the traditional ruling elite. He now had to look to those below the level of the gentry to provide him with a support base. He appalled his fellow nobles by negotiating with the rebel captains, even paying some, such as Latimer of Kent, to act as go-betweens, ferrying messages from the court to various rebel groups.[25] On Somerset's part, this ploy was undoubtedly prompted primarily by pragmatism rather than principle. In a letter to the diplomat Sir Philip Hoby written on 24 August 1549, Somerset had described the rebellion as 'no other thing but a plague and a fury among the vilest and worst sort of men'. He believed that many of the rebel complaints concealed a simple lust for power and wealth:

Some crieth, pluck down enclosures and parks, some for their commons, others pretend religion. A number would rule another while, and some direct things as gentlemen have done, and indeed all have conceived a wonderful hate against gentlemen and taketh them as their enemies. The ruffians among them and the soldiers, which be the chief doers, look for spoil.[26]

Yet, if he held conventional upper-class views about the motivations behind popular rebellion, Somerset was nonetheless influenced by some of the 'Commonwealth' ideas circulating at this point. Like other enormously wealthy noblemen, he may have been concerned about the conspicuous display of his wealth and power – his unfinished protectoral palace required some two million bricks for its construction – but he also instituted reforms on his own estates which considerably reduced the burdens of villeinage, replacing many customary dues with reasonable cash payments. More significant in broader terms were the policies that Somerset implemented in 1548–9 to deal with the crisis unfolding across the nation. Armed resistance remained anathema to the protectoral regime, but it proved willing to negotiate with the rebels if they would drop the threat of force and communicate via the device of suitably framed petitions. Somerset also put in place, as we have seen, enclosure commissioners who, drawn from below gentry level, would be empowered to review and, if necessary, remove recent enclosures. In short, Somerset's government entered into negotiations with the people and offered them a significant share of power at the obvious expense of the major landowners.[27]

The response of the commons to these overtures was also very revealing and tells us much about the sophistication of popular politics. Somerset had initially believed that the risings in East Anglia and southern England, like those in Cornwall and Devon, were linked to residual loyalty to the Catholic Church. He blamed the stirrings in Norfolk on 'papist priests', although the rebels were very quick to assure him of their enthusiasm for the new religion. Certainly, there is some evidence that the Norfolk rebels were genuinely attached to the idea of maintaining an active, preaching ministry. The chronicler Neville acknowledged that the rebel camps had made use of chaplains for morning and evening prayers, though he claimed this was a piece of hypocrisy meant only to give their cause the veneer of sanctity. Somerset's regime was itself suspicious of the depth of sincerity behind the rebels' stated religious views. The Privy Council responded positively to the Essex rebels' demands for recourse to 'sondrie textes of scripture' and were pleased that the articles in their petition 'acknowledge the Gospell whiche ye saye ye greatlie hunger'. Yet they remained unsure whether these demands proceeded 'from the harte', or were 'only a recytall of textes' for their 'present purpose'.

The evidence was contradictory. The Northaw rebels had rejected Edward's authority on the grounds of his minority, whereas the Essex articles presented by 'William Essex' had acknowledged the boy-king as a 'Josiah' who, like the biblical monarch, because of his attachment to the faith, was better suited to rule than a man many years his senior.[28] Equally, that evocative phrase from the Norwich articles calling for the manumission of all serfs on the grounds of Christ's sacrifice may have owed less to the influence of evangelical teaching than it initially appeared. Villeinage was by this point relatively uncommon in East Anglia, but bondmen (those bound to give service to the lord of the manor as part of their tenancy) were to be found on most of the estates of Thomas Howard, Duke of Norfolk. What seemed at first a religiously inspired call for universal freedom may in fact have been a targeted attack on the power of a hated local magnate. Deducing the degree to which religious beliefs were sincerely held by the populace is a thorny historical problem and one that many historians of the Reformation find virtually impossible to resolve conclusively. What we can ascertain from the rebel petitions is that those who rose and formed encampments in 1549 understood that framing their demands in the language of the Reformation was a good way of getting themselves heard. If their own religious beliefs remain elusive, the strategic nous of those below gentry level was clearly on display.

*

The potential partnership between Crown and commons was never fully realised. After 1549, rebellions were suppressed with even greater severity than before. In the wake of the revolt of the northern earls against Elizabeth I's government in 1569, her agents, eagerly egged on by the Virgin Queen, summarily executed rebels by the hundreds. Writing in January 1570, Sir Thomas Gargrave stated that in the North Riding of Yorkshire 'ther ys by marcyall lawe alredy executyd, above 500 of the poore sorte'. The Earl of Sussex especially singled out those 'constables and other officers' whom he saw as the common people's seducers.[29] Hostile accounts of the rebellions of 1549, foremost among them Alexander Neville's *De Furoribus Norfolciensium* (1575), a text given to schoolchildren as part of their education in Latin rhetoric, rammed home the evils of revolt and the harsh punishments that would befall those foolish enough to engage in insurrection. Deeper social changes during the Elizabethan era further diminished the chances of another popular rebellion as widespread as the 'commotion time'. Many of those petty officers, such as Robert Kett, who had earlier been leading rebels were increasingly integrated with those wealthy vested interests that promoted enclosure and sought to stifle popular resistance. The energies of many prosperous yeomen were now directed at engrossing the estates of their less well-off neighbours, not in coming to their aid. Thomas Dillamore, a yeoman of Chippenham, Cambridgeshire, in 1636 was in sole possession of land that in 1544 had been in the hands of fifteen men.[30] The serious threat that popular rebellion had once posed authority appeared to have been permanently negated. The so-called 'Oxfordshire Rising' of 1596 was a case in point: the 'rising' consisted of no more than the meeting of a carpenter and two millers on a hilltop in a preparation for a march on London. Despite the fact that no one else appears to have heeded this call to arms, the three men were taken into custody, tortured and then executed.[31] Serious uprisings in the late sixteenth and early seventeenth centuries, such as the Northern Rebellion of 1569 and Essex's revolt in

1601, were led by the aristocracy (a trend which the civil war, at its opening at least, confirmed).

Yet 1549 did more than facilitate the further enrichment of some better-off yeomen and ensure their gradual assimilation into the political elite. It did more, even, than hold out the brief promise of a new form of government based on the cooperation of Crown and commons (a promise that was, in many respects, to be fulfilled during the 1640s). In the same way that the memory of 1381 and 1450 had clearly influenced the rebels of 1549 and provided a geography of rebellion, so the 'commotion time', despite its transformation by Neville and later writers into merely 'Kett's rebellion', retained a powerful force in the popular memory.

Much of what historians have been able to recover about the much wider scale of the 1549 rebellions has been gleaned from statements from individuals about the 'commotion time' made fifty or even sixty years after the event. These were the words of ordinary men and women who remembered the 'merry world' of the camp at Mousehold Heath and viewed Robert Kett as an 'honest man'.[32] While Neville gloated that Kett's mouldering bones had provided Norwich citizens with a grim reminder of the penalties for rebellion well into the early seventeenth century, for some, the daily sight of his body on the walls of the castle may instead have brought a reminder of a brief time in which the grasp of landholders had been loosened, long-standing injustices righted and popular government established. Similarly, the decision to celebrate the anniversary of the city's relief on 27 August with special sermons every year, originally meant as a thanksgiving for Norwich's deliverance from the rebels, was gradually transformed over the centuries into a commemoration of Kett. By the nineteenth century, historians were revising the unsympathetic picture of the rebel leader painted by Neville and Sotherton, and by the early twentieth, as we have seen, he was even being claimed as an early socialist.

Today, the visitor to Norwich has hardly arrived in the city before he or she comes upon some street or park named after Kett. The fabled 'oak of reformation', propped up by stakes, remains a tourist attraction. Even the 'ungracious boy' who bared his back-side to the royal herald was, until very recently, preserved for posterity in a mural in the shopping centre. Beyond Norfolk, Kett's oak of reformation is celebrated in sculpture outside Kett House in Cambridge, a legacy of the fact that one of Robert Kett's descendants, George Kett, became the Tory Mayor of the city in late Victorian times. Today, it is Kett and his rebels who are remembered and celebrated and the Earl of Warwick who has been consigned to historical oblivion. As George Kett put it, perhaps the greatest evidence that Kett was a committed Christian can be seen in his reverence for Christ's example: 'This forerunner of Rousseau followed the teaching of his Master in giving up his life for the people whom God had made free, but who were yet found everywhere in chains.'[33]

In a book published in 1883, H. M. Hyndman, the founder of the Social Democratic Federation, Britain's first fully fledged Marxist party, placed his organisation within a British tradition of class struggle:

> Tyler, Cade, Ball, Kett . . . read to me like sound English names: not a foreigner in the whole batch. They all held opinions which our capitalist-landlord House of Commons would denounce as direct plagiarism from 'foreign revolutionists'. We islanders have been revolutionists, however, and will be again, ignorant as our capitalists are of the history of the people.[34]

That the names of Wat Tyler, Jack Straw, John Ball, Jack Cade and Robert Kett are so familiar to us is a legacy of the enduring power of hostile contemporary sources. These were the work of medieval and early modern chroniclers intent on producing propagandist narratives warning the monarch's subjects of the evils of rebellion and the harsh penalties for revolt. Writers such as Jean Froissart, Thomas Walsingham, Nicholas Sotherton and Alexander Neville presented the uprisings as the work of ambitious and unscrupulous upstarts, who manipulated the gullible commonalty into supporting their schemes. These narratives set out a simple morality play in which the vaulting ambition and pride of Tyler, Cade and Kett were followed by their inevitable fall and just and exemplary – meaning brutal – punishment. Their supporters likewise received the providential rewards of rebellion: death by hanging, drawing and quartering. After the aberration of popular revolt, the natural order of society was restored, the lower orders reduced to silent passivity.[35]

Unfortunately, these chronicles and histories remain our main sources of information about the revolts. Some historians and writers on the left have at times adopted a rather too literal approach to these texts, accepting uncritically the calls for class war sometimes placed in the mouths of Tyler, Ball and Cade, as if the rebel captains intended a mass slaughter of the aristocracy and gentry and the 'levelling' of all social distinctions.[36] At the other extreme, some historians have adopted an overly cautious approach to these sources, effectively glossing over any social or political radicalism in medieval and early modern English rebellions. For such academics, these uprisings never challenged the dominant idea of a 'society of orders', a supposedly natural hierarchy of aristocracy, gentry and clergy, beneath whom lay the commons, 'those who did not rule'; medieval rebels, it is argued, sought only to remedy abuses perpetrated by certain individuals within this system, not to overthrow the system itself.[37]

It is often claimed, partly as a result of this alleged inherent conservatism, that popular rebellion in this period had little tangible political, social or economic impact.[38] But we seriously underestimate the importance of these revolts if we see them as essentially futile. In three keys ways, the Peasants' Revolt, Cade's rebellion and the 'commotion time' of 1549 were radical events.

In the first place, the 'inevitability' of the defeat of these revolts is deeply questionable. The element of contingency was central to the ultimate suppression of all of them. In the case of the Peasants' Revolt, the actions of the young Richard II were crucial to averting a potential catastrophe for the English ruling elite. As Alistair Dunn has pointed out, had the monarch not acted so decisively, the implementation of the Kentishmen's demands for total manumission of England's serfs would have seen 1381 ranked with other world-historical events, such as the abolition of private serfdom in the Russian Empire in 1861 and the emancipation of the slaves in the United States in 1865, as a vital stage in ending human bondage. On the other hand, if the Peasants' Revolt did not see the immediate liberation of the serfs, it unquestionably hastened the decline of bound labour. The years that followed 1381, rather than being characterised by brutal repression by the elite, represented a historic high in terms of wages, living conditions and life expectancy for the English peasantry. Subsequent popular rebellions were launched not out of desperation but as a result of the growing confidence of the commons. The assertive yeoman class, in particular, forced a grudging recognition from the elite of the important role of the commonalty in politics.

Second, popular rebellion had important intellectual as well as social consequences. As most of Wat Tyler's men were *not* serfs, their demands for freedom were symbolic as well as practical: manumission represented the lifting of all oppressive burdens. 'Freedom' already meant something more than just a legal status.[39] This language of English liberty resonated down through the demands of the Norfolk rebels to the Parliamentarian rhetoric of the 1640s. By the time of the civil war, 'slavery' was clearly understood not merely as a legal status or an economic system, but as a metaphysical state, meaning any situation where the liberty of the individual was ultimately subject to the caprice of a superior. Such, Parliamentarian propagandists alleged, was the case of the English people under the government of Charles I.

Far from being creatures of habit, bound by the political and social conventions of their day, ordinary people in late medieval England were capable of making sophisticated and strategic use of political and religious language. It is not just that some rebels may have been influenced by contemporary radical ideas, whether Lollard heresy, evangelical Protestantism or the arguments of mid-Tudor 'Commonwealthsmen', though there is certainly some evidence that this was the case. Rather, the political conventions of the day were ambiguous enough to be open to more radical readings. Propagandists may have repeatedly insisted upon the naturalness of the 'society of orders', but lordship placed obligations on the lord as well as on the serf. Rebels were often quick to seize upon the implicit social contract inherent within this vision of society. Moreover, many of those who did rebel, such as Robert Kett, were not men excluded from authority but men who governed at a local level. Other terms, too, could be stretched. 'Commonwealth' might be interpreted as meaning the whole realm, as when royal ministers formulated schemes for the reform of the 'Commonweal', but it could equally be read as meaning the commons, without the gentry or the lords.[40] Historians have occasionally presented such interpretations of established ideas as 'misunderstandings' or 'misreadings', by sub-gentry groups, of concepts articulated by the ruling elite. Rather, they are evidence of the ability of ordinary people to use political ideas in sophisticated, strategic ways.

These medieval and early modern rebels created a memory of resistance in revolt that was preserved first orally and later through print. That memory also reverberated through the physical landscape. It was no coincidence that Jack Cade's rebels, like those of 1381, formed their camp outside London on Blackheath, or that the Norfolk rebels of 1549 followed their East Anglian ancestors of 1381 in choosing Mousehold Heath. In spite of the severe repression experienced, and the efforts of the Crown's propagandists, the memory of these rebellions, for the people at least, remained profoundly empowering. In 1642, as England moved from rebellion to outright revolution, it seemed that the ghosts of Wat Tyler, Jack Cade and Robert Kett were walking abroad once more.

PART THREE

'THE POOREST HE . . . THE GREATEST HE': RADICALISM IN THE ENGLISH REVOLUTION

The Levellers were defeated. Two hundred years later, however, the working class, the Chartists, put forward similar demands which, as the result of hard prolonged struggle, have been substantially realised.

Daphne May, 'The Putney Debates', *Communist Review*, January 1948[1]

The Levellers . . . anticipated by a century and a half the main ideas of the American and French Revolutions

Tony Benn[2]

The Roots of Civil War Radicalism: The Revolution before the Revolution

On the morning of 17 May 1649, Corporals Perkins and Church and Cornet Thompson were executed by firing squad in the churchyard at Burford.* The three condemned men had been identified as the ringleaders of a mutiny of over a thousand troops (a fourth soldier sentenced to death, Cornet Henry Denne, 'howling and weeping like a crocodile', repudiated the mutiny and was reprieved through the intervention of General Sir Thomas Fairfax).†[1] While Thompson expressed contrition for his part in the mutiny and Perkins, petrified by the sight of his dead comrade lying at his feet, could only cry 'Shoot, shoot',

---

* Another corporal implicated in the rising, William Eyre, was a volunteer member of the irregular militia that the republican MP Henry Marten had raised in Berkshire and was not deemed to be under military discipline. He was imprisoned in Oxford and then Warwick Gaol until 1650; see W. Eyre, *The Serious Representation of Col. William Eyre* (1649).

† As commander of the Parliamentarian New Model Army, Fairfax was personally involved in suppressing the Leveller mutinies of 1649. He showed leniency at Burford, but a month earlier, over Cromwell's pleas for clemency, he had had Robert Lockyer executed for leading a mutiny in Colonel Whalley's regiment.

Church strode to the place of execution and 'without the least acknowledgment of errour or shew of feare' pulled off his doublet, looked his executioners in the eye and bade them do their duty.[2]

The soldiers had broken with military discipline on 1 May at Salisbury, refusing to be sent to Ireland to fight the Royalist coalition there until their grievances, especially over indemnity for their actions in war and arrears of pay, now amounting to £1.3 million, had been met. Some of the mutineers were influenced by so-called 'Leveller' ideas, which, as mentioned earlier, promoted a new constitutional settlement for England based on a wider male electoral franchise, greater political accountability and religious toleration. Thompson's brother Corporal William Thompson had drafted a printed declaration that combined the soldiers' demands with the text of the Leveller manifesto, the 'Agreement of the People'. A number of those involved in the mutinies of 1649, including William Thompson, William Eyre, Robert Everard and Robert Lockyer, had already been implicated in earlier Leveller-inspired mutinies.

The 'Burford business', as it came to be known, might have remained a footnote to accounts of the demise of the Leveller movement of the seventeenth century were it not for the efforts of the Oxford Workers' Educational Association, and in particular Alan Hicks. In 1975, Hicks organised a meeting to commemorate the deaths of Thompson, Church and Perkins. In its first year 'Levellers' Day', as it came to be known, was a relatively low-key affair. This all changed in 1976 when Hicks decided to invite the then Energy Secretary, Tony Benn, to come and speak. The presence of a government minister (and an increasingly outspoken one, at that) not only attracted greater attention for the event from the left-wing press but also raised Tory hackles both locally and nationally. Burford's Conservative MP, the future Cabinet minister Douglas Hurd, complained that the WEA was misusing public funds to support what was essentially a party-political event, noting sardonically that he doubted that the minister was coming to the Cotswolds to talk about North Sea oil. Locals took more direct action, daubing the side of the church with the words 'Bollocks to Benn', picked out in yellow paint (the graffiti were hastily removed with wire brushes). Although the Vicar of Burford had supported the event, a local nonconformist minister, Raymond Moody, complained that local residents did not want the day to become a regular left-wing jamboree 'like the Durham miners' gala'.

Despite the efforts of the local Conservative Association, who in 1983 tried to scupper Levellers' Day by booking the church hall for a nonexistent jumble sale, Moody's nightmare came true. The annual event has been running successfully for over thirty years and has attracted a 'Who's Who' of left-wing speakers and activists: Labour luminaries including Ken Livingstone, Michael Foot and a pre-Blairite-makeover Peter Hain, prominent peace campaigners such as Bruce Kent, environmentalists such as George Monbiot, and the Marxist historians E. P. Thompson and Christopher Hill. The day has long featured appropriately right-on entertainment as well as speeches, from artists like the 'Bard of Barking', Billy Bragg, and Mark Chadwick from the Levellers folk-rock group. Occasionally, the odd cabaret act has performed too ('David Blunkett and his dog Nelson').[3]

Why has the suppression of the mutiny at Burford become such a celebrated part of England's radical history? Undoubtedly, some of this is due to the setting itself. The magnificent Church of St John the Baptist at Burford is a living monument to the divisions rent in English society by the civil war. At one end of the church is the font where Antony Sedley scrawled his name as he and his fellow mutineers waited to learn their fate, while at the other lies the memorial to Lucius Cary, 2nd Viscount Falkland, a leading Royalist born in Burford, killed at the Battle of Newbury in 1643. There is something slightly incongruous about an event that celebrates political radicalism taking place in a chocolate-box tourist town within the Tory Cotswolds. Even so, Burford's honeyed sandstone buildings provide an undeniably fitting backdrop as the local civil war re-enactment societies march along its streets.

But this is only part of the reason that Levellers' Day has been an enduring success. The continued commemoration of the suppression of the mutiny at Burford also tells us much about how and why we remember the Leveller movement as a whole. It is now, perhaps, the most celebrated of all English radical movements – though, as we will see, its elevation to the historical pantheon has been a recent phenomenon. What is commemorated at Burford, however, is the nadir of that movement, not its zenith, and some historians question whether the Burford mutineers should really be regarded as Levellers at all.[4] The palpable pathos of Levellers' Day, with its annual musket salute to the executed soldiers, reveals a preference for memorialising the movement as a heroic failure. Like the eighteenth-century radical republican William Godwin, husband of Mary Wollstonecraft and father of Mary Shelley, twentieth-century historians and writers have admired the Levellers as a movement that anticipated the modern political ideals of civil rights, mass suffrage and freedom of conscience, but who were too far 'ahead of their time' to see their ideas come to fruition.[5] Instead, historians such as Christopher Hill and E. P. Thompson and politicians including Tony Benn have argued that Leveller ideas were driven back into a radical underground, to re-emerge in the late eighteenth century in the thought of English 'Jacobins' and Painites.

Recently, historians have seriously questioned the prominence given to the group in the history of the English Revolution. They have even queried whether there was a meaningful 'Leveller' movement at all, at least before the autumn of 1647, noting that the term was one of abuse, fastened on John Lilburne and his associates by their critics.[6] It has been argued that Leveller ideas only appear 'modern' when viewed through the distorting lens of a Marxist/socialist historiography that wishes to place them within a 'tradition' of British radicalism. In fact, some recent scholars contend that the main Leveller spokesmen, because of their own intensely heterodox religious views, were more preoccupied with liberty of conscience than with the vote. The Levellers, these historians argue, only loom large in contemporary historiography because of the present-centred, ideologically driven concerns of left-wing historians. In their own time, the Levellers had little impact and were deemed unworthy of comment by most historians of the civil war until the late nineteenth century.[7]

New research, however, demonstrates that the key Leveller writers, Lilburne, Richard Overton, William Walwyn and John Wildman, were at the centre of the political turmoil of the civil war and the revolution. Far from being marginal figures, individuals like Wildman were, in fact, well connected to radical MPs within the Commons such as Henry Marten and Thomas Rainborowe.[8] By cautioning against seeing their politics as reflecting a simple dichotomy between radicals and conservatives, recent work has also directed our attention to those moments when the army grandees themselves seriously considered radical solutions, such as the Levellers' various Agreements of the People, for settling the nation. These moments demonstrate that in pragmatic terms, radical thought did exert a significant influence at the time. More than this, they remind us that the failure to achieve more radical political settlements was a result of contingent factors; it was not inevitable.

Unquestionably, though, hostile pamphleteers were successful in smearing men such as Lilburne, Walwyn, Overton and Wildman with accusations of 'levelling' – wishing to do away with private property and 'level' the social hierarchy – charges that stuck in part because of the emergence of groups such as the 'Diggers', who did advocate communal living and the abolition of the private ownership of land. The success of this propaganda campaign against the Levellers made it politically dangerous to exploit publicly the work of Lilburne *et al.* Consequently, the acknowledged influence of these writers was minimal until their 'rediscovery' in the nineteenth century. That process of historical erasure has obscured the extent to which the political world of the seventeenth century was profoundly shaken, and shaped, by radical thought and action.

Any attempt to discuss the phenomenon of radicalism in the English Revolution must also tackle the nature of that revolution itself. The leading 'revisionist' historian of the civil wars, John Morrill, has stated that the events of the 1640s did not constitute the first modern revolution, but in fact, 'the last and greatest of the European wars of religion'.[9] Other historians have suggested that the English Revolution should be re-termed 'a Second Reformation' or its own 'radical reformation'.[10] By the late sixteenth century, Protestantism was entrenched as the official religion of the state and was now the dominant religion among those individuals who normally constituted the core of the 'political nation' – the aristocracy and gentry. However, this ascendancy conveyed no sense of security to English Protestants. Many reformers (perhaps with some justification) were convinced that most people were indifferent to the Christian religion and would prefer to spend their Sundays fishing, gaming or drinking. The Reformation's shallow roots were especially worrying when placed in a European context of rapid Protestant retreat in the face of the forces of an aggressive Catholic counter-Reformation. While the fear of the threat of 'Popery', of a Vatican-inspired insurrection and assassination, undoubtedly lurched at times into frenzied paranoia, the threat was nonetheless real, as demonstrated first by the danger of foreign invasion posed by the Spanish Armada in 1588, and second by the possibility of domestic conspiracy posed by the Gunpowder Plot of 1605.

Worse still, English Protestants were internally divided, between those contented to conform to the Elizabethan Church settlement and those, known by their critics as 'puritans', who believed that the established religion was still only 'half-reformed', retaining too much doctrine and discipline that smacked of the old religion.

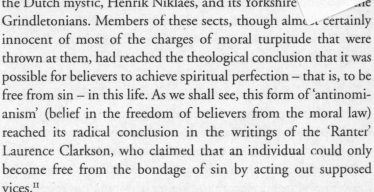

Puritanism, nonetheless, remained a reform m
within the Church rather than one seeking to s

Outside of the established Church and viewe
and hostility by conformists and puritans alik
number of religious sects, such as the Family of Lov
the Dutch mystic, Henrik Niklaes, and its Yorkshire
Grindletonians. Members of these sects, though almost certainly
innocent of most of the charges of moral turpitude that were
thrown at them, had reached the theological conclusion that it was
possible for believers to achieve spiritual perfection – that is, to be
free from sin – in this life. As we shall see, this form of 'antinomianism' (belief in the freedom of believers from the moral law)
reached its radical conclusion in the writings of the 'Ranter'
Laurence Clarkson, who claimed that an individual could only
become free from the bondage of sin by acting out supposed
vices.[11]

Always fragile and contested, the Elizabethan religious settlement
began to break apart in the last years of the reign of James I. In the
eyes of many British Protestants, the Thirty Years War was part of an
apocalyptic conflict between the forces of Christ (Protestantism) and
Anti-Christ (the papacy and the Catholic Habsburg emperors).
Domestic attacks on James's pacific foreign policy convinced him
that Calvinist critics, including his Archbishop of Canterbury,
George Abbot, were politically dangerous, and James began to
favour a group of churchmen led by William Laud, whose vision of
religion was less overtly anti-papal and placed a reassuringly heavy
emphasis upon order and obedience. These changes within the
Church accelerated after the accession of Charles I in 1625. Charles
strongly favoured the style of worship offered by Laud and his associates, which elevated ceremony above the puritan emphasis on
preaching. Laud believed in the 'beauty of holiness', the importance
of celebrating God through the material fabric of churches, stained
glass, altar rails and more elaborate clerical dress, and of separating
the sacred from the profane.

...iewed puritanism as essentially schismatic and regarded vir-
...lly all aspects of the social networks established by puritans,
such as the establishment of lectureships via voluntary subscriptions, as fundamentally seditious. He was made Bishop of London
in 1628, then Archbishop of Canterbury in 1633, following the
death of the long-sidelined George Abbot. The rise of the Laudian
faction was viewed with growing horror and dismay by many
English Protestants. Coupled, through Charles's French queen
Henrietta Maria, with the increasing Catholic presence at court,
Laudian innovations seemed to indicate that, in the words of the
Earl of Bedford, Laud was 'that little thief put into the window of
the church to unlock the door to Popery'.

Laud's rigorous campaign against nonconformity was most
notoriously evidenced by the brutal punishments meted out first
to Alexander Leighton in 1630 and then to William Prynne, John
Bastwick and Henry Burton in 1637 for distributing anti-episcopal
literature. Leighton was placed in the pillory for two hours in the
middle of a snowstorm. His ear was nailed to the pillory before
being cut off and he was then whipped thirty-seven times before
being branded with the letters S.S. (for 'sower of sedition').
Prynne, Bastwick and Burton received similarly grisly punishments – this was the second time that Prynne had had his ears
trimmed: he had been given the same treatment in 1633 for a work
that had denounced female actors as 'notorious whores', an unfortunate choice of words, given the Queen's fondness for acting in
court entertainments.

Laud's determination to root out puritan sedition had the reverse
effect: it radicalised Protestants who had previously seen themselves
as orthodox members of the Church of England. For example,
Stephen Denison, a lecturer at All-Hallow's, Thames Street,
London, had in 1627 vigorously attacked from the pulpit one John
Hetherington, a 'Familist' box-maker, and presented him to the
Ecclesiastical Court of High Commission for his allegedly heretical
views. By the 1630s, however, Denison was himself in trouble with

the Laudian authorities for preaching against the religious pictures and stained glass that had been installed in the newly restored St Katherine Creechurch, Aldgate. In 1635, Denison was brought up before the Court of High Commission and suspended from his ministry.[12] For some, such as John Cotton of Boston, Lincolnshire, the pressure of Laudian persecution was so severe that it could only be relieved by emigration to the New World. Others, including the Cheshire minister Samuel Eaton, fled to the Dutch Republic.

It was as part of this campaign against Laudian persecution that two of the leading Levellers, John Lilburne and Richard Overton, first came to prominence. Lilburne, born in Sunderland in 1615 to a minor gentry family of modest means, had been exposed to puritan ideas through his apprenticeship with a London clothier, Thomas Hewson. By 1636, Lilburne's enthusiasm for the puritan cause saw him regularly visiting Dr John Bastwick in prison, and the following year he was a tearful witness to his friend's brutal punishment. The cruelty of the Laudian regime catalysed Lilburne's political awakening. He became heavily involved in printing illicit anti-episcopal tracts, travelling to and from England and the Netherlands to oversee their production and distribution. By 1638, these activities had come to the attention of the authorities and in April of that year, by order of the prerogative court of Star Chamber, Lilburne was flogged all the way from Fleet Prison to Westminster and then placed in the pillory before finally being gaoled. Prefiguring his later pamphlets which dwelt on his many subsequent trials and imprisonments, he was quick to publicise his sufferings in print. In November 1640, through the efforts of a new MP, Oliver Cromwell, Lilburne was released from prison. By now, he had become something of a celebrity: an engraving by George Glover from 1641 depicts a raffishly handsome young man with an aquiline nose, well-trimmed moustache and chiselled cheekbones.

Richard Overton too began his public career as a key part of the campaign against Laudian 'prelacy'. His early life remains obscure. He may have been university-educated – a Richard Overton matriculated at Queens' College, Cambridge, in 1631 – but we cannot be certain that this was the future Leveller.[13] Unlike the self-publicist Lilburne, Overton, especially in his early career, hid behind the cloak of anonymity. By 1640, however, he was certainly involved in illicitly printing radical religious works. Recent research has demonstrated that Overton was the leading figure behind the secret 'Cloppenburg Press', a printing operation that, before the lifting of ecclesiastical censorship, disseminated radical religious literature, including works by the puritan 'martyr' William Prynne. These works, though, went much further than attacks on the Laudian regime: they called for the utter destruction of the repressive state Church, anticipating Overton's later support for very broad religious toleration.[14]

Religious controversy in the pre-civil-war era was clearly deeply divisive, and capable of dissolving other bonds – of kinship, of fealty – that held communities together. Conversely, religious belief could also unite individuals who otherwise existed in very different social worlds: the poor London wood-turner Nehemiah Wallington and Robert Greville, 2nd Baron Brooke, were both convinced that Parliament was fighting a war for godly reformation. However, we miss something if we view the English civil war as being caused only by 'religion' interpreted in a very narrow sense. The religious struggle was also a political and cultural struggle. The fortunes of England's Reformation had waxed and waned with the royal succession, from the caesaro-papalism of Henry VIII to the evangelical Protestantism of Edward VI, to the counter-Reformation Catholicism of Mary and the less distinctly Calvinist Protestantism of Elizabeth I. Importantly, this top-down dynastic Reformation was confirmed by parliamentary statute. It was a Reformation legitimised not by popular action or mere royal will, but by the law of the land. In 1642, Parliament justified its resistance to the King on legal as well as religious grounds, as Thomas May, the official historian of the Long Parliament that sat from 1640 from 1649, explained:

That frequent naming of religion, as if it were the only quarrel, hath caused a great mistake of the question in some . . . to abuse the parliament's cause . . . as, instead of disputing whether the parliament of England lawfully assembled . . . may by arms defend the religion established by the same power, together with the laws and liberties of the nation: they make it the question, whether subjects, taken in a general notion, may make war against their king for religion's sake.[15]

May's point can be illustrated further by looking at some of the constitutional flashpoints of Charles I's reign. The King's decision to rule without parliaments after 1629 forced him to rely on a number of 'fiscal expedients', based on his prerogative powers as monarch, in order to raise enough revenue to make up the shortfall produced by the loss of parliamentary subsidies. The most notorious of these, and the most financially successful in the short term, was 'ship money'. A traditional emergency levy on maritime counties that required each county to raise the cost of the hire of one ship, ship money was first levied by Charles in 1634. Controversy over it intensified in October 1636, when it became clear that Charles intended to levy the tax on all counties, and on a regular, not emergency, basis. His right to do this was famously challenged by the wealthy Buckinghamshire landowner John Hampden, who made clear that his stance was based on principle, not financial self-interest, by paying all of his ship-money assessment on his property in the county, bar the sum of twenty shillings. The King finally obtained a legal decision in his favour on 12 June 1638, but the judges ruled for the Crown only by the narrowest possible margin, seven to five.

The dispute over ship money was more than just an argument over the principle of 'no taxation without representation'. To understand the core of the controversy we need to look at a speech made by Hampden in Parliament in 1628, eight years before he decided to take his stance. Then, according to contemporary accounts, he had stated that if '[the King] be no papist, papists are friends and kindred to him'.[16] Hampden was clearly convinced that there was a 'popish plot' to alter the government of both Church and state, and that the origins of that conspiracy lay very close to the King himself. He was not alone in his view, and had contacts with the godly peer Viscount Saye and Sele, a fellow ship-money refuser, and the Earl of Bedford. In court, Hampden was represented by Oliver St John, later one of the leading 'political Independents' in the Long Parliament, an advocate of religious toleration and close associate of Oliver Cromwell.

So opposition to Ship Money was based not just on financial self-interest nor on the constitutional principle that taxation could only be levied with parliamentary approval, but also on the belief that if Charles could successfully support himself via fiscal expedients of this kind, he would have no need to call Parliament ever again. And, without Parliament to stop him, there would be nothing to prevent him completing the process already begun by his archbishop, William Laud, in reverting England to 'Popery'.

Finance, politics and religion were, then, deeply intertwined. 'Popery' itself signified not only the reintroduction of Catholic forms of worship but also its political analogues, the increasing power of the clergy – seen in the elevation of Laud and other bishops to the Privy Council – and the weakening of the authority of representative institutions, especially Parliament.[17] The anti-episcopal works circulated by Richard Overton suggested that Charles's government was not just infected with Popery but was an evil tyranny. As early as 1640, the pamphlets coming from his Cloppenburg Press were suggesting that this tyrannical government could only be stopped by force.

As the key role of the mere apprentice Lilburne suggests, it was not just Protestant gentlemen such as John Hampden who were engaged in this battle against the forces of Popery. Indeed, if our focus is restricted to Westminster alone, it can appear as if events hung solely on the actions of the great Parliamentarian peers Essex,

Warwick, Bedford and Saye and Sele, plus their clients in the Lower House, Hampden, John Pym, Oliver St John and Sir John Clotworthy.[18] In fact, this was an analysis of the initial cause of the civil war later favoured by the Levellers, as Overton and William Walwyn explained in *A remonstrance of many thousand citizens* (1646): 'This nation and that of Scotland are joined together in a most bloody and consuming war by the waste and policy of a sort of lords in each nation that were malcontents and vexed that the king had advanced others, and not themselves, to the managing of state affairs.'[19] However, if our perspective is broadened out to include not only England, but Europe as a whole, these peers appear less impressive figures. A sixteenth-century Italian visitor to England, Giovanni Botero, commented:

> In England the nobility possess few castles or strong places environed with walls and ditches, neither have they jurisdiction over the people. The dignities of dukedoms, marquesses and earldoms are no more but mere titles, which the king bestoweth on whom he pleaseth, and peradventure they possess never a penny of revenue in the place from whence they take their titles.[20]

As we have already seen, even before the great aristocratic conflagration of the Wars of the Roses, aristocratic and royal armies had struggled to suppress rebel hosts. From the late fifteenth century onwards, every aristocrat-led rebellion had to depend upon a successful appeal to the commons in order to raise sufficient military strength. As Overton and Walwyn noted, the civil war was 'a mighty work and [the nobles] were nowise able to effect it themselves'.[21] Those appeals had to chime with popular concerns. It was patently not enough simply to expect the commonalty to rise in support of a local magnate out of a residual sense of deference. Increasingly, the gentry and the nobility had to frame their demands for support on the grounds not of their status but of their commitment to Protestantism, to their locality and to the nation. Even the King was forced to engage in this sort of bargaining, in August 1642 promising Derbyshire miners extensive financial and legal concessions in return for their allegiance.[22] In Yorkshire, the Fairfax family was co-opted into a popular Parliamentarian uprising raised in their name but actually led by local constables and lesser gentry. The irregular forces raised by the Bradford 'club-men' defended the town from the assault of the Royalist troops commanded by Sir William Savile and Colonel George Goring with terrifying ferocity: it was reported that the local men had unhorsed one Royalist officer and, when he pleaded for quarter, told him, 'Aye, they would quarter him' – and cut him to pieces.[23] Thus successful rebellion in seventeenth-century England involved cooperation between nobles, gentry and the commons. When conflict broke out in 1642, war was fought not between the armed retinues of the nobility, but over control of the military resources of the monarchical state – a fact displayed in Sir John Hotham's famous refusal in April of that year to grant the King access to his royal arsenal at Hull.

The military weakness of the English nobility also reminds us that revolution in England could not have taken place when it did without foreign intervention. By the late 1630s there was certainly a steady stream of criticism, from behind closed doors, of Charles I's government. The King's religious policies had divided and angered many, but for the most part this discontent did not go much beyond talk (and talk in private, at that). The risks involved in raising a domestic insurrection were too high. It was the fact that Charles was King of Scotland and Ireland as well as of England that resulted in the eventual downfall of his regime. The revolt of Scottish Covenanters in 1638, provoked by the imposition of a new, anti-Calvinist prayer book, forced Charles to recall his English Parliament after eleven years of personal rule. The rebellion raised by Irish Catholics in October 1641 prevented him from dissolving that Parliament and sent England into a state of mass hysteria, as the Irish rebels' (fraudulent) claim to be fighting under the King's commission seemed to fulfil long-standing beliefs in a 'popish plot' to overthrow Church and state. Coordination between the King's opponents in each of the three kingdoms meant that he was unable to deal with each of his rebellious dominions in turn. By the beginning of 1642, it was less remarkable that a party within Parliament was willing to take up arms against their King, and more surprising that Charles had been able to muster enough support to make a fight of it.

The radical groups that emerged in the 1640s in England developed from a society that was already religiously divided and in which social relations were severely strained. But it was the events of the 1640s themselves that would have the greatest radicalising impact on these movements. Three moments in particular served to inspire radical thought and action. The first was the assault on the apparatus of Charles I's personal rule, undertaken by the Long Parliament between 1640 and 1642 ('the revolution', in the words of the historian David Cressy, 'before the revolution').[24] The second was the impact of the first civil war itself and the search for means to settle the kingdom following its resolution in 1646. The third was the trial and execution of the King and the establishment of a republic in 1649. Though radical hopes were disappointed, first by political stagnation under the Rump Parliament and the return to old forms of government under the Cromwellian protectorate, there was a revival of radical pamphleteering and political activity after the downfall of the protectorate of Richard Cromwell in 1659. Even under the restored monarchy, radicals continued to speak, write and conspire with a view to the establishment of new forms of government in Church and state.

The first two years of the Long Parliament saw a sustained and at first virtually unchallenged attack on the King's capacity to govern by his prerogative. The Courts of High Commission and Star Chamber, which had been responsible for the landmark royal legal victories of the 1630s and for the brutal punishments of

Leighton, Burton, Bastwick and Prynne, were abolished. The assault on the machinery of Laudian persecution had the unintended consequence of ushering in de facto freedom of the press. Even before these shackles were removed, a flood of Scottish Covenanter propaganda combined with illicitly published radical works had made direct and forceful criticisms of the King's regime, even of Charles himself. Many of these came from the secret press operated by Richard Overton. The London bookseller George Thomason, whose collection of pamphlets provides us with much of the evidence for radical activity in the 1640s, bought only 22 titles in 1640, compared with 1966 in 1642. This massive increase was, in part, a product of the massive public hunger for news. For example, titles dealing with the Irish rebellion of October 1641 accounted for 22 per cent of works published between then and April 1642.

The fiscal expediencies of ship money, forest fines and fines for 'distraint of knighthood' were declared illegal.* Laudian innovations in the Church were condemned and parliamentary orders were issued, such as the one of 8 September 1641 against religious images in churches – orders that in many parts of the country were seen to legitimise direct action. One of the churchwardens of Woolchurch in London, it was reported to a Commons committee, had rather overzealously interpreted the order: 'he had taken up divers brass inscriptions which tended to idolatry: and defaced some statues on tombs which were in the posture of praying and the like, and desired direction how he should raise to defray the charge with other particulars to the same effect'. The committee, though cognisant of the honesty of the man's intentions, informed him that tombs were not included within the purview of the

---

* Forest fines and 'distraint of knighthood' were ancient fines revived by Charles to prop up his prerogative rule. The former were fines for encroachment on the boundaries of royal forests – as defined by their area in the reign of Edward I (1272–1307). 'Distraint of knighthood' was a fine imposed on all men with landed income worth £40 or more per annum who had failed to present themselves for knighthood at the King's coronation.

Commons' order – not least because the more substantial tombs were likely to be those of the ancestors of the most wealthy members of the parish community.[25]

The 'evil counsellors' Laud, Sir Francis Windebank, Lord Keeper Finch and Thomas Wentworth, Earl of Strafford, were arrested. In the case of Wentworth, Charles's Lord Deputy in Ireland, when charges of treason refused to stick, Parliament resurrected the medieval device of a bill of attainder, whereby an individual could be condemned to death simply by a majority vote in favour passing through the two Houses. The vote in both was conducted in an atmosphere of outright political intimidation, with hostile mobs surrounding Parliament. Those who were accused of stirring up popular demonstrations went unpunished. The now well-known radical agitator John Lilburne was called before the Commons on 4 May 1641 to answer the charge of having said: 'This day there are but 7,000 come to crave judgement against the Lord Strafford, without weapons, but tomorrow there will be 40 or 50,000 in arms who if they cannot have the Lord Strafford they will have the king's person.' Despite these inflammatory comments, Lilburne was 'utterly and freely discharged'.[26]

Fear of reprisals led the vote to be won in the Commons by 204 to 59 in favour, but the majority was less conclusive than it appeared, given that the House was half empty. While Charles would regret his assent to Strafford's execution for the rest of his life, and view his failure to defend his trusted servant as a gross stain upon his conscience, he appears to have suffered few qualms in abandoning Laud to his fate. However, the hated Archbishop would not be executed until 1645, after a humiliating trial in which the prosecuting attorney, his old adversary William Prynne, would employ evidence from the prelate's diary, including accounts of erotic dreams involving the Duke of Buckingham, to devastating effect.

The dismantling of Charles I's personal rule received almost unanimous support in both Houses of Parliament. Future Royalists such as Viscount Falkland and Edward Hyde as well as future Parliamentarians including Hampden and John Pym voted for the Triennial Bill, which established mechanisms whereby Parliament would be called every three years whether summoned by the monarch or not, and could not be dissolved without its own consent. However, while few, not even the King, attempted to defend the Laudian innovations in the Church introduced during the 1620s and 1630s, few, equally, were agreed on the form the national Church should take instead. It was here, on the issue of England's religious settlement, that the fault lines which would finally result in the formation of two armed camps began to crack. If the constitutional changes enacted by Parliament between 1640 and 1641 could be described as fairly conservative, constituting an attempt to turn the political clock back to the Jacobean era, the same could not be said in the religious sphere, where petitions for root-and-branch reform in the Church sought not to restore the Elizabethan settlement but to dismantle it completely.

The movement for root-and-branch reform in the Church initially gathered considerable support within Parliament. Some of this enthusiasm was fuelled by a sense that the purging of Laudian 'Popery' heralded the downfall of 'Babylon' and the establishment of a new Jerusalem. Apocalyptic enthusiasm, however, was gradually tempered by growing concern about the rise of radical sects and the threat to social order posed by this popular reformation. Some of those who initially supported reform, such as Sir Edward Dering, came under pressure from constituents worried about its consequences. Robert Abbott, Vicar of Cranbrook in Kent, on 15 March 1641 complained to Dering about the increasing number of sectarian churches in his county that would have 'every particular congregation to be independent, and . . . the votes about every matter of Jurisdiction to be drawne up from the whole body of the church . . . both men and women . . . They would have none in the commission but by solemne Couenant.'[27] Abbott alleged also that he was under pressure from some of his other parishioners to abandon the use of the Book of Common Prayer, bell-tolling at funerals and the churching of women – all of this, he added, was to the detriment of the incumbent's income.

Works that attacked English religious sects appeared, recycling scare stories about Anabaptist groups from the early Reformation in Germany. Hostile 'news-books' recorded the activities of 'mechanic' preachers – unordained, often self-educated men, including John Durant, a soap-maker, John Spencer, coachman to Lord Brooke, and John Green, a felt- or hat-maker, who took it upon themselves to preach.[28] Religious radicals were accused of sexual transgressions. It was claimed some women preachers, with their male colleagues, worked 'in a joynt labour for the procreating of young Saints to fill up the numbers of the new faith'. To many conservatives, acts of popular iconoclasm came to look indistinguishable from class-motivated rioting. In the Church of St Olave, Southwark, on 6 June 1641, members of the community disrupted a communion service, shouting, 'Why do you suffer Baal's priest to give you the communion and serve you so? Kick him out of the church; kneel to a pope, hang him. Baal's priest, get you home and crum your porridge with your bread.'[29] At St Thomas the Apostle, also in London, after the taking of the Protestation (an oath defending the Protestant religion against Popery, subscribed to in churches across the land), the altar rails around the communion table were torn down and set on fire, the people saying that 'they would make them a burnt offering, and that Dagon [the idol of the Philistines] being now down, they would burn him ... And further one of them said, that if the parson came to read the service in a surplice, they would burn him and the surplice with the rails.'[30]

For many conservatives, monarchy, episcopacy and the social order were deeply interconnected: remove one, they believed, and the others would also soon be torn down. Sir Thomas Aston's *Remonstrance against Presbytery*, presented to Parliament on 27 February 1641, stated that, for the puritans, 'Freedom of their consciences and persons is not enough, but they must have their purses and estates free too . . . Nay they go higher, even to the denial of the right to proprietie in our estates.' The root-and-branch petitioners, Aston argued, wished to get rid of '26 bishops and set up 9324 potential Popes', one in each parish.[31] Outbreaks of rioting against fen-drainage schemes in East Anglia and disorder in Windsor Forest, though largely unconnected with the pressure for root-and-branch reform, were also co-opted into conservative propaganda. Dr Edward Layfield, minister of All Hallows, Barking, linked the disturbances of 1640–1 to an earlier tradition of popular rebellion: 'They are . . . like Jack Straw and Wat Tyler that speak against ceremonies of the church.' One Dr Rogers of Hertfordshire recalled John Ball's text, 'When Adam delved and Eve span, who was then the gentleman?' The same connection between the Long Parliament, religious reform and popular rebellion would be made in Charles I's answer to Parliament's *Nineteen Propositions* of 1642. Agreeing to Parliament's proposals would, Charles suggested, 'end in a dark, equal chaos of confusion, and the long line of our many noble ancestors in a Jack Cade or a Wat Tyler'.[32]

Some of the most radical voices in favour of reform, such as John Milton (albeit writing anonymously), even made this connection between monarchy and prelacy explicit. In his *Of Reformation*, Milton, then working as a schoolmaster to the children of a London tailor, employed a corporeal metaphor, describing episcopacy as the 'Huge and Monstrous Wen little lesse than the Head [monarchy] itself'. Radical surgery was required upon the body politic to support the 'floating carcase of a crazy and diseased Monarchy'.[33] While he was not yet a fully fledged republican, Milton's antiepiscopal tracts demonstrated not only hostility to the bishops but clear contempt for Charles I's kingship.[34]

Charles might have exploited the growing divisions over religious reform and dissolved this troublesome Parliament, had it not been for events outside England. In August 1641, he went north to Scotland to negotiate with the Scottish Covenanters. Had peace been successfully concluded, it would have removed the financial shackles that forced him to keep the Long Parliament in session. However, any faith that his opponents might have placed in his sincerity was dashed by the King's complicity in a plot, called 'the Incident', to seize the Covenanter leaders Archibald Campbell, 8th Earl of Argyll, James, Duke of Hamilton and his brother, William, Earl of Lanark. Charles's reputation was not further enhanced by his decision to plead his innocence, accompanied by armed men, before the Edinburgh Parliament on 12 October.

The repercussions of 'the Incident' were as nothing, however, compared with the impact of the rebellion that began in Ireland that month. A reaction to the hated rule of Strafford, the revolt was sparked by economic as well as religious causes. However, as viewed through the eyes of many English pamphleteers, it was nothing less than a Catholic war against Protestants. News-sheets were filled with stories of atrocities committed by the rebels: foetuses ripped from their mothers' wombs while still alive, wives raped and husbands murdered in the sight of their spouses – indeed, killings were reported in the tens of thousands, numbers so high that, had they been correct, exceeded the actual numbers of Irish Protestants. These scare stories generated panic across the country. The nonconformist autobiographer Joseph Lister recalled that as a teenage boy in Pudsey, Yorkshire, he was present when the church service was interrupted by a man crying, 'Friends, we are all as good as dead men, for the Irish rebels are coming; they are come as far as Rochdale . . . and will be at Halifax and Bradford shortly.' Lister recalled that the news put the congregation 'all in confusion, some ran out, others wept'. The panic only subsided once riders were sent to Halifax and returned to confirm that the 'Irish rebels' were, in fact, Protestant refugees.[35]

The Irish rebels claimed to be fighting under a royal commission from Charles I. Trust in the King had sunk so low that John Pym, the veteran MP who had made a political career of calling for tougher measures against Popery, could press for stronger security measures which included limitations on Charles's powers of appointment. Pym urged that the King should employ only councillors approved by Parliament. The vote on this 'additional instruction' was won, but only by 151 to 110. Meanwhile, the kingdom was placed on an increasingly warlike footing. An Impressment Bill was passed, removing the King's power to order men to serve outside their own counties. The Earl of Essex was placed in command of the trained bands south of the Trent.

The assault on the King's prerogative, which was drawing opposition from constitutional moderates, including Edward Hyde and Sir Symonds D'Ewes, together with the populist means by which Pym was attempting to secure his goals helped gather a party around the King. Although Pym narrowly succeeded in getting the Grand Remonstrance, a lengthy indictment of Charles I's rule, passed through the Commons – by 159 votes to 148 – the most heated debate occurred after it had been approved, namely, over the question of whether the Remonstrance should be published. Sir Edward Dering famously complained: 'When I first heard of a Remonstrance, I presently imagined that like faithful councillors we should hold up a glass to His Majesty . . . I did not dream that we should remonstrate downwards and tell stories to the people.' The irony was that Dering's own speech was later published with his consent. Dering, however, argued that whereas he continued to represent the true freeholders of Kent, the propertied male householders whose 'voice' had made him their MP, Pym stooped to appeal to the vulgar mob thronging the streets of London.[36] The King's answer to the Grand Remonstrance made clear that he felt that the appeal to popularity was providing him with the ammunition to build a Royalist party. Only he himself, the King's declaration claimed, stood between the fundamental law and the Church and the 'irreverence of those many schismatics and separatists, wherewith of late this kingdom and this city [London] abounds, to the great dishonour and hazard of both Church and State'.[37]

The fears of the moderates were compounded when the govern-

ment of the City of London effectively lost control to Pym's 'junto'.*
On 27 December citizens and apprentices, including John Lilburne,
stormed Westminster Abbey, damaging the monuments, before surg-
ing around the royal palace at Whitehall.[38] On 3 January 1642, perhaps
convinced by impeachment proceedings issued against twelve bishops
that he was next in line, Charles chose to seize the initiative. In a
repeat of 'the Incident', he planned to arrest his leading parliamentary
opponents, including Sir Arthur Haselrig, John Hampden, Denzil
Holles, John Pym and William Strode, and their principal ally among
the peers, Viscount Mandeville. On the 4th, the King entered the
Commons, accompanied by troops, only to find that his 'birds' had
already flown. His actions caused the volatile City to erupt in angry
demonstrations, now clearly targeted at Charles and not at his 'evil
counsellors'. The next day, after being cold-shouldered by the City
government, Charles found his coach surrounded by the mob, one of
whom, the future Parliamentarian journalist Henry Walker, threw
into the carriage a copy of his incendiary pamphlet, *To your tents, oh
Israel*, which praised the deposition of the biblical King Rehoboam.[39]

Charles, accompanied by a pitifully small band of followers, left
his capital, fearful that he would become the victim of crowd violence. England now moved into a state of low-level armed hostility as
each side attempted to cajole, persuade or force the broadly neutral
majority to support them in the impending civil conflict. Even before
the King raised his standard at Nottingham on 22 August 1642, small
groups of his supporters had already begun to resort to plunder, as
evidenced by a parliamentary order of the same month which permitted communities to 'join together, to defend themselves and others
from rapine and force'. New propositions for peace were presented
to the King by Parliament that June, but already these appeared to
be designed as propaganda for recruiting supporters to the Parliamentarian cause rather than genuine terms aimed at avoiding conflict.

---

* A common seventeenth-century term for a political clique or faction, derived from a
misspelled Anglicisation of the Spanish *junta*.

ALL COMMANDED AND YET WERE UNDER COMMAND

Following the first pitched battle of the conflict, at Edgehill on 23 October 1642, the country moved from guerrilla fighting to hot war. What has often been romanticised as a chivalrous 'war without an enemy' was, in fact, the bloodiest civil conflict that the British Isles has ever known. As a proportion of the adult population, more men died during England's civil wars than during the First World War. It has been estimated that some 85,000 men fell in the fighting itself, with a further 100,000 dying from wounds or disease. In addition, some 120,000 were made prisoners of war. In Scotland and Ireland, the human costs were even higher. Incidents of atrocity where the accepted rules of war broke down were not unheard of, though they were far less frequent than in the wars in Ireland, where religious animosities and ethnic hatred fuelled the violence. On Christmas Day 1643, at Barthomley in Cheshire, Lord Byron's troops murdered twenty captured Parliamentarian soldiers in cold blood. In February 1644 at Hopton Castle, Shropshire, surrendering troops were murdered and their bodies tossed into the moat. During the Royalist sack of Bolton that May, both combatants and non-combatants were killed by Prince

Rupert's men: estimates of the number of fatalities range from 200 to 1800. One reason for the greater violence shown at both Barthomley and Bolton may have been that the Royalist troops involved had recently returned from the much more intense fighting taking place in Ireland.[1]

The impact of the civil war was felt across much of the nation. Although it is the great pitched battles of Edgehill, Marston Moor and Naseby that are best remembered, these were uncharacteristic of most of the fighting, which mainly comprised widely dispersed, low-level skirmishes between small garrison forces. These garrisons were generally poorly supplied and forced to support themselves by resorting to plunder. It has been calculated that the cash value of goods plundered amounted to more than that taken in war taxation, and taxation itself reached levels that would not be matched again until the 1690s. The presence of soldiers within towns placed greater strains on communities' limited resources. Garrison towns had a higher incidence of disease, mainly typhus and cholera, with the death rate in Berkshire doubling in the years 1643–4 as a result of the influx of military personnel via the important inland port of Reading. The familiar consequence of modern-day conflicts, the growth of refugee populations, was a major feature of the civil war, and individuals who had fled to temporary accommodation during the 1640s could still be found living there in the Restoration period. The war even etched itself into the English landscape. A country that, unlike its European neighbours, was remarkably unmilitarised was suddenly littered with siege fortifications. Rich grazing land was reduced to expanses of churned mud as turf was cut to shore up earthworks. Trees and houses (and in the case of Brampton Bryan, Herefordshire, even a whole town) were uprooted and flattened to remove potential cover for the besieging forces.

Many leading radicals experienced this bitter conflict at first hand. John Lilburne enlisted as a member of Lord Brooke's troop and fought at Edgehill and Marston Moor; the future 'Ranters'

Laurence Clarkson and Abezier Coppe both served as army preachers; while the early Quaker leader James Nayler served as a soldier for some nine years, winning praise for his service from the Parliamentarian general John Lambert. In broader terms the war politicised the army, and not simply in the sense that the army leadership came, through force of arms, to have a greater role in securing a constitutional settlement once the fighting was over. While bread-and-butter issues of indemnity and pay were core concerns of the rank and file, they were not divorced from apparently more abstract demands for freedom of conscience, as the Levellers recognised: indeed, Leveller pamphlets linked freedom from conscription with freedom of conscience. As Thomas Rainborowe would point out during the Putney Debates of 1647, impressment was also linked to wealth and power: 'We do find in all presses that go forth none must be pressed that are freehold men. When these gentlemen fall out among themselves they shall press the poor scrubs to come and kill one another for them.'[2]

The Parliamentarian New Model Army, formed in 1645, the first army in the civil war not to be tied to a particular region or garrison, had a reputation – stoked by its critics – of being a nursery for radical political and religious ideas. Though the puritanical zeal of its soldiers may have been exaggerated, as the presence of Baptist ministers such as Coppe and Clarkson indicates, the rank and file was certainly exposed to the thought of radical preachers. Of the seventeen chaplains appointed to the army between 1645 and 1647, fifteen were Independents – favouring independent congregations organised and directed by the communities concerned – and two were Baptists. More conservative Presbyterian ministers such as Richard Baxter were gradually being pushed out. To the disgust of Baxter and his fellow ministers Thomas Edwards and Edmund Calamy, some of the soldiers themselves, such as Captain Paul Hobson, became lay preachers.[3] The presence of lay preachers divided the army command as well. The staunch

Presbyterian commander Sir Samuel Luke had Hobson arrested for breaching orders against unlicensed preaching, only to find himself thwarted by Sir Thomas Fairfax and Hobson's immediate commander, Charles Fleetwood. Many officers were also MPs, including Fleetwood, Henry Ireton, Oliver Cromwell's son-in-law, Rainborowe, Thomas Harrison and Philip Skippon.* The army itself, especially after 1646, seems to have developed a sense of corporate political identity. This can be seen most powerfully in the famous remark of Cornet Joyce: when required to justify his seizure of the King from his parliamentary captors on 3 June 1647, Joyce defended his actions to the Parliament by saying 'all commanded and yet were under command'.[4]

The notion that authority in the army was ultimately the result of the popular sovereignty of its rank and file was enshrined in the 'Solemn Engagement', an agreement signed by the officers and the troops' agents at the general rendezvous at Newmarket on 5 June. The 'Engagement', almost a covenant between the officers and the agents, stated that the army would not be disbanded, nor the officers separated from their men, until the army's conditions had been satisfied. The document was produced in reaction to the attempts of the Presbyterian-dominated Parliament to disband the army without fully recompensing arrears of pay or offering guarantees concerning the soldiers' immunity from prosecution for their actions during wartime. Soldiers were also concerned that the Parliament seemed intent on agreeing to a 'cheap peace' with Charles that would make all the New Model Army's hard-fought victories seemingly worthless. In the words of Edward Sexby, an agent for the rank and file at Putney, the soldiers had 'ventured our lives, and it was all for this: to recover our birthrights and privileges as Englishmen . . . I wonder we were so much deceived. If we had not right in this kingdom we were mere mercenary soldiers.'[5]

* The famous self-denying ordinance that prohibited members of the Lords and Commons from also being army officers did not prevent reappointment after resignation.

One of the soldiers' core demands, a product of the de facto toleration within the army itself, was for freedom of conscience. But the puritan alliance that had brought down the Laudian Church was now utterly destroyed. The outbreak of the Irish rebellion had seen the establishment of a fragile religious truce between the Presbyterians (those who favoured a restrictive national Church settlement) and Independents (Congregationalists). However, as the war progressed, that peace came under great strain, and by late 1643 a pamphlet war had broken out between Presbyterians and defenders of the congregational way. One of the leading Presbyterian polemicists, Thomas Edwards, had already entered into the fray against the Independents in 1641, before the peace accord of November that year, with his *Reasons against the Independent Government of Particular Congregations*. That pamphlet had elicited a doughty riposte from Katherine Chidley, one of the most strident writers of the civil wars and later a leading figure in the Leveller movement. Chidley, aside from raising seven children, was also a member of a Shrewsbury 'conventicle', and had been actively involved in the campaign against Laudian innovations in the Church, mixing with figures such as John Lilburne and the radical separatist minister John Duppa. For Edwards, the horror of Independency was that it would lead to religious tolerance, and thence to religious and political anarchy and social disorder. Chidley's response, however, was not to dispute the social challenge inherent in separatist religion. The unbelieving husband, she asserted, though he might command her body, could have no authority over the believing wife's conscience.

Despite the humiliation Edwards had suffered in being so effectively dressed down by a woman, he had kept to the truce agreed in November 1641. However, the publication of the *Apologeticall Narration* in late 1643, a pamphlet authored by leading Independents Thomas Goodwin, Philip Nye and Sidrach Simpson calling for Parliament to accept the congregational way, signalled the effective end of the peace between Presbyterians and

Independents. Conservative writers such as Edwards entered the fray once more to decry the evils of religious toleration and the perverted practices of the separatist churches. It was in response to these Presbyterian attacks on the sects that leading Levellers Richard Overton and William Walwyn came to public prominence – Overton had until now successfully kept his role in illicit printing secret. Both emerged as staunch defenders of religious toleration, though self-interest undoubtedly played a part in their stance.

Overton's earliest attributed works fitted with Puritan attacks on the Laudian Church, although displaying an unusual satirical edge. However, in *Mans Mortalitie*, published anonymously in January 1644 and officially condemned by Parliament on 26 August that year, he revealed for the first time his radical theology. In this pamphlet, Overton laid out his belief in the doctrine of thnetopsychism, the 'mortalist' heresy that the soul died with the body and would only be miraculously restored at the Last Judgement. The heresy had political implications too, as advocates often suggested that the kingdom of God would be established on Earth, not in heaven. This was a gross affront to orthodox Christian understanding, in which the soul was judged immediately after death. So-called Presbyterian 'heresiographers', including Thomas Edwards, latched on to the idea of the 'soul sleeping' as evidence of the grotesque opinions that de facto toleration was allowing to flourish.*

In contrast to Overton's flagrantly heretical opinions, Walwyn's personal religious views were more obscure. The eldest of the leading Levellers and the son of a well-respected and well-to-do Worcestershire gentleman, Walwyn had until the early 1640s lived the life of a seemingly contented London merchant and family man (he claimed to have twenty children). An engraving from the late seventeenth century shows an avuncular, ruddy-cheeked character,

---

* Overton, though, was not an advocate of 'soul sleeping' but of the mortality of the soul. The distinction was lost on most of his opponents.

with something of the well-fed country squire about him. He supported Parliament at the outbreak of the war, gathering money from his parish to support the Parliamentarian troops. But it was his break with the Calvinist doctrine of predestination, and his acceptance of the idea of Christ's free grace, that brought him into public controversy with the Presbyterian Thomas Edwards. Walwyn emerged with Overton as one of the most far-reaching advocates of religious liberty in Britain, arguing for the toleration of groups such as Jews, Catholics and atheists who would still face discrimination in the Victorian era.

Overton's and Walwyn's arguments went far beyond the pragmatic defence of a limited toleration supported by most Independents, which offered the only protection against the Presbyterians' tendency to persecute. They went further, even, than more famous advocates of toleration, such as the New England separatist Roger Williams in his *The Bloudy Tenent of Persecution* (1644) and the poet and pamphleteer John Milton in his *Areopagitica* (1644). For Williams and Milton, the danger of intolerance was not so much that it oppressed human consciences but that, because of degenerate human reason, magistrates were as likely to suppress divine truth – in Williams's words 'Christ Jesus in his servants' – as to correct error.

Overton and Walwyn, though, like Williams and Milton, men with deeply held religious beliefs, presented their arguments for toleration differently. For the former, it was a civil as well as a spiritual good: tolerant societies, they argued, with an eye to the example of the Dutch Republic, were more prosperous, more unified, more stable, and thus more successful in war than nations that persecuted some of their subjects.[6] Overton's first and most famous tract, issued under his 'Martin Mar-Priest' pseudonym, *The Arraignement of Mr Persecution* (1645), placed England's current struggles within the European context of a continent ravaged by confessional warfare. Holy wars, even against 'infidels', slaughtered only the innocent: 'To kill the unbeleever, as *Turke, Pagan, Jew &c.* is to slay such as Christ *would have to live to repent.*'

In the midst of a war that was seen by many as a struggle between the forces of Popery and those of the godly, Overton made a remarkable plea for Catholic–Protestant reconciliation: 'If the Papist knew the Protestant, the Protestant the Papist, to love one another: and would not molest, or at least injure one another for their *Conscience*, but live peaceably and quietly one by another, bearing one with another . . . What man would lift up his hand against his Neighbour?'[7] Likewise, Walwyn denied the efficacy of persecution, even in the case of one 'whose mind is so mis-informed as to deny a Deity'.[8] Neither the Fleet Prison nor the Bedlam Hospital had the power to change a man's mind, he said. In a clear jibe at Edwards and his fellow Presbyterian polemicists, he noted that it was often the 'most weak and passionate men, the most unable to defend truth or their own opinions', who were 'the most violent for persecution'.[9] Again, toleration's role as a panacea for civil strife was commended: 'the way to foster love and amity in a family as in a state being an equal respect from those in authority'.[10] For Walwyn, God was love; what was not borne of love, like persecution, could not be good.

Thomas Edwards, however, was scarcely overflowing with the milk of human kindness. Undeterred by a second, published, debate with Katherine Chidley in which she taunted him that his argument was so weak that it was 'a task most befitting a woman . . . to answer it', Edwards had spent much time amassing information from a variety of godly informants on his sectarian and Independent opponents. The result of all this research was *Gangraena*, published in 1646 in three parts. The metaphor of bodily corruption deployed by Milton in *Of Reformation* was now redirected from the bishops to the sects. As Edwards saw it, in the wake of the King's defeat in the first civil war, the Presbyterian cause, set upon by an unholy alliance of the army, the Independents and the heretical sects, was faltering both in Parliament and in the country as a whole. The sects, nourished by de facto toleration, were growing like a canker upon the body politic. If the gangrenous limb were not cauterised and toleration ended, the result would be not only the death of a national Church, but also the end of civil society.

Gangraena, despite its length (over eight hundred pages), lack of structure and hectoring style, became a publishing sensation, going through three printings in three months. The book focused not on what Presbyterians would have regarded as intellectual heresy – there was very little discussion here of antinomianism or free grace – but upon the evil moral and social consequences of toleration. If one believed Edwards, there was scarcely a Baptist minister who had not fondled one of his young female believers during the course of an adult immersion. When they were not baptising comely young maidens, religious radicals were baptising horses in derision of the ordained clergy. The ministers of the sects themselves, according to Edwards, were uniformly uneducated, being shoemakers, milliners and soap-boilers who had had the presumption to think that they could preach with the same authority as the university-educated ministry. (In fact, many of Edwards's targets had been to university, or at the very least, had considerable schooling.[11])

Edwards was not a mere fantasist or an outright liar. He was, however, highly selective when quoting from his targets' works, 'source-mining' their pamphlets for the most controversial passages, and often severely distorting their meaning by wresting them free from their context. The vision of England's religious landscape that he produced proved deeply influential. *Gangraena* both presented and helped create two distinct and opposing groups: the godly, Presbyterian opponents of heresy and schism on the one hand, and the unholy alliance of Independents, sectaries and army men on the other. This radical conspiracy had its headquarters in London. As the centre of radical activity, the capital predominated over all other areas in Edwards's discussion – a diseased metropolitan heart that pumped error and sin into the provinces.

This image of two diametrically opposed camps was reinforced by the tendency of some of Edwards's victims, such as John Goodwin, an independent minister whose church had connections with the Levellers, especially William Walwyn, to come to the defence of other targets of the heresiographer's ire. The identities constructed glossed over the differences between individuals and lumped them in the same camp. For example, there was much disagreement among Presbyterians over the precise form of Church government. Equally, Edwards greatly diminished the theological, social and political gulf between 'respectable' Independents such as Jeremiah Burroughes and 'mechanick' or 'tub' preachers such as the hatmaker Thomas Webbe.[12]

Along with other heresiographical works, Edwards's contributed to the sectarianisation of radical religion in the 1640s. While, in reality, the religious identity of individuals could be extremely fluid – Laurence Clarkson, for example, moved from being an Independent to a Baptist, to a 'Ranter' and finally to a Muggletonian – Edwards and his fellow conservative polemicists presented taxonomies of heresy in their works, giving loose-knit groups of individuals clear corporate identities, such as 'Dippers' (Baptists), 'Seekers', 'Adamites' (an alleged sect of naked radicals) and 'Divorcers' (another fabricated sect, in this case designed to lampoon Milton's divorce tracts). In fact, most of the names of radical groups with which we are now familiar, such as Quaker and Ranter, came to us from these hostile commentators, rather than from the groups themselves. The term 'Leveller' itself, first used with reference to the participants in the Midland rising of 1607, was, according to John Lilburne, imposed upon the group by Henry Ireton at the Putney Debates. The Levellers themselves repeatedly disowned the term, knowing that it was intended to link their arguments with a sweeping 'levelling' of the social hierarchy and with an attack on private property. In one of their last collaborative works, *A Manifestation* (1649), Lilburne, Overton and Walwyn complained that they 'never had it in our thoughts to level men's estates, it being the utmost of our aim . . . that every man may with as much security as may be enjoy his propriety [proper state and condition, including property]'.[13]

Edwards's picture of radical activity in the 1640s has strongly influenced historians as well as contemporaries. As a result, the connections between the army, the sects and the Levellers have, to a degree, been exaggerated. The Levellers constituted a looser, broader and more influential coalition than the sectarianised picture of radical activity allows. Lilburne, Overton and Walwyn had all come to prominence before they were ever labelled 'Levellers'. The Levellers were individuals with connections in Westminster as well as among the army and the sects. The youngest of their four leading writers, the lawyer John Wildman, even had links with leading Royalists, having twice married into the Berkshire aristocracy. (Both matches seemed unusual choices for a political radical – Wildman's first wife was the daughter of a Catholic nobleman, his second the daughter of the Royalist Lord Lovelace.) Edwards presented religious and political divisions in the late 1640s as a simple dichotomy between radical (the Independents, the army, the sects) and conservative (Presbyterian MPs and clergymen). However, as we shall see, the political centre, itself fast-shifting over the course of the decade, at times adopted the agenda of the radicals, while radicals themselves sometimes consorted with Royalists.

Thomas Edwards wished more than simply to smear his rivals with accusations of sexual impropriety or religious ignorance. *Gangraena* was in part a piece of propaganda designed to help mobilise a counter-revolutionary movement that would deal with the threat posed by the New Model Army and Independent MPs within Parliament. After the end of the first civil war in 1646, English politics had become like the endgame of a chess match, with all political activity focused on the King. By the summer of 1647, tensions between the army and Parliament came to a head, as Parliament attempted to disband the army without full pay. The army, increasingly concerned at the overtures that Presbyterians within Parliament such as Denzil Holles were making to the King, chose to seize the political initiative, first in the daring capture of Charles by Cornet Joyce (with the probable knowledge of Cromwell) and then by accusing eleven Presbyterian MPs of treason.

In July, the army met at Reading, the first of several meetings of that year, to discuss whether it should move on London. The product of these discussions was a set of peace terms, the *Heads of the Proposals*, drafted largely by Henry Ireton, a document that betrayed some influence of Leveller ideas. As Ireton would later point out to his critics at the Putney Debates, in the *Heads of the Proposals* he had already publicly advocated biennial parliaments and a 'more equall distribution of Elections'. Leveller writers such as John Wildman heavily criticised Ireton for going in person to Charles, to 'kneele and kisse and fawn upon him' in order to get his approval of the terms – an attempt that proved fruitless as Charles once again preferred to play his opponents in Parliament and in the army against each other.[14] At the same time as the army was considering alternative peace terms with the King, counter-revolutionary mobs threatened MPs sympathetic to the army, forcing them to flee the House. The following month, the army marched on London to prevent the capital from falling under the control of the Presbyterians and restore the Independent MPs to Parliament.

However, as the attacks on Ireton indicated, army unity itself was now disintegrating, as the leadership and the new 'Agitators', elected in September 1647 to act as delegates for the lower ranks, disagreed over how best to settle the kingdom. The grievances of some of the rank and file were expressed in a pamphlet, *The Case of the armie truly stated*, published in October 1647 and probably largely written by Edward Sexby, originally a trooper in Fairfax's regiment. The pamphlet accused the 'Grandees', as Cromwell and Ireton were known, of betraying the 'Solemn Engagement' signed in June 1647 by their independent negotiations with the King. *The Case* called for the dissolution of the Long Parliament and the election of a new 'representative' (future Parliament) by all 'freeborn' men. The Grandees reacted by attempting to soothe discontent within the army. They called the new Agitators and their civilian associates, the Levellers John Wildman and Maximilian Petty (a member of an Oxfordshire gentry family), to a meeting at St Mary's Church, Putney, where the terms of *The Case* and a new manifesto produced by the civilian Levellers, the Agreement of the People, would be discussed.

The Putney Debates, which began on 28 October 1647, now represent the most famous event in the history of the Leveller movement. At the time, Putney was a small town of fewer than a thousand people on the outskirts of London. It was chosen because of its closeness to the City and its good transport links both by land and by water – the church itself was close to the river. Also, it was there that the Independent minister, close friend of Oliver Cromwell and participant in the Debates, Hugh Peters, had regularly preached. Thus geographical convenience and an army connection via Peters led Putney to be chosen as the site for one of the most remarkable political discussions in English history.

In 2006, the Putney Debates were voted the most overlooked radical event in British history in a competition sponsored by the *Guardian*. But the prominence given to the Debates both in academic histories of the civil war and in 'public history' is a recent phenomenon. The text of the discussions held was not published until 1891. Until then, the little-known manuscript had gathered dust in the archives of Worcester College, Oxford. For over two hundred years, references to the Putney Debates and the Levellers were few and far between. Although a permanent record of the discussions was kept by the general secretary of the army, William Clarke, they were barely mentioned in contemporary news-sheets and pamphlets.

This secrecy was unsurprising. Discussion of the franchise, the most celebrated element of the Debates for recent historians and commentators, were not, at the time, the most controversial subject on the agenda and so not the one to which most attention was paid. The focus instead was on settling the kingdom: in particular, the King's role in any future peace negotiations. During the Debates, two soldiers referred to Charles I as a 'man of blood', a tyrant who had waged war against his people and must be brought to retributive, divinely willed justice. Religious language suffused the talk at Putney; those attending also gathered for prayer meetings charged with apocalyptic language. Putney saw a major shift from the pursuit of a negotiated settlement with the King to the decision to bring him to trial. In the chaotic political circus that followed the first civil war, few of the participants in the discussions, Cromwell least of all, were prepared to leave hostages to fortune by letting the proceedings be reported in public.

Indeed, some elements of the Putney Debates look positively archaic to modern eyes. The focus of earlier historians on the question of the extension of the franchise led them practically to ignore the first half of the Debates, which concerned the obligations placed on the army by previous covenants and agreements, such as the 'Solemn Engagement' of June 1647.[15] When the question of franchise finally came up for discussion, the Leveller spokesmen all called for a very broad extension. The irony, however, was that this was one element in the debate in which the participants were able to reach a compromise. It was also a point that was fudged in the Levellers' first Agreement of the People, in which they attempted to set out their ideas for a post-civil war settlement.

The Putney Debates are now most famous for the apparently irreconcilable clash between Colonel Thomas Rainborowe, MP for Droitwich, vice-admiral of the English navy and an implacable opponent of Oliver Cromwell, and Cromwell's son-in-law Henry Ireton: a clash between a view of politics based on a commitment to equal rights and one based on 'interest' and property. Rainborowe expressed his belief that all men who signed the Agreement should be eligible to vote: 'For really I think that the poorest he that is in England has a life to live as the greatest he . . . every man that is to live under a Government ought first by his own consent put himself under that government.' Ireton responded: 'No person has a right to an interest or share in the disposing or determining of the affairs of the kingdom . . . that has not a permanent fixed interest in this kingdom.'[16]

At Putney, the Levellers presented a consistently radical position on the franchise. The civilian Leveller Maximilian Petty, along with John Wildman and Thomas Rainborowe, defended the idea of universal male suffrage.* Wildman's response to Ireton was essentially the same as Rainborowe's: 'Every person in England has as clear a right to elect his [note the masculine pronoun] representative as the greatest person in England.'[17] Petty concurred, arguing that '*before* there was a government, every man *had* such a voice'.[18] The arguments advanced by Wildman, Rainborowe and Petty were consistent with those promoted by John Lilburne in several pamphlets published in 1646 that called for democratic elections for the government of the City of London.[19]

However, the Levellers' manifesto, the Agreement of the People, was noticeably less clear-cut in its discussion of the franchise. Point one of the Agreement stated:

> That the people of England being at this day very unequally distributed by counties, cities and boroughs for the election of their deputies in parliament, ought to be more indifferently proportioned according to the number of the inhabitants: the circumstances whereof, for number, place, and manner, are to be set down before the end of this present parliament.[20]

If we can detect a clear statement about the franchise here, it was to argue more for a moderate revision along the lines of the Great

---

* It is worth noting that no participant at Putney argued for the rights of women, despite the prominence of figures such as Katherine Chidley within the Leveller movement.

Reform Act of 1832, with the equalisation of the number of constituencies on the basis of population, rather than the kind of mass enfranchisement enacted by the 1918 Representation of the People Act. Indeed, as far as elections were concerned, the text of the Agreement was markedly similar to that of Ireton's *Heads of the Proposals*.

At the Putney Debates, Ireton's reaction to the Agreement's discussion of the franchise seems, consequently, disproportionate. The Agreement did not say that every man should have an equal voice in elections, as Ireton implied. That position was only clearly taken in the *The Case of the armie*, a document originating from the soldiers, not the civilian Levellers: 'all the freeborn at the age of 21 yeares and upwards be the electors'.[21] Ireton may have wished to push the civilian Levellers into supporting the more radical proposal in a bid to scupper the Agreement. However, it is also possible that he may simply have been trying to clear up the apparent inconsistency between the two documents. The relationship between the *The Case* and the Agreement was not clear, a confusion increased by the fact that at Putney there appeared to be two political discussions going on at the same time: one strand of the debate, the one targeted by Ireton and noted by most historians, referred to the franchise, the other, addressed by Rainborowe and later Petty, referred to the process for ratifying the new constitution.

We should look again at those famous words of Rainborowe's, now painted in gold on the walls of St Mary's Church, Putney. Though Rainborowe spoke movingly of the rights due to the 'poorest he', neither he nor any of the other leading Leveller spokesmen was firmly wedded to universal male suffrage. Rather, they were arguing that the new form of government created by the Agreement had to be established by plebiscite. Petty brought the discussion round to the idea of the origins of government in a 'state of nature', before the creation of the state and the control of behaviour by positive law. Arguably, by dissolving the old Parliament and erecting a new form of government, the Levellers were proposing to return England, if briefly, to that original state.[22] In that quotation, Rainborowe did not mention the vote, or even the broader term 'franchise'. Instead, he went on to claim that 'every man that is to live under a Government ought first by his own consent put himself under that Government'. Rather than dwelling on elections, as is usually assumed, Rainborowe was speaking of the moment when the Agreement, like an oath of loyalty to the new regime, would be tendered to the nation for subscription, when all men would choose whether to put themselves 'under that Government'.

By focusing on the most apparently 'modern' aspect of the Putney Debates, the franchise discussion, we have omitted to mention that there appeared to be plenty of room for compromise between the officers and the Levellers. Hugh Peters's suggestion that the discussion of the franchise should be moved to a committee and settled by it was accepted. Ireton seemed willing to compromise on the formula of the franchise, allowing 'That all soldiers and others, if they be not servants or beggars, ought to have voices in electing those which shall represent them in Parliament, although they have not forty shillings per annum in freehold land.' And we know that Ireton sat on a committee which recommended that the Commons should decide on the franchise 'soe as to give as much inlargement to Common freedome as may bee, with a due regard had to the equality and end of the present Constitution in that point'. That committee's recommendations also made it clear that all who had fought for Parliament ought to have the vote. The Levellers themselves largely kept to this compromise position in subsequent Agreements of the People.[23] This consensus should not surprise us: constitutional arrangements that gave large numbers of adult male inhabitants the vote were not unusual in early modern Europe or America.[24]

As mentioned earlier, the narrow focus on the franchise obscures the most significant part of the Agreement: not its rather

vague pronouncements on the vote, but the 'reserves', those rights
with which the new elected representative would not be able to
tamper. This was a momentous development. For the first time in
British history, the Agreement, probably the work of the legally
trained John Wildman – or John Lawmind, as he sometimes ana-
grammatically liked to style himself – set down a number of
rights that could not be abrogated by government. This marked
an evolutionary leap forward from earlier charters and petitions,
which could claim only the (often temporary) acquiescence of the
monarch as their source of authority. Here were freedoms, liberty
of conscience, equality before the law, that no power in the land
could encroach upon.

The Agreement sought to deal with the potential political problems of the present, as well as to remedy the shortcomings of
the past. The heavy emphasis in Parliamentarian rhetoric on the
political sovereignty of the Commons threatened to replace royal
absolutism with parliamentary tyranny. This danger became
particularly acute for the army, as Parliament came to be dominated in the later 1640s by a hostile Presbyterian faction, bent on
counter-revolution. The reserved rights detailed in the Agreement
would be protected from parliamentary infringement. These
'reserves' included the right to freedom of worship, freedom from
conscription, indemnity from prosecution, equality before the law
and a commitment that the content of the law itself must be fair:
'That as the laws ought to be equal, so they must be good and not
evidently destructive to the safety and well-being of the people.'

The committee appointed in October 1647 also found common
ground here, as with the franchise. Many other elements of the
Leveller programme gained assent: the present parliament would
be dissolved by September 1648; biennial elections would be introduced; Parliament would sit for at least six months, and a council
of state would govern between parliaments; the monarchy and
lords would remain, but with reduced powers. The idea of a set of
reserves – rights protected from assault by either the executive or

legislature – can be found not only in the Agreement but also in the 'Instrument of Government', the first protectoral constitution, drafted by Major-General John Lambert, who also had a hand in writing the *Heads of the Proposals*.[25] In the autumn of 1647, no longer at loggerheads, agitators, Levellers and Grandees had achieved a remarkable degree of consensus.

But the main sticking point between the Grandees and the Levellers remained: what to do with the King. Possibly the most radical element of the Agreement was that it proposed coming to a settlement without involving the monarch. It was not an overtly republican document, but it envisaged a procedure whereby Charles would effectively be left out of the decision-making process (a pragmatic suggestion, given what was to follow). While the Putney Debates were taking place, Wildman accused Ireton and Cromwell in print – not without some justification – of going behind the army's back and continuing to press for a negotiated settlement with the King. On 11 November, matters were thrown into greater confusion by Charles's escape from his army captors at Hampton Court – where he had been under house arrest since August – and his flight to the Isle of Wight, where he hoped the governor of the island, Robert Hammond, would let him take a ship to the continent.* The King was to be disappointed, however, as Hammond chose instead to obey the orders of his cousin Oliver Cromwell: he put the King into custody in Carisbrooke Castle. Nonetheless, Charles was now less closely confined than he had been at Hampton Court, and once again started negotiations with Presbyterian MPs in the Commons.

The army, meanwhile, was increasingly divided. On 15 November, the first of three scheduled rendezvous took place at Corkbush Field near Ware in Hertfordshire. Some of the soldiers

---

* Charles's break for freedom was reputedly inspired by reports of the hostile references made at Putney to the King as a 'man of blood'. Despite the effective ban on reporting, information about the debates reached the King via Royalist prisoners in the Tower of London, who in turn received their news from a fellow prisoner, John Lilburne.

were in a mutinous mood, Colonel William Eyre and Major Thomas Scott leading calls for the army to support the Agreement over a newly drafted Remonstrance presented by General Fairfax. Rainborowe handed the General a copy of the Agreement and a petition supporting it. Two more regiments, Thomas Harrison's and Robert Lilburne's, now appeared, though they had not been summoned to the rendezvous. These soldiers wore copies of the Agreement, bearing the slogan 'England's freedom and soldiers' rights', like totems in their hats. The mutineers were dealt with forcefully, some of Fairfax's officers riding among them and pulling the pamphlets from them. Eight or nine men identified as ring-leaders were court-martialled on the spot, but only one, Private Arnold, was shot. Arnold was appropriated as a martyr to the Leveller cause, although, given the usual exercise of military discipline at the time, Fairfax's response was remarkably lenient. Moreover, the general's own manifesto repeated his commitment not just to the core issues of pay and indemnity but also to regular parliaments, elected on such terms as to 'render the House of Commons . . . an equal representative of the people that are to elect'.[26]

With the suppression of the army mutinies came worse news for the Leveller cause: the London Independent and Baptist churches issued a declaration distancing themselves from the movement. It 'cannot but be very prejudicial to human society, and the promotion of the good of commonwealths, cities, armies or families, to admit of a parity, or all to be equal in power,' they stated.[27] Two key bases of support for the Levellers, the army and the Independent and Baptist churches in London, appeared to be seriously wavering in their commitment to the radicals' programme.

At this point both the army Grandees and the majority in Parliament were continuing to pursue a settlement with the King. They were unaware, however, that Charles was signing an 'Engagement' with former Covenanters to use a Scottish army, combined with English pro-Royalist risings, to recover his kingdom on the most generous terms possible. News of the King's treachery and his failed attempt to escape from the Isle of Wight led Parliament to pass a 'Vote of No Addresses' on 3 January 1648, declaring that it would no longer receive overtures from the King, nor would it make any. Plotting, subterfuge and double-dealing had been the hallmarks of Charles I's political behaviour from the beginning of the first civil war. The second civil war constituted the last in a long line of disastrous attempts on his part to reverse the revolutionary process by force. The Royalist risings in England and Wales occurred before the Scots had raised an army, and the New Model Army was consequently able to deal with its enemies in turn, rather than simultaneously.

The notion that the King must be brought to justice had first been mooted at Putney. By the time of the army prayer meeting at Windsor Castle, held from 28 April to 1 May, the officers' attitude to Charles had clearly hardened. The agitator William Allen recalled their resolution to 'call Charles Stuart, that man of blood, to an account for that blood he had shed, and mischief he had done to his utmost, against the Lord's cause and people in these poor nations'.[28] There was a hardening, too, in the attitude of the army towards those who once again took up the Royalist cause – in Cromwell's words, 'their fault who have appeared in this summer's business is certainly double to theirs who were in the first [civil war] because it is the repetition of the same offence against all the witnesses God has borne'.[29] The Royalist commanders of Colchester, Sir Charles Lucas and Sir John Lisle, were executed without trial after the town fell to Fairfax's forces.* The rout of the Royalist forces was completed by Oliver Cromwell, as his soldiers utterly crushed the Scottish army at the Battle of Preston, killing a thousand of their men and taking nearly two thousand prisoner.

---

* Lucas and Lisle were executed on the grounds of breach of parole – they had both earlier sworn never to take up arms for the King again.

Faced with a supremely victorious army sweeping all before it, Parliament reacted to the news of the 'Engagers" routing by reopening negotiations with the King, though Charles was no more sincere about his intentions to honour the new peace proposals, the Treaty of Newport, than he had been about any of the many previous attempts at settlement. As he explained to a confidant, his only desire was to buy time so that he might escape. For Ireton, the King's readiness to wage war once more against his own people made him a criminal who had to be brought to justice. The rest of the officers were almost certainly won over to this position once it became clear that Parliament was ready to reach a settlement with the King that was indistinguishable from the one for which the Royalist participants in the second civil war had been fighting.

It was at this point, in the winter of 1648, that the Levellers came closest to achieving their political goals, as the army leadership now strove for a settlement that did not require the consent of Charles Stuart. Leading Levellers, including Lilburne, Wildman and City Independents, met at the Nag's Head tavern and secured amendments to a draft Remonstrance put together by Ireton. The final version was laid before the Commons on 18 November. It made clear that 'exemplary justice . . . in capital punishment' should be meted out to the 'principal author' (the King) of the 'late wars'.[30] The document's hostility towards the reigning monarch was clear for all to see, but this was not yet a republican manifesto. Instead, it projected a political settlement in which a new monarch would be elected by the representative body and not admitted to the throne until he had subscribed to a new version of the Agreement of the People. This version, far more detailed than the original, looked more like a pragmatic programme for political settlement than an abstract statement of principle. It nonetheless retained the core idea of the 'reserves', though these were more limited in scope than in the first Agreement.

The officers' engagement with the idea of an Agreement is often presented as if it were a sham, designed to divert radical energies while the army leadership got on with the main business of bringing the King to justice. Lilburne accused the officers of talking with the Levellers 'meerly to quiet and please us (*like children with rattles*) till they had done their main work'.[31] Some of the leading Levellers even turned on each other, Richard Overton accusing Wildman of 'selling out' his principles for the promise of preferment under the new regime. Yet, in viewing events in late 1648 and early 1649 in this way, historians have been guilty again of privileging the Putney Debates above all other attempts to arrive at a solution. The discussions that took place at Whitehall in December 1648 were arguably much more significant. At Putney, as Ireton had reminded the participants, the army was merely discussing its own plans for the settlement of the kingdom. At Whitehall, with the New Model Army now firmly in control of the capital and with Parliament purged, by Colonel Thomas Pride and his men, of those MPs who wished to continue negotiating with the King, there was a real possibility that the debates would determine the shape that any new government would take.

The officers presented their amended version of the Agreement to the Commons on 20 January, the day that the King's trial opened at Westminster Hall. Aside from their rejection of the religious reserve, one stumbling-block remained for the Levellers, and for Lilburne in particular: they continued to insist that any Agreement had to be tendered to the people for approval before a new government could be established. The timing of the submission of the 'Officers' Agreement', as it came to be known, has led to suggestions that, like modern-day politicians choosing to bury unpopular announcements on 'bad-news days', Ireton and Cromwell saw an opportunity to let the Agreement die a quiet death while the nation's attention was fixed upon the fate of their monarch. Certainly, Parliament did not seem to take up the Agreement with any great alacrity, merely thanking Ireton and Cromwell for their efforts while simultaneously counselling them on the need for the army to stay out of politics. By March 1649 Lilburne, Overton, Walwyn and Thomas Prince (the Levellers' treasurer, formerly a cheese-maker) were in prison, arrested for their attack on the new military regime contained in *The Second Part of England's New Chaines Discovered*, a follow-up to Lilburne's pamphlet of 26 February.

However, evidence suggests that there was more genuine commitment to, and public enthusiasm for, the notion of a new government established on the basis of the Agreement than previously assumed. Manuscript copies of the 'Officers' Agreement' exist that were clearly being circulated for subscription in local communities, presumably in preparation for the creation of a new administration.[32] Indeed, before Pride's purge Ireton had attempted to get well-disposed MPs to agree to dissolve Parliament rather than continue to sit as an attenuated version of the Long Parliament that had been in session since November 1640. The failure to establish a new government on the basis of the Agreement almost certainly has more to do with the extreme political volatility of the years 1649–51, as the fate of the fledgling republic hung in the balance, threatened by both Irish and Scottish Royalist risings, than with any Machiavellian plot by Ireton to pull the wool over the eyes of Wildman, Lilburne and their associates.* The vehemence of Lilburne's attacks on the officers, and the tendency of historians to view the politics of the 1640s in terms of a simple dichotomy between Leveller 'radicals' and 'conservative' Grandees, has obscured the fact that in 1649 the Levellers had come within a whisker of seeing their projected settlement for the government of England reach fruition.

---

* Charles II was proclaimed by the Scots as King of Great Britain, not merely of Scotland, on 5 February 1649, just six days after the execution of his father, effectively signalling that the Scottish Convenanters were intent, once again, on intervening militarily in English political affairs.

THE EARTH A COMMON TREASURY

On 30 January 1649, Charles I was executed on a platform erected outside his Banqueting House in Whitehall, the 'royal actor', as the poet Andrew Marvell described him, performing one last role, this time tragic, upon the world's stage. Eyewitnesses spoke of a great groan emanating from the crowd as the executioner's axe fell upon him. Charles's dignified conduct in his final hours, and his careful repackaging by Royalist writers as a martyr for the Anglican Church, meant that the regicide paradoxically became a great propaganda coup for the Stuart cause. Rid of a king who in life was a constant political liability, Charles's old supporters were now left with a monarch who in death had been transformed into a Christ-like figure, having given his life in a bid to save his people.

If the execution provoked deep shock among the population at large, there is also considerable evidence that execution may not have been the outcome that was desired of the King's show trial at Westminster Hall. There was never any chance that Charles would be acquitted, but it is possible that the purpose of the trial was to get him to accept publicly his responsibility for the wars of the

1640s and to step down in favour of one of his sons, probably the youngest (and presumably the most malleable), Henry, Duke of Gloucester. These schemes might have been merely diversionary tactics to draw attention from the true objective of the trial, but in any case, they were rendered useless by the King's resolute refusal to recognise the authority of the court and therefore to answer the charges that were laid against him. Whether it had been their original intention or not, the members of the High Court of Justice were pushed into recording a capital judgement against Charles.

England's new rulers were as hesitant to declare themselves a republic as they appear to have been to kill their king. It took two months for the 'Rump', as the remainder of the Long Parliament came to be known, to declare that the office of king and the House of Lords had been abolished, and it was not until May 1649 that the Rump declared that England was now a 'Commonwealth and Free State . . . governed by the representatives of the people in parliament . . . without any king or House of Lords'.

The regicide was deeply unpopular, and the socially and politically conservative majority in the Rump could barely bring themselves to describe the new regime as a 'commonwealth'. It was government without a king, not a republic. But in spite of this reluctance and the gradual regression to constitutional conservatism at the centre, the King's death and the acts establishing a commonwealth served to inspire many to call for more radical political and religious settlements. To a significant proportion of the population, Charles's death was a prophetic moment, signalling the coming of the new millennium and the reign of Christ and his saints on earth. Prominent among these were the individuals who later became known as the Fifth Monarchists, as a result of their close reading of the prophecies of the Book of Daniel, in which the fall of the four earthly empires (Assyrian, Persian, Greek and Roman) would be followed by the rule of 'King Jesus' and his saints. In Fifth Monarchist readings of the regicide, Charles I was identified as the 'little horn' of the fourth beast – the fourth empire – discussed in Daniel's prophecy (Daniel 7:8): 'And behold in this horn were eyes like the eyes of man, and a mouth speaking great things.'

The most remarkable of the many prophecies to be inspired by the execution of Charles I and the establishment of the Commonwealth came from an obscure petty gentleman, Gerrard Winstanley, who, with William Everard and several others, began to dig the common land on St George's Hill, Walton, Surrey, on 1 April 1649, in preparation for sowing it with peas, beans and carrots.

Until 1648, when he began publishing his mystical works, Winstanley had done little to attract public attention. He was relatively well connected in London society. His kinsmen in London included the lawyer James Winstanley (whose daughter, after the Restoration, would be made a Lady of the Privy Chamber in Ordinary to the Queen), and a prosperous merchant taylor, also James Winstanley, connected to the London Whig and City Chamberlain, Sir Thomas Player. Gerrard Winstanley also married well. His first wife, Susan, was the child of a leading London surgeon, William King, who became master of the Barber-Surgeons Company in 1650. However, Winstanley's textile business in London, like many others, suffered during the war, and in late 1643 he was forced to declare himself bankrupt. The experience was a bitter one: in his later works, he declared his hatred of 'the theeving art of buying and selling' which generally involved 'oppressing fellow-creatures'. By the end of the year, he had moved to Surrey, possibly because his father-in-law owned property there, at Ham; by 1646 he was working as a grazier in the nearby community of Cobham. Though he was not one of Cobham's wealthiest inhabitants, neither was he living in abject poverty. On manorial court rolls from this time he was listed as a 'gentleman'. On 10 April 1646, in an early presage of his later activities, Winstanley and five others were up before the manorial court for digging on the commons and taking peat and turf in what was probably a protest over restrictive tenancy agreements.[1]

Winstanley's later works indicate that he sided with Parliament during the first civil war, though his activism does not appear to have gone beyond taking the Parliamentary loyalty oath, the Solemn League and Covenant, in London in 1643. Towards the end of 1648, though, he became publicly involved in defending William Everard, a former New Model Army soldier and now prophet, against charges of blasphemy. Everard was a shadowy and volatile character, a one-time Parliamentarian spy who had been first imprisoned, then cashiered, for his part in an earlier plot to kill Charles I.[2] Winstanley answered the blasphemy charges in print in *Truth Lifting up Its Head above Scandals* (October 1648). Depending on how you looked at it, the pamphlet was either a very brave or a very naive attempt at refuting the charges, for the beliefs that Winstanley admitted he himself held could scarcely be called anything other than deeply heterodox. *Truth Lifting up Its Head* was the culmination of the three other spiritual works that he had published that year, *The Mysterie of God*, *The Breaking of the Day of God* and *The Saints' Paradise*. In these works he had equated God with the spirit of 'pure Reason', which, he said, was 'that living power of light that is in all things: it is the salt that savours all things: it is the fire that burns up dross and so restores what is corrupted'.[3]

Like some other radicals, Winstanley believed the regicide heralded the ushering-in of the new millennium. However, whereas the Fifth Monarchists saw the Second Coming as being the literal rule of Christ with His saints – a fundamentally undemocratic vision, as the unregenerate could not be permitted a role in the government of 'King Jesus' – Winstanley interpreted the millennium as the rising of Christ's spirit in all. The promise of salvation was universal and all would be saved, though for the sinful, the process by which the 'dross' would be burnt up would necessarily be painful.

Winstanley directly attacked traditional religion. Heaven and hell were not real, physical places: those who worshipped a God in some celestial heaven kept Him 'at a distance'. This Christ at a distance would save no one: only 'Christ within is thy saviour'.[4] Heaven was living under 'true magistracy', the spirit of love and charity; hell was living under the 'kingly' power of covetousness, the spirit of oppression.[5] As the true essence of God was the spirit, the university-educated clergy, to whom Winstanley directed *Truth Lifting up Its Head*, had no better claim to it than anyone else. To worship other men's interpretations of the Bible, rather than follow the spirit, was to worship the Devil. Winstanley's emphasis on the spirit diminished the importance of the historic Christ. He denied the traditional Christian account of the resurrection, asserting that Christ had not physically risen after crucifixion.

This denial was important to his belief system and to explain the actions that he later took in Surrey. For Winstanley, the Fall of Man had had serious material, as well as spiritual, consequences. It was the Fall, itself precipitated by an act of covetousness, the taking of an apple, that had rendered the earth barren and unfruitful in places. Christ's essence, however, would cleanse and purge the 'poysoned' earth. His spirit would rise 'like a corne of wheat' from under 'the clods of earth'.[6] Pastoral metaphors can be found throughout Winstanley's early writings. In *Truth Lifting up Its Head* he described the spreading of the spirit of righteousness in these terms: 'The Thorne bush is burning; but the Vine is flourishing. The Ashes of the Thorne bush is laid at the root and feet of the Vine, and it growes abundantly.'[7]

There were clear similarities between Winstanley's religious thought and that of other religious radicals. The emphasis on practical Christianity, charity and the 'golden rule' linked his work with the writings of Overton and Walwyn. The emphasis on the spirit connected him with earlier antinomian writers and prefigured the centrality of the spirit to the Quaker movement, a sect that Winstanley would gravitate towards in later life. The attack upon formal religion and the spiritual monopoly of the clergy was common to the works of many radicals. However, Winstanley always denied being influenced by other religious writers (the only reference to a religious work in his writings other than the Bible is to John Foxe's *Book of Martyrs*), claiming that what he wrote came from 'a free discovery within'. There is also no clear evidence that he had contact with other radical figures until he came to the defence of Everard in the autumn of 1648, though there is a suggestion in some of his works that he may have briefly been involved with Baptists and 'dipped' (undergone adult re-baptism).[8]

Historians who have discussed Winstanley's thought have often struggled to reconcile his 'mystical' works published in 1648 with the 'political' works that began to appear in 1649. This has led some to offer various arguments about his character as a thinker: that he was either essentially a mystical writer and that the later Digger experiments were symbolic; that he was really a political writer, and that he dressed up his writings in the language of visions, trances and prophecy, as did some female 'prophets', as a means of attracting an audience for his work; or that he was intellectually schizoid with his life falling into two distinct periods, mystical and then political.

None of these arguments is correct. Winstanley was at one and the same time a mystic and a communist. His theology was deeply political: he always associated sin with covetousness – meaning, for him, private ownership of the land and economic domination. Likewise, his communism drew strength from his theology. The experiment of digging on the common land would work, he believed, because the spirit of righteousness rising in men and women would make wastelands fertile. But Winstanley was no crackpot: he also advocated in his works, and practised on Digger settlements, sound techniques for agricultural improvement such as manuring the land, planting beans and pulses so as to fix nitrogen in the soil, or the practice known as 'Devonshiring', in which undergrowth was burnt and the ashes spread to fertilise poor soil.[9]

The first of Winstanley's works to fuse the religious and the political into radical praxis, *The New Law of Righteousness*, emerged at the height of revolutionary fervour in England. Completed just four days before the execution of the King, it was in this pamphlet that he first declared the message given to him while in a trance:

> Worke together. Eat bread together ... Whosoever it is that labours in the earth, for any person or persons, that lifts up themselves as Lords and Rulers over others, and that doth not look upon themselves equal to others in the Creation, the hand of the Lord shall be upon that labourer: I the Lord have spoke it and I will do it; Declare this all abroad.[10]

The common land was to be worked by the people, who were to withdraw their labour from the landowning classes. But Winstanley's vision saw no need for a class war against the rich. If they wished to keep their enclosed lands, he said (with his tongue lodged firmly in his cheek), the gentry and aristocracy could plough them themselves. In time, the spirit of righteousness would make all mankind act in one spirit.

There was, however, a progression over the course of 1649 in the weight Winstanley gave to human agency in effecting this transformation. While the voice in the trance was clearly a call to action, *The New Law* also intimated that the new society would not be created by human efforts alone. Instead, 'Everyone is to wait, till the Lord Christ do spread himself in multiplicities of bodies, making them all of one heart and one mind.'[11] This stance had shifted by the time the first Digger manifesto, *The True Levellers Standard*, was published on 20 April 1649, a work defending the establishment of the first commune on St George's Hill.*

---

* The Diggers defined themselves as 'true Levellers' to distinguish themselves from 'sword Levellers' like Lilburne, Overton, Walwyn and Wildman, who were now, in the wake of the Burford incident, too heavily linked to the use of force.

The religious language of Winstanley's earlier works was still very apparent in *The True Levellers Standard*. Here he revisited his discussion of the Fall, explaining, via a dreadful pun, that Adam's actions had dammed up – 'A-dam' – the spirit of righteousness. He justified the establishment of the Digger community with many biblical references, especially to the Book of Acts, whose vision of Christian charity had also proved an inspiration to earlier communitarian religious movements.

Now, though, the prophetic language was combined with specific reference to the immediate political context of the 1640s and to current political ideas. Like the leading Leveller writers, Winstanley reinterpreted the Parliament's Solemn League and Covenant (to which, as already mentioned, he had himself subscribed) as a social contract between the Commons and the people 'to endeavour a reformation and to bring in liberty every man in his place', which Parliament had now defaulted upon by 'imprisoning and oppressing' men who attempted to fulfil the Covenant's true ends.[12] He also deployed the concept of the 'Norman yoke', which had been a feature of Leveller writing. According to this argument, the Norman Conquest had replaced England's fair and equitable Anglo-Saxon constitution with oppressive and unjust laws. Moreover, it had imported into England a new political elite and it was this same 'Norman' class that continued to oppress the English. For Winstanley, England's 'Norman' laws were no more than legal equivalents of the 'cords, manacles and yokes' worn by 'Newgate prisoners'.[13] However, he went further than Lilburne in arguing that the crucial element of this oppressive system was the private ownership of land: 'England is not a free people till the poor that have no land have a free allowance to dig and labour the commons, and so live as comfortably as the landlords that live in their enclosures.'[14]

The anger directed at the landowning class is much more evident in *The True Levellers Standard*: 'those that buy or sell land, and are landlords have got it either by oppression or murder or theft'.

Winstanley clarifies the plan to use the establishment of Digger com-
munes to institute a strike of all agricultural labourers: 'All labourers
or such as are called poor people . . . shall not dare to work for hire
for any landlord or for any that is lifted up above others: for by their
labours they have lifted up tyrants and tyranny; and by denying to
labour for hire they shall pull them down again.'[15] Human activity
was now clearly central to Winstanley achieving his prophetic vision.
But in spite of the growing stridency and overt political engagement
of his writings, he disavowed public disorder or the use of violence
to achieve his ends: 'There is no intent of tumult or fighting, but
only to get bread to eat with the sweat of our brows.'[16]

   Although he did not directly acknowledge its influence,
Winstanley's stance in *The True Levellers Standard* was similar to that
adopted in a pamphlet published in December 1648, *Light Shining
in Buckingham-shire*. This anonymous work, like Winstanley's,
linked the Fall of Man with enclosure, and landownership and private property with theft and murder. Although it was far more
explicitly anti-monarchical – 'Kings are the root of tyranny . . .
Kings are of the beast'[17] – than Winstanley's writings, *Light Shining*
also called for a 'just portion for each man to live' and employed the
Book of Acts to justify establishing a 'public maintenance and stock'
for the poor. *Light Shining* demonstrates that Winstanley's was not
an isolated voice, and that there were elements of the Leveller movement calling for social as well as political reform.

   The hostility to the rich evident in his writings from 1649
onwards is also clearly present here, reminding us that civil war
could also be viewed as class war. Indeed, the sequel to *Light
Shining in Buckingham-shire*, published in March 1649, anticipated
Marx's theory of the appropriation of surplus labour value: 'the
flower of those industrious mens labours are boulted out from
them, and only the Bean left them to feed on'.[18] However, whereas
A Light and *More Light Shining on Buckingham-shire* only advocated the redistribution of Crown and Church lands among the
poor, Winstanley's Diggers called for the utter transformation of

English society – not merely for some of the land to be portioned out to the needy but for private ownership of the 'common treasury' of the earth to be abolished altogether.

The True Levellers Standard was presented as a multi-authored work and signed by thirteen others besides Winstanley and Everard. The historian John Gurney has demonstrated that about a third of those identified in Digger pamphlets were Surrey residents and most of them came from Cobham, explaining in part the less marked local hostility to the Digger settlement on Little Heath at Cobham than to the one first established on St George's Hill, Walton. Perhaps more remarkably, given the latter commemoration of the Diggers as champions of the rural poor, many of these individuals were not rootless, homeless 'peasants' at all but local householders who retained their original Cobham homes at the same time as taking part in establishing the Digger community. There is something here reminiscent of the Buckinghamshire pamphlets: *More Light* complained that the 'successful' tenant farmers were overburdened with official duties; their 'reward' for hard work was more unpaid hard work. Again, what comes through is the voice of the overburdened ratepayer, not that of the poorest sections of the community.[19]

The Digger settlements, and Winstanley's political writings, were, then, a radical response to longer term economic changes, namely, the transformation of a feudal society to a form of agrarian capitalism. Labour services had, by and large, been replaced by cash rents, fens had been drained and more and more common land enclosed. However, instead of the sporadic resistance to these changes offered by enclosure rioters, such as placing checks on the encroachment of landlords on the commons, Winstanley and the Diggers proposed instead the common ownership of all land. This would have been anathema to most early Stuart anti-enclosure rioters, who believed that in defending the commons they were defending their personal property.[20] Certainly the Digger movement matched other forms of direct action in meeting the crisis of subsistence provoked by the civil war, such as the taking of wood for fuel from enclosed forests. However, the radical approach of the Diggers, to cultivate the commons both as an example of the future form that the ideal society would take and as a means of freeing labourers and tenant farmers from the 'tyranny' of landowners, could also antagonise their social equals, who viewed these communal settlements as a threat to 'their' land. Here we can see a significant change from the nature of rural politics a hundred years earlier. In 1549 Kett, a wealthy yeoman farmer, had supported and led the rebels. Now, in Surrey, men of the same class were vehement in their opposition to this new communal movement.

The original Digger settlement at St George's Hill soon attracted opposition from locals, many of whom were from the same middling background as the Diggers themselves and were concerned about the implications for their own use of the commons.[21]

The settlement at Walton was attacked almost as soon as the community was established. There is evidence that some of the Diggers, most likely the eccentric and occasionally violent William Everard, may have responded in kind. A yeoman of the parish, Henry Saunders, formally complained to the Council of State, the executive body of the republic, on 16 April 1649 about the activities of twenty to thirty Diggers who had burnt about ten acres of heath. Lord General Fairfax was ordered by the Council to investigate. However, his agent, Captain John Gladman, saw little at Walton to concern the Council, viewing the activities of the Diggers 'not worth the writing nor yet taking nottis of'.[22] Gladman suspected that the Council's time was being wasted with what was little more than a local land dispute. Everard and Winstanley were nonetheless summoned to Whitehall on 20 April to be interviewed by Fairfax, who treated the two men with leniency, allowing them to keep their hats on in his presence.*

---

* The refusal of 'hat honour', the removing of headgear in the presence of a social superior, was usually viewed as a profound affront to noble dignity.

From this moment on, Fairfax was identified, rightly or wrongly, as a potential ally by Winstanley and became the target of further appeals from the Digger leader. In May, Fairfax visited Cobham and had another amicable exchange with Winstanley, who repeated his assurances that the Diggers were not violent.

However, hostility from some of the Walton community continued unabated. On 11 June that year, four Diggers were badly hurt in an assault led by Starr and another yeoman, John Taylor, accompanied by fellow male villagers dressed as women in order to further humiliate and shame the Diggers. In the same month, actions were brought against the Diggers at Kingston Assizes for trespass, which Winstanley appealed against in a pamphlet directed at the Rump Parliament, *An Appeal to the House of Commons* (24 July 1649). The appeals were unsuccessful, and it was at this point, in the face of ongoing attacks, that the Diggers were forced to move their settlement to Little Heath, Cobham, closer to where many of the Diggers themselves had originated.

The parish of Cobham was more polarised socially. Local gentry had aggressively attacked rights to commons and timber, which had led to greater solidarity among the yeoman class. Initially, the settlement at Cobham appeared to meet with less resistance than the one at St George's Hill. But towards the end of the year hostile gentry, including Sir Anthony Vincent, Thomas Sutton and John Platt, Rector of West Horsley, were pressing the Council of State to deal with the Diggers. On 28 November, local soldiers tore down some of their dwellings, took away wood and cast three or four elderly squatters out into the open.

In the face of this opposition, Winstanley redoubled his efforts to promote the Digger movement, both in person and in print. A missionary tour conducted over the winter of 1649–50 seems to have met with some success. Settlements were established at Wellingborough in Northamptonshire, Cox Hall in Kent, Iver in Buckinghamshire, Barnet in Hertfordshire and Bosworth in Leicestershire, as well as in Gloucestershire and Nottinghamshire.

Class hostility ran through the declarations produced by the Iver and Wellingborough Diggers: 'Rich men's hearts are hardened, they will not give us if we beg at their doors; if we steal, the Law will end our lives, divers of the poor are starved to death already, and it were better for us that are living to dye by the Sword than by the Famine.'[23] The only remedy was for the poor to fertilise and farm the common and waste ground.

In his pamphlets Winstanley renewed the demand that the republic intervene to support the Diggers' programme. In *A New Year's Gift for the Parliament and Armie* published on 1 January 1650, he attacked the government for failing to carry through the work begun by the regicide. Kingly power could not be destroyed simply by cutting off the King's head, but was like a 'great spread tree' that 'would grow again and recover fresh strength' if not removed root and branch.[24] While laws protecting private land-ownership remained, regal power too survived. Winstanley stressed, though, that the Diggers were for good government, not anarchy. The acts abolishing kingship and establishing the Commonwealth had made 'a firm foundation' but needed to be followed up by attacks on the power of the lawyers and the clergy, and, most of all, by granting the people the right to cultivate the commons. Winstanley repeated his commitment to non-violent means of pursuing the Diggers' goals, but he warned Parliament that if they did not fulfil their promise to abolish kingly power, then there would be no 'law but club law amongst the people'.[25] The *Appeale to All Englishmen* produced by the Little Heath Diggers in March 1650 went further, instructing copyholders that they were now freed from obedience to their lords of the manor and should not attend their 'Court-Barons' (manorial courts).

By the spring of 1650, however, Winstanley's community at Cobham had been destroyed. John Platt, accompanied by fifty men, had set fire to half a dozen of the Diggers' shelters and set a watch on the area for three days and nights to ensure that the squatters did not return. At Wellingborough, the Council of State on 15 April expressed support for one Thomas Pentlow's campaign against the 'Levellers' (as his letter described them).

The Digger experiment was over, and Winstanley and his followers were forced to find work threshing wheat on the estate of the Hastings family in Pirton, Hertfordshire, where the prophetess Lady Eleanor Davies (she published almost seventy largely unreadable prophetic tracts) owned the rectory and manor. Winstanley had a difficult relationship with the unstable female mystic. While adopting the persona of Melchizedek King of Salem, Lady Eleanor confronted him about the threshing accounts in the tithe barn on 3 December. Winstanley, for his part, refuted the claim that he had ever taken the work for money, saying that his aim was 'the convertion of your spirit to true Nobilitie, which is falne in the earth'. This was a clear dig at Davies's social pretensions, for despite her support for the republic and her repeated pleas of penury, she continued to make much of her aristocratic lineage. But Winstanley too was guilty of holding on to traditional prejudices, finding her adoption of male roles absurd. Lady Eleanor, Winstanley said, had 'lost the Breeches, which is indeed true Reason, the strength of A man'.[26] Despite these problems, he promised to do what he could for her business and draw up a clear set of accounts.

Meanwhile, his fellow Digger William Everard had joined the household of the English Behmenists John and Mary Pordage at Bradfield rectory in Berkshire.* Also rumoured to be present at Bradfield at this time was the prophet Thomas Totney. Everard's appearance heralded a series of unusual events. John Pordage was reported to have fled the local church in a 'Trance . . . bellowing like a Bull'. The previous week, a thirteen-year-old boy had begun making strange prognostications about the appearance of the Lord Jehovah. The 'conjuror' Everard was reportedly responsible for the disturbances and in December of 1650 he was committed to

---

* Behmenists were followers of Jakob Boehme, a German Lutheran mystic and shoemaker.

Bridewell Prison before being moved, due to his 'distracted' state, to Bethlem Hospital in March 1651. No more was heard of him.[27]

While his former comrade languished in a lunatic asylum, Winstanley completed his last and best-known work, *The Law of Freedom in a Platform, or, True Magistracy Restored*, published in February 1652 and dedicated to Oliver Cromwell. Here, the Digger leader laid out his most systematic vision of the new society. The earth would be worked in common, but individual families would continue to live apart rather than in communal dwellings. Private ownership of goods was not outlawed and families might keep animals for their own use, but most commodities, whether agricultural produce or manufactured goods, would be kept in storehouses. From the storehouses families could take what they needed, whether corn, meat, draught animals or household items.

What is most remarkable about *The Law of Freedom*, in contrast to Winstanley's other works, is the prominent role given to the system of overseers and to the law in ensuring that all worked the earth for the common good. This has led some historians to suggest that Winstanley had shifted from being England's 'first socialist' to becoming its 'first Stalinist'.[28] Elements of his system certainly seem repressive. Those who repeatedly refused to join the others in farming the land would be made slaves of the Commonwealth. Those who practised the law for money, or who engaged in trade for profit, or demanded money for preaching or praying, or who committed rape would be put to death.[29] The belief in the imminent rising of the spirit of Christ in everyone seemed to have been replaced with a pessimistic belief in the need for a strict penal code to coerce a recalcitrant public into working for the common good.

However, before we depict Winstanley as a seventeenth-century Pol Pot, offering the people the choice between hard agricultural toil and death, we must remember that, in comparison to the existing system of criminal law, his penal code considerably reduced the number of crimes that carried the death penalty. Winstanley himself justified the exercise of capital punishment only on the grounds that it was a 'kinder' punishment than imprisonment, which, given the state of early modern prisons, especially as experienced by the poor, was not unreasonable. Death as a result of 'gaol fever'– typhus – commonly killed off inmates before they finished their sentences. Even if they avoided death, many left gaol physically shattered – one woman accused of witchcraft had to be carried to the assizes in a wheelbarrow as her toes had rotted off.[30] Moreover, though the vision presented in *The Law of Freedom* paid much greater attention to law and institutions, it remained a millenarian vision nonetheless. The 'spirit of universal Righteousness dwelling in Mankind' was 'rising up to teach every one to do to another as he would have another do to him'.[31] It was also a broadly democratic vision. Government was to be founded on a contract with the people. There were to be regular elections and individuals were to hold office only for short periods in order to check corruption. Utopian optimism, rather than totalitarian power-hunger, continued to dominate Winstanley's thought.

It is also important to remember the specific circumstances that prompted him to write his last work. In 1651, the Independent minister Hugh Peters had initiated a debate about the reform of the law, education and the clergy in his *Good Work for a Good Magistrate*. Cromwell himself was at this time encouraging such proposals and attempting to court radical opinion. Winstanley appears to have wanted to contribute to the debate stimulated by Peters's work; indeed, portions of *The Law of Freedom* are a direct commentary on *Good Work for a Good Magistrate*. So Winstanley's last work was intended less as a summation of all his earlier Digger pamphlets and more as a contribution to a specific contemporary debate. In this regard, it was only partially successful. A number of other contributors to the controversy poached elements of his work, but, like modern historians, they tended to concentrate on the coercive elements of his vision rather than those that stressed community.

Aside from its alleged repressiveness, *The Law of Freedom* has also been attacked for its moral conservatism. Winstanley continued to see the traditional patriarchal household as the basis of his new Utopian Commonwealth. The Digger leader, like the Leveller spokesmen, has been criticised for the lack of attention given to women in his work. In answering Lady Eleanor Davies, Winstanley had resorted to deploying the orthodox separation between masculine authority and female submission. However, there were some good political reasons for his apparent moral conservatism. Apart from being smeared as violent anarchists, the Diggers were also accused by their opponents of holding women in 'common' and living in 'bestialness'.[32] In his last mystical work, *Fire in the Bush*, Winstanley condemned 'Lust of the flesh' as part of covetousness.[33] His concern here was with the association of his Digger movement with the activities of so-called 'Ranters', religious radicals who were said to advocate, among other things, free love, drinking, smoking and swearing.

As we have already seen, the association of religious radicalism with libertinism was neither unusual nor unique to the years 1649–50. However, these accusations were especially problematic for Winstanley for two reasons. First, patriarchal theory and English law held that wives were essentially the property of their husbands. If, the Diggers critics argued, they wished to abolish private property, surely this included men's property in their wives? If the land became common, then it must follow that women became common too. Second, at the time the Digger colonies were being established, England was in the grip of a moral panic, spread by contemporary news-sheets and pamphlets, concerning the activities of the supposed 'Ranters', whose activities the equivalent of an early modern tabloid press spent much time and energy in detailing. The pamphlet *The Ranters Religion*, published on 11 October 1650, claimed they held that:

All Women ought to be in common, and when they are assembled together (this is a known truth) they first entertaine one another, the men those of their own sex, and the Women their fellow females: with horrid Oathes and execrations, then they fall to bowzing, and drinke deep healths (Oh cursed Caitiffes!) to their Brother God, and their Brother Devill; then being well heated with Liquor, each Brother takes his she Otter upon his knee, and the word (spoken in derision of the sacred Writ) being given, viz. *Increase and Multiply*, they fall to their lascivious embraces, with a joynt motion &c.[34]

Other pamphlets alleged that Ranter meetings consisted of 'mixt dances of men and women stark naked'.[35] The leading reputed Ranter Abezier Coppe was accused of lying in bed 'with two women at a time'.[36] Yet other publications accused Ranters of making a mockery of the Eucharist:

one of them took [a piece of beef] in his hand, tearing it asunder said to the other, *This is the flesh of Christ*, take and eat. The other took a cup of Ale and threw it in the chimney corner, saying *There is the bloud of Christ*. And having some discourse of God it was proved that every one of these said, *That he could go into the house of Office, and make a God every morning*, by easing his body.[37]

It was said that one woman Ranter, the almost certainly fictitious 'Mary Adams', proclaimed that she was the reincarnation of the Virgin Mary and was pregnant with Jesus Christ. Pamphlets reported that for these blasphemies she was kept under close confinement until she gave birth. When the baby was born it proved not to be the Messiah but a hideous misshapen monster, with no hands or feet but claws like a toad. Adams herself became covered in boils, blotches and putrefying scabs; shortly afterwards, she compounded her sins by committing suicide.[38]

The Rump Parliament took the 'Ranter scare' very seriously,

passing a new law against blasphemy in 1650 that was designed to counter the threat to public morals posed by this sect (a law which Milton, that famous advocate of liberty of conscience, praised as 'that prudent and well deliberated act').[39] However, some historians have questioned whether the Ranters existed at all or were in fact mere phantoms created by the popular press both to satiate puerile public interest and to act as a check on real radical movements such as the Diggers. In time, accusations of descending into 'Ranterism' became a means by which the sects themselves could exercise internal discipline over their members.

It is certainly true that the popular press recycled images and stories that had already appeared in print to spotlight the activities of religious radicals. Images of supposed naked 'Adamite' meetings published in 1641 were reprinted in 1650 with a new text claiming that they were depictions of 'Ranter' gatherings. The press also co-opted cases involving generally irreligious behaviour, such as the mock communion in the alehouse described above, into accounts of the particular sect, the 'Ranters'. There was no real theological coherence to this picture. At one and the same time, 'Ranters' were depicted as libertines, pseudo-Christs and anti-formalists. The 'Ranter scare', it has been suggested, reminds us that the real influence of 'radicalism' in the English Revolution was essentially negative, in that it acted as an ideological bogeyman that conservatives could use to rally support.[40]

However, if we dismiss the Ranters as simply the creation of the popular press, we ignore an important facet of the radicalism of the English Revolution. The alehouse radicalism that pamphlets like *Strange Newes from Newgate* detailed, for instance, was not a fabrication, something we can see from the autobiography of Lodowick Muggleton, the co-founder, with his cousin John Reeve, of a sect bearing his name that would survive in an underground existence until the late 1970s. Muggleton recounted frequent arguments in London pubs in the Minories between himself, Reeve and various Ranters over the spiritual authority of

the Muggletonian prophets.*⁴¹ Moreover, while there was no identifiable organised sect of Ranters – and given the anti-formalism
ascribed to them, why should we expect to find one? – there were
certainly individuals who advocated the kind of rejection of orthodox morality depicted in the popular prints. Foremost of these
was Laurence Clarkson, who had already attracted attention as a
target of Thomas Edwards's ire in his *Gangraena*. Clarkson's work,
A Single Eye, published June 1650, may have been responsible for
fuelling the whole Ranter scare. In this work, Clarkson infamously
stated: 'Therefore till acted that so called Sin, thou art not delivered from the power of sin, but ready upon all the Alarms to
tremble and fear the reproach of thy body.'⁴² Clarkson's call to
enact sinful behaviour in order to free oneself from sin was the
radical extension of the antinomian belief that the moral law was
no longer binding upon God's 'saints'. Clarkson was not alone
in advocating such behaviour. The anonymous author of the
pamphlet *A Justification of the Mad Crew* stated that among their
community 'to every woman is their wife, not one woman apart
from another, but all in one, and one in all'.⁴³

Winstanley feared the Ranters not simply because accusations
of 'Ranterism' were used to tar all religious and political radicals,
but also because elements of supposed Ranter writing sounded
similar to the programme of the Diggers.⁴⁴ The vision of the

---

* Muggletonian beliefs were unusual, to say the least. Unitarians, they believed that God
was a man between five and six feet tall who lived in a real, physical heaven about six miles
above the Earth. The death of Jesus – God – had caused a power vacuum in heaven, with
Elijah and Moses having to deputise for the Almighty until the resurrection.
Muggletonians, like their bitter rivals the Quakers, rejected traditional forms of worship
and Muggletonian religious meetings were often little more than informal gatherings in
pubs. In addition, they initially held that the solar system was geocentric – revolving
around the Earth. On a more enlightened note, because Muggletonians rejected the separation of matter and spirit they believed that there could be no such things as witches,
ghosts or other spectral phenomena. This remarkable little sect survived until at least 1979,
when the last known Muggletonian believer, a Kent apple farmer called Philip Noakes,
died. Given Muggletonians' ambivalence about evangelising, and its rather secretive
nature, it may be that some living followers remain, either in the UK or the USA.

author of *A Justification of the Mad Crew* was communitarian as well as libertine: 'Come give me your mony, your land, your wives and children, let it be their land, mony, wives and children as well as yours, and yours as well as theirs; call it our mony, our wives, our children, our Table, our meat, our drink.'[45] The same radical interpretation of Christian charity was evident in the work of Abezier Coppe, who believed that the world was entering its last days and those who did not cast their gold and silver into the common treasury would be condemned at the Last Judgement. Only those who accounted 'All things common' partook in 'true communion'.[46] Conservatives saw in the Ranters not just a convenient rhetorical stick with which to beat their political and religious opponents, but also the most extreme manifestation of a society in which traditional values had been seriously undermined, the greatest expression of a world turned upside down.

The years after the death of Charles I have been seen to witness a steady process of conservative retrenchment. By 1649, some of the most outspoken radicals were already dead. Apart from the army mutineers, the Leveller cause had also lost one of its most eloquent spokesmen in Thomas Rainborowe, killed by Royalists in 1648 in a botched hostage-taking at Doncaster (the Cavaliers had planned to exchange Rainborowe for Sir Marmaduke Langdale, then a prisoner of the Parliamentarians). The Leveller newspaper *The Moderate* reported Rainborowe's heroic death. He had desired his would-be captors to

> give him a sword, that he might die like a man, but one ran him again through the belly, he boldly with both hands pulled the sword out of his body, bending the point back almost to the hilt, endeavouring to have forst it from him, with which they cried, pistol the rogue, but that failing to go off, one threw his pistol violently at him, bruised his forehead very much and made him stagger . . . being again ran through the body, [Rainborowe] fell,

having before flung one of them upon the ground, they rid away from him, he got up and followed him some 12 yards, which they seeing swore the dog was following them, and returned again upon him, but with faintnesse he was faln before they came back yet then they ran him some 8 times thorow the body; the last words the maid of the house heard him say before appearing in the street, either for his rescue, or to revenge him on them, not so much as a musket shot off, or an alarm by drum, though his struggling with them was above a quarter of an hour.[47]

Other Levellers, including John Lilburne, languished in prison; or, in exile, men such as Edward Sexby and John Wildman resorted to pursuing conspiracies against Cromwell's protectorate. Gerrard Winstanley returned to a life of relative obscurity – though in 1654 a Winstanley was reported to be in contact with the Quakers, telling one of their leaders, Edward Burrough, that they were carrying on the work of the Diggers. The civil war, which had started with declamations by its pamphleteers of the 'slavery' endured by the people under Charles I's personal rule, had now produced a regime that regularly transported large numbers of its subjects to become bound labourers on the plantations of the West Indies.[48] The limits of religious tolerance during the protectorate were clearly displayed by the trial of the Quaker James Nayler for blasphemy in 1656, a trial that concluded with penalties – physical mutilation, branding, imprisonment – that were remarkably similar to those handed out to Burton, Bastwick and Prynne in 1637. The new republic could clearly be as tyrannical and cruel as the old monarchy. A year after Nayler's trial, Lilburne was dead, having earlier rejected his former life of political activism by laying down 'the temporall sword' to become a Quaker.[49]

There was a brief revival of radical fortunes with the downfall of Richard Cromwell's protectorate in 1659 (he had succeeded to the title following his father's death in 1658) and the recall of the Rump. Levellers and classical republicans returned to the political fray, including John Milton in *The Ready and Easie Way to establish a free commonwealth* – a pamphlet produced when it was already clear that the newly restored Commonwealth was failing – and there was an increase in Quaker political pamphleteering, partly as a result of the illness of the group's more conservative founder, George Fox. This radical activity, however, also acted to galvanise moderates within Parliament to move for the restoration of the monarchy. The republic did not simply collapse: it was forced out by organised conservative opposition and, most importantly, by the intervention of General George Monck and his troops.[50]

The restoration of Charles II saw Richard Cromwell and the regicide Edmund Ludlow fly into exile, while radicals such as Henry Marten and John Lambert were imprisoned. The restored monarchy displayed a vindictive thirst for vengeance. Even the carpenter who had erected Charles I's gallows was executed. Those regicides who had fled the country, such as John Okey, were hunted down – Okey was dragged from his pregnant wife in Delft. Not even death could obstruct the restored monarch's desire for retributive justice. The bodies of Henry Ireton and Oliver Cromwell were exhumed and hanged, drawn and quartered. The retribution ended simply because there were no more regicides left to kill and because the executions themselves were becoming politically counterproductive. The dying speeches in which these traitors were expected to display their contrition for their horrible crimes instead became platforms for declaring their unyielding support for the 'Good Old Cause'. In his scaffold speech, John Cook, the prosecuting counsel at Charles I's trial, declared, 'We are not traitors, nor murderers, nor fanatics, but true Christians and good Commonwealth men, fixed and constant to principles of sanctity, truth, justice and mercy.'[51]

The commitment of those who escaped Royalist clutches also remained undimmed. The republican Algernon Sidney left his response to the execution of his friend Sir Henry Vane – not a regicide, but viewed as too politically dangerous by the restored monarchy to be allowed to live – in the visitors' book at the Calvinist Academy in Geneva in 1663: 'Sit Sanguinis Ultor Justorum [Let there be revenge for the blood of the just].'[52] Radicals both aristocratic and plebeian continued to plot and fight against the restored monarchy, as evidenced by Venner's rising in 1661 and the Northern Rising of 1663, both insurrections involving large numbers of ex-New Model Army soldiers. The ideals of the 'Good Old Cause' were voiced even in a rebellion ostensibly in support of a royal pretender, the Duke of Monmouth against the reigning King, the Catholic James II. The one-eyed former New Model Army soldier Richard 'Hannibal' Rumbold was captured after the failure of the Scottish rebellion, led by the Earl of Argyll, in 1685, the counterpart to Monmouth's rising in Dorset and Somerset. His last words on the scaffold were a rousing affirmation of political equality (later to be immortalised by Thomas Jefferson): 'I am sure there was no man born marked of God above another; for none comes into the world with a saddle upon his back, neither any booted and spurred to ride him.'[53]

In November 1688 another Protestant challenger to James II landed in the West Country. However, unlike the Duke of Monmouth's rag-tag army, the Dutch Stadtholder William of Orange was accompanied by an invasion force four times the size of the Spanish Armada of a century earlier. And in contrast to Monmouth's rebellion, which drew its support largely from impoverished cloth-workers and farmhands, the Prince of Orange could rely on the backing of most of the English political elite, including members of the royal family such as James's Protestant daughter, Anne, alienated by the King's pro-Catholic policies and authoritarian rule.

These high-profile defections weakened the King's resolve and, instead of meeting William's army in battle, he turned back towards his capital. London, however, was no longer a safe haven for James. The atmosphere in the City, which had largely stayed loyal during the Monmouth rebellion, was deeply hostile to the King and his ministers: mobs attacked Catholic chapels and homes, and the hated Lord Chancellor, George Jeffries, was incarcerated in the Tower for his own safety. Terrified that he too might fall victim to crowd violence, James fled London on 11 December but was captured by Kent fishermen near Sheerness as his boat took on ballast. The King's capture was an inconvenience for William, now looked upon as the only individual capable of restoring order to the nation through his disciplined army, and on 23 December, with the Prince's connivance, James left the country. With the King gone, and after considerable pressure from the Prince of Orange himself, the hastily summoned Convention Parliament – so named because it was called by an ad hoc council of peers rather than by the King – agreed that William would rule as joint monarch with his wife Mary, the eldest daughter of James II, rather than act merely as her consort. On 13 February 1689, William and Mary formally accepted the throne.

As the Restoration regime finally met its end in the Glorious Revolution of 1688–9, a number of the surviving radicals returned to England, including, as an active member of William's invasion party, John Wildman. He was appointed Postmaster General and though soon dismissed from this post – under something of a cloud, he was accused both of consorting with James II and with blackening the names of Tories with fraudulent letters – he was still enough in royal favour to be knighted the year before his death, in February 1691. Wildman had remained a staunch advocate of popular sovereignty and limited monarchy, but his politics were more overtly Whig than republican or Leveller. Radical hopes were largely disappointed by the outcome of the Glorious Revolution. Revealingly, others whose politics had mellowed less, such as Edmund Ludlow, were no more welcome in post-revolutionary England than they had been after the Restoration. Ludlow was once again declared a traitor and orders were sent for his arrest.

In some respects, the world of 1688 can look like the realisation of the world of the Levellers, with religious toleration enacted through legislation, regular elections secured via the Triennial Act, greater accountability of the executive, and a declaration of the subjects' rights (including, significantly for later radical movements, the right to petition Parliament) on the statute books. Certainly, for most eighteenth-century radicals, 1688 was a crucial moment in the defining of British liberty. However, what looks similar is not necessarily the same, as the case of Edmund Ludlow reminds us. The Levellers had wisely acknowledged the need to limit the power of representative institutions, ring-fencing key rights against abridgement by the legislature. The Bill of Rights of 1689 featured no 'reserved' powers equivalent to those contained in the Agreement of the People, and though it did clip the wings of the monarchy, it placed no similar limitations on the sovereignty of Parliament. The absence of such controls would subsequently allow the Whig Party under Robert Walpole to undermine important elements of the revolution settlement, such as the 1694 Triennial Act. The extension of the life of parliaments after 1716 from three to seven years allowed Walpole to subdue the vibrant electoral politics of the age of Queen Anne and ushered in the long rule of a political oligarchy.

It was, in any case, unlikely that many in 1688–9 would have looked back to the Levellers for models of constitutional reform. The era of the civil war and revolution was viewed, from the perspective of the 1680s, as a national catastrophe that all sides were desperate not to revisit.* Consequently, it was dangerous to make positive reflections on the civil wars. 'Leveller' itself remained a term of opprobrium into the eighteenth century and was attached as a smear term to a number of eighteenth-century radical groups, most prominently in its use by 'loyalists' in the 1790s in John

---

* The revolution of 1688–9 was known as 'Glorious' not because it was achieved without violence, but because it was comparatively bloodless when viewed in the context of the events of the 1640s.

Reeves's Association for Preserving Liberty and Property against Republicans and Levellers, a national political society aimed at suppressing 'seditious' activity.

The propaganda appears to have worked. Though we know that some members of the radical London Corresponding Society owned copies of Leveller pamphlets, they did not advertise the fact, as to do so would have been very politically damaging. When radical writers such as Catharine Macaulay and William Godwin revived interest in the history of England's seventeenth-century revolution, they preferred to laud the 'republicans', men like John Hampden, Henry Vane and Algernon Sidney, rather than the Levellers. Of the major Leveller writers, Lilburne alone received some attention from Godwin, but it was largely negative. Godwin saw the Leveller leader as essentially self-interested and self-obsessed, pursuing his own personal quarrels to the detriment of the wider struggle, contrasting Lilburne, to his disadvantage, with the more 'public-spirited' Oliver Cromwell.[54] In his novel *Sybil*, published in 1845, the young Benjamin Disraeli could confidently declare that not 'one man in a thousand . . . has ever heard of Major Wildman: yet he was the soul of English politics in the most eventful period in this kingdom . . . and seemed more than once to hold the balance which was to decide the permanent form of our government'.[55]

The Levellers, then, remained largely forgotten until the late nineteenth century, when the work of Charles Firth recovered the text of the Putney Debates from the original manuscripts kept in Worcester College, Oxford. But Firth's transcriptions of the Debates were mainly perceived as interesting only to military historians. It took a non-British scholar, the German democratic socialist Eduard Bernstein, to draw serious attention not just to Putney as a crucial part of the English Revolution, but also to the importance of Winstanley and the Diggers, who had sunk even further from view than Lilburne, Walwyn, Overton and Wildman.

In the English-speaking world it was not until the publication in 1938 of A. S. P. Woodhouse's provocatively titled *Puritanism and Liberty* that Putney was established as a milestone in British constitutional history. His edition of the Debates had an explicitly political aim: to provide ideological ammunition for the public in the battle against the forces of fascism and, later, Soviet totalitarianism. It is his reinterpretation of Putney as a crucible of democratic thought that has proved most influential to the present day. In the era of the attempted left and centre-left 'popular front' against appeasement, the liberal reading of Putney offered by Woodhouse was adopted by British Marxist historians, most prominently Christopher Hill but also A. L. Morton and Brian Manning and, in a wider context of establishing an English radical tradition, E. P. Thompson. As a soldier, Thompson had carried a copy of *A Handbook of Freedom* (1939) in his knapsack, an anthology of radical English historical documents by the communist poets and writers Edgell Rickword and Jack Lindsay that included the Putney Debates. The Army Bureau for Current Affairs had encouraged discussion of the Debates among army education units, seeing in this a means of giving soldiers a sense of the historic purpose of the British army in defending liberty.

By the 1940s, the Putney Debates had clearly entered into the consciousness not only of historians, but also of politicians. The campaigning journalist Frank Owen adopted the name 'Thomas Rainsborough' in a number of articles on the conduct of the Second World War in *Tribune* magazine. Putney also served as an inspiration to modern radicals outside of England. The Trinidadian Trotskyite C. L. R. James found inspiration for his anticolonial cause not only in the activities of the Haitian revolutionaries, the subjects of his most famous work, *Black Jacobins*, but also in debates between seventeenth-century Englishmen.[56] Putney had become part of the language of political debate in the postwar era – most notably in Tony Benn's *Arguments for Socialism*. The Levellers and Diggers were also entering into popular culture. Winstanley's life was celebrated in David Caute's novel *Comrade Jacob* and in Andrew Molo and Kevin Brownlow's film *Winstanley*. The Diggers at Iver in Buckinghamshire were commemorated in Caryl Churchill's play *Light Shining in Buckinghamshire* (first performed in 1976), and celebrated in song by Leon Rosselson.

The Diggers and Levellers have been celebrated outside England as well. In Alexander Garden, Moscow, a column commemorating revolutionary heroes bears Winstanley's name at number eight on the list after Marx and Engels. As the Green movement gathered strength in the 1990s, in part through the actions of squatters such as the famous 'Swampy', celebrations of the three-hundred-and-fiftieth anniversary of the Digger settlements were accompanied not only by an academic conference but also by 're-enactments' of the original settlement: anarchist activists briefly reclaimed for the common people the land currently occupied by the millionaire residents of present-day St George's Hill, including entertainers such as Cliff Richard and Rolf Harris. The popularisation of the radicals of the seventeenth century has most recently been seen in the opening of a new exhibition centre at St Mary's Church, Putney, to celebrate the three-hundred-and-sixtieth anniversary of the Debates, lauded as a major step forward in disseminating 'our inspiring radical history' to a wider public.[57]

Without the pioneering Marxist, socialist and liberal historiography of the late nineteenth and early twentieth centuries, we would not have recovered the history of English radicalism in the seventeenth. The Levellers have now become the most potent symbol of Britain's 'democratic tradition', their work celebrated in print, on stage, in film and in song. While professional historians of the seventeenth century may complain, legitimately, that the history curriculum currently taught to our students remains too chronologically narrow, they can scarcely say that the Levellers are likely to disappear from the public consciousness. Now, in fact, we face the opposite problem: that the image of the Levellers as the 'first socialists' or 'first democrats' is the dominant one, and one that is now being institutionalised at Putney through permanent exhibitions and plaques. If the Levellers are part of a 'democratic tradition', though, it is a tradition that has largely been invented by twentieth- and twenty-first-century historians, journalists and politicians, not one created by radical movements themselves. In 1649, the imprisoned John Lilburne defiantly predicted that 'posterity . . . shall reap the benefit of our endeavours whatever shall become of us'.[58] But until the late nineteenth century there was very little reference to them and there is scant evidence that their works influenced any subsequent radicals, whether in Britain, America or France.

The commemoration of the execution of the Leveller mutineers at Burford illustrates the problems inherent in the left-wing celebration of the movement. Essentially, 'Levellers' Day' presents it as a heroic failure. However, the Levellers were far more influential and far better connected in terms of the politics of their own time than was previously recognised. That the Agreement of the People did not become the new constitution for the republic was a matter of contingency: indeed, it seems to have been abandoned only once the process of subscribing to the Agreement had already begun. Nonetheless, the idea of reserved rights became incorporated into the constitution of the first protectoral government. The notion of inalienable, natural rights was, for the first time, being publicly recognised. The tactics that the Levellers pioneered – mass petitioning, cheap-print pamphleteering and large-scale public demonstrations – also had an important afterlife, informing feverish party-politicking from the Restoration to the death of Queen Anne.

It may be harder to detect an immediate legacy bequeathed by Gerrard Winstanley. Certainly, his work had less of an impact on his contemporaries than that of the Levellers. However, his perceptive analysis of the connections between landed wealth and political power, and his radical solution to the inequality this relationship produced – the abolition of the private ownership of land – would resonate with subsequent radical thinkers and movements, from Thomas Spence in the 1790s to the Chartists in the 1830s and 1840s.

It is not that the importance of radicalism in the English Revolution has been exaggerated, though it is certainly true that many of the present-day champions of the Levellers and Diggers are guilty of misrepresenting their objectives. Rather, the experience of the 1640s was so traumatic both for the common people, and, most importantly, for the political elite that it had largely to be expunged from public memory – only to be invoked, like the 'commotion time' of 1549, in negative terms, as a warning of the evils of rebellion. As Winstanley said, in 1649 it really did appear as if the old world was 'burning up like parchment in the fire'. The impact of that period in English political life was so profound that merely raising the spectre of the civil wars was enough to induce public anxiety. It was by a constant process of historical revision that the radicals were increasingly marginalised until they were almost obliterated from histories of the period. Individuals themselves were repackaged: the millenarian Edmund Ludlow, for instance, in the hands of his eighteenth-century editor John Toland, was transformed into a secular republican. If the ideas of seventeenth-century radicals lingered on in print, it was only in a half-life; their thoughts, a lasting testament to their radicalism, still too dangerous to deploy in public. Consequently, the radicalism that emerged as a potent force in the late eighteenth century, at least publicly, would owe remarkably little to the political movements of the English Revolution.

PART FOUR

THE AGE OF PAINE: BRITISH RADICALS AND THE FRENCH REVOLUTION

It is an age of revolutions, in which every thing may be looked for.

Thomas Paine, *Rights of Man* (1791)

TOM: . . . I want freedom and happiness, the same as they have got in France.

JACK: What, Tom, we imitate them? We follow the French! Why they only begun all this mischief at first, in order to be just what we are already. Why I'd sooner go to the Negers to get learning, or go to the Turks to get religion, than to the French for freedom and happiness.

Hannah More, *Village Politics* (1792)

Wilkes, Paine, and 'Liberty Restored'

The passage of the Septennial Act ended the frantic party politics of the reign of Queen Anne, but this did not represent the death of popular political participation. Though the relatively broad electorate of the late seventeenth and early eighteenth centuries gradually shrank as the terms of the franchise failed to keep step with population growth, the public could still exert a powerful political influence. As Hogarth's 'election' series indicated, the main impact of the Septennial Act was not to alter the boisterous, carnivalesque nature of English elections but to increase the power of the aristocracy and gentry as political power brokers, thereby inflating the cost of fighting seats fivefold from the beginning to the end of the eighteenth century. This in turn made contested elections less and less likely – in 1761 for example, only 17 per cent of constituencies were presented with a choice of candidates. But even in this stagnant political landscape, as the rising cost of electioneering indicated, 'treating' (bribing) the electorate remained very important, especially in the bigger borough and county constituencies. In Hull, the electorate's customary two-guinea bribe at polling time was seen as a sort of local birthright.

Public opinion continued to be influential in other ways too. In comparison to most Western European countries, Britain had an extraordinarily vibrant national and local press, with a literate population to match. By 1753 there were thirty-two provincial newspapers in the country, with a total circulation of around thirty thousand copies a day. Where it could not be effected through the polls, the press helped oust unpopular political leaders, first Sir Robert Walpole in 1742 and then, later, the Duke of Newcastle. Mass petitioning and addressing also continued unabated in the eighteenth century, providing the British public with a direct means of communicating with and complaining about their largely unelected governors.

Even so, popular pressure tended to be brought to bear most heavily on unpopular individuals, such as Walpole, rather than upon parties or the political system as a whole. The two-party politics of the reign of Queen Anne had been fundamentally altered by the connections between the Tory Party and support for the exiled Catholic Stuart dynasty. As a result of this link, the Tory Party's share of seats at Westminster dwindled to under one-fifth of the Commons by 1750. The Whig ascendency was justified by the continued threat of Jacobite-sponsored insurrection: this was the party that would defend the legacy of the Glorious Revolution from the return of 'Catholic tyranny'. But, as the threat of rebellion subsided in the second half of the eighteenth century, the period's vibrant popular politics became more focused and critical of the political establishment. Electoral reform, an integral part of the Levellers' programme, once more became a hot topic.[1]

During the 1760s and 1770s, agitation for political reform in England centred on the figure of John Wilkes. A notorious libertine – he was accused of having a relationship with the Chevalier d'Éon, a reputed French male-impersonator who turned out, confusingly, to be a man pretending to be a woman pretending to be a man – Wilkes made an unlikely champion for electoral reform, having heavily bribed the Aylesbury electors to win his first

parliamentary seat. Wilkes's feelings about some of his new constituents were less than generous. After his election he wrote, 'I . . .
have given . . . orders to keep away from the house and gardens all
the rabble at A[ylesbury]. If any of the better sort choose at any
time to walk in the gardens, the gardener shall attend them . . .
and then I shall get rid of the numbers of women, children, dogs
&c. You wou'd stare at the number of little thefts they make.'[2]

Despite Wilkes's obvious failings as a popular champion, in the
early 1760s he and his newspaper the *North Briton* offered virtually
the only serious opposition to the government of the Scottish Lord
Bute. Wilkes savaged Bute's ministry for the cheap peace that it
had agreed with France to terminate the Seven Years War. These
attacks were deeply scurrilous: Wilkes accused Bute of owing
his position to a sexual relationship with the Queen Mother. In
November 1763, the Commons decided that issue no. 45 of the
North Briton constituted seditious libel – a crime, the House
deemed, not covered by parliamentary privilege. Wilkes, who had
recently been badly injured in a pistol duel with a fellow MP, was
now left open to legal proceedings. He fled for France on
Christmas Day 1763.

Wilkes recalled his exile fondly: much of his time abroad was
devoted to the amorous attentions of his nineteen-year-old Italian
mistress, Gertrude Corradini (of whom he said '[her] conversation
[is] childish and weak but in bed she could not be call'd *fatui
puella cunni* [a girl with a lazy cunt]').[3] By 1767, however, his
money was running out. Consequently, he was strongly motivated
to stand in the general election of March 1768; having previously
used parliamentary privilege to evade paying his debts, he needed
to escape his creditors and to annul his convictions for libel of 1764
by means of a royal pardon.[4] Nonetheless, Wilkes was an important figure, not only in the movement for electoral reform but also,
through his ability to protect London printers, as alderman for
Farringdon Without, in the ongoing struggle with the House of
Commons to defend the printers' right to report proceedings in

Parliament in their newspapers. (Until this point, debates and votes in the Lords and Commons remained officially secret.*)

Though still an outlaw, Wilkes returned to England in 1768 to stand first, unsuccessfully, as a parliamentary candidate for the City of London and then, to popular acclaim, as MP for Middlesex. His attempt to win the latter seat by popular vote rather than by the usual eighteenth-century routes of patronage or purchase was self-interested; at the time he had neither the money nor the influence to adopt alternative tactics. But Middlesex's relatively open franchise would make it a popular battleground for radical candidates into the nineteenth century, and an important showcase for the principle of popular election. Under the eighteenth-century electoral system there was little relationship between population and political representation. Before the 1832 Great Reform Act, Middlesex, with a population of around one million, elected just eight MPs, while Cornwall, with barely a hundred thousand, had forty-two. About half of all MPs in the Commons stood for seats whose electorates were so small that results could easily be secured by bribery.[5] The Commons' repeated rejection of Wilkes's election (he 'won' the seat in three separate by-election contests) on the grounds of his outlawry was an open affront to the electorate and caused a popular outcry.[6] In one notorious incident, the 'massacre' of St George's Fields, seven of Wilkes's supporters were killed by troops sent to suppress the mass meeting.

Wilkes's imprisonment in June 1768 appeared no impediment to his political career, since in January of the following year he secured election as a city alderman. By June 1771, the Wilkite members of the Society of the Supporters of the Bill of Rights

---

* Since the mid-seventeenth century these 'secrecy norms' had been regularly breached, but it remained officially a criminal offence to report votes or debates. It was not until the nineteenth century, when the Palace of Westminster was rebuilt, that galleries and seats for journalists were installed in Parliament.

(SSBR) were pushing a far-reaching programme of political reform. The Society appealed to the idea of a British 'ancient constitution' and sought to recover the reputedly 'lost' rights of English freeholders. It called for parliamentary inquiries into public expenditure, the appointment of judges to redress the grievances of the Middlesex electors, compensation for the wrongful arrest of the Lord Mayor in the printers' case, close scrutiny of the whole range of maladministration in Ireland, and the virtual withdrawal of all the contentious legislation concerning the American colonies since 1763. Candidates were also to support the return of annual parliaments (claimed as a 'Saxon' institution), the establishment of a 'full and equal representation of the people' and the exclusion of all 'placemen' (government pensionaries), without exception, from the House of Commons. This concern with the corrosive influence of the court was in line with the themes of Wilkes's earlier journalism in the *North Briton*. Here, he had accused the court of being captured by a malign pro-French faction, centring on Bute, who, as a Scotsman, inevitably favoured the revival of the Auld Alliance. The fear of foreign influence was likewise evident in the rhetoric of the Bill of Rights Society, created to guard 'native' freedoms vigilantly.[7]

In the summer of 1770, John Wilkes undertook a tour of the South East in support of reform. He was warmly received in Lewes, in Sussex, an open borough with a history of political and religious dissatisfaction.* Lewes was then the home of a young excise officer, Thomas Paine. (Wilkes is alleged to have met Paine on this visit, but unfortunately there is no firm evidence to corroborate the story.) His American biographer, Eric Foner, has described Paine's time in Lewes as 'a period of almost unrelenting

---

* In Lewes, all male householders who rented property worth £10 or more a year were permitted to vote.

failure'.[8] However, though his life in the town ended with domestic and professional failure, it was also, as George Hindmarsh and Colin Brent have demonstrated, crucial to his political education.[9]

Paine had taken up lodgings in the High Street with an innkeeper, Samuel Ollive, and his family, and later joined Ollive in another business venture, running a tobacco mill from the premises. Paine, for a time at least, threw himself successfully into the town's social life. Aside from his involvement in the Headstrong Club, a debating society, he was a very active member of St Michael's parish vestry, helping administer poor relief, and was reputed to be a keen bowls player and ice skater. In spite of all this activity, his time in Lewes has left frustratingly little trace in the town's archives. There remain only two letters by him in Lewes Record Office, dealing with a mundane property dispute with his neighbours in the Dissenting meeting house.[10]

In 1771 Paine was married for a second time, to Samuel Ollive's daughter Elizabeth. (Her father had died in 1769.) Elizabeth was only twenty-two, ten years younger than her husband. The couple opened a shop together but Paine was now being regularly drawn into London society, having been nominated by his fellow excisemen to press their case for better pay and conditions with their employers. Paine liked to portray his literary career as beginning only in the New World, falsely claiming that it 'was the cause of America that made me an author' and that *Common Sense* was 'the first work I ever did publish'.[11] However, two years before he arrived in Philadelphia, he had already published his first political pamphlet, *The Case of the Officers of the Excise*. It is a reflection of how much he wished to erase the memory of the failures of his early life that he did not make a freer acknowledgement of this work, which despite its limited purpose addressed broader themes that would dominate much of Paine's later writings.[12] Speaking from his own experience, he argued that the poor salaries of the excise officers, who had not seen a rise for nearly a century, were a recipe for peculation and corruption. Poverty would make thieves and liars of all men:

> true honesty is sentimental, and the practice of it dependent upon circumstances . . . The rich, in ease and affluence, may think I have drawn an unnatural portrait; but could they descend to the cold regions of want, the circle of polar poverty, they would find their opinions changing with the climate.[13]

There was, however,

> a striking difference between dishonesty arising from want of food, and want of principle. The first is worthy of compassion, the other of punishment. Nature never produced a man who would starve in a well-stored larder, because the provisions were not his own: but he who robs it from luxury of appetite deserves a gibbet.[14]

Paine distributed four thousand copies of his pamphlet, paid for by his fellow officers and produced with the tacit support of the Excise Board. But though the publication raised his public profile further, bringing him into contact with literary figures such as Oliver Goldsmith and with leading scientific virtuosi such as John Bevis and George Lewis Scott, the time away from Lewes had seen his business affairs fall into disarray.

In April 1774 he was dismissed from his job by the Excise Board, ostensibly for being absent without leave. In the same month, he was forced to sell all the goods and effects of his tobacco business. By May, not just his professional but also his personal life lay in tatters. Paine and his wife separated, signing a formal document acknowledging the fact in June 1774. In eighteenth-century England the social stigma attached to separation was considerable, and hostile biographers later made much of the failure of this marriage, suggesting that it was the result of his impotence, his drinking, violent abuse of his spouse or a

combination of all three. Loyalist writers contrasted the failure of
Paine the husband with the firm and faithful regard shown by
George III for both his own wife and children and his wider
family, the nation.[15] For his part, Paine adamantly refused to offer
an explanation for the dissolution of his marriage, stating only,
'I had cause for it, but I will name it to no one.' Elizabeth received
her full inheritance from her father as a result of the settlement
and was free to trade independently, but the separation left her in
an even more difficult position than it left Paine. While he was
conspicuously able to resume a public life, his erstwhile wife was
now consigned to a dreadful social limbo, enjoying neither the
prospects of a young single woman nor the independence offered
by widowhood.

It was Paine's scientific interests that rescued him from this personal nadir. Via his contacts in London he made the acquaintance
of Benjamin Franklin, the inventor, philosopher, diplomat and
later leading American revolutionary. Franklin provided him with
a letter of introduction, and with this and a ticket for a berth on
a ship to America Paine left his old life behind to seek fresh pas-
tures in the New World. He nearly didn't make it. In a letter to
Franklin dated 4 March 1775, he described the outbreak of 'putrid
fever' (lice-borne typhus) that had broken out on board ship:

> We buried five, and not above that number escaped the disease. By
> good Providence we had a Doctor on board, who entered himself
> as one of the servants, otherwise we must have been in as
> deplorable a situation, as a passage of nine weeks could have ren-
> dered us. Two cabin passengers escaped the illness but suffered
> dreadfully with the fever. I had very little hopes that the Captain
> or myself would live to see America.[16]

On arriving in America, Paine was so weak that he had to be
brought ashore on a stretcher. Franklin's letter got him some
accommodation, provided by the doctor who had dealt with the

passengers on their arrival in Philadelphia. Nonetheless, it was a further six weeks before Paine was well enough to make contact with Franklin's son-in-law, Richard Bache, who set about trying to find the immigrant some work as a teacher.

In many respects Paine was right to say that he only really became the author Thomas Paine in America (the 'e' itself found its way on to the end of his surname only once he had crossed the Atlantic). Even his most famous work published in England, *Rights of Man*, was dedicated to an American, George Washington, and its text (beyond the references to his polemical Aunt Sally, Edmund Burke) was littered with transatlantic metaphors and allusions.[17] However, though his early life in England had been blighted by personal and professional catastrophes, that experience was vital to the formation of his political outlook. His time in Lewes and London provided Paine with a political education via his exposure to Wilkite reform, his work as a vestryman and his involvement in the Headstrong Club. It was in England, though he denied the fact, that he first became a political writer, arguing on behalf of his fellow excise officers.

More importantly than all this, though, the experience of failure marked him out from other radical luminaries. His *Case of the Officers of the Excise* shows a writer not simply placing himself in the shoes of the oppressed and the poor, but one who had felt the terrible pressure of poverty himself. Unlike William Godwin, Mary Wollstonecraft or William Blake, Paine had not been singled out as a precocious talent and carefully nurtured by parents and patrons to fulfil his artistic or literary potential. Until 1774, his life had promised to unfold as a banal, everyday tragedy: financial failure in an unglamorous trade leading to marital failure, destitution and a pauper's death. It was that knowledge of the bitterness of everyday life, as well as its occasional rewards, that made him the writer he was. While Godwin wrote *Political Justice* and Wollstonecraft *A Vindication of the Rights of Woman* – radical classics, certainly, but, to their core, middle-class books for middle-class readers – only Paine could have written *Rights of Man*, a work targeted at and in sympathy with a readership that could barely afford bread, let alone books.

The Philadelphia that Paine found himself in was no less socially divided than the England he had just left. The richest 10 per cent of the population owned over half of the wealth of the city; the poorest 40 per cent only 4 per cent. The American rich aped the fashions of the English aristocracy, which included maintaining large landed estates outside Philadelphia. The rich also dominated the municipal government. One visitor remarked that among the 'uppermost circles in Philadelphia . . . it seems as if nothing would make them happier than that an order of nobility should be established by which they might be exalted above their fellow citizens, as much as they are in their own conceit'. However, the middling sorts in the colonies were developing their own political organisations with the creation of the first artisan party, the Patriotic Society. There was great anxiety among the North American upper classes about the politicising and democratising effect of the evolving revolutionary struggle. Gouverneur Morris, the lawyer and later leading revolutionary, witnessing a mass meeting in New York in 1774, noted that now 'the mob begin to think and reason'.[18]

Paine had come to an America that was on the brink of outright revolt against British colonial overlordship. The first Continental Congress had met in Philadelphia at the beginning of September 1774 and resolved to boycott British goods unless the British government honoured their rights (the deadline for this ultimatum passed the day after Paine arrived). He took lodgings in the heart of the city, in a building with a clear view of the Philadelphia slave market. He regularly frequented the nearby bookshop of Robert Aitken. The two struck up a friendship and Aitken soon offered Paine the opportunity to renew his writing efforts by becoming executive editor of a new journal, the *Pennsylvania Magazine*, which he planned to publish. Paine accepted, though his literary offerings were initially constrained by Aitken's insistence that he steer clear of controversial topics. One exception to this was an essay on the evils of slavery, which has earned Paine the undeserved title of 'the first American [sic] abolitionist'.[19]

Paine was not the first writer in America to condemn slavery. He did, however, underline the inherent hypocrisy in the white colonists' repeated claim that they were being made slaves by the government of George III, pointing out that 'they hold so many hundred thousands in slavery; and annually enslave many thousands more, without any pretence of authority, or claim upon them'.[20] Yet, like many eighteenth- and nineteenth-century abolitionists, Paine's comments appear far less enlightened once we examine the substance of them. Although he suggested that old or infirm slaves be cared for by their former masters and the healthy and productive be paid for their labours, he thought that freed slaves 'might sometime form useful barrier settlements on the frontiers. Thus they may become interested in the public welfare, and assist in promoting it; instead of being dangerous, as now they are, should any enemy promise them a better condition.' The destiny of emancipated slaves was, it seemed, to serve as a 'human shield' to protect white Americans.[21]

The nature of Paine's contributions to the *Pennsylvania Magazine* was fundamentally changed by one event: the Battle of Lexington on 19 April 1775, when British troops opened fire on American militiamen, killing eight and injuring ten. From this moment on, as he later declared in *Common Sense*, he became increasingly committed to the struggle of the American colonists against the British government:

> No man was a warmer wisher for a reconciliation than myself, before the fatal nineteenth of April, 1775, but the moment the event of that day was made known, I rejected the hardened, sullen-tempered Pharaoh of England for ever; and disdain the wretch, that with the pretended title of FATHER OF THE PEOPLE can unfeelingly hear of their slaughter, and composedly sleep with their blood upon his soul.[22]

A dispute with Aitken over his contract, still unwritten, led Paine to seek an alternative literary outlet for his attacks on British tyranny. At this point, the colonies' public communications with the British government continued to be couched in loyal terms: talk of 'independence' or of a republic was seen as deeply dangerous. But Paine was convinced that the time had come for a pamphlet that would destroy the tissue-thin fiction that Americans were nothing more than transplanted subjects of George III. Publishing *Common Sense* – as it was eventually titled – was not without difficulties. At first no printer would agree to sell it, until finally Robert Bell, a Scot of some ill-repute, agreed. The pamphlet was revised with the assistance of Franklin, Samuel Adams, the astronomer David Rittenhouse and Benjamin Rush. On 10 January 1776, at the price of two shillings, *Common Sense* went on sale.

Paine estimated that it sold 150,000 copies, going through twenty-five editions and reaching hundreds of thousands of readers. Compared with contemporary colonial papers, which had a circulation of about 1000 to 2000, this constituted an enormous publishing success.[23] However, we need to take some care with these figures, which historians have freely cited despite the fact that they were supported only by Paine's own testimony as author. In-depth research into the dissemination of *Common Sense* suggests that its actual sales figures were less impressive, if still very high by colonial standards. Paine's real success was not merely to produce a pamphlet that sold well, but as a skilled self-publicist convincingly to present the image of his book as articulating the feelings of the majority of Americans.[24]

His abilities as a self-promoter should not distract us, though, from the revolutionary content of *Common Sense*. Dispensing with the usual cautious colonial rhetoric, here was a clear, energetic and republican voice calling for independence. The true novelty and radicalism of Paine's pamphlet came in its opening passages, where he challenged the commonplace assumption that human society necessitated government. Indeed, a long tradition of writers on government had treated society and government as interchangeable terms. Not so, Paine countered. Nature dictated that people form societies as a concomitant of the inherent human values of sociability and solidarity. It was only when human beings ignored their consciences and common sense that they required the 'necessary evil' of government.[25] On this basis, the way forward for the colonists was to resist the encroachments of the British state by forming a 'civil society' to protect their interests, by associating together in a 'Continental Congress' that would secure 'freedom and property' and 'free exercise of religion' for all.[26]

Paine's work was not written exclusively for an American audience. As he clearly stated, the 'cause of America is, in great measure, the cause of all mankind'.[27] *Common Sense* was widely circulated in England and translated into several European languages. It represented a stark break from the propaganda of the Wilkite reform movement. Its searing attack on the hereditary principle clearly prefigured the arguments of part one of *Rights of Man*. With a sharp dig at George III's mental infirmity, Paine argued that 'One of the strongest natural proofs of the folly of hereditary right in kings, is that nature disapproves it, otherwise she would not so frequently turn it into ridicule, by giving mankind an *ass for a lion*.'[28]

Monarchy was, then, unnatural, if not plain idiotic. Paine also dispensed with the appeals to history that had been such a common tactic of previous radical writers. The much vaunted English 'ancient constitution' was a myth, supported more by 'national pride' than by 'reason'. Far from being a well-balanced parliamentary monarchy, England's constitution was an ugly hotch-potch of republicanism (the Commons) and absolutism (the King). This politically eclectic arrangement was worsened by the fact that the ultimate veto was in the hands of the most antiquated part of the whole apparatus: the monarch.[29] Republics, on the other hand, prospered everywhere, as in the cases of Holland and

Switzerland.[30] Paine also took a swipe at the rhetoric of the 'free-born Englishman'. America, not Britain, was the home of liberty, for the original settlers had fled 'not from the tender embraces of the mother, but from the cruelty of the monster; and it is so far true of England, that the same tyranny which drove the first emigrants from home, pursues their descendants still'.[31] For this reason, it was necessary that there be a clear and inviolable separation between Church and state: 'As to religion, I hold it to be the indispensable duty of government to protect all conscientious professors thereof, and I know of no other business which government has to do therewith.'[32]

Paine's pamphlet provoked much hostile reaction, from both English and American writers, and started a spat with John Adams that lasted for the rest of Paine's life. Transformed by his American experience, his politics now had little in common with the reform movement in England. By now, Wilkes was no longer the figurehead of electoral reform but a loyal courtier of George III.* The cause of reform in England had nonetheless continued to gather pace, revived by the developing crisis over the colonies. In *Take Your Choice!* (1776), Major John Cartwright, an advocate of separate legislatures for the American colonies but not full independence, had argued for universal manhood suffrage, the secret ballot and annual parliaments. However, the radicalism of this position was less pronounced than it seemed at first. For Cartwright, universal male suffrage was mainly a bargaining position by which he hoped to barter down the government towards something like the concessions that would be offered by the Great Reform Act of 1832. His plans for the payment of MPs sought less

---

* The transformation was encapsulated in the – quite possibly apocryphal – story of the elderly woman who called out to him in the street, 'Wilkes and liberty!' only to receive the response, 'Be quiet you old fool! That's all over long ago!' Wilkes's reputation as an advocate of reform nonetheless stayed with him. In 1794 a loyalist mob smashed the windows of his house. His reponse was characteristically phlegmatic: 'They are only some of my pupils, now set up for themselves.'

to open the Commons to men without wealth than to limit the dangers of corruption and peculation. Similarly, the abolition of property qualifications was meant to allow merchants and businessmen to become MPs, not to open up politics to working-class men.

Cartwright, in any case, was on the 'extreme' wing of domestic reform in the 1770s and 1780s. The mainstream was represented by the 'association' movement of the clergyman and landowner, Charles Wyvill. He was no democrat: according to him, the British electorate should ideally be made up of independent men of property. Moreover, Cartwright and Wyvill, like many other eighteenth-century gentlemen reformers, essentially believed that reform constituted not the creation of a new political system but the restoration of an Anglo-Saxon political Arcadia. As Wyvill put it, the aim was 'the preservation of our constitution on its genuine principles'.[33] England's 'ancient constitution' and key post-1066 reaffirmations of it, in the form of Magna Carta and the Bill of Rights of 1689, which Paine had brusquely dismissed in *Common Sense*, were at least as, if not more, important to their conception of liberty as the example of the Americans and, later, the French. In broader terms, the backward-looking nature of their idea of reform was reflected in the developing interest in the history of English liberty, exemplified by Catharine Macaulay's radical Whig *History of England*, the final volume of which was published in 1783.

Macaulay had a direct connection with the reform movement. Her brother, one Alderman Sawbridge, promoted thirteen motions for annual parliaments in the House of Commons between 1771 and 1786 – efforts that first Lord North, then Pitt the Younger, were content to 'conquer . . . by silence and by sleep'. Macaulay's *History* was overtly republican in its sympathies, invoking the memory of hallowed seventeenth-century names such as Milton, Algernon Sidney and James Harrington, and late seventeenth- and early eighteenth-century 'commonwealthsmen' including William Molyneux, Robert, 1st Viscount Molesworth, and John Toland (all men with

Irish roots), as well as Walter Moyle, John Trenchard, Thomas Gordon and Anthony Ashley Cooper, 3rd Earl of Shaftesbury.[34] However, this republican strain was very much of the classical variety: the ideology of well-educated, literate gentlemen (and women). Moreover, eighteenth-century radical historians such as Macaulay and Godwin were uninterested in the Utopian imaginings of the English Revolution, whether plebeian (Winstanley) or aristocratic (Harrington). For them, figures like Milton and Sidney stood as examples of political virtue in an age of corruption, not as republican theorists. In any case, as we shall see, for most of the radical Whigs and some 'country' Tories, the true English Revolution had happened in 1688, not 1649.[35]

If Paine was out of step with the reform movement in England, in America he proved an unerringly accurate political prophet. Events moved inexorably along the path that he had mapped out in *Common Sense*. The Declaration of Independence was finally agreed by Congress on 5 July 1776. While Paine had had no part in writing this or the constitution approved later that month, he demonstrated the strength of his allegiance to the new nation by volunteering for military service.* Though his military contribution to the Revolutionary War effort may have been minimal, his interventions in the propaganda campaign remained decisive. In *The American Crisis* he attempted to rouse the American public, at a low ebb after the retreat of Washington's forces back to Philadelphia, and demand their allegiance to the cause of independence:

These are the times that try men's souls. The summer soldier and the sun-shine patriot will, in this crisis, shrink from the service of his country: but he that stands it now, deserves the thanks of man and woman. Tyranny, like hell, is not easily conquered: yet we have

---

* The extent of Paine's bravery should not be exaggerated. One fellow soldier reportedly remarked, 'Paine may be a good philosopher but he is not a soldier – he always kept out of danger.'[36]

this consolation with us, that the harder the conflict, the more glorious the triumph. What we obtain too cheap, we esteem too
lightly; it is dearness only that gives everything its value.[37]

Aside from such stirring rhetoric – legend has it that
Washington ordered this passage be read to his troops before the
Battle of Trenton – *The Crisis* offered glimpses of the mordant wit
that would be so brilliantly displayed in the *Rights of Man*. Writing
of George III's face-saving speech in the wake of the humiliating
defeat of the British forces at Yorktown on 19 October 1781, Paine
remarked, 'One broken leg is better than two, but still it is not a
source of joy.'[38]

In January 1784, after the peace had been concluded, Paine
was rewarded for his literary efforts by the state of New York with
the gift of a farm in New Rochelle. He decided to rent out this
property, and instead took up residence in Bordentown, New
Jersey, near his friend and fellow patriot Colonel Joseph Kirkbride.
Supported by a cash gift of $3000 from Congress and a further £500
from Philadelphia, Paine spent much of his time in Bordentown
furthering his scientific interests, in particular his plans to develop
a single-span iron bridge. With the assistance of an English carpenter and mechanic, John Hall, his eventual design was modelled
on a spider's web. The model, however, was very expensive to
produce and met with little enthusiasm when Paine displayed
his designs to the Pennsylvania Assembly in December 1786.
Convinced that the project would never get off the ground in
America, and increasingly feeling that he was being inade-
quately rewarded for his war efforts, he decided to take his model
to France in a bid to secure support and financial backing. He
set sail in April 1787 with letters of introduction from the
French court.

Landing at Le Havre a month later, Paine soon made contact
with Thomas Jefferson, then American minister in Paris. His
bridge received a favourable response from the French Academy of

Sciences, but despite the efforts of his friends Jefferson and Lafayette, no money was forthcoming. Having returned to England to visit his parents, Paine decided instead to concentrate on securing funding in his homeland. Between the summer of 1788 and that of 1790 much of his time was devoted to overseeing the construction of a 110-foot bridge, based on his model. The arch was forged in Rotherham and shipped down to London, eventually arriving in May 1790 to be assembled on a field somewhere between Paddington and Marylebone. Although the bridge attracted considerable public interest, and some public criticism, it quickly began to deteriorate as its wooden supports started to give way and the iron began to corrode.

Though preoccupied with his bridge, Paine had retained a close watch on the revolutionary events unfolding across the Channel, his interest fuelled by regular reports from Jefferson. He had also continued to write, producing *Prospects on the Rubicon*, which warned Britain of the dangers of renewing war with France. As his scientific schemes sank into the London mud, his attention turned back to political matters.

A large number of Whig political clubs had long met to celebrate the birthday of William III and commemorate the achievements of the revolution that he had inaugurated. In 1788, the centenary of England's own, allegedly bloodless, revolution seemed to prophesy that a similarly painless political transformation might occur in Bourbon France.*

Attending the Revolution Society meeting on 4 November 1788 at the London tavern in Bishopsgate Street were Dr Andrew Kippis, a well-known Unitarian minister and William Godwin's classics tutor at Hoxton Academy; Lord Stanhope, the Duke of

* Of course, the idea that the revolution was 'bloodless' was nonsense, especially when events in Ireland and Scotland were included in the discussion. See Vallance, *Glorious Revolution*, especially chapter 7.

Portland, the Marquess of Carmarthen and the Lord Mayor of London; and the MPs Henry Beaufoy, William Smith, Sir Watkin Lewes and Joshua Grigby.

As they processed towards the tavern they bore King William's original standard, flown when he landed at Torbay. In front of the tavern, a painting 'emblematic of the glorious event' carried the legend 'A TYRANT DEPOSED AND LIBERTY RESTORED'. During the dinner forty-one toasts were drunk to desirable reforms, including the total abolition of the slave trade, the reform of the criminal law code, the abolition of the press gangs and the revision of the game laws. It was declared that the day on which the Bill of Rights was carried through Parliament, 16 December, should be made a day of national thanksgiving. In addition, the Society composed a statement expressing the hope for a rapprochement between England and France so that 'two nations, so eminently distinguished in arms, and in literature, instead of exhausting themselves in sanguinary wars for no valuable purpose, may unite together in communicating the advantages of freedom, science and the arts to the most remote regions of the earth'.

Dr Richard Price, Dissenting minister, pioneer of life insurance and supporter of the American Revolution, had been invited to deliver the oration that year but had to decline, owing to illness.[39]

However, the following year, as the Revolution Society met once again to celebrate King William's birthday, Price did accept the invitation to speak. In the intervening twelve months, events in France had moved on apace. The Third Estate of the Estates-General, summoned in May of 1789, had by June of that year declared itself the National Assembly and sworn, on 20 June, the 'tennis court oath', not to dissolve until they had given France a new constitution. On 14 July, the Paris mob attacked the Bastille Fortress, great symbol of absolutist tyranny, storming its defences and killing the governor whose decapitated head was paraded around the city (though they freed only seven prisoners – four forgers, two noblemen and a murderer). On 26 August the

National Assembly published *The Declaration of the Rights of Man and of the Citizen*, like the American Declaration of Independence a statement of general principles designed to pave the way for a full written constitution. The first article of the French Declaration stated that 'men are born and remain free and equal in rights'. (Women would not be placed on a par with men until the constitution of the Fourth Republic in 1946.)

In his sermon, Price expressed his excitement at having lived to see these events unfold (he was only fifty but had been in poor health for some time):

> What an eventful period is this! . . . I could almost say, *Lord now lettest thou thy servant depart in peace for mine eyes have seen thy salvation.* I have lived to see a diffusion of knowledge which has undermined superstition and error. I have lived to see the rights of man better understood than ever, and nations panting for liberty, which seemed to have lost the idea of it. I have lived to see thirty millions of people, indignant and resolute, spurning at slavery and demanding liberty with an irresistible voice.[40]

Price's sermon, published as *A Discourse on the Love of our Country*, was a call for a radical reinterpretation of the values of patriotism. For him, patriotism meant not attachment to land or soil but loyalty to a community of shared values, ideals and traditions. True patriotism was not jingoism, the automatic belief that your country was inherently superior to all others. Only false patriots were content to value 'their own liberty while idly allowing that precious condition to be crushed elsewhere – or happily celebrating conquest and domination if on the winning side'. Instead, people should consider themselves as 'citizens of the world, and take care to maintain a just regard to the rights of other countries'.

Price was not a republican and his sermon contained the wish that George III's recovery from his recent bout of mental illness would be swift. However, his understanding of the values for which 'true patriots' should perish certainly did not include unqualified obedience to the monarch. For him, the legacy of the revolution of 1688–9 was threefold: it had guaranteed liberty of conscience, it had confirmed the right to resist power when it was abused and it had established that the people had the right to choose their governors. The right to resist unjust power included a clear legitimisation of the use of force:

> For it has oftener happened that men have been too passive than too unruly, and the rebellion of Kings against their people has been more common and done more mischief than the rebellion of people against their Kings . . . Civil governors are properly the servants of the public and a King is no more than the first servant of the public, created by it, maintained by it, and responsible to it.[41]

The freedoms established by the Glorious Revolution needed to be not just maintained but also expanded. The Test Acts, which barred Dissenters from holding public office, needed to be repealed. The system of political representation needed to be reformed and the Tory doctrines of passive obedience and non-resistance in the face of tyranny firmly repudiated. Heady with the excitement generated by Price's sermon, the members of the Revolution Society adjourned to the London tavern, where Price moved that a vote of thanks be sent to the French National Assembly; another member, less cautiously, urged a toast to the 'Parliament of *Britain* . . . may it become a National Assembly'.[42]

Price's sermon became the catalyst for the most celebrated British controversy of the French Revolution era. It was such a heated debate in no small part because his main opponent, Edmund Burke, had previously been seen as one of the most reform-minded Whig politicians in Parliament. Burke had been an opponent of the British war against the American colonists in the

1770s, a fierce critic of the impact of the court upon the independence of Parliament, and he had bitterly inveighed against the current form of British colonialism in India: 'Were we to be driven out of India this day,' he remarked in a 1783 parliamentary committee report, 'nothing would remain, to tell that it had been possessed, during the inglorious period of our dominion, by any thing better than the ouran-outang or the tiger.'

Burke was now, though, an increasingly isolated figure: the fearless young scourge of the corrupt had slowly transformed into a grumpy old man. His conduct during the Regency crisis of 1788, as the allies of Charles James Fox pressed for the Prince Regent to be given full powers on account of the King's mental incapacity, managed to alienate both his Foxite allies by suggesting that 'Prinny' needed to clean up his act before assuming the powers of a king, and the Crown, through his blunt assessment of George III's state of mind. Previously sympathetic to the pleas for toleration from both Catholics and Dissenters, Burke had become increasingly disenchanted with the so-called movement of 'Rational Dissent', which men like Price represented. He viewed them as politically pusillanimous for their failure to support the Foxite Whigs in the wake of the court party's massive victory in 1784.

More importantly, by 1789 Burke was convinced that some spokesmen for Dissent were moving towards advocating sedition. Price's assertion that the 'first concern' of true 'lovers of our country must be to enlighten it' evidently rankled with him. Instead of keeping within his proper sphere of activity, Price, thought Burke, was offering a dangerous incitement to mob violence. Dissenting ministers like Price, 'debauched by ambition', were no longer the mere instructors of the people: now they sought to be their masters. Burke felt that the result of Price's intervention in public debate would be that learning would be cast 'into the mire, and trodden down under the hoof of a swinish multitude' (a comment that would later be wittily appropriated by radicals such as Thomas Spence in his *Pig's Meat, or Lessons for the Swinish Multitude* (1793–5)).[43]

Where Price saw a France throwing off tyranny and moving towards liberty, Burke saw only a people who had shaken free from the 'yoke of Laws and morals'; for him, *The Declaration of the Rights of Man* was a '*digest* of anarchy'.[44] These public statements were already bringing Burke criticism from his old Whig allies before he published his *Reflections on the Revolution in France*: friends to whom he showed the manuscript warned him that its overheated prose and occasional forays into quixotic whimsy – most notably his fawning over the loveliness of Marie Antoinette – would ruin his reputation. Burke persisted nonetheless. Despite its title, the main target of his work was Price's reinterpretation of the English Revolution of 1688, not the events that were unravelling in France. Burke denied that the Glorious Revolution had wrought the changes attributed to it by Price. In fact, it was not really a revolution at all, but a 'small and temporary deviation from the strict order of a regular hereditary succession'. The leading men of 1688–9 had effectively given the kiss of life to an old constitution, not fathered a new one.

> [They] regenerated the deficient part of the old constitution through the parts which were not impaired. They kept these old parts exactly as they were, that the part recovered might be suited to them. They acted by the ancient organised states in the shape of their old organisation, and not by the organic *moleculae* of a disbanded people.[45]

In 1688–9, England had not exchanged a hereditary monarchy for an elected one: the hereditary succession had only been interrupted by the exceptional abdication of one monarch, James II, and his necessary replacement by another. There had been a reformation, not a revolution. Rejecting the Whig notion of a constitutional monarchy, Burke portrayed kingship as essentially depending on an emotional, even mystical, bond between ruler and people.[46] He felt societies should follow Britain's example:

evolve gradually and organically, along lines dictated by custom and tradition. In this sense, the freedoms and liberties enjoyed by future generations would always be largely circumscribed by their historic predecessors. Though a slower process, this was a far safer way to progress than to build a constitution from scratch from abstract principles of reason and natural law.[47]

Reflections was a best-seller, shifting seven thousand copies in its first week and going through eleven editions by September 1791. It has since been celebrated as a classic work of conservative political thought, invoked by Margaret Thatcher among others.[48] At the time, however, it provoked a torrent of ridicule and abuse from radicals, with the loose-living gentleman reformer John Horne Tooke* calling it 'the tears of the priesthood for the loss of their pudding'.[49] The pamphlet provoked a paper war between reformers and loyalists, prompting over seventy hostile replies. One of the first of these came from a young novelist and educationalist, Mary Wollstonecraft, a friend and protégée of Richard Price. Wollstonecraft's *Vindication of the Rights of Men*† railed against Burke's obliviousness to the plight of the poor and his obsession

---

* Tooke's appetite for women almost put Wilkes to shame. On being told by Wilkes's attorney that it was high time he settled down and took a wife, Tooke replied, 'Whose wife?' His capacity for alcohol was similarly impressive. He once settled an argument with a guest at one of his celebrated Sunday dinners by challenging his antagonist to a brandy-drinking contest. By the second quart bottle, Tooke's opponent had literally been drunk under the table.[50]

† Wollstonecraft's work was written in some haste. Her future husband, William Godwin, later recalled that she had sent the pages to the printer as she wrote them. Halfway through the work she was seized by 'a temporary fit of torpor and indolence, and began to repent her undertaking'. She called in on her printer Joseph Johnson and told him about the impasse: 'Mr Johnson immediately, in a kind and friendly way, entreated her not to put any constraint upon her inclination, and to give herself no uneasiness upon the sheets already printed, which he would cheerfully throw aside, if it would contribute to her happiness.' This was not what Wollstonecraft had expected to hear. If Johnson's comments had been intended to encourage his writer to abandon her project, they had quite the reverse effect. 'Her friend's so readily falling in with her ill-humour, and seeming to expect that she would lay aside her undertaking, piqued her pride. She immediately went home; and proceeded to the end of her work, with no other interruptions but what were absolutely necessary.'[51]

with the sanctity of private property: 'Where is the eye that marks these evils, more gigantic than any infringements of property, which you piously deprecate? Are these remediless evils? And is the humane heart satisfied with turning the poor over to *another* world, to receive the blessings this could afford?'

Wollstonecraft's view of the English working classes was nonetheless a deeply negative one, seeing them as degraded and brutalised by the tyranny of the rich: 'I have turned impatiently to the poor . . . but, alas! what did I see! a being scarcely above the brutes . . . a broken spirit, worn-out body, and all those gross vices which the example of the rich, rudely copied, could produce.'[52] *A Vindication of the Rights of Men* made Wollstonecraft a celebrity. She was fêted by fellow radicals – the *Analytical Review* wrote: 'How deeply it must wound the feelings of a *chivalrous knight* [a reference to Burke's mourning of the death of the 'Age of Chivalry'], who owes the fealty of "proud submission and dignified obedience" to the fair sex, to perceive that two of the boldest of his adversaries are women!',[53] and it was seen as important enough to warrant vicious attacks in the loyalist press, some of which suggested that Wollstonecraft's sympathy with the working classes was a result of her intimacy with a number of 'honest mechanics'.[54]

RIGHTS OF MAN, THE RIGHTS OF WOMAN AND POLITICAL JUSTICE

The attention given to Wollstonecraft's intervention in the debate paled in comparison to that generated by Paine's intellectual assault on Edmund Burke. *Rights of Man*, part one, utterly dwarfed the sales of Burke's *Reflections* and of all the subsequent radical replies to it. It was published by Wollstonecraft's printer Joseph Johnson on 21 February 1791, then withdrawn for fear of prosecution, before being published again in March the following year by J. S. Jordan. Paine's leading English biographer, John Keane, has estimated that about one in ten literate people in England owned a copy (and this figure is probably an underestimate, as it does not include the many pirated editions of Paine's work that were in circulation).[1] Paine himself claimed that the sales of his work far exceeded the number of signatories to the loyal addresses that were produced in response, denouncing it as seditious.[2]

Though he had considerable form as a phrase-maker, having coined the term 'United States of America', Paine was not the first English radical to speak of 'the Rights of Man'. These words were first written down in English in a manmade cave in South Shields

Alfred the Great by Hamo
Thornycroft. Veneration of the
Anglo-Saxon king reached its
peak in the late Victorian era.
CORBIS

The Great Charter was signed with the King's seal, from *Our Island Story*. In this popular
Edwardian re-imagining, a suitably peeved King John sets his seal to Magna Carta.

TOP LEFT: The Magna Carta memorial at Runnymede. This memorial, paid for by the American Bar Association, celebrates the Charter's defence of 'Freedom Under Law'. ALAMY

TOP RIGHT: The John F. Kennedy memorial at Runnymede. In recognition of the 'special relationship' between Britain and the USA, and in memory of the 35th President, the land of Runnymede Hill was gifted to America. ALAMY

The death of Wat Tyler, the leader of the rebels of 1381, as depicted by Froissart in his *Chronicles*. The exact sequence of events leading to Tyler's death remains unclear. MEPL

An eighteenth-century representation of Robert Kett dispensing justice beneath the 'oak of reformation', which still stands to this day. MEPL

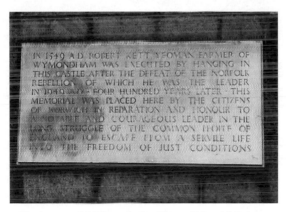

IN 1549 A.D. ROBERT KETT YEOMAN FARMER OF
WYMONDHAM WAS EXECUTED BY HANGING IN
THIS CASTLE AFTER THE DEFEAT OF THE NORFOLK
REBELLION OF WHICH HE WAS THE LEADER
IN 1949 A.D. FOUR HUNDRED YEARS LATER - THIS
MEMORIAL WAS PLACED HERE BY THE CITIZENS
OF NORWICH IN REPARATION AND HONOUR TO
A NOTABLE AND COURAGEOUS LEADER IN THE
LONG STRUGGLE OF THE COMMON PEOPLE OF
ENGLAND TO ESCAPE FROM A SERVILE LIFE
INTO THE FREEDOM OF JUST CONDITIONS

Kett's memorial. Through the efforts of Norwich Labour
alderman Fred Henderson, this plaque in honour of the rebel
leader was erected in 1949.

An image of the Putney Debates taken from a contemporary pamphlet. As many as a hundred officers, soldiers and civilians may have been present at this seminal debate over English liberty. MEPL

Unusually among the Leveller leaders, John Lilburne, an inveterate self-publicist, remained a significant figure in histories of the civil wars produced in the eighteenth and nineteenth centuries.

William Walwyn, the oldest of the leading Levellers and a well-to-do London merchant of Worcestershire gentry stock, was radicalised by his conversion to the doctrine of free grace.

John Wildman's extraordinary political career stretched from the 1640s to the 1690s. He was knighted by William III and briefly held the office of postmaster-general after the Glorious Revolution. MEPL

Thomas Paine. A rather flattering print of Britain's most famous radical export, taken from the portrait by George Romney. MEPL

Fashion before Ease by James Gillray. This anti-Paine print mocks the radical's humble origins (he began his career as a manufacturer of ladies' underwear) and alludes to both to his heavy drinking and allegations of domestic violence (he separated from his second wife in 1774).

William Godwin by James Northcote. Godwin was the author of *Caleb Williams* and *Political Justice*. Thomas De Quincey despised Godwin's cold, rational intellectualism, comparing him to Godwin's daughter Mary's fictional creation, Frankenstein's monster.

Mary Wollstonecraft by John Opie. This sympathetic portrait captures Wollstonecraft's preference for plain dress and no make-up. Other observers were less kind, one commentator describing her as a 'philosophical sloven'.
PRIVATE COLLECTION/ BRIDGEMAN ART LIBRARY

The Belle-Alliance by George Cruikshank. Women's reform societies are depicted as the preserve of a feminine underclass of dubious morality. BRITISH MUSEUM

by the radical Newcastle schoolteacher and bookseller, Thomas Spence. Like Gerrard Winstanley, Spence had become politicised by local struggles over land rights – in this case, the Newcastle corporation's attempts to make money by enclosing part of the Town Moor, thereby threatening the grazing rights of freemen. The dispute led Spence to develop his 'land plan', which for the rest of his life would constitute the core of his political philosophy. The plan was reminiscent of Winstanley's thought, in that it identified the private ownership of land as the source of all inequality and evil in the country. However, rather than proposing, as Winstanley ultimately did, that this inegalitarian system should be replaced with a centralised, communitarian state, Spence – like most eighteenth-century radicals an opponent of 'big government' – argued that all land should be held in trust by each parish and apportioned by the parish for the benefit of each of its inhabitants. He first publicly discussed his ideas in a lecture to the Newcastle Philosophical Society on 'the real Rights of Man' in November 1775. The lecture was not well received, and the Society subsequently stripped him of his membership for hawking printed copies of it on the streets of Newcastle.

Nothing daunted, Spence continued his radical activities in the North East. He later recounted (in the third person) how he had first come to write the phrase that would become an integral part of political discourse by the 1790s:

A man who had been a farmer, and also a miner, and who had been ill-used by his landlords, dug a cave for himself by the seaside, at Marsdon Rocks, between Shields and Sunderland, about the year 1780, and the singularity of such a habitation, exciting the curiosity of many to pay him a visit; our author as one of that number. Exulting in the idea of a human being, who had bravely emancipated himself from the iron fangs of aristocracy, to live free from impost, he wrote extempore with chaulk above the fire place of this free man, the following lines:

Ye landlords vile, whose man's peace mar,
Come levy rents here if you can;
Your stewards and lawyers I defy,

And live with all the RIGHTS OF MAN

With his wife, the former miner known as Jack 'the Blaster' Bates had excavated his new home in the rocks at the ripe old age of eighty. Marsden Grotto, as it became known, soon developed into a popular tourist destination and Jack and his wife supplemented their income by providing the visitors with refreshments which were often, not unreasonably, alleged to have been procured by smuggling. The grotto was taken over and greatly expanded in the early nineteenth century by a Whitburn publican, Peter Allan, also seeking, like Jack, a means of running a business without paying ground rent. Allan excavated a 'ballroom', a dining-room and a gaol in the rocks, extra space that was much needed as, besides his family, the grotto accommodated two pigs, a beehive, a greyhound, a one-legged raven called Ralph and a lovelorn sailor whose hermit-like existence and unkempt appearance led him to be known as 'Peter Allan's hairy man'. The Allan family were eventually forced to pay rent to the farmer who owned the land above the grotto. Despite these additional costs, it has continued to operate as a successful pub (claiming to be Europe's only cave bar) to the present day.[3]

In contrast to Spence, Paine did not initially use the phrase 'the Rights of Man' to include economic or property rights. But he used part one of *Rights of Man* to undertake perhaps the most successful literary demolition job ever perpetrated in the English language. As the radical *Manchester Herald* neatly put it on 28 April 1792, '[Burke] was the *flint* to Mr Paine's *steel*.'[4] In the *Reflections* Burke had contended not only that the people (contrary to the assertion of Price) had no right to choose their own governors, but also that the English would resist the assertion of this right 'with their lives and fortunes'. Paine revelled in exposing these Burkeian absurdities: 'That men should take up arms, and spend their lives and fortunes, not to maintain their rights, but to maintain they have not rights, is an entirely new species of discovery, and suited to the paradoxical genius of Mr Burke.'[5] He then set about destroying the two main props of Burke's argument: his conservative interpretation of the revolution of 1688 and his negative reading of events taking place in France. On the former, Paine took a quite different approach from that of Richard Price, not offering a radical reworking of the Glorious Revolution but instead arguing that both it and the idea of a tradition of British liberty were irrelevancies. He himself, he said, was 'contending for the rights of the *living*, and against their being willed away, and controlled and contracted for, by the manuscript assumed authority of the dead; and Mr Burke is contending for the authority of the dead over the rights and freedom of the living'.[6]

Paine asserted, quite wrongly as it turned out, that the Glorious Revolution would sink into insignificance as a world-historical event:

As the estimation of all things is by comparison, the Revolution of 1688, however from circumstances it may have been exalted beyond its value, will find its level. It is already on the wane, eclipsed by the enlarging orb of reason, and the luminous revolutions of America and France. In less than another century, it will go, as well as Mr Burke's labors, 'to the family vault of all the Capulets'. Mankind will then scarcely believe that a country calling itself free, would send to Holland for a man [William III], and clothe him with power, on purpose to put themselves in fear of him, and give him almost a million sterling a year for leave to *submit* themselves and their posterity, like bond-men and bond-women for ever.[7]

The 'ancient constitution' that Burke venerated was no more than a chimera, he claimed. England's government was based upon naked power, the military conquest of the nation by Duke William of Normandy in 1066. Key elements of this English constitution, Magna Carta and the Bill of Rights (which Paine styled a 'Bill of Wrongs'), were no more than 're-conquests': they did not throw off the usurpation of popular sovereignty but merely set new bounds to the exercise of royal tyranny. The much vaunted liberties extended by the Glorious Revolution offered the people no more than the largely useless right to petition their tyrannical governors.[8] 'Can then Mr Burke produce the English Constitution? If he cannot, we may fairly conclude, that though it has been so much talked about, no such thing as a constitution exists, or ever did exist, and consequently that the people have yet a constitution to form.'[9] If any further evidence were needed, Paine went on, people had only to look at the ease with which the electoral arrangements put in place in 1688–9 had been largely obliterated by the 'despotic legislation', such as the Septennial Act of 1716, of the Whig oligarchy which fatally weakened the revolution settlement's commitment to regular elections.[10]

If Burke's description of the English constitution were a fabrication, his narrative of the French Revolution, for Paine, was a histrionic travesty that chose to pity 'the plumage [the French royal family]' and forgot 'the bird [the French people]'.[11] Burke's sympathies, he argued, were not only misdirected but rested on a misapprehension of the aims of the French Revolution. At this stage at least, Paine believed that Louis XVI was 'favourable to the enterprise': 'Perhaps no man bred up in the style of an absolute king ever possessed a heart so little disposed to the exercise of that species of power as the present King of France.' The revolutionaries were not aiming at the person of the King, but at the evils associated with the monarchical system: 'The monarch and the monarchy were distinct and separate things; and it was against the established despotism of the latter, and not against the person or principles of the former, that the revolt commenced, and the Revolution has been carried.'[12] If there had been, as Burke had keenly noted, atrocities committed by the revolutionaries, this was a consequence of the cruelties of the legal system under which the French people operated. It was these 'sanguinary punishments' that corrupted mankind: 'In England, the punishment in certain cases, is by *hanging, drawing and quartering*; the heart of the sufferer is cut out and held up to the view of the populace.' In France, under the former government, the punishments were no less barbarous. 'Who does not remember the execution of Damien, torn to pieces by horses? The effect of those cruel spectacles exhibited to the populace, is to destroy tenderness, or excite revenge, and by the base and false idea of governing men by terror, instead of reason, they become precedents.'[13]

The National Assembly had already made important moves towards correcting the evils of French law. Freedom of conscience was declared a natural right, which, Paine said, had abolished the 'presumption' inherent in the English Toleration Act of 1689, which perversely assumed that legislators could interpose themselves 'between the divine and the worshipper'.[14]* The Assembly had also reformed the game laws so that farmers could take game caught on their land without prosecution, whereas in England 'game is made the property of those at whose expense it is not fed'.[16] Most importantly, the French constitution, unlike the English, was not illusory: it was the product of a convention of the people, not the usurpation of Norman conquerors.

In contrast, England's government remained the mishmash that Paine had described in *Common Sense*. The principle of hereditary succession, which Burke saw as largely unaffected by the events of 1688–9, was also savaged (though it would receive a more extensive mauling in part two of *Rights of Man*). Not only monarchy, but also aristocracy and, especially, the legislative role of the House

---

* Here Paine was alluding to the contemporary meaning of 'toleration' as a statutory indulgence of certain groups outside the state Church, as prescribed licence rather than a general liberty.[15]

of Lords were absurdities: 'the idea of hereditary legislators is as inconsistent as that of hereditary judges, or hereditary juries; and as absurd as an hereditary mathematician, or an hereditary wise man; and as ridiculous as an hereditary poet-laureate'. Legislators who were elected by no one were accountable to no one and, consequently, should be trusted by no one. Moreover, he continued, whatever qualities their distant ancestors might have had, they had been frittered away among the English aristocracy as a result of centuries of inbreeding.[17] These monarchical and aristocratic elements of the government were essentially parasitic on its 'republican' parts. In a passage reminiscent of sixteenth- and seventeenth-century analyses of the English state, Paine argued:

> All that part of the government of England which begins with the office of constable, and proceeds through the departments of magistrate, quarter-session, and general assize, including the trial by jury, is republican government. Nothing of monarchy appears in any part of it, except the name which William the Conqueror imposed upon the English, that of obliging them to call him 'their Sovereign Lord and King'.[18]

However, though he made a frank criticism of the current electoral system in England, with its 'pocket' and 'rotten' boroughs, he did not yet extend this championing of republican government to call for universal male suffrage – perhaps because it would have embarrassed his French comrades, who at this point restricted the franchise to male property-holders.[19]

The publication of the first part of Paine's *Rights of Man* was a strong impetus to the formation in major British cities of the so-called 'corresponding societies', whose aim was constitutional reform. The first of these societies was established in Sheffield at the end of 1791. At its inception, it benefited from the support of men like Joseph Gales, editor of the *Sheffield Register*, a pro-reform, anti-slavery paper.[20] The Sheffield Society also acted as a distribution centre for Paine's work. In January 1792, it had sixteen hundred subscribers to the sixpenny edition of part one of *Rights of Man*. The dissemination of *Rights of Man* was greatly assisted by Paine's own willingness to let provincial societies make their own copies, and by his readiness to allow the profits from sales to go to the corresponding societies themselves rather than be made over to the author.

The London Corresponding Society was established in January 1792 and led by a forty-year-old Scottish shoemaker, Thomas Hardy (the LCS would retain strong Scottish connections throughout its history). Hardy's own interest in reform had been piqued by the free pamphlets produced by the Society for Constitutional Information set up at the height of the gentry-led reform movement in 1780. Like Joseph Gales, Hardy also had connections with the movement for the abolition of slavery: Olaudah Equiano, a former slave turned abolitionist, wrote part of his autobiography while living in Hardy's house.[21] Together with the events of the French Revolution and the publication of Paine's work, these radical abolitionist and SCI pamphlets convinced Hardy of the need for a political organisation to represent the 'humble in situation and circumstances'.[22] His aim was reflected in the minimal cost of subscription to the Society, a penny a week, affordable for the artisans and journeymen who came to make up the majority of the LCS's membership. But though the corresponding societies have often been touted as 'the first working-class political organisations', it is important to note that there was a significant minority of members who came from gentry stock and the professional classes, and that this group played an influential role in the leadership of the LCS. Gentlemen reformers such as John Horne Tooke and Major John Cartwright gave advice and attended meetings. Its members also included barristers and lawyers like Maurice Margarot and Joseph Gerrald, and even a Scottish peer, Basil William Douglas, Lord Daer.

The championing of Paine's work by the corresponding societies has sometimes obscured the differences between his arguments, based on the rejection of the notion of specifically Anglo-Saxon liberties and legitimised by appeals to reason and natural law, and those voiced in the LCS's addresses to the nation. The declaration of the Society made on 19 December 1791 made clear that its aims were non-violent, and also expressed belief in an 'ancient constitution': 'First, as our Constitution was, from the earliest periods, founded in Liberty, it should not be destroyed, as if it were the Government of Despotism.'[23] Further addresses spoke of seeing 'our liberties restored', rather than established anew – these included social as well as political reforms – and as late as 1793 spoke of 'the spirit of the Constitution . . . confirmed by the Revolution of 1688'.[24] Even as the LCS began to make common cause with more radical movements in Ireland and Scotland, its public pronouncements continued to ground its actions in the language of Magna Carta and the Bill of Rights.[25] While Paine had argued for the English to follow the example of the French revolutionaries and replace Westminster with a truly representative National Assembly, the LCS continued to speak publicly only of a reformed Parliament, with elections on the basis of franchise for all adult males.[26]

Moreover, some of the corresponding societies were inspired by local rather than national struggles, as in Sheffield. Here the catalyst had been the attempt by the Duke of Norfolk and other leading gentry such as the Reverend James Wilkinson, the fox-hunting squire of Broomhall, to enclose six thousand acres of common land, for which the poor were to be compensated with a derisory two acres in total. The men and women of Sheffield responded by breaking into the debtors' gaol on 27 July 1790 and releasing the prisoners, then converging on Wilkinson's residence, where they set his library on fire along with several hayricks. Although the riot was eventually suppressed by the swearing-in of many special constables, the following Friday the barn of Norwood Hall, owned by James Wheat, clerk of the town trustees and a prime mover in the enclosure acts, was also mysteriously burnt down. One William Broomhead, explaining the reason behind the setting-up of the Sheffield Constitutional Society when pressed by the prosecution during the treason trials of 1794 (see page 264), said its aim was

> To enlighten the people, to show the people the reason, the ground of all their complaints and sufferings; when a man works hard for thirteen or fourteen hours of the day, the week through, and is not able to maintain his family; that is what I understand of it; to show the people the ground of this; why they were not able.[27]

The difference in emphasis between the publications of the LCS and those of Paine grew wider with the printing of the second part of *Rights of Man* on 16 February 1792. The original title planned for the work, 'Kingship', gave a clearer indication of Paine's current preoccupations. Influenced by events in France – most notably the flight of the royal family to Varennes on 20–1 June 1791, which turned the popular tide against the monarchy of Louis XVI – this latest was a far more starkly republican pamphlet than part one.

In part two, Paine described 'the history of all monarchical governments' as 'but a disgustful picture of human wretchedness, and the accidental respite of a few years' repose'.[28] Nature herself, he railed, appeared to disown hereditary government, seeing 'that the mental characters of successors, in all countries, are below the average human understanding; that one is a tyrant, another an idiot, a third insane, and some all three together, it is impossible to attach confidence to it, when reason in man has power to act'.[29] While it required some talent to be 'a common mechanic . . . to be a king, requires only the animal figure of a man – a sort of breathing automaton'.[30] Monarchy, as it existed in eighteenth-century Europe, was a mere sham or fraud, put upon the public: 'monarchy is all a bubble, a mere court artifice to procure money'.[31] Rather than maintaining order, it had been this monarchical system that had caused the 'riots and tumults' of recent years (here Paine singled out the violent anti-Catholic Gordon Riots of the 1780s as a particular example). It was the monarchical state that left society divided, depriving it of its 'natural cohesion'.[32] Instead of leading to anarchy, the dissolution of this government would only bring society closer together, as demonstrated by the example of those voluntary associations that men made for trade or other concerns without the interference of government. For, he continued, government was 'nothing more than a national association acting on the principles of society'.[33] This faith in national conventions was clear evidence of the debt owed in Paine's thought to his American experience. While it was England that gave him a connection with the labouring poor, it was the United States that convinced him of the potential of mass political action.

The frankness of this attack on monarchy contrasted with the LCS's publications, which continued to speak of 'preserving the people's love' for the King.[34] More importantly, the corresponding societies as a whole had restricted their demands to the vote and more regular parliaments. Though he continued to attack the inequality of the current system of representation (without, again, saying anything specific about the franchise), Paine's arguments in the second part of *Rights of Man* went much further. Reflecting on the state of the poor in England, his comments were not unlike those of other middle-class radicals such as Mary Wollstonecraft. 'Why is it', he asked, 'that scarcely any are executed but the poor? The fact is a proof, among other things, of a wretchedness in their condition. Bred up without morals, and cast upon the world without a prospect, they are the exposed sacrifice of vice and legal barbarity.'[35] Here, though, followed an important difference. Whereas other radicals, in a vein not dissimilar to their loyalist opponents, continued to stress moral reformation via education as the remedy for the 'barbarity' of the poor, Paine argued that the way to put an end to the criminality of the English underclass was to end poverty itself.

He pointed to the unequal distribution of the tax burden. The value of the revenue from taxes on land had declined markedly in relative terms when compared with that raised from taxes on commodities – taxes that all were forced to pay, irrespective of income. A case in point was the excise tax on beer, which the landed wealthy could avoid paying as their estates were large enough to contain their own breweries, and which now, Paine claimed, exceeded the entire revenue from taxes on land.[36] To remedy this inequality, he proposed a sliding scale of inheritance tax, which would be imposed on landed estates worth £13,000 or more. This was in fact a very limited proposal for redistributive taxation, given that the estates subject to the tax were only the very wealthiest in the country; and Paine did not propose taxing wealth generated from industry or commerce as it 'would be impolitic to set bounds to property acquired by industry, and therefore it is right to place the prohibition beyond the probable acquisition to which industry can extend'.[37]

Nonetheless, combined with the 'peace dividend' that he argued would result from ending the war with France (which would allow for a significant cut in the general level of taxation), he believed that this tax on land would raise sufficient funds to pay for a system of old-age pensions and child-support payments for poorer families.[38] Children would be provided with free schooling and lump sums would be paid to families on births and deaths – this as a means of doing away with the grotesque dragging of the poor 'from place to place to breathe their last, as a reprisal of parish upon parish'.[39] For the large population of migrant workers who came to London seeking their fortunes, public hostels would be built to provide food and shelter until they could find paid employment, for hunger 'is not among the postponable wants, and a day, even a few hours, in such a condition, is often the crisis of a life of ruin'.[40]

Paradoxically, it was the essence of Paine's success as a writer – his ability to appeal to ordinary people – that also prepared the way for his downfall and that of the movement for radical reform as a whole. In the second part of *Rights of Man* he had shifted his focus from attacking the British *ancien régime* and advocating democratic change to calling for greater social equality. The so-called 'social chapter' of the second part of *Rights of Man* provided his opponents in the loyalist press with the opportunity to smear him and his fellow radicals with the label 'Levellers'. Reform, the loyalists argued, would not be satisfied until it had not only gained the vote for all working men but also appropriated the property of their social betters. The threat of social revolution helped drive a wedge between middle-class and working-class reformers, leading the former essentially to abandon agitation 'out-of-doors' while leaving the latter, in frustration, to turn to increasingly desperate measures to achieve their goals.

Shortly after the publication of the second part of *Rights of Man* there appeared another work whose arguments were clearly at odds with those of the corresponding societies, though for rather different reasons. The members of the LCS grounded their demands on their masculine birthright: 'Are we Men, and shall we not speak?'[41] There was little discussion here of extending the franchise to women. Indeed, in general, most radical and reformist discourse was grounded in values and faculties that were deemed to be almost exclusively masculine, the veneration of 'reason' being the most obvious.

Into this largely male-dominated debate came Mary Wollstonecraft's *Vindication of the Rights of Woman*. Its title was somewhat misleading. Wollstonecraft's work was neither a reply to Paine's (her targets were the French *philosophes* Talleyrand and Rousseau) nor a call for women's political emancipation (though her work has since been appropriated by modern feminists). Indeed, her interest was not in demanding the same natural and civil rights for women as Painite reformers claimed pertained to men but in suggesting ways in which women could be brought to exercise masculine 'public virtue' – the classical notion of virtue as the pursuit of the public good.[42] Wollstonecraft's incipient republicanism is on show from the start:

> Surely it is madness to make the fate of thousands depend on the caprice of a weak fellow creature, whose very station sinks him *necessarily* below the meanest of his subjects! But one power should not be thrown down to exalt another – for all power inebriates a weak man; and its abuse proves that the more equality there is established among men, the more virtue and happiness will reign in society.[43]

She also touched, albeit briefly, on the issue of women's right to vote:

> I really think that women ought to have representatives, instead of being arbitrarily governed without having any direct share allowed them in the deliberations of government. But as the whole system of representation is now, in this country, only a convenient handle for despotism, [women] need not complain, for they are as well represented as a numerous class of hard working mechanics, who pay for the support of royalty when they can scarcely stop their children's mouths with bread.[44]

But the main body of her work was directed at the upbringing of women, focusing mainly on the education, or lack of it, given to gentlewomen. Wollstonecraft frankly admitted that her book was addressed to the 'middle class', and the list of women that she admired was also distinctly posh, including Catharine Macaulay and the Empress of Russia.[45] As she saw it, at present, the daughters of the gentry were raised only for the marriage market. This infantilised them, thereby making them, paradoxically, wholly unsuited for their future role as wives and mothers:

strength of body and mind are sacrificed to libertine notions of beauty, to the desire of establishing themselves, – the only way women can rise in the world, – by marriage. And this desire making mere animals of them, when they marry they act as such children may be expected to act: – they dress; they paint, and nick-name God's creatures. – Surely these weak beings are only fit for a seraglio! – Can they be expected to govern a family with judgment, or take care of the poor babes whom they bring into the world?[46]

She compared the attitudes of men and women to travel. While a man would set out with an objective, a clear end in view, a woman would have her mind fixed only on incidentals, especially 'the impression she may make on her fellow-travellers'. The only question in women's heads, she said, was: will I 'make a sensation'? 'Can dignity of mind,' Wollstonecraft sternly asked, 'exist with such cares?'*[47] The only way to deal with the insipidity of most middle-class women, she said, was through education. She proposed national co-educational day schools that would include 'the rich and poor'. Her work reveals that she felt that class, as much as gender distinctions, was an impediment to the exercise of virtue. Consequently, children within these schools, to 'prevent any of the distinctions of vanity . . . should be dressed alike, and all obliged to submit to the same discipline'. However, this attentiveness to the distorting power of the social hierarchy did not lead her to advocate a truly egalitarian education system:

At the age of nine, girls and boys, intended for domestic employments, or mechanical trades, ought to be removed to other schools, and receive instruction, in some measure appropriated to the

* Wollstonecraft revealed her contempt for the conventional accoutrements of feminine beauty – elaborate clothes, make-up and extravagant headgear – by wearing her hair unadorned, using no cosmetics and clothing herself in cheap, rough dresses and the sort of black worsted stockings worn by milkmaids – giving her the appearance, according to one hostile commentator, of a 'philosophical sloven'.

destination of each individual, the two sexes being still together in the morning; but in the afternoon, the girls should attend a school, where plain-work, mantua-making, millinery, &c. would be their employment

The young people of superior abilities, or fortune, might now be taught, in another school, the dead and living languages, the elements of science, and continue the study of history and politics on a more extensive scale, which would not exclude polite literature.[48]

Wollstonecraft's attitude to class can at best be described as ambivalent. She spoke of finding most 'virtue' in 'low life', among those women who supported their families through the sweat of their brows, but, almost in the same breath, she reiterated the orthodox piety that in order for the poor to be rendered 'virtuous' 'they must be employed'. She suggested that middle-class women could prevent the poor from falling into a vicious indolence by employing them as servants.[49]

Nonetheless, despite these obvious debts to the values of the day, *A Vindication* remains a remarkably bold statement in favour of the fundamental equality of the sexes:

A wild wish has just flown from my heart to my head, and I will not stifle it though it may excite a horse-laugh. – I do earnestly wish to see the distinction of sex confounded in society, unless where love animates the behaviour. For this distinction is, I am firmly persuaded, the foundation of the weakness of character ascribed to woman.

When we read passages like these, it is not so hard to see why Wollstonecraft was designated by later writers a pioneering feminist. In her own time, too, she was lauded for *A Vindication*, especially by other women writers. The poet Anne Seward called it a 'wonderful book' while a woman reader from Glasgow complained that the text was in such high demand that it was difficult to get a look at it.[50] It received glowing reviews from most of the reformist press and may have sold as many as three thousand copies in its first five years in print.

Not all reviewers were so enthusiastic, however. Hannah More, the bluestocking philanthropist, writer and abolitionist, described the title alone as 'fantastic and absurd' and refused to read it.[51] More was opposed to teaching poor children to read as this would only make them dissatisfied with their lot. In contrast to Wollstonecraft's emphasis on fostering independence, she preferred to promote Sunday schools, intended to inculcate obedience and deference in children – institutions which Wollstonecraft's future husband, William Godwin, accurately satirised as teaching only 'a superstitious veneration for the church of England, and how to bow to every man in a handsome coat'.[52]

If Paine's work was the popular publishing success of the 1790s, William Godwin's *Enquiry Concerning Political Justice*, published in February 1793, was the radical work that gathered most praise from the reform-minded intelligentsia. William Hazlitt famously wrote that, in contrast to Godwin, in literary circles 'Tom Paine was considered for the time as a Tom Fool to him, [William] Paley an old woman, Edmund Burke a flashy sophist'.[53] By this point Godwin, who, like his father, had trained to be a schoolteacher and nonconformist minister, had turned his back on those vocations and was well established as a writer on historical subjects for George Robinson's *New Annual Register*. *Political Justice* was a long and expensive book – necessarily so, perhaps, since his publisher Robinson, for this work too, had paid him a considerable advance for it – a fact that was rumoured to have saved Godwin from prosecution for sedition. The Prime Minister, William Pitt, was reported to have said that a book costing three guineas was unlikely to be of interest to radical artisans, who could barely find three shillings.[54] All the same, demand for the work appears to have been high, with Robinson having to purchase pirated copies printed in Dublin to sell in London in order to keep up with demand.[55] But as we shall see below (p. 252), there were other, more substantive, reasons as to why Godwin evaded prosecution while Paine was found guilty of seditious libel *in absentia* in September 1792.

Political Justice unquestionably contained strong criticism of the existing political, legal and religious structures of late eighteenth-century England. The preface to the work explicitly stated Godwin's republican credentials: 'monarchy was as a species of government unavoidably corrupt'.[56] The education of a prince made him profoundly unfit to rule: 'Above all, simple, unqualified truth is a stranger to his ear. It either never approaches; or if so unexpected a guest should once appear, it meets with so cold a reception, as to afford little encouragement to a second visit.'[57] This was in no small part, Godwin went on, because monarchy was such a fragile sham that its workings had to be hidden from public view as far as possible: 'The most fatal opinion that could lay hold upon the mind of their subjects is that kings are but men. Accordingly they are carefully withdrawn from the profaneness of vulgar inspection; and, when they are exhibited, it is with every artifice that may dazzle our sense and mislead our judgment'.[58] They were not, then, as the members of the Revolution Society suggested, the servants of the people, because, rationally, the people could never have chosen freely such poor trustees to exercise their power: 'A king of England therefore holds his crown independently, or, as it has been energetically expressed, "in contempt" of the choice of the people' – this last referring to Edmund Burke's comment in his *Reflections* that George III 'holds his crown in contempt of the choice of the Revolution Society, who have not a single vote for a king amongst them'.[59]

As far as private property was concerned, Godwin was a greater 'Leveller' than Paine. Godwin viewed all ownership as essentially fiduciary: property was held in trust, exclusively for the purpose of serving the public good. Man had no right to dispose of even a shilling of his wealth at his mere caprice. Those 'philanthropists' (perhaps Godwin was speaking with Hannah More and her ilk in mind), '[so] far from being entitled to well earned applause' for their efforts, were, in fact, in the eye of justice delinquents if they withhold 'any portion from that service'.[60] One benefit of the eventual equalisation of property, he said, would be the end of the indolent and bloated rich. All, in this Utopia, would need to take part in some manual labour in order to sustain themselves: 'The mathematician, the poet and the philosopher will derive a new stock of chearfulness and energy from the recurring labour that makes them feel they are men.'[61] It is somewhat ironic that these comments concerning the moral benefits of physical activity should come from Godwin, an author whose temperament was so delicate that he could write for only three hours a day before he had dizzy spells.[62]

This romantic image of an egalitarian Utopia constructed by thinking, working men inspired the poets Samuel Taylor Coleridge and Robert Southey's schemes for 'pantisocracy' (from *pan* and *socratia*, 'all governing equally'). They planned to establish a community on the banks of the Susquehanna River in Pennsylvania, made up initially of twelve couples who would provide £125 in capital each and live lives combining three hours of manual labour a day – based on Adam Smith's calculation that only one-twentieth of workers' time was actually spent in productive labour – with extensive intellectual contemplation. Goods (and also, Coleridge hoped, women) would be held in common. The aim was to create a community that would raise children unpolluted by the distorted values of contemporary society. Southey daydreamed to Coleridge in a letter of 3 September 1794 as he described life in their ideal society: 'Past sorrows will be obliterated in anticipating future pleasure. When Coleridge and I are sawing down a tree we shall discuss metaphysics; criticise poetry while hunting a buffalo, and write sonnets whilst following the plough.' The impoverished poets didn't have the money for the journey, only getting as far as Bristol, where they fell out over women. In later life, both would repudiate their earlier flirtation with radical Utopianism, Southey describing Godwin's mind as 'like a close-stool pan, most often empty, and better empty than when full'.[63]

In many respects, Godwin's language was similar to that of other late eighteenth-century radicals in its gender-loaded references to 'manly' labour and 'unmanly' poverty. However, his belief in the fundamental evil of inalienable private property led him to challenge directly the key institution of patriarchal society: marriage. Marriage was, after all, at this point essentially a form of property ownership in which the wife was the chattel of the husband. It was 'an affair of property and the worst of all properties'.[64] Consequently, marriage should be abolished. Men and women would continue to propagate the species as 'reason and duty' dictated, but they would no longer be corrupted by the vicissitudes of the marriage market (a conclusion markedly similar to Wollstonecraft's).[65]

All of this was controversial enough, as too were Godwin's comments on English justice (or the lack thereof), which will be discussed later. However, these elements of *Political Justice* were undercut by his core political philosophy. This uniquely rejected both the appeal to a history of English liberty (which, like Paine, Godwin believed was a fiction) and the natural rights-based arguments of *Rights of Man*. Instead, Godwin believed in the spirit of 'universal benevolence', a moral obligation incumbent on all men to use their wealth, resources and talents for the public good. To use these resources for other ends was simply pernicious. Equally, as men had no right to property either in men or, more pertinently, in women, no one had the right to exercise dominion over anyone else.

This vision of 'universal benevolence' was starkly utilitarian, allowing little room for sentiment. In a famous passage, Godwin rehearsed the example of a fire at the palace of the celebrated Archbishop of Cambrai, François Fénelon, author of the stinging attack on divine-right monarchy, *The Adventures of Telemachus* (1699). The good Archbishop and his chambermaid are trapped inside the burning building, but there is only time to save one of them. Few, Godwin believed, would disagree that the life of the Archbishop was more worthy of saving than that of a servant girl. But what if the chambermaid was 'my wife, my mother or my benefactor'? This did not alter the case:

> justice, pure, unadulterated justice, would still have preferred that which was most valuable. Justice would have taught me to save the life of Fénelon at the expense of the other. What magic is there in the pronoun 'my', to overturn the decisions of everlasting truth? My wife or my mother may be a fool or a prostitute, malicious, lying or dishonest. If they be, of what consequence is it that they are mine?[66]

This kind of cold rationalism, rejecting all emotional ties, later led Thomas De Quincey, author of *Confessions of an English Opium-Eater* (1822), to describe Godwin as 'a ghoul, or a bloodless vampyre, or the monster created by Frankenstein'.[67] Not without reason, either. Godwin was apparently partly inspired to write *Political Justice* by the example of the Houyhnhnms, the ultra-rational horse-like creatures depicted in the final book of Jonathan Swift's *Gulliver's Travels*, describing the latter as 'one of the most virtuous, liberal and enlightened examples of human genius that has yet been produced'. Godwin seems to have missed the point that Swift meant the Houyhnhnms, with their utter contempt for all other species, to be just as objectionable as the grotesque, human-like Yahoos.[68]

The most remarkable feature of this Utopian vision of slowly spreading 'universal benevolence' was Godwin's musings on its end point, a world in which death itself had been conquered. In contrast to the theory of demographic catastrophe later outlined by Thomas Malthus, which essentially posited only natural disasters (war, plague, famine) and human 'vices' (in which he included the use of contraception and homosexuality) as possible checks on population outstripping global resources, Godwin believed that the exercise of 'moral restraint' would prevent such a disaster taking place: 'The men . . . who exist when the earth shall refuse itself to a more extended population, will cease to propagate, for they will no longer have any motive, either of error or duty, to induce them'. His next words will cause modern readers to raise an eyebrow: 'In addition to this they will perhaps be immortal. The whole will be a people of men, and not of children. Generation will not succeed generation, nor truth have in a certain degree to recommence her career at the end of every thirty years.'[69] Once man (it was not clear whether women were implicitly included in this ultimate prospect of humanity) had acquired full control of his reasoning faculties, his mind would be powerful enough to control every aspect of his body, preventing what had seemed its inevitable degeneration. This interest in immortality was not a mere blip in Godwin's intellectual career. He would return to the theme in *St Leon*, published in 1799, a historical fiction that traced the adventures of the titular French knight who had found the fabled philosopher's stone.

Godwin's belief in the 'perfectibility' of man is a reminder that though many leading radical intellectuals had rejected Christianity and organised religion in general, radicalism continued to have a deep ideological taproot in Protestant nonconformity. Godwin's education in Norwich had been undertaken by the Sandemanian tutor Samuel Newton. Sandemanianism, an ultra-Calvinist off-shoot of Presbyterianism, held that grace was achieved neither through good works nor through faith but 'only by the rational perception of divine truth'.[70] This was a creed (also followed by the scientist Michael Faraday) that Godwin later ridiculed as 'after Calvin had damned ninety-nine in a hundred of mankind . . . a scheme for damning ninety-nine in a hundred of the followers of Calvin'.

By the time he came to write *Political Justice*, like Paine and Wollstonecraft he had moved towards deism. But just as Paine still remained indebted to his Quaker upbringing, so Godwin's belief in human perfectibility and reason spoke of the legacy of his Sandemanian past. His remarks about immortality also remind us that as much as being an 'Age of Reason', the 1790s, like the 1640s, were an era of religious expectation. This visionary element to radical activity was no better displayed than in William Blake's poems, 'A Song of Liberty' (1790) and *The Visions of the Daughters of Albion* (1793). Blake had had some connections with the radical Swedenborgian New Jerusalem Church in 1789, but by the time that political agitation for reform was at its peak, he had already abandoned this brief dalliance. Like other, now largely forgotten figures such as the millenarian prophet Richard Brothers, Blake continued, nonetheless, to place his politically engaged poems within an apocalyptic framework.[71]

Most importantly, as far as the government reaction to *Political Justice* was concerned, Godwin did not believe this rational Utopia to be imminent: indeed, it would best be achieved by a very gradual process of enlightenment. Looking back on the English civil war, of which he would later write a sympathetic, pro-republican history, Godwin stated that, admitting 'these objects [the overturning of monarchy] to have been in the utmost degree excellent, they ought not, for the purpose of obtaining them, to have precipitated the question to the extremity of a civil war'.[72] He rejected not only the use of violence to achieve political ends – as did most other English radicals – but also collective action as a whole. Political associations such as those formed by the Yorkshire reformer Charles Wyvill were ineffective, if not dangerous: 'revolutions', Godwin pompously declared, 'less originate in the energies of the people at large, than in the conceptions of persons of some degree of study and reflection'.[73] Associations had to be treated with great care, for the 'conviviality of a feast may lead to the depredations of a riot . . . There is nothing more barbarous, cruel and blood-thirsty than the triumph of a mob.'[74] Only 'a few favoured minds' were perceptive enough not just to conceive of an alternative structure for human society but also to grasp the means by which this change could be brought about:

When these advantages have been unfolded by superior penetration, they cannot yet for some time be expected to be understood by the multitude. Time, reading and conversation are necessary to render them familiar. They must descend in regular gradation from the most thoughtful to the most unobservant. He, that begins with an appeal to the people, may be suspected to understand little of the true character of mind. A sinister design may gain by precipitation; but true wisdom is best adapted to a slow, unvarying, incessant progress.[75]

Elsewhere in *Political Justice*, Godwin indirectly criticised Paine for the intemperate haste with which he had denounced injustice and oppression.[76] Though Godwin would personally intervene to help defend members of the LCS when they found themselves on trial for treason in 1794, this was motivated by his anger at the injustice of the prosecution and the barbarity of the possible punishments (hanging, drawing and quartering). It did not represent an approval of the corresponding societies' methods. As the LCS began to organise mass meetings and demonstrations in the mid-1790s to press for electoral reform, Godwin became more and more outspoken in his criticism. Regarding the use of these tactics, he remarked that the radical lecturer John Thelwall's remonstrations to members against the use of violence were like 'Lord George Gordon preaching peace to the rioters in Westminster Hall' or 'Iago adjuring Othello not to dishonour him by giving harbour to a thought of jealousy'. Godwin later bluntly stated, in an apparent endorsement of government surveillance and suppression of radical activity, that the LCS was 'a formidable machine; the system of political lecturing is a hot-bed, perhaps too well adapted to ripen men for purposes, more or less similar to those of the Jacobin Society of Paris. Both branches of the situation are well deserving of the attention of the members of the government of Great Britain.'[77]

THE REIGN OF TERROR

While Godwin's rejection of collective action was unquestionably an extension of his core political philosophy, it
may well also have been in part a reaction to the immediate circumstances in which *Political Justice* was written. Radical and
reformist activity was already coming under increasing popular
pressure. In July 1791, over two and a half days, 'Church and King'
rioters in Birmingham had attacked Dissenting meeting houses
and the properties of leading nonconformists, including that of
Joseph Priestley, scientist, founder of modern Unitarianism and a
leading figure in the movement for the repeal of the Test and
Corporation Acts, which banned Catholics and Dissenters from
holding public office. The atmosphere in the city was already
heated, with both ultra-radical and reactionary handbills circulating and hostile graffiti daubed on walls calling for the destruction
of 'Presbyterians'.

The pretext for the riot itself was a dinner celebrating the
second anniversary of the storming of the Bastille, to be held at
Thomas Dadley's hotel in Temple Row. As the diners arrived for
the event, which had been advertised in the Birmingham press,

they were jeered by a crowd of seventy or so people. Although these hecklers soon dispersed, by the time the dinner was nearly over at eight o'clock a mob several hundred strong had gathered outside. As the diners left the hotel, the rioters pelted them with stones and then set about sacking the hotel. Next, they turned their attention to the New Meeting House, where Priestley was minister, reducing the building to a burnt-out shell, then setting alight another Dissenting chapel, the Old Meeting House, before moving on to Priestley's own home, Fairhill. Priestley, who had wisely heeded warnings to stay away from the dinner, fled his house before the mob could seize him, but he was able to watch the first part of the attack from a distance. Anticipating that the dinner might be the catalyst for mob violence, he and his son had removed all flammable materials from their home, leaving the mob so bereft of means to spark the conflagration that they reportedly tried to use, with little success, one of Priestley's 'electrical machines'. Priestley's precautions, however, proved only a temporary obstacle to the rioters, who looted his home before razing it to the ground. His pioneering laboratory, library and papers were all lost.

The rioters' activities met with notably little official response. Unsatiated by the demolition of Fairhill and unfettered by police or military action, they continued on to the homes of leading Birmingham Dissenters, destroying Bakerville House, the home of John Rylands, and draining its substantial wine cellar dry. William Hutton, the Dissenting historian, who had actually declined an invitation to the dinner and was viewed by Priestley as politically and religiously conservative, attempted to buy off the rioters with beer. He was dragged to the Fountain tavern, where he was presented with the bill for the 329 gallons consumed. This display of enforced largesse didn't save his home, which was first looted and then burnt. It took two years for Hutton to receive compensation and, even then, it only partially covered his losses. Despite their attack on this moderate nonconformist, the crowd's actions were not indiscriminate: when they arrived at the home of John Taylor, they carefully removed to safety the furniture and possessions of its current occupant, the Dowager Lady Carhampton, a minor royal, before destroying the house.

In all, the rioters destroyed twenty-seven homes and four non-conformist meeting houses. The scale of the destruction – contemporary engravings show once grand dwellings reduced to shattered husks – was almost certainly exacerbated by the actions of local magistrates, who actively encouraged and directed the mayhem. Two leading figures, Dr Benjamin Spencer, Vicar of Aston, and Joseph Carles, a JP, were among the hostile crowd baying outside Dadley's hotel. When a nonconformist did manage to apprehend one of the rioters and bring him to the gaol, he was informed by the keeper that the gaol was under orders not to take any prisoners that night.[1] If Pitt's government did not directly orchestrate the riot, it and the Crown nonetheless took considerable pleasure in its outcome. George III expressed his satisfaction: 'I cannot but feel better pleased that Priestley is the sufferer for the doctrines he and his party have instilled, and that the people see them in their true light.'[2] The compensation paid to those who had lost their property in the riots was less than generous and slow in coming. The vast majority of the rioters also got off scot-free.

When the trial finally got under way in August 1791, only twelve men were arraigned. The jurors were hand-picked by John Brooke, Under-Sheriff of Warwickshire and, along with Carles and Spencer, another likely orchestrator of the riots. Unsurprisingly, the jury acquitted most of the prisoners. Of the four who were convicted, one was pardoned. The remaining three, who were ultimately executed, were all notorious local criminals and it was strongly suspected that the trial had simply provided the authorities with a convenient way of getting rid of them on minimal evidence. As William Hutton bitterly remarked: 'The world will be apt to draw this conclusion, *None were executed for the Riots.*'[3]

Official repression followed locally coordinated intimidation. By the time *Political Justice* was published in January 1793, the government of Pitt the Younger had already begun to take stringent measures against both individual radicals and the London Corresponding Society. On 21 May 1792, the government had issued a royal proclamation urging magistrates to prosecute printers and booksellers found to be producing or distributing seditious material, and warned the public to be on their guard against seditious writings. When this failed to check radical activity, a second proclamation was issued that December, which increased the pressure on local officials to take action against any such writings. The meetings of the LCS itself were increasingly surveilled by government spies and the minutes of the Society became (with good reason) more and more paranoid about loyalist infiltration and eavesdropping.

An orchestrated loyalist campaign came to fruition under the direction of John Reeves, a one-time commissioner for bankruptcy, barrister and legal writer. Reeves's role as clerk to the Board of Trade provided him with government connections and he had already contributed to the framing of new police legislation for Ireland and England. Alarmed by the radical activity he saw going on in London, on 20 November 1792 at the Crown and Anchor pub in the Strand he formed the first Association for Preserving Liberty and Property against Republicans and Levellers. His initiative was excellent news for Pitt's administration. It provided the veneer of spontaneity to the exercise, while the government could surreptitiously bankroll and coordinate the new associations. Their popularity – some two thousand had been formed by the time Reeves wound up his activities in July 1793 – should not obscure the fact that these societies were not meant to encourage popular political participation. Reeves's own committee advised

that the business of such Societies should be conducted by a Committee, and that the Committee should be small, as better adapted for the dispatch of business; for it should be remembered, that these are not open Societies for talk and debate, but for private consultation and real business. The societies at large need not meet more than once a month, or once in two or three months, to audit the accounts, and to see to the application of money.

Also, the membership of the committees was drawn almost exclusively from the gentry.[4]

Similarly, questions surround the genuine popularity of the 'Paine burnings' that took place in towns across England and whose timing coincided neatly with Reeves's association movement. It has recently been estimated that close to half a million people attended these burnings of effigies of Paine, approximately one-sixth of the total adult population of England and Wales at the time – making them probably the most witnessed public events of the eighteenth century. It is worth noting, though, that the local committees that organised them, again mainly drawn from the wealthier sections of the community, laid on large amounts of free food and alcoholic drink to ensure good attendance. At Shrewsbury, members of the crowd were even paid to shout 'Church and King'.[5] The most recent study of these political carnivals has also concluded that they were less common in major towns and cities, where the authorities were more wary about their ability to control crowd behaviour.[6] In any case, it is a moot point as to how far attendance at a 'Paine burning' should be seen as representing genuine commitment to Church and King. Besides the obvious draw of complimentary food and drink, these were pieces of political theatre that cleverly aped the form of a much older type of popular festivity, the charivari. Descriptions of the burnings point up the parallels:

The Effigies of Tom Paine having been Burnt at Wooburn, Bedford, Ampthill etc; I believe put it into the Heads of the Wheelwrights Apprentices and Journeymen and some shoemakers and other Lads in Silsoe to do the same, they carried him round the Vilage, and to Flitton, siting upon an Ass, with his Face to its Tail, and when they Returnd they Hung him and then shot at Him, afterwards Burnd Him they Beggd round the Vilage and got a five shillings which they Expended in Gun Powder and Beer – the meeting was quite orderly, and without any Riot, the Fire-Arms they had were no other than three or four old Fowling pieces they borrowed in the Vilage.[7]

Rather than being a ringing endorsement of the government of George III or of a modernising commercial society, these public performances might, in fact, be evidence of the survival of a more traditional worldview, in which moments of licensed disorder had an important place.[8]

Equally, the government's extensive propaganda efforts acknowledged that they required public support to resist the radical threat, and that such support could not be won simply by bribery or intimidation. In the first years of the French Revolution, the government was funding loyalist periodicals to the tune of £5000 a year, including a new daily newspaper, the *Sun*, from October 1792.[9] Nor were the arguments of loyalist writers, as is sometimes alleged, simple appeals to the hearts of the people over their heads. In fact, rather like the appeal of Thatcherism to some sections of the British working class in the 1980s, loyalism succeeded by suggesting that radicals threatened an English constitution that defended not only liberty, but also property. In adopting this line, loyalist writers fixed on a small portion of radical writing, the so-called 'social chapter' of the second part of Paine's *Rights of Man*, and the arguments of Thomas Spence and William Godwin, ignoring the essentially Whiggish rhetoric of the corresponding societies.

Loyalists took Paine's emphasis on the separation between government and civil society and transformed him from an enthusiastic advocate of trade and scientific innovation into a backwards-looking primitivist.[10] Radicals like Paine, the loyalists alleged, wished to return a successful, commercial Britain to the 'state of nature'. One parody of the *Rights of Man, Buff, or a Dissertation on Nakedness* (1792), claimed that 'the more perfect civilization is, the less occasion *has the human body for covering*, because the more does it regulate its own affairs and govern itself'.[11] Satirising Paine's reading of English history as the story of successive conquests, *Buff* claimed that clothing had been imposed on men by nefarious sheep rustlers. By these criminals 'the human mind was deceived into a belief of the utility of skins for a cover-ing, and the bodies, and limbs of man till then, free and unrestrained, were doomed to imprisonment within walls of wool'.[12] Similarly, Paine's modest schemes for an inheritance tax on large estates were presented as a demand for the equalisation of all property.[13]

With the exception of *Rights of Man*, such loyalist publications outsold their radical competitors several times over. A telling com-parison could be made between Wollstonecraft and her fellow writer, Hannah More. While *A Vindication* sold fairly well, its sales were dwarfed by More's *Cheap Repository Tracts* – her antidote to the 'fatal poison' of Thomas Paine – which allegedly reached over two million people, a quarter of the whole population in the 1790s.[14] More's highly didactic work stressed the evils of idleness, drunkenness, gambling and atheism, each a sure path to hell. Her work stressed the need for order and obedience, and the role of marriage and family in forging social cohesion.[15] The roaring success of these tracts was not quite evidence of wide popular endorsement, however, since multiple copies were often purchased by the gentry to distribute free to the poor. Along with her fellow abolitionist, William Wilberforce (who like More strenuously opposed working-class political emancipation at the same time as he fought for the freedom of slaves), More initiated a Christian mission against Jacobinism, in 1796 founding the Society for Bettering the Condition and Increasing the Comforts of the Poor, which set up soup kitchens and gave information on producing cheap and nutritious food.[16]

Radicals were aware of the latent power of some of the loyalists' charges. Godwin remarked: 'No idea has excited greater horror in the minds of a multitude of persons, than that of the mischiefs that are to ensue from the dissemination of what they call levelling principles.'[17] Awareness of this may have encouraged some radicals to steer clear of advocating ideas that would leave them open to charges of social 'levelling'. Nonetheless, it was arguably the lack of caution demonstrated by the corresponding societies in their public activities that allowed Pitt's government to step up its campaign against them. As the character of the French Revolution became more pronouncedly republican and increasingly violent, some English radicals, such as Blake, withdrew from direct involvement in politics. The corresponding societies, on the other hand, continued to offer addresses of congratulation to the fledgling French republic in its victories over its enemies, raised subscriptions for the 'soldiers of liberty' and praised the National Convention, the successor to the National Assembly. After France had formally declared war on Britain in December 1792, these activities allowed the government to portray the societies as not only seditious but also treacherous.

By late 1793, Scotland had become the focus of radical activity. Here, the franchise was even narrower than in England: one in a hundred men possessed the vote, compared with roughly one in ten south of the border. Scottish reformers met at a national convention in Edinburgh that was consciously modelled on French revolutionary practice and imitated Jacobin language, including referring to members as 'citizens'. On 6 December 1793 the Edinburgh authorities closed the meetings. They had already prosecuted two members, Thomas Muir, a young lawyer, and the Reverend Thomas Fyshe Palmer, a Dissenting minister, before an openly hostile judge and a packed jury. Other leaders of the convention followed, including William Skirving, its secretary, and Maurice Margarot and Joseph Gerrald, two delegates from the

LCS, all of whom were found guilty and sentenced to transportation to Botany Bay in Australia.

The fate of the 'Scottish martyrs' became a *cause célèbre*. The LCS issued an address warning the English public that the judgement visited upon its members in Edinburgh might soon be extended to those who called for reform in England, too: 'Can you believe that those who send virtuous Irishmen and Scotchmen fettered with felons to Botany-Bay, do not meditate and will not attempt to seize the first moment to send us after them?'[18]

The convicts' voyage to Australia was packed with incident. Dissension arose among the fellow radicals. Palmer and Skirving allegedly participated in an attempt to kill the captain and take control of the ship. They then claimed that Margarot had revealed their scheme to the captain, leading him to mete out severe punishments to Palmer and Skirving. Only one of the 'martyrs', Margarot, returned to England. Gerrald died of tuberculosis six months after landing in Australia. Skirving died of dysentery soon after, at his small farm in Port Jackson. Palmer died, also of dysentery, in a Spanish prison hulk off the island of Guguan in 1802, having been forced by a storm to make a landing there on his return journey to England – his sentence had expired in 1800 – though he knew that Spain and England were then at war.

Thomas Muir's escapades were the most remarkable. He managed to escape from Australia on board an American trading ship, the *Otter*, in January 1796. After a series of voyages on various vessels up and down the coast of America, he finally secured passage to Europe aboard a Spanish frigate bound for Cadiz. On 26 April 1797, his ship was attacked by two British warships. Muir was severely and painfully disfigured when a wood splinter blown out by a cannon-ball blinded him in one eye and almost cut off his cheek. This mutilation proved, ironically, to be his salvation, ensuring that the boarding British troops did not recognise him and instead took him for another Spanish prisoner of war. Sent ashore, he was then detained by the Spanish authorities as a British prisoner, only to secure release eventually through the efforts of the French Directory later that year. Muir then moved to Paris, where he exaggerated the role he had played in British radical politics to secure funds from the French government. He died in Chantilly, north of Paris, in 1798.

The trials of the 'Scottish Martyrs' were soon followed by legal proceedings against English radicals. On 12 May 1794, Thomas Hardy and Daniel Adams were arrested following reports from government spies of movements to arm the members of the LCS. A parliamentary committee of secrecy was formed to investigate the constitutional societies, while legislation was rushed through Parliament to suspend the Habeas Corpus Act, thereby allowing the government to imprison radicals without charge. Henry 'Redhead' Yorke, a West-Indian-born mixed-race northern radical journalist and lecturer, was arrested on 16 June and gaoled for over a year before being tried and found guilty; he was sentenced to a fine of £200 and two years' imprisonment.* In all, thirteen members of the LCS were indicted for treason, though only Hardy, Tooke and Thelwall were brought to trial. Ever the gourmand, Tooke supplemented his fellow prisoners' diets with strawberries, peaches and artichokes from his garden, while his friends kept him supplied with essentials such as snuff, partridges, turtle soup, Madeira and hock.[19] Tooke recorded in his diary that his time in prison only confirmed his radical politics: 'I cannot find any one Action that I have committed, any word that I have written, any syllable that I have uttered, or any single thought that I have entertained, of a political nature, which I wish either to conceal or to recall.'[20]

Tooke believed that the government had miscalculated in trying the three men, instead having gifted a propaganda victory to the

---

* In Dorchester Gaol, Yorke met the governor's daughter, whom he later married. By the time of his release, he had fully repudiated his radical principles and turned his propagandist efforts to supporting the unreformed constitution.

cause of reform. Hardy was tried first and acquitted on 5 November 1794. Tooke's and Thelwall's trials followed, with the jury taking just two minutes to acquit Tooke, who had leapt at the opportunity to grill prosecution witnesses with great gusto. The acquittals were wildly celebrated and seemed a public repudiation of the bullying tactics of Pitt's ministry. The reasons behind the acquittals were almost certainly more complex than this, though. The juries were being asked to sentence these men to a grisly death not on the grounds of incontrovertible participation in treasonous conspiracies, but on a 'constructive' interpretation of treason (meaning that the general conduct or actions of Hardy, Tooke and Thelwall could be imputed to be treasonable). The prosecution's case was also far less well presented than the radicals' – the prosecutor's opening speech took nine hours – whereas Thomas Erskine, the Foxite MP who acted for the defence, was widely praised for his brilliant performance. Furthermore, some of the evidence against the three had been patently tissue-thin: Tooke had been arrested on the strength of an intercepted letter which read 'Is it possible to get ready by Thursday?', which was almost certainly to do with the preparation of a pamphlet, but which the government presented as setting the timetable for an insurrection.[21] Finally, the jury was almost certainly reluctant to sentence the men to the full punishments for treason merely on the grounds of the possible consequences of their actions.

However, though the acquittals made Hardy, Tooke and Thelwall popular heroes, Tooke was almost certainly wrong in believing that it had been the radical societies rather than the government that had benefited most from the trials. Membership of the LCS continued to grow over the next year, but divisions within its ranks were increasingly evident. Many members, seriously frightened by the treason proceedings, retreated from political engagement. Others found the outspoken radicalism of some of the 'acquitted felons' (as William Windham, the pugnacious MP for Norwich, described them), especially John Thelwall, dangerous and repellent. The process of separating middle-class reformers from working-class institutions, which had already begun as a result of the injudicious congratulations the LCS had addressed to the French for their constitutional achievements, gathered pace. The Society broke into myriad splinter groups: among them, the London Reforming Society, the Friends of Liberty and the Friends of Civil and Religious Liberty, which advocated a more moderate and gradualist path to reform. Another group, the Friends of Peace, led by the Liverpool lawyer and later abolitionist William Roscoe, attempted to offer a middle way between loyalism and Jacobinism, advocating peace with France, moderate parliamentary reform and measures against political corruption.[22]

The terrible pressure put on radicals by the combination of loyalist propaganda and the threat of prosecution was reflected in William Godwin's most famous novel, *Caleb Williams* (1794), or, to give it its more revealing, original title, *Things as They Are*. In contrast to *Political Justice*'s abstract theorising and cool rationality, *Caleb Williams* dealt with the faulty exercise of reason in the real, unjust, unequal world.[23] The book's bleak atmosphere was reflected in Godwin's original preface, written in May 1794 but withdrawn from subsequent editions on account of 'the alarm of booksellers': '"Caleb Williams" [stepped into] the world in the same month [as] the sanguinary plot broke out against the liberties of Englishmen [the trials of Hardy, Tooke and Thelwall] . . . Terror was the order of the day: it was feared that even the humble novelist might be shown to be constructively a traitor.'[24]

A brilliant novel of pursuit, and perhaps the first 'thriller', *Caleb Williams* tells the story of its eponymous hero's flight, or attempted flight, from the clutches of his master, one Mr Falkland, a once noble gentleman turned tyrant by a dark personal secret. The book ruminates on the deleterious effects of social hierarchy on the human spirit, captured in Falkland's famous speech to Williams: 'Do not imagine I am afraid of you! I wear an armour, against which all your weapons are impotent. I have dug a pit for you; and, whichever way you move, backward or forward, to the right or the left, it is ready to swallow you. Be still! If once you fall, call as loud as you will, no man on earth shall hear your cries.'[25] The novel also examines the English justice system at length, and attacks it.

In *Political Justice*, Godwin had already spoken of his opposition to gaol as an effective means of curbing criminal activity: 'Jails are to a proverb seminaries of vice; and he must be an uncommon proficient in the passion and the practice of injustice, or a man of sublime virtue, who does not come out of them a much worse man than he entered.'[26] In his novel he uses the central character, Caleb, as a fictional guinea-pig, forced to endure all the torments that the English system of trial and retribution can invent. The impressive detail that he marshalled in his account of Caleb's sufferings in prison was built on extensive research in court records and his reading of the works of John Howard, the leading prison reformer.[27] The state of English prisons was, to Godwin, a shameful monument to a nation that prided itself on having given liberty to the world:

> We talk of instruments of torture; Englishmen take credit to themselves for having banished the use of them from their happy shore! Alas! he that has observed the secrets of a prison, well knows that there is more torture in the lingering existence of a criminal, in the silent intolerable minutes that he spends, than in the tangible misery of whips and racks ... Our dungeons were cells, 7½ feet by 6½, below the surface of the ground, damp, without window, light, or air, except from a few holes worked for that purpose in the door. In some of these miserable receptacles three persons were put to sleep together.[28]

In this dank and fetid hell-hole Caleb is forced to wait out the best part of a year before he is even brought to trial. When he finally does get his day in court, it is clear that the law is the servant of property, as the magistrate plainly tells him: 'A fine time of it indeed it would be, if, when gentlemen of six thousand a year take up their servants for robbing them, those servants could trump up such accusations as these, and could get any magistrate or court of justice to listen to them!'[29] The power of Godwin's novel, though, lies in the fact that it offers no trite moral conclusions to comfort its readers. He does not offer a simple tale of a just, honest lad confounded by the forces of property and authority. The true dénouement of the work comes not with its rather implausible reconciliation of Falkland with Caleb – a dramatically unsatisfactory ending that Godwin had wisely left out of the original version – but in Caleb's interview with his father. As the latter makes clear, Caleb's experiences, on the run and in prison, have turned him into a sort of monster: 'I regard you as vicious; but I do not consider the vicious as proper objects of indignation and scorn. I consider you as a machine: you are not constituted, I am afraid, to be greatly useful to your fellow men: but you did not make yourself; you are just what circumstances irresistibly compelled you to be.'[30] Furthermore, Williams's relentless desire to clear his reputation has not just crushed his own humanity – it also results in the destruction of another man, Falkland. As Caleb finally realises: 'I began these memoirs with the idea of vindicating my character. I have now no character that I wish to vindicate.'[31]

The 'English Jacobins' have been accused of over-dramatising both their sufferings in the 1790s and the harshness of the measures used by Pitt's ministry. A young member of the LCS and future parliamentary radical, Francis Place, described the late 1790s as Pitt's 'Reign of Terror': 'A disloyal word was enough to bring down punishment upon any man's head; laughing at the awkwardness of a volunteer corps was criminal, people were apprehended and sent on board a man of war for this breach of decorum, which was punished as a terrible crime.'[32]

Comments of this kind have been portrayed as histrionic by some historians. It is certainly true that fewer members of radical societies were executed for treason than 'loyalists' were condemned to death for their part in 'Church and King' riots. In broader terms, it has been argued that the radicals' attack on the penal code of the time was misguided. The number of capital offences had increased since the Glorious Revolution to over two hundred by the late eighteenth century, but historians have pointed out that the exercise of pardons meant that only a small minority of those convicted were sentenced to death. Moreover, the so-called 'bloody code' was not a consciously developed system of judicial tyranny. Most penal legislation was constructed piecemeal and was very specific: catch-all statutes like the infamous 'Waltham Black Act' of 1723, which made it a hanging offence to appear with a blackened or disguised face in or near any park or warren, were highly unusual.[33] In any case, many of those sentenced to death suffered under legislation drawn up by the Tudors and Stuarts: the inflation in the number of felonies was more a measure of more regular parliamentary sessions in the eighteenth century than of the intrinsic bloodthirstiness of the Hanoverian legislators.[34] The law was not simply the tool of the ruling classes, but a 'multi-use right', frequently resorted to by a large proportion of the English population. By the Napoleonic era, the legal system was collapsing under the weight of the litigation being instigated by the public, and 90 per cent of those convicted of felonies were pardoned, turning justice into a lottery.[35]

Yet the fact that the eighteenth-century penal code was less murderous than has sometimes been assumed does not detract from the fact that it was a remarkably efficient tool of the governing classes. Moreover, the ready use of the law by so many members of the public helped legitimise a system that was heavily weighted in favour of the propertied but which continued, successfully, to proclaim that its protections benefited all. The rhetoric used by supporters of the system was remarkably similar to that deployed to defend the unreformed constitution. As Hannah More's carpenter sang:

British laws for my guard,
My cottage is barr'd,
'Tis safe in the light or the dark, Sir;
If the Squire should oppress,
I get instant redress:
My orchard's as safe as his park, Sir.[36]

Again, the dream of sacrosanct personal property was held out to all, even though the reality was available only to a tiny minority of the population. Even the habitual use of pardons themselves, as William Godwin recognised, worked to foster loyalty to the monarchical state:

> A system of pardons is a system of unmitigated slavery. I am taught to expect a certain desirable event, from what? From the clemency, the uncontrolled, unmerited kindness of a fellow mortal. Can any lesson be more degrading? The pusillanimous servility of the man who devotes himself with everlasting obsequiousness to another, because that other, having begun to be unjust, relents in his career; the ardour with which he confesses the rectitude of his sentence and the enormity of his deserts, will constitute a tale that future ages will find it difficult to understand.[37]

And, of course, not all criminals convicted of felonies were pardoned. A large number of men and women went to their deaths for what now seem trivial offences. The logic of the Hanoverian penal code was, as Judge Burnett reminded a horse thief at Hertford Assizes, remorselessly clear. When the plaintiff complained that it was hard to hang him only for stealing a horse, Burnett replied, 'Man, thou art not to be hanged *only* for stealing a horse, but that horses might not be stolen.'[38]

The undoubted gift of some British radicals for self-dramatisation should not obscure, either, the very real suffering of some of the leading 'Jacobins'. Though Thomas Hardy was eventually acquitted of treason, his time in prison left him a broken man. While he was still in custody, his home was attacked by a loyalist mob. His pregnant wife managed to escape and seek the protection of friends, but two months later, with Hardy still in prison, she died giving birth to their child. The infant was stillborn. Hardy blamed the King and his ministers for his wife's death and that of their child. His first act after his acquittal in November 1794 was to visit his wife's grave. *The Times* reported:

> On approaching the grave [Hardy] immediately fell and embraced the cold earth . . . he was lost in the agony of his grief; it was with difficulty that he could be removed; and such was the effect upon his wounded feelings and dilapidated frame and most 'constructively' destroyed prospects, that for a considerable time there were entertained apprehensions regarding his own life.[39]

Hardy's imprisonment struck him financially as well as emotionally. Although he remained involved in radical politics, the seizure of his goods by the Crown – never returned, despite his acquittal – drove him to return to his former business as a shoemaker. When this proved unsuccessful, as a result of the attacks of loyalist mobs and the general depression of trade, he was forced to rely on the charity of fellow radicals, especially Sir Francis Burdett.

Hardy's fate demonstrated the success of the Pitt ministry's tactics. Judicial punishments were arguably unnecessary when public intimidation, mass propaganda campaigns and restrictions on freedoms of speech and association wrought the same effects. By the mid-1790s, the membership of the LCS was in decline. Its leaders had attempted to reverse this trend by co-opting some of the tactics employed by the loyalists, moving from the medium of print to organising mass meetings. Also, like the loyalists, they employed a little bribery to encourage attendance: at the mass meeting held by the Society on 29 June 1795 at St George's Fields, London, biscuits were distributed among the poor, stamped on one side with the inscription 'unanimity, firmness and spirit' and on the other, 'freedom and plenty, or slavery and want'.[40]

On 26 October 1795, somewhere between 40,000 and 100,000 people gathered in a field in Islington to hear speeches by Thelwall, John Gale Jones, a surgeon and man-midwife, and John Binns, an Irish-born plumber. Three days later, George III's coach was attacked as he rode in state to open Parliament. Pitt's government responded with the 'two bills', or 'Gagging Acts'. The first bill made actions against the King's person or his heirs capital offences, and extended the law of treason to include inciting hatred of the King, his heirs, his government or the constitution, though the punishment for this lesser treason was transportation, not death. For the first time since the days of Henry VIII, treason had been turned into a 'thought crime'.[41] The second bill restricted public meetings to fifty people, unless a magistrate had given permission in advance; it also gave magistrates wide powers over the use of public lecture rooms, curtailing the activities of radical lecturers. LCS members soon fell foul of the new legislation, with Binns and Gale Jones arrested in 1796 for attempting to keep up correspondence with other societies. John Thelwall tried to continue his radical lectures, but found loyalist mobs ready to break up such gatherings, apparently with the tacit approval of local magistrates. In Great Yarmouth, he narrowly escaped being press-ganged by a hostile crowd and put on to a Russian ship to Siberia. Though he dodged their clutches, the repeated harassment that he faced on his lecture tours eventually led Thelwall to abandon politics.

The LCS's legal costs and declining membership were putting it into a financial tailspin. The government remained, nonetheless, in a state of high alert. Harvest failures, coupled with the impact of naval blockades on trade, led to serious food shortages, escalating prices, even famine. Agitation for reform looked as if it might also become a dangerous conduit for more general public disaffection. Anonymous letters and handbills were dropped in the street or posted on doors, threatening dire consequences if the price of food were not lowered. One found in Bath read:

> Peace
> and Large Bread
> or
> a King without a Head[42]

Dissatisfaction was also brewing among the thousands of seamen cooped up below decks on the battle fleets. In April 1797, crews mutinied over pay and conditions. The mutiny at Spithead ended in May after concessions from the government, but crews at the Thames anchorage of the Nore, worried that they were excluded from this agreement, began their own action, which was much more militant and included a blockade of the river. Public declarations by the Nore mutineers betrayed the influence of radical ideas on the sailors:

> Shall we who have endured the toils of a tedious, disgraceful war [against the French], be the victims of tyranny and oppression which vile, gilded, pampered knaves, wallowing in the lap of luxury, choose to load us with? Shall we, who amid the rage and tempest and the war of jarring elements, undaunted climb the unsteady cordage and totter on the topmast's dreadful height, suffer ourselves to be treated worse than the dogs of London Streets? Shall we, who in the battle's sanguinary rage, confound, terrify and subdue your proudest foe, guard your coasts from invasion, your children from slaughter, and your lands from pillage – be the footballs and shuttlecocks of a set of tyrants who derive from us alone their honours, their titles and their fortunes? No, the Age of Reason has at length revolved. Long have we been endeavouring to find ourselves men. We now find ourselves so. We will be treated as such.[43]

When the mutiny finally ended in mid-June, the government responded with ferocity: thirty-six men were executed, and ten times that number flogged or sentenced to transportation.

Some of the Nore mutineers had spoken of sailing their ships over to the enemy, and by 1798 some English radicals also appear to have been flirting with the idea of using force to secure their goals. The Newcastle radical and LCS member Thomas Spence had already aroused suspicions by allowing members of the shadowy Lambeth Loyal Association to practise military drill in a large room above his London bookshop. By 1798, some radicals in England appear to have been corresponding with the United Irishmen, led by Wolfe Tone and by then engaged in a mass rebellion against English rule, and dabbling with plans for a domestic insurrection. On 28 February that year, John Binns was arrested in Margate seeking a ship bound for France. He was accompanied by four Irishmen, notably Arthur O'Connor, a fiery leader of the UI, and the Reverend James Coigley, a Catholic priest. A treasonable address to the French was found in Coigley's pocket. All five men were tried for treason. Charles James Fox, Richard Brinsley Sheridan and other leading Whigs appeared in court to act as character witnesses for O'Connor, who now shifted the blame on to Coigley, who was found guilty and executed. Binns was also acquitted, but, like many other radicals, fell foul of the second suspension of the Habeas Corpus Act in 1798. In March the next year, he was arrested and imprisoned without charge in Gloucester Gaol. He would not be released until February 1801.

Mass arrests of radicals in Manchester and London in the spring of 1798 had already crippled the corresponding societies. Finally, in July 1799, legislation formally outlawed the LCS and its more shadowy splinter groups, the United Scotsmen, United Britons and United Englishmen. Radical activity after this point took on a more underground existence, coming to the surface only occasionally in rumours of risings and in the anonymous bills posted featuring the language and imagery of the French Revolution.

The 'Despard conspiracy', uncovered in 1802, set the tone for other early nineteenth-century plots in both its desperation and its extremely limited chances of success. Edward Marcus Despard, a former colleague of Horatio Nelson (who would give a character reference at his trial) and Superintendent of Honduras – dismissed under a cloud in 1790 – was arrested at the Oakly Arms, Lambeth, in November 1802, while apparently planning a coup designed to coincide with the opening of Parliament. During his trial the next year, the government preferred to present Despard as a maverick operator, largely so as to continue to conceal the depth to which its spies had penetrated London radical circles. Historians remain divided as to the seriousness of the conspiracy, but the government, despite pleas for clemency on the grounds of Despard's earlier service, was committed to pushing for the full penalties of law. He was found guilty and on 21 February 1803 carried on a hurdle to his place of execution, the Surrey county gaol at Newington. From the scaffold, he told the waiting twenty thousand spectators that he was innocent of treason and had ever been 'a friend to truth, to liberty, and to justice . . . to the poor and the oppressed'. Despard was hanged and then decapitated, his skull lifted for all the crowd to see: 'This is the head of a traitor.'[44]

The later 1790s were not kind to the leading lights of English radicalism. At the beginning of his French exile, Paine had been fêted by the Convention and in August 1792 he was named an honorary French citizen. The following month, he was elected as a deputy for Calais. However, the pace of revolutionary events in France was quickening, the orderly process that he hoped would lead to the creation of a new French constitution descending instead into violence and dictatorship. Paine, whose French was very limited, was left floundering.

Power was slipping out of the hands of his allies, the Girondins, into those of the Jacobins led by Marat and Robespierre. A key dividing line between the camps was their respective attitudes to the fate of Louis XVI. The Girondins reluctantly agreed to his trial on the strength of incriminating evidence found among the King's papers, but Paine in particular argued in the Convention, in a speech read out in French translation, against passing a capital sentence. He was shouted down. Increasingly hostile noises were made in Paine's direction: a delegation from Arras proclaimed that they no longer wished him to represent them in the Convention. On 27 December 1793, on the orders of Robespierre, he was arrested, and was given just enough time to hand over the English manuscript of his classic attack on organised religion, *The Age of Reason*, before being escorted to prison. There he languished for two years, at one point contracting a severe fever that left him in a state of semi-consciousness for several weeks.

Paine was finally released in November 1794, through the intercession of the new American ambassador to Paris, James Monroe. Paine continued to be active in writing, publishing *Agrarian Justice* in 1796, which revisited, but in a more radical vein, the redistributive schemes of the 'social chapter' of *Rights of Man*. He also used his pen as an outlet for the bitter sense of betrayal he felt at his treatment in Paris, for which he held the American government responsible. From Paine's perspective, his service to the American republic and his US citizenship ought to have afforded him better protection. An open letter to Washington, once the recipient of Paine's highest praises, was filled with anger and bile. Monroe distanced himself from Paine and would not allow him to return with him when he was recalled to Washington in November 1797. Paine continued to write: he became embroiled in the intrigues aimed at facilitating a French invasion of the British Isles; but his heart no longer appeared to be in these struggles, his attentions increasingly reverting to his scientific and technological interests.

In March 1802, peace between Britain and France finally allowed Paine to return to America, his adopted homeland. He was, though, no more warmly welcomed there than in France. Federalists saw him as a useful bogeyman with which to smear

Jefferson by association: a tactic assisted by Paine's own habit of making public private correspondence between himself and Jefferson. The Federalist press pulled no punches in its assault on his character, the *General Advertiser* calling him 'that living opprobrium of humanity . . . the infamous scavenger of all the filth which could be raked from the dirty paths which have been hitherto trodden by all the revilers of Christianity'. The *Baltimore Republican* called him a 'loathsome reptile', the *Philadelphia Port Folio* 'a drunken atheist, and the scavenger of faction'; while Boston's *Mercury and New-England Palladium* described him as a 'lying, drunken brutal infidel, who rejoiced in the opportunity of basking and wallowing in the confusion, devastation, bloodshed, rapine, and murder, in which his soul delights'.

The hostility was so great that Paine was forced to register under a pseudonym in order to secure a hotel room in Washington. When his whereabouts were discovered, one Federalist wrote: 'He dines at the public table, and, as a show, is as profitable to Lovell [the hotel owner] as an Ourang Outang, for many strangers who come to the city feel a curiosity to see the creature.' Equally, for those caught up in the religious revival of the Second Great Awakening, Paine's deist views, frankly expressed in *The Age of Reason*, were unconscionable. A seed merchant who had deigned to shake the hand of the author of *Rights of Man* was suspended from singing for three months by his Presbyterian church.[45]

In 1804 Paine retired to his farm in New Rochelle, but he was increasingly beset by financial problems, which he dealt with by selling portions of his property. The farm seems, in any case, to have become too much for an elderly man in need of company and care. From spring 1806 he lived in a series of inns and rented apartments, and was looked after by his remaining friends. In January 1809, he set out his will, leaving most of his remaining estate to the children of Mme Bonneville, the wife of a friend and now a close companion of his as well. In May, he and Mme Bonneville moved into his last residence, in Greenwich Village, New York. Paine died on the morning of 8 June 1809, resolutely refusing the attempts of local ministers to get him to acknowledge his sins and commit his soul to God. His will had instructed burial in the local Quaker cemetery but the Society of Friends, perhaps mindful of Paine's attacks on the sect during the Revolutionary War, refused. Instead, his remains were interred on his New Rochelle farm. They did not rest in the ground long. In 1819 his former Federalist antagonist William Cobbett, now a convert to radicalism, dug up his bones and returned them to England for a more fitting burial, but the project was never fully realised and they were scattered, the skull supposedly finding its way to Australia.[46]

After disastrous liaisons with the Swiss bisexual painter Henry Fuseli and the American fraudster, adventurer and novelist Gilbert Imlay, Mary Wollstonecraft had become one half of the most celebrated radical couple in London. William Godwin had become entranced with Wollstonecraft, after an initially frosty meeting five years earlier, through reading her *Letters from Norway*: 'If ever there was a book calculated to make a man in love with its author, this appears to me to be the book. She speaks of her sorrows in a way that fills us with melancholy, and dissolves us in tenderness, at the same time she displays a genius which commands all our admiration.'[47] Their love affair developed first through writing, enabling the inexperienced Godwin to overcome his social awkwardness. In July 1796, he wrote to Wollstonecraft: 'I love your imagination, your delicate epicurism, the malicious leer of your eye, in short everything that constitutes the bewitching *tout ensemble* of the celebrated Mary.'[48]

When their relationship did finally come to be consummated, the methodical Godwin recorded their love-making via a code of dashes and dots in his journal. Nonetheless, in keeping with his belief in the evils attendant on cohabitation, they continued to live, work and socialise more or less separately. Yet despite both writers' public condemnation of the institution of marriage, Godwin and Wollstonecraft did eventually marry, on 29 March

1797. The impetus was almost certainly Wollstonecraft's pregnancy: though a doughty flouter of convention herself, Mary had no wish for another of her children (she already had a daughter by Imlay) to endure the stigma of bastardy.

Their living arrangements remained essentially the same. Although they now rented a house together at 29 Polygon Buildings, Somers Town, London, Godwin also rented rooms to work in near by and stayed there until dinnertime each day; this arrangement, he said, combined 'the novelty and lively sensation of a visit, with the more delicious and heart-felt pleasures of domestic life'. Mary, for her part, teased Godwin: 'A husband is a convenient part of the furniture of a house . . . I wish you, from my soul, to be riveted in my heart, but I do not desire to have you always at my elbow.'[49]

On 31 August 1797 she gave birth to a daughter, Mary Wollstonecraft Godwin. The pregnancy and the birth had been uncomplicated, but during labour a small part of the placenta had broken off in the womb. Attempts to remove it led to bleeding and infection. Wollstonecraft developed a high fever. Godwin sought the best medical advice he could get, including consulting John Gale Jones, the man-midwife and LCS member. But it was too late. Eleven days after giving birth, Mary Wollstonecraft died. Godwin told a close friend that he never expected to find happiness again.

Godwin's grief could not even be endured in private. Loyalist writers crowed that Wollstonecraft's death was punishment for an immoral life. The Reverend Richard Polwhele, in his *Unsex'd Females: A Poem* (1798), wrote:

I cannot but think, that the Hand of Providence is visible . . . [in the way] she was given up to her 'heart's lusts', and let 'to follow her own imaginations', that the fallacy of her doctrines and the effects of an irreligious conduct, might be manifested to the world; and as she died a death that strongly marked the distinction of the sexes, by pointing out the destiny of women, and the disease to which they are liable.[50]

Godwin threw himself into the effort of writing a memoir in vindication of his wife. His work remains the starting point for all subsequent biographers; but it was not an easy task, nor one for which Godwin was praised. Fuseli callously refused Godwin's request for letters that Wollstonecraft had written to the painter, taunting him by showing him the drawer in which they lay, many unopened, and then shutting it again with a sneer. Godwin's readiness to detail his wife's earlier affairs also brought criticism from friends that he was only further tarnishing her reputation. Southey felt that Godwin's memoir had stripped 'his dead wife naked'; Roscoe accused him in poetry of mourning her 'with a heart of stone'. Godwin's frankness about his wife's previous sexual relationships was lapped up gleefully by the anti-Jacobin press, which used Wollstonecraft's example to demonstrate the connection between 'promiscuity' and revolutionary politics.[51] Godwin's own status as the leading philosopher of radicalism was on the wane. He wrote several novels after *St Leon*, but these became increasingly conventional in substance and tone. By 1812, his future son-in-law, Percy Shelley, was surprised to find that Godwin was still alive.

In the twenty-first century, Godwin, Wollstonecraft and Paine have all been rehabilitated: Paine as the tireless advocate of the rights of man; Godwin as the intellectual founder of modern anarchism and brilliant novelist of human psychology; and Wollstonecraft as a proto-feminist in both her life and her writings. The most remarkable turnaround has been in the reputation of Paine, now transformed into the darling of both the right and the left, especially in the United States, where to date, through the efforts of the Friends of Thomas Paine, no fewer than nine state legislatures have declared 'Thomas Paine Days'.[52]

The tributes to each of them represent a combination of half-truths and convenient appropriations. Thomas Spence was labelled an early socialist because of his concern with the redistribution of landed property. Yet Spence, like most eighteenth-century radicals, fundamentally distrusted the idea of the 'big state' that appeals to many modern socialists. The distrust was hardly surprising. In the eighteenth century the so-called 'fiscal-military' state had no interest in the welfare of its subjects: its essential concerns were waging war and raising and collecting the taxes to pay for it. Similarly, Tom Paine was in favour of measures to assist the young and the old, paid for by redistributive taxation, but he was no opponent of emergent capitalism or of the acquisition of personal wealth from trade and commerce. Wollstonecraft was certainly a fierce advocate of the equality of the sexes but her notion of equality, with its emphasis on the exercise of republican virtue, has little in common with modern feminism. Nevertheless, these eighteenth-century radicals remain tempting sources for political inspiration. Their writings seem so deceptively modern – shorn, we wrongly think, of the religious preoccupations of the seventeenth century. But Godwin genuinely believed in the possibility of immortality and Joseph Priestley thought the French Revolution heralded the Second Coming. The 'Age of Reason' had not yet come to pass (nor, perhaps, has it ever).

By the time of Wollstonecraft's death, the sense of millenarian excitement and feverish anticipation that had marked the early 1790s had dissipated, to be replaced with feelings of dread and terror. The political gains of British radicalism appeared minimal. Fewer men, as a proportion of the population, now enjoyed the vote than in 1640. Attempts to get reform bills through Parliament had repeatedly failed. The government's power had been consolidated through repressive legislation. Working-class political organisations disintegrated, torn between desperate insurrectionary splinter groups and the more respectable reform organisations established to fill the corresponding societies' place.

Even to historians sympathetic to the aspirations of radicals, it has often seemed hard to pick out real radical achievements from the era of the French Revolution. E. P. Thompson famously claimed that this decade was seminal in the formation of working-class identity, but organisations like the LCS were dominated by a

Whiggish ideology of gradual reform that was largely bereft of the language of class. Their membership, too, was heterodox and some of their most prominent members came from wealthy landed or professional backgrounds. Some historians have sought consolation in the argument that radicalism was only beaten by the resort to an appeal to the people through popular loyalism. Yet, loyalism did not emerge out of thin air. Loyalist rhetoric and loyalist organisation – via addresses and associations – had been a key feature of political life for nearly a century. The Paine burnings, Reevesian associations and loyalist chapbooks and pamphlets hardly constituted the creation of a new 'public sphere' for rational debate.

The 1790s were nonetheless a critical period in the history of English radicalism. The decade saw as bright a florescence of radical thought as had been witnessed during the civil wars. It also saw the formation, in the form of the corresponding societies, of the first working-class-initiated and -dominated political organisations. These societies would establish many features of the radical agenda over the next half-century: agitation for parliamentary reform and an expanded franchise by means of mass political meetings, political parties and a radical press. It was the working-class radicals in particular who pushed the issue of the vote to the forefront of British radical politics. In contrast, in the writings of the radical luminaries of the revolutionary era, Paine, Godwin and Wollstonecraft, the issue of the franchise had been largely neglected. Yet the 1790s also represented a missed opportunity. The success with which loyalists had attacked the 'levelling' and 'republican' principles of radicals during that decade meant that social reform, the redistribution of wealth and thoroughgoing constitutional change, the most radical elements of the agitation of the 1790s, were now marginalised. This was despite the fact that the early decades of the nineteenth century saw a steep decline in the living standards of the poor. Reform had become more respectable, but also distinctly less 'radical'.

PART FIVE

The Mask of Anarchy: Radicalism from Waterloo to the Great Reform Act

For reets o'mon, for liberty to vote, an' speak an' write, an' be eawrsels [ourselves] – honest, hard-workin' folk. We wanted to live eawr own lives an' th' upper classes wouldn't let us. That's abeawt it, lad.

Handloom-weaver and Peterloo veteran Joseph Wrigley speaking in the 1870s to journalist James Haslam about the St Peter's Fields meeting[1]

A ROPE OF SAND

The term 'radical' began to be used in its more modern sense, meaning relating to thoroughgoing progressive constitutional reform, during the French Revolutionary Wars. This was a period of intense popular political agitation, a time when mass meetings, marches and demonstrations became key components of public life. Yet, though this was the first time that the term 'radical' was actively appropriated by contemporaries, rather than fastened on groups and individuals by subsequent historians, it was also arguably in this period that the British radical agenda narrowed, to focus predominantly on electoral reform.

The issue was undoubtedly pressing: the electoral system had noticeably failed to keep track of population growth, such that the electorate had declined as a proportion of the population from 5.2 per cent in 1715 to 3.2 per cent on the eve of the Great Reform Act.[1] Nonetheless, the character of British radicalism overall was undoubtedly changing. In the face of the ongoing threat (until 1815) of French invasion, pressure from the loyalist press and government censorship, radicalism took on a more patriotic, more 'Anglo-Saxon' hue. The Painite emphasis on universal human rights, and on the need for social as well as political reform, now smacked too much of French influence or dangerous 'Levellerism'. Talk of inalienable natural rights and interventionist social policy on the part of government, except with regard to prisons, was also anathema to the emerging radical philosophical creed of utilitarianism, founded by Jeremy Bentham. At the same time the anticlericalism of English radicalism became more subdued. The mainstream of radicalism thereby became paradoxically less 'radical' just at the moment that it began to embrace the term enthusiastically.

As we shall see, there continued to be a violent, insurrectionary strain to radicalism, though the strength of the 'physical force' wing was exaggerated by the activities of government agents provocateurs. That aspect of radical activity could look more threatening when combined with serious industrial unrest – the waves of machine-breaking that occurred mainly between 1811 and 1814, and which, in the North West in particular, betrayed the influence of radical political ideas and rhetoric. The government responded with a swift, severe and largely effective repression, utilising both the law and force of arms. In negative terms, the most significant impact of popular radicalism may have been in eventually convincing the Whig Party in Parliament (and some moderate Tories) to support reform in order to consolidate power and stave off the threat of revolution.

But this period was significant in the history of English radicalism for more positive reasons too: it largely established the platform of political reform – universal male suffrage, secret ballots, annual parliaments, and equal electoral districts – advocated later by the Chartists; it established, too, the methods for achieving this goal – mass political meetings, petitions and propaganda disseminated through pro-reform newspapers. It saw the emergence of the first women-only reform organisations and the increasing public involvement of women in politics, as well as the first thoroughgoing critiques not simply of the unreformed constitution, but of the capitalist economic system that was driving British industrialisation.

Early nineteenth-century radicalism, then, set the agenda for reformers for much of the next fifty years. Its most enduring and powerful legacy, however, came from its greatest tragedy: the massacre by yeomen cavalry and professional soldiers of unarmed demonstrators on 19 August 1819 that came to be known as 'Peterloo'. This atrocity created a powerful memory of working-class political activism that inspired not only future British radicals but liberation movements the world over.

Although popular radical movements had not been completely snuffed out (especially in the capital), during the first decade of the nineteenth century efforts were targeted at Westminster and at achieving reform through parliamentary means. Hopes in this regard peaked when Pitt resigned in 1801, ostensibly over the issue of Catholic emancipation, but perhaps also because of his increasingly poor health (not helped by his daily consumption of six bottles of wine). Radical hopes within Westminster were fastened upon Sir Francis Burdett, a gentleman reformer whose father-in-law Thomas Coutts, founder of the banking dynasty, had bought him the pocket borough of Boroughbridge.

Despite owing his place in the House entirely to the corrupt nature of the unreformed constitution, Burdett was one of the most outspoken figures in the Commons in opposing the repressive measures of the first Pitt ministry – the Combination Acts,* the suspension of Habeas Corpus and the exclusion of reporters from the House. In the general election of 1802 he was invited to stand as candidate for the county of Middlesex; he won the contest, but the election was voided on the grounds of voting irregularities. However, as his opponent William Mainwaring had also engaged

---

* The Combination Acts of 1799 and 1802 prohibited trade unions and all levels of collective bargaining by workers.

in electoral sharp practice, 'treating' (bribing) voters, a new election was called in 1804.

William Cobbett, one-time author of the anti-Jacobin periodical the *Porcupine*, now turned his new journal, the *Political Register*, to the cause of reform, partly out of personal pique for having been convicted of libelling the Lord Chancellor of Ireland. More important, though, was Cobbett's belief that the victory of the banker Mainwaring would represent a triumph of parasitic 'new money' over a man of unimpeachable noble lineage. (Here Cobbett overlooked the fact that most of Burdett's money came from his banker in-laws.) Though Burdett again triumphed in the popular vote, the action of the sheriffs in discounting all votes cast after 3 p.m., even though the poll itself closed at five, gave the seat to Mainwaring. Burdett took pleasure in the sheriffs' decision, sensing an opportunity to turn this contested election into a wider controversy over the fairness of the electoral system itself. With the help of the veteran reformer Major John Cartwright, Burdett's disgruntled supporters had by November 1804 formed the Middlesex Freeholders' Club to raise funds for his campaign to overturn Mainwaring's election. The campaign ultimately proved successful; but only a year after taking his seat, Burdett was voted out, unable to bear the costs of another election campaign.[2]

Nonetheless, hopes that the parliamentary road to reform might prove successful remained high. The death of Pitt in January 1806 had brought Charles James Fox into government, a change that veterans of the radical struggles of the 1790s such as Thomas Hardy viewed with optimism. In this, his last year, however, Fox was preoccupied with other issues beyond electoral reform, namely Catholic emancipation – the same cause over which George III had blocked Pitt – and the abolition of the slave trade. Fox's focus on these concerns was seen as something of a betrayal by London radicals, even though he had, in fact, always expressed ambivalence about electoral reform.

The Whig Party as a whole, including its more progressive

wing, existed in a rather uneasy relationship with popular radical-ism. The 'people' were often invoked in Whig rhetoric, but this did not make it a party of democrats. For the Whigs, parliamen-tary, not popular, sovereignty was what was important. Indeed, public opinion, in the shape of popular anti-Popery, seemed a threat to some cherished Whig objectives – most obviously, Catholic emancipation. These differences between Whiggery and radicalism emerged in distinct attitudes towards the monarchy and British history. Whigs believed in constitutional monarchy, in which a legally bound Crown worked in partnership with Parliament. Most radicals, on the other hand, were not republi-cans, but believed in a form of popular monarchism which saw a direct, even emotional, connection between monarch and people. That link could prove very important when Parliament was deemed to be deaf to the people's wishes. So whereas Whigs con-tinued to venerate the supposedly bloodless Glorious Revolution of 1688–9 as a key moment in British constitutional history, radi-cals could favour more violent episodes, like the Peasants' Revolt of 1381, when the aristocracy was bypassed and politics consisted of a negotiation between King and commons.[3]

Fox did not live to see either abolition or Catholic emancipa-tion achieved. A notorious rake, gourmand and imbiber, he died in September 1806 of dropsy. The post-mortem revealed a severely hardened liver, thirty-five gallstones and over seven pints of fluid in his abdomen. Though the short-lived 'Ministry of All the Talents' had done next to nothing for reform, Fox's passing was mourned by leading radicals, including John Thelwall and William Godwin. There were certainly both positive and negative repercussions for radicals in Fox's death: on the one hand, it seemed to weaken the possibility of an alliance between reformers outside of Parliament, but on the other, it necessitated another general election, which appeared to offer radicals the chance to elect members sympathetic to reform, especially within Fox's old constituency Westminster, with its broad 'scot and lot' franchise.

The reform candidate, James Paull, was defeated, but polled an encouraging number of votes. When another general election was called in April 1807, after Parliament had been dissolved when the King refused to give his assent to a bill allowing Catholics to become officers in the army, Paull – whose relationship with other London radicals was seriously strained – was rather unceremoniously dumped by the Westminster Freeholders' Club and replaced with Burdett.*

The dispute demonstrated the fissiparous nature of London radicalism and foreshadowed later splits and disagreements, but the divisions were obscured by Burdett's convincing victory. It was met with an ecstatic response, the religious writer and actuary William Frend warning the Whigs and Tories that a third party, 'the Public', would now have 'some share in the game'. The Whig candidate, the playwright Richard Brinsley Sheridan, reportedly polled so badly that the sherrifs allowed him to double-count his votes in order to save some face.[4] The former London Corresponding Society member John Gale Jones called the final day of the election, 23 May, a 'day sacred to Freedom'.[5]

By the summer of 1807, radical hopes were firmly fixed on securing greater parliamentary influence. The future leader of the marchers at Peterloo, Henry Hunt, a gentleman farmer with an estate of over three thousand acres in Wiltshire and, like his fellow farmer William Cobbett, a late convert to reform, attempted, unsuccessfully, to follow Burdett's example in Bristol.[6] Cartwright also tried to gain a seat in the Commons, and shifted his literary energies from producing populist works like *Take Your Choice* to targeting ministers and MPs sympathetic to reform in *England's Aegis, or the military energies of the Constitution*.[7] Cartwright was nonetheless disappointed with

---

* Paull had fought a duel with Burdett a mere two days before his deselection. Paull's vengeful behaviour at the duel – he had demanded that the pistols be reloaded and fired again after the first shots missed – alienated many metropolitan reformists. The dishonoured reformist committed suicide a year later. Paull's request that his body be returned to the East Indies – he had made his fortune as a trader in Lucknow, India – and then blown up was not honoured.

Burdett's inactivity in Parliament, especially his refusal to sponsor a reform bill immediately. Burdett responded that he needed to win over his parliamentary colleagues first by 'not making violent motions and acting the savage'.[8] However, events in Europe soon gave fresh impetus to reform. The decision of the British government to intervene militarily to support the Spanish and Portuguese people in their uprising against Napoleon in the summer of 1808 recast British foreign policy as a crusade for freedom against French tyranny. In this context, liberty and reform could scarcely seem unpatriotic. The Peninsular War, too, provided background for the successful campaign against Prince Frederick, the Duke of York, George III's second (and favourite) son and the Commander-in-Chief of the British army, who was charged with having sold promotions to officers who had paid bribes to his mistress, Mary Anne Clark. After intensive pressure from the Whigs, along with Burdett, the Duke was forced to resign on 17 March 1809.

The Duke's resignation seemed to open up the opportunity for Foxite Whigs like Samuel Whitbread, Thomas Brand, Samuel Romilly, Henry Brougham and Lord Folkestone to unite with the more populist radicals, Burdett and Thomas, Lord Cochrane (whose naval successes against the French had raised his public stock). Cartwright engineered a number of dinner meetings under the auspices of the Committee of Friends to Parliamentary Reform (founded in 1808). At the triumphal dinner held at the Crown and Anchor tavern on 1 May 1809 and attended by over twelve hundred people, many leading reformers were present, including Cartwright, Cochrane and Francis Place. However, Whitbread and Lord Folkestone did not attend. Gwyllym Lloyd Wardle, MP, who had led the attack on the Duke of York, informed the attendees that there was widespread support across the country for reform, citing fifteen thousand signatures in support from Sheffield and another four thousand from Paisley. However, the prospect of cooperation between the Whigs and more radical reformers was weakened by the public animosity expressed by some, such as the linen draper Robert Waithman, who called them 'professed lovers of Places, Pensions and Reversions'.[9]

Despite the evident tensions within the movement for reform, the 1 May meeting did finally get reform bills placed before Parliament. The first of these was moved by Burdett on 15 June, an auspicious date, chosen because it was the date of the 'signing' of Magna Carta: Burdett was keen to assure the House that the bill was nothing more than a confirmation of England's 'ancient constitution'. There was nothing in it, he said, that could not already be found in 'the Statute Book and recognised by the Common Law of the Land'.[10] The bill called for annual parliaments, the equalisation of constituencies and a taxpayer franchise. Despite the evident moderation both in the substance of the bill and in the rhetoric used to promote it, Burdett's motion was discussed by a very sparsely attended House and the bill was defeated by seventy-nine votes to fifteen.

Not only was Parliament as a whole apparently unmoved by the cause of reform, it also continued to guard the privacy of its proceedings jealously. On 2 February Charles Yorke, MP for Cambridgeshire, had brought in a motion for the enforcement of the standing order expelling strangers (meaning reporters) from the Commons. John Gale Jones was then brought before the bar for allegedly placarding the House with bills calling Yorke's motion a 'public outrage'. Despite offering an apology, Gale Jones was sent to Newgate Prison. Burdett petitioned before the Commons for his release and, significantly, when this failed, published a letter in Cobbett's *Political Register* denying the House had the power to imprison English subjects. The response of the Commons was to vote to commit Burdett to the Tower until the end of the parliamentary session. Fittingly for a man who had made his stand for reform on the basis of the liberties granted by England's 'ancient constitution', he was arrested while at home listening to his son, just down from Eton, translate Magna Carta from Latin into English.[11]

Burdett's imprisonment raised his popularity among radicals to a pitch not seen since his election victory in 1807. However, the aspirations now invested in him frequently far exceeded the baronet's own essentially Whiggish political ideology. He was depicted as the slayer of tyrants and despots, the 'pilot' who would lead England to an egalitarian Utopia. One handbill read:

> When the LION gets out of the Tower
> How Happy will ENGLISHMEN BE
> He'll the RATS of the NATION *DEVOUR*
> And Britons, from Thraldom set Free – !!![12]

Cartwright and other London radicals hoped to exploit Burdett's release, scheduled for 21 June 1810, as a great propaganda victory for the cause of reform. Crowds were to wear blue cockades and carry banners saying 'Magna Carta', 'The Constitution' and 'Burdett For Ever!' However, he proved unwilling to take on the mantle of popular champion, preferring to slink away on a Thames riverboat, thereby earning himself the nickname 'Sir Francis Sly-Go' from Henry Hunt.[13] Burdett claimed that his no-show was borne out of fear of bloodshed, should the crowd's behaviour get out of hand. He may also have been concerned about his own personal safety. Perhaps influential too was the advice of his mentor, John Horne Tooke, that courting popularity by implication left a politician's reputation at the mercy of the mob.

Another possibility is that Burdett was encouraged by the success that Foxite Whigs had already had in promoting more limited reform bills through Parliament. (Tellingly, it was another moderate reformer, William Frend, who had brought the vessel that had taken Burdett from the Tower unobserved.) A bill introduced in the Commons in May by Thomas Brand, an opposition Whig, which substituted triennial for annual parliaments and the gradual, compensated elimination of rotten boroughs rather than immediate equalisation, had secured 115 votes in favour, the best showing by a reform bill since the 1780s.[14] The success was, however, deceptive. The Whig leadership was never in any sense committed in principle to the cause of reform, and Brand's relative success was not followed up. Meetings engineered by Cartwright between Brand, Burdett and their supporters petered out in the spring of 1811. As John Disney, Cartwright's cousin, remarked, 'We have nothing but general principle to unite us – and the moment specific propositions are named, we become a rope of sand.'[15]

But even Disney's sense that there were core principles uniting Whigs and London radicals was illusory. Francis Jeffrey, editor of the *Edinburgh Review*, in an article of January 1810 argued that a dangerous confrontation was building up between the 'courtiers' and the democrats, while the 'constitutional Whigs' in between were becoming increasingly powerless. He felt the democrats should ally themselves with more respectable bits of the popular party, 'to temper its violence and moderate its excesses, till it can be guided in safety to the defence, and not to the destruction of our liberties'. Jeffrey urged figures like Sir Francis Burdett to stand behind a moderate reform programme aimed at eliminating rotten boroughs and extending the franchise to respectable citizens – exactly the kinds of proposal that Brand had had some success with in May of that year, and that would eventually become enshrined in law in 1832. In this formulation, as in 1832, Jeffrey proposed reform as offering a safety-valve that would release some of the popular hostility towards the political establishment. Reform, as Jeffrey indicated, was about consolidating 'ancient liberties', not winning new freedoms.

Many Whigs were not even prepared to go this far. John Allen, confidant of Byron's friend Lord Holland, stated: 'When the country is decidedly for it, the object [reform] is so great that it might be worth while to break up the party to obtain it – but to take it up prematurely would divide opposition without advancing the cause of reform.'[16] The exploitation of the revelations of corruption in the Duke of York's case, while productive in the short term, carried fundamental problems for more radical reformers. It made the case for electoral reform as a measure that would cleanse the Augean stables of English politics, not as a means of bringing democracy to the people.*

Away from Westminster, radical activity was also being squeezed as libel laws were broadened to allow ex-officio information – accusations filed by the Solicitor-General, Attorney-General or some other Crown officer – to be used in such cases. Now, the accusation of libel did not have to be approved by a grand jury. This new power caused Jeremy Bentham to conclude that 'by law there exists no more liberty of the press in England than in Morocco'.[17]

From late 1809, the radical press came under sustained attack in a spate of libel prosecutions. Daniel Lovell of the *Statesman* was sentenced on three counts of seditious libel, fined £1000 and imprisoned for three years, with a further three years on a good-behaviour bond after his release. John Drakard of the *Stamford News* was imprisoned for eighteen months for publishing an article against severe flogging in the army, even though John and Leigh Hunt had been acquitted for publishing exactly the same piece in their *Examiner*. (The government nonetheless managed to get them on another charge at the end of 1812.) Cobbett too was tried and convicted for libel: the government's success, it was widely believed, signalled the death knell for his *Political Register*.[18] Burdett's reputation was tarnished further when it was revealed that he had been conducting an adulterous relationship with Lady Oxford, which had resulted in at least one love child. (The dubious paternity of the Oxford children meant they were widely known as

* The anti-corruption strain to reformist rhetoric was nonetheless a persistent one, even within popular radicalism. A great deal of Hunt's rhetoric in favour of reform was based on the notion that it would overturn the corrupt 'court party' and thereby reduce waste, leading in turn to a reduction in taxation.

the 'Harleian Miscellany', after the collected volumes of rare pamphlets in the library of the 1st and 2nd Earls of Oxford.) Burdett's description of the Duke of York as 'a picture of hypocrisy and profligacy truly revolting to propriety and decency' was gleefully thrown back in his face by loyalist writers.[19]

Cartwright's tactic of encouraging cooperation between Foxite Whigs and parliamentary radicals through gentlemanly dinner meetings was also proving a dead end. Some radicals were losing patience with the idea that reform would come from within the Commons itself. Henry Hunt described the notion of Parliament reforming itself as 'contemptible and ridiculous'.[20] Burdett talked of politics at Westminster as a 'low farce'. It was hoped that the King's insanity, and the installation of his son as Prince Regent, would usher in a new ministry more sympathetic to reform. However, the general election of 1812, despite significant radical efforts to put up candidates, resulted in a convincing Tory victory, even in areas like Bristol where there was considerable reformist activity.

Cartwright began to think that exerting pressure from outside of Parliament was the only realistic means of putting reform back on the political agenda. The previous year his friend, the Devon reformer, geologist and inventor (of unsinkable lifeboats, semaphore telegraphs and schemes for naming the bones of the body) Thomas Northmore, had proposed a reform society to be called the Hampden Club. The first of these opened in May 1811. Its subscription of three guineas and requirement of a £300 property qualification for full membership indicated that it was not designed to be a working-class institution like the old LCS. The aged Cartwright was opposed to the socially restrictive terms of the Hampden Clubs, seeing them as indicative of the lukewarm Whig approach to reform as a whole. He worked to establish more popular societies under the banner of the Union for Parliamentary Reform, launched in June of the same year.[21] To spur the growth of these clubs, he went on extensive tours of the country. On his second tour of 1813 he travelled more than nine hundred miles in twenty-nine days and visited three hundred communities. By 1817, in no small part as a result of his efforts, 150 Hampden Clubs had been formed in the North West. Unlike the original, these clubs were far more socially inclusive, with much lower subscription rates. Aside from establishing political reform clubs, Cartwright's tours were aimed at gathering signatures for mass petitions. To this end, he would print multiple copies of the petition in question, ready to be signed – an advance on the old method of affixing signatures to one long roll of manuscript. His tour of 1813 gathered 130,000 signatures in support of a taxpayer franchise and annual parliaments.

Cartwright's model for his tours had been the successful petitioning campaign that had contributed to the ending of British involvement in the slave trade in 1807. However, for all the names that had been gathered in support of them, Cartwright's petitions received scant attention from the Commons. Indeed, despite Cartwright's apparent intention to educate people in the provinces in the ways of correctly addressing the Commons, most of his petitions were rejected on the grounds that they were inappropriately framed. The implication, as the historian Olivia Smith has noted, was that 'the disenfranchised could not write in a language which merited attention'.[22]*

More importantly, Cartwright's pro-reform campaign chimed with another, more threatening, popular movement. Between 1803 and 1814, Parliament repealed most of the Elizabethan paternalist legislation that had offered protection to weavers and clothworkers. Regulations that forbade the use of machinery and the employment of unskilled or semi-skilled workers, and required the enforcement of a minimum wage in certain industries were swept away.[24] At the same time, the Combination Acts enthusiastically

* Petitioning continues to this day to be regulated by an act of 1661 against 'tumultuous' petitioning, and by eighteenth-century notions of 'decent and respectable language'.[23]

supported by that lover of liberty William Wilberforce, severely limited workers' ability to defend their rights by collective action. Although the terms of the act applied to combinations of employers as well as to trade unions, a legal action against four hosiers initiated by Gravener Henson, the leader of the Nottinghamshire framework knitters, failed in 1811. Whatever the letter of the law, it clearly applied only to employees. When stockingers in Nottingham succeeded in forming a union of 2390 members with a common fund of £195, their organisation was broken up by an employers' committee that was equally illegal under the strict terms of the Combination Acts.[25]

Partly inspired by Cartwright's tours, the textile workers began petitioning campaigns of their own, which were equally successful in securing signatures and equally unsuccessful in having any influence on Parliament. The indifference of the Commons was clearly demonstrated by the repeal of the Elizabethan Statute of Artificers, which defined the conditions of apprenticeship, despite petitions signed by some 300,000 people urging retention. Between 1811 and 1812, a committee of trades representatives in the Manchester area, encouraged by John Knight, a small manufacturer who was to have a long career in radical politics, was trying to arrange a petition to the Commons to bring both peace and reform. The idea was scotched in June 1812 when the Deputy Constable of Manchester raided a meeting and arrested those present on a charge (subsequently refuted in court) of administering unlawful oaths. Economic grievances and political reform appeared to be becoming increasingly intertwined, as an address published in October 1811 complained:

They, the Members of that House, can make arrangements which advance the price of provisions – increase your taxes – introduce such a state of things as diminishes your business and employment, and reduces your wages, and when you state to them that you cannot exist under these accumulated and accumulating evils, they

then coolly tell you they *cannot* relieve you. Had you possessed
70,000 votes for the election of Members to sit in that House,
would your application have been treated with such indifference,
not to say inattention? We believe not.[26]

Cartwright, himself no social radical – he once told Thomas
Hardy that he was opposed to 'any attempt to excite the poor to
invade the property of the rich'[27] – had journeyed north on his
first tour in 1812 in part to support the thirty-nine Manchester
reformers, including John Knight, indicted over links with
machine-breaking activities.[28] Cartwright's willingness to appeal to
working-class groups led some moderate reformers, such as the
Reverend Charles Wyvill, to denounce him as an incendiary.[29] His
decision to tour areas suffering from industrial unrest also brought
him into conflict with the authorities. He was arrested at
Huddersfield on 22 January 1813 at a meeting held only a week
after the execution of fourteen machine-breakers, but managed to
avoid any further punishment.[30]

KING LUDD

The problem for reformers such as Cartwright who were willing to court popularity and attempt to bring to Parliament
political pressure for reform was that petitioning was not the sole
tactic employed by the depressed textile workers of the North West
and the Midlands. Indeed, what is surprising, given its ineffec-
tiveness, is how long workers persisted with mass petitioning as a
means to influence the government. (Admittedly, as we shall see,
this petitioning was not as humble as tradition required: it was
often accompanied by the threat of violence.) Alongside petitioning, textile workers in these two areas used a combination of the
anonymous – or, rather, pseudonymous – threat of damage to
machinery and physical harm to employers, and the perpetration
of real acts of violence against property and persons. A letter from
one 'Mr Pistol', written in Nottingham in January 1812, warned

all Persons what soever from takeing out work Called the Single
Preess, or the two Course [hole]* which is Condemn by Law, any

* Cheap stockings that could be mass produced with less skilled labour.

Persons Found so doing to the great _____ injuries of our Trade such People so found out shall be shot any Persons will bring me information of the offenders shall receive a reward of one Guinea to be Paid be me, Mr Pistol.[1]

The news of the assassination of the Prime Minister, Spencer Perceval, in the lobby of the House of Commons on 11 May 1812 by a bankrupt merchant, John Bellingham, bearing a grudge against the British government, was received with joy in many depressed parts of the country. In a town in the Potteries, 'A man came running down the street, leaping into the air, waving his hat round his head, and shouting with frantic joy, "Perceval is shot, hurrah! Perceval is shot, hurrah!"'[2] The Vicar of St Mark's, Liverpool, the assassin Bellingham's local church, received a threatening letter signed 'Jenkins, Lt de Luddites', for giving a sermon deploring the 'melancholy event'. 'Jenkins' poured scorn on the Vicar's sermon and added, 'Had it been in any other place than the church, my pistol would have silenced the blasphemy.' The radical overtones of the letter were made clear by the author's reference to the 'brave and patriotic Bellingham' and the threat of death to the 'depraved George the Prince'.[3]*

The pseudonym adopted by 'Jenkins, Lt de Luddites' linked Perceval's assassination with the wave of machine-breaking that swept the North West and the Midlands in the 1810s. 'Luddite' is a term now associated with an indiscriminate technophobia. The Luddites reputedly took their name from the apocryphal story of a village idiot, Ned Ludd, who, when told to 'square his needles' (adjust the mechanism of his frame loom), had instead smashed the loom to pieces with a hammer.[5] There has been a tendency, reflected in the work of some historians, to regard Luddite activity as essentially apolitical, or, at best, conservative

---

* Before his murder, Perceval had himself received anonymous letters threatening his death if he continued to pursue a bill to make frame-breaking a capital offence.[4]

in its outlook – seeking the restoration of a paternalistic 'moral economy' that the industrial revolution was inevitably consigning to the past.[6] It is certainly true that there was nothing new about machine-breaking; nor, indeed, was there anything peculiarly English about it. Already in 1675, Spitalfields weavers had destroyed 'engines' that could do the work of several people, and in 1710 a London hosier employing too many apprentices in violation of the Framework Knitters' Charter had his machines broken by angry stockingers. As a result of this unrest, by 1727 the breaking of machines had been made a capital felony.[7] There had also been serious outbreaks of Luddite-like activity in France in the wake of the revolution of 1789.[8]

The first Luddite attack took place in the Nottinghamshire village of Arnold. The workers' grievances were to do, first, with the use of wide stocking frames to produce large amounts of cheap, shoddy stocking material that was merely cut and sewn rather than completely fashioned, and, second, with the employment of 'colts' – workers who had not completed the seven-year apprenticeship required by law. Further disturbances broke out in the Midlands in the spring and autumn of 1811. By January 1812, frame-breaking had spread to Manchester and its environs; it continued into the winter and spring of 1812, resurfaced in 1814, then again in Leicestershire in the autumn of 1816. The different nature of weaving in the North West, with looms located in large factories, affected the form the machine-breaking took, with attacks involving larger numbers of people and, as factory owners had often made preparations for the defence of their property, frequently accompanied by acts of violence. In Yorkshire, it was not weaving frames but shearing machinery, used to finish wool, that was targeted. Attacks were made on gig mills (prohibited by law since the era of Edward VI), which raised the nap on woollen cloth to make it easier to finish, and on the shearing frames that mechanised the process of shearing itself. (Shearing had traditionally been done with very heavy hand-shears that required a great deal of skill and physical strength to use – the average pair weighed around eighteen kilos.⁹)

Some historians have pointed to the fragmented nature of Luddite activity – the main areas of unrest in the Midlands and the North West were separated by a distance of over fifty miles – suggesting that the outbreaks were essentially unconnected, with the sense of mass insurrection more a phantom of government paranoia than a reality.¹⁰ The notion that these were distinct, localised actions seems to be supported by the differences between Luddite rhetoric in the Midlands, in Yorkshire and in the North West. In Nottinghamshire, Luddites justified their actions on the basis of customary rights, enshrined in documents like the charter of the Company of Framework Knitters. This has often been con-trasted with the more radical, Jacobin language found in Luddite letters from Yorkshire and the North West.¹¹ Even this more clearly politicised language has sometimes been dismissed as empty posturing.

The problem with viewing Luddism as essentially conservative, or simply apolitical, is that both Luddites themselves and their opponents saw them as members of a nationwide conspiracy. Whether machine-breaking took place in the Midlands, Yorkshire or Lancashire, 'General Ludd' was seen behind it all. As the ballad 'Well Done Ned Ludd' cautioned hostile readers, 'Deface this who dare/Shall have the tyrants fare/For Ned's Everywhere/To both see and hear.'¹² Government spies firmly believed that a real 'General Ludd' existed, an insurrectionary mastermind orchestrating machine-breaking across the country. Abraham Kaye, a private in the Bolton militia, reported that he saw 'one called General Ludd, who had a pike in his hand, like a serjeant's halbert; I could not distinguish his face, which was very white, but not the natural colour'.¹³ A number of leading working-class radicals were identi-fied as Ludd, most notably Gravener Henson, Jem Towle and George Mellor (though Henson pointed out that at the time of the alleged insurrectionary activity he had the cast-iron alibi of being in prison).[14]

Real or imaginary, the figure of Ludd gave a sense of unity to the movement of industrial unrest. That feeling of community offered moral support to those engaged in or supportive of machine-breaking. Luddite letters and ballads helped reinforce this sense of a common cause. A letter from John and Maria Middleton in the town of Haughton to their son James in Nottingham reported their happiness at the news of a 'Luddite victory': 'We have enjoyed ourselves over a pot or two of beer and heared Mr Lud's song.'[15] Unquestionably, some of this Luddite literature was openly hostile to the government and the monarchy. A leaflet distributed in Yorkshire early in 1812 called on 'all Croppers, Weavers &c. & Public at large . . . to shake off the hateful Yoke of a Silly Old Man [George III]'.[16] Some letters were clearly revolutionary in tone. One from 'Eliza Ludd', dated 30 April 1812, stated: 'Doubtless you are well acquainted with the Political History of America, if so you must confess that, it was ministerial tyranny that gave rise to that glorious spirit in which the British Colonies obtain'd their independance by force of arms, at a period, when we was ten times as strong as now!'[17] This was almost certainly much more than mere talk. Failed attempts to effect a revolution by force emerged in former Luddite strongholds and involved personalities with past connections with Luddite activity.[18]

In response to the Luddite threat, there were few figures in authority willing to challenge the repressive measures imposed by Lord Liverpool's government. When the bill making frame-breaking a capital offence became law in 1813, it was condemned in the Lords by Byron: 'When a proposal is made to emancipate or relieve, you hesitate, you deliberate for years, you temporize and tamper with the minds of men; but a death-bill must be passed off hand, without a thought of the consequences.'[19] Byron's essentially eighteenth-century Whig political ideology allowed him more faith in the jury system than in his fellow peers:

Suppose [the bill] passed. Suppose one of these men, as I have seen them – meagre with famine, sullen with despair, careless of a life which your lordships are perhaps about to value at something less than the price of a stocking-frame – suppose this man (and there are a thousand such from whom you may select your victims) dragged into court to be tried for this new offence by this new law, still there are two things wanting to convict and condemn him; and these are, in my opinion, twelve butchers for a jury and a Jeffreys for a judge.[20]

This stirring rhetoric fell on deaf ears. The House of Lords, accustomed to speakers who observed official norms of politeness, was unused to hearing the Prime Minister compared to 'that Athenian lawgiver [Draco] whose edicts were said to be written . . . in blood'. Byron's speech was deemed too impertinent even to be worthy of a reply. Though the Whig Party's limited proposal for a commission to investigate measures to alleviate distress in the textile industry had been accepted, the resulting bill was hobbled by both Tories and opposition Whigs (including Byron's political mentor Lord Holland). The affair served to convince Byron to give up his brief political career, his pessimism clearly reflected in a poem to Lady Melbourne written on 21 September 1813:

> 'Tis said – *Indifference* marks the present time,
> Then hear the reason – though 'tis told in rhyme –
> A King who *can't* – a Prince of Wales who *don't* –
> Patriots who *shan't* – and Ministers who *won't* –
> What matters who are *in* or *out* of place,
> The *Mad* – the *Bad* – the *Useless* – or the *Base?*[21]

With the new legislation in place, prosecutions of Luddites proceeded quickly. The Cheshire judges of the special commission sentenced fourteen men to death, two of whom were actually executed. In Yorkshire, seventeen were hanged and one transported for life. In Lancashire, four people were sentenced to death, not for machine-breaking but for forcing dealers to sell bread, butter and cheese at lower prices. The destruction of Haughton Mill led to the conviction and sentencing to death of three men and one boy, Abraham Charlson, who had acted as a watchman: 'He was young for his age, and when he was brought to the scaffold, he "called on his mother for help, thinking she had the power to save him".'[22] The garrisoning that had been part of the repressive measures of the 1790s was increased. One hundred and fifty-five new barracks were placed in industrial districts between 1792 and 1815. The numbers of troops sent to quell the Luddite disturbances – twelve thousand – exceeded the total number of men under the Duke of Wellington's command on the Iberian peninsula.[23]

The scale of the military forces deployed against the Luddites is less surprising when it is borne in mind that some Luddite activity was more akin to mass armed insurrection than limited industrial sabotage. The attack on Rawfolds Mill in the Spen Valley was the most violent clash of this kind. The mill owner, William Cartwright, had responded to the wave of machine-breaking by turning his factory into a fortress, defended by soldiers and armed workmen and protected by barricades of spiked rollers. Undaunted, on 11 April 1812 some hundred and fifty Luddites, led by George Mellor, a young Huddersfield cloth-dresser, attempted to storm the mill. As some tried to pin down the defenders with covering fire, others, armed with hatchets and hammers, tried to break down the armoured doors. These men suffered heavy casualities, and two were mortally wounded. In the wake of the bloody raid on Rawfolds, a local minister, Hammond Roberson, tried in vain to secure a deathbed confession from one of these men, John Booth. As Booth slid towards death he motioned to Roberson to come over. 'Can you keep a secret?' 'Yes, yes,' replied the eager Roberson, 'I can.' 'So can I,' replied Booth and promptly died.[24]

The same code of silence protected the ringleader, Mellor, who now turned his thoughts to avenging his fallen comrades and shifting the target of Luddite attacks from the masters' machines to the masters themselves. The mill owner at Marsden, William Horsfall, was singled out as a potential target. On 27 April, Mellor and two associates, hiding behind a wall, shot and killed Horsfall as he rode by. Horsfall's murder, followed shortly after by the assassination of Prime Minister Perceval, sent the region into panic. The actions of extremists such as Mellor weakened the overall local support for the Luddites while hardening the resolve of mill owners and magistrates. Nonetheless, it was not until October of that year that Mellor was finally arrested, a sign that there remained some in the community willing to protect even homicidal Luddites. Mellor was tried by special commission, convicted and executed along with his two associates at York on 8 January 1813. Fourteen men were also executed for their part in the raid on Rawfolds Mill.

The impact of Luddite activity on the reform movement as a whole was considerable. It made middle-class reformers distance themselves from the Hampden Clubs, which, according to one Derbyshire magistrate, came to be dominated by the Luddites who formed clubs 'in almost every village in an angle between Leicester, Derby and Newark'.[25] Although this was an exaggeration, the popular reform platform of universal suffrage certainly came to be more appealing in Luddite areas, if only because other avenues – petitioning, union organisation and direct action – had one by one been closed off.[26]

Luddism may have been crushed by a heavy-handed government, but it was in the wake of Luddite activity that an uneasy alliance was formed between some of the radical reformers, led by Henry Hunt, and the Society of Spencean Philanthropists, which emerged from a murky underworld of brothels, cheap London taverns and Dissenting meeting houses.[27] Not only ideologically, but culturally and socially, these two strands of radicalism had little in common. The movement for radical parliamentary reform was dominated by gentlemen like Hunt, Cartwright and Burdett.

Hunt's status as a leader of the movement was built to a considerable extent on his 'natural' authority as a major landowner, his immaculate dress (including his trademark white hat) and his stentorian voice. The Spenceans represented the diametric opposite of Hunt's 'John Bull' figure. Their members were poor artisans, cabinet-makers, cobblers and butchers. The behaviour and appearance of some the Society's leading lights deliberately flouted convention. Robert Wedderburn, a mixed-race tailor, and Samuel Ferrand Waddington, a four-foot-high shoemaker given to cross-dressing (respectively known as the 'Black Prince' and the 'Black Dwarf'), played out a bawdy, profane and grotesque political theatre at Spencean meetings that was directly at odds with the studied orderliness and respectability of Hunt's brand of radicalism. (Later, Waddington would take to wearing a huge white hat in derision of the 'gentleman radical'.[28]) Hunt, an orthodox Anglican, could scarcely have had a more different religious outlook from the ultra-radicals, either. The radical underground in London had exploited the broadening of toleration in 1813 to include Unitarians, allowing them to take out licences as Dissenting ministers since the harsh legislation against political debating societies did not cover religious meetings. This was not, though, merely a pragmatic tactic, as many of the ultra-radicals were influenced by prophetic or millenarian groups: blasphemy as well as sedition was the substance of the sermons of men like Wedderburn and Waddington.

These two disparate strands of English radicalism were brought together at the mass meetings organised by the Spenceans at Spa Fields in London on 15 November and 2 December 1816. The main organisers, the surgeon apothecary Dr James Watson, the shoemaker Thomas Preston and the professional plotter Arthur Thistlewood, had invited most of the leading figures in reform to attend a meeting of 'Distressed Manufacturers, Mariners, Artisans and others'. The lapse of the Seditious Meetings Act of 1795 had made mass public meetings, briefly experimented with by the

LCS, a possibility once more. However, with the exception of Hunt, none of the leading gentlemen reformers was prepared to accept the Spenceans' call. For men like Burdett and Francis Place, it was not politicians like Hunt, prepared to whip up the mob, who were needed, but strong leaders in the shape of 'men of consequence and talent'.[29] However, it was not just the lack of gentry leadership that concerned men such as Burdett. At a Hampden Club meeting on 15 June 1816, he had conceded to Gale Jones that there was indeed an 'essential power in the people'; but there was also, he noted, 'an essential power at Hyde Park, at Knightsbridge, at the Tower, at Woolwich, at Hounslow, at Deptford and at Chatham. We are in fact, in this metropolis, in the midst of a circumvallation of fortresses.' Burdett saw that beneath some of the talk of popular political agency lurked justifications for the use of physical force; but such talk, even in peacetime, was deeply reckless, the language of 'desperation and bloodshed'; in such a heavily militarised society, it was madness.[30] Yet it was exactly this kind of action that the Spenceans had in mind as James Watson trawled London's docks and alehouses looking for demobbed soldiers, navvies and other hard men to provide the muscle for their projected insurrection.

Hunt, for his part, was clear that his participation in the Spa Fields meetings came at a price: the abandonment of the Spenceans' revolutionary agenda. In a private meeting with Watson, he demanded that the public platform for the meeting be universal male suffrage, annual parliaments and the secret ballot. There would be no mention of the redistribution of property and no attempt would be made to incite the crowd to riot.

The first meeting, on 15 November, passed without incident. Hunt addressed around ten thousand people from the window of a nearby public house. His speech concentrated on now-familiar themes in radical rhetoric: the oppressive burden of taxation that resulted from the corruption of the court, and its bloated, useless employees:

What was the cause of the want of employment? Taxation. What was the cause of taxation? Corruption. It was corruption that had enabled the borough-mongers to wage that bloody war which had for its object the destruction of the liberties of all countries but principally of our own ... Everything that concerned their subsistence or comforts was taxed. Was not their loaf taxed? was not their beer taxed? was not everything they ate, drank, wore, and even said, taxed? ... [The taxes] were imposed by the authority of a borough-mongering faction who thought of nothing but oppressing the people, and subsisting on the plunder wrung from their miseries.[31]

These problems were to be addressed by petitions, remonstrations and loud public calls for reformation. Only when such avenues had been utterly exhausted should the people resort to physical force. However, if that 'fatal day should be destined to arrive', Hunt promised the crowd that he 'would not be found concealed behind a counter, or sheltering himself in the rear'.[32] The meeting concluded with the signing of a petition in support of radical electoral reform, which was to be presented to the Prince Regent. The original plan was for Hunt and Burdett to offer the petition in person, but Burdett refused, signalling once again his disapproval of the 'rabble-rousing' tactics deployed by Hunt. Hunt then tried to deliver the petition to the Regent, but was not allowed into his presence.

The Spenceans felt this worked to their advantage. The Prince's refusal to receive the petitions would raise public anger to the point where a spontaneous uprising would be on the cards. Their chance soon came. At the second meeting on 2 December, again attended by a crowd of ten thousand or so, James Watson's drunken and unhinged son – he had already been treated in Bath for insanity – in an echo of Camille Desmoulin's exhortation to the Paris crowd before the storming of the Bastille, asked the crowd, 'If they will not give us what we want, shall we not take it?'[33]

Grabbing one of the red, white and green tricolours (the projected flag of the future British republic), Watson Jr called on the crowd to follow him and headed off towards Clerkenwell. However, most of the audience stayed to hear Hunt speak and passed a resolution to meet again in the New Year, once Parliament had reassembled. The group that had followed the younger Watson raided a gunsmith's shop in Skinner Street near Newgate, then splintered off, some heading up the Strand, others moving towards the Minories and the Tower. By nightfall, however, order had been restored and most of the ringleaders of the riot were already languishing behind bars.[34]

For the middle- and upper-class reformers of the London Hampden Club, the debacle of the second Spa Fields meeting provoked a disastrous split. Burdett, who had been due to lead a new reform bill drafted by the Club in the Commons, absented himself from proceedings. Hunt, along with deputies from the more radical provincial clubs and later William Cobbett, denounced the other members of the London Hampden Club for rejecting the platform of annual parliaments and universal suffrage and for placing the cause of reform in the hands of such a pusillanimous friend of the people as Burdett. It was necessary to 'draw a line of separation between the real and sham friends of reform', he declared.[35]

For Lord Liverpool's government, the Spa Fields riot seemed to provide both the firm evidence of an insurrectionary conspiracy in the capital and the necessary pretext for the legal crackdown that would thwart both it and reform in general. However, such measures had been easier to pass through the Commons during wartime than while the country was at peace, as it now was. On 28 January 1817, though, the government was provided with the grounds that it required for new 'gagging acts'. On the way to the opening of Parliament, a window of the Regent's coach had been broken by a stone thrown from the crowd. By inflating this incident into an attempt on the Prince's life, Liverpool secured the suspension once again of Habeas Corpus; the renewal of the act against seditious meetings; a law making attempts on the Regent as treasonable as those against the King; and the revival of measures making it treason to 'seduce' soldiers and sailors from their oaths of loyalty – this last aimed at the recruiting tactics of the Spenceans. The radical bookseller and satirist William Hone pictured Liverpool's ministers thanking the stone that hit the Regent's carriage in his cheap-print parody *The Bullet Te Deum with the Canticle of the Stone*. 'We praise thee O stone: we acknowledge thee to be a Bullet . . . We believe that thou art a pretext: for rejecting Reform.'[36]

The government was soon given more evidence of insurrectionary activity via the investigations of a Lords' secret committee on sedition. The committee not only condemned the Spencean programme of land reform but pointed to the connections between ultra-radicals and advocates of thorough parliamentary reform. It condemned the platform of universal male suffrage and annual parliaments as 'a project which . . . would involve the total subversion of the British Constitution'.[37] Parliament's hostility to the reform programme made Cartwright's continued use of mass petitioning to the Commons completely ineffective, if not counterproductive. By March, his campaign had amassed 514 petitions in support of universal suffrage, featuring a total of one and a quarter million signatures; but Parliament saw the size and scale of the petitions as evidence of a conspiracy against the government. They were rejected wholesale.[38]

The legacy of Cartwright's provincial petitioning campaigns lived on, nonetheless. On 10 March 1817, some twelve thousand people gathered outside St Peter's Church in Manchester for a brief meeting before beginning the first protest march in English history. But unlike later 'hunger marches', most notably the Jarrow Crusade, there was an implicit threat of insurrection in the behaviour of the 'Blanketeers' – so called on account of the 'blankets, rugs, or large coats, rolled up and tied, knap-sack like, on their backs' for sleeping rough en route. The Blanketeers planned to march from Manchester to London in order to present petitions to the Prince Regent, thus appealing over the head of a seemingly corrupt Parliament.[39] The week before the meeting, Parliament had suspended Habeas Corpus again. The marchers attempted to respond to this by following very closely the strict letter of the law with regard to correct petitioning. Their leader, John Bagguley, directed them to form themselves into groups of ten, each with a leader who was to tie to his wrist a petition signed by twenty people. This they duly did.

However, Bagguley did not interpret the right to petition as purely supplicatory, declaring, 'the law says that [if] the King did not give an Answer to the Petition within the space of 40 days, He was liable to be seiz'd & all his Family and confined in prison till he give an Answer'. The Salford tailor John Johnston warned that if the Prince 'will not harken to our Petition, but we will punish him by taking his head off as was formerly by Charles 1st'. As well as invoking the memory of the regicide, the Blanketeers also marshalled England's history of popular rebellion to their cause. William Benbow reminded his fellow marchers that 'a blacksmith in the reign of Richard 2nd went to London with 20,000 men and got their Liberties which remained till they were destroyed by Tyranny'.[40] The threat of violence was not a hollow one: at the same time as the marchers were engaged in exercising their rights to petition, ultra-radicals in London and Lancashire were planning nationwide uprisings, should the march fail.[41]

The vast majority of the petitioners got no further than St Peter's Fields, the starting point for the march, where Bagguley along with twenty-seven other ringleaders was arrested. As Samuel Bamford, secretary of the Middleton Hampden Club, had presciently warned, the plans for the march had easily been detected by government spies, who had had two of the leading organisers, including the aged printer William Ogden, arrested the day before. In the confusion, significant numbers of people set off on the march anyway. Most got as far as Stockport before the military overtook them and dispersed them with force, wounding several.

One unfortunate old man, who happened to be watching the mêlée from his cottage door, was shot dead. A few escaped to struggle on towards London, but only one, Abel Couldwell of Stalybridge, made it to the capital to present his petition.

As a consequence of the disturbance, the Manchester magistrates decided they needed their own military force ready to suppress any future popular demonstrations. They created the Manchester and Salford Yeomanry, a militia force recruited from the ranks of shopkeepers and tradesmen which would later commit the butchery at Peterloo. The Blanketeers had marched under Cartwright's slogan, 'Hold Fast by the Laws'. Their treatment at the hands of the Manchester magistracy demonstrated how misplaced that trust had been. In Parliament, the constitutionalist mottos of the march – described as a 'foolish and absurd expedition' by one MP – met with ridicule.* Henry Brougham, once seriously considered as a reform candidate to pair up with Sir Francis Burdett, told the Commons:

> Sir, I would not be a party in telling the people, (monstrous assertion!) that twelve hundred years ago this country enjoyed a free and perfect constitution. (*Hear, hear, hear!*) This, sir, is a specimen of the historical knowledge, – of the antiquarian research, – of the acquaintance with constitutional law of these wiseacres out of doors, who, after poring for days and nights, and brooding over their wild and mischievous schemes, rise up with their little nostrums and big blunders to amend the British Constitution! (*Laughter and loud cheers.*)[42]

The same month as the Blanketeers' march was forcefully dispersed, the government turned its attention to the radical press.

---

* *The Times*, 10 February 1818, in a speech by a Mr Phillips, condemning the violence used by the Manchester magistrates – a reminder that sympathy for the casualties of major demonstrations did not equate to support for the cause of those demonstrations.

Lord Sidmouth, the Home Secretary, issued a circular to magistrates reminding them of their power to imprison any writer, publisher or bookseller believed to be guilty of writing or distributing seditious or blasphemous works and urging them to take action against 'hawkers and pedlars' without a licence to sell books. Mass arrests of members of provincial reform societies under the Suspension Act sent other radicals into exile. Cobbett publicly declared his disapproval of all conspiratorial activity before fleeing to America. This left the leading radical publishers William Hone, T. J. Wooler (whose *Black Dwarf* had a circulation of twelve thousand copies an issue) and W. T. Sherwin (who changed the name of his *Republican* to *Sherwin's Weekly Political Register* in a bid to avoid prosecution). Hone was arrested for blasphemy and sedition on 3 May 1817. Importantly, he was charged only with blasphemy. A very high bail was set, forcing him to remain in prison until his trial, scheduled for December. Hone had in fact been assiduous in avoiding any taint of involvement in seditious activity, advising the Spa Fields crowd not to carry arms, withdrawing sensitive parodies from sale and even turning in seditious materials when they were planted on his premises by government agents.[43]

The Crown had vindictively decided to hold all three trials for blasphemy on consecutive days, hoping to grind Hone, who was representing himself, into the ground. The tactic, and the decision to prosecute him for blasphemy as the charge that would stick, failed disastrously. Hone's 'blasphemy' consisted of publishing three parodies of the Church catechism, litany and creed. There was nothing at all unusual about this kind of parody. Indeed, as Hone cleverly pointed out, it had been used by George Canning, now a member of the ministry, in his former career as an anti-Jacobin poet. Moreover, as the parody was directed against the government and not against religion, the trials gave Hone the opportunity to renew his attacks within a packed courtroom – with a crowd of twenty thousand waiting outside, it was said. His brilliant defence speeches have been described as the finest ever uttered in an English courtroom. Hone's defence was based on showing the ubiquity and orthodoxy of religious parody as a literary form. As he regaled them with one ridiculous parody after another, the court descended into hysterics, with the sheriff vainly threatening to arrest 'the first man I see laugh'.[44] The prosecution was no match for Hone's encyclopedic knowledge of print culture, and the sources he used to support his case ranged so widely – he referred to over eighty texts – that at one point the Attorney-General suggested that Martin Luther, another author of religious parodies, might have been charged with blasphemy too.[45] The government's humiliation was completed by the calamitous decision of the Lord Chief Justice, Lord Ellenborough, to preside over the last two trials personally.

The jury acquitted Hone of all three charges. Ellenborough tendered his immediate resignation, though it was not accepted, and the Chief Justice was forced to head up the Crown's equally unsuccessful prosecution of James Watson for high treason, a task which so wearied him that he had to call on another justice to sum up the evidence. Hone's victory in the courts had been preceded by Wooler's acquittal at one of two trials for seditious libel in June 1817. The other verdict, one of guilty, which was later overturned on procedural grounds at King's Bench, was damaging, too. Three jurymen entered a demur to the verdict that was effectively an indictment of the government: 'As *truth* is declared by the law of the land to be a libel, we three are *compelled* to find the Defendant guilty.'[46]

The trials of Wooler and Hone were, in the short term, propaganda victories for the radicals, but their importance should not be exaggerated. The targeting of the radical press with charges of seditious libel and blasphemy had already had the effect of driving the most significant reformist writer, William Cobbett, out of the country. Wooler had only got off on a technicality, and Hone's prosecution had failed not merely because of his own brilliant

defence but also because he was one of the most circumspect radical writers and publishers.*

The pressure exerted by the government also had the effect of
turning the leading radicals against each other, as Hunt recorded
in his memoirs:

Mr Wooler, as well as Mr White, of the *Independent Whig* [another
radical journal], lashed Mr Cobbett most unmercifully for his cowardice in flying his country, and abandoning the Reformers at such
a critical moment. Mr Wooler was excessively severe, and he laid it
on with an unsparing hand. I lost no opportunity to vindicate the
character of my absent friend, and in doing this I attacked Mr
Wooler as violently as he attacked Mr Cobbett, for which Mr
Wooler denounced me as a spy of the Government![47]

* He had withdrawn the offending parodies from sale and had only been prosecuted
because Richard Carlile, the Painite writer and publisher, had reissued them without his
permission.

PETERLOO

Harrying the press was not enough for Lord Liverpool's administration. The Spa Fields riots had failed to provide sufficient clear evidence of insurrectionary goings-on and the 'attempt on the Regent's life' had too quickly become an object of public scorn. As Cobbett wrote of the administration in late 1816: 'Oh, how they sigh! They are working and slaving and fretting and stewing; they are sweating all over; they are absolutely pining and dying for a plot.'[1]

Evidence of potential insurrection was uncovered in the wake of the Blanketeers' march. Later that month, a meeting was broken up at the Royal Oak in Ardwick Bridge near Manchester, where an attack on the city was being planned. The insurrectionists, probably encouraged by a spy called 'Ackers', aimed to free the imprisoned Blanketeers and 'make a Moscow of Manchester'. Government spies reported that speakers were making inflated claims for the level of support for the rising: 'two or three thousand would be sufficient to do what they had to do, for no doubt they would be fifty thousand strong by Daylight'. Another claim was that men in Leeds and Huddersfield were ready to rise too, and had been arming themselves since the Luddite machine-breaking episodes.[2]

The Ardwick 'conspiracy', though, barely merited the term. If it demonstrated anything, it was the successful penetration of working-class organisations by government informers. The Lords' secret committee had already identified the provinces, again the North West and the Midlands, as the main breeding grounds for rebellion. It reported that songs were being sung and speeches made in alehouses that were 'destructive of the social order, recommending the equalisation of property'. Oaths were frequently administered, but worst of all, said the report, 'arms were being collected in some areas'.[3]

The actual threat to security posed by this activity was, however, minimal. Although Blanketeers and ultra-radicals often alluded to the historical precedent of the Peasants' Revolt, the contrast with the danger represented by popular rebellion in earlier periods is telling. As we have seen, in the late medieval period, a heavily armed populace had often posed a serious military challenge to royal armies. By the early nineteenth century, though, not only did the government possess a very large permanent army with which to suppress revolts, it also subjected the manufacture of arms in the country to close scrutiny. When a parcel of daggers arrived at a public house in Hinckley, Leicestershire, for collection by the secretary of the local Hampden Club, London soon knew about it. When a rural carpenter near Stamford received an order from 'the East India Company' for three thousand pike handles, the Home Office, quickly informed, enquired of the company's chairman 'how far you may be led by the circumstances . . . to believe the transaction to be a genuine one'. Spies were ubiquitous – they even reported to the Home Office seditious conversations overheard in the privy.[4]

In June 1817, the full-blown popular insurrection that Liverpool's government had been hoping for finally happened. One of its key orchestrators was Thomas Bacon, a sixty-four-year-old stockinger and veteran republican from Pentrich in

Derbyshire, who had been a delegate to the Hampden Club rally in London in January and had taken a leading role in forming the Pentrich branch. The other was W. J. Richards, a.k.a. William Oliver and later better known as 'Oliver the Spy', a former surveyor employed by the Home Office as an informer and agent provocateur. In May, Bacon was already making enquiries with contacts at the Butterley ironworks near Ripley, Derbyshire, about supplying arms and munitions for a planned rising and telling of his plans to establish a republican government, headed (rather implausibly) by the gentlemen reformers Sir Francis Burdett, Lord Cochrane and Sir Robert Wilson. By this point, the government already knew about Bacon's plans. Rather than jump the gun, however, as had happened at Ardwick, they wanted to allow this rising to come to fruition. By 4 June, the date set for it had been revealed, and a march on Nottingham to meet other revolutionary forces announced.

Only on 5 June did the prospective leader of this rebellion, the 'Nottingham Captain' Jeremiah Brandreth, a dark, forbidding figure (some said of gypsy stock), enter the picture. At the rebels' final meeting on 8 June at the White Horse in Pentrich, Brandreth promised his followers that each would receive a hundred guineas, bread, beef and ale once they reached Nottingham, where they would be joined by sixteen thousand other rebels. Brandreth's fulsome promises, straight from the 'land of Cockayne', were given some credibility by the supporting testimony of Oliver, who was not present at the Pentrich meeting but had claimed at an earlier one at Thornhill on the 6th, at which other Pentrich rebels were present, that London was about to rise and Burdett was ready to head a new English republic.

The rising had been known to the government for a while via its network of spies (two special constables had been present at the meeting at the White Horse), and it had now become public knowledge in Pentrich itself. The hand of the local magistrates was, though, stayed by the government. As the Lord Lieutenant of

Nottingham, the Duke of Newcastle, explained to Lord Sidmouth three days after the rising:

> As Your Lordship is aware the plot had been hatching for some time, which we knew, and were prepared accordingly. We thought it much more desirable to let the matter come to a Crisis, than to endeavour to crush it before the Designs were openly disclosed – I am very glad that we adopted this mode, as we have now not only become acquainted with what the bad People will do, but we have ascertained that the Country People are not of their way of thinking.[5]

Unaware that the authorities were completely cognisant of their designs, the Pentrich rebels, in total only about fifty men, set off at ten o'clock on the night of 9 June. Despite the attempts to secure arms from the local ironworks they were poorly armed, with only a few old muskets between them. As they marched, they attempted to force men living in nearby houses to join the rising. This led to the first fatality: a servant, Robert Walters, was shot through a window by Brandreth when his mistress refused to allow the rebels entry.*

At three o'clock the following morning, the marchers reached the Butterley ironworks but found it heavily guarded – another sign that the rising had been anticipated. As the owner, Goodwin, reported, the marchers came out very much the worse in the clash with the cavalry and pikemen stationed outside:

> nothing could exceed the zeal & activity shown by the Cavalry & pikemen, they had made a race after the Insurgents, several of whom took refuge in the woods between Butterley & Swanwick, the Pikemen went in & beat them out & the Cavalry stationed on

---

* Brandreth would not be tried for this murder. Instead William, Joseph and Robert Turner, and William Ludlam and William Barker, were convicted of it.

the outside took them prisoners. In the afternoon two Troops of Yeomanry from Derby & several Magistrates arrived – One troop remained at Ripley till noon on Wednesday the 11th when they left us escorting 15 more prisoners which had been taken.[6]

The marchers who escaped the forces at the foundry continued on towards Nottingham. En route they stopped at several inns, demanding food, beer and weapons. The rising was finally brought to an end at Gilt Brook, the valley between Eastwood and Kimberley. Here, the revolutionaries came upon the soldiers of the 15th Regiment of Light Dragoons, only eighteen mounted men, but enough to make them flee across the fields in terror. Some of them managed to get back to Pentrich, where they were hidden in a hayloft and supplied with food by a local nonconformist minister. They would later be uncovered by soldiers, but one, Miles Bacon, managed to escape by leaping across the Cromford canal. He eventually reached a farmhouse at Whitwick in Leicestershire, staying on as a farmhand and marrying Elizabeth Griffin, the daughter of the house, in March 1821. (He named his first son Jeremiah, after Brandreth, and died aged eighty-four in 1879.)

About forty men were seized, in addition to those taken prisoner at the ironworks. Brandreth managed to escape and stayed on the run for a month, twice stowing away on ships bound for America, only to be discovered and thrown off. He was finally captured on 22 July in Nottingham, having sought refuge in the home of his 'old friend' Henry Sampson, in fact another government informer. Thomas Bacon was captured the following month in St Ives, then in Huntingdonshire.

The Pentrich rebels were tried by special commission at Derby. The main problem for the government was how to avoid William Oliver's role in the rising being discussed (his identity had already been revealed, though too late to help the Pentrich men, by the *Leeds Mercury*). The role of another government informer, John Castle, brought to light by the evidence of Henry Hunt, had

helped persuade the jury to acquit Arthur Thistlewood, Dr James
Watson, John Hopper and Thomas Preston at their trials for treason in June.[7] However, Oliver's role posed problems for the
defence too, as his testimony would have confirmed the existence
of revolutionary cells in the Midlands and in Yorkshire. Oliver had
certainly helped bring the rising forward, but he had not conjured
the insurrectionary mood out of thin air. In the end, the defence
contended that the marchers were simple men after bread, beer
and cash, not revolution. The argument did not save Brandreth,
who along with his lieutenants, William Turner and Isaac Ludlum,
was executed at Nuns Green, Derby, on 17 November 1817. In a
gesture of princely clemency, the Regent remitted the usual punishment of hanging, drawing and quartering, and Brandreth and
his associates were merely hanged and beheaded. A further eleven
Pentrich men were sentenced to transportation for life, another
three for a period of fourteen years.

Although Oliver played a key role in ensuring that the Pentrich
rising unfolded as it did, as the earlier Ardwick conspiracy
showed, insurrectionary plotting was ongoing in the North and
Midlands. There are hints of connections between Luddism and
revolutionary activity, but the taciturn Brandreth, despite the
efforts of the prison chaplain, gave little away in the days before
his execution (his last letters display no more than a reasonable
level of literacy, a love for his wife and firm faith in God) More
significant was the role that Oliver unwittingly played in eliciting
sympathy for the Pentrich men from middle-class and gentlemen
reformers.[8] His involvement transformed the Pentrich rising from
a dangerous proletarian revolt into a shameful government-
orchestrated sham. Burdett, no friend of revolution, complained
in the Commons that nothing 'could be more atrocious, especially in these times of wretchedness and distress, than for the
government to hire and pay people to excite sedition'.[9]
Caricatures showed Oliver and Castle as rapacious foxes tricking
the poor chickens – the London Spenceans and the Pentrich

men – into their lair. Percy Bysshe Shelley's bitter pamphlet, *An Address to the People on the Death of the Princess Charlotte* (better known by its Painite subtitle, *We Pity the Plumage but Forget the Dying Bird*), contrasted the public outpouring of grief at the death of the Princess, a day before the execution of Brandreth, with the lack of sympathy for the Pentrich men:

> The news of the death of the Princess Charlotte, and of the execution of Brandreth, Ludlam, and Turner, arrived nearly at the same time. If beauty, youth, innocence, amiable manners, and the exercise of the domestic virtues could alone justify public sorrow when they are extinguished for ever, this interesting Lady would well deserve that exhibition. She was the last and the best of her race. But there were thousands of others equally distinguished as she, for private excellences, who have been cut off in youth and hope.
>
> The execution of Brandreth, Ludlam, and Turner, is an event of quite a different character from the death of the Princess Charlotte. These men were shut up in a horrible dungeon, for many months, with the fear of a hideous death and of everlasting hell thrust before their eyes; and at last were brought to the scaffold and hung. They too had domestic affections, and were remarkable for the exercise of private virtues. Perhaps their low station permitted the growth of those affections in a degree not consistent with a more exalted rank.
>
> They had sons, and brothers, and sisters, and fathers, who loved them, it should seem, more than the Princess Charlotte could be loved by those whom the regulations of her rank had held in perpetual estrangement from her. Her husband was to her as father, mother, and brethren. Ludlam and Turner were men of mature years, and the affections were ripened and strengthened within them.
>
> What those sufferers felt shall not be said. But what must have been the lone and various agony of their kindred may be inferred from Edward Turner, who, when he saw his brother dragged along upon the hurdle, shrieked horribly and fell in a fit, and was carried

away like a corpse by two men. How fearful must have been their agony, sitting in solitude on that day when the tempestuous voice of horror from the crowd, told them that the head so dear to them was severed from the body! Yes they listened to the maddening shriek which burst from the multitude: they heard the rush of ten thousand terror-stricken feet, the groans and the hootings which told them that the mangled and distorted head was then lifted into the air.

For Shelley, the Pentrich rising was solely the work of government spies, 'the most worthless and infamous of mankind', whose aim was to prop up a corrupt and oppressive administration:

> It was their business if they found no discontent to create it. It was their business to find victims, no matter whether right or wrong. It was their business to produce upon the public all impression, that if any attempt to attain national freedom, or to diminish the burthens of debt and taxation under which we groan, were successful, the starving multitude would rush in, and confound all orders and distinctions, and institutions and laws, in common ruin.
>
> To produce this salutary impression, they betrayed some innocent and unsuspecting rustics into a crime whose penalty is a hideous death. A few hungry and ignorant manufacturers seduced by the splendid promises of these remorseless blood-conspirators, collected together in what is called rebellion against the state.[10]

Immediately after the Pentrich rising, the government had been able to exploit the fear of insurrection and pass the act suspending Habeas Corpus. As the details of the rising and the role of the spies emerged, the news of the plot worked against the administration, leading to some rapprochement between popular and middle-class radicalism.[11] However, the extent of this closing of the gap should not be overstated. In metropolitan circles, 1818 was a year of unseemly squabbles over political precedence between Burdett and

Hunt in particular, as a great deal of radical effort remained focused on the election of MPs to Parliament and the sponsorship of moderate reform bills in the Commons. The internecine conflict between the reformers in London led Hunt and Cartwright in particular to look to the provinces, and to mass meetings, as the best means of achieving their goals. With mass petitioning clearly ineffective, even when reformers followed the letter of the law, as had the Blanketeers, Cartwright and Hunt believed that the most effective way to exert pressure for reform was to put the unrepresented communities on show in vast popular assemblies. In Hunt's case, this took the form of a plan for a union of non-represented people; in Cartwright's, the idea of elected 'legislative attorneys' who would personally petition the Commons.[12] With the lapsing of the Seditious Meetings Act, Hunt, in cooperation with some of the Spenceans, began to organise mass meetings. The first, held at Palace Yard, Westminster, in September 1818, remonstrated with the Regent, asserted the sovereignty of the people and demanded their rightful share in the fruits of their toil – a remonstrance that indicated Hunt's rhetoric had become more flexible since the Spa Fields meeting.

The Regent's predictable refusal to accept the remonstrance prompted an escalation of the campaign. Mass meetings were arranged in the North and the Midlands in the summer of 1819 – those attending would constitute a significant part of Hunt's projected union of the unrepresented. More meetings followed at Smithfield and in Birmingham, where Cartwright received a public vote of thanks. The final provincial meeting was set for Manchester, which would be followed by a vast open-air rally on Kennington Common in London, where it was imagined Hunt would be received as the conquering hero.

The Manchester meeting, scheduled for 9 August, was banned by the local magistrates under advice from the acting Home Secretary, Henry Hobhouse. He informed them that the plan for the crowd to elect pseudo-MPs constituted a criminal offence.

However, following clarification from Lord Sidmouth that only the action, not the intention, of electing such MPs was illegal, the meeting was rearranged for 16 August to take place on St Peter's Fields, the scene two years earlier of the dispersal of the Blanketeers. Aware of the unfortunate precedent, and stung by loyalist propaganda that portrayed the mass meetings as assemblies of the great unwashed, the organisers took pains to ensure that the local reform societies presented an orderly meeting. In the rural areas around Manchester such as Samuel Bamford's Middleton, which supplied many of the contingents that would be present at St Peter's Fields, the preparations borrowed from older festive traditions, such as that of the rush-bearings, a pre-Reformation ritual that took place in Lancashire and involved the renewing of rushes on the church floor. (Ironically, rush-bearings had also played a part in anti-Jacobin 'Paine burnings' during the 1790s.[13]) Seen through the eyes of watching spies and special constables, however, the organisational activities of the radicals were sinister and suspect. The authorities received reports of night-time drillings on the moors; what reformers such as Bamford excused as 'periods of healthful exercise and enjoyment' looked to hostile observers like a 'military array'.[14]

The 16th of August 1819 was a fine, clear summer's day. At first light, the area of St Peter's Fields had been cleared of as many objects as possible that could be used as potential weapons. In any case, the processions of men, women and children that came in from the villages and towns surrounding Manchester had fully heeded Hunt's instruction to bring no weapon other than that of a 'self-approving conscience'. Samuel Bamford disagreed, arguing that there 'could be no harm whatever in taking a score or two of cudgels, just to keep the specials at a respectful distance from our line'.[15] But Hunt's order prevailed: even when the military intervened, the crowd largely followed his direction from the platform not to resist.

By mid-morning, a crowd had begun to gather. When finally amassed, it probably amounted to around sixty thousand people, then equivalent to about 6 per cent of the population of Lancashire. Groups had come from as far afield as Wigan to the west and Saddleworth to the east, plus a substantial number from Manchester itself. The crowd was largely, then, a mixture of the urban and the rural poor. Perhaps the most distinctive contingents, and to some the most threatening, were those from the female reform societies, the women all decked in white – the colour of virginity and the colour often associated with rush-bearings, but also the colour of the French 'festivals of reason' in the 1790s.[16] Although women-only friendly societies had emerged during that decade, the overtly political female reform societies were a very recent phenomenon, the first having been established in June 1819 in Blackburn, quickly followed by others in Stockport, Oldham, Manchester, Royton, Failsworth and Leigh. In some areas, like Bamford's Middleton, no separate female reform societies existed because women were already granted full membership rights in the existing reform club.[17]

The role of women at the St Peter's Fields meeting, as at other reform meetings, was prominent but also largely silent and ceremonial. When Henry Hunt arrived at one o'clock to the strains of 'God Save the King' and 'Rule Britannia', he was accompanied by the women of the Manchester Female Reform Society. Its president, Mary Fildes, sat beside Hunt in his carriage. Along with Hunt, Richard Carlile, the *Times* reporter John Tyas and the local organisers John Knight and Joseph Johnson, the women of the Society took the platform, proudly carrying their flag. Women did not speak at reform meetings, however: their main role was to present male leaders like Hunt with the symbolic 'cap of liberty', an emblem with Saxon as well as French connotations. At Peterloo, Fildes was to present Hunt with the 'colours' of the Manchester Female Reform Society. Cobbett patronisingly equated this action with the role of queens at jousts in blessing the participants.[18]

Hunt's arrival prompted the local magistracy into action. They were clearly prepared for a violent confrontation: present were 600 professional soldiers from the 15th Hussars, plus several hundred infantrymen, 400 men from the Cheshire Yeomanry, 400 special constables, 120 cavalry from the Manchester and Salford Yeomanry and a Royal Artillery force with two six-pounder guns.

The specials' blood was already up, according to Bamford, as one of their number had been severely beaten for spying on the Middleton men drilling the night before.[19] The magistrates swore and signed an affidavit for Hunt's arrest and that of other leading radicals, on the grounds that an immense mob had collected and they considered the town in danger. Joseph Nadin, the Deputy Constable, claimed that he could not serve the affidavit without using military force. 'Then you shall have military force. For God's sake don't sacrifice the lives of the Special Constables,' William Hulton, the chairman of the magistrates, replied. These orders were then passed to Colonel Guy L'Estrange – in charge of the professional soldiers in the absence of General Byng, who was busy enjoying himself at York races – as well as to Major Trafford, commander of the Manchester Yeomanry. Eyewitnesses reported that the yeomanry were already drunk by this point. 'He could hardly sit on his horse, he was so drunk, he sat like a monkey,' it was reported of one of them.

The orders were received first by the yeomanry, led by Hugh Birley, a local factory owner. They set off into Cooper Street, heading towards the house where the magistrates were sitting, to receive fuller orders. Their hasty advance brought the first casualty of the day: a baby in the arms of one Mrs Ann Fildes was wounded when she was knocked down by a horse.[20] The Chief Constable now informed Birley that he had an arrest warrant that required military assistance to execute. He ordered Birley to take his cavalry to the hustings so that the speakers could be removed.

By this point, around 1.40 p.m., Hunt had just begun to address the crowds. They were now all so tightly packed around the hustings that one eyewitness, Elizabeth Healey, recalled she had to get out as she was struggling to breathe in the crush. She had a lucky escape. Hunt's words were soon drowned out by the noise of approaching horses. He ordered the crowd to stand firm: 'They are in disorder already. This is a trick. Give them three cheers.' Hunt was right about the disorder: the inexperienced cavalry, with their freshly sharpened sabres unsheathed, had lost all composure, the troops fragmenting as each man pressed on towards the hustings, hacking, beating and trampling the crowd out of the way. As Bamford recalled,

> [the cavalry] were in confusion: they evidently could not, with all the weight of man and horse, penetrate that compact mass of human beings; and their sabres were plied to hew a way through naked held-up hands, and defenceless heads; and then chopped limbs, and wound gaping skulls were seen; and groans and cries were mingled with the din of that horrid confusion.[21]

Once they had cut their way through the crowd, the yeomanry and special constables quickly set upon those on the platform. Mary Fildes was dragged from the hustings, her white dress catching on a nail. As she tried to free herself, she was slashed across the body with a sabre. Thirty-five people were dragged before the magistrates, including the reporter John Tyas and a heavily pregnant woman, Mrs Elizabeth Gaunt. Gaunt was badly beaten and later thrown into the New Bailey Prison, where she was kept in solitary confinement and physically abused.[22] Henry Hunt alleged that, having been taken down from the hustings, he was abandoned by Officers Nadin and Andrew so that the yeomanry might cut him to pieces:

> But I stuck to Nadin as my shield and buckler. They reached over his head and cut my hat; and my hand was also slightly cut. They then wheeled round and came again; but I wheeled round also,

and still presented Nadin in front. When I got to the door I found my hat thrust off; I put my head on one side, and instantly there came upon my shoulder a blow from a bludgeon, which would have murdered me if it had come upon my bare head.[23]

With the speakers off the platform, the yeomanry went on the rampage, kicking up a cloud of dust that obscured the goings-on from the eyes of the magistrates peering down from 6 Mount Street. At 1.50 p.m., the Hussars, led by Colonel L'Estrange, were ordered to assist them, the chairman of the magistrates William Hulton telling him '[the protesters] are attacking the Yeomanry. Disperse them.' (Some witnesses had seen stones and sticks being hurled at the yeomanry, but only after they had charged the crowd with swords drawn.) L'Estrange obeyed, forming his men into a line across the eastern end of the field, who then charged the crowd. They were joined by the Cheshire Yeomanry, attacking from the south. The fleeing crowd, trapped between these advancing troops, found their escape through Peter Street blocked by the 88th Infantry's bayonets. Meanwhile, the yeomanry were warming to their task, hurling insults between blows: 'Damn you, I'll reform you' – 'I'll let you know I'm a soldier today' – 'Spare your lives? Damn your bloody lives.' The worst carnage occurred by the Friends' meeting house as the demonstrators were hemmed in by the infantry and pursued by the Hussars. 'The people came in great crowds past my door, and a parcel of them beat down the fence,' a woman living near by reported.

The people were so pressed they could not get away. They kept cutting them in the corner, and the shrieks would astonish you, and they were laying on them all the time as hard as they could, and an officer belonging to the soldiers came up and said, 'Gentlemen, gentlemen, for shame forbear. The people cannot get away.' Just as he was saying so the rail broke and let a whole number of people into my cellar.

The woman at the bottom of this human avalanche, Martha Partington from Eccles, was 'took up dead'.[24]

Samuel Bamford recalled the hideous scene in the wake of the carnage:

> The sun looked down through a sultry and motionless air . . . over the whole field, were strewed caps, bonnets, hats, shawls, and shoes, and other parts of male and female dress; trampled, torn, and bloody. The yeomanry had dismounted – some easing their horses' girths . . . some wiping their sabres. Several mounds of human beings still remained where they had fallen, crushed down and smothered. Some of these still groaning – others with staring eyes, were gasping for breath and others would never breathe more. All was silent save those low sounds, and the occasional snorting and pawing of steeds.[25]

As a direct or indirect result of the actions of the yeomanry and the professional soldiers at Peterloo, fifteen people were killed and 654 are known to have been wounded, the majority seriously. The aftermath of the meeting was grimly recorded in the press. The *Observer* noted six coaches, three carts and three litters carrying away the wounded. The *Star* reported:

> All the roads leading from Manchester to Ashton, Stockport, Cheadle, Bury, Bolton are covered with wounded stragglers, who have not yet been able to reach their houses after the events of Monday . . . There are 17 wounded persons along the Stockport Road; 13–14 on the Ashton Road; at least 20 on the Oldham Road; 7 or 8 on the Rochdale Road, besides several others on the roads to Liverpool.[26]

The violence did not end with the dispersal of the meeting. Rioting in the deprived New Cross area on the evening of the 16th led to two deaths. Two days later, a special constable, Robert Campbell, was killed in a revenge attack.[27]

Thanks to the pioneering work of Michael Bush, we now know perhaps as much as we ever will about the human cost of Peterloo. The surviving casualty lists that he has collated make for grim and revealing reading and explode a number of myths concerning the events of 16 August 1819.

For one, they make it impossible to challenge the label 'massacre'. The number of injured used to be accepted as around four hundred persons out of a total of sixty thousand. We now know the number to be far higher, and Bush suggests that a figure of over seven hundred injured is not unrealistic. The imprecision is partly due to the incompleteness of the casualty lists (some known to have been compiled no longer survive), but also to the fact that those with minor – and even some major – injuries feared the repercussions of admitting that they had attended the meeting. William Marsh of Chorlton Row in Manchester received a sabre wound to the back of the head; his body was crushed and his left leg broken when he was trampled by horses. His three children worked at the cavalry leader Hugh Birley's factory. When Birley found out that their father had been at the meeting, he sacked them.[28] Jonathan Clarke, a hatter of Reddish near Stockport with seven children, one newly born, was unable to work and so unable to pay the rent on account of his injuries. His landlord, branding him a reformer, seized his goods and chattels in lieu of the unpaid rent, selling them for £2 4s.

James Lees of Delph, a twenty-five-year-old weaver, was admitted to the Infirmary with two severe sabre wounds to the head, but dismissed untreated when he refused to say, as required by the chief surgeon, that 'he had had enough of Manchester meetings'.[29] The danger of revealing one's presence at the meeting was such that some probably died in secret rather than seek medical help.[30] John Rhodes, of 3 Pits Hopwood, who also received a severe sabre wound to the head, was found 'wandering about bloody' by a woman who 'took him into her house, shaved off the hair and put on a plaister. He was dreadfully bruised internally so that he has not since held up his head and died about 18 November.' The coroner's inquest, presided over by the inappropriately named Kinder Wood, found that the cause of death was 'the diseased state of the belly and chest, and so due to "natural causes and not external injury"'.[31]

Women feature prominently among the lists of those injured: though they made up only one in eight of the crowd, they constitute one in three of the recorded casualties. Apologists for the yeomanry and magistracy have argued that a high proportion of women were injured because they were more liable to be crushed by the crowd. However, this is contradicted by the evidence from the lists, which shows that most of the injuries sustained by women were the result either of sabre or truncheon blows or of being trampled by cavalry.[32]

What is more, women were clearly singled out for particularly brutal treatment by the yeomanry. Elizabeth Farren was attacked by a yeoman called Tebbutt. She received a deep sabre wound to the forehead and fell to the ground. Tebbutt continued his attack as she fell, causing her to drop her child, who was also struck by a blow from his sword. What made the attack even more horrific was that Tebbutt was not a stranger, but one of Farren's neighbours.[33] Elizabeth, Ellen and Isabella Harvey were all badly beaten, crushed and cut. Elizabeth was 'Thrown down and trampled on, the flesh trod off her neck and face; shoulders, knees and ankle hurt severely'. Ellen was struck so hard by a sabre blow that it cut through her quarter-inch-thick whalebone stays. No relief was awarded to any of them because their family were 'respectable people' who would not accept charity.[34] Mary Heys of Rawlinson Buildings, a mother of six children, her husband almost blind, was trampled under foot by a cavalry horse, ripping the flesh off her legs and feet. She was pregnant at the time. Following Peterloo, she suffered from almost daily seizures. Her child was born two months prematurely; Mary died during labour.[35]

The attacks on women at Peterloo clearly breached norms of masculine behaviour. The violence meted out to female reformers had been encouraged before that event by loyalist propaganda and, indeed, even by some reformist literature that viewed women's participation in politics with disdain. In populist loyalist works like Hannah More's *Cheap Repository Tracts*, female reformers were presented as revolutionary termagants who had abandoned their domestic duties for politics. In one such tract, a male radical complains, 'Why I must own that since our Debby has turned speechmaker, the children [are] all in rags, and I can't get a clean shirt.'[36] Female reformers were portrayed not just as neglectful of their matrimonial and maternal responsibilities but as sluts and whores. The *Manchester Exchange Herald* recorded: 'The Public scarcely need to be informed, that the females are women well known to be the most abandoned of their sex.' The *New Times* stated: 'We cannot conceive that any but a hardened and shameless Prostitute would have the audacity to appear on the hustings on such an occasion and for such a purpose.'

This misogynistic invective was accompanied by similarly vicious popular prints. George Cruikshank's *The Belle Alliance: or, the Female Reformers of Blackburn* depicted the women on the platform as sub-human, grotesques, barely clothed in shabby undergarments.[37] The print is loaded with crude sexual innuendo. One female reformer holds a cap of liberty on a pole coming out from between a man's legs. The women's banner carries an image of St George besting the dragon – a clear reference to the slang term for sex with the woman on top, 'riding St George' – a literal sign of a sexual world turned upside down.[38] A similar image by J. L. Marks, *Much Wanted, a Reform among Females*, presented female reformers as empty-headed, rosy-cheeked slatterns. Here the sexual imagery is even more blatant than in Cruikshank, with women holding obviously phallic rolled petitions and remonstrances. One woman has her hands clasped downwards in front of her in the form of a vagina. In the crowd, a woman carrying a washing-tub on her head appears unperturbed by a male hand groping her breast.[39]

Unfortunately, male reformers were not much more enlightened than loyalist propagandists and printmakers. Wooler's *Black Dwarf*, in an 1818 editorial, reacted to 'female politicians' with an elaborate fantasy about women lawyers and clergymen, archly insinuating, 'Gladly we would embrace such legislative bodies.' Returning to the familiar theme of 'the world turned upside down', the editor speculated that if women were given political rights, men would only be allowed to be nurses and milkmaids.[40]

In the aftermath of Peterloo there was some sympathy for the women victims and in some cases, such as that of the radical publisher Richard Carlile, the event converted some male reformers to the cause of female political emancipation. However, compassion for the women reformers' suffering was most often tempered by the persistence of conventional patriarchal attitudes. Cruikshank famously performed a dramatic pictorial about-face with his post-Peterloo print, *Britons Strike Home*, which depicted corpulent, drunken yeomen cavalry cutting down and trampling defenceless women, some with babes-in-arms. While we know that incidents of this kind did happen at Peterloo, women were presented here as passive victims and returned to traditional, motherly roles.[41] This representation contrasts with the testimonies of eye-witnesses, which suggest that women forcibly resisted the military. Bamford recalled 'a young married woman, with her face all bloody', presumably from having suffered a sabre cut. Her bonnet had 'slipped off her head and was hanging from her neck by the string'. Cradled in her apron was a supply of stones which she hurled at the cavalry until, according to Bamford, 'she fell backwards and was near being taken; but she got away covered with severe bruises'.[42] Equally, though *The Times*'s John Tyas may have indicted the yeomanry for their behaviour on 16 August, he also criticised women for being present at all. Ventriloquising his own feelings through the mouths of 'local women' who abused the female reformers, Tyas told his readers that it would have been better if they had stayed at home and left politics to their husbands.[43]

The government itself was utterly unapologetic, reiterating the loyalist commonplace that a female reformer was barely a woman at all. Lord Castlereagh, in his defence of the repressive 'Six Acts', stated that there was no provision for a law against women's political participation because 'when the French republicans were carrying on their bloody orgies, they could find no female to join them except by ransacking the bagnios and public brothels'.[44]* Of course, dehumanisation via hostile propaganda has historically been an important precondition for massacre, and even genocide: the root of the word 'massacre' itself is related to the Old French word for a butcher's block. A year before the Great Reform Act, for instance, the British authorities in Tasmania instituted a 'pheasant drive' against the remaining aboriginal population, thereby bringing off the only totally successful genocide in human history.[45] Similarly, the yeomanry at Peterloo had been consistently encouraged through loyalist imagery and print to see female reformers as less than women, less than human. E. P. Thompson described Peterloo as a 'class war', but it was also a vicious battle of the sexes.[46]

A habitual refrain of conservative writing on Peterloo has been that the 'tragedy' was only an 'unfortunate' consequence of the panicked actions of non-professional soldiers and cavalry. This is unsupportable. The casualty lists present many instances in which the actions of the yeomanry clearly moved beyond 'dispersing' the crowd to gratuitous acts of violence. One man, Patrick Reynolds, was separated from the crowd and chased by the cavalry into a lime pit, receiving severe chemical burns.[47] William Cheetham of Little Bolton was badly cut on the back of the neck by a yeoman

---

* The 'Six Acts' prohibited drilling and military training (a law that has only recently been removed from the statute books) and meetings of over fifty people; authorised justices to enter and search houses without warrants to look for arms; raised the stamp duty on periodicals; and extended the powers of magistrates to deal with seditious action and libel.[48]

called Meagher, who appears in other depositions as a particularly nasty piece of work. In this instance he had ordered the crowd to disperse, to which Cheetham had responded, 'Give us room to pass.' Meagher then moved his horse a little and, as Cheetham went betwixt him and the wall, cut him, saying: 'I will cutt off your damn'd head.'[49] Neither were the professional soldiers, the Hussars, any more restrained. They feature less prominently on the casualty lists only because they entered the fray later than the yeomanry. Peter Warburton was pinned to the Quaker meeting house wall, sustaining seven cuts to his head and body from the sabres of the 15th Hussars. Charles Washington described how the Hussars had entered the chapel yard, hacking down people who had sought refuge within its walls. The soldiers of the 88th Infantry contributed to the bloodshed by cutting off escape routes from St Peter's Fields. They stabbed people in the stomach, back, arms and head with their bayonets, or clubbed them to the ground with the butts of their muskets. Joseph Ogden was attempting to get home when he was stabbed in the head with a bayonet, then clubbed with the musket butt, leaving him disabled for six weeks.[50]

The most persistent myth concerning Peterloo is that it turned the tide of opinion towards political reform. Leaving aside the problem with the chronology here – it took another thirteen years for a very limited reform bill to pass through Parliament – this idea is not supported by the response to the event either by loyalists or by those sympathetic to reform. In the wake of Peterloo, a compensation fund was established by national and regional relief committees. These committees were run by 'respectable' reformers like the Manchester businessman Archibald Prentice. The sums dispensed are a telling reflection of the value placed by middle-class radicals on the lives of those who suffered at Peterloo. Seventy per cent of the payments made were for sums under £2 – pitifully small amounts in cases where the injuries meant that individuals were unable to work for weeks or even months on end. Owen McCabe received a mere £9 compensation, though he was condemned to walk on crutches for the rest of his life.[51] Joshua Whitworth's father, a man of seventy who was largely supported by his son, who was killed by a musket shot on the night of the 16th, received just £4 from the relief committee.[52] In fact, though these committees raised thousands of pounds, most of the money went not to the largely poor casualties of Peterloo but to pay legal fees for the defence of the reform leaders. The contrast could not be greater between the suffering of Elizabeth Gaunt, thrown into the New Bailey, and the 'tribulations' of Henry Hunt in Ilchester Gaol. While the severely beaten Gaunt languished in solitary confinement, Hunt was enjoying convivial evenings with the gaoler and his wife, dining on fine turbot 'presented by the radicals of Plymouth' – other gifts included bottles of wine and gin, sugar loaf, grapes, apricots and pears – and listening to piano recitals by his ward, Miss Grey.[53]

The casualties of Peterloo were certainly seen as fitting objects for middle-class pity, but in most of the press this did not extend to sympathy for the cause for which they had suffered.[54] *The Times* condemned the conduct of the authorities at Manchester, but it also complained of the 'inflammatory manner' in which that conduct was being described in reformist literature. The lesson of 16 August was that the magistrates should operate with more restraint, lest their actions contribute to the 'poison' spread by 'those wretches', the radicals.[55] This had been largely the substance of Tyas's account of Peterloo, which concentrated as much on subsequent rioting in Macclesfield and Oldham as it did on the events in Manchester. As James Wroe dryly noted in the first part of *The Peter Loo Massacre!* (1819), Tyas appeared to be more frightened by the looting of 'new hats and tea kettles (dreadful emblems of civil commotion)' by the Macclesfield mob than by the 'newly-sharpened swords' of the Manchester Yeoman Cavalry.[56]

Some of the treatments of Peterloo in the reformist press itself scarcely amounted to searing indictments of either the Manchester magistracy or Lord Liverpool's government. John Edward Taylor, founder of the *Manchester Guardian* (launched in May 1821) and a witness at the meeting, in his pamphlet *Notes and Observations*

Critical and Explanatory (1820), avoided the word 'massacre' and claimed, despite clear evidence to the contrary, that many of the yeomanry were 'incapable of acting with deliberate cruelty'.[57] However, such caution was not ill-advised. Booksellers who promoted strident indictments of the magistracy, like Wroe's seminal *Peter Loo Massacre!*, risked conviction for seditious libel. At Salford Sessions, John Chorlton was charged and found guilty of 'bringing the soldiers of Our Lord the King into discredit and disgrace by charging them with murder and cruelties' , when he was merely guilty of selling Wroe's pamphlet.[58] In total, there were seventy-five prosecutions for seditious or blasphemous libel in 1819.[59]

People could find themselves in trouble for simply discussing such literature. John Jenkins, an ex-weaver and Royal Marine, had taken to touring the country with one of the many radical engravings of Peterloo, giving his audiences a running commentary of the massacre while picking out details with the aid of a magnifying glass. In November 1819, Jenkins was showing his print in Chudleigh, Devon, when his activities came to the attention of Gilbert Burrington, the vicar of the village and also a local magistrate. He committed Jenkins to the Exeter house of correction as a vagrant and passed information concerning his seditious conduct to the Home Secretary.[60]

Of course, we often associate the radical response to Peterloo with the rousing lines of Shelley's 'Mask of Anarchy', especially its stirring exhortation to the people to 'Rise like lions after slumber'. The events of 16 August certainly stirred deep emotions in the poet: 'The torrent of my indignation has not done boiling in my veins . . . I wait anxiously [to] hear how the Country will express its sense of this bloody murderous oppression of its destroyers. "Something must be done." . . . What yet I know not.'[61] Shelley's wife Mary wrote of his conviction that 'a clash between the two classes of society was inevitable, and he eagerly ranged himself on the people's side. He had an idea of publishing a series of poems adapted expressly to commemorate their circumstances and wrongs.' But the plan to produce a volume entitled *Popular Songs* was never achieved in Shelley's brief lifetime, and it is often forgotten that Leigh Hunt did not publish 'The Mask of Anarchy' in his *Examiner*. The libel laws ensured that it did not emerge in print until 1832.[62] Engels may have described Shelley as the poet of the proletariat, but he only became so several decades after his death.[63]

Some of the radical commentary on Peterloo was wildly popular. Hone's *Political House that Jack Built* (1819), with illustrations by Cruikshank – including the memorable portrait of the Prince Regent as a 'dandy of sixty, / Who bows with a grace / And has *taste* in wigs, collars, cuirasses, and lace' – reputedly sold over a hundred thousand copies in a few weeks. As biting as this satire was, true radicalism in Hone's work had only a liminal presence, lurking, for instance, in his nods to classical republican accounts of tyrannicide in *The Man in the Moon* (1820). He might have been implying that the Prince Regent and his chief ministers, Canning, Castlereagh and Sidmouth, were worthy of the assassin's bullet; but if so, he gave no more than a sly, cautious nod to his audience.[64]

The problem was that those few, like Richard Carlile, who were prepared to run the gauntlet of the libel laws and openly advocate armed resistance were spouting a rhetoric that had been proved hollow by the Pentrich rising. Carlile, in *Sherwin's Political Register*, urged: 'The People have now no recourse left but to arm themselves immediately, for the recovery of their rights, and the defence of their persons, or patiently to submit to the most unconditional slavery.' Burdett was probably being more realistic when he said, 'it is useless to prompt people to resistance when they have no arms'.[65] Carlile himself was imprisoned for publishing his unambiguous rallying call to resistance. The alternative, promoted by Hunt and Wooler, was to continue with a policy of peaceful demonstration, the futility of which had been clearly shown at St Peter's Fields.

In the immediate aftermath of Peterloo, it was the administration of Lord Liverpool that emerged as the real winner. Those who were prosecuted were the victims, the radical leaders and their followers, not the perpetrators of the violence. The latter were not only exonerated, but richly rewarded by the government. Hay, one of the Peterloo magistrates, was gifted the £2000 living of Rochdale. Liverpool publicly stated that the actions of the magistrates had been 'substantially right'. The government's critics, Carlile, Wroe, Hunt, Burdett and Cartwright, were imprisoned. Moderates such as Earl Fitzwilliam who expressed their disgust at the massacre were removed from office. The 'threat' posed by this peaceful demonstration was enough to allow the ministry to get the 'Six Acts' through Parliament.

THE CATO STREET CONSPIRACY
AND THE BATTLE FOR REFORM

After Peterloo, some did follow Carlile's call to arms. The reformer Ethelinda Wilson carried pistols with her to political meetings and spent much time in London attempting to secure weapons for a projected popular insurrection.[1] A letter from Manchester posted on 4 December 1819 reported a conversation in an apothecary's shop between the shop assistant and 'a man of rough appearance'. When the assistant became aware of the man's radical politics, he warned the customer that the soldiers in the city would be 'very severe' in the event of any disturbance. The man replied, 'They'll not Peterloo us again this time', at which point he produced a long dagger from his coat, along with two pistols. That night, shots were fired in the street. The letter finished, 'Reports of guns or pistols are heard every evening, in all directions in the town, to the great terror of the inhabitants.'[2]

Peterloo was the catalyst to the last major insurrectionary plot of the Georgian era. As we have seen, the ultra-radical London Spenceans had been fomenting plans for a general rising of the people since 1816. However, Henry Hunt's successful co-option of the Spa Fields meetings as his democratic platform had made the use of such mass gatherings as a springboard for revolution an apparent dead-end. This prompted a shift of tactics on the Spenceans' part vis-à-vis organising a *coup d'état*. An attempt at just such a plot in August 1817 at Bartholomew Fair was thwarted by last-minute government intervention. Under the leadership of Arthur Thistlewood, the Spenceans now looked to a mass assassination of the Privy Council as the best means to achieve their goals. Coups were planned for late 1817 and early 1818, but on each occasion had to be aborted.

The idea of an assassination plot was well established by the time that the government informer and agent provocateur George Edwards, a Fleet Street model-maker (he had been commissioned to execute busts of Thomas Paine and Richard Carlile) and brother of William, bona fide Spencean and London police officer, became involved in the conspiracy. Edwards reported back to the Home Office that the violent suppression of the Manchester meeting was stirring the Spenceans to action. They viewed Peterloo as 'the revolution begun in blood': Allen Davenport, a shoemaker, was reported as saying, 'I compare the present time to the French Revolution, we must arm ourselves as they did.'

Having squashed the mass platform, the government now saw an opportunity to flush out ultra-radical insurrectionists. Edwards's key role was to feed the group the false information that the Cabinet was meeting for dinner on 23 February 1820 at the Grosvenor Square home of the President of the Privy Council, the Earl of Harrowby. (Wellington's suggestion that the Cabinet actually meet for dinner that evening, but with soldiers masquerading as servants, ready to seize the plotters, had been rejected as being too risky.) With the death of the old King, George III, on 29 January, the time appeared ripe for ultra-radicals to exploit the uncertainty within the government. The plan, such as it was, was for the conspirators to butcher the Cabinet *en masse*, decapitating Lord Sidmouth and Castlereagh and taking their severed heads around the slums of London on poles in order to whip up support for a general insurrection. Their misplaced confidence was revealed in their preparation of propaganda announcing the formation of a provisional republican government.

However, the trap was well set. On the evening of the 23rd, the Cato Street loft in which the conspirators gathered was raided by police and guardsmen. In the struggle that followed, one policeman, Richard Smithers, was killed with a sword by Thistlewood. The candles were knocked out and shots fired in the dark of the hayloft. Thistlewood and three other conspirators managed to escape through a back window, but William Davidson, a Jamaican mixed-race cabinet-maker, and the rest of the ultra-radicals were captured. Just as the soldiers were escorting their prisoners back to Bow Street, the Covent Garden theatre crowds were emptying out into the street. According to the *Courier*:

> The Police Office surrounded by the military, their arms gleaming in the glaring light of the torches, many of them carrying muskets and other spoils taken in the affray, the roar of the coaches in consequence of the Theatres being just closed, and the confused buzz of the multitude drawn together by the appearance of the military, gave altogether a very un-English complexion to the night.[3]

The following day, Thistlewood was also turned in by Edwards, who knew the location of his bolt-hole. Edwards claimed, but never appears to have been paid, a £1000 reward for his arrest. Although the number of conspirators brought to justice remained small, the nationwide anger that Peterloo had provoked meant that the support for this latest insurrection came from more than just a small cadre of metropolitan zealots. Subsequent searches revealed that the assassination plot had received considerable material support from artisan friendly societies, and several caches of arms were also uncovered.

In all, eleven men were charged with high treason. Two of them, Robert Adams and John Harrison, turned King's evidence, which allowed the prosecution to avoid having to rely on the testimony of Edwards, whose role, like that of Castle and Oliver in earlier treason trials, was already causing an outcry in reformist circles. In the Commons, Matthew Wood, the former London Mayor, now radical City MP, accused the government of entrapment, while the *Observer* flouted ministerial instructions not to report the trial. Adams was let off, thanks to his cooperation with the prosecution, though shortly afterwards he was imprisoned for debt. Harrison, along with four others, was transported for life to Australia.* Thistlewood and Davidson, along with John Brunt, John Ings and Richard Tidd, were all sentenced to death.

The condemned men met their end with defiance and revolutionary resolve. Ings wrote to his wife that he was sorry to leave her 'in a land full of corruption, where justice and liberty has taken their flight from'. He hoped she would 'bear in mind that the cause of my being consigned to the scaffold was a pure motive. I thought I should have rendered my starving fellow-men, women and children, a service.' Brunt declared in court that he 'had joined the conspiracy for the public good . . . He would die as the descendant of an ancient Briton.' On the scaffold, Thistlewood resolutely maintained that he died for liberty. Byron's friend, John Cam Hobhouse, noted in his diary that the 'men died like heroes'.[4] The five were hanged at Newgate on 1 May 1820. Their decapitated bodies were buried in quicklime inside the gaol. Though the revolutionary intent of the Cato Street conspiracy was undoubtedly more serious than that of the Pentrich rising, the involvement of government agents provocateurs continued to arouse public opposition. Matthew Wood's call for an inquiry into the prosecution of the plot forced Edwards into hiding and, finally, into exile in the Cape Colony, South Africa (coincidentally, also the final destination of 'Oliver the Spy').[5]

* He later opened a bakery in New South Wales, while two of his co-conspirators went on to become policemen.

The Cato Street conspiracy may have been a government-engineered trap, but the violent mood of many radicals was real enough. The sense of a nationwide conspiracy was fuelled by the discovery of plots in Glasgow and Yorkshire. On 5 and 6 April 1820, groups of armed weavers rose in the vicinity of Glasgow, leading to a violent clash with the military at Bonnymuir. One of the leaders of the rising, John Baird, fought ferociously:

> after discharging his piece [musket] he presented it at the officer empty, and told him he would do for him if he did not stand off. The officer presented his pistol at him, but it flashed and did not go off. Mr Baird then took the butt end of his piece and struck a private on the left thigh, where upon the sergeant of Hussars fired at him. Baird then threw his musket from him and seized a pike, and while the sergeant was in the act of drawing his sword, wounded him in the right arm.[6]

They had, however, been betrayed by another government spy, named King, and after the arrival of other troops the rebels were forced to surrender. Several were sabred by the yeomanry after they had put down their arms. Baird and Andrew Hardie (an ancestor of Keir Hardie) were sentenced to death and executed on 8 September that year. Like Thistlewood and the other Cato Street conspirators, they went to their deaths protesting the justice of their cause. The magistracy had to use considerable force to prevent a riot by sympathisers at their executions. Over twenty other rebels were transported for life.[7]

These risings and conspiracies helped justify the government's repressive 'Six Acts', but they were not fatal to popular radicalism. The Cato Street trial revived, if to a lesser extent, the concerns about the use of spies and agents provocateurs, which played well to pro-reform members of the middle class. Popular radicalism also enjoyed a brief resurgence thanks, paradoxically, to the royal family. One of George IV's first acts as King was to initiate divorce proceedings against his wife Queen Caroline, from whom he had long been separated. His first step was to have her excluded from public prayers for the royal family. The Queen, exiled in Europe, incensed at this insult, determined to return to England to reaffirm her position as royal consort. By the time she reached England, her cause had been co-opted by leading London radicals, in particular Matthew Wood, who rightly saw the potential here to embarrass the government and drum up support for the cause of reform. Bootle Wilbraham, a Yorkshire landowner and MP, wrote in September 1820: 'Radicalism has taken the shape of affection for the Queen, and has deserted its old form, for we are all as quiet as lambs in this part of England, and you would not imagine that this had been a disturbed county twelve months ago.'[8] Mass petitioning and addressing were revived: a laudatory address from 'the married ladies of London' carried 17,642 signatures.[9]

Overall, the Queen Caroline affair proved a spur to the growth of middle-class female political activism.[10] In total, Caroline received over 350 of these supportive loyal addresses, many of them from groups of women who saw their own domestic difficulties reflected in the royal drama. Campaigning came to a head over the so-called 'trial' of the Queen in August 1820, when a divorce bill was put before Parliament. The affair briefly revived the radical press, under severe pressure from the extended libel laws and raised stamp duty. The 'trial' saw the production of massive numbers of scurrilous libels and prints concerning the King – so many, in fact, that the Crown expended over £2500 to buy up and suppress them. Some ultra-radical broadsheets even used the tribulations of the Queen to justify regicide. A broadsheet called *The Pig of Pall Mall* threatened the King's death. There were reports of seditious words being spoken to the effect that 'if there was no necessity of a queen . . . they would have no king'. Rumours also circulated of men arming in the North in preparation for an insurrection.[11] This radical pressure effectively stymied the divorce bill in Parliament.

Though it passed the Lords on its third reading, Liverpool was forced to concede on 10 November that it would proceed no further. In celebration at Caroline's 'acquittal', a massive thanksgiving service was held at St Paul's Cathedral; the psalm sung was 'Deliver me, O Lord, from the evil man'.

The capital that radicals were able to make out of the Queen Caroline affair was short-lived. The Queen herself had no real commitment to reform, and the public, it seemed, quickly lost interest in her case once it became clear that the King would not be able to divorce her. Caroline's triumph soon turned into humiliation. She was refused entry to George IV's coronation on 21 July 1821 and, on being turned away from the Abbey, was jeered by the assembled crowd. A fortnight later she was taken seriously ill, and died on 7 August. Briefly, the Queen's 'trial' had allowed radical writers and politicians to focus on familiar unifying themes: corruption and waste, as personified in the body of the dissolute King himself. In some ultra-radical circles, this had extended to arguments for doing away with the King altogether. However, following the 'trial' episode, the divisions between metropolitan radicals became more and more pronounced. Carlile and Hunt publicly traded shots, Carlile even repudiating the label 'radical':

> It is my intention to call upon every man who stiles himself a Reformer to come up to the Political Principles of Thomas Paine, as laid down in the Second Part of his 'Rights of Man'. I know they are secretly admired by you all. I shall call upon you to substitute the word Republican for the unmeaning and hacknied word Radical . . . The boasted *white hat* [Hunt] teaches no useful principles. We will disavow all badges, and resort to the declaration of some well-defined and well understood principles. Badges are too often the converts of treachery.[12]

Hunt, for his part, was increasingly turning his attention to business ventures, albeit ones with a radical tinge. He manufactured a 'radical Breakfast powder', a nutritious start to the day which had the benefit of being untaxed and therefore contributed nothing to the propping-up of 'Old Corruption'. He also produced shoe-blacking adorned with the slogan 'Equal Laws, Equal Rights, Annual Parliaments, Universal Suffrage and the Ballot'. Burdett, who had been imprisoned for his condemnation of the actions of the yeomanry at Peterloo, directed his political efforts away from the cause of constitutional reform and towards Catholic emancipation. Cartwright, now into his eighties, was busying himself writing his last political will and testament, another lengthy exposition of England's 'Saxon' liberties, *The English Constitution Produced and Illustrated* (1823). The similarly aged Thomas Jefferson wrote to Cartwright to congratulate him on his work, joking that they would soon have an eternity to discuss political reform together; Cartwright died on 23 September 1824. Some radicals rejected reform altogether. The publisher William Hone moved away from controversial works to focus on collections of folklore and natural history. Formerly a deist, in the 1830s he converted to evangelical Christianity.

Increasingly concerned about the 'despotism' of the Tory administration and worried that without a change in the franchise they would never be able to retake power, some elements of the Whig Party did eventually move to a more committed attachment to limited electoral reform. J. G. Lambton, later Lord Privy Seal, wrote to his father-in-law Lord Grey that it was 'insanity to think that we have any chance of turning the Ministers out while the House of Commons is constituted as it is'.[13] In 1819, Lord John Russell successfully moved for the disenfranchisement of the rotten borough of Grampound, Cornwall. In 1821, he put forward proposals for limited reform that were rejected by the narrow margin of only 155 to 124, and the following year he presented a bolder scheme whereby 100 new members, 60 representing counties and 40 representing large towns, would be added to the House, while each of the

100 smallest boroughs would lose one of its two members. By this point, two leading Whig politicians, the Dukes of Devonshire and Grafton, had already declared their support for reform. Aside from the threat of government tyranny, the weakening of the cause of universal suffrage suggested that advocating reform would no longer mean opening the door for more radical constitutional change.

Some of the arguments for limited reform in the 1820s were informed by the emerging political philosophy of utilitarianism, epitomised in the thought of Jeremy Bentham, who believed that the first principle of government should be to pursue the 'greatest happiness of the greatest number'. As he also believed that individuals were essentially self-interested, democratic reform was important in making the country's governors accountable to the will of the majority. In his early, unpublished writings on reform from the 1790s, Bentham had, in fact, advocated a very extensive expansion of the franchise, even suggesting that women and former slaves should enjoy the vote: 'As to the Negro and the Woman, were they by some strange accident to overcome the body of prejudice which combats their admission with so much force, there could not be a stronger proof of a degree of merit superior to any that was to be found among whites and among men.'[14] In his *Plan for Parliamentary Reform*, written in 1809 and published in 1817, Bentham continued to argue for a broader franchise than most Whigs in Parliament would have been prepared to accept. He advocated annual parliaments, the secret ballot and a franchise of all literate males. He conceded that many women too were now literate, but still did not advocate their enfranchisement as it would have been too controversial at the time.

But it was in the much watered-down form of James Mill's *Essay on Government* (1820) that Bentham's ideas reached their greatest audience. Here, the franchise was limited to male taxpayers over the age of forty, a form of suffrage which would give prominence to the middle classes, 'the wisest part of the community'. Although utilitarianism essentially rejected both the idea of innate natural rights (an insupportable fiction, according to Bentham) and the notion of an 'ancient constitution', he appeared quite prepared to allow his ideas to be popularised in radical periodicals such as John Wade's *Gorgon*, which he helped to fund, and Wooler's *Black Dwarf*.[15] Bentham was equally willing to allow authors to intersperse borrowings from his texts with references to Anglo-Saxon liberties. He collaborated with John Cartwright on works that bore the latter's trademark faith in the rights gifted by the 'ancient constitution'.[16] Even Bentham's intellectual disciple, Francis Place, spent considerable time researching parliamentary history, believing that many were 'led more by authority than by reason'.[17]

Bentham's political philosophy was attractive to respectable reformers: he was not an advocate of direct, participatory democracy like Henry Hunt. For Bentham, the role of a free press and a broadened franchise was to give vent to public opinion, which would act as an important check on governmental corruption.[18] Wade's periodical, in particular, emphasised Bentham's belief in the essentially parasitic nature of the landowning class – 'they are in a word, idlers not labourers, not the many but the few'.[19] These arguments appealed to middle-class, pro-reform merchants and industrialists such as Archibald Prentice, who promoted a bowdlerised version of Bentham's beliefs in his *Manchester Gazette*.[20] Benthamite arguments also fitted in with the dominance of Ricardian economic ideas, which claimed that it was vital to support trade and manufacturing to avoid the stagnation that was an 'inevitable' feature of primarily agricultural societies.[21]

One significant impact of so-called 'philosophical radicalism' – indeed, perhaps the only meaningful victory for radicalism as a whole during the 1820s – can be attributed to the eventually successful campaign to repeal the Combination Acts. Orchestrated by the radical MP Joseph Hume inside Parliament and by Francis Place without, the campaign was not an attempt to reassert the right of working people to form trade unions (which may explain why Hume and Place were ultimately successful). In fact, the Benthamite Place viewed unions as a social evil, like employers' cartels an unnecessary and damaging interference in the operation of the free market. He had argued in favour of the repeal of the paternalistic Tudor labour legislation, noting in the *Statesman* on 8 March 1815 that

> among the many calamitous circumstances arising from the want of a real Representation of the People . . . is to be reckoned the evil of excessive Legislation; or, in other words, the interference of Parliament in matters which cannot advantageously be regulated by law, and in which, therefore, the exertions of individuals ought to be left free and unrestrained.[22]

Place's antipathy to unions was revealed fully in an 1825 letter to Burdett:

> Combinations will soon cease to exist. Men have been kept together for long periods only by the oppression of the laws; these being repealed, combinations will lose the matter which cements them into masses, and they will fall to pieces . . . He knows nothing of the working people who can suppose that, when left at liberty to act for themselves, without being driven into permanent associations by the oppression of the laws, they will continue to contribute money for distant and doubtful experiments, for uncertain and precarious benefits.[23]

Nonetheless, the work of Place and Hume allowed union organisers, most prominently John Gast, to begin working openly again for a general combination of trade organisations. By the late 1820s, Gast had established the first trade union paper, the *Trades' Newspaper*, and successfully defended attacks on local friendly societies, which in turn helped provide the foundation for the new 'cooperative movement'. At this stage, however, the 'guild socialism'

of Robert Owen, the intellectual founder of the cooperative movement, remained anathema to most radicals, popular or otherwise.
Owen, a Lanark mill owner who had introduced fairer working
practices into his firm, including shops where employees gained a
share of the profits, was viewed as a threat to individual self-reliance.
T. J. Wooler described Owen's plans for self-supporting communities established on the cooperative principle as an assault upon
'those proud feelings of self-reliance and estimation, which in a
sound and healthy state of things constitute the support of free
states'.[24] For most radicals, including the surviving Spenceans like
Thomas Preston, social evils remained the creation of excessive taxation and the corrupt oligarchy that fed off it: they were not
products of industrial capitalism itself.

Although Lord Russell's reform bills were a testimony to the
growing impetus behind moderate reform, it was the contingency
of Lord Liverpool's resignation in 1827, as a result of a severe
stroke, that opened the path for the ultimate success of limited
reform. Following the brief premiership of Canning, the Duke of
Wellington's second ministry – appointed partly on the grounds
of political neutrality – succeeded in alienating both liberal and
Canningite Tories by refusing to transfer the seats of nearby
East Retford to Birmingham, and Tory devotees of the established
Church by conceding Catholic emancipation. These develop-
ments actually moved some Tories towards reform. The Marquess
of Blandford made limited reform proposals in Parliament in
February 1830, in the belief that anti-popish sentiment would
help shore up the Anglican Church. Conversely, Catholic emancipation (the Catholic Relief Act was passed in April 1829) may
have eased Whig anxieties about broadening the franchise: with
this secured, they no longer had to worry about the threat of
unleashing popular anti-Catholicism.

Agitation within Parliament was accompanied by extensive
reform activity outside, fed by public discontent arising from the
severe economic recession that hit the country in 1829–30. After a

period of relative stability (if not prosperity) for labourers in the late eighteenth century, the living standards of the lower classes in Britain had gone into a significant decline. If the nation avoided the mass starvation that occurred in Ireland, it was as much by luck as design. The people of mid-Victorian England were nonetheless noticeably undernourished compared to their predecessors: the average height of army recruits fell by some two inches after 1845 and did not recover to former levels until thirty years later.[25] The massive increase in the nation's population (from thirteen million in 1783 to nearly twenty-seven million by 1841) was a result of an increase in the birthrate, not a decline in the horrific levels of infant mortality. In some urban areas, such as Liverpool, the life expectancy of labourers at fifteen was less than half of what it had been for agricultural workers in 1450. In that city, many working families lived in dank cellars into which the effluent from communal privies freely flowed: one family's bed was reported as precariously positioned over a four-foot ravine filled with human waste.[26]

In January 1830, the Birmingham Political Union was established by the wealthy Tory industrialist Thomas Attwood. He strenuously avoided making any public commitment to universal suffrage, but he was successful nonetheless in gathering mass support for his campaign for limited electoral reform: by 1831 he was regularly addressing crowds numbering tens, even hundreds, of thousands. In the July and August 1830 elections after the death of George IV, the government was challenged in many constituencies and failed to strengthen its majority. In southern England, the 'Captain Swing' riots, a wave of rick-burning that bore comparison with the Luddite activity of the 1810s, created a very unsettled atmosphere. The government responded harshly against the rioters: Henry Cook of Micheldever in Hampshire, a lad of nineteen, was hanged for knocking the hat off the head of a member of the Barings banking family during an altercation.[27]

The weakened Tory government, undermined further by the Prime Minister's unadvisedly robust rejection of reform, lost a hostile vote on subjecting its civil list to public scrutiny, and Wellington was forced to resign in November 1830, to be replaced by the Whig Lord Grey, who publicly affirmed that reform would be a key priority for his ministry. In March 1831, Lord Russell introduced the first reform bill in the Commons, where, in a packed chamber, it passed its second reading by only one vote. However, the bill was amended in committee with a proviso that, against the wishes of government, retained the original number of MPs.

Seeking a mandate for Russell's original bill, Parliament was again dissolved. The general election in the spring of 1831 increased the Whig majority in the House and the reintroduced bill passed its second reading by a majority of 136, only to be rejected by the Lords in October. This affront to the cause of reform led to serious rioting in Derby, Nottingham – where the homes of the Duke of Nottingham and the Earl of Middleton were attacked – and Bristol, where the Bishop's palace and Lord Mayor's house were set on fire. There was a palpable sense that the outright rejection of reform would lead to revolution. Some advocates of reform realised this feeling was strategically useful. James Mill wrote, 'The people . . . should appear to be ready and impatient to break out into action, without actually breaking out.'[28] Mill's comment echoed the thoughts of his mentor, Bentham, who also believed that the threat of popular violence could be a useful weapon in the battle for reform.[29]

As chaos reigned outside Parliament, dissension ruled within. The failure of the bill in the Lords led to the resignation of Grey in May 1832. The King recalled Wellington, but with a commission to form a government committed to some degree of electoral reform, an undertaking that neither the Duke nor his Tory supporters felt able to meet. In the absence of an alternative, Grey returned to office, this time successfully persuading William IV to threaten the creation of new Whig peers if the Lords persisted in obstructing the bill. With success in the Upper House inevitable, the bill eventually passed into law in June 1832.

Historians remain divided as to whether the Reform Act represents a political or constitutional watershed. The opinions of contemporaries reflected the continuities rather than the changes. The political diarist Charles Greville noted, 'A Reformed Parliament turns out to be very much like every other Parliament . . . except that the Whigs have got possession of the power which the Tories have lost.' John Cam Hobhouse, now a prominent Whig politician, claimed that Grey looked upon reform as 'a mere trick of state for the preservation of power'. In crude terms, the Reform Act did expand the size of the electorate considerably, from around 400,000 potential electors to 656,000 (about one in five of the adult male population). This was not, though, a staggering advance for democracy, and in fact these male electors constituted a smaller proportion of the population than had enjoyed the vote in 1640.[30] What is more, in eliminating the rotten boroughs, the 1832 Reform Act also largely swept away the broadly democratic ratepayer 'scot and lot' franchise that had existed in some thirty-seven boroughs, including seats like Westminster that had been key battlegrounds for radical reformers. By opting for a £10 property qualification instead of a ratepayer franchise, the Reform Act actually disenfranchised large numbers of working-class men. Conversely, it enfranchised so-called 'opulent serfs', the £50 'tenants-at-will' whose lack of security of land tenure made them easy targets for manipulation by landowners.

Numerically, more could vote; but it was more of the wealthy, making the electoral system arguably less 'democratic'.[31] And it was not only men who suffered under the 'Great' Reform Act. For the first time, women were explicitly forbidden to vote in national elections and, after 1835, in local elections too. Hitherto, some female property holders had exercised the vote. Now they could not.

There is no better illustration of the winners and losers under the act than in the contrasting fortunes of Henry Hunt and his Peterloo nemesis, Sir Hugh Hornby Birley, factory owner and leader of the Manchester Yeomanry. In 1830, Hunt had won the seat of Preston, a constituency with a broad 'potwalloper' (householder) franchise. As MP, he campaigned on an unashamedly populist, pro-working-class platform, attacking the Whig reform bill's exclusive, property-based franchise and thereby earning the anger of some fellow radicals. He even presented a petition in favour of female suffrage in the Commons. Partly as a result of this uncompromising stance, Hunt lost his seat at the first elections held under the new system.[32] The campaign also ruined his health and his wealth. He suffered a stroke in February 1835 and died soon after. Birley, on the other hand, was one of many wealthy businessmen and industrialists who were Tory in their political sympathies but who increasingly recognised the value of moderate reform as a means of ensuring that trade and manufacturing interests were represented at Westminster. It was through the efforts of Birley and his Tory colleagues that the seats of the two rotten boroughs of Grampound and Penryn were finally transferred to Manchester in 1832. (His son, also named Hugh, would serve as MP for Manchester between 1868 and 1883.) Birley made clear that he did all of this in the cause of business interests, not out of any regret for his actions against the 'unrepresented people' at Peterloo in 1819.

Peterloo did not, then, lead inexorably to the reforms of 1832, limited though even these were. It was the leader of the yeomanry, Birley, not the radical spokesman, Hunt, who emerged the 'winner' in that year. Between 1830 and 1832, popular political action mainly had a negative, if significant, impact on events in Westminster, convincing MPs that reform was necessary to stave off revolution, via an alliance of the upper and middle classes.

Yet Peterloo was important in a number of positive ways, too. It heralded the emergence of women-only political societies, while female involvement in politics would not be thwarted by the terms of the 1832 act. Women would play a significant role in Chartism, which in turn would provide an inspiration to the female suffrage movement. Hunt, the hero of Peterloo, had longer-term significance, too: though his political career ended in failure, his model of charismatic leadership arguably provided the template for every successful populist politician up to the twentieth century, when the advent of radio and television diminished the importance of oratorial magnetism. Hunt's 'mass platform' also established the broad terms on which radical activity, most notably through the Chartist movement, would be conducted over the next twenty to thirty years, a platform that focused on universal male suffrage, annual parliaments and the secret ballot.

Whether such objectives were the best means of bettering the conditions of the industrial working class is another matter, but for the most part, radical political language and ideas continued to be dominated by a constitutionalist outlook. The critiques of capitalism advanced by Owen and others sustained the interest of only a small minority. Yet, even shorn of social and economic critique, the basic elements of the mass platform remained transformative. Moreover, the adoption of radical tactics during the reform agitation of 1830–2 demonstrated that this programme could be successful, particularly when it gathered more respectable supporters.

Most important, though, was the powerful memory that Peterloo conveyed of working-class solidarity. The memory of the demonstration, particularly Shelley's poetic re-imaging of it in 'The Mask of Anarchy', proved a powerful spur to various liberation movements. Shelley's words inspired Mohandas K. Gandhi's campaigns for the rights of the Indian community in South Africa and, through him, Martin Luther King and the American civil rights movement. In China in 1989, in a chilling replay of the events of 1819, the students in Tiananmen Square reportedly chanted the words of Shelley's poem as government troops bore down on them.[33] In Britain, too, the sense of radical identity created by Peterloo helped sustain popular radicalism in the 1830s and

1840s through difficult times. It became a seminal moment in the political education of many future radicals. As the Lancashire dialect writer and Chartist Ben Brierley recalled:

My father was not only a Waterloo veteran, but he was at Peterloo in 1819, when that bloody massacre took place, and when many were cut down for peacefully agitating for freedom. At that time Radicals were not allowed to mix in bar-parlour company. The tap-room was the only place where they could give vent to their views, and they had to be careful of what they said even there, as there were so many spies going about in those days . . . I was then five years of age. I was sent with a can for some soup which was being given out to the people in the district. When I presented myself the person who was doling it out remarked: 'That lad mun ha' noan, his gronfeyther were a Jacobin' . . . I went away without soup, but those words have rung in my ears ever since. They set me a-thinking, and I wondered what sort of an animal a Jacobin was that his little starving grandson could have no soup. This treatment had much to do with the formation of my political character, and as I grew up I felt determined I would never belong to a party which made me suffer for what my grandfather believed.[34]

PART SIX

A KNIFE-AND-FORK QUESTION?
THE RISE AND FALL OF CHARTISM

MR WEBB – What is the child to be called?

MRS KING – James Feargus O'Connor King.

MR WEBB – Is your husband a Chartist?

MRS KING – I don't know, but his wife is.

Reported conversation between Mrs King, a Manchester
Chartist, and Richard Webb, public registrar of the district[1]

The Tolpuddle Martyrs and the People's Charter

On the morning of 24 February 1834, six farm labourers were arrested in the Dorset village of Tolpuddle. They were marched in chains to the gaol at Dorchester where, according to one of the prisoners, George Loveless, 'we were ushered down some steps into a miserable dungeon, opened but twice a year, with only a glimmering light . . . The smoke of this place, together with its natural dampness, amounted nearly to suffocation: and in this most dreadful situation, we passed three whole days.'[1]

The men were charged, under legislation ostensibly meant to tackle oath-bound conspiracies, with administering unlawful oaths during an agricultural labourers' friendly society meeting. The guilty verdict in the trials was certainly dubious: it was doubtful that the oath that Loveless administered to his fellow labourers really amounted to the kind of sworn conspiracy that the Georgian legislation aimed to prevent.[2] As Daniel O'Connell, the Irish nationalist leader and MP for County Clare, later remarked, if the Dorset labourers were guilty of swearing illegal oaths, then so were all the members of Britain's Orange Lodges.[3] The government of Lord Sidmouth was under little illusion that the Dorchester labourers were really plotting a violent insurrection. Rather, the case presented an excellent opportunity to curb the resurgence in union activity. Trade combinations, as we have seen, were already in existence in the late eighteenth century and by 1824, with the repeal of the Combination Acts, they were legal once again. In 1834, there were significant moves afoot by the Owenite GNCTU (the Grand National Consolidated Trades Union) to expand unionisation in the agricultural sector. The brutal sentences in the Tolpuddle case certainly helped Sidmouth's government to put a damper on trade union expansion in this area.[4]

The Dorset men were found guilty at Dorchester Assizes on 17 March. They each received a sentence of seven years' transportation – considered harsh even at the time. Five of them set sail for Australia from Portsmouth on 11 April (Loveless's departure was delayed because of illness), reaching Sydney in August of that year. A month later, Loveless landed in Tasmania and was put to work on a government farm. Conditions in the Australian penal colonies were appalling: one of the men, James Brine, had to go six months without shoes, fresh clothes or bedding, sleeping on the bare ground each night. The others fared a little better, though hunger, hard labour and the constant threat of brutal corporal punishment for minor offences were familiar to all six men.[5] Transportation was certainly a long way from Lord Ellenborough's ludicrous description in the 1810 penal reform debate – 'a summer airing by an easy migration to a milder climate'.[6]

The trial of the 'Tolpuddle Martyrs', as they came to be known, quickly became a *cause célèbre* in radical circles. Feargus O'Connor, the firebrand MP for Cork, denounced the government for its treatment of the men: 'Earl Grey, Lord Brougham, the noble Lord, the Paymaster of the Forces, and the right honourable Secretary for the Colonies, should be on board the hulks in place of those unfortunate men.'[7] Petitions and public demonstrations, including a forty-thousand-strong rally in Copenhagen Fields, London, demanded that the sentences be reversed. In the face of this considerable pressure, Lord Melbourne's new government granted the men conditional pardons in June 1835; after further campaigning, they were made unconditional the following year.

However, the men found out about their pardons only by chance, despite the fact that news of the quashing of their sentences had reached Australia in August 1836. Loveless was the first to return to England, gaining free passage in January 1837. The men were welcomed back as heroes. Funds had been raised to support them and their families, and a London committee had attempted to raise enough money to buy them farms of their own.

Hailed, then and now, as heroes of the trade union movement, the Tolpuddle Martyrs were also integral to the development of nineteenth-century radicalism. Loveless, a pacific Methodist, had been radicalised by the experience of transportation: soon after his return, he was actively engaged not only in union activity but in agitation for the vote. He was soon involved with Chartism, the largest and most significant popular radical movement of the 1830s and 1840s. His pamphlet, *The Victims of Whiggery*, was widely read at Chartist meetings, and the Martyrs also established a Chartist committee at Greensted, Essex, where the London committee had secured for them a leasehold farm.[8]

Chartism took its name from the 'People's Charter', the movement's founding manifesto. The Charter's 'Six Points' demanded universal male suffrage, annual parliaments, the secret ballot, the equalisation of constituencies, salaries for MPs and an end to property qualifications for parliamentary candidates. In the context of the 1830s and 1840s, these demands remained radical in the sense that they went far beyond what the vast majority in Parliament was willing to consider. Indeed, five of the Six Points would not be fulfilled until the 1918 Representation of the People Act, while annual or even fixed-term parliaments have never been realised. However, the basic elements of the Charter were hardly innovative: they constituted the substance of the Peterloo

marchers' platform of twenty years earlier. This was no coincidence. Feargus O'Connor, the dominant figure in the movement
from 1839 to 1848, like many other Chartists, was a great admirer
of Henry Hunt, calling himself a 'Huntite' and proclaiming that
'[Mr Hunt] was the great architect who taught the people what
that edifice [meaning the reformed political system] should be;
[Mr O'Connor] was only a humble workman endeavouring to
raise that edifice to its completion.'[9]

It used to be suggested that what was truly radical about
Chartism was the methods advocated by some of its supporters
for achieving its political programme, namely violent insurrection.
A distinction was made between 'physical force' and 'moral force'
Chartists, epitomised by the contrast between the slight, bookish,
bureaucratic founder of the London Working Men's Association,
William Lovett, and the beefy, bombastic, belligerent leader of
the Marylebone Radical Association, Feargus O'Connor. However,
whatever the obvious differences between O'Connor and Lovett in
style and personal appearance, the two men, as we shall see, shared
a common belief in the ultimate right to use force to defend liberty.
In fact, the concentration of historians on the Six Points, and
especially the vote, in discussions of Chartism has obscured the
genuinely innovative nature of the movement, which lay in
Chartism's strong claim to be the first truly modern British political party: unlike earlier radical movements, it drew its strength from
Ireland, Scotland and Wales as well as England. It established many
of the basic forms and structures that would be fundamental to
political organisations right up to the present day. Tactics pioneered
by the Chartists – hijacking the public meetings of political opponents, establishing election funds, staging mass demonstrations –
were all later exploited by the militant women's suffrage movement,
among others. Even Chartism's more ridiculed initiatives – particularly O'Connor's 'Land Plan', in the light of a growing global food
crisis – appear increasingly prescient. Like Peterloo, however, the
movement's significance lies in far more than the bare facts of its

aims and organisation. Chartism became an integral part of the cultural life of local communities, offering, despite many historians' verdicts of ultimate 'failure', a powerful morale-boosting memory of working-class political activism and solidarity.

Chartism was seen by both contemporaries and later historians as a reaction to economic distress and widening social inequality. The 1830s and 1840s were decades of intense industrial, technological and demographic change. Nowhere was this more evident than in the rapidly expanding conurbations of the North: Manchester, Sheffield and Leeds. Speaking of the Manchester region, one contemporary observer recorded:

> The country has undergone a change scarcely to be credited, except by those who have witnessed it. Villages have sprung into towns, and ordinary sized towns have become rivals in population and wealth of the great capitals of nations; gigantic factories, vomiting their dense clouds of poisonous smoke, have obliterated from the face of a large part of the kingdom every vestige of nature's beauty, while the plastered, tinselled, and gaudy palaces of the princes of commerce have sprung up, left and right, as if at the beck of an enchanter's wand.[10]

Early nineteenth-century Britain was a noticeably more connected, more informed and more urbanised nation than it had been one hundred years previously. By the 1840s, railways were replacing turnpikes and telegrams the penny post. These new forms of communication and improved transport links effectively 'shrank' the nation: in 1710, news of the trial of Henry Sacheverell had taken three days to travel just from London to Shropshire. In 1820, news of the 'trial' of Queen Caroline took the same length of time to get to the Isle of Skye. Coupled with rising levels of literacy, reflected in a buoyant provincial press, these changes arguably made the general British public the most politically informed in Europe (if not the most politically emancipated.)[11]

But in terms of the working and living conditions of the British poor, the benefits of this process of 'modernisation' were hard to see. While most of the population continued to work the land, the balance was quickly shifting, as more and more people gravitated towards the industrial centres in search of work. The nature of the workforce was also changing, with mechanisation making the cheaper labour of women and children more and more attractive – a fact that caused no little anxiety among radicalism's male leadership. For factory hands, these were decades of severe hardship. Wages were low and hours long. Wheat prices rose from 39 shillings a quarter (28 pounds) in 1836 to 68 shillings in 1840, while in the cotton mills of Manchester conditions steadily worsened.[12] The rapid pace of urban growth, and the inevitable desire to cut costs, meant that housing for workers was usually shoddily built, with poor sanitation and ventilation.

European visitors were shocked by the gaping gulf between rich and poor in England's rapidly expanding industrial towns. Friedrich Engels, then working for his father's textile firm in Manchester, recalled a conversation with one of the town's gentlemen:

> I spoke to him about the disgraceful unhealthy slums and drew his attention to the disgusting condition of that part of the town in which the factory workers lived. I declared that I had never seen so badly built a town in my life. He listened patiently and at the corner of the street at which we parted company he remarked: 'And yet there is great deal of money made here. Good morning, Sir.'[13]

At the time that he wrote these comments in 1844, Engels believed that the stark social divisions made a revolution by the proletariat imminent and inevitable. If that prediction proved false, it was nonetheless true that such blatant social inequality had a politicising effect on some workers, as the Chartist George Flinn, a leading conspirator in the 1840 Bradford rising, recalled:

[Flinn] was charged by his mill master with having a little more knowledge than most of his fellow workmen; and in the eyes of a mill master that is a crime of no small degree. Well, how was he situated in order to get this knowledge? He lived in a cellar, nine feet by seven. *This dwelling was his workshop, his bed-room, his kitchen, his study,* AND NOT UNFREQUENTLY HIS HOSPITAL. Could any man live thus and not 'acquire knowledge'. Was he to close his eyes to the fact, that while he was obliged to toil in such a position, the fruit of his labour was filched from him, and splendid mansions arose in every direction around him, inhabited by those that mock him with expressions of sympathy?[14]

There is certainly some correlation between peaks of Chartist activity and troughs of economic depression. However, the relationship is not a straightforward one. For one thing, Chartism remained a resolutely political movement. While the great Chartist preacher Joseph Rayner Stephens, may have described universal suffrage as a 'knife and fork question' in 1838, and the old Chartist Thomas Dunning referred to his early view of politics as 'a-bread-and-cheese question', yet the remedies prescribed for grumbling bellies were political, not economic.[15] Even its most apparently 'economic' endeavour, O'Connor's Land Plan, was directed at creating independent, self-sufficient smallholders, thereby fostering the political autonomy of the working classes. The Land Plan was not designed to abolish private property of any kind or to 'level' social distinctions. The economic distress of the 1830s and 1840s could have inspired fresh waves of Luddite activity or 'Swing' riots. That it did not suggests that, rightly or wrongly, the millions who supported the Chartist cause saw the political agenda of the Six Points as the remedy to their problems.[16]

Chartism coalesced out of three movements clearly rooted in the depression of the 1830s: the 'ten-hours movement', which aimed at limiting the working day; the movement for factory reform; and the opposition to reform of the Poor Law. Yet the underlying problems were seen as products of political despotism, a Whig 'tyranny' represented not only by the Poor Law Reform Act of 1834 but also by the Irish coercion bill of 1833 which gave the Lord Lieutenant of Ireland extensive powers to suppress political meetings, and the severe repression of the largely non-violent 'Swing' rioters who had attacked threshing machines across southern England in the summer of 1830.[17] Lord John Russell's famous speech, which earned him the nickname 'Finality Jack', declared that the 1832 act represented the end, not the beginning, of England's political reformation. This betrayal of the cause of reform seemed to be followed by an attack upon the remnants of paternalism, which alarmed both traditionalist Tories and many radicals.

The Poor Law Reform Act, whose evils were so vividly portrayed by Dickens in *Oliver Twist*, proposed to abolish outdoor relief for the able-bodied poor, who were to be forced to find work or face the horror and shame of the workhouse. Opposition to the new Poor Law was not led solely by working-class activists. Initial leadership came from Sir Robert Peel and Robert Owen, both capitalist cotton mill owners, though of very different political stripes. Similarly, the ten-hours movement in Yorkshire in the 1830s was led by a Tory land steward, Richard Oastler, and was promoted in Parliament by his friend Michael Sadler, until the latter lost his seat as a consequence of the Reform Act. In Lancashire, the Owenite trade union leader John Doherty and the radical factory master from Todmorden, John Fielden, campaigned for even shorter hours, their supporters whipped up by the impassioned and increasingly incendiary preaching of J. R. Stephens. The imposition of the new Poor Law was fiercely resisted in the North, with Tories and working-class radicals lining up together against the regime of the 'bloody Whigs'.

Public pressure, and not infrequently the resort to physical force, bore positive results. The outrage of the North spilled over into violence as attempts were made to prevent the new Poor Law unions from electing their boards of guardians, and then, once defeated, to prevent the boards from electing their secretaries and getting to work. Led by Lawrence Pitkethly, Oastler's right-hand man, the Huddersfield crowds used controlled violence to delay the implementation of the act for over a year, while in Fielden's Todmorden the existing workhouses were closed and no new ones built. Many of those who had taken part in the anti-Poor Law movement became Chartists in 1838–9. Indeed, there was a great deal of overlap between membership of trade unions, the various campaigns for shorter working hours and action against the new Poor Law.

However, the initial steps towards the creation of the Chartist organisation were made in the old radical hotbed of London. There were continuities of personnel as well as of geography with an earlier phase of radicalism. Agitation out-of-doors for electoral reform in 1830–2 had seen an unlicensed, cheap radical press emerge, led by Henry Hetherington's *Poor Man's Guardian*, issued from July 1831. Hetherington was supported in his work by James Watson (no relation to the orchestrator of the Spa Fields meetings of 1816) and the already mentioned William Lovett, a Cornish cabinet maker. Both Lovett and Watson were heavily influenced by the work of the veteran republican Richard Carlile. Lovett was also, like O'Connor, an acolyte of the hero of Peterloo, Henry Hunt, joining his Friends of Civil and Religious Liberty in 1827. All three men had also joined the Owenite London Mechanics' Institute where Thomas Hodgskin, the intellectual critic of capitalism, was a lecturer. They were leading members, too, of the British Association for the Promotion of Cooperative Knowledge and its offspring, the Metropolitan Trades Union.

However, though influenced by Owenite socialism, Hetherington, Lovett and Watson were convinced, unlike Owen, that socialism could be achieved, not only by the principle of cooperation, but also by radical political change at a national level. Lovett, in particular, is often associated with the 'moral force' wing of Chartism which supposedly repudiated the use of violence. Lovett, with his thin frame and weak constitution, certainly did not look like a violent revolutionary. Yet, when young, he had been branded 'a dangerous man' by government spies, and was known to have advocated the use of force and pledged his (admittedly limited) strength in the fight against the aristocracy. In 1830 he would publicly resist Hunt's initiatives to purge 'revolutionaries' such as Carlile from his Radical Reform Association (the renamed Friends of Civil and Religious Liberty).

After the reform bill crisis of 1831, when the rejection of the bill by the Lords had seen major riots in Derby, Nottingham and Bristol, Lovett, Hetherington and Watson formed the National Union of the Working Classes to spearhead the working-class campaign for a real reform bill. Hetherington's paper was joined at this time by an Irish radical and law student, James O'Brien, who shortly became editor of the *Poor Man's Guardian*, publishing his comments under the pseudonym of 'Bronterre'.* The academically brilliant O'Brien – he had won the gold medal for science at Trinity College, Dublin, the highest honour awarded to undergraduates – brought a broader perspective to the paper: he was widely read in the history of the French Revolution and his editorials spoke of class struggle in a wider European context. Like Lovett, O'Brien was not a physically imposing figure (O'Connor would later call him a 'starved viper') and his health was increasingly undermined by his unstinting workload and, some alleged, alcoholism.[19] However, again like Lovett, he was also an advocate of armed insurrection, though he was very careful about voicing such opinions in print. Unlike Lovett, he did not repudiate this position in later life but remained one of Chartism's most daring and original thinkers.

At the peak of its popularity, the *Poor Man's Guardian* sold sixteen

---

* The name was probably a compound of the Gaelic *Bron* – meaning 'sorrow' – and the French *terre* – earth – and designed to reflect the young radical's early interest in land reform.[18]

thousand copies a week. Along with the struggle over the unlicensed press, it played a seminal role in the formation of the early Chartist organisation. In 1834, the paper won an important case, when it was upheld as a lawful publication by a London jury. The government responded by reducing stamp duty on newspapers to 1d (½p), enabling the 'respectable' press to compete with the unstamped, thus pricing the latter out of the market. Radicals in turn argued for the abolition of all 'taxes on knowledge'.

It was from this largely successful campaign – stamp duty on pamphlets was abolished in early 1836 – that the People's Charter eventually emerged. In June that year, the Association of Working Men to procure a Cheap and Honest Press became the London Working Men's Association, for Benefitting Politically, Socially and Morally the Useful Classes. However, the LWMA, led by Lovett, was a distinctly elitist association. Its membership rate was a hefty shilling a month, out of reach for most workers, and it further restricted admission exclusively to 'persons of good moral character'. Moreover, a clear olive branch was extended to middle-class reform: gentlemen were admitted as honorary members; these included Augustus Beaumont, Colonel Perronet Thompson, MP, William Carpenter and Feargus O'Connor (though like many of the other 'honorary' members, O'Connor played no real part in the LWMA).

By October 1836, the Association had already adopted resolutions containing five of the Six Points of the Charter, and all six were embodied in a petition prepared for submission to the House of Commons in January the following year. Public meetings were held, associations in the provinces were urged to cooperate, and on 31 May 1837 a meeting was arranged at the British Coffee House in Cockspur Street, Charing Cross, between members of the LWMA and radical MPs to consider the petition, which had already been signed by three thousand people. The meeting led to a joint committee of six MPs (Daniel O'Connell, J. A. Roebuck, J. T. Leader, Charles Hindley, W. Sharman Crawford and Colonel Perronet Thompson) and six working-class members (Hetherington, Watson and Lovett, plus John Cleave, Richard Moore and Henry Vincent). The committee issued a statement of the Six Points and set about preparing draft legislation on the subject. The People's Charter's status as draft legislation is often forgotten but, at least initially, the tactics of metropolitan radicals in the 1830s represented a revival of the strategy of the 1810s: to put reform bills before Parliament with the encouragement of pressure exerted out-of-doors through the press and public petitioning.

The draft bill was scuppered when Roebuck, Thompson and Crawford lost their seats in the 1837 general election. Most dramatically, O'Connell turned his back on the working class, attacking unions and supporting the new Poor Law, a shift that would bring him into direct conflict with his fellow Irishman O'Connor. The People's Charter itself, though fully in draft by spring 1837, was not published until May the following year. Though largely the work of Lovett, the aged Benthamite Francis Place also had a hand in drafting the printed version.

In the meantime, the economic depression of 1837 had led the Tory industrialist Thomas Attwood to revive the Birmingham Political Union. Though formerly an organisation advocating only limited electoral reform, based on household suffrage and triennial parliaments, by November of that year the BPU had moved towards advocating universal suffrage. Like the LWMA, in the spring of 1838 it was sending out groups of missionaries to proselytise on behalf of radical reform. On 14 May, the BPU adopted a national petition for reform; the following week, a delegation attended a Glasgow reform meeting which attracted an audience of 150,000.

With representatives of the LWMA also present, the BPU men now endorsed the full Six Points of the Charter. The LWMA was still slow to produce propaganda to meet the upsurge in radical support: at the Glasgow meeting, Arthur Wade, the Grand National Consolidated Trades Union chaplain who had led the campaign to pardon the Tolpuddle Martyrs, was reduced to waving page proofs of the Charter in front of the audience. This was not such a disaster, perhaps, when one reflects on the text of the Charter itself, as opposed to the shorthand of the Six Points. The document betrayed Lovett's influence in its attention to minutiae: the text even included diagrams and elaborate descriptions of automatic voting machines. Each box would feature a series of 'apertures, with the Candidates' names opposite, through which each voter drops a brass ball, which falling in a zig-zag direction, touches on a clock-work spring, which moves a pinion on which the hands are fastened, and thus registers one, each time a person votes'.[20] Arguably, it was the impassioned platform oratory of men like O'Connor and Stephens that drew working-class supporters to the Chartist movement, rather than the dry fare dished up by Lovett and the LWMA.

The LWMA and the BPU, both reform movements prepared to reach out to the middle classes, were now being challenged by other more distinctly working-class organisations. In September 1835 Feargus O'Connor, having lost his Irish seat at Parliament for having failed to meet the necessary property qualification, founded the Marylebone Radical Association. O'Connor, the son of wealthy Irish Protestant landowners, had already established a reputation for defending radical causes even before intervening in the case of the Tolpuddle Martyrs. In this he was following family tradition, both his father and uncle belonged to the United Irishmen. During the reform debate of 1831-2, O'Connor had come forth as an outspoken advocate of Irish rights and democratic change. Once elected MP for Cork in 1832, he was also active in the campaign for freedom of the press. His split with the Irish nationalists, led by Daniel O'Connell, 'the Liberator', was also precipitated by O'Connor's increasingly radical political outlook, namely his opposition to O'Connell's laissez-faire economics and anti-union stance.

In December 1835, O'Connor went on a tour of the North, founding more radical associations. When he returned to London in autumn the following year he was already established as an English leader. His unsuccessful candidacy in Oldham had opened his eyes for the first time to the scale of degradation in the North: 'I saw England for the first time with the naked eye . . . I then for the first time saw the Rattle Boxes [the rattles used by watchmen to wake factory workers] and their victims. I was up betimes every morning, and watched the pallied face, the emaciated frame, and the twisted limbs, wending their way to the earthly hell.'[21] By November 1837 he had established the *Northern Star* newspaper in Leeds under the initial editorship of William Hill, a minister of the radical Swedenborgian sect. The paper quickly became a commercial success, turning a profit after its first month in business.

The attention that O'Connor had given to cultivating support in the industrial North would prove crucial when contrasted with the artisan-led and London-based LWMA. Despite his honorary membership, he had a strong dislike for the LWMA because of its middle-class links. O'Connor had come from a wealthy family, and in all respects he appeared the antithesis of the sober, moralistic, radicalism-by-committee epitomised by Lovett. Unmarried, of no particular religious faith and on occasion a very heavy drinker, O'Connor made a poor fit with the LWMA's idealised membership of temperate, respectable, orderly artisans. His political style was also at odds with the cautiousness of the LMWA's public pronouncements. While his imposing physical presence, booming voice and skill on the platform echoed his political hero Henry Hunt, he flirted with the use of physical force in ways that the 'Orator' would have found both foolhardy and insupportable. By early 1838, O'Connor and Lovett were openly trading insults, the former accusing the LWMA leader of complicity in setting up a hostile parliamentary committee looking into trade union action in Glasgow following the murder of a 'blackleg' worker. Lovett responded in kind, calling O'Connor 'the great "I AM" of politics, the great personification of Radicalism'.[22]

Aside from setting up the *Northern Star* to promote his activities,

O'Connor also aligned himself with radical groups urging change beyond the Six Points of the LWMA's Charter. In January 1837 Bronterre O'Brien and George Julian Harney, a radical who, like O'Brien, idolised the French revolutionaries, formed a rival party, the East London Democratic Association, with the help of the biographer of Thomas Spence, Allen Davenport, and the radical tailor Charles Neesom. In contrast to the LWMA, the BPU and O'Connor's Marylebone Radical Association, this was an explicitly republican organisation that worked to disseminate 'the principles propagated by that great philosopher and redeemer of mankind, the Immortal Thomas Paine'. Reorganised in May 1838 as the London Democratic Association, the LDA set itself in direct opposition to the LWMA.

The fragmentation of London radicalism, another echo of the 1810s, was by the summer of 1838 reduced to a sideshow as provincial organisations sprang up across the Midlands and the North. The Great Northern Union held its first meeting in Leeds to rally the North, while the members of the LWMA were in constant demand as lecturers.

The first explicitly Chartist meeting took place at Kersal Moor near Manchester on 24 September 1838. Estimates of the crowd vary between 100,000 and 250,000. The meeting was ostensibly held to elect delegates to a national convention, not yet touted as an 'anti-Parliament' but designed to organise the Chartists' national petition and see it through Westminster. Again, the tactics adopted by the Chartists, most notably mass petitioning, seemed a throwback to an earlier era. However, as the LWMA lecturers toured the country during the winter of 1838–9, drumming up support for the petition, they saw that some of their followers were already considering more desperate measures should the petition, as was strongly suspected, be rejected. Harney found ironworkers in Winlaton, Newcastle upon Tyne, making weapons. The Kersal Moor meeting was followed by another at

Hartshead Moor on 15 October, where the speeches touched on the necessity of using physical force, to which O'Connor gave ambiguous support.

The delegates to the convention finally met on 4 February 1839 at the British Hotel in Cockspur Street, London. In total, there were supposed to be fifty-three of them, but because of a few absentees the numbers did not exceed the maximum fifty persons prescribed by the Six Acts. Although the LWMA was well represented (Lovett operating as secretary of the meeting), the largest caucus came from the North, with twenty delegates led by O'Connor. There was only one representative of the agricultural labour force, George Loveless, the Tolpuddle Martyr, but he never took his seat. (Loveless seems to have been nominated without his knowledge, but in any case he could not attend as he was unable to pay someone to tend his Greensted smallholding for him.) In fact, only about half the delegates could be called working men, with the convention's number including even one clergyman, Arthur Wade.

The meeting was told that the petition had already been signed by over half a million people, but this cause for congratulation was quickly overshadowed by a number of potentially divisive questions. Was the convention an anti-Parliament, or merely concerned with the petition? Should Chartists oppose the middle-class Anti-Corn Law League, which threatened to siphon off some of their membership? Was physical violence to be contemplated? What should they do if Parliament rejected the petition? The militancy of some Chartist supporters was already attracting the attention of the government. John Frost, delegate for Newport and a JP, was ejected from the magistracy, Henry Vincent was arrested, and Major General Sir Charles Napier (whose letters reveal a sympathy for the plight of the poor if not with Chartism) was put in charge of six thousand troops in the Northern District, which included Yorkshire and Lancashire.

On 14 June 1839, the first national petition was finally presented to the Commons. It was three miles long and contained 1,280,000 signatures, over 50 per cent more people than had voted in the 1837 election. The petition did not fare well in the House: the initial reaction when it was wheeled into the Chamber was not hushed awe but derision. Attwood, although he presented it, would not give it his unqualified support on the grounds of concerns over the advocacy of physical force by some Chartists, but also because he didn't want two hundred of the seats of a reformed Parliament to go to the Irish – an early indication of the problems that the 'British' dimension of Chartism would provoke. The BPU's commitment to the cause of reform had, in any case, been seriously weakened by the incorporation of Birmingham as a parliamentary borough that year. When a motion for the petition to be discussed by a parliamentary committee was eventually brought before the House almost a month later, MPs scarcely seemed involved in the debate at all: Disraeli spent his time leisurely eating oranges. The motion was defeated by 235 votes to 46.

Given the fate of Cartwright's petitioning campaign in the 1810s, we need to ask why the Chartists resorted to a political tactic that had seemingly proved such a failure in the past. For a start, it was one of the very few legitimate means of political communication open to a working-class political organisation. The polls were, after all, largely closed to labouring men in the wake of the 1832 Reform Act, and property qualifications excluded all but gentlemen from standing as MPs. For a movement with a considerable amount of female support, petitioning also had the advantage of being a political activity in which women could participate legitimately. In fact, O'Connor encouraged both women and children to sign the national petition: 'Let every man, woman and child sign the petition . . . Go on, good men! Go on, virtuous women! . . . we are engaged in the cause of justice which is the cause of God. Sign the petition!'[23] Chartists also stressed that they would not petition in the obsequious style demanded by parliamentary custom. Speaking of petitioning in favour of the repeal of the new Poor Law, Bronterre O'Brien wrote:

In my opinion petitions for the mere repeal of the new Act would be useless. – They would be disregarded and thrown contemptuously under the table, as all petitions from the oppressed classes are . . . I would recommend that instead of petitioning for a mere repeal of the Act, we should petition –

THAT THE POOR OF ENGLAND SHALL BE HEARD BY COUNCIL AT THE BAR OF THE HOUSE OF COMMONS AGAINST THE LATE TYRANNICAL AND INHUMAN ENACTMENT MISCALLED THE POOR LAW AMENDMENT ACT.

A petition of this sort, accompanied to the House by 200,000 people and headed by all the popular leaders of good repute throughout the country, would be worth ten thousand of the ordinary kind.[24]

However limited its influence on Parliament, petitioning did help to bind together the Chartist membership (Attwood described the national petition as a 'holy league').[25] In some instances, whole communities subscribed to the petition. Overall, mass petitions presented a powerful, physical representation of the popular will. As O'Connor would say of the last 'monster' petition of 1848: 'Did [O'Connor] ask them to petition parliament in the hope of this grievance being redressed? (no, no) Did he ask them to petition parliament in the hope of its having any effect on the legislature? (no) No; it was in the confidence that five millions of men were strong in the knowledge that they were fraternizing together.'[26] Nonetheless, many Chartists questioned the usefulness of petitions, which could seem, in the words of some Yorkshire Chartists, 'like throwing a feather into the wind'.[27] More ominously, many said this was the last petition that they would deign to sign.

THE NEWPORT RISING – CHARTISM REINVIGORATED

The summer of 1839 was a time of considerable political uncertainty. Fears about a political vacuum at the centre were raised by the so-called 'Bedchamber Crisis' when, following the resignation of Lord Melbourne, the young Queen Victoria refused to dismiss her Whig ladies in waiting as a condition of Sir Robert Peel accepting the offer to form a government. The Chartist convention itself, having relocated to Birmingham's Owenite Lawrence Street Chapel, was considering what 'ulterior measures' could be used if the petition should be unsuccessful: proposals included the withdrawing of bank deposits, the holding of a 'sacred month' of strike action and the use of 'exclusive dealing' (buying goods only from shopkeepers known to be sympathetic to reform). Then, Parliament's overwhelming rejection of the petition, though scarcely unexpected, acted as a catalyst to all these combustible elements.

More mass meetings were held at Newcastle Town Moor (20 May), Hartshead Moor (21 May) and Kersal Moor (25 May). At some Chartist meetings, the political preaching of J. R. Stephens made an uncompromising argument for the use of force:

resistance, active resistance, the resistance by force, to unjust oppression, is as high a virtue in the sight of God as obedience is when the enactments of the Parliament or the country are in accordance with the laws of God. We are to obey when the laws are good, and to disobey when the laws are bad – we are to yield up our homage to the rulers and governors of the land when the rulers and the governors are a terror to evil doers, and a praise to them that do well.[1]

The convention reassembled in Birmingham on 1 July and resolved to return to London in a week. However, these plans were thrown into disarray when, on 4 July, a posse of police came by train from London to clear a crowd that had gathered in the Bull Ring to hear John Fussell, a jeweller and a Birmingham convention delegate, speak.

Fussell had been arrested back in May for making inflammatory speeches advocating the use of force, but released due to lack of evidence. The attempt to arrest him a second time led to a serious riot. The police were severely outnumbered and lacked additional support. The crowd routed them within twenty minutes. Several officers were injured, three with serious stab wounds. Additional troops were called in and two leading Scottish Chartists and doctors, John Taylor and Peter McDouall, both prominent advocates of physical force, were arrested. The arrests flew in the face of eyewitness accounts, which recorded that both Taylor and McDouall had urged the crowd to disperse peacefully. The apparent injustice drew comparisons with Peterloo, though at Birmingham the crowd unquestionably gave as good as they got.

The convention issued resolutions the following day, protesting against the actions of the authorities and deploring the arrests of McDouall and Taylor. Unwisely, these resolutions were then placed on placards with William Lovett's name on them. The following day, Lovett and the Birmingham delegate John Collins, who had taken the manuscript of the resolutions to the printers, were arrested. With these arrests and with the rejection of the national petition, the convention, which had relocated to London, began to disintegrate as an effective governing body. Votes on motions became more sparsely attended until the convention was prorogued on 6 August and finally dissolved a month later by its remaining twenty-three delegates. The dissolution represented the formal end of the LWMA's leadership of the Chartist movement.

In the late summer and autumn of 1839, violence and insurrection, in the words of George Harney, were very much 'in the air'.[2] There were rumours of risings being prepared in the West Riding, but only in South Wales did anything happen. The area had a recent history of industrial violence: in the mining districts militant cells of workers, known as the 'Scotch Cattle', handed out beatings to 'black-leg' workers and set fire to the homes of anti-union shopkeepers. In the spring of 1839, there had been heated confrontations between Chartist demonstrators and police. On the night of 3–4 November, seven thousand colliers and ironworkers marched on Newport at the beginning of what was to have been a rising in the valleys to capture key towns and, some alleged, establish a republic.[3] They were led by John Frost, now ousted as a magistrate for his obvious support for insurrection, Zephaniah Williams, a free-thinking innkeeper and collier, and William Jones, a travelling actor from Bristol and flamboyant radical speaker. What followed represented the most fatal clash between radicals and the authorities in modern British history, worse even than Peterloo. One of the rebels, nineteen-year-old George Shell, left this note for his mother: 'I shall this night be engaged in a struggle for freedom, and should it please God to spare my life, I shall see you soon; but if not, grieve not for me. I shall fall in a noble cause.'[4]

The planned night attack on the town was botched as the marchers, delayed by poor weather, did not reach Newport until after daybreak. Alerted to the rising, the town authorities had already enlisted hundreds of special constables, as well as a small contingent of regular soldiers. The main focus of the rising was the Westgate Hotel, where a number of Chartist prisoners were already being held. The hotel was heavily protected by both constables and soldiers, and the Chartist assault quickly became a bloodbath, with soldiers delivering a devastating barrage of rifle fire into the crowd that had thronged around the building, before turning their guns on the few militants who had broken in. Twenty-four people were killed or later died from their injuries, including young Shell, who was shot several times; he took over three hours to die. A further fifty were seriously injured. As with Peterloo, the actual numbers of casualties and fatalities will probably never be known, as wounded rebels slunk into hiding to avoid detection and subsequent prosecution. One hundred and twenty-five were arrested and twenty-one charged with high treason, including Frost, Williams and Jones. Eyewitness reports of the carnage convey the severity of the injuries incurred:

> There was a dreadful scene, dreadful beyond expression – the groans of the dying, the shrieks of the wounded, the pallid, ghostly countenances and the bloodshot eyes of the dead, in addition to the shattered windows and passageways ankle-deep in gore.

One special constable recalled many

> who suffered in the fight, crawled away, some exhibiting frightful wounds, and glaring eyes, wildly crying for mercy, others, desperately maimed, were carried in the arms of the humane for medical aid; and a few of the miserable objects that were helplessly and mortally wounded, continued for a some minutes to writhe in tortures, crying for water.[5]

The Newport rising accelerated the government's judicial campaign against Chartism, leading to the last mass treason trials in

British history. Between June 1839 and June 1840, at least 543
Chartists were detained, for periods of between a few weeks and a
few years. Lovett and Collins were sentenced to a year in prison in
August 1839 and Stephens to eighteen months, as was O'Connor
in March 1840. Harney was one of the few to escape, when a grand
jury refused to indict him for one of his milder speeches, also in
March that year. Frost and the other Newport leaders were sentenced to death but, anxious not to create political martyrs, the
government commuted this to transportation for life. The Chartist
ringleaders were taken from gaol in the dead of night, leaving no
opportunity for their families to see them before they were sent to
the other side of the world. For some, this would have been the
last time they would have been able to see their relatives alive:
Williams and Jones would die in Tasmania.[6]

Capital punishment was also eschewed in the trials of other
insurrectionists too. Robert Peddie of Edinburgh, who was identified as the leader of an abortive rising in West Yorkshire, was
sentenced to three years' imprisonment. At Beverley Gaol, Peddie
spent six weeks in total silence, working a treadmill in full view
of spectators outside the prison. He was then placed on stone-
breaking duty for another three months until it was reduced to
half-time on health grounds. After sixteen months of this back-
breaking work he was allowed to do some tailoring. Samuel
Holberry, the leader of a planned rising in Sheffield, was sentenced
to four years' imprisonment. The poor diet, hard labour and terrible conditions proved too much for him and his fellow conspirator
John Clayton. Both men died in prison. Holberry's pregnant wife
Mary was rigorously examined by the authorities about her knowledge of the uprising: the stress proved too much, and she
miscarried. At Chester Castle, Chartist prisoners were placed in
cells below ground level, at one point with water running down the
walls. At Monmouth, the Newport prisoners slept three to a bed. In
York Castle, conditions were so bad that they cost Barnsley Chartist
Peter Hoey the use of his leg. In contrast, O'Connor's incarceration

was relatively pleasant: his cell was made comfortable with his own furniture, he was allowed his books and newspapers and was even permitted to keep caged birds for company.

Historians used to portray the dissolution of the convention and the subsequent Newport rising as evidence of Chartism's gradual drift from 'moral' to 'physical' force, with O'Connor eclipsing Lovett as the movement's human totem. In fact, no such transition took place. Of course, O'Connor was a more belligerent character than Lovett, occasionally willing to use his fists to convince his opponents where argument would not, but here their differences ended. The justification of the use of armed force was almost a constant in Chartist rhetoric, simply becoming more pronounced at moments of particular tension, as in the summer and autumn of 1839. The right to bear arms had been discussed and defended in the convention's debates. Lovett's own *Manifesto of the General Convention* was a clear endorsement of the use of ulterior measures, including armed resistance. Nonetheless, it would be a mistake to suggest that Chartism was at core an insurrectionary movement. In fact, the Newport rising was the only significant Chartist-inspired action of this kind.

Instead, we should understand the Chartist rhetoric of physical force as an argument that developed from some mainstream elements of Whig political thought. Even when they seemed most radical, the Chartists' arguments were deeply constitutional. Those who publicly defended the right of resistance did not support their claims with reference to the French or even the American Revolution, but rather employed English legal precedents. The clear assertion in the English Bill of Rights of 1689 of the right of Protestant subjects to bear arms for their defence was central to arguments in defence of physical force, but so too were a whole slew of other historical examples, from the 'code of Alfred' to the works of the seventeenth-century republican Algernon Sidney.[7]

Most telling was J. A. Richardson's use of Major John Cartwright's arguments in his speech to the convention on the right to bear arms, given in April 1839.[8] Cartwright was hardly a revolutionary, even if loyalists had occasionally tried to smear him as such. His political ideology grew out of the ideas of the 'true' or 'honest' Whigs of the eighteenth century. Yet Richardson was not distorting Cartwright's words: he had, like his Whig predecessors, acknowledged the right of the people ultimately to resist tyrannical government. To Cartwright, the early nineteenth-century British state, with its overwhelming military power, was tyrannical. One of the ways its power could be challenged, apart from political reform, was by the creation of a new citizen militia. In 1808, Cartwright had called for laws to establish definitively the right of subjects to bear arms.[9] The difference among most British radicals on this question was not between those who advocated and those who repudiated the right to use force, but over what constituted tyranny and at what point it could only be resisted by resort to arms.[10] Radicals, like their Whig predecessors, acknowledged the ultimate right of the people to resist tyranny by force. The question was whether the British government in the 1830s and 1840s was a tyranny: if so, could it be said that all other remedies had been exhausted?

In the wake of the Newport rising and the mass arrests that followed, Chartism was forced to reorganise. With O'Connor and Lovett both in gaol, it was left to new figures to take the lead. Chief among these was the Manchester trade union activist and mill owner, James Leach. It was Leach who chaired the meeting held at the Griffin Inn in Manchester on 20 July 1840 that founded the National Charter Association of Great Britain. For the next eighteen years, the NCA would provide direction, leadership and organisational structure to the Chartist movement, though it was most effective in its first two years. The NCA was no mere substitute for the now defunct convention: it was established on quite a different basis, building upon local Chartist branch organisations, not mass meetings. With a constitution, an elected president, a national executive, local divisions and a subscription-paying membership, Chartism under the direction of the NCA could lay claim to be the first modern British political party. By December 1841, it could boast 282 branches and 13,000 card-carrying members; a year later, this had grown to 401 branches and 50,000 members.

The aims of the NCA were clearly delineated in the *Northern Star* on 1 August 1840. It sought to obtain a 'Radical Reform' of the House of Commons, meaning 'a full and faithful Representation of the entire people of the United Kingdom'. The principles embodied in the Six Points of the Charter would be achieved through 'peaceable and constitutional means', namely the familiar tactics of public meetings and petitioning. In addition, the NCA listed other ways in which the great aims of the Charter might be met. It would encourage local associations to follow Bronterre O'Brien's plan to field as many Chartist candidates as possible in national elections. Given the nature of the post-1832 electorate, this was not aimed, naively, at putting only Chartist MPs in Parliament. Members were instructed to attend as many 'public political meetings' (similar to election hustings) as possible, to ensure that there was a widespread discussion of 'our rights and claims'. They were urged to set a positive example by observing 'strict sobriety', while 'Political Knowledge' would be diffused by 'missionaries' and through the active Chartist press.[11]

As well as the sophistication of the political tactics it advocated, and its well-developed organisation, the NCA had one other revolutionary feature: unlike any previous national political party, it granted women members the same voting rights as men. (Its membership cards even carried images of both male and female workers.) In its statement of aims, of course, it continued to limit itself to fighting for universal suffrage for men over the age of twenty-one. Increasingly, though, it appeared as if the concentration on manhood suffrage came from a conviction that the public at large was not ready to support women's political emancipation.

Women, as we have seen, were encouraged to sign the monster petition of 1839 – John Collins claimed that twenty-four thousand Birmingham women signed it. William Lovett alleged that initial drafts of the People's Charter had actually called for the enfranchisement of women, but this had had to be dropped for fear of setting back the cause of gaining votes for men. By 1840, however, some male Chartists, most prominently R. J. Richardson, were arguing that women were the political equals of men (though in Richardson's case, this was undermined by his assumption that a wife resigned her political rights to her husband after marriage). The same point was made in John Watkins's *Address to the Women of England*, which advocated the vote only for single women and widows, again, on the basis that they, unlike married women, could exercise political independence. Quite apart from all this, it was not always clear that the later Chartist press was in touch with its female audience. In O'Brien's *National Reformer*, one editorial warned its women readers:

> As long as you continue to rear up your daughters as mere dolls for admiration; as long as you are content to educate them after the present doltish system, with a little dancing, a little French, a little sampler work and other little etceteras . . . with a great deal of attention to curls, the looking-glass, and fine clothes . . . so long will you find [man] content with his supremacy.[12]

It is doubtful that the daughters of many mill workers had time, after an eighteen-hour working day, for dancing, French lessons or sampler work.

Even those male writers who were more realistic about the challenges facing working women often couched their arguments more in terms of the impact of female labour on women's 'natural' vocation as wives and mothers. Underlying a lot of Chartist writing was an understandable anxiety about the erosion of the traditional role of the man as breadwinner and head of the household. These were men who were no longer able to support their families themselves and were forced to watch their wives and children, now often working long hours to support the adult male of the household, going about their labours clad in no more than rags. J. R. Stephens urged the men in the crowd at Hyde, Manchester, on 17 February 1839, to support the Charter in order to keep their wives from having to work:

> You husbands! unless your minds be made up that your wives ought not and shall not work; that rather than kill your views by allowing them to work, you will allow God to take their lives by gradual starvation, – and that is what I should do; for before I would allow my wife to go to a mill and be worked there, that wife should stay at home, and die in her chair or on the floor, and the verdict should be 'Died by the Visitation of God' – she should not die by the visitation of the factory demon.

Stephens retold the story of a doctor's visit to a nearby mill:

> There was a stream of blood all the way from the factory door across a considerable piece of ground to the cottage where the woman lived. There was no limb broken; the machinery had not torn her. It was the most awful sight that an English father, or an English husband can imagine. It was the lawfully wedded wife of a hard-working English husband, who had been standing in that mill fifteen hours in the day (including meal times) in the last stage of pregnancy till nature could endure no longer, and had burst the over-charged vessels of her over-worked frame; and there the woman was bleeding to death in consequence . . . Now, until you, as husbands, say to yourselves, 'I will work willingly, I will sweat freely, I won't spare my own body, I will apply myself diligently and industriously to labour, but by the God that said "for this cause shall a man leave his father and mother, and cleave unto his wife", by that God, and by that dear woman whom he gave to be

my crown and my glory, by that God, and by that woman, my wife shall never work at all'; until you do this, and refuse to sell the bodies of your wives and children to the mill owner, all the acts of Parliament that ever could be passed would not prevent it.[13]

Conditions in the mills for women workers, as for men and children too, were undoubtedly dire, but the emphasis in Stephens's story was the way that the 'factory demon' had destroyed a wife and mother. He believed that the remedy for this evil was greater male industry and diligence, not better working conditions for all. His portrayal of women as wives and mothers who had been wrenched into the unnatural sphere of labour ignored the important role they played in Chartist organisation and activism. By the early 1840s, there were over a hundred local women's Chartist associations. They were often heavily involved in the collection of signatures for the Chartist mass petitions. As managers of their households, women had a key part to play in campaigns of 'exclusive dealing'. Mary Savage, secretary of the Nottingham Female Political Union, instructed her members: 'Let every shop and shopkeeper be noted in a book kept for the purpose, stating name, residence, trade and whether Whig or Tory; also another book containing the names of those friendly to the cause of the people.'[14] Those deemed 'unfriendly' could expect a sharp decline in their trade in areas where Chartist support was strong. Some Chartist women went further, following their menfolk in resorting to the use of force. Elizabeth Cresswell of Mansfield was arrested carrying a loaded revolver and several spare bullets. She was sentenced to a month's hard labour for unlawful assembly, despite having a young baby.

While the NCA's structure and the rights it accorded to women members were certainly radical, the relative moderation of its aims and objectives should not be overlooked. Writing at the time when the Association was at its most effective, Engels had spoken of the typical English Chartist as 'a republican, though he seldom, if ever, uses the term. He prefers to describe himself as a democrat, although he gives his sympathy to republican parties all over the world. Indeed, he is more than a republican, because the democracy he supports is not only political but social and economic as well.' The Six Points of the Charter might look 'innocent enough', but, Engels contended, they would undermine the whole English constitution, including the position of the Queen and the House of Lords.[15] In 1852, in an article in the *New York Tribune*, Karl Marx wrote that, due to the growth of working-class consciousness in England, 'universal suffrage in England would . . . be a far more socialistic measure than anything which has been honoured with that name on the Continent'.[16] This was a viewpoint shared by Chartism's political opponents: in 1841, Disraeli promised to defeat 'Chartists and socialists' and 'Jesuits and infidels'.[17]

Many subsequent commentators have also contended that the Chartist movement was republican through and through.[18] Much of the evidence, however, points in quite the opposite direction. Both the NCA's constitution and the earlier Declaration of Rights adopted by the convention in September 1839 essentially endorsed the existing 'mixed government' of monarch, Lords and Commons. The Chartist Declaration of Rights, while it defined monarchy as a public trust, with the royal prerogative subservient to Parliament, defined the legislative power as 'essentially and rightly vested in the monarch, the peers, and the duly elected commons of the realm, in parliament assembled'.[19] The Declaration may have countenanced some reform of the Lords, but it kept the monarchy firmly off the agenda. This fact wasn't lost on the veteran republican Richard Carlile, who contended that there could 'be no reformed House of Commons, of popular representation, with a House of Lords'.[20] Some Chartists may have agreed with Engels (prefiguring the interpretation of Walter Bagehot in his influential *English Constitution* of 1867) that the monarchy was a 'sham', having only the 'outward semblance of authority' while real power resided in the House of Commons, dominated by the middle classes.[21] As Thomas Doubleday, the editor of the major Chartist newspaper in the North East, the *Northern Liberator*, revealed, 'under the *present system* neither King nor Queen has a particle of political power! That power is BEHIND THE THRONE and not *upon it!*'[22]

However, comments like these, which were not essentially republican either, need to be set against the frequent appeals to the Crown made by Chartists after the failure of the mass petitions of 1839, 1842 and 1848. If Parliament proved deaf to the people's demands, it was hoped that Queen Victoria would exert her authority on their behalf, a belief sustained by the apparent flexing of royal muscles during the Bedchamber Crisis. Chartists' faith in the monarchy's ability to supplement Parliament's defects should not surprise us too much, given the extent to which many Chartist writers idolised 'good' kings and queens, especially Alfred and Elizabeth. Some held an utterly unfounded belief that Victoria was sympathetic to Chartism, on the grounds of a spurious rumour that it was her intervention that had spared Frost and the other Newport rebels from execution. In fact, the Queen's political sympathies fell clearly on the other side: a mere six weeks after the rising, she invited the Mayor of Newport, Thomas Phillips, to stay with the royal family at Windsor, relaxing strict court etiquette by permitting him to dine with her in private. During the same stay, she also knighted him. Her consort, Prince Albert, was equally unsympathetic, saying after O'Connor's unsuccessful trial for seditious conspiracy in March 1843, 'I am sorry that Feargus escaped, still the effect of the trial is satisfactory.'[23]

Chartism was re-energised not only by the creation of the NCA but by Feargus O'Connor's release from York Prison at the end of August 1841. Ever the showman, he emerged from gaol dressed in a suit of fustian, the rough fabric worn by working men. Having continued to contribute regularly to the *Northern Star* while in prison, he swiftly threw himself back into political activity, touring

the country promoting the Charter. He also responded vigorously
to a number of challenges to his leadership of the movement.

Lovett had remained in prison until July 1840, refusing to be
bound over for good behaviour in order to secure an early release:
'we have been about the first political victims who have been
classed and punished as misdemeanants and felons because
we happened to be of *the working class* . . . to enter into a bond
for our future good conduct would at once be an admission of
guilt'.[24] While incarcerated, he had written his *Chartism: A New
Organisation of the People, Embracing a Plan for the Education and
Improvement of the People, Politically and Socially; Addressed to the
Working-Classes of the United Kingdom, and more especially the
Advocates of the Rights and Liberties of the Whole People as Set Forth
in the 'People's Charter'.* As the title suggests, Lovett's work recon-
figured Chartism, replacing the emphasis on political campaigning
with a highly detailed programme, including mapped-out lesson
plans, of morally and socially improving working-class education.
As he had with the London Working Men's Association, he also
stressed the importance of weaning British workers off the
immoral and destructive pastimes of drinking and gaming:

> Many of those who frequent public-houses in their houses of relax-
> ation, are not so much induced by the love of drink, as to spend
> their hours in cheerful society; and if places were provided (*unas-
> sociated with the means of intoxication*) where they could spend a
> pleasant and agreeable evening, we should have little cause for
> lamenting the prevalence of intemperance, and its demoralizing
> consequences. Those who could not join in the dance might be
> amused with the games of chess and drafts, which are both rational
> and instructive; but cards, dice, and all kinds of gambling, should
> be scrupulously excluded.[25]

However, alongside his concentration on reforming working-
class education and culture, there was a potential cause for

confrontation with the NCA in Lovett's plan for a 'National Association of the United Kingdom for Promoting the Political and Social Improvement of the People'. He had already pointedly refused to join the NCA, making his split from O'Connor clear. The latter responded bullishly to the apparent threat, attacking Lovett's plan as 'Knowledge Chartism' and suggesting, without foundation, that it represented a surreptitious return to the Benthamite idea of intellectual qualifications for the franchise.

The threat inherent in Lovett's plan was indicative of a wider movement to link Chartism with temperance or teetotalism. Around the same time the *Northern Star* published an address that called for teetotal Chartist societies to be established, given that 'NO GOVERNMENT CAN LONG WITHSTAND THE JUST CLAIMS OF A PEOPLE WHO HAVE THE COURAGE TO CONQUER THEIR OWN VICES.'[26] O'Connor was resist-ant to this new movement, as he had been to Lovett's plan, complaining, 'I object to Teetotal Chartism, because all who do not join in, and I fear there are many, will be considered unwor-thy of their civil rights.'[27] His hostile remarks were not simply the response of a man who was himself fond of a drink or two. He was increasingly concerned about the threat posed to the cohesion of Chartism as a movement by an alliance of middle- and working-class radicals forming in the *Northern Star*'s home city of Leeds. The city was more broadly based economically than its neighbours Manchester and Sheffield, and consequently less susceptible to their severe booms and busts. A softer form of Chartism emerged from this environment, more accommodating to the local middle-class reform movement headed by Samuel Smiles, now best known as the author of *Self-help* (1859) but then editor of the *Leeds Times*. In September 1840, Smiles established the Leeds Parliamentary Reform Association (LPRA), which included several notable tex-tile magnates and Anti-Corn Law League activists.

The LPRA urged working men to unite around an agenda of household suffrage and triennial parliaments. It invited several radical MPs, including Daniel O'Connell, to speak at its 'Great Reform Festival', to be held in the Temple Works, at Holbeck, Leeds, in January 1841. (This extraordinary building was based on the Temple of Horus at Edfu in Egypt, and was said at the time to house the largest single room in the world.) The *Northern Star* published a number of hostile editorials in the run-up to the meeting. The NCA also organised a meeting, which ended just before the LPRA's started. NCA members took the opportunity to speak at every available 'public political meeting', and, not surprisingly, they moved on to the Temple Works where the LPRA meeting was taking place. O'Connell, delayed en route, failed to show up, so the radical MP Joseph Hume took his place. Hume gave a speech that was ambiguous enough to hint at universal suffrage without making any clear commitment to it. However, his talk was followed by a number of speeches from Chartists who welcomed class cooperation but also insisted on the terms of the Charter. The mealy-mouthed pronouncements of Hume were thrown into sharp relief by the frank rhetoric of Chartists such as Robert Lowery:

> I know you will tell me that as Chartists, we have been violent, we have uttered language no honest man would ever assent to – but middle men, I ask you, have you ever stepped into the huts of poverty? Have you ever seen your wives in rags and your children without food? If you have not, then I ask you to bear in mind the causes why those of whom you complain have been violent, to keep in mind that those who have been violent have drained degradation to its bitterest dregs . . . What is the extent of representation that will truly represent the people, and secure to them their rights? I say no representation short of that which admits every man arrived at a mature age to a vote – that is to say Universal Suffrage.[28]

The successful Chartist subversion of the 'Reform Festival' was a humiliation for the LPRA: it continued as an effective political force only until October.

The same tactic was used at meetings held by the Anti-Corn Law League, now seen as Chartism's main political rival. One such meeting, held in Dundee in May 1841, was placarded with reminders of the plight of John Frost, the 'murder' of John Clayton, the extent of the national debt, the disgraceful compensation paid 'to the owners of Black Slaves', and the £70,000 recently spent on the royal stables. By March 1842, the League was responding by disrupting Chartist meetings. At a Manchester Hall of Science meeting on the repeal of the Irish Union, 'League assassins' attempted to force a chairman of their own upon the participants. O'Connor, according to his own account, knocked out one of the League members but was hit on the head with a large stone 'just above the right eye, which knocked me down, the blood gushing out copiously'.[29]

At the National Charter Association's formation, Bronterre O'Brien had suggested another tactic: if Chartist candidates stood at local parliamentary hustings, they could demonstrate the unrepresentative nature of the franchise by overwhelmingly winning the show of hands. This measure was employed for the first time during the 1841 election. In terms of votes, Chartism's performance at the polls was an unqualified disaster: many candidates gathered only a handful. However, Chartists successfully exploited the hustings by making public speeches and convincingly demonstrating the unfairness of the electoral system: at the West Riding hustings, one observer noted that 'there were in that crowd nine non-electors for [every] one elector'.[30] The tactic was deployed by Chartists throughout the 1840 and 1850s. When Ernest Jones stood for election at Halifax for the second time in 1852, the contrast between the tens of thousands who gave their support to him at the hustings and the five hundred voters who eventually elected the Whig candidate Sir Charles Wood spoke for itself.[31]

Despite the failure of the first great petition and the oft-made assertion that it would be the last, Chartists continued to utilise mass petitioning as a political tactic. John Frost's conviction for high treason proved to be a great rallying point. A petition for his pardon gathered 1,339,298 signatures. On 25 May 1841, it was presented to the House by Thomas Slingsby Duncombe, radical MP for Finsbury, who would be the most important spokesman for the Chartist cause in the Commons during the 1840s – indeed, for most of the decade he was its lone supportive voice.

Duncombe was a remarkable character: an impeccably dressed former Guards officer educated at Harrow, the grandson of a bishop and nephew of 1st Baron Feversham, his upbringing and experiences could hardly have been more different from those of the average Chartist. Nonetheless, he was the most consistent supporter of parliamentary reform in the House, and regularly raised other issues such as the opening of Chartists' mail for evidence of seditious activity and the raising of Church rates. In a fine piece of political theatre, he managed to convince the Commons to allow the petition to be carried into the Chamber on the shoulders of a team of stonemasons dressed in fustian. Of all the mass petitions submitted by the Chartists, this was the most successful, largely because it was only tangentially related to the Six Points of the Charter. It was voted down only when the Speaker cast his vote against, arguing that it infringed the royal prerogative of granting pardons.

John Frost would not receive a pardon until 1854, again through the efforts of Duncombe in the Commons, and then only partial. He was unable finally to return to England under a free pardon until 1856. Nonetheless, the success of the petitioning campaign seemed to bode well for a revival of mass petitioning in support of the Charter. At a Chartist meeting in Birmingham in September 1841, Peter McDouall proposed a plan for another national petition and convention. The NCA took up the proposal, and plans were made for a convention to meet in London in February the following year. The new petition reflected both the growth of Chartism as a British political force and also some of the problems that this raised. The president of the Irish Universal Suffrage

Association, Patrick O'Higgins, spoke of his members as 'the Prussians whose coming up will enable their English brethren to win the great moral Waterloo'. The importance of the IUSA to the movement as a whole was reflected in the text of the petition: 'your Petitioners complain of the many grievances borne by the people of Ireland; and contend that they are fully entitled to a repeal of the Legislative Union'.[32]

However, the involvement of Irish politicians in the Charter cause had provoked some consternation in England, as witnessed by Thomas Attwood's equivocal stance on the 1839 petition. In the same year Carlile complained, with O'Connor obviously in mind:

> I dislike the sound of these Irish O's, in connection with the question of English Reform, and look upon an Irish *Protestant* as a base and bastard Irishman, a traitor to his persecuted country, without the apology of philosophical dissent from the Romish Church. If this be an unsound prejudice of mine, I feel, express and submit it to correction. I count such men obstacles to the public good of this country, and that the temper of an Irishman is best suited to the state of Ireland. I wish them all at home and happy, reforming themselves and Ireland. They are not solid and steady enough, not sufficiently philosophical, for the necessities of English Reform. I dislike the mixture, and think it does not work well.[33]

In 1842, the apparent sop to Irish nationalism caused some disagreement in Scotland, where there was little support for the repeal of the Union. Sectarian divisions were also involved: Chartism had considerable strength among Scottish Presbyterians, who were less than ecstatic at the thought of political cooperation with Irish Catholics.

In terms of the gathering of subscriptions, the 1842 petition was, however, an unqualified success. In all, 3,317,752 people subscribed to it, more than two and a half times the total who had signed the 1839 petition. When it was delivered to the Commons on 2 May, it was accompanied by a crowd of some fifty thousand workers. The petition itself had been carried on a decorated box by relays of workmen. However, the box was so big that it could not be brought through the members' entrance: despite the Chartists' efforts, not only the box and parts of the door frame had to be disassembled, but the petition itself had to be split up into sections.

Once again, it fell to Duncombe to present the petition to the Commons. Though the House refused his request to allow six representatives of the Chartists to speak at the Commons bar, the petition nonetheless prompted a heated debate. Lord Macaulay laid out the dire consequences if Parliament allowed the Chartists to succeed:

> The Government would rest upon spoliation . . . What must be the effect of such a sweeping confiscation of property? No experience enables us to guess at it. All I can say is, that it seems to me to be something more horrid than can be imagined. A great community of human beings – a vast people would be called into existence in a new position; there would be a depression, if not an utter stoppage of trade, and of all of those vast engagements of the country by which our people were supported, and how is it possible to doubt that famine and pestilence would come before long to wind up the effects of such a state of things. The best thing which I can expect, and which I think everyone must see as a result, is, that in some of the desperate struggles which must take place in such a state of things, some strong military despot must arise, and give some sort of protection – some security to the property which may remain.[34]

In contrast to the extremely close division on Frost's pardon, the House decided not to receive the petition by 287 votes to 49.

In the wake of the failure of the second great petition, a spate of direct industrial action caught the national leadership off guard. Strikes erupted across the country, beginning among coalminers in

Staffordshire in July 1842 and spreading to fourteen English counties, eight Scottish and one Welsh. One anonymous Ashton mill
worker gave a vivid description of the spread of the unrest:

> Tuesday 9th Met at 5 o'clock went to Oldham, Hyde, Manchester,
> Stockport, & Newton lees – Hurst and all other places round about
> and stopt every Mill in them – Soldiers and police trying to stop us,
> took a sword from one of the Soldiers, broke it in pieces made
> bloody noses for the policemen. Wednesday 10th went to Glossop
> dale Stopt every Mill there. Masters thought to stop us got knocked
> down . . . the Shop keepers are going hand in hand with us giving
> £5, £4, and £2 a piece for men to go to preston, Hull & every
> Manufacturing town in Great Britain and Ireland to stop them –
> now is the time or never – lose this opportunity and we are lost! lost!
> Lost!!!! We get plenty of something to eat the Shops are open they
> give us what we want. Today Augt 11th to Stockport, they are stopt
> but we go parading the Streets like Soldiers 6 a breast. News from
> Manchester Bloody fights Soldiers ready to fight for the people
> police the same Now's the time for Liberty we want the Wages paid
> 1840 if they wont give it us Revolution is the consequence. We have
> stopt every trade – Tailors, coblers – Brushmakers – Sweeps, Tinkers,
> Carters – Masons – Builders – Colliers &c and every other trade.
> Not a Cart is allowed to go through the Streets.[35]

By 11 August, over a hundred cotton factories, many dyeworks
and machine shops and about fifty thousand workmen lay idle. A
conference of eighty trade delegates met at Carpenters' Hall in
Manchester, appealed for law and order and endorsed the Charter.
The strikes then spread across the Pennines to Yorkshire, where
gangs of strikers pulled out the boiler plugs to put out the fires and
halt the works (lending the name 'the Plug Plot' to the episode),
while in Manchester the trades delegates continued to meet. The
unrest was marked by greater violence than had accompanied
the strikes of 1839. A bloody confrontation occurred at Salterhebble,

Yorkshire, on the road to the nearest station, at Elland, where strikers attacked cavalry who were returning from dropping arrested demonstrators there. One of the ambush party, a carpet weaver named Charles Greenwood, returned home having spent a night hiding in a drain only to find that his sixteen-year-old son had died 'of tuberculosis and want of food' during his absence. Eight men who were thrown from their horses were robbed as they lay semiconscious on the road. Fighting broke out in Halifax on 16 August, soldiers using their bayonets and firing shots to disperse the crowd. At least three people, one a soldier, were killed in the attack.

The liberal press unhesitatingly linked the unrest to Chartism, but at the national level it appeared that the Chartist leadership was essentially caught unawares by the strikes. At the same time as trade unionists were meeting in Manchester, the NCA was gathering there to commemorate the anniversary of Peterloo and unveil a statue of Henry Hunt. Most members had received little information about the strike activity, and George Harney and William Hill opposed Peter McDouall's motion to give it official support. The *Northern Star* itself remained under the editorship of Hill, and the 20 August issue stayed focused on the commemoration of Peterloo. What little comment the *Star* made on the strikes offered a pessimistic verdict on their chances of success. Belatedly, most members of the NCA followed O'Connor in giving the so-called 'Plug Plot' their support. However, connections between the trade union action and Chartism only really existed at the local level. The NCA did little more than offer the strikers its sympathy. As one Wiltshire Chartist grumbled: 'the general complaint is that there is no public body sitting, either in London or Manchester, to direct the Movement'.[36]

Indeed, many Chartists suspected that the unrest was actually being provoked and orchestrated by the Anti-Corn Law League. Derided by Chartists as the 'mill owners' ramp', the League was alleged to be stirring up strike action in order to allow industrialists, suffering in the economic depression, to shut down factories and lay off workers. The government too had its suspicions, ordering that the ACLL leader Richard Cobden's post should be watched and read. These suspicions were not without foundation. The ACLL in Derby distributed leaflets to households praising 'the determination of the people' and advising that 'you have a moral right to subsistence . . . you receive misgovernment instead'.[37] Worried about the repercussions of the strike, some Chartists signed up as special constables to help contain the disorder.

But the militancy of some of the strikers and their attachment to Chartism were indisputable. Looking back on the Plug Plot from 1887, Joseph Lawson of Pudsey recalled how he had watched a striker stand directly in front of a troop of cavalry, shouting out that he was

> determined that no more work should be done till the 'People's Charter' was the law of the land. He bared his breast as he spoke, and told both the magistrates and soldiers, they might pierce his heart with bullets or lances, but the people were moved to no longer starve when there was an abundance in the land, kept from the producers of all wealth by bad and unjust laws.[38]

Similarly, strikers in West Yorkshire promised 'Not to work again until the charter was established'.[39]

However, by the end of August, the strikes had dissipated. The resources that the strikers could call upon were minimal. Some accounts reported that they were close to starving to death. One eyewitness recalled seeing one of the marchers drop down dead as they passed through Ovenden, between Bradford and Halifax. Many had little choice but to give in and take what scant relief they could get under the new Poor Law, or die. In addition, though the strikes were serious, they were also localised. Some areas, such as Birmingham, London, Monmouthshire and Tyneside, were largely unaffected.

The government also had powerful military resources at its disposal, made even more effective by the development of the railway system. Regular troops were supplemented by England's developing local police forces, which in turn were supported by large numbers of special constables: thirteen hundred were drafted in Halifax alone. As the industrial action weakened, the government returned to the tactics of 1839–40 and a wave of mass arrests began. In October, 274 cases were heard in Staffordshire: 54 men were transported and 154 imprisoned. The Chartist leadership was again targeted. McDouall went into self-imposed exile and O'Connor was arrested and indicted in September for seditious conspiracy. He was tried, along with fifty-eight others, at Lancaster on 1 March 1843. The Attorney-General made clear his intention to paint O'Connor in the blackest light possible:

> I propose to charge O'Connor as a general conspirator with the others and not to proceed against him for libel merely, or for acting as a Delegate, or taking part at the meeting of Delegates – I propose to try him in the same indictment with the worst of the defendants who headed mobs, made seditious speeches, and stopped mills and factories. I shall blend in one accusation the head and the hands – the bludgeon and the pen, and let the jury and the public see in one case the whole crime, its commencement and its consequence.[40]

The trial, however, was a failure. Fifty-nine prisoners were acquitted, the juries recording not-guilty verdicts on all the major charges. Those that were found guilty of minor offences were never called for sentencing.

THE LAND PLAN, O'CONNOR
AND THE LEGACY OF CHARTISM

On 20 January 1843, Daniel McNaughtan, a Scottish wood-turner, shot and killed Edward Drummond, Sir Robert Peel's private secretary, mistaking him for the Prime Minister. McNaughtan escaped the death penalty through a successful plea of insanity.

However, the killing, and McNaughtan's acquittal, caused considerable public alarm, coming as it did soon after the turmoil of the summer of 1842. The links between political radicalism and Drummond's murder may have been more than the product of politicians' nightmares. Drummond had managed to acquire a large amount of cash (£750 – over £50,000 in today's money) in the two years before the incident when he had been travelling around Britain and France. The leading Glasgow Chartist Abram Turner had worked in McNaughtan's shop. More suspicious still was the fact that McNaughtan's reader's ticket for the Glasgow Mechanics' Institute library showed that he had recently been reading works on insanity. As both a former actor and a medical student, it may not have been beyond his skill to feign the symptoms of a lunatic. However, whether his subsequent fate was better than execution is debatable. He spent most of the remainder of his life in solitary confinement in a tiny cell in Bethlem Hospital in London, and died in 1865, a year after being moved to the Crowthorne Asylum for the Criminally Insane in Berkshire.[1]

Madness and confusion also characterised the next four years of the Chartist movement in Britain: the former in the shape of the folly that was the Chartist Land Company, the latter as the party splintered and weakened into a variety of factions, no longer under the effective control of the NCA.

The threat from middle-class reform organisations had not been fully countered in 1841. A new challenge was mounted by the National Complete Suffrage Union, formed by the wealthy Quaker philanthropist and abolitionist Joseph Sturge. In April 1842, Sturge succeeded in organising a convention bringing together members of the NCSU and NCA to agree a common programme. However, his attempts to get the delegates to drop the party label 'Chartist' because of its associations with physical force were opposed by Lovett and other Chartist delegates. With the debate inconclusive, it was agreed to adjourn until a second meeting in December that year. Cooperation between Chartists and the NCSU nonetheless continued.

At Nottingham, O'Connor supported Sturge's candidacy at the election against the Tory nominee John Walter, editor of *The Times*. The atmosphere at the hustings was poisonous. It was the first time that J. R. Stephens had appeared in public since his trial and subsequent repudiation of Chartism. Angry Chartist supporters responded to his presence by tearing up prints of him from the *Northern Star* before his face. Stephens, who had come to support Walter's candidacy, was given protection by Tory 'lambs', who started to move towards the hostile Chartists. At this point, Sturge and Henry Vincent, another Chartist won over by the NCSU, wisely fled the platform. O'Connor now stepped into the breach. According to Thomas Cooper, the Chartist shoemaker, schoolmaster and poet,

Britain Strikes Home by George Cruikshank. This famous print represented a seeming political volte-face by Cruikshank, who would later collaborate with the radical publisher William Hone on a proposed memorial to the victims of Peterloo. However, women continue to be rendered here as passive victims of violence. BRIDGEMAN ART LIBRARY

Henry Hunt by J. Wiche. 'Orator' Hunt, the 'hero' of Peterloo, shown here without his famous white hat. TOPHAM

THE PEOPLE'S CHARTER:

Being the Outline of An Act to provide for the Just Representation of the People of Great Britain and Ireland in the Commons' House of Parliament:

EMBRACING THE PRINCIPLES OF

Universal Suffrage; No Property Qualification; Annual Parliaments; Equal Representation; Payment of Members; and Vote by Ballot.

Prepared by a Committee of Twelve Persons: Six Members of Parliament, and Six Members of the "London Working Men's Association;" and addressed to the People of the United Kingdom.—Re-printed from the Third Edition, Revised and Corrected, from Communications made by many Associations in various parts of the Kingdom.

The Chartists' plans for electoral reform even extended to devising elaborate mechanised ballot boxes.

Slight and bookish, William Lovett, a former cabinet-maker and founder of the London Working Men's Association, seemed an unlikely revolutionary.

Feargus O'Connor. Despite being described by his nemesis, Lovett, as 'the great "I AM"' of politics', the egotistical O'Connor was largely responsible for holding the Chartist movement together. ISTOCK

The Kennington Common meeting by William Kilburn. This remarkable photograph captures the scale of the last great Chartist meeting, which was attended by a crowd of around 150,000.

Suffragettes photographed under duress in prison. The Suffragette tactic of giving false names to avoid the full penalties of the so-called 'Cat and Mouse Act' forced the police to adopt more underhand means to ascertain their true identities, including doctoring photos. NATIONAL ARCHIVES

Leading WSPU activists Emily Wilding Davison, Christabel Pankhurst, Sylvia Pankhurst and Emmeline Pethick-Lawrence in 1910. Davison would commit the most dramatic instance of suffragette militancy, throwing herself under the King's horse, Anmer, at the 1913 Derby. NATIONAL PORTRAIT GALLERY

Emmeline Pankhurst, the WSPU leader, pictured near the end of her life. She would die in June 1928, just as the bill equalising suffrage passed through Parliament.
NATIONAL PORTRAIT GALLERY

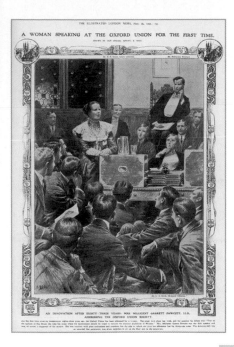

Millicent Fawcett. The role of her constitutionalist National Union of Women's Suffrage Societies in gaining the vote for women has been grossly underestimated. Not only this, the Liberal Fawcett's pre-war alliance with Labour did much to turn the fledgling political party into a serious electoral force. MEPL

Annie Kenney. Derided as 'the blotter' – a mere cipher for Christabel Pankhurst's orders – Kenney's unwavering loyalty to the WSPU cause and working-class credentials nonetheless made her an important figure in the union. MEPL

Keir Hardie. 'His eyes two deep wells of kindness, like mountain pools with the sunlight distilled': Sylvia Pankhurst's description of Hardie on their first meeting (when she was eleven) was clearly coloured by their much later love affair.
NATIONAL PORTRAIT GALLERY

David Lloyd George. 'The contrast between the buoyancy of the girl and the depression of the statesman was almost painful': the Liberal Chancellor came out the worst in the courtroom battle with Christabel Pankhurst. MEPL

William Morris, an occasional dinner guest at the Pankhursts' London home, was a giant figure in early British socialism, his romantic idealism proving more popular than orthodox Marxism. MEPL

The Battle of Cable Street. East End Jews, trade unionists and socialists put Mosley's British Union of Fascists to flight. However, the Labour leadership and the TUC worked to suppress such militant anti-fascist activity. TOPHAM

The Jarrow Crusade. Disowned by the Labour Party and the TUC, the unemployed men from Jarrow returned to the north-east with little more than their rail fares back. TOPHAM

The largest public demonstration in British history – as many as two million people marched through London to protest against the imminent war in Iraq in February 2003.
KIRSTY WIGGLESWORTH/PA PHOTOS

[O'Connor] fought like a dragon – flooring the fellows like ninepins – was thrown – forty men upon him – tore him down (Stephens and the rest had cut) and then mounted the Tory wagon! What a shout then rent the air, amidst throbbing hearts! I shall never forget it! McDouall and others then crowded the wagon and it was dragged alongside ours – we stepped on to it and, successively, addressed the meeting.[2]

After this drama, the election ended in a moral victory for the Chartists and the NCSU. Sturge overwhelmingly swept the hustings and Walter won the poll by just eighty-four votes. Shortly afterwards, he lost the seat when corruption charges against him were upheld.

The alliance between the pacifist Sturge and the belligerent O'Connor was predictably short-lived. When the convention of 374 delegates assembled at the Birmingham Mechanics' Institute on 27 December, the meeting quickly broke up over the NCSU's proposal to replace the Charter with a new 'bill of rights'. Lovett, a member of the NCSU's council, had been purposely kept in the dark about this. Indignantly, he proposed on the morning of the 28th that an amendment be passed, stating that the People's Charter retained precedence over all other documents. O'Connor, usually Lovett's implacable opponent, seconded the motion. The amendment was carried by 193 votes to 94. Sturge and his supporters responded by walking out of the conference. For now, the prospect of cross-class cooperation was negligible.

The failure to reach a compromise with the NCSU was a reminder of both the strength and the weakness of the Charter. The Six Points provided Chartism's foundation stones, principles on which even O'Connor and Lovett could agree. By 1842, however, as a result of the Newport rising and the Plug Plot, the Charter was closely associated with the threat of 'physical force'. Perhaps more importantly, it threatened a thorough transformation of the political landscape, not merely the reform of one component, the franchise. If Chartism was not the 'socialist' or 'republican' organisation that Engels and later Marx took it to be, it was nonetheless a good deal more radical than single-issue pressure groups like the Anti-Corn Law League and the National Complete Suffrage Union. Yet, by 1843, even the attachment of the Chartists themselves to the Six Points appeared to be weakening. George Julian Harney, subeditor of the *Northern Star* from 1843 as well as a member of the NCA executive, met Engels at the *Northern Star* offices in Leeds, and through him came into contact with a lot of European republicans. Following a meeting with the German communist Wilhelm Weitling in 1844, Harney formed the Democratic Friends of All Nations. The following year saw the emergence of a more extreme group, the Fraternal Democrats, whose members included Marx, Engels, Karl Schapper, Harney and a newcomer to British radicalism, the poet and barrister Ernest Jones.

Jones's background was scarcely typical among the Chartists: the son of an army officer and his wife, a daughter of a leading Kent landowner, Jones had received an expensive private education and was fluent in a number of foreign languages. A sequence of bad property deals, however, forced him to declare for bankruptcy in 1844. In part, as with Thomas Paine, it seems to have been Jones's financial misfortune that awakened his interest in radical politics. By 1846, he had produced his first collection of political poems, *Chartist Songs*, which became very popular within the movement. O'Connor recognised that Jones's intelligence and literary talents would be a great asset, and quickly brought him in as an intellectual collaborator. Through his opinion pieces in the *Star*, however, O'Connor made it clear that he saw alliances with European socialists as a threat to the movement's national unity, writing a xenophobic article in July 1847 urging followers to have 'nothing whatever to do with any foreign movement'.

By 1843, O'Connor had appeared increasingly detached from the political objectives of the Charter. The new constitution

ratified by the NCA that year removed references to the Charter
and instead aimed first 'by peaceful and legal means alone to better
the condition of man, by removing the causes which have produced
moral and social degradation'; and, second, 'to provide for the
unemployed, and [provide the] means of support for those who
are desirous to locate upon the land'.[3] The new, depoliticised constitution was a tactical move reflecting the new aim of registering
the NCA as a friendly society. Once approved by the official registrar, it would be able to buy and sell land with relative ease.
Subscribers would contribute to a land fund that would purchase
country estates and divide them into smallholdings. Through a
lottery, these would then be allocated to individual subscribers.

O'Connor was keen to differentiate this scheme from Owenite
socialist communities, such as the one established under the name
of Queenwood in Hampshire, even though a number of Chartists,
including Thomas Wheeler, the drafter of the 1843 constitution,
were influenced by Owenism. Queenwood was remarkable in a
variety of ways: the buildings were lavishly furnished and equipped
with the latest technological advances, including a conveyor belt
that took dishes from the kitchen to the communal dining room
and back again. Future plans included central heating for all
rooms, hot and cold running water and artificial lighting. The cost
of creating this Utopian vision of a supremely comfortable socialist future bankrupted the Owenite Rational Society.

More important than Queenwood's high specifications, however, was Owen's longstanding opposition to organised religion
and the traditional nuclear family which was, in his opinion, its
product. At Queenwood, all members of the Society lived com-
munally, rather than in individual family units. The *Northern Star*
criticised Owenism's deist outlook, condemning the 'infidelity
[with] which Mr OWEN and all the principal leaders of Socialism
interlard their system'. O'Connor was even more forceful in
declaring that Chartism, unlike Owenite socialism, was a friend
and supporter of traditional family values:

There is no sight . . . which can be presented to my eyes so beautiful, so cheering, so natural and becoming, as that of the
husbandman tilling the ground for his own and his family's sole
use, behoof and benefit. When I see a man with his foot on his
spade, I think I recognise the image of his God and see him in that
character which even the Malthusian deigns to assign him – A
MAN STANDING ON HIS OWN RESOURCES.[4]

There is some irony in the fact that this eulogy came from the
bachelor O'Connor, whose later years were blighted, in all proba-
bility, by the symptoms of syphilis, while Owen, who derided the
family as a poisonous social institution breeding competition and
cruelty, was a happily married man and father of eight children.

O'Connor was adamant that the Land Plan was no threat either
to accepted social institutions or to private property: 'there should
be nothing in common, save and except the public institutions
and the 100 acres of land. Every man should be the master of his
own house, his own time and his own earnings.'[5] Nonetheless,
underneath O'Connor's vision of independent smallholders still
lurked an understanding of the land that figures like the Digger
Gerrard Winstanley and Thomas Spence might have understood
and sympathised with:

the land of a country belongs to society; and that society, according to its wants has the same right to impose fresh conditions on
the lessees, that the landlord has to impose fresh conditions upon
a tenant at the expiration of his tenure. Society is the landlord: and
as society never dies, the existing government are the trustees . . .
Society looks on the performance of all requisite duties as the only
condition on which its lessees can make good that title.[6]

The Land Plan is often seen as Feargus O'Connor's greatest mistake and the biggest blemish on his career as leader of the Chartist
movement. But Chartism was in the doldrums by 1843. The second

national petition had come to nothing, the elections had failed to increase Chartist representation in Parliament and, in the provinces, local Chartist newspapers were folding at an alarming rate. The Land Plan helped reinvigorate a movement that was in danger of fizzling out or splitting into innumerable different radical groupings. It would eventually prove more popular than the NCA itself, with seventy thousand shareholders at its peak and over six hundred local branches. During a severe economic downturn, the prospect of living self-sufficiently was deeply enticing. The coalminers' strike of 1843–4 revealed the scale of the desperation. In County Durham, the major landowner Lord Londonderry evicted scores of striking miners' families from the housing that he controlled, forcing them to sleep rough among the rocks and caves of the north-east coast, foraging for food along the shoreline. Chartism itself had abandoned the equivocal stance of 1842 and now more openly embraced and supported the trade union movement. In 1844, the *Northern Star* changed its subtitle from the *Leeds Advertiser* to the *National Trades Journal* and in 1845 it expended considerable column inches in publicising the creation of the National Association of United Trades for the Protection of Labour.

Though the Land Plan fitted into a longer tradition of radical thinking about the land, more important than that legacy was the interest in the 1840s, across the political spectrum, in the land as a means of reversing the social and moral ills of industrialisation. The Labourers' Friendly Society, Home Colonization Societies and benevolent societies formed by labourers themselves all looked to small garden plots of land as a means of lifting workers out of abject poverty and cultivating wastegrounds that lay idle. The idea appealed to Parliament as well. A select committee of the House of Commons endorsed the idea of allotments for workers, and major newspapers not known for being pro-Chartist endorsed the Commons' plan. The Tory backers of the Labourers' Friendly Society did not want to create a new class of small farmers, but rather ameliorate the worst effects of urbanisation and the factory system, which included the boost – from a Tory perspective – that these gave to political radicalism. As the Society's poet put it:

> How delightful to see them gain competence, health
> And while they increase agricultural wealth
> improve in their morals; their sovereign obey . . .
> their energies roused, they are slothful no more
> They have almost deserted the publican's door.[7]

But the differences between this vision of the land and O'Connor's should not be overstated. At a fundamental level, O'Connor may have believed that the land was a public trust, but the Chartist Land Plan was not designed to convert workers into independent small farmers any more than it was intended to make all land common. Apart from the notion that toiling in the soil would inculcate deference, loyalty and political placidity, the Tory schemes and the Chartist Land Plan were actually quite similar. If anything, the Land Plan seemed to move Chartism back towards the agenda of Lovett's LWMA, emphasising education, moral reform and self-help. Though the absence of the Charter from the 1843 constitution might have been strategic, it also helped to imply that Chartism had moved away from advocating radical political change to a more gradualist stance.

The attempt to get the NCA registered as a friendly society had, however, proved a failure, the registrar continuing to view Chartism, not unreasonably, as an overtly political movement. A new tack was adopted when the NCA convention meeting in London approved the repackaging of the Land Plan as a cooperative. The Chartist Cooperative Land Society, as the new organisation was called, established its first site at Heronsgate (renamed O'Connorville) near Watford in March 1846. At the end of the year, a Land and Labour Bank was launched to gather funds. However, O'Connor had been forced, secretly, to buy the Heronsgate estate under his own name (existing laws concerning building societies did not permit them to run lotteries) and the land itself was heavily mortgaged to release more capital. Legal complications arose over the status of the company and O'Connor's ability as an MP to administer it and the bank at the same time. After a series of drawn-out cases, the Lord Chief Justice ruled out all possibility of this in 1850, and O'Connor petitioned for a bill to dissolve the company, which was finally done in August 1851. These difficulties were largely kept from *Northern Star* readers, who heard only of the successful acquisition of a second estate at Lowbands, in Worcestershire, in August 1847; and then at Charterville, in Minster Lovell in Oxfordshire, Snigs End in Gloucestershire and Great Dodford in Worcestershire.

Only two hundred and fifty tenants ever settled on the land. Many of these, as we shall see, were unable to make their allotments provide enough food either to support their families or to provide an income. However, none of this was evident from O'Connor's editorials in the *Star*, where he painted O'Connorville as a bucolic workers' paradise: 'My pale face is turned into a good, sound, sun-burnt ruddy complexion. I can jump over the gates without opening them. I am up every morning at 6 o'clock, and when I look out of my window at the prospect, and think of the number my labours will make happy, I feel myself a giant.'[8] O'Connorville was thrown open for inspection on the Chartists' jubilee, Monday, 17 August 1846 (an event heavy with symbolism: the biblical jubilee was the day when the land would be returned to its original owners). Twelve thousand toured the estate, inspected the ongoing building work and petted Rebecca the cow, named after the Rebecca Riots against high tolls on turnpike roads in Wales. Ernest Jones was among the visitors that day. He shared O'Connor's enthusiasm for the project:

When I left London this morning I thought I was only going some seventeen or eighteen miles out of town: I now begin to think I must have made a very long journey indeed, for I have come to a land that at one time I scarcely ever expected to see. I have come

from the land of slavery to the land of liberty – from the land of
poverty to the land of plenty – from the land of the Whigs to the
great land of the Charter! This is the promised land, my friends![9]

The Land Plan had briefly taken prominence over the Charter.
However, it was always hoped that its success would contribute to
the attainment of Chartism's political goals. It was even suggested
that it would help Chartist supporters gain representation under
the existing electoral system, with successful male allottees securing enfranchisement. But the Land Plan on its own was not
enough to revive Chartism as an overtly political movement. Its
brief, and final, resuscitation was the culmination of several factors, none of which was the direct result of Chartist agitation.

The first of these was the surprise election of Feargus O'Connor
as MP for Nottingham in 1847. Attempts at enfranchising Chartist
voters at the election had proved frustratingly difficult, despite
rising property values. The movement was hindered as well by the
obstructive behaviour of election officers: the revising barrister for
Manchester rejected 450 claims by Chartists; similarly, most of the
three thousand claims put forward in Birmingham were also dismissed. In September 1846, the Chartists set up a National Central
Registration and Election Committee (NCREC) under Thomas
Duncombe's presidency to coordinate its election strategy.
Although this could be seen as the first modern party election
campaign, candidates did not have to stand as Chartists in order to
receive the NCREC's support. Colonel Perronet Thompson
received a £5 donation towards his registration expenses at
Bradford, although he was now a supporter of the NCSU, not
a Chartist. Such candidates were, though, pledged to agree to
support the implementation of the Charter in any parliamentary
division.

The strategy did produce some successes, with the election of
nine radical-Liberal candidates endorsed by the NCREC. Again,
there were propaganda triumphs at the hustings. Harney sealed his

reputation as a politician of substance at Tiverton, confronting the Foreign Secretary Lord Palmerston with a dissection of his foreign policy that forced Palmerston to improvise a lengthy and detailed rebuttal. In Swansea, the Chartist candidate used the hustings to taunt the Liberal candidate (who had been returned unopposed at every election from 1832 to 1842), saying, 'I see this will be a one-sided Parliament, a rich man's Parliament.'[10] However, overall the election was a disappointing show for the Chartists. They had achieved nowhere near the twenty to thirty sympathetic MPs they had hoped for, and the lack of any Chartist candidates in Scotland indicated that the movement's reach was shrinking. The contrast with the Land Plan was an eye-opener: the NCREC's total income of £470 was minuscule compared to the Land Plan, which raised over £1420 in the first week of publication alone.

The one outstanding success, almost completely unexpected, was O'Connor's election at Nottingham. He spent little personal energy campaigning, preferring to dig and manure his Lowbands estate for 'swedes and white turnips'. Two hours before the election closed, he had polled fewer votes than all the other candidates. However, his opponents were even more blasé, neither of the Whigs bothering to speak before the hustings. The Tory candidate didn't even turn up. O'Connor's victory was, in large part, due to a lot of Tory voters determined to keep out the Whigs. If the other Tory candidate had bothered to stand, O'Connor would certainly have lost. Even if he himself seemed uninterested in the Nottingham contest, he at least, in contrast to his opponents, had a strong local election team behind him, led by one James Sweet, well versed in the running of local elections and up to speed with the key issues in the area. Sir John Cam Hobhouse, President of the Board of Control and one of the Whig candidates at Nottingham, noted the universal shock at O'Connor's win and the humiliation that followed for the losers: 'O'Connor's people were astonished at his success & the shabby dissenters affected to be equally surprised and vexed. The bells of the Churches rang and bands of music paraded the town & stopt under my windows to shout and play "Johnny so long at the fair", "Oh dear what can the matter be."'[11]

However, O'Connor's election was less of a triumph than it appeared to be. First and most obviously, it was more a product of his opponents' mistakes than anything else. More importantly, with Duncombe seriously ill, it left Chartism in the Commons in O'Connor's hands. His failure as an MP has sometimes been exaggerated. When time and opportunity allowed, he was an effective and able parliamentarian. Unlike many MPs, he viewed himself as the delegate of his constituents, holding an annual informal 'election', open to the disenfranchised, into his conduct as MP, and promising to resign if the majority disapproved of his actions. Unquestionably, though, he spread himself too thinly: in addition to his work as an MP, he retained oversight of the Land Plan, continued to make regular contributions to the *Northern Star*, and undertook considerable public speaking duties. After 1850, as his mental illness became evident, his conduct in Parliament became a great embarrassment to the movement. His erratic behaviour included sitting in the Speaker's chair, randomly offering his hand to some MPs, and physically assaulting others. Arguably by this point, Chartism was spent, anyway, as an effective political force.

O'Connor's election may have been an unanticipated bonus, but the more general revival in Chartist fortunes was a product of a pan-European economic and political crisis that brought political systems tumbling down. In England, commodity prices, especially wheat, had risen to levels not seen since the year of Peterloo. Overall, prices were at a level unequalled since 1841 and the cotton industry was in a deep depression: barely a third of Manchester's factory labour force was in full-time work by November 1847. But the suffering in England was nothing compared to the famine that was now gripping Ireland and would eventually claim over two million lives. It was Ireland that prompted the resignation of Peel as Prime Minister on 29 June

1846 over the new Irish coercion bill, granting emergency powers to quell disturbances caused by the famine, and his replacement by Lord Russell.

The death of the Irish nationalist leader Daniel O'Connell once again opened up the possibility of cooperation between English Chartists and Irish nationalists. By 1847, an alliance had developed between the Chartists and the Irish Confederation, a nationalist organisation headed by the Limerick MP William Smith O'Brien. While this union might have been convenient for Chartism, it revived fears of imminent insurrection, especially in cities with large Irish populations such as Liverpool, Manchester and Birmingham. The growth of confederation clubs in these conurbations seemed to confirm Thomas Carlyle's words in his *Chartism*: 'Crowds of miserable Irish darken all our towns . . . sunk from decent manhood to squalid apehood . . . the ready-made nucleus of degradation and disorder.'[12]

Such fears were heightened further by events outside the British Isles. The *Northern Star* reported the Krakow rising of 1846 under the headline, 'Springtime of the Peoples'. The Chartist press itself, which had endured a slump in the mid-1840s that only the *Star* had really survived, underwent a renaissance, with the number of titles doubling from ten in 1847 to twenty the following year. These publications fed a public hunger for news of the revolutionary events unfolding on the Continent. January 1848 saw anti-Austrian riots in Milan and an uprising against the King of Naples in Sicily. In the second week of February, there was serious rioting in Munich; in the third week, the French government's attempts to suppress the reform movement led to massive crowd actions in the streets of Paris and large-scale desertions from the army. On 24 February came the most dramatic news, as a revolutionary mob sacked the Tuileries Palace, forcing the abdication of Louis Philippe in favour of the infant Comte de Paris. That night at Sadler's Wells theatre, the occupants of the cheap seats forced the performance to stop, and ordered the orchestra to play the

'Marseillaise' instead. The following day, the *Northern Star* declared, 'The Revolution has been accomplished.' One Barnsley radical recalled the excitement with which the news was received:

> One Sunday night I read, for a houseful of listeners, ten columns of the proceedings on the banks of the Seine which culminated in the deposition and flight of Louis Philippe, king of the French. Of course the Chartists in England and the Young Irish Repealers in the sister isle were jubilant, for they nursed the delusion that the revolutionary waves would soon beat up against the White Cliffs of Dover.[13]

But it was only with the benefit of hindsight that this expectation proved premature. In the spring of 1848, it seemed very possible that England would undergo a revolution equivalent to the one that had erupted in France. On 6 March, a reform meeting in Trafalgar Square was taken over by the Chartists. The crowd remained on the streets and was dispersed with difficulty by the police. That same evening, some of them marched to Buckingham Palace, smashing lamps and windows on the way. The mob ran free for some three days. On the same day that rioting broke out in London, looters raided shops in Glasgow, calling for 'bread or revolution'. The army was called in and shot five of the looters. In Manchester the following day the workhouse was stormed, but the crowd was dispersed by police after a four-hour struggle. In reprisal, the police station in Oldham Road was attacked.

Across the country, more peaceful meetings were being organised by local Chartists, with speeches delivered by O'Connor, Jones, Samuel Kydd, George White and Joseph Barker. On St Patrick's Day, a fraternal meeting of Chartists and Irish met at the Free Trade Hall in Manchester to be addressed by O'Connor. The meetings supported a new national petition, which was already gathering signatures by the thousand. These local meetings would be followed by a peaceful rally on Kennington Common in

London on 10 April, after which a mass procession would present the petition to the House of Commons. If the petition were rejected, the Queen was to be called upon by a newly elected NCA national assembly to dissolve Parliament, and the assembly would remain in session until a new government had agreed to make the Charter the law of the land. This was a far more explicit and forceful endorsement of 'ulterior measures' than had accompanied any previous Chartist petitioning campaign.

Given the sobering precedent of events in Europe, the British government was taking no chances. The Queen was safely removed to Osborne House on the Isle of Wight (though Lord Palmerston was concerned that the island's defences were inadequate). On 7 April, the Chief Commissioner of Police banned the procession from Kennington Common, and the government began to rush the Crown and government security bill through Parliament – a far-reaching measure that redefined and extended the offence of treason to include 'open and advised speaking'. It was made law within twelve days, causing the black Chartist activist William Cuffay to wonder drily 'how anything to abridge the rights of the working classes can be passed in a few hours'. The Duke of Wellington put himself forward to organise London's defences, and 85,000 special constables were enrolled (including one W. E. Gladstone). If we accept a moderate estimate of the Kennington Common crowd as close to the 150,000 given by Chartism's first historian, Robert Gammage – somewhere between the gross overestimate of 500,000 made by O'Connor or the blatant underestimate of Lord Russell at 15,000 – this probably amounted to one constable for every one and a half marchers.[14] The philosopher Alexander Bain, then at the Board of Health, recalled the extent of the government's preparations:

In our office and all other offices of Government, the windows of the ground floors were fitted with iron bars running up and down, like a lunatic asylum; there were, besides, barricades of deal boxes full of papers built up at each window to be a protection to the people within while firing out upon the mob through narrow openings between the sides of the boxes. Each man in the office mustered between eight and nine in the morning, and had a musket given him with twenty rounds of ball cartridge in a belt for going round the middle. I sat the whole day with my belt about me, snuffing up the smell of new leather.[15]

According to the author Charles Mackay, 'There was scarcely a merchant, a banker, or shopkeeper, or clerk in London, except the very old, who did not take the oath and carry a truncheon, to crack the skull of a Chartist if it became necessary.'[16] Backing up this massive police presence was the military, only to be used if the Chartists attempted to cross over the Thames into Westminster.

This show of force led some Chartists to advise against going ahead with the Kennington Common meeting. On 9 April, Bronterre O'Brien spoke against it and resigned from the convention. Duncombe urged the convention to 'Think! Think! Think! And remember – one false step may seal the fate of millions.' Others, though, were less cautious, Ernest Jones suggesting that petitioning should be abandoned but that the leaders should not 'damp a fine enthusiasm'. Despite the clear reservations of some, the meeting went ahead and a large crowd assembled. O'Connor was visibly in a state of high anxiety, the Metropolitan Police Commissioner Sir Richard Mayne noting that he was 'deadly pale' with 'perspiration running down'. The next day, O'Connor would have to miss both convention and Parliament, complaining 'my chest in great pain'. Some historians have read into this early signs of his later illness, but given the rumours of insurrection and the massive police presence, stress and fear are the most plausible explanations for his behaviour.

The petition was loaded into three cabs and taken to Parliament. O'Connor, having told the crowd to disperse, took another cab to the Home Office to assure Sir George Grey, the

Home Secretary, of the legality of the day's proceedings. By two o'clock, the Prime Minister was able to inform the Queen that the crisis was over. Russell wrote to her, 'the Kennington Common Meeting has proved a complete failure', yet in the same letter could add, 'At Manchester, however, the Chartists are armed and have bad designs.'[17]

If O'Connor is often condemned for his apparent loss of nerve at Kennington, it should be remembered that, given the scale of the government's preparations, the alternative – to allow the crowd to remain in situ or even encourage them to march with the petition towards Westminster – could have led to a bloodbath that would have made Peterloo seem like a minor altercation. He should, rather, be applauded for having acted quickly to diffuse a highly volatile situation. Likewise, the attacks on O'Connor's handling of the petition ignore both the actual strength of support demonstrated for the petition and the weakness of the government's case against it. He is frequently blamed for inflating the number of signatures, claiming that there were over five million. The official figure given by the clerks of the Commons was 1,975,467, fewer than half that number. They also revealed that the petition contained a number of obviously fraudulent signatures: it was unlikely that 'Victoria Rex', 'the Duke of Wellington' or 'Mr Punch' had actually appended their names to it.

However, it needs to be pointed out that the number that the Commons clerks offered was an estimate, too. The calculation down to a single unit might give the impression that they had pored over the petition's pages day and night, counting the signatures one by one. This, as O'Connor pointed out, was not possible in the time that they had actually taken to examine the document. They would have had to count 150 signatures a minute. Instead, the clerks would have followed standard Commons practice in estimating the size of mass petitions by counting the number of signatures on one yard of petition and then multiplying that figure by its full length. Also, in this case, the discovery of a number of bogus signatures would have led them to revise their estimate downwards, assuming that the same proportion of false names appeared on each yard of petition. The clerks also dismissed a lot of signatures that were perfectly legitimate. For example, they deemed fraudulent multiple signatures given in the same hand, even though this was almost certainly evidence that illiterate Chartist supporters had had literate individuals sign for them. They also discounted the signatures of women – estimated at 8000 in every 100,000 – despite the fact that the right of women to petition had been upheld by Parliament in 1829. These decisions, clearly, favoured a conservative estimate of the number of names on the petition as a whole.

We will never be able to gain an exact figure for those who signed the 1848 petition, as, like many both before and after, the papers were not kept but probably went straight into the Commons' furnace after the clerks had done their work. Even so, the estimate of just under two million signatures represented a considerable proportion of an adult population of just over seventeen million, and was several times the size of the electorate. This is the fact that is often overlooked: every one of the Chartists' mass petitions gathered more supporters than there were electors under the existing franchise. Moreover, though the Commons rejected every one of them, on each occasion the Chartists succeeded in forcing a lengthy debate within Parliament, thereby pushing the Charter on to the political centre stage.

Undoubtedly, though, it was the government and not the Chartists who had greater cause for happiness in the wake of the Kennington Common meeting. Chartism appeared in disarray. O'Connor refused to be part of a national assembly that gathered in May. Harney was also absent: leadership, significantly, passed to Ernest Jones. The new security law was used to clamp down on the radical press. John Mitchel, editor of the *United Irishman*, was sentenced to transportation to Australia for fourteen years. His conviction led to rioting in Bradford and London. In Bradford on

28 May, a crowd of two thousand routed police and special constables; the troops had to be called in to restore order. The following day a massive silent march of eighty thousand workers through London appeared deeply threatening, and a further meeting in the East End on 4 June was broken up on instructions of the Home Office; sporadic street fighting followed.

Jones's first period as leader of the Chartist movement was brief. The planned day of protest agreed by the provisional executive of the national assembly led to his arrest and subsequent sentencing to two years in prison. As Ben Wilson recalled, the conditions of Jones's incarceration were harsh:

Mr Jones was suffering from dysentry at the time, and he was consigned to a dark cell from which a man dying from cholera had just been removed; their efforts, however, were in vain, as the prison authorities never succeeded in making him perform the degrading task [i.e. commit suicide]. In the second year of his imprisonment Mr Jones was so broken in health that he could no longer stand upright, and was found lying on the floor of his cell and only then was he taken to the hospital. He was told then that if he would petition for his release and promise to abjure politics the remainder of his sentence would be remitted, but he refused his liberty on those conditions and was again sent to his cell. During his imprisonment and before writing materials were allowed him he wrote some of his most admired poems, making pens from the quills that occasionally dropped from the wing of a passing bird in the prison yard, these he cut secretly with a razor that was brought to him twice a week to shave with; an ink bottle he contrived to make from a piece of soap he got from the washing shed, and this he filled with ink from the ink bottle when he was allowed to write his quarterly letter; paper was supplied by those quarterly letters, the fly leaves of a bible, prayer book, and any books he was allowed to read. One poem 'The New World' was composed before he had succeeded in securing ink and written almost entirely in his own blood![18]

If the authorities had hoped to break Jones's spirit as well as his body, they were not successful. When he finally emerged from prison in 1850 he had become a convinced socialist, no longer wedded to the language of the 'ancient constitution' but fully a disciple of Marx and Engels.

Chartist meetings on Whit Monday, 21 June 1848, which included a small demonstration outside Osborne House on the Isle of Wight, were taken as signs that a mass rising was being prepared. A large meeting in London was dispersed as soon as Peter McDouall heard that the magistrates and police intended to put it down. That same afternoon in the Albion beer shop, McDouall chaired a large and disaffected group of London Chartists who agreed to form a committee to 'appoint the day and hour when the final struggle is to take place'. However, two Chartists, George Davis and T. R. Reading, contacted the Home Office, alerting them to these designs, almost certainly out of genuine concern over the shift towards conspiratorial violence. When the conspiracy took renewed shape in July, following the suspension of Habeas Corpus and the arrest of Patrick O'Higgins on charges of high treason, no NCA executive member remained involved.

McDouall having absented himself, the leading figures were now William Cuffay and the Irishman Daniel Donovan. Cuffay, born in Chatham, Kent, but the grandson of an African slave, had been noted for his militancy in the weeks leading up to the Kennington Common demonstration. Following the dispersal of the crowd, he had denounced O'Connor and the rest of the Chartist leadership as 'cowardly humbugs'. The rising was finally set for the night of Wednesday 16 August, but plans for a coordinated rising in Manchester were smashed by police raids the preceding night. The London conspirators were arrested on the 16th as they assembled at the Orange Tree pub near Holborn. Cuffay had managed to flee to his lodgings but reportedly refused to make good his escape 'lest it should be said that he abandoned his associates in the hour of peril'.[19]

Six of the conspirators were sentenced to transportation, while fifteen others received sentences of eighteen to twenty-four months. McDouall was sentenced to two years in prison. Cuffay spent the rest of his life in Tasmania. Though he eventually died in the workhouse, he was not buried in an unmarked pauper's grave. A headstone was provided by the authorities in the belief that his supporters might want to honour his memory. As we have seen, Chartists who moved to Australia, whether through free emigration or penal transportation, made a significant contribution to the reform movement in the colony. Cuffay was no exception. A radical to his dying breath, he took an active part in the campaign against Tasmania's 'law of master and servant' and worked for universal manhood suffrage.[20]

According to Henry Solly, the founder of English working men's clubs and a former Chartist, 'Chartism was practically at an end on the night of 10 April, and all attempts to resuscitate it were only the old story of flogging a dead horse.'[21] If that remark was somewhat sweeping, it was nonetheless true that 1848 marked the end of Chartism as an effective mass political movement. It was Robert Gammage, writing his history six years after the Kennington Common meeting, who first identified O'Connor as the chief culprit behind Chartism's failure. By 1852, O'Connor had been committed to a lunatic asylum. When Ernest Jones visited him in 1853, he found a pathetic spectacle. The former radical leader sat playing with the toys brought by Jones's children, singing 'The Lion of Freedom', the song written to celebrate his release from prison in 1841. Jones noted that he was well cared for, but he would not see out another two years, dying in 1855. Even in death, O'Connor proved controversial: a proposed memorial in Nottingham was the subject of a protracted local dispute – opponents feared that celebrating him would sully the city's reputation. Two days after the statue was finally unveiled in the Arboretum (where it stands to this day), it was daubed with ink, and on a later occasion tarred and feathered.[22]

Before he was committed to the asylum, it was already clear that O'Connor's greatest scheme, the Land Plan, was a dismal failure. The rural idyll that he had presented in the pages of the *Northern Star* had turned sour for most of those few subscribers who had received allotments. In 1850, sixty-eight eviction orders had to be served against those who had failed to pay their rent. The problems with the Land Bank were fully revealed by the select committee investigation into its operation. The Commons declared that it was 'an illegal scheme, and will not fulfil the expectations held out by the directors to the Shareholders'.[23] According to the estimate of the government actuary, it would have taken a hundred and fifty years for the scheme to make back their investments. Neither were the small plots of two, three and four acres sufficient both to maintain a family and to produce enough surplus to pay the ground rent.

The select committee investigation revealed the high hopes and commitment of subscribers to the scheme, and, at the same time, how many of them had no idea how to make their allotments a success. One allottee reported that his 'Peas and the Beans got the Blight and the Great Part of the Potatoes Got the Disease, the Land is the only Remedy for the working man but it wants A Little Capital to begin.' Nonetheless, he noted, 'With my trade on Strike in London I would not think of Nobing it [giving it up] I would sooner eat Potatoes tops.'[24] Many of these industrial workers had little understanding of what to plant when and how. Charles William Stubbs, an Oxfordshire clergyman and later Bishop of Truro, reported that a friend of his had visited the Chartist allotments at Minster Lovell. There he heard that one of the allottees had 'actually inquired what he was to plant in order to make bread another sowed his turnips as thick as mustard and cress, and refused to thin them because they looked too nourishing; another wished to known how many *bushels* of the same seed to sow to the acre'.[25]

Yet, without O'Connor's leadership, the movement rapidly

fractured into a variety of political leagues and unions, including Bronterre O'Brien's National Reform League and Thomas Cooper's People's Charter Union. The flagship of the Chartist press, the *Northern Star*, declined in sales to only five thousand copies a week, compared to forty thousand in 1839, as the paper floundered without the guiding hand of Harney, who left to produce his own paper, the *Red Republican*. Harney himself now saw Chartism divided between those interested in developing a social programme, 'Chartists and something more', and those prepared to compromise the Charter in order to win over middle-class reformists – 'Chartists, or something less'. A clear shift towards the former by the NCA was indicated by the much broader social and economic programme agreed at the London convention on 31 March 1851. This represented less a realistic political manifesto and more a wish-list of almost every radical demand made from the 1790s onwards.

Chartists performed very poorly at the 1852 election: their one electoral victory at Tavistock in Devon, where Samuel Carter was elected, proved short-lived as Carter was later disqualified for failing to meet the property qualification required of MP's. As the *Star* commented on 20 March, 'The Charter is no more to be had now by asking for, than next year's apples are – like them they must grow and ripen first.'[26]

By this point, the NCA had been infiltrated by the international-socialist Fraternal Democrats. As 'Howard Morton' (probably Helen MacFarlane) wrote in Harney's *Red Republican* in June 1850:

> Chartism in 1850 is a different thing from Chartism in 1840. The leaders of the English Proletarians have proved that they are true Democrats, and no shams, by going ahead so rapidly within the last few years. They have progressed from the idea of a simple *political reform* to the idea of a *Social Revolution*.[27]

It was MacFarlane who produced the first translation of *The Communist Manifesto* for publication in the *Red Republican*. But whereas Harney moved away from socialism during the 1850s, Ernest Jones did not, promoting the ideas of Marx and Engels through his periodicals, the *People's Paper* and *Notes to the People*. However, even the ideologically committed Jones eventually bowed to political pragmatism when, in 1858, he called an NCA conference (the last under the NCA umbrella) to promote co-operation with the middle-class reformers. This resulted in the formation of the Political Reform Union, which in turn contributed to the new liberal reform movement that culminated in the Second Reform Act of 1867. In his last significant political act, Jones stood as an unofficial Liberal in Manchester in November 1868, polling a very respectable ten thousand votes. When he died on 26 January 1869, he was on the brink of being selected as the official Liberal candidate.

The career of Ernest Jones arguably serves as a better indicator of the successes and failures of the Chartist movement than that of the more famous Feargus O'Connor. Ending the narrative in 1848 leaves us with a movement that appears an unqualified failure. However, as the historian Edward Royle has reminded us, in the face of a political system stacked heavily against them and a similar imbalance in firepower when it came to the exercise of physical force, it is fairer to ask how Chartism succeeded for as long as it did. Indeed, looking at it from the perspective of 1867, we can see legacies of ideology and organisation that informed a more successful reform movement, eventually leading to the enfranchisement of at least some of the male working class.

However, as with the history of most of British radicalism, evaluating Chartism on the basis of a simple historical balance sheet of gains and losses tells us very little about the true impact of the movement. This lay in its powerful legacy to working-class historical memory, community and culture. The connections were repeatedly made by later reformers. 'The blood of the Chartists of forty-eight is the seed of the Reform movement of 1866,' announced the *English Leader*, reporting a West Riding reform demonstration addressed by Ernest Jones that year.[28] In 1884 the Third Reform Act was celebrated at Maude's Temperance Hotel, Halifax, by twenty-two former members of the old Chartist Association, as a fulfilment of their political faith. The secret of the movement's long afterlife was its success in reaching far beyond English radical groups' traditional roots in London artisan society and out into the towns and villages of the provinces. Here, the role of the *Northern Star*, which knitted together the local and the national, was crucial. In later life, many Chartists recorded the central importance of reading the *Star* in their communities. As Ben Brierley recalled, the communal reading of the Chartist paper habitually sparked off excited discussions:

> The *Northern Star*, the only newspaper that appeared to circulate anywhere, found its way weekly to the Cut side, being subscribed for by my father and five others. Every Sunday morning these sub-scribers met at our house to hear what prospect there was of the expected 'smash up' [revolution] taking place. It was my task to read aloud so that all could hear at the same time; and the com-ments that were made on the events apparently foreshadowed would have been exceedingly edifying to me were I to hear them now. A Republic was to take the place of the 'base, bloody, and brutal Whigs,' and the usurpers of all civil rights, the Lords. The Queen was to be dethroned, and the president of a Republic take her place. This would be a very easy task. Ten thousand trained pikemen would sweep England through; and Hollinwood [a nearby Lancashire town] could furnish a contingent of at least a thousand.[29]

The *Star* gave people who had never written before an outlet to discuss their political beliefs. And Chartist meetings were occa-sions for conviviality as well as serious talk, as Thomas Dunning recalled: 'we held open-air meetings in Wood Street on evenings during the week, and on Sunday evenings we sang Chartist hymns, and Mr William Cooper delivered political sermons from scriptural texts'.[30]

If Chartists failed, beyond the election of O'Connor, to secure representation at a national level, they were far more successful in gaining influence in local government – in Sheffield, even gaining control of the council. Even the Land Plan, so often seen as the downfall of the movement, was viewed through rose-tinted spectacles by some old Chartists, Ben Wilson claiming, 'the scheme was before its time; yet I believe the day is not far distant when it will be successfully carried out'.[31] Once, Wilson's comments might have been dismissed as wishful thinking. Today, smallholdings farmed by family groups are once again being seen as a solution to the global food crisis. This is especially true in the developing world, where farming for cash crops has led to serious environmental damage while, through the inequities of the food distribution system, delivering minimal financial returns to the farmers themselves.[32]

The achievement of Chartism in etching itself into the memory of local communities is even more remarkable. Chartism lacks a national feast day like that dedicated by the TUC to the Tolpuddle Martyrs.[33] Successive political movements, Liberalism and then Labour, attempted to appropriate the memory of Chartism with varying degrees of success: the Chartists' essentially political ideology and ambivalent relationship with the unions made them harder to incorporate into a narrative of the 'rise of Labour'.[34] In the late twentieth century, the Chartist homesteads were co-opted by the heritage industry with the acquisition of the last unimproved Chartist cottage at Great Dodford in Worcestershire by the National Trust in 1997. As the age of New Labour dawned, the National Trust, that 'ethereal . . . holding company for the dead spirit of the nation', to quote Patrick Wright, was also seeking to change its image, away from a preserver of stately homes, perhaps to a 'People's Trust'.[35] It was fitting that in the year of Blair's triumph, the model town of O'Connorville should become, as Paul Barker acerbically put it in the *New Statesman*, 'a leafy, Arcadian village, much sought after by the Mercedes-owning classes'.[36] Simon Schama's televised *History of Britain* (2001) reinforced the image of Chartism as the movement of an urban working-class hankering for a pastoral paradise by using the Dodford cottage as a location, ignoring the grittier filming opportunities in Kennington Park in South London.[37]

If the media's use of such chocolate-box imagery threatens to obscure the more complex reality of the movement, an antidote is provided by the longer-standing commemoration of Chartism in the communities where it took strongest hold: South Wales, the North West and the Midlands. Here, local people have fought for and preserved Chartist memorials and celebrated key dates in Chartist history, such as the Newport rising. The success of Chartism at the level of families and individuals is perhaps no better demonstrated than in the growth of societies dedicated to Chartist family history, which has crossed over into cyberspace with searchable Chartist databases and dedicated historical blogs offering more information. A political movement that touched the lives of millions is now being rediscovered by the twenty-first-century ancestors of those ordinary, yet extraordinary, Victorian men and women.[38]

Some historians have accused Chartism of having become essentially a political anachronism by the 1840s, its constitutionalism ill-suited either to the increasingly class-based nature of politics in Victorian Britain or to the growing political sophistication of the parties in Westminster, no longer dominated by hard-edged politicians like Liverpool and Castlereagh but by men like Peel, whom O'Connor himself admired as a 'great man'. Yet this supposedly outdated political movement bequeathed a remarkably resilient historical legacy. Radical liberalism displayed obvious debts to Chartist tactics, personnel and style, as Gladstone took on the mantle of charismatic leadership from O'Connor. Later, the mixture of constitutionalist language and militant action proved a potent combination for radical suffragists, some of whom, including a Manchester barrister called Richard Pankhurst, would trace their political awakening to the influence of Chartists like Ernest Jones.

PART SEVEN

THE BLOODLESS REVOLUTION

The true and inner secret of the Militant Movement was that we were an autocracy. No committee ever has, or ever will, run a revolution. Whether that revolution be bloodless like the women's, or dripping with tears and blood like the Russian, they may say a committee runs it, but probe deeply enough and you will find one head that towers above all others.

Annie Kenney[1]

The Pankhursts, the Suffrage Movement and Socialism

In the summer of 1866, following the fall of the reformist Russell–Gladstone administration and the coming to power of the Derby–Disraeli minority Tory government, agitation for the vote threatened to spill over into mass insurrection. The public mood had never been so hostile since the days of the great Chartist demonstration on Kennington Common in 1848. Members of the Reform League, the working-class organisation that had pared down the Chartist programme to the single issue of manhood suffrage, moved for a mass demonstration in Hyde Park on 23 July. The park was then a public space tailored for genteel amusement, designed for leisurely canters in horse-drawn carriages. It was also, unlike rougher, proletarian Kennington Common, closer to Westminster and unprotected by the natural barrier of the Thames. The government's response was to ban the demonstration, arguing that it was 'opposed to the purpose for which the parks are open to the public'.[1]

In the face of vacillation by some of the more timorous members of the Reform League, the majority followed the decision of the atheist lawyer Charles Bradlaugh, who argued that they should proceed to the park and if they were obstructed by the police, lead the procession peacefully towards Trafalgar Square instead. On the day, the way was indeed barred at Marble Arch, by a force of sixteen hundred police and barricades of omnibuses, and the leaders of the procession instructed the crowd to change course and follow them to Trafalgar Square. However, a minority remained and, discovering that the railings around the park were poorly secured, tore them down, circumventing the blockade. With the perimeter breached, contingents from the march were joined by bystanders, the numbers within the park swelling to an estimated two hundred thousand. Stones were hurled at the police and military support was summoned. Wisely, after receiving a deputation from the Reform League headed by the former Chartist John Bedford Leno, the Home Secretary, Spencer Walpole, urged police restraint. The crowds were eventually dispersed after speeches announcing another meeting the following day, which passed peacefully, in Trafalgar Square.

Mass meetings agitating for manhood suffrage continued throughout that year, spreading out from the metropolis to other major British cities. The autumn saw crowds of 300,000 in Birmingham, 250,000 in Manchester and an 'incredible number' in Glasgow, all pressing for one man, one vote. Now pressure was also now being exerted for the franchise to be extended to women. In Manchester, members of the more middle-class Reform Union, including the former Chartist Ernest Jones, pressed for women's suffrage. Also on this committee was a young lawyer called Richard Marsden Pankhurst.[2]

Further reform meetings were staged in the spring of 1867, including another mass demonstration on 1 May in Hyde Park which flew in the teeth of another official ban by the Home Secretary. A week after the demonstration, Walpole resigned, protesting unconvincingly that his decision had nothing to do with his abject failure to prevent the Hyde Park meeting. The park's reputation as a site for unrestrained political speech, today institutionalised in Speakers' Corner, had been established. On 20 May in the Commons, J. S. Mill, the philosopher and Liberal MP, gathered a respectable seventy-three votes for his amendment in favour of women's suffrage, but the motion was nonetheless heavily defeated. In fact, the resulting householder franchise established by the Second Reform Act, if much more radical than anticipated (increasing the number of borough voters by 138 per cent to 1.22 million and county voters by just under 46 per cent to 791,253), actually disadvantaged women householders by making the convenient and cost-effective practice of 'compounding' (combining) rates into rent illegal.[3]

The name Pankhurst is now synonymous with the struggle for votes for women. The reduction of the history of the fight for women's suffrage into the story of the Pankhurst family (Richard and Emmeline, and their daughters Christabel, Sylvia and Adela) has been a feature of recent accounts and dramatisations of the movement, both sympathetic and hostile. For some historians, such as June Purvis, Emmeline and Christabel are the true heroines of this story, with Mrs Pankhurst the brilliant political strategist and her beautiful eldest daughter the visionary thinker and captivating public speaker.[4] For others, however, such as the journalist Melanie Phillips, Emmeline and Christabel were manhating harridans whose rhetoric, and the 'terrorist' action it sanctioned, was ultimately responsible for the breakdown of the traditional family and, with it, the disintegration of society as a whole.[5] For left-wing writers and historians, especially male ones, Sylvia is the star: less hostile to men – indeed, in awe of Richard, her father, the radical lawyer – and, unlike Emmeline and Christabel, a lifelong socialist and peace campaigner.[6] Poor, frail Adela, the youngest of the Pankhurst daughters, who emigrated to Australia in 1914, is usually only mentioned in relation to her belated conversion to far-right politics in the 1940s.[7]

The centenary of the foundation of Emmeline Pankhurst's Women's Social and Political Union in 2003 was treated largely as if it were the centenary of the suffrage cause as a whole. However, the campaign for votes for women stretched back to the Victorian era.[8] As we shall see, the campaigns initiated by Victorian feminists encompassed much more than just the franchise: they also fought for changes to marriage and divorce laws, promoted women's education and professional development, and attacked the 'sexual double standard' that victimised female prostitutes but viewed their male clients as simply relieving 'natural' impulses. Moreover, the WSPU was arguably neither the most popular nor the most politically effective women's suffrage organisation. The 'suffragettes' (a term coined by the hostile *Daily Mail* in 1906 to differentiate the followers of the WSPU from less militant 'suffragists') were only part of a much wider movement for female suffrage, including many other groups, most prominently Millicent Fawcett's suffragist (constitutionalist) National Union of Women's Suffrage Societies (NUWSS).

Portraying the suffrage movement as a Pankhurst personality cult also falsely detaches it from earlier movements for political reform. In fact, both the WSPU and the NUWSS had their roots in nineteenth-century radicalism, specifically the agitation leading up to the passage of the Second Reform Act in 1867. Suffragette and suffragist tactics consciously echoed the activities of male reformers in order to confer legitimacy on their actions. As Mrs Pankhurst argued in a speech delivered in New York on 21 October 1913:

> The extensions of the franchise to the men of my country have been preceded by very great violence, by something like a revolution, by something like civil war. In 1832, you know we were on the edge of civil war and on the edge of revolution, and it was at the point of the sword – no, not at the point of the sword – it was after the practice of arson on so large a scale that half the city of Bristol was burned down in a single night, it was because more and greater violence and arson were feared that the Reform Bill of 1832 was allowed to pass into law.[9]

Like the Chartists, they used mass petitioning, large-scale public meetings and 'anti-Parliaments' as devices to muster support and exert political pressure. The first signs of suffragette militancy, the interrupting of Liberal Party meetings, mimicked the Chartist ploy of invading Anti-Corn Law League gatherings.

Ideologically, the movement for women's suffrage also shared the radical belief that it was part of a tradition to defend British freedom. For suffragists like Millicent Fawcett, this tradition could be seen to stretch back even to Celtic warrior heroines such as Boudicca. For militants like Sylvia Pankhurst, it was of a more recent vintage, written in the pages of Mary Wollstonecraft's *Vindication of the Rights of Woman*, defended in blood at Peterloo and preserved in the hearts of radical republicans and socialists. Like many male radicals, feminist writers often spoke longingly of an Anglo-Saxon 'ancient constitution' that guaranteed the rights of freeborn men and women. In a variant on the notion of the 'Norman yoke', however, many feminists saw the seventeenth century as a key period when these Anglo-Saxon rights were overridden, when Sir Edward Coke refined the concept of legal coverture – the idea that a married woman's legal rights were merged with her husband's – which underwrote Britain's unequal marriage laws.[10] Along with so many radical movements, place as well as history was significant for the advocates of women's suffrage. As the working-class suffragette and socialist Hannah Mitchell noted, the first act of WSPU militancy took place on the site of the Peterloo massacre of 1819.[11]

The expectations that advocates of women's suffrage placed on the franchise also bore comparison with earlier radical movements. Like the Chartists, suffragettes and suffragists alike believed in the transformative power of the vote. Enfranchisement would not only lead to political emancipation but to the transfiguration of a male-dominated society into a different mould. In this sense, the WSPU and NUWSS continued the tradition of Victorian women's suffrage movements in arguing for sexual, social and economic emancipation, as well as political liberation. As we have seen, historians have often criticised the Chartists for offering largely political solutions to what were essentially social and economic problems, and for placing a 'naive' trust in the capability of the ballot box to effect significant change. Yet, if the consequence of the 1918 and 1928 Representation of the People Acts was not the feminine millennium envisaged by Christabel Pankhurst, it nonetheless came close to the 'bloodless revolution' described by the working-class suffragette, Annie Kenney. In this regard, the movement for women's suffrage was the most successful of all the British radical movements and the most influential in terms of its broader social impact.

The suffrage movement had strong roots in nineteenth-century Manchester radicalism. As the youngest Pankhurst daughter Adela wrote: 'The very stones of Manchester might have cried out to [Christabel] how political reforms were gained, for the blood of the Chartists . . . had flowed over them in days not long gone by.'[12] Several leading suffragists and suffragettes had family connections with early nineteenth-century radicalism. Mrs Pankhurst asserted that her paternal grandfather had narrowly escaped death at Peterloo, while Anne Cobden Sanderson and Jane Catherine Cobden Unwin, the daughters of Richard Cobden, the leader of the Anti-Corn Law League, both gravitated towards the suffrage cause.[13]

Despite these claims to a shared political lineage with male radicals, historians have often looked to demographic factors to explain the rise of the women's suffrage campaign. In comparison to the early twentieth century, the latter half of the nineteenth saw marriages produce very high numbers of children. For those women who married between 1841 and 1845, the live birth rate was 5.71, while one-third of marriages around 1860 led to eight or more children. For women who married between 1925 and 1929, the average birth rate was only 2.19. Certainly, women's letters and biographies of the time show that the onerous burdens of child-birth and child-rearing were felt across the class divides. Queen Victoria could complain to her uncle, the King of Belgium,

> I think, dearest Uncle, you cannot *really* wish me to be 'maman d'une nombreuse famille' for I think you will see with me the great inconvenience a *large* family would be to us all, and particularly to myself; men never think, at least seldom think, what a hard task it is for us women to go through this *very often*.[14]

While Hannah Mitchell remarked:

> One Friday, having done my weekend cleaning and baked a batch of bread during the day, I hoped for a good night's rest, but I scarcely had retired before my labour began. My baby was not born until the following evening after twenty-four hours of intense suffering which an ignorant attendant did little to alleviate . . . My baby was brought into the world with instruments and without an anaesthetic . . . Only one thing emerged clearly from much bitter thinking at that time, the fixed resolve to bring no more babies into the world. I felt it impossible to face again either the personal suffering, or the task of bringing a second child up in poverty.[15]

Mitchell's comments were no exaggeration: in the 1880s, hospital records showed working women continuing to turn the mangle after their waters had broken, and returning to the same task a few hours after giving birth.[16]

As Mitchell's autobiography made clear, the crucial difference between working-class and middle-class women was not the negative response to the repeated pain, confinement and drudgery of childbirth and child-rearing – in itself a marked shift from the attitude of eighteenth-century female radicals, notably Mary Wollstonecraft, who had assumed motherhood was a natural and inevitable part of a woman's life.[17] Those experiences were shared across social classes. Rather, the difference lay in the contrast between the lives of poor women, dominated by a ceaseless round of factory labour and domestic work, and those of their middle-class counterparts, governed by societal norms of feminine 'respectability', values that effectively cut out most gainful employment.

Besides its high birth rate, the other significant demographic fact of mid-Victorian England was the large number of unmarried women. Of the ten million women of all ages resident in England and Wales in 1861, there were 1.5 million unmarried women aged twenty and over and 750,000 widows aged twenty and over. Occupations open to these single women were limited in terms of both their earning power and their intellectual reward. For middle-class women, the only respectable occupations beyond that of wife and mother were those of teacher and governess. In 1861, 72.5 per cent of teachers were women, but teaching was ill-paid, of low social status, and offered no chance of advancement. Spinsters could also become governesses, but being a governess carried all the disadvantages of teaching plus significant pitfalls of its own, not least the precarious position of an unmarried female in another woman's house.[18]

In general, the number of women *officially* in work was in decline in the late nineteenth century: women as a percentage of the workforce diminished from 34.1 per cent in 1861 to 31.1 per cent thirty years later. Moreover, the majority of these women were young and single. The rhetoric of reformers who complained that the 'factory monster' was taking mothers away from their children overlooked the essential demographic truth about the female industrial workforce: in 1851, only a quarter of women factory workers were married, and of these only one-fifth had children younger than a year old.[19] What that rhetoric about the damaging effect of the factory system on the family really demonstrated was that women workers continued to be viewed with moral disgust. These attitudes seem to have been internalised by 'respectable' working-class women too, for whom the ability to stay completely confined to the domestic sphere was a badge of success. It was, after all, in this period that the affectionate term 'mum' came to be a coveted title among would-be late Victorian domestic goddesses. Indeed, even suffragettes could be found extolling women's fitness for public life on the grounds that management of the home was ideal practice for managing that grander domicile, the nation.

The lack of alternative outlets for women's intellectual energies has been seen as a major underlying cause behind the growth of the female suffrage movement. Certainly, unmarried middle-class women were prominent in the first feminist organisations that emerged in the latter half of the nineteenth century. Of the first eleven members of the Kensington Society that met in London in 1865, nine were unmarried. Although in part inspired by the national agitation surrounding the Second Reform Act, the Society's concerns were much broader than the vote, encompassing marriage reform, women's right to work and, especially, the need for decent education for girls and young women.[20] Many of the Society's members had a strong interest in education: Barbara Bodichon and Emily Davies went on to found Girton College, Cambridge; Frances Mary Buss founded the North London Collegiate School; and Dorothea Beale founded Cheltenham Ladies' College. Other occupations were also well represented, particularly journalism – for instance, by Frances Power Cobbe and Sophia Dobson Collet. Another member, Elizabeth Garrett, became famed as one of the first recognised female doctors in England, while some, such as Helen Taylor, the outspoken stepdaughter and amanuensis of the Liberal philosopher and recently elected MP John Stuart Mill, had connections with politics.* The

---

* Mill's election as MP for Westminster in 1865 had been an important spur to the cause of women's suffrage: he had made a clear commitment to securing women's voting rights in his election address of 28 April 1866. Three years later, his *Subjection of Women* would emerge as a classic liberal argument for equality of the sexes.

Kensington Society was responsible for the first women-sponsored petition for female suffrage, signed by fifteen hundred people and delivered to Parliament on 7 June 1866 as the House debated the Second Reform Act. The petition, drafted by Bodichon, Davies and Jessie Boucherett, called for the enfranchisement of 'all house-holders, without distinction of sex, who possess such property or rental qualification as your Honourable House may determine'.[21] Though it was greeted with derision in the Commons, such peti-tioning helped form the basis for subsequent women's suffrage societies.[22]

While it is important to stress the initial leadership given to the suffrage movement by well-connected middle-class women, its growth should not be solely attributed to the frustrations borne of the limited opportunities for unmarried women in Victorian England. Not least, such an explanation skirts dangerously close to contemporary anti-suffragist propaganda, which inaccurately por-trayed the movement as a political parlour game for well-to-do women (although, ironically, the WSPU did at one stage produce its own board game, called 'Pank-a-Squith').[23] More importantly, by the late nineteenth century, as we have seen, there was already a considerable prehistory of women's activity within other politi-cal movements, much of it emerging from working-class communities. From the women's reform societies that sent con-tingents to Peterloo to the thousands of women who signed the Chartist petitions, women had been very active participants in the radical agitation of the early part of the century. Some of that activity had already taken a militant bent: women had been involved in securing arms for a possible insurrection.[24] As we shall see, towards the end of the century, with the emergence of women's trade unions and the Women's Cooperative Guild, female working-class activism was revived.

Connections with broader reform movements were also impor-tant to middle-class suffrage societies. The Manchester Society for Women's Suffrage, formed shortly after Parliament's rejection of the petition for enfranchising women in February 1867, was chaired by Jacob Bright, younger brother of John Bright, the tireless campaigner for parliamentary reform (though the elder Bright was opposed to women's political emancipation – according to his sister Priscilla, he 'could never bear women to assist themselves').[25] As a young man Jacob Bright had had Chartist affiliations, and after Mill's failure to gain re-election he took over the leadership of the suffrage cause in the Commons. On 6 November 1867, the National Society for Women's Suffrage was formed from the Manchester, London and Edinburgh suffrage societies. Its creation led to a split in the women's suffrage movement, with the departure of Conservative members of the London Women's Suffrage Society, concerned about alienating public opinion by pushing too soon and too hard for the vote. This was despite the fact that the newly created NSWS had rather limited aims: these were, as its letterhead declared, the 'Enfranchisement of Unmarried Women & Widows Possessing the Due Property Qualification'. Lydia Becker, a prize-winning botanist and the secretary of the Manchester Society, described the aims of the NSWS as 'to see men and women of the *middle classes* stand on the same terms of equality as prevail in the working classes – and the highest aristocracy. *A great lady* or a *factory woman* are independent persons – personages – the women of the middle classes are *nobodies*, and if they act for themselves they lose caste!'[26]

It was within this milieu of radical Manchester Liberalism that Dr Richard Pankhurst first came to prominence. Pankhurst had been awarded his LLD (with a gold medal) from London University in 1863, but after being called to the Bar he practised as a barrister on the northern circuit. Shortly after qualifying, he had joined the Manchester Society for Women's Suffrage, although women's suffrage was only one of many radical causes that he espoused. In November 1868 his legal expertise was drawn upon in support of women's political rights in the case of Chorlton vs Lings, which concerned the right of female ratepayers to vote in local elections.

Pankhurst argued that the 1867 Reform Act enfranchised women, as the word 'man' was habitually interpreted in both Roman and English law as encompassing both sexes. He contended that the famous words of the twenty-ninth chapter of Magna Carta, though framed in the masculine, held good for women too.[27] The Court of Common Pleas, however, ruled that the uninterrupted customary usage of centuries with regard to the franchise had greater weight than the specific statutes Pankhurst cited.[28]

Pankhurst had more success with the amendment that he helped to draft in 1869 to the municipal corporations bill. Led through the Commons by Jacob Bright, the amendment permitted women householders to vote in municipal elections. Pankhurst assisted Bright again the following year, drafting the women's disabilites removal bill, which attempted to secure by statute what Pankhurst had failed to achieve through the courts. The bill would have made it law that in all acts relating to the franchise, 'wherever words occur which import the masculine gender, the same shall be held to include females for all purposes connected with and having reference to the right to be registered as voters, and to vote in such elections, any law or usage to the contrary notwithstanding'. This, effectively the first women's suffrage bill, was no more successful than the court action, which was not very surprising given the very broad female electorate it would have created. The dispute over whether to press for equal suffrage or accept a more limited female franchise would soon become a key bone of contention among the members of the NSWS.

But Dr Pankhurst's politics were very soon moving beyond the 'radical Liberalism' of Bright. Not only an advocate of equal voting rights for men and women, Pankhurst was also a republican who advocated the abolition of both the monarchy and the House of Lords and, as befitted the son of Baptists, he was a staunch opponent of the national Church. His speeches were filled with violent rhetoric and bloody metaphors. In one, he described the Lords as

'A public abattoir where the liberties and interests of the people have been butchered like cattle of the field, for the profit of the privileged few . . . no more a legislative assembly than was Procrustes with his den of blood and his bed of mutilation.'[29] In Sylvia Pankhurst's history of the suffragette movement, her father is clearly given the most sympathetic treatment of any member of her family. To Sylvia, he was a political hero, fearlessly championing the cause of the downtrodden and the disenfranchised. She recalled that he had admired the Chartist Ernest Jones so much that he had purchased his papers when he had seen them being hawked on the street, only to gift them back to Jones's impoverished widow.

To Dr Pankhurst's Manchester Liberal contemporaries, however, his open conversion to radical republicanism was repulsive. One leading Liberal, the Reverend Philip Harris, attacked him as one who was 'passing through a phase of Red Republicanism . . . such a torrent of abuse, expressed in the most shrieking tones against every cherished institution in this country'.[30] To others, Richard Pankhurst appeared more ludicrous than threatening, his extreme politics jarring with his gentle temperament, slight frame and high-pitched voice. In a posthumous description of him, the *Manchester City News* stated:

There were two characteristics of Dr Pankhurst which beyond all others stick in the memories of those who knew him, his smile and his voice . . . The smile that was not the smile of gaiety, nor of amusement. It was not the twinkle of the humorist. It was a smile of universal kindliness and goodwill – such a smile as the visage of St Francis may have worn. The voice was a natural alto, a thin piping treble, heaven knows how many octaves above the normal pitch.

It used to be amusing, in a way, to hear the Doctor, with that smile and in that voice, propounding the most blood curdling theories of government, and denouncing the wrath to come on Kings, and Priests, and Aristocrats. You knew that he would not hurt a fly, much less a fellow creature.[31]

Dr Pankhurst had founded the Manchester Republican Club in 1873 and his views now placed him increasingly in opposition to both the Manchester Society for Women's Suffrage and the local Liberal Association. He broke with the more pragmatic suffragists by refusing to support the bill promoted by the Conservative MP William Forsyth in 1874, which would have enfranchised only widows and unmarried women. In July 1883, Pankhurst formally broke with the Manchester Liberal Club and later the same year stood for election as an Independent Radical Liberal, on a platform of universal male and female suffrage, Irish Home Rule, the disestablishment of the Church of England, secular national education and land nationalisation. He lost heavily to his Conservative opponent, who secured the votes of many Liberals.

While Dr Pankhurst's fledgling political career failed to take flight, the cause of women's suffrage was also stuttering to a halt nationally. A series of private members' bills on the issue, promoted by Jacob Bright, had come to nothing and the NSWS was itself increasingly divided, both over the issue of whether to plump for limited women's suffrage or hold out for equal voting rights, and over the involvement of suffragists in the campaign against the Contagious Diseases Acts (CDAs) passed in 1864, 1866 and 1869. These acts aimed at tackling the spread of venereal disease among British troops by targeting infected prostitutes in garrison towns. Opponents saw a threefold problem with this legislation. First, it continued the sexual double standard by focusing on the prostitutes rather than dealing with their customers. Second, it threatened innocent women with arrest by plainclothes police and then compulsory medical examination, simply for passing through suspect areas. Third, these mandatory examinations and the forced internment in secure hospitals of infected women seemed even to many who were generally unsympathetic to women's rights to be a flagrant assault on civil liberties.

However, the stance of suffragists on these acts was not uniform. Many leading suffragists were members of the Ladies'

National Association for the Repeal of the Contagious Diseases Act, including Elizabeth Wolstenholme Elmy, a founder member of the Manchester SWS, Harriet Martineau, the campaigning journalist, and Ursula Bright, wife of Jacob and another key member of the MSWS. The head of the Ladies' National Association, Josephine Butler, had also signed the petition for women's suffrage delivered to Mill in 1866. Butler always cast the struggle over the CDAs as a political as well as a moral cause. She presented the police powers conferred by the acts as a violation of the British constitution and the rule of law, and the campaign for their repeal as part of a tradition of radical protest that stretched from Wat Tyler to John Wilkes and on to the Chartists.[32]

Other suffragists were opposed to the repeal of the Contagious Diseases Acts. Elizabeth Garrett Anderson, whose younger sister Millicent sympathised with the campaign, believed that the acts were the only effective medical means of stopping married men from infecting their unsuspecting wives. More significant was the opposition from Mill and Helen Taylor. Both were initially sympathetic to the movement for repeal, but wished to keep the issue separate from that of suffrage. For Mill in particular, the moral-crusade aspect of the campaign for repeal jarred with his secular liberalism. Mill was appalled at what he saw as the 'fanaticism' of some anti-CDA activists, including Butler, who described the struggle over the acts in apocalyptic terms. He was also repulsed by what he felt was the unnecessarily prurient detail in which some repealers discussed sexual matters. Mill went so far as to campaign to have anti-CDA campaigners removed from the executive of the NSWS.[33]

These divisions were significant not just in their impact on the short-term success of the women's suffrage movement but also in the way they prefigured later tensions. Was Victorian feminism a moral crusade or a political campaign? Was the transformation of a patriarchal society the fulfilment of divine providence as well as natural justice? What was most important, securing the vote, gaining educational and employment rights, or altering the laws relating to sex, marriage and divorce? These questions would come to the fore during the most intense period of suffragette militancy, 1912–14. For the moment, the campaign against the CDAs helped foster the development of women's political organisations and brought women further into the sphere of public life. The moral campaign against prostitution eventually scored some victories in the passage of the Criminal Law Amendment Act of 1885 and the repeal of the Contagious Diseases Act of 1886, though the repeal campaign's increasing association with repressive 'moral purity' movements, such as the National Vigilance Association, disquieted libertarians such as Butler and feminists like Elmy.[34]

The Victorian campaign for women's suffrage culminated in the attempt of William Woodall, a Liberal MP, to tack a women's-suffrage amendment on to Gladstone's Representation of the People bill on 10 June 1884. But Gladstone himself was unsympathetic to the issue of votes for women, declaring it to be 'One of those questions which it would be intolerable to mix up with purely political and Party debates. If there be a subject in the whole compass of human life and experience that is sacred, beyond all other subjects, it is the character and position of women.'[35] In a letter to Samuel Smith, MP, published in 1892, he revealed his fear that granting a woman the vote would invite her 'unwittingly to trespass upon the delicacy, the purity, the refinement, the elevation of her own nature, which are the present source of its power'.[36]

Woodall's amendment was defeated by 156 votes, 104 of which were of reported 'friends' of suffrage who had not wished to vote against Gladstone. The efforts of the NSWS suffered a further setback when payments to election canvassers were banned as part of the Corrupt Practices Act of 1883. Suddenly, the large numbers of otherwise unoccupied middle-class women looked like a good human resource for the main political parties. Auxiliary leagues of women supporters were formed, including the Conservative Women's Council of the Primrose League in 1885 and the Women's Liberal Association in 1886. These associations drew members and funds from the NSWS. As a clear indicator of the impasse the suffrage movement had reached, no bills for female enfranchisement were debated in Parliament between 1886 and 1892.

Richard Pankhurst lived with his parents until 1879 when, at the age of forty-four, he married Emmeline Goulden, the twenty-year-old daughter of Robert Goulden, a Manchester manufacturer, amateur actor and, for a time, owner of the Prince of Wales Theatre in Salford. The Gouldens shared Pankhurst's passion for radical causes: Mrs Goulden subscribed to the *Woman's Suffrage Journal*. Emmeline accompanied her mother to MSWS meetings, and it was through her work for the Society that she met and fell in love with Richard Pankhurst. The couple had five children: Christabel, Estelle Sylvia, Henry Francis Robert (who died aged just four), Adela Constantia Mary and Henry Francis. Though all but the last of these births came in the first six years of her marriage, they did not restrict Mrs Pankhurst's political activities. She was elected to the committee of the MSWS, co-opted into the married women's property committee, and campaigned on behalf of her husband when he unsuccessfully stood for Parliament in 1883.

Though it failed, Richard Pankhurst's candidacy in Manchester had raised his public profile, and in 1885 he was invited by the Rotherhithe Liberal and Radical Association to stand as their candidate in the general election of that year. Mrs Pankhurst again campaigned on her husband's behalf, but to no avail: his defeat was sealed by the opposition of Irish voters, who had been instructed by the Irish nationalist leader Charles Parnell to vote against all government candidates, whether they were in favour of Home Rule or not.

But the Rotherhithe election introduced Dr Pankhurst into the vibrant radical socialist culture of late Victorian London. The following year, the family relocated to the capital. Mrs Pankhurst opened a fancy goods shop, 'Emerson's', which she hoped would provide her with financial independence and allow her husband to concentrate on his political career. However, the shop soon proved only an additional drain on Dr Pankhurst's resources. As his daughter Sylvia drily recalled:

> The estate agent had told Mrs Pankhurst that the Hampstead Road was a rising neighbourhood; undoubtedly it was, but that part of it had not yet risen so far as to support the elegant estab-lishment Mrs Pankhurst intended . . . squalid market stalls were pitched in the gutter, butchers loudly shouted: 'Buy! buy! buy!' on Saturday nights, whilst ill-dressed women, their baskets laden with vegetables, jostled each other upon the densely thronged pavements.[37]

The first years after the move were overshadowed by a family tragedy. Their son Frank became ill while the Pankhursts were away on one of Richard's many business trips to Manchester. He died of diphtheria in 1888, probably brought on by the defective drains at the Pankhursts' London home. Emmeline's shop was closed and the family moved to a new, more sanitary home in Russell Square. It was here, in 1889, that Emmeline gave birth to her last child, named Henry (Harry) Francis in memory of his dead brother. Harry's birth and the closure of the shop signalled Emmeline's return to active politics. The Pankhursts' Russell Square home became a centre for radical activity: their guests included William Morris, the author, designer and visionary socialist, Tom Mann, the leader of the great London dock strike of 1889, and Annie Besant, the crusading radical journalist who helped organise the Bryant & May matchgirls' strike in 1888. Besant was a doughty campaigner not only for the rights of women workers but also for birth control, freedom of speech and freedom of conscience, and had a reputation as a dynamic public speaker, a talent aided by her wonderful speaking voice and good looks: the Irish journalist T. P. O'Connor recalled her 'full and well-shaped figure, her dark hair, her finely chiselled features . . . with that short upper lip that seemed always in a pout'.[38]

The matchgirls' strike was a seminal moment in the rise of the 'new unions' and in women's economic organisation. The girls' working conditions had been abysmal: they worked fourteen-hour days for terrible wages – often reduced further by a system of fines for 'offences' such as going to the toilet – and many suffered from health problems linked to working with yellow phosphorus, especially 'phossy jaw', a form of bone cancer that led to horrific facial disfigurement and then death. Within three weeks of going on strike, with the help of the Liberal press, the newly formed matchgirls' union – the first women-only union – had forced Bryant & May to re-employ the strikers and abandon its system of fines.

Dr Pankhurst's rather old-fashioned radicalism was increasingly influenced by the emerging socialist movement and by William Morris in particular. As he told a conference sponsored by the Fabian Society in June 1886: 'Let Mr Morris . . . train up among his socialistic young fellows a handful of men to go to parliament in that spirit [the spirit of the Irish nationalists] and they would do noble work.'[39] Morris's uniquely British reading of socialism was deeply influential, arguably because it fitted better with domestic traditions of radicalism and religious nonconformity than did classical Marxism. As Hannah Mitchell recalled, his brand of socialism was particularly appealing to the Christian Socialists of the 'Labour Churches', first established in Manchester in 1891:

> The Labour Church attracted a type of Socialist who was not satisfied with the stark materialism of the Marxist school, desiring warmth and colour in human lives: not just bread, but bread and roses too. Perhaps we were not quite sound on economics as our Marxian friends took care to remind us, but we realized the injustice and ugliness of the present system. We had enough imagination to visualize the greater possibility for beauty and culture in a more

justly ordered state. If our conception of Socialism owed more to Morris than to Marx, we were none the less sincere, and many found their belief strengthened by the help and inspiration of the weekly meetings held in these Northern towns.[40]

Yet Morris was an unlikely revolutionary. Three years before his 'conversion', as he called it, to revolutionary socialism, his firm, Morris & Co., had been commissioned to decorate the throne room in St James's Palace. In 1883 he had joined H. M. Hyndman's Social Democratic Federation (SDF), the first organised British Marxist party. This was no act of youthful hotheadedness on Morris's part. He was nearly fifty (eight years older than Hyndman), and with a considerable professional reputation as a designer and artist at stake. The SDF certainly gained a lot more than did Morris by the association.[41] It was then, and remained, a tiny political organisation, never mustering more than a few hundred supporters. There were connections with the campaign for women's suffrage through the involvement in the SDF of Helen Taylor, while Mrs Pankhurst, along with Sylvia, attended SDF meetings. Sylvia's memory of these was not particularly positive:

> The Socialist movement was then so impecunious that its meetings were generally held in the meanest of mean streets in miserable premises, and frequently over foul-smelling stables. The chairman had scarcely finished speaking when Mrs Pankhurst rose up and insisted on leaving the hall. Outside she told us that she had found a bug on her glove, and therefore could not bear to remain any longer.

Equally, Hyndman struck an unimpressive figure as a popular leader: he 'always seemed to me like an old-fashioned china mantelpiece ornament – the head and chest disproportionately large and prominent for the lower limbs, and everything from the back view small and unfinished'.[42]

For the Pankhursts, though, more important than the intellectual influence of William Morris was their connection with the emerging Independent Labour Party, and in particular Keir Hardie. The illegitimate son of a Lanarkshire farm servant, Hardie had known genuine poverty in his youth. He was fired from his job as a bakery delivery boy for being late for work when he was tending his dying brother. Having successfully formed and led a coalminers' union in Lanarkshire, he stood for election as a socialist MP for mid-Lanark. He came last in the contest, but, undeterred, in 1888 went on to form the Scottish Parliamentary Labour Party. The president of the party, Robert Cunninghame Graham (known as the 'gaucho laird' for his extensive travels in South America), became the UK's first socialist MP, and Hardie himself gained election to the Commons as an Independent Labour candidate for West Ham in 1892. In the Commons, he refused to observe the official dress code of black frock-coat, black silk top-hat and starched collar, dressing in tweed suit, red tie and deer-stalker hat. In 1893, he founded the Independent Labour Party in Bradford and rose to further prominence by controversially attacking the monarchy in a speech in 1894, in which he lambasted the royal family for refusing to allow a message of condolence to the victims of the Pontypridd mining disaster to be attached to an address of thanks for the birth of the future Edward VIII.

Sylvia Pankhurst first met Hardie in 1893 when she was just eleven. Her later description of the meeting was clearly coloured by the love affair that subsequently developed between the two: 'There he was; his majestic head surrounded by ample curls going grey and shining with glints of silver and golden brown; his great forehead deeply lined; his eyes two deep wells of kindness, like mountain pools with the sunlight distilled they always seemed to me . . . I felt that I could have rushed into his arms.'[43] Hardie was a staunch supporter of women's suffrage but, unlike many leading figures in the Labour movement, viewed the 'adult suffragist' position – that the only desirable electoral reform was universal adult enfranchisement – as impracticable in the short term. As he presciently observed: 'If the workers were prepared to lay every other reform on the shelf, and begin an agitation for adult suffrage they might, if specially fortunate, be successful and get it about the year 1929.'[44]

Hardie's public commitment to women's suffrage was relatively unusual among British socialists at this time. Indeed, his close association with the 'genteel' Pankhursts and advocacy of the 'middle-class' cause of votes for women often brought him criticism from within the ranks of the ILP. This reflected a broader ambivalence within the British socialist movement as to the status of women. Some socialist organisations appeared far in advance of most mainstream parties. The Fabian Society, whose members included such literary luminaries as H. G. Wells and George Bernard Shaw, had declared itself in favour of women's suffrage from its inception, making it one of the first British political organisations, if not the very first, to do so. One of its early political tracts, published in 1884, declared that the 'sexes should henceforth enjoy equal political rights'.[45] This policy was reflected in the very high number of Fabian members who were women, just under a quarter of the total membership in 1906.[46]

However, other socialist organisations were less welcoming. Ernest Belfort Bax, a leading member of the Social Democratic Federation and later of the Socialist League, in his book *The Fraud of Feminism*, asserted the physical and mental inferiority of women, using the 'evidence' of a leading member of the medical profession, Sir Almroth Wright, to demonstrate that menstruation and the menopause rendered women periodically insane and therefore unfit to exercise political functions.[47] James Ramsay MacDonald, who later overtook Hardie as the leading figure in both the ILP and the Labour movement as a whole, described the suffrage cause as a 'very great menace'.[48]

Especially within the trade unions, chauvinistic attitudes of this kind supported male economic self-interest. Female 'sweated labour' threatened the incomes of male workers, as well as attacking firmly established ideals about the role of the man as the breadwinner and provider for his family. There were resonances with the Chartist rhetoric of J. R. Stephens in the frequent refrain of male trade unionists that they sought better conditions for their members so that women could be returned from the factory floor to their rightful place in the home. Hannah Mitchell noted that her male socialist counterparts did not appear to think that domestic workers, too, needed to lose their chains: 'I soon found that a good deal of Socialist talk about freedom, was, Well, just talk and these Socialist young men expected Sunday dinners and huge teas with home made cakes, potted meats and pies, exactly like their reactionary fellows.'[49] She noted with irritation that when she was first imprisoned for suffragette activity, her husband had posted bail for her, against her wishes, so that she could come home and cook his dinner.[50]

According to Henry Broadhurst, secretary of the parliamentary committee of the TUC, 'It was [male unionists'] duty as men and husbands to use their utmost efforts to bring about a condition of things, where their wives would be in their proper sphere at home, instead of being dragged into competition for livelihood against the great and strong men of the world.' However, as Clementina Black, secretary of the Women's Trade Union League, noted in a speech to conference in 1887, male trade unionists were noticeably less eager to interfere in the case of trades like needlework and match-making:

Why not? There is no need to ask. Men do not work at these trades and suffer nothing from the competition of women. The real point to be complained of is the low rate of payment earned by the women; and the way to prevent the employment of women in any trade they are unfit for is for men to join in helping them to combine in order that they may receive the same wages for the same work. If employers have to pay women the same prices as men, there would be no temptation to them to employ women to do what they are less fit to do than men. But the women are not represented here to speak for themselves, and protest against the attempt of one class of workers – especially a class whose interests are concerned – to impose restrictions upon another class of workers.[51]

But the comfortable world of the 'labour aristocracy', dominated by men like Broadhurst who enjoyed a cosy relationship with the British establishment, was being increasingly shaken by more militant union activity. Much of it, like the matchgirls' strike, was led by unskilled women workers. The same year as the Bryant & May strike, 1888, there were strikes by women cigar workers in Nottingham, by blanket weavers in Yorkshire and by cotton and jute workers in Dundee.[52] These workers were beginning to learn the lesson taught by the old-established male-dominated unions: that political influence was the route towards raising workers' standard of living. As Selina Cooper, the millworker, trade unionist and radical suffragist, noted: 'Those well-organized industries had the ballot box as a lever to raise their standard of life, but the women workers, however well they combined, had no such lever to help them in their demands for the redressing of their grievances.'[53] Working-class women, as well as the middle-class suffragists, were becoming increasingly aware of the importance of securing the vote.

The rhetoric of many within the Labour movement tended to overlook the fact that the most powerful unions represented only some of the workers, and, indeed, pursued interests that were antagonistic to the needs of other sections of the working class. They tended to present the suffrage movement as essentially a bourgeois political cause that would serve merely to enfranchise the workers' class enemies. Even some female trade unionists attacked suffragists for replacing 'class antagonism' with 'sex antagonism'.[54] There was some truth to this position: despite the

Pankhursts' claims to the contrary, equal suffrage would predominantly enfranchise middle-class women who were widely – and probably correctly – believed to be predisposed to vote Tory. And this evaluation of the political costs of equal suffrage revealed a more deep-seated problem. The adult-suffrage position maintained by the ILP and affirmed by socialist women's groups at an international conference at Stuttgart in 1907 would, of course, have represented a much more far-reaching act of political emancipation than mere equalisation of the existing franchise. But it is debatable whether many male Labour activists were actually attached to the idea in principle. Adult suffrage served as a useful delaying tactic, allowing the Labour movement to argue that other issues were more pressing and achievable, and Hannah Mitchell was probably right when she quoted Shaw's witticism in summing up the position: 'If a man owes you a sovereign and being able to pay you fifteen shillings, refuses to do so, depend upon it, ladies, he never intends to pay the lot.'[55]

This lack of intellectual commitment to adult suffrage reflected a wider absence of interest in constitutional reform among British socialists. There was a strong sense that, with the enfranchisement of a large section of the male working class under the 1884 Reform Act, British democracy was practically the finished article. As Christabel Pankhurst would later put it, 'Labour men cared relatively little for franchise reform even for men, because already the working-men voters were in a majority.'[56] Of course, some residual attachment to radical republicanism remained, but it was outweighed by a rather complacent constitutionalism. As the Fabian Society remarked, the nation's constitutional apparatus required only a little tinkering, not radical surgery:

When the House of Commons is freed from the veto of the House of Lords and thrown open to candidates from all classes by an effective system of Payment of Representatives and a more rational method of election, the British Parliamentary system will be, in the opinion of the Fabian Society, a first-rate practical instrument of democratic government.[57]

By the 1890s, the Fabians had publicly repudiated republicanism, Shaw rehearsing the shop-worn argument that a hereditary monarchy was better than the elected alternative, fearing that if the royals were done away with, the people would only 'idolize some British Boulanger and worship the honour of the army. For my part I prefer the Queen.'[58] Though the initial ILP programme put together by Hardie and MacDonald had demonstrated continuity with an earlier tradition of British radicalism in its demand for more frequent parliaments, payments for MPs, abolition of the House of Lords and adult suffrage, MacDonald later denigrated the pursuit of constitutional reform as mere 'will o' the wisps'.[59] This would be a dominant argument within Labour circles throughout the twentieth century. The advocacy of constitutional reform was presented either as a species of antiquated radical Liberalism or as an ulterior means by which the establishment could inoculate itself against the spread of socialism. (For example, Labour intellectuals argued against a new British bill of rights on the grounds that it would empower unelected, upper-class judges.[60])

For democratic socialists, then, further electoral or constitutional reform in what was already a mass male democracy was often perceived as an unnecessary diversion from the main business of creating a socialist society, a project that would largely be conducted via economic, not political, change. But even revolutionary groups such as Morris's Socialist League that viewed parliamentary democracy as an irrelevancy were increasingly pessimistic about the radical potential of the British working class. Although the late 1880s were years of great social unrest, when revolution once again appeared to be in the air, the turmoil of the decade ultimately sealed the defeat, not the success, of revolutionary socialism. Meetings of the unemployed in London culminated in two major incidents: window-smashing in Pall Mall on 'Black Monday', 8 February 1886, which was followed by the arrest of H. M. Hyndman, Henry Hyde Champion and John Burns of the SDF; and 'Bloody Sunday', 13 November 1887, when Burns, Cunninghame Graham and Besant led a demonstration in Trafalgar Square in defence of the right of public assembly, after the government's refusal to allow a meeting in protest at a new Irish 'coercion bill'. In a wider international context, the march took place at a point when socialism globally was being brutally repressed. The British right-wing press applauded Bismarck's anti-socialist laws in Germany, and papers like *The Times* supported the execution of eleven anarchists on 11 November in the wake of the Haymarket Riot in Chicago, when a rally in support of striking workers descended into bloody mayhem after a pipe bomb was thrown at the police lines.

In Trafalgar Square, the two thousand waiting police, backed up by four hundred troops and four squadrons of cavalry, responded with violence. At least three people died as a result of assault by the police or army, and some two hundred were injured.[61] Cunninghame Graham and Burns were arrested, the former badly beaten by police *after* he had been seized:

> one policeman after another, two certainly, but I think no more, stepped up from behind and struck him on the head from behind with a violence and brutality which were shocking to behold. Even after this, and when some five or six other police were dragging him into the Square, another from behind seized him most needlessly by the hair . . . and dragged his head back, and in that condition he was forced forwards many yards.[62]

At a meeting held to protest against the outrages on the following Sunday in Hyde Park, mounted police knocked down a young radical writer, Alfred Linnell, who subsequently died from his injuries.

The crushing of the demonstration, the rejoicing and gloating of the Conservative press at the police action, and the notable silence of the Liberal opposition all profoundly shook the faith of revolutionary socialists. Morris wrote a powerful 'Death Song' for Linnell's funeral in which he warned 'the rich': 'Not one, not one, nor thousands must they slay, / But one and all if they would dusk the day'.[63] Even Morris had been disturbed by the ease and severity with which the marchers had been scattered. If a revolution were to come, it did not look as if the British working class would lead it.

DEEDS NOT WORDS[1]

After the birth of her fifth and last child, and with the failure of her retail enterprise, Mrs Pankhurst, as Sylvia's history testifies, had returned to politics. In 1889 she helped to form the Women's Franchise League, on whose council sat Jacob Bright, Jane Cobden, Josephine Butler and the American suffragist Elizabeth Cady Stanton. This organisation expanded the terms of the narrow suffrage advocated by the National Society for Women's Suffrage to include married women, and demanded equal divorce and inheritance rights. It also embraced some of Dr Pankhurst's political radicalism, publishing a pamphlet in favour of the abolition of the House of Lords. However, the WFL was wound up in the 1890s because of the ill-health of some of its leading members, including Pankhurst, who was suffering from gastric ulcers, probably exacerbated by his growing financial difficulties. The costs of Emmeline's unsuccessful shop and the terms of their lease on the Russell Square house exacted a heavy toll.

No longer able to afford either, the Pankhursts returned to Victoria Park, Manchester, where they joined the local Independent Labour Party Association. As we have seen, they had become heavily involved in socialist activity in London and had already made contact with the leading ILP figure of the time, Keir Hardie. And the ILP held other attractions for a couple devoted to the cause of women's suffrage. Though some of its members were equivocal on the issue, the ILP itself, like the Fabians, allowed women full roles within the party as lecturers and as members of its national administrative council, rather than relegating them to an auxiliary association. A number of women already held important posts within the party, including Katherine St John Conway, later editor of the *Labour Leader*, Caroline Martyn and Enid Stacy, who were both council members.

The Pankhursts soon made their mark within the local ILP. Emmeline was elected to the Chorlton Board of Poor Law Guardians, a reminder that though women were not able to vote in national elections until 1918, they were already making inroads into local government. In May 1895 Dr Pankhurst was adopted as ILP candidate for Gorton, an industrial suburb of Manchester. He lost to the Conservative candidate – no Liberal stood – but polled an impressive 4300 votes. Despite the fact that his election platform contained many Liberal elements, though, it was clear that local Liberals had abstained from voting for him: his affiliation to the ILP was becoming professionally costly.

In 1896, in his role as a barrister, Richard Pankhurst unsuccessfully defended a number of local socialists who had been fined for speaking at the Boggart Hole Clough, a natural amphitheatre that was regularly used by the ILP for open-air meetings. The Clough, formerly part of the Carill-Worsley estate, had recently been acquired by the Corporation of Manchester. Although there were no specific by-laws to prevent public meetings, driven by the obvious political animus of Councillor George Needham – who aimed to stop the gatherings of a 'certain party' – the council used a law of 1868 against disorderly behaviour to prosecute ILP speakers. Mrs Pankhurst was prominent at the meetings, collecting money for the imprisoned men. On the evening of 3 July, a crowd of ten thousand gathered to protest at the prosecution of Mrs Pankhurst and other socialists. Speakers at the meeting included Keir Hardie and Tom Mann.* The following Sunday, the Pankhursts, accompanied by Christabel and Sylvia, drove to the Clough in an open barouche. They were greeted by a crowd of between twenty-five and forty thousand people. They had clearly become ILP celebrities: the following week's *Labour Leader* carried sketches of Christabel, Sylvia and Emmeline. The savvy Emmeline had noted the considerable publicity that ILP figures such as Leonard Hall and Fred Brocklehurst had garnered for the party by choosing prison in preference to paying fines. This kind of coverage was invaluable for a party that was so poor in its early stages that its members had to advertise its meetings in chalk, on paving stones. The value of imprisonment as a publicity stunt would later inform suffragette tactics in its militant years.

However, for all the Boggart Hole Clough dispute's worth to the ILP, it only added to the financial pressures on Richard Pankhurst. He continued to act as the advocate of progressive causes, securing one final legal victory when he won the right to a public footpath over Kinder Scout in the Peak District. But the stress of these high-profile cases and the accompanying loss of lucrative official legal business proved too much: he died on 5 July 1898 of a perforated ulcer. His death was a crushing blow to his devoted wife, and Emmeline retired from political activity. This seclusion was the product of financial necessity as well as personal grief. Richard's pursuit of politically worthy rather than financially rewarding cases had left the family considerably in debt. Robert Blatchford, editor of the popular socialist paper the *Clarion*, offered to raise a subscription to help support the Pankhursts, but Emmeline refused to accept money for her own family from a working-class readership

---

* The case against Emmeline Pankhurst was dismissed without her coming to trial, Hardie scuppering the proceedings by informing the prosecution that he had over four hundred witnesses ready to testify for the defence.

that often struggled to meet its own needs. Instead, she took up paid employment as registrar of births and deaths for Chorlton, an experience that also brought her a greater appreciation of the problems faced by working-class women.

Though the political career of Emmeline Pankhurst was temporarily on hold, the late 1890s saw a grass-roots resurgence in the women's suffrage movement. Middle-class women's suffrage societies had been reorganised under the umbrella of the National Union of Women's Suffrage Societies, led by Millicent Garrett Fawcett. Fawcett, the well-connected widow of a Liberal Cabinet minister, according to legend was marked out by Emily Davies as a future suffrage leader when she was still a teenager. Like other Victorian suffragists, Millicent had become politically active during the debates over the Second Reform Act in 1867. Her marriage to Henry Fawcett that same year marked the beginning of a close and loving personal and political partnership. Aside from running the household, Millicent acted as guide and secretary to her blind husband. He, in turn, was an outspoken and principled supporter of women's suffrage in Parliament. In the wake of his sudden death in 1884, Millicent had thrown herself into, first, the campaign for moral reform, then the cause of women's suffrage. The formation of NUWSS led in 1897 to a private member's bill in favour of women's suffrage receiving a second reading in the Commons for the first time.

Working-class political organisations too were undergoing a period of growth. Esther Roper, the bespectacled daughter of a poor factory worker turned Christian missionary, as secretary of the Manchester Society for Women's Suffrage, began the first campaign for the vote directed specifically at working women. Roper correctly saw that the large numbers of women trade unionists were an as yet untapped source of strength for the suffrage movement, and she went about recruiting female unionists by deploying women workers as speakers and organising visits to factories. With her close friend and possibly lover Eva Gore-Booth, the poet and daughter of the Anglo-Irish landowner and Arctic explorer Sir Henry Gore-Booth, Roper did much to attract working-class women to the suffrage movement. The success of their efforts, and those of other working-class activists such as Selina Cooper of the Women's Cooperative Guild, can be gauged by the near-thirty thousand signatures that the North of England Society for Women's Suffrage managed to gather for a petition in 1901, when the membership of the NUWSS as a whole was only ten thousand.

The petition, though, was unsuccessful, and before the election of 1903 attempts at getting suffrage bills through the Commons were largely stillborn, as parliamentary politics continued to be dominated by the Boer War. Nonetheless, the growth of female trade unionism posed questions about the representation of women. The recently created Labour Representation Committee – which later became the Labour Party – left the funding of parliamentary candidates to individual constituency organisations.

The textile unions that affiliated to the LRC in 1902 were dominated by women, with close to 100,000 female members compared to only 70,000 men. Under the terms of their agreement with the LRC, the unions agreed to an affiliation fee of ten shillings per thousand members, in addition to which fourpence was levied each year on each member, women included, for Labour representation. Thousands of women trade unionists were therefore paying for candidates, but could not vote for them. Gore-Booth and Roper responded to this injustice by forming the Lancashire and Cheshire Women's Textile and Other Workers Representation Committee, to campaign for the first women's suffrage candidate to stand in an election.* The move demonstrated the growing frustration that many suffragists, who also shared a socialist political philosophy, felt at the Labour movement's lack of

* The candidate, Thorley Smith, stood for Wigan in the 1906 election, losing to the Conservatives but coming ahead of the Liberal candidate.

commitment to votes for women, despite the important financial support given by women trade unionists.

The growth of a working-class women's suffrage movement in the North of England was crucial to the re-engagement of the Pankhursts with the cause. This time, however, the leading figure was Mrs Pankhurst's eldest (and favourite) daughter, Christabel. Emmeline had tried to engage her bright but dreamy child in opening a new fancy goods shop, but Christabel hated the work, and this venture, like Emerson's, proved a financial failure. Striving to find something else to occupy Christabel's restless mind, Emmeline suggested that she attend some classes at Manchester University. It was here that Christabel came into contact with Esther Roper and, through her, Eva Gore-Booth. Within a year, Christabel was giving talks for the North of England Society for Women's Suffrage across northern England and Scotland. She was not yet the mesmerising public speaker of the high years of suffragette militancy – one observer of her early performances noted that she was rather hesitant.[2]

As early as 1902 it was clear that Christabel, like her mother a member of the ILP, was having misgivings about the alliance between the suffrage and Labour movements. In an article in the *ILP News* published that year, she complained:

> As a rule, Socialists are silent on the position of women. If not actually antagonistic to the movement for women's rights, they hold aloof from it. One gathers that some day, when the Socialists are in power, and have nothing better to do, they will give women votes as a finishing touch to their arrangements, but for the present they profess no interest in the subject . . . Why are women expected to have such confidence in the men of the Labour Party? Working-men are as unjust to women as are those of other classes.[3]

Some suffragettes who broke away from the Pankhursts later claimed that Christabel's brief involvement in Labour politics had only ever been based on a self-interested search for a platform. As Teresa Billington-Greig, a stormy agnostic who remained a committed socialist throughout her career as a radical suffragette, claimed: 'Mrs Pankhurst believed there was hope for this Labour conversion policy, while Christabel only endured it till her time came.'[4]

Recent research adds some weight to the argument that the Pankhursts' split from the ILP was premeditated. Most histories of the suffrage movement trace it to a dispute over the use of Pankhurst Hall, a meeting room established in the memory of Dr Pankhurst through subscriptions raised by the *Clarion* newspaper. The Pankhursts allegedly claimed that they broke with the party after hearing that the local ILP branch that used the hall would not admit women as members. Yet there is no evidence that this was the case and, indeed, all of the Pankhurst daughters would later speak at the hall, surely an odd decision if it had been such a serious snub.[5] Rather than being a reaction to a perceived insult to the memory of Dr Pankhurst, it is more likely that the decision to form the Women's Social and Political Union, as the Pankhursts' organisation came to be known, was a considered political choice made on similar grounds to Roper and Booth's formation of the Lancashire and Cheshire Women's Textile and Other Workers Representation Committee: namely, the very slow progress in getting a clear commitment to women's suffrage from the male Labour leadership. Like Roper and Gore-Booth, the Pankhursts hoped to create a ginger group which, without splitting completely from the ILP, would pressurise the party into taking a firmer line and supporting pro-suffrage parliamentary candidates. Indeed, Mrs Pankhurst had initially planned to call her organisation the Women's Labour Representation Committee, to be prevented only by the similarity to the name of the group already founded by Roper and Gore-Booth.

The Women's Social and Political Union was formed on 10 October 1903 at a meeting at Pankhurst's home. Most attendees were female working-class supporters of the ILP. The WSPU's position on the franchise mirrored that of Mrs Pankhurst's late husband: that the terms of the 1884 Representation of the People Act should be changed to include women. Despite the strong ILP presence, the WSPU eschewed any political affiliation and, unlike other suffrage organisations, advertised itself as a women-only party. It was also keen from the beginning to attract supporters from across the social spectrum. The recruitment of Annie Kenney, 'the little factory girl' as Emmeline Pethick-Lawrence (the WPSU's treasurer) later called her, was a notable propaganda coup for the WSPU.[6] In fact, Kenney had only briefly worked in a factory and her father, a cotton minder, had generally been able to provide a more comfortable and 'respectable' home than most mill-hands enjoyed, but when it was important for the WSPU to advertise its working-class credentials, Kenney willingly donned her mill-girl's shawl and clogs. She had been drawn to socialism through reading Blatchford's *Clarion*, but his failure to tackle the inequalities faced by women led her to the suffrage movement. Kenney first met Christabel when the elder Pankhurst daughter, with Teresa Billington, was addressing a meeting of the Oldham Trades Council. Kenney initially found Billington the more persuasive speaker, but she liked Christabel more.

It was the beginning of both a close working relationship and a deep friendship. Kenney was often presented by hostile observers as Christabel's unquestioning acolyte, and the closeness between the two has even led some historians to allege (on scant evidence) that the relationship was sexual.[7] There was more than a twinge of jealousy in Sylvia Pankhurst's description of Kenney's 'abundant, loosely-dressed golden hair' as 'the most youthful thing about her', and her 'twinkling, bright blue eyes' surrounded by 'crow's feet'.[8] Her bitterness again surfaced in this allusion to the differing impacts of the suffrage movement on the lives of activists: 'Movements for liberation bring with them, to some, opportunities of personal advancement and release from uncongenial drudgery; to others, loss of livelihood, lowering of status, a double load of toil.'9 For middle-class Sylvia, political activism brought poverty, stress and, eventually, the effective breakdown of her relationship with her sister and mother. For respectable, working-class Annie Kenney it brought contact and friendship with wealthy WSPU activists like Lady Constance Lytton and the Pethick-Lawrences, whom she helped bring into the movement; the excitement of foreign travel – she acted as go-between when Christabel was in exile in Paris and later toured America; and personal fame. As a paid WSPU activist, the movement also gave Kenney a reasonable living.

The root of Sylvia's unhappiness unquestionably lay in the prominent role, during the key militant years, that Kenney played in the WSPU compared to her own limited contribution. Kenney freely admitted that she was no great thinker, but her contribution was more than mere poster-girl for working-class activism or mouthpiece for Christabel. Her physical frailty, as even Sylvia conceded, masked a considerable mental toughness, and it was her readiness to undertake dangerous activities that saw her, alongside Christabel, involved in the first expressions of WSPU militancy.

Lady Frances Balfour, younger sister of the Conservative Prime Minister Lord Salisbury and a leading member of the National Union of Women's Suffrage Societies, described the parliamentary treatment of the issue of women's suffrage between 1897 and 1906 as being 'always shoved onto a siding to let express trains go by, and even the slowest train was an express to those who wished the matter shelved'.10 The derision with which another private member's bill in favour of women's suffrage was talked out of the House in 1905 – one MP stated that women did not warrant the vote as they were 'nervous, emotional and had very little sense of proportion'11 – convinced Mrs Pankhurst that the lobbying tactics of the NUWSS would not be enough to achieve their goal.

The first inklings of suffragette militancy came in February 1904, when Christabel interrupted a free trade meeting at which

Winston Churchill was the main speaker to demand the alteration of the Representation of the People Act to include women. This intervention was largely ignored by the press, but the next year, a repeat performance garnered far more impressive results. On 13 October 1905, this time accompanied by Annie Kenney, Christabel interrupted a meeting at the Free Trade Hall, Manchester, again featuring Churchill as a speaker. During the time set aside for questions, Annie asked whether the Liberal Party would give votes to women. When the question was ignored, Christabel repeated it. Police dragged the two women out of the hall. Deliberately courting arrest, Christabel spat in the face of both Superintendent Watson and Inspector Mather, hit Mather in the mouth and said that she *wanted* to assault a policeman. Mather, slapped once more by Christabel, ejected them from the building and asked them to leave, but the women refused and he was forced to arrest them. The next morning Christabel explained their conduct:

> We cannot make any orderly protest because we have not the means whereby citizens may do such a thing; we have not a vote; and so long as we have not votes we must be disorderly. There is no other way whereby we can put forward our claims to political justice. When we have that you will not see us at the police courts; but so long as we have not votes this will not happen.[12]

The lessons learnt from the Boggart Hole Clough affair were put into effect. Both women refused to pay their fines and were sent to Strangeways Prison. The hoped-for media attention duly followed, with coverage from significant local papers such as the *Manchester Guardian* and the national press, including *The Times*.

The recycling of an old ILP strategy from the 1890s is a reminder that, at least at this stage, the WSPU's 'militancy' was very similar to the tactics of civil disobedience practised by earlier radical groups. The shock value came from the fact that it was women who were the agents of violence (if, at this stage, largely symbolic). Until 1908, the suffragettes' strategy was not obviously distinct from the suffragists', and mirrored earlier movements in its use of marches, mass meetings and petitions.[13] Indeed, the device of heckling or otherwise interrupting the political meetings of other parties was itself an established tactic, regularly deployed by the Chartists in the 1830s and 1840s. Given these continuities with the past, it was fitting that the first act of suffragette militancy took place near the site of the Peterloo massacre and in the Free Trade Hall so often used for meetings of the Anti-Corn Law League.

At this stage, though its activities were beginning to gain national attention, the WSPU remained an essentially northern organisation. Now unquestionably one of its leading activists, Christabel had had to return to the North regularly in any case in order to complete her studies at the University of Manchester. She graduated in 1906 with first-class honours in law, one of only two students that year to do so. Sylvia recalled that when her sister went up to collect her degree, she was met with a protest by male students, one of whom, Walter Newbold, went on to be the first avowedly communist British MP.[14] Though excluded from the Bar because of her sex, Christabel would soon put her legal expertise on display in defending WSPU members, including herself.

That same year, the Pankhursts decided to move the WSPU's headquarters to London. Sylvia, a talented artist, had won a two-year scholarship to the Royal College of Art and was living in lodgings in Chelsea. Isolated from her family and often lonely, she took increasing comfort in the company of Keir Hardie, frequently visiting him in his bedsit at number 14 Neville's Court.* Hardie impressed her with his frugality and self-sufficiency, cooking for himself on an open range in his room, though his culinary repertoire was hardly varied – he subsisted largely on a diet of

---

* Hardie subsisted on a meagre income of £150 a year from the ILP, which barely met his expenses as an MP.

drop-scones, bread and tea. When she visited, he would puff away on his pipe, writing letters for the *Labour Leader*. Occasionally he would read aloud to her from one of his favourite authors: Keats, Scott, Burns, Byron, Shelley or Morris.[15]

Sylvia helped bring the teetotal, puritanical Hardie out of his shell, taking him to the theatre to see his first play, an appropriately improving Shavian production, and dining out occasionally in restaurants, where he tried the exotic luxury of black coffee for the first time. The support was mutual, Sylvia recalling a particularly low point in relations with her family, when she had moved into new digs shortly after the death of her brother Harry in 1910:

> all unexpected, Keir Hardie came knocking at my door. With quick discernment and practical kindness, he took command of the situation. He lifted the heavy things into position, and when all was, so far as it could be, in order, took me out for a meal at the little Italian restaurant where Harry and I had lunched on many a happy Sunday. I was immensely cheered.[16]

Though Hardie was already married – his wife Lillie stayed in Ayrshire and was offered, unsurprisingly, no encouragement from her husband to venture south – his close friendship with Sylvia had almost certainly become a love affair.[17]

It was through Hardie that the Pankhursts were first introduced to Emmeline and Frederick (Fred) Pethick-Lawrence, a wealthy Liberal couple who had devoted themselves for several years to philanthropic work in the East End. At the entreaty of Annie Kenney, Emmeline Pethick-Lawrence agreed to act as treasurer of the WSPU. It was a momentous decision, for a number of reasons. Hitherto, the WSPU had been a poor organisation, occasionally dependent on handouts from the ILP (itself a pretty cash-strapped party), rustled up by Keir Hardie. Now the Pethick-Lawrences would provide real financial support for the Union, as well as a home for Christabel for the next six years. More than this, the well-connected Mrs Pethick-Lawrence was able, in her role as treasurer, to encourage other wealthy women to contribute, creating the beginnings of the Union's lucrative donor base in Kensington and Chelsea. This increased financial security raised the prospect of political independence from the Labour movement. The Pethick-Lawrences also set up the WSPU's first newspaper, *Votes for Women*. Finally, their charitable efforts in the East End meshed with work that Sylvia and Teresa Billington had undertaken in winning working-class women in London to the suffrage cause.

It was widely anticipated that the Liberal landslide of 1906 would lead to a shift in the government's stance on women's suffrage. Millicent Fawcett believed that the election had brought four hundred MPs sympathetic to the suffrage campaign into the Commons. The march organised by the WSPU on 19 February that year saw large numbers of working-class women take part who had joined the unemployment demonstrations of the previous year. The poverty of the East End, however, shocked even Annie Kenney, whose own background was scarcely middle-class:

> I have travelled through all the great European cities, but I have never seen such drabness, such hopeless despair, such agonizing poverty, as I saw in the East End of London. I felt it was like one big long funeral, but the dead who were being buried were not the human dead – they were the dead of lost endeavour, of lost hopes, aspirations, faith, courage, and of all the qualities that go to make a consciously free man.[18]

The Pethick-Lawrences' money was essential to providing supporters like these with transport and food. As the WSPU's militant campaign progressed, its ability to use the cash of its wealthy supporters to pay its working-class activists would be a powerful engine to sustain its intensity.

The march, like the earlier arrests of Christabel and Annie Kenney, proved successful in gathering more publicity for the movement, making the *Mirror*'s front page. A similar propaganda coup was won the next month when a deputation of thirty women went to 10 Downing Street requesting a meeting with the Prime Minister, Sir Henry Campbell-Bannerman. The women were asked to leave but two of the contingent, Irene Fenwick Miller and Mrs Flora 'General' Drummond, managed to rush back inside, where they were arrested. Annie Kenney then jumped into the Prime Minister's car and began to address the crowd that had gathered outside. Campbell-Bannerman ordered that the women should not be prosecuted as this would only give their cause greater publicity: the first sign that the government was getting wise to the WSPU's tactics. Even so, the *Mirror* again led with coverage of the Downing Street incident.

In the summer of 1906 the WSPU continued to advertise itself as a movement for working women with socialist ideological sympathies. An editorial in the *Labour Record* written by Mrs Pethick-Lawrence called for 'volunteers for what we call Danger-work', who would engage in 'active agitation . . . regardless of the risks or consequences which may be entailed, in the spirit with which they so often sing the well-known song – The Red Flag . . . This is a people's movement. It is the awakening of the working women of this country to their need of representation.'[19]

Proselytising of this kind overlooked the growing tensions between the Pankhursts and the Labour movement. At the Cockermouth by-election later that year, Christabel announced that the WSPU, in addition to opposing all Liberal candidates – hardly surprising, given the off-hand way the new government had dismissed representations from both the WSPU and the NUWSS – would also adopt a sceptical attitude to all other political parties. In a joint statement with Teresa Billington, Christabel wrote: 'Labour MPs tell us candidly that they are sent by the Trade Unionists to the House of Commons to promote reforms which must take precedence of [sic] women's suffrage.'[20]

For the time being, there was little public opposition to the non-alignment statement, even though most of the WSPU's governing committee remained paid-up ILP members and the Union as a whole had owed much of its initial support to the Labour movement. The internal divisions within the WSPU had, however, been visible at the Union's first conference that same year. Leading socialists such as John Bruce Glasier, husband of the radical suffragist Katherine St John, had already grown tired of what they saw as the increasingly domineering attitude of the Pankhursts. As Glasier recorded in his diary, he had had to endure

> A weary ordeal of chatter about women's suffrage . . . belabouring me as Chairman of the Party for neglect of the question. At last, get roused and speak with something like scorn of their miserable individualist sexism; and virtually tell them that the ILP will not stir a finger more than it has done for all the women suffragettes in creation. Really the pair [Christabel and Emmeline Pankhurst] are not seeking democratic freedom, but self-importance . . . They want to be ladies, not workers, and lack the humility of real heroism.[21]

The influx of upper- and middle-class supporters was also a cause for concern: Glasier's wife Katherine took to mocking the WSPU as now 'the Society Woman's Political Union'.[22]

The draft constitution affirmed at the 1906 WSPU conference attempted to assert both the Union's socialist credentials and its democratic organisational structure. The stated aims of the WSPU were to 'secure for Women the Parliamentary Vote as it is or may be granted to men; to use the power thus obtained to establish equality of rights and opportunities between the sexes, and to promote the social and industrial well-being of the community'.[23] Under the sections on 'organisation', a system for electing the executive was put in place, modelled on the democratic structure of WSPU local branches in Scotland, which Teresa Billington had helped to organise. However, though the conference ratified the constitution, the structure it had laid out for the national Union was never implemented. True control of the WSPU lay in the hands of Mrs Pankhurst, her eldest daughter and the Pethick-Lawrences. Historians have often noted the paradox that, as Emmeline Pethick-Lawrence put it, 'a society that was founded upon a desire for the extension of democracy [turned] into an enthusiastically supported dictatorship'.[24]

For the time being, this dispute brewing between the Pankhursts and the large numbers of members who continued to sympathise with the ILP was muted by the WSPU's success with militant tactics. On 23 October, it mounted a demonstration at the opening of Parliament. A delegation of women demanded that the Liberal Chief Whip give them assurances that women's suffrage would be discussed before the end of the parliamentary session. When this was, as anticipated, refused, women mounted seats in the Commons' lobby and made protest speeches, while other suffragettes linked arms and closed around the speakers to protect them. Arrests inevitably followed, including Mary Gawthorpe, who had climbed on to a settee to make her speech, Mrs Pethick-Lawrence, Annie Kenney, Mrs Montefiore, Adela Pankhurst, Teresa Billington, Edith How-Martyn, Irene Fenwick Miller, Mrs Baldock and Mrs Anne Cobden Sanderson. The prisoners refused to recognise the authority of the 'male' court. All were found guilty of breach of the peace, and when they refused to be bound over for good behaviour were sentenced to two months' imprisonment.

This was undoubtedly the most successful militant action that the WSPU had mounted so far. It garnered praise and support from both the national press and the constitutional suffragists. The *Daily News* noted the action in Parliament approvingly, claiming, 'No class has ever got the vote except at the risk of something like revolution.' The *Daily Mirror* compared the suffragettes' actions with those of male reformers: 'By what means, but by screaming, knocking and rioting, did men themselves ever gain what they were pleased to call their rights?'[25] When these predominantly middle-class women were categorised as second-division prisoners ('common' criminals), it provoked uproar. Correspondents reflected on the different treatments meted out to female reformers and male:

> Charles Stewart Parnell, Charles Bradlaugh, Leigh Hunt, Edmund Yates, and other men in like case – that is, who were not criminals, though imprisoned under the laws – were treated differently. They had books and the use of writing materials, they lived in decent rooms, and were allowed to receive letters and occasional callers. But your women political prisoners are being treated like the commonest of criminals, merely for protesting in the hearing of your legislators against the inequality of men and women under our Constitution.[26]

This public pressure forced the Home Secretary to change tack, announcing that the women would be placed in the first division, the category reserved for political prisoners or those convicted of perjury or contempt of court and which allowed them considerable freedoms and a better diet. A prison warder at Holloway, Agnes Resbury, explained the difference:

> First Class Misdemeanours . . . are allowed special treatment, and if they have the means and wish it, they can have a large cell, furnished to their own liking. I have seen these special cells furnished by Maple's, the walls hung with pretty drapery, floors covered with rugs, side-board, easy chairs, pretty bedstead, their own bedding from home – eiderdown etc. – also the photographs of their friends standing about; all food sent in from outside restaurants – hot breakfast, lunch and dinner in the evening; they exercise by themselves and do not see or associate with other prisoners and are allowed to be visited every day, by their friends. You will think it no punishment to them, but I've seen them very depressed; the confinement to this class of prisoner, in the one cell for months,

taken from a Home of luxury and from Society, where their life is usually a whirl of pleasure, must mean suffering to them far more than to the ordinary prisoner coming in and out. Those coming in for the same offence [who] are not able to afford these privileges ... are allowed the best treatment the Prison affords; an ordinary furnished cell, small wash-stand and mirror etc., and the best diet, fourth class diet.[27]

The experience of incarceration brought Mrs Pethick-Lawrence close to a nervous breakdown, and she was released after giving an undertaking to keep the peace for six months. She immediately left the country for Italy to begin her recuperation.

The spectacle of middle-class women treated, at least initially, as common criminals for what were clearly political offences served to elicit a great deal of sympathy and backing from the well-to-do supporters of the NUWSS in London. Alice Milne, secretary of the Manchester Branch of the WSPU, wrote that she had arrived at the London office in October 1906 to find 'the place full of fashionable ladies in silks & satins. Tea & cakes were handed round & then the organisers each made a speech ... The ladies were much impressed & promised to return the following Monday with friends ... What a fever our Union Members in Manchester would have been in if such ladies made a de[s]cent on us.'[28] The suffragist leadership threw itself behind the cause of the imprisoned suffragettes, Fawcett writing to *The Times* to declare that the activities of the WSPU had given a boost to the suffrage movement as a whole. When her old friend Anne Cobden Sanderson was eventually released, Fawcett held a special celebratory feast in her honour at the Savoy.

WSPU militancy at this point had undeniably re-energised a movement that, even if it was growing in strength, especially in the North, had stalled at the level of national politics. The success of its tactics could be seen in the extent to which the National Union of Women's Suffrage Societies itself now copied them. It shifted from being a group that largely restricted itself to lobbying Parliament to a broader campaigning organisation.[29] By the beginning of 1907, both organisations were arranging mass meetings and marches in support of women's suffrage. In February of that year, the NUWSS organised a procession through London (christened the 'Mud March' because of the terrible weather conditions on the day), which involved some three thousand participants. Later in the spring, the WSPU organised successive marches on Parliament in which activists repeatedly tried to breach police lines, leading to further mass arrests and imprisonments. As the militant activity grew, so did the size of the WSPU's coffers: the Union enjoyed a total income of £2959 in the fiscal year March 1906 to February 1907.[30]

However, the tensions that had emerged between the Pankhursts and leading socialist members of the WSPU now came into the open. At the 1907 Labour conference, Emmeline Pankhurst reaffirmed Christabel's stance that the WSPU would not align itself with any political party. In response, Anne Cobden Sanderson and Charlotte Despard, the wealthy socialist philanthropist, stated their personal commitment to supporting ILP candidates. Mrs Pankhurst and Christabel responded to this 'disloyalty' by resigning from the ILP, the former heading off attempts to wrest control of the Union from her and her daughter by cancelling the annual conference and dramatically tearing up the democratic constitution passed the previous year. The reaction of the dissidents, led by Teresa Billington-Greig – she had married earlier that year and, like Mrs Pethick-Lawrence, added her husband's name to her own to indicate the equal nature of their marriage – was to form a new organisation, the Women's Freedom League. The WFL skimmed off perhaps as much as a fifth of the WSPU membership, and though it remained committed to militant action, this would take a slightly different form from that increasingly pursued by the WSPU: less violent and destructive, more theatrical and spectacular, like Muriel Matters's showering of

London with leaflets from a hot-air balloon, later parodied in the classic Ealing comedy *Kind Hearts and Coronets*.

The split caused great heartache to some former WSPU members, such as Hannah Mitchell. Mitchell never repudiated the militant campaign but was hurt by the Pankhursts' decision, to her eyes unnecessary, to force WSPU members to choose between socialism and suffrage. But whatever their private feelings, the split gave Mrs Pankhurst and Christabel unchallenged leadership of the Union as well as control of a movement whose wealth and political success went on increasing. Continued militancy seemed to be further justified by political changes in Westminster. Campbell-Bannerman had been replaced as Prime Minister in April 1908 by Herbert Asquith, who, along with his wife, was an out-and-out opponent of women's suffrage. According to Asquith,

> The inequalities which democracy requires that we should fight against and remove are the unearned privileges and the artificial distinction which man has made, and which man can unmake. They are not those indelible differences of faculty and function by which Nature herself has given diversity and richness to human society.[31]

Asquith deployed two arguments in support of his denial that women's suffrage was an issue of immediate political concern. First, he pointed out that all of the main political parties were divided on the issue. There was considerable truth in this. Asquith led a party that was predominantly sympathetic to suffrage. In contrast, the Conservative leaders Balfour and Bonar Law were privately in favour of giving women the vote, but most of their party was not. Labour, as we have seen, was divided between a few committed advocates of women's suffrage such as Hardie, some genuine supporters, and large sections of both the leadership and the rank and file that viewed the franchise as low on their list of political priorities. The WSPU was, at times, insensitive to these complexities.

Second, Asquith argued that women's suffrage was a minority cause without even the support of the majority of the nation's women. Christabel took this as an invitation to organise a mass demonstration (planned for 21 June 1908), to prove once and for all that public opinion was on the side of the suffragettes. Meanwhile, acts of militancy continued. Asquith's government proved itself less lenient than Campbell-Bannerman's. When Flora Drummond and four other women were sent to prison for padlocking themselves to the railings outside 10 Downing Street on 17 January 1908, they were categorised as second-, not first-, division prisoners. When Emmeline Pankhurst was arrested for the first time a month later during another march on Parliament, she too was sentenced – to six weeks – as a second-division prisoner.

The preparations for the mass demonstration were substantial. Seven hundred banners were made up in the WSPU's colours of white, green and purple. Enormous posters were produced with portraits of the twenty women speakers who would address the crowds that day. A steam launch was hired which, a few days before the event, called in at the terrace of the House of Commons at 4 p.m., while MPs were taking tea. Mrs Drummond, who stood on the cabin roof, invited the MPs to attend the demonstration and assured them that there would be no arrests. On the day itself, thirty thousand WSPU marchers wended their way to Hyde Park. At the head of the procession were horse-drawn coaches carrying the Labour luminaries Hardie, George Bernard Shaw, the Jewish writer and humorist Israel Zangwill, Mrs Thomas Hardy and Mrs H. G. Wells. The crowd was the largest for any pro-reform demonstration in British history and the largest for any British public meeting until the march against the war in Iraq in 2003. Even the usually unsympathetic *Times* wrote, 'Its organisers had counted on an audience of 250,000. That expectation was certainly fulfilled; probably it was doubled; it would be difficult to contradict anyone who asserted that it was trebled. Like the distance and numbers of the stars, the facts were beyond the threshold of perception.'[32]

Not all of the WSPU organisers were convinced that everyone assembled was sympathetic to the cause. Helen Fraser, a Scottish delegate, recalled that 'the vast mass of people were simply curious – not sympathetic – not opposed. Simply indifferent.'[33] Christabel nonetheless felt that the demonstration had made an unanswerable case: 'What would Mr Asquith say? We had eclipsed every peaceful demonstration made by men when asking for votes. What was the breaking of the Hyde Park railings in the 1860s [during the agitation over the Second Reform Bill] compared to the women's mighty manifestation?'[34]

Asquith, however, saw nothing to make him change his earlier stance. Further mass meetings took place later in the summer, with crowds of 20,000 on Clapham Common, 150,000 at Heaton Park in Manchester and 100,000 on Woodhouse Moor in Leeds. But these mass demonstrations were short-lived. The success of the Hyde Park showing had perversely backed the WSPU into a corner. It would be virtually impossible to mount a bigger demonstration of public support than had taken place in June; subsequent ones could only give the impression that backing for the cause was falling off. For an organisation that had made its mark with daring and innovative political interventions, the alternative for the WSPU of adopting the more orthodox campaigning methods of the NUWSS was scarcely appealing. A return to militant action seemed to be not only justified by Asquith's intransigence, but also the only viable option on the table if the WSPU were to continue as a distinct political organisation.

Militancy was already taking an increasingly violent turn. On the afternoon of 30 June, a group of thirteen women, including Mrs Pankhurst, left Caxton Hall to carry a women's suffrage resolution to Asquith. When it was rejected, predictably, that same evening a large crowd filled Parliament Square. This only partly comprised suffragettes and their supporters: there was also a sizeable number of men, who had come just to jeer or jostle the women. The increasing risk to their members from hostile elements in the crowd

would be another crucial reason for the WSPU's eventual abandonment of large-scale public meetings. Recalling it later, Hannah
Mitchell wrote that in those groups of male 'roughs', she could
'visualize the sadism of the Nazi young men. We saw it there in the
minds of those youths. They were encouraged by the inactivity of
the police, who just stood round, some of them openly grinning
and to whom we appealed in vain.'[35]

Twenty-five women were arrested that night, again trying to
break a police cordon around Parliament. Exasperated by their failure, two WSPU members, Mary Leigh and Edith New, took a cab
to 10 Downing Street and smashed Asquith's windows. At the
police station, Leigh warned, 'It will be a bomb next time.' The
following day, the women were sentenced to two months as third-
division prisoners, a fate reserved for the worst class of offenders.

The culmination of these marches on Parliament took place on
12 October 1908, this time with the objective of breaking into the
Commons Chamber itself. The WSPU printed up thousands of
handbills calling on both men and women to 'rush the House of
Commons'. These were distributed openly: once again, the objective was deliberately to court arrest. Christabel even showed one to
a police inspector; that day, summonses for the arrest of
Christabel, Mrs Pankhurst and Mrs Drummond were duly issued.
The women finally presented themselves for arrest at six o'clock
the following evening, just before the demonstration was due to
start. A crowd of sixty thousand had assembled near Parliament
Square, confronted by five thousand police, who had cordoned off
the area. In all, twenty-four women and thirteen men were
arrested for trying to break police lines, though only one woman,
Mrs Travers Symons, Keir Hardie's secretary, managed to get into
the Commons Chamber.

The trial of the Pankhursts and Mrs Drummond for the hand-
bill incident was a considerable propaganda coup for the WSPU.
They managed to subpoena both David Lloyd George and Herbert
Gladstone as witnesses, giving Christabel the opportunity to finally

display her talents as a lawyer. By now, she had already established a keen reputation as a combative platform speaker. Hecklers often found themselves mercilessly dispatched: 'Many times she was asked: "Wouldn't yer like to be a man, Miss?" Christabel would look steadily and sweetly at the heckler before replying: "Yes, wouldn't *you* like to be a man?"' Emmeline Pethick-Lawrence recalled how one recipient of a deadly Pankhurst putdown 'began to bluster and blare, when, to his indignation and utter astonishment, the other men in the audience . . . turned to him and said: "Shut up!" That was the reward for trying to maintain the supremacy of man! One member of the audience said: "We've come to 'ear 'er – not you, see!" and threatened to cop him one on the jaw.'[36] As the *Daily Mail* noted, 'the hecklers find themselves heckled, twitted, tripped, floored. I think they like it. She does, and shows it. She flings herself into the fray, and literally pants for the next question to tear into shreds.'[37]

Lloyd George also had a considerable reputation as a mesmerising public speaker. But Christabel had developed a special hatred for the Liberal Chancellor, conceiving him to be her political nemesis, and in the courtroom she proceeded to tie him into a series of knots with an unrelenting barrage of questions. Did the Chancellor really think that the suffragettes were dangerous? If so, why had he brought his young daughter along with him to the meeting at Hyde Park in June? Perhaps hoping to rescue the floundering Lloyd George, the magistrate intervened to tell her that she was not entitled to cross-examine her own witness. Christabel, however, had not got a first in law for nothing: 'I rather anticipated this difficulty and I looked up *Taylor on Evidence* and I saw words which I thought gave me a good deal of latitude.'[38] The magistrate let her proceed. Turning to Britain's history of constitutional struggle, Christabel defended the suffragettes' actions to the jury on the grounds of Magna Carta and the use of violence in other struggles for electoral reform.[39] The court encounter was neatly summed up by Max Beerbohm: 'The contrast between the buoyancy of the girl and the depression of the statesman was almost painful. Youth and an ideal on the one hand, and on the other, middle age and no illusions left over!'[40]

Yet, though she won the verbal battle, Christabel lost the case. Mrs Pankhurst and Mrs Drummond were given three-month prison sentences, Christabel ten weeks. Lloyd George, for his part, had certainly had enough of the Pankhursts, and Christabel in particular. When the WSPU demanded that he either pledge government action on votes for women or resign, he retorted that he had 'no desire to speak by Gracious permission of Queen Christabel'.[41]

'IT IS NO LONGER A MOVEMENT, IT IS A WHIRLWIND'[1]

The 'rush the Commons' case was a significant moment in the progression of WSPU militancy. It was the point at which the Union publicly declared that it had reached the limits of civil disobedience and moved towards a new position advocating active law-breaking and violent resistance. As far as Christabel was concerned, in the rush on the Commons the WSPU had kept within the letter of the law on public petitioning. The guilty verdict indicated that there was nothing to be gained from 'male' justice. As with Chartist justifications for the use of 'physical force', the suffragettes deemed they had been pushed to the point were violent direct action was the only alternative left open to them. The WSPU now moved away from more established radical tactics to new strategies: hunger-striking, window-smashing, physical assault, and later arson and bombing. Seen from within the organisation, these ploys appeared a success. Its income continued to grow rapidly and its activities remained headline news. Outside the Union, however, militancy, once undeniably the catalyst that had revived a moribund suffrage movement, now threatened to fragment it. As the NUWSS moved from collaborating with the

WSPU to distancing itself from 'militancy', so the government dug in, becoming ever more intransigent and repressive in its response to the suffragettes' activities.

Mrs Pankhurst increasingly referred to the WSPU's actions as a military campaign. Certainly, the militarism of the Union was on display at the Women's Exhibition at the Princess Skating Rink in Knightsbridge, held between 13 and 26 May 1909. Women were given lessons in ju-jitsu (a martial art that Sylvia Pankhurst practised) while other members performed drill exercises under the direction of NCOs. Resistance continued to be defended, as it had been by the Chartists, on the grounds that it was a constitutional right. With another march on Parliament scheduled for 29 June, WSPU propaganda followed Christabel's rhetoric at her recent trial by stressing the legitimacy of the suffragettes' actions, quoting the right to petition embodied in the Bill of Rights of 1689:

'It is the right of the subjects to petition the King, and all commitments and prosecutions for such petitioning are illegal.' Mr Asquith, as the King's representative, is bound, therefore, to receive the deputation and hear their petition. If he refuses to do so, and calls out the police to prevent women from using their right to present a petition, he will be guilty of illegal and unconstitutional action.[2]

The first suffragette hunger-striker was actually sent to prison for asserting the people's right to petition Parliament.[3] On 24 June, Marion Wallace Dunlop, an artist, illustrator of children's books, Fabian and suffragette, stamped the words of the Bill of Rights on to the walls of St Stephen's Hall in the Palace of Westminster with indelible ink. At her trial on 2 July, she was sentenced to one month's imprisonment and denied classification as a first-division prisoner. Apparently without the knowledge of the WSPU leadership, she then began a hunger strike.[4] After refusing food for nearly four days she was released. The tactic was unprecedented, though it would be taken up by later political movements across the world, both violent and non-violent.

The WSPU quickly latched on to the powerful propaganda value of the hunger strike. On 29 June, Mrs Pankhurst, along with eight elderly women, came to the Commons where they were met by one Chief Inspector Scantlebury who presented Pankhurst with a letter from Asquith's private secretary declaring that the Prime Minister would not receive the deputation. Pankhurst threw the letter to the ground and struck Scantlebury in the face, first lightly and then with more force when the initial assault failed to procure her arrest. When the delegation was taken into custody, it precipitated a riot in which 106 women and fourteen men were arrested. At nine o'clock that evening, another weapon was added to the suffragette armoury as thirteen women began to stone the windows of the Home Office, the Privy Council and the Treasury. At this stage the WSPU was still anxious to minimise the risk of injury, so the stones were attached to pieces of string so as not to hurt the people inside. The window-breakers, also refused status as political prisoners, went on hunger strike on 14 July, and six days later they were released.

In the late summer of 1909, seemingly without provocation, the WSPU's tactics changed quite dramatically. The window-breaking continued, but now with noticeably less regard for public safety. On 20 August, members hurled stones through the windows of Sun Hall, Liverpool, where the War Minister, Richard Haldane, was delivering a speech. When a policeman tried to stop them, a brick was hurled at him. Mary Gawthorpe, one of the Manchester organisers and a member of the WSPU's central committee, later told an impromptu meeting: 'The attack on Sun Hall was premeditated. Whether people liked it or not the stone-throwing epoch had been reached, and there would be a good many more stones thrown before the fight was over if the government did not give women what they wanted.' These violent actions reached their climax on 17 September, with an attack on Bingley Hall in

Birmingham, where Asquith was speaking. Two days earlier, Jennie Baines, a local activist whose husband George and son Wilfred assisted her in her militant activities, delivered this warning at an open-air gathering: 'We warn every citizen attending the meeting in Bingley Hall to beware. He may not only get crippled, he may lose his life eventually.'[5]

When the day arrived, Mary Leigh and Charlotte Marsh equipped themselves with axes and climbed on to the roof of a nearby building. They then proceeded to chop slates from the roof to hurl at Asquith's car and at policemen below. The assault caused not only physical damage but personal injury – one of the policemen was badly hurt by a piece of slate, while a detective who attempted to reach the women on the roof was knocked down to a lower building. Leigh and Marsh were finally brought down from the roof with a high-powered water hose. On the ground, another suffragette, Mary Edwards, assaulted policemen. At her trial on 20 September she declared unrepentantly, 'I had the opportunity, had I chosen to take it, of seriously injuring Mr Asquith. I am now sorry I did not do it. As he will not listen to words I think it is time that blows should be struck . . . I was two yards from him.'[6]

In all, the WSPU committed some thirty militant actions over the course of 1909. As the comments of Mary Gawthorpe indicated, the militancy of that late summer could not be described as merely a reaction to the incarceration of WSPU members, not least because no suffragettes were imprisoned at this time. Moreover, as recent research has shown, nearly half of those involved in the militancy could be defined as paid employees of the WSPU, and the same proportion were involved in more than one incident.[7] This indicated that rather than resulting from the spontaneous initiative of individual suffragettes, much WSPU militancy was the work of a hard core of salaried activists with clear links to the leadership. What had brought about this shift towards a more violent and directed campaign?

Two reasons have been identified. The first was relatively long-standing, though it was exacerbated in 1909 by the emerging crisis over Lloyd George's 'people's budget'. Suffragettes had already complained of the danger of becoming the subjects of crowd violence during the mass meetings of 1908. In 1909, suffragettes who attempted to interrupt pro-budget meetings often received harsh treatment. As the *Manchester Guardian* reported of the Birmingham demonstration:

> An enormous crowd of men, many of whom were of the roughest class, possessed [Broad Street] . . . Nothing but the hoofs of the policemen's horses could make them give an inch of ground, but whenever a woman came along and made for the gate into King Alfred's Place they parted before her, gave her a clear approach, and when she had got into her stride closed up around her and bore her forward into the arms of the police . . . Each time the woman, who was acting the part of the football in this unseemly scrimmage, was driven back until she was lost in the crowd, but she would reappear in a few moments and the same process would go on again.[8]

At the same meeting, the suffragist Laura Ainsworth complained that the police had driven them into a back alley where they were left at the mercy of a mob who hurled everything they could find at them. Misogyny was, perhaps, not the only motivation for these attacks. For the first time in British history, Lloyd George's budget promised some system of social security for the people, offering old-age pensions and a national insurance scheme that would help the unemployed. When, in the autumn of 1909, the Lords rejected his budget, Lloyd George denounced them as merely 'five hundred ordinary men chosen by random out of the ranks of the unemployed' on the principle of 'the first of the litter'.[9] It was now Lloyd George, not Christabel Pankhurst, who was seen as the champion of the downtrodden.

Second, the dispute over the 'people's budget' threatened seriously to overshadow suffragette activity. The initial publicity that the first WSPU hunger-strikers had achieved had given way to some public scepticism about these tactics, especially when they repeatedly secured the prisoners an early release. Pressure was being exerted at the highest level for the Liberal government to take a harsher line. On 15 August 1909, Gladstone had received a letter from the King requesting to know why 'the existing methods which must obviously exist for dealing with prisoners who refuse nourishment' were not being employed.[10] Similar questions were being raised in the press. Shortly after the Bingley Hall assault, an editorial in the *Pall Mall Gazette* demonstrated the cynical response the suffragettes' activities were provoking in some parts of the media:

> We shall wait to see whether the women secure their release from prison like some of their predecessors by the simple expedient of a two days' fast. If they do, it will be time to let the Home Secretary understand that his supine sentimental methods involve taking liberties with the public safety, which should not, and will not, be tolerated.[11]

That month, the most infamous government response to the militant campaign yet seen began. When seven women in Winson Green Prison in Birmingham again went on hunger strike, medical officers began forcibly feeding them. Within government, there had already been extended discussions concerning force-feeding prisoners. Gladstone had listened to evidence from asylum doctors, where forcible feeding was used to nourish patients too mentally incapacitated to swallow food properly. Feeding patients through tubes inserted in the nose had been practised very successfully in asylums for several years, with little in the way of medical complications. However, forcibly feeding healthy, mentally competent women who did not want to be treated in this way would clearly be a very different case. For the time being, Gladstone and Asquith had followed medical advice in resisting its use.[12]

The events of the late summer of 1909 left the Crown, the courts and a significant section of the press feeling that the suffragettes were clearly abusing their privileges as first-division prisoners, effectively thumbing their nose at the judicial system. The government responded by reminding prison medical officers that they were legally responsible for the well-being of their inmates and that assisting in the suicide of prisoners was a crime. The WSPU prisoners could not be allowed to starve, nor could they be released, so forcible feeding must be used.

The horrors of forcible feeding are vividly detailed in suffragette accounts, and the resonances with torture are not hard to appreciate. It is a moot point whether it was really a medical procedure used to prevent inmates from starving themselves to death, or rather an invasive punishment used to compel suffragettes to submit to the prison regime. Some prison officers clearly began forcible feeding long before the prisoner was in any danger of causing harm to herself by refusing to eat.[13] Whatever the government's motivation, the physical and mental suffering endured by suffragette prisoners cannot be denied. Mary Leigh wrote:

> I was . . . surrounded, forced back on the chair, which was tilted backwards. There were about ten of them. The doctor then forced my mouth so as to form a pouch, and held me while one of the wardresses poured some liquid from a spoon; it was milk and brandy . . . on Saturday afternoon, the Wardresses forced me on to the bed and two doctors came in with them, and while I was held down a nasal tube was inserted. It is two yards long with a funnel at the end – there is glass junction in the middle to see if the liquid is passing. The end is put up a nostril, one one day, and the other nostril, the other. Great pain is experienced during the process . . . the drums of the ear seem to be bursting, a horrible pain in the

throat and the breast. The tube is pushed down 20 inches. I have to lie on the bed, pinned down by Wardresses, one doctor stands up on a chair holding the funnel at arm's length, so as to have the funnel end above the level, and then the other doctor, who is behind, forces the other end up the nostrils.[14]

Leigh reported feeling faint afterwards and vomiting the first time the tube was withdrawn.

Case reports reveal the mental as well as physical trauma that the procedure inflicted on the women. Prison medical officers noted that Jessie Lawes, Mrs Pethick-Lawrence's cousin, was

nervous and hysterical, and in much nervous dread amounting to horror at any artificial feeling. Dr Cory thought it wise not to feed her again today, knowing by experience how much this comparatively simple proceeding appears to upset her. General condition good. She takes no food, and yet needs it; yet the operation profoundly upsets her and the looking forward to it seems to be a mental torture.[15]

Sylvia Pankhurst recalled how Emily Wilding Davison had been so terrified by the procedure

that when, by accident, the wardress locked her into a cell where there were two plank beds, she conceived the idea of using them to fasten herself in. She laid them on the floor, end to end, jammed the wooden stool and her shoes into the intervening space, and crouched down, holding all in position. Threats and coaxing failed to move her. By order of the visiting Magistrates who happened to be in the prison at the time, the cell window was broken, the nozzle of a hose pipe poked in, and the great stream of water turned on. Already weak from five days' hunger strike and three days' forcible feeding, she clung to the bed boards, gasping for breath. When the water was six inches deep a voice cried: 'Stop!'[16]

The WSPU also alleged, probably with good cause, that forcible feeding was used only against the lower-profile working-class inmates. The wife of H. N. Brailsford, the leading Liberal journalist, was sent to prison for attacking barricades outside a meeting in Newcastle being addressed by Lloyd George, with an axe hidden in a bunch of chrysanthemums. Mrs Brailsford began a hunger strike, but unlike her fellow prisoners was not forcibly fed. The WSPU alleged that this was because of her privileged position. A more celebrated case occurred when Lady Constance Lytton was imprisoned, having assumed the identity of a working-class suffragette, 'Jane Wharton'. When she had been taken into custody under her own identity, Lytton had been carefully examined by two prison doctors and another external medical authority, who had confirmed that she had a heart condition and ordered her release. However, Christabel Pankhurst recalled,

> [as] 'Jane Warton', the working woman, she had no heart examination at all, and was forcibly fed. Four wardresses held her down, a fifth helped in the forcible feeding processes. The doctor offered a choice of a steel or a wooden gag, explaining that the steel gag would hurt. The prisoner was silent. After an effort with the wooden gag, the steel gag was used. Her jaws were forced painfully wide, the large tube pushed far down her throat and food very quickly poured down but returned in a few seconds after, in a bout of sickness, while doctor and wardresses held down her retching body. Then they left her – no clean clothing could then be supplied, it seemed, and she lay as she was, until the next morning. From the next cell the distressing sounds of the forcible feeding of Elsie Howey could be heard.

According to Pankhurst, Lytton was repeatedly force-fed, though the assistant medical officer tested her heart 'and cheerfully pronounced it a "splendid heart"'.[17] Shortly after her release from prison she suffered a heart attack, and two years later a stroke which left her paralysed.

The horrors of forcible feeding, which Lytton herself did much to publicise both immediately after her release and in her book *Prisons and Prisoners* (1914), led to a public outcry. One hundred and sixteen doctors signed a memorandum against the practice, and H. N. Brailsford and H. W. Nevinson, another journalist, resigned as writers on the *Daily News* in response to its support for the practice. However, their resignations told a story. Public denunciation of forcible feeding was largely limited to the pages of the WSPU's *Votes for Women*. Even newspapers such as the *Nation* and *Daily News*, which had been sympathetic to the suffrage cause, refused to condemn it. The medical establishment, despite the protests of some – predominantly female – doctors, when it discussed the practice at all, tended to support it. Letters and articles in the *British Medical Journal* reassured the public that the procedure was relatively simple and free of complications, despite later cases such as that of Lilian Lenton, who developed pleurisy after being forcibly fed. The *Lancet* showed how seriously it took the dispute by publishing a parody of the force-feeding controversy by one Dr Charles Mercier, which referred to the complications of 'forcible bathing' for prisoners who refused to wash.[18]

The WSPU responded by upping the ante with further assaults on people as well as property. On 15 November 1909, Winston Churchill was attacked leaving a train at Bristol by Theresa Garnett, who beat him with a riding crop, screaming, 'Take that, you brute!'[19] The government was now seriously worried that Asquith himself might become the subject of an assassination attempt, fears that were exacerbated by (almost certainly false) reports of Women's Freedom League members practising with firearms at 92 Tottenham Court Road in London. Indeed, it was ultimately the activities of the WFL, though misconstrued, and not the WSPU, that would drive a wedge between 'constitutional' suffragists and militants. In October, Millicent Fawcett had publicly criticised militant activity when it was mistakenly reported that a WFL member had thrown acid at an election official at the

Bermondsey by-election. In fact, in keeping with the WFL's increasingly non-violent brand of militancy, the activists had merely poured some non-toxic liquid into a ballot box.[20]

The criticism of the Women's Freedom League was misplaced, given not only the different nature of their militancy, but also the fact that WFL members themselves were increasingly critical of the suffragettes' tactics. Dora Marsden, a recent convert to the WFL from the WSPU, condemned the Pankhursts' militancy as 'puerile'. Teresa Billington-Greig dismissed the WSPU for relying on 'cheap sentiment'.[21] Within the organisation's leadership, questions about the militant campaign were starting to be raised. A letter to *The Times*, purporting to be from working-class activists, complained:

> It is not the fact of demonstrations or even violence that is offensive . . . it is being mixed up and held accountable as a class for educated and upper class women who kick, shriek, bite and spit. As far as importance in the eyes of the Government goes where shall we be if working women do not support us? . . . It is not the rioting but the kind of rioting.[22]

Frederick Pethick-Lawrence felt that it was foolish to antagonise the public when no sustained propaganda effort had been made to convert them to the cause.[23] Militancy, which had first served to reignite the smouldering embers of the women's suffrage cause, now threatened to dampen them completely.

Divisions among the suffrage societies, the intransigence of Asquith and the constitutional crisis precipitated by Lloyd George's budget had combined to marginalise the issue of votes for women. The deadlock was broken by the January 1910 election, which left the Liberals with only two more seats than the Conservatives, and which, at least the National Union of Women's Suffrage Societies claimed, had produced a Commons with 323

MPs in favour of women's suffrage. A petition in favour had also managed to attract 280,000 signatures, as well as a more than usually sympathetic reception in the House. When the Women's Social and Political Union announced a truce on 31 January, the main political parties felt able to discuss the franchise without seeming to give in to intimidation. Mrs Pankhurst's retrospective explanation of the Union's reasons for agreeing to a truce revealed the impasse that had been reached:

My own strongest, but unspoken, reason for welcoming the Conciliation movement was that it might avert the need for stronger militancy and would at least postpone the use thereof. Mild militancy was more or less played out. The Government had, as far as they could, closed every door to meetings. Cabinet Ministers had shown their contempt for the mildness of our protests and had publicly taunted us on that score.[24]

The WSPU had to choose, then, whether to cooperate with the newly formed conciliation committee or to move towards more extreme forms of militancy in the hope of forcing the government's hand.

The committee was chaired by the Conservative Lord Lytton, brother of Constance, the suffragette. Brailsford, whose wife Jane had been on hunger strike, acted as an informal liaison officer with the NUWSS. The committee's challenge was to find a middle way between universal suffrage proposals, which alienated Conservative suffragists, and the equal-votes solution, which Liberals and Labour worried would simply strengthen the power of the propertied. The resulting bill aimed to reproduce the same franchise as then existed for women on the local government registers. It met with the general approval of both the NUWSS and the WSPU, which remained publicly in favour of equal suffrage – though as far as the NUWSS was concerned, the growing influence of socialist activists was leading to calls for it to endorse universal suffrage.

Initial signs for the bill were very hopeful: it passed its first reading by 299 votes to 189. Though this forced even Asquith to consider providing the bill with further facilities for amendment in the next session of Parliament, the Cabinet's discussions indicated that some of the bill's firmest opponents were among those, like Lloyd George, who wished to see more sweeping franchise reform. Its limited terms meant that it received only lukewarm support from the People's Suffrage Federation and the Women's Cooperative Guild. The Labour Party also failed to press for further amendments, although some thirty-two Labour MPs voted for it.

The truce, which had held for just over nine months, ended on 18 November when Asquith announced that Parliament would be dissolved but made no reference to the conciliation bill. A renewed attempt to rush Parliament was met with a ferocious police response, completely unlike that previously experienced by WSPU activists. Up to this point, police given the task of cordoning off Parliament from demonstrators had acted with considerable restraint. This all changed on 'Black Friday'. The three hundred women, led by Princess Sophia Duleep Singh, the daughter of the Maharaja of Lahore, were kicked, punched in the nose, and had their hair pulled and their breasts grabbed as they tried to break through police lines. In all, 115 women and four men were arrested, but charges were later withdrawn, only adding to allegations of police brutality. Brailsford and Jessie Murray, a leading female doctor, took depositions from women about their injuries. These confirmed accusations of sexual assault. A Mrs H. testified: 'One policeman . . . put his arm round me and seized my left breast, nipping it and wringing it very painfully, saying as he did so, "You have been wanting this for a long time, haven't you."'[25] The police brutality has been explained by the fact that the usual Commons guard of A Division had been replaced by new men drafted in from Whitechapel and the East End, who had had no experience of dealing with political demonstrations, but were used to administering rough justice to poor people whose complaints were less liable to make headlines.

In the short term, militant activity did not appear to have harmed either the WSPU's membership or its popularity with suffrage activists. The circulation of *Votes for Women* had grown from 16,000 in 1909 to 30,000 the following year. There was no sign, either, in the immediate aftermath of 'Black Friday' that the WSPU would change its tactics. On 22 November, two hundred women marched on Downing Street in response to Asquith's announcement that facilities for an amendment to the conciliation bill would be provided in the next parliament but not in the next session. During the course of the 'Battle of Downing Street', Augustine Birrell, the Chief Secretary for Ireland, was pushed about by a crowd of angry women and slipped, damaging his knee, which left him confined to bed for several days. This now-familiar scene of a Cabinet minister beset by angry suffragettes concealed a shift in WSPU strategy. Marches on Parliament, which had formed a key component from 1906 to 1910, were now judged too risky. Instead, the Union moved towards a campaign of widespread property destruction, first through window-breaking and then arson and bombing.

In this next phase of the WSPU's militant campaign, its activists would often see themselves as engaged in a war against not only an obdurate Liberal government but also an unsympathetic general public, which would be shaken from its apathy to the suffrage question by violent action alone. The irony was that there was clear evidence that the public at large was increasingly being won over to the enfranchisement of women. The general election of December 1910 made virtually no difference to the make-up of Parliament, but, outside of Westminster, eighty-six city and town councils passed resolutions supporting the second conciliation bill. These included five of the largest provincial cities in England and the three largest cities in Scotland. Its promoters proposed several modifications to the bill in its 1911 version, leaving it open to widening amendments.

The WSPU itself had shifted from the anger of Black Friday to

an incautious optimism. Christabel Pankhurst had already, prematurely as it turned out, announced that the Union would not
oppose Liberal candidates at forthcoming by-elections. Its members were in celebratory mood at the suffragette Women's
Coronation Procession in which forty thousand women walked
from the Embankment to the Albert Hall. Behind the scenes,
though, the bill was seriously threatened, not by staunch antis like
Asquith, but by those, especially Lloyd George, who saw this version of the female franchise as effectively spelling political suicide
for the Liberal Party. He remarked in private: 'We seem to be playing into the hands of the enemy. The Conciliation Bill would, on
balance, add hundreds of thousands of votes throughout the country to the strength of the Tory Party.'[26]

A survey of the views of local Liberal associations conducted by
the party's Chief Whip confirmed that the party as a whole agreed
with the Chancellor's assessment. Lloyd George's pivotal role in
the defeat of the second conciliation bill only reinforced
Christabel's conviction that he, and not Asquith, was the suffragettes' worst enemy in Parliament. Such a view overlooked the fact
that Lloyd George's position was actually the same as the WSPU's:
that the Liberal Party needed to bite the bullet and accept equal
suffrage. He was simply unwilling to accept a compromise that
would only have benefited his political opponents.

On 7 November, Asquith announced that in the next session
the government would introduce a bill providing for manhood
suffrage based on residency and which would be open to amendment in the future to include the enfranchisement of women. The
announcement brought a swift and furious reaction from the
WSPU: they would not trust the government to bring in such an
amendment, and they considered the proposal an insult to their
collective intelligence. They were not alone in viewing Asquith's
proposal with suspicion. Even *The Times* was sceptical about the
administration's intentions: 'experience warns us against inter-
preting Mr Asquith's words in their plain and obvious sense'.[27]

The WSPU, as ever, was not inclined to wait and see. On 21 November, it began a mass window-breaking campaign, targeting the offices of the *Daily Mail* and the *Daily News*, the Guards' Club and Dunn's Hat Shop as well as government buildings. Two hundred and twenty women were arrested, along with three men. These attacks revealed the broader, transgressive nature of suffragette militancy. By destroying clothes and hat shops, the suffragettes simultaneously destroyed the objects the male world expected them to venerate. The target of the militants' hostility was not simply a government that denied them their rights as citizens: it was a patriarchal culture, exemplified by men-only institutions such as the Guards' Club which saw them as submissive adornments.[28]

Lloyd George now announced to a public meeting of five thousand people in Bath that the conciliation bill had been 'torpedoed'. Breakfasting with C. P. Scott a week later, he declared that the WSPU's leadership had lost its senses: 'Christabel Pankhurst has lost all sense of proportion and of reality . . . It's just like going to a lunatic asylum . . . and talking to a man who thinks he's God Almighty.'[29] The WSPU's conduct was certainly becoming more extreme. In December, Emily Wilding Davison began the arson campaign, setting fire to postboxes by inserting paraffin-soaked rags through the slots. She received six months in prison, though the WSPU denied that her actions had received the sanction of its leadership – a claim which increasingly smacked of 'plausible deniability' rather than the truth. In March the following year, 150 women armed with hammers smashed shop windows on Oxford Street in London, causing £5000 worth of damage and leading to 124 arrests. Four days later, more windows were broken in Knightsbridge and Kensington High Street.

The timing of the action was questionable, to say the least. Such militancy provided a convenient pretext with which to deny women the vote. The *Morning Post* declared, 'Nothing could indicate more plainly their lack of fitness to be entrusted with the exercise of political power.' Lord Robert Cecil, a leading Unionist supporter of the conciliation bill, saw militancy as fundamentally counterproductive:

> If the deplorable outrages committed by the so-called Suffragists were devised for the purposes of advancing the cause of Women's Suffrage, they can only be described as senseless. But if their object was to put all possible difficulties in the way of the Constitutional Suffragists, and particularly in the way of the Conciliation Bill, then the proceedings, however unscrupulous, were exceedingly well designed.[30]

Some MPs may have been concerned that a vote in favour of the bill would look like an endorsement of vandalism, but for many Liberals it provided a convenient excuse for ditching a bill that they feared would only aid their political rivals. The third conciliation bill was defeated by 208 votes to 222, assisted by Liberal defections and also by the opposition of Irish MPs who, with the encouragement of Churchill and Lewis 'Loulou' Harcourt, thought that the suffrage issue was destabilising a Liberal government that would shortly deliver them Home Rule.

The reaction of the government was now to pursue a policy of 'decapitation' against the WSPU. They arrested the Pethick-Lawrences at the Union's headquarters at Clement's Inn but found that Christabel Pankhurst was not there, having already moved to a flat of her own near by. Alerted to the police action, she went into hiding before fleeing to Paris the next day. Both the Pethick-Lawrences and Mrs Pankhurst were given lengthy prison sentences.

If the WSPU appeared temporarily in disarray, the NUWSS seemed only to have gained strength from the struggle over the conciliation bills. At grass-roots level, there were many NUWSS members who were politically sympathetic to Labour. The vacillations of the Liberals over the bills had weaned their leadership off their natural affiliation with the party. The Labour Party had become more flexible on the issue of the franchise, encouraged by the likelihood of a government-sponsored adult-suffrage bill raised by Asquith's mooted compromise of 7 November.

The alliance was practically sealed by the firm commitment given to women's suffrage at the Labour Party's January 1912 conference, in a statement which affirmed that though adult male suffrage remained the ultimate goal, no vote would be given to a bill that did not include women. This move was followed in May by a statement from the NUWSS confirming its policy of supporting Labour candidates. The statement was neutrally worded so as not to alienate those leading NUWSS members who were dyed-in-the-wool Liberals: 'In recommending that preference be given at elections to candidates who were not only themselves in favour of women's suffrage, but belonged to a party which also identified with it, they were acting simply in the interest of women's suffrage, and they were perfectly ready to extend the same principle to other political parties which might in the future offer similar conditions.'[31] The noncommittal wording belied the energy with which the NUWSS threw itself into supporting Labour candidates. Through the Election Fighting Fund it not only gave Labour its backing in principle, but effectively put at its service the resources of a much better-organised, -supported and -financed political pressure group. In 1910, the NUWSS had over two hundred branches and a membership of 21,571. Even the less well-supported WSPU could, thanks to its wealthy donors in West London, command party funds twice the size of those at the disposal of the Labour Party.[32] It was the Election Fighting Fund that effectively transformed Labour from a party dependent for electoral success on backroom deals with the Liberals into a genuine national political force.

The partnership very quickly brought results. In the 1912 Crewe by-election, the EFF helped to defeat the Liberal candidate. At Midlothian, the Liberal candidate was again thwarted: the

Unionists overturned a large majority and the EFF garnered 2413 votes for Labour. Nonetheless, some leading Labour figures remained sceptical about the alliance, especially Ramsay MacDonald, who saw his role as the Lib-Lab wire-puller-in-chief under threat. He continued to denigrate the suffrage movement as essentially a middle-class cause and refused EFF assistance in his own constituency of Leicester.

The compromise tabled by Asquith back in November 1911 on the suggestion of Lloyd George, however, was no more successful than any of the three conciliation bills. A point of order from Bonar Law, the pro-suffrage Conservative, noted the exclusion from the final form of the bill of the occupier franchise, which had been present at the second reading. The Speaker let the Liberal Party know that, as a result of this error, he was considering ruling the bill incapable of containing the proposed women's suffrage amendments. Asquith publicly expressed shock at the ruling, though in private it caused him much amusement: 'the Speaker's *coup d'état* has bowled over the Women for this session – a great relief'.[33] In any case, the news was not the 'bombshell' that Asquith claimed: the civil servant in charge of drafting the bill, Arthur Tring, pointed out on 8 January 1913 that there was a procedural question mark over the women's suffrage amendments.

The NUWSS, emboldened by its new alliance with Labour, responded by rejecting the consolation prize of an offer to support a private member's bill with facilities for further amendments. The reaction was significant. W. H. Dickinson's private member's bill failed largely on the grounds that it was too democratic for most Conservative MPs, as it enfranchised the wives of householders as well as single-women property-owners. But, conversely for the NUWSS, the bill was not now democratic enough. Philip Snowden, then MP for Blackburn and later chairman of the ILP, believed that the shift in both the Labour and the NUWSS's positions was deeply significant for the fate of women's suffrage in general. It had now put 'into the region of the impossible',

Snowden wrote to Millicent Fawcett, any attempt to introduce a male franchise bill into the Commons that did not at the same time enfranchise women.[34] For the WSPU, predictably, the defeat of the government's bill was taken only as evidence, once again, of women's betrayal by Parliament. It was the catalyst for a renewed and ever more violent wave of militant activity. But the danger was that the WSPU's brand of militancy was now not merely politically counterproductive, it was becoming irrelevant.

THE SPECTACULAR PAGEANT
DRAWS TO A CLOSE

In the wake of Christabel Pankhurst's flight and the imprisonment of her mother and the Pethick-Lawrences, Annie Kenney
was placed in ostensible charge of the WSPU. In reality, she was
simply the cipher for Christabel's orders, becoming known as
'blotting paper for Christabel', a title that Kenney found amusing,
signing her letters to Christabel 'the blotter'.

Emmeline and Christabel Pankhurst were now in total control
of the movement. The government attack on the WSPU's leadership had prompted an internal power struggle that by the end of
1912 had been conclusively resolved in favour of their 'duumvirate'.
On 22 May, Mrs Pankhurst and the Pethick-Lawrences were
found guilty of conspiracy, though the jury urged leniency on
account of the political motives behind their crimes. The judge
nonetheless sentenced them as second-division prisoners and, in
response, Mrs Pankhurst and the Pethick- Lawrences announced
they would go on hunger strike in a week if their status were
not changed. Their case brought an appeal to Asquith signed
by a hundred MPs and leading international socialists including Jean Jaurès, Eduard Bernstein, Romain Rolland and Marie

Curie, urging that the suffragettes be recognised as political prisoners.

On 10 June, all three were transferred to first-division status. This was not enough for the WSPU: at a meeting at the Albert Hall five days later, it was announced that all WSPU prisoners would go on hunger strike if not placed in the first division. In another indication of the government's selective application of forcible feeding, on the grounds of both her social status and her political influence Mrs Pankhurst was never forcibly fed, but she was released on 24 June, seriously weakened by fasting. Mrs Pethick-Lawrence was released the same day, having been forcibly fed once; while her husband came out three days later, having been forcibly fed five times. Perhaps it was thought that subjecting a man to the ordeal would be less likely to provoke public indignation. By 6 July, all WSPU hunger-strikers had been freed, forty-five before their sentences had expired. For some of the lower-profile figures, the suffering had been almost too much. Emily Wilding Davison had attempted suicide in prison by throwing herself off a banister, only to be caught by a wire-mesh screen below.

The Pethick-Lawrences, Christabel and Mrs Pankhurst now met in Boulogne to discuss tactics. The Pankhursts were determined to continue with window-smashing. Perhaps for the first time, the Pethick-Lawrences offered a serious challenge to the Pankhursts' strategy for the WSPU, by suggesting that continuing these attacks was counterproductive. Targeting the general public before they had been won over to the cause would, they argued, only antagonise them and make it harder for the WSPU to achieve its political objectives.

The Pankhursts, and Christabel in particular, were not prepared to accept this challenge both to their authority and to the militant campaign. On their return to the UK in early October 1912, the Pethick-Lawrences were informed that their association with the WSPU was at an end. The total control that Mrs Pankhurst and

Christabel now held over the movement was confirmed by the move of the WSPU's HQ from Clement's Inn, where the lease had been in the name of the Pethick-Lawrences and the building had adjoined their private apartments, to Lincoln's Inn House. A deal was agreed whereby, in return for retaining full control of *Votes for Women*, the Pethick-Lawrences would not oppose their ejection from the WSPU. With the Union's newspaper out of the Pankhursts' hands, Christabel produced a new journal, the *Suffragette*, which she edited herself. The first issue featured an editorial by Mrs Pankhurst explaining the split, and ending with a powerful rallying cry to the WSPU's followers:

> Those of you who can express your militancy by facing Party mobs at Cabinet Ministers' meetings when you remind them of their falseness to principle – do so. Those of you who can express your militancy by joining us in our anti-Government bye-election policy – do so. Those of you who can break windows – break them. Those of you who can still further attack the secret idol of property so as to make the Government realise that property is as greatly endangered by Women Suffrage as it was by the Chartists of old – do so. And my last word to the Government: I incite this meeting to rebellion. I say to the Government, You have not dared to take the leaders of Ulster for their incitement to rebellion, take me if you dare.[1]

Ireland loomed increasingly large as a point of comparison for the WSPU militants. The month before Mrs Pankhurst had issued her call to arms, the Ulster loyalists had signed the 'Solemn League and Covenant', a pledge to resist Home Rule, which attracted eighty thousand signatures in one day. Shortly afterwards, the Ulster Unionist Council, headed by Edward Carson, MP, formed the paramilitary offshoot, the United Volunteer Force, to defend the Union by force. The WSPU viewed the Liberal government's treatment of the Ulster loyalists as markedly more lenient than its approach to suffragette militants. Irish nationalists did not escape WSPU condemnation either, being viewed as backsliders who had reneged on earlier commitments to women's suffrage in order to protect a Liberal government and, thereby, the prospect of Home Rule. Clear evidence of the suffragettes' anger at the nationalists' 'betrayal' had come on 18 July 1912 in Dublin, when Mary Leigh hurled an axe into a carriage in which Asquith and the nationalist leader John Redmond were riding. Having fled the scene, that same evening Leigh and Gladys Evans tried to set fire to the Theatre Royal, where Asquith had just seen a performance, setting alight curtains, hurling a flaming chair down into the orchestra and setting off small bombs in tin cans. Neither woman made any attempt to evade arrest and each was sentenced to five years in prison. After hunger strikes, they were released, having served no more than sixteen weeks.

The actions of Leigh and Evans were only part of a series of dramatic and increasingly violent incidents in the summer of 1912. The most revealing, in terms of both its nature and the arguments used to justify it, was perpetrated by Helen Craggs, a teacher at Roedean and daughter of Sir John Craggs, a chartered accountant.[2] Craggs was found on the morning of 13 July in Nuneham Courtenay, Oxfordshire, with flammable materials ready to torch the house of 'Loulou' Harcourt, the leading Cabinet 'anti'. Along with this paraphernalia was found a note that read

Women . . . see around them the most appalling evils in the social order; they see children born into conditions which maim them, physically and mentally, for life; they see their fellow-women working in the sweated industries at a wage which makes their life a living death – or sacrificed as white slaves to a life which is worse than death.[3]

Craggs was arrested and later sentenced to nine months' imprisonment in Oxford Gaol. Like the other WSPU prisoners, she was released after going on hunger strike, having been forcibly fed once.

Craggs's abortive attempt to set fire to the home of a Cabinet minister was the first of a series of major arson attacks mounted by the WSPU in the coming two years. As well as indicating the path that future militant action would take, the note found with Craggs indicated a significant change in the tone of the militant campaign. The emphasis was shifting away from the depiction of the suffrage movement as a political crusade towards a moral one. The leading WSPU activist 'General' Flora Drummond now defined the Union's aims as bringing an end not only to 'sweated labour' but also to the 'White Slave Traffic', paedophilia and male predation on young girls. This was a campaign, Mrs Pankhurst now publicly declared, directed at antagonising the public, not just targeting anti-suffrage ministers: 'We are not destroying Orchid Houses, breaking windows, cutting telegraph wires, injuring golf greens, in order to win the approval of people who were attacked. If the general public were pleased with what we are doing, that would be a proof that our warfare is ineffective. We don't intend that you should be pleased.'[4]

The number of militant incidents escalated over 1913–14, to 337.[5] Bombing now joined the list of WSPU tactics. At six o'clock in the morning on 18 February 1913, Emily Wilding Davison and accomplices set off a bomb that destroyed five rooms in Lloyd George's new house near Walton Heath, Surrey. In July of the same year, Edith Rigby planted a pipe bomb in the Liverpool Exchange building. There were even some men involved in the campaign: the young Harold Laski, later a leading British socialist intellectual, planted a bomb in Oxted railway station.[6] The use of high explosives brought with it an increased risk of causing death or serious injury to the general public, and it was certainly more through luck than judgement that no one was killed as a result of WSPU actions.[7]

It is important to remember, however, that throughout the

militant campaign, it was the WSPU activists themselves who were most in danger. Their most famous act of militancy resulted in the death not of a Cabinet minister or member of the public, but of a suffragette. On 3 June 1913, Emily Wilding Davison and her flatmate decided to attend the Derby, to be held the following day, and disrupt the race by suddenly waving the WSPU colours before the horses at Tattenham Corner. But instead, Davison dashed on to the course and was run down by the King's horse, Anmer, fracturing her skull. She died five days later, never having regained consciousness.

Debate still rages as to whether Davison intended all along to give her life for the cause. She had bought a return ticket, and inside her jacket were found the WSPU's colours, indicating that she may have intended first of all to follow the original plan, her martyrdom only the product of a sudden impulse. However, she had attempted suicide once before and was clearly preoccupied with morbid visions long before Derby Day. In an unpublished article she spoke of 'a grim holocaust to Liberty' in which the 'the surrender of Life itself [was] the supreme consummation of sacrifice, than which none can go higher or greater'.[8] Sylvia Pankhurst, for one, believed that her actions were deliberate.[9]

Davison's funeral was attended by tens of thousands of mourners, but the show of public sympathy here masked the otherwise steep decline in the WSPU's support. The situation was deceptive. Large amounts of money continued to pour in from wealthy donors and a hard core of activists kept up an almost unrelenting campaign of militant action. Yet, by 1913, membership had gone into a steep decline, numbers dropping from 4459 in 1909–10 to 923. This loss of support contrasted with the growth of the National Union of Women's Suffrage Societies,[10] whose membership was rising by about 1000 a month in 1913, reaching a peak of nearly 100,000 on the eve of the First World War, with five times the number of local branches as the WSPU. This expansion was at the expense not only of the Pankhursts' suffragettes, but also of the

Women's Liberal Federation, which lost 18,000 members and sixty-eight local branches between 1912 and 1914.[11] The NUWSS had even succeeded in winning over the most masculine bastion of the trade union movement, the miners. A meeting held on 14 February 1914 to seek donations to the new Women's Suffrage Mandate Fund raised some £6000, mainly from union sources.[12] Whereas the NUWSS was able to step up mass meetings and 'pilgrimages', on the increasingly rare occasions that WSPU associations held public meetings its members were attacked by hostile groups of men and pelted with mud, stones and rotten fruit.

The WSPU was losing ground not just because of its continued advocacy of violent militancy, but also because of its interlinking of the suffrage cause with the ongoing campaign against the evils of prostitution and venereal disease. Christabel's contributions to the *Suffragette* were now dominated by these themes. As she wrote on 11 April 1913: 'The chief fruits [sic] of woman slavery is the Social Evil [prostitution]. As a result of the Social Evil, the nation is poisoned morally, mentally, and physically. Women are only just finding this out. As their knowledge grows they will look upon militancy as a surgical operation – a violence fraught with mercy and healing.'[13] Her ideas relating to prostitution, sex and marriage were collected in *The Great Scourge and How to End It*, published in 1913.[14] In this work, Christabel made the extraordinary claim that between 75 and 80 per cent of men were infected with gonorrhoea before marriage and that, as a consequence, humanity (at least, British humanity) was faced with the prospect of 'race suicide', caused by the sterility the disease wrought in women.[15]

According to Christabel, the remedy for the twin evils of prostitution and venereal disease was abstinence and moral purity for men, and the vote for women. In this sense, *The Great Scourge* was very much a political tract, albeit in the broadest sense. Christabel saw man's domination over woman as slavery, and marriage as essentially a form of sex-slavery. Only the vote would allow women to break this bondage. 'Those who want to have women as slaves,' she wrote, 'obviously do not want women to become voters.'[16] The redefinition of the suffrage movement as a sex war and the feminist separatism suggested by *The Great Scourge* were certainly radical, though they had their antecedents in the campaigns against the Contagious Diseases Acts of the 1860s.

However, in many respects Christabel's portrayal of masculinity was deeply conventional. She shared the assumption of many male medical authorities on sexuality that men were barely restrained sexual predators. Many contemporary discussions of sex portrayed civilised man as forced into a continual struggle against his animal urges. Women, on the other hand, were depicted as having almost no sexual desires whatsoever. Christabel accepted the received wisdom that excess sex degraded men, reducing them to their bestial core: 'it not only soils and debilitates a man's body, but also contaminates his mind'.[17] But she did engage in a radical assault on the idea that male sexual desire was unconquerable. Self-control, she chillingly assured her male readers, was perfectly possible, and for those who could not master it themselves there was the option of chemical castration, already practised in prisons.[18]

Within the movement *The Great Scourge* went uncriticised, a sign not only of Christabel's and Mrs Pankhurst's control over the WSPU but also of the change in its membership. Long a female-only society, it had now even excluded its 'honorary' male members and had lost many of its married-women followers as well. What was left was a rump of young, single-female activists less disturbed by the sexual segregation Christabel advocated. Outside of the WSPU, however, *The Great Scourge* attracted much criticism. The feminist journalist Rebecca West wrote in the *Clarion* that Christabel's comments on venereal disease were 'utterly valueless and are likely to discredit the cause in which we believe'.[19] Sylvia Pankhurst included lengthy criticisms of Christabel's work in her history of the suffrage movement.[20] The book even outraged traditional moralists. While the moral conservatism of *The Great Scourge* might have had a broad appeal –

Lord Kitchener had issued similar warnings to soldiers to safe-guard their health and 'avoid excesses' – the book's clear attack on the institution of marriage did not.[21]

The main beneficiary of the WSPU's change in approach was, as we have seen, the NUWSS. The Liberal government made little capital from the narrowing base of support for the suffragettes. Its solution to the heightened militant campaign was to step up its policy of pressurising the organisation's leadership and repressing rank-and-file activity. Gladstone, a Home Secretary who had been personally sympathetic to the suffrage cause, was replaced by the hard-liner Reginald McKenna. It was McKenna who devised the Discharge of Prisoners Act (given the royal assent on 25 April 1913), better known as the 'Cat and Mouse Act'. This provided for the release and later rearrest of prisoners staging hunger strikes. The measure was designed to answer complaints in the Conservative press that the suffragettes were successfully flouting the law by securing early release through fasting. On 30 April, the offices of the *Suffragette* were raided and leading staff arrested. Papers found there provided more information of a centralised conspiracy to commit arson, and research has shown that local militant incidents during 1913–14 were closely linked to the presence of key activists.[22] Even with this information, the Special Branch's attempts to thwart the arson campaign had something of the Keystone Kops about them. Officers complained to the Home Secretary that suffragette activists were avoiding tails by switching cars in mid-pursuit and by employing high-speed motorbikes to get from one arson target to another. One officer was paid to use his own high-performance motorcycle to pursue the WSPU riders, but caught nothing other than the smell of burning suffragette rubber in his nostrils.[23]

The spate of arson attacks continued almost unabated, but this is not to suggest that the Home Office's efforts against the WSPU were futile. Forcible feeding had been resumed in the wake of the clear violation of licence terms by suffragettes such as Mary

Richardson, caught red-handed in the vicinity of a flaming mansion. There was clear evidence now that the Home Office was using forcible feeding not so much to keep prisoners alive as to ensure that they made their court hearings; it was also drugging them so that they would not struggle when undergoing the procedure.[24] Furthermore, police surveillance techniques were becoming increasingly sophisticated, not to say devious. As the case of Lady Lytton demonstrated, ascertaining the identity of suffragettes was not always straightforward. This was particularly important after the passage of the Cat and Mouse Act, in order to discover whether any 'mice' had broken their licence terms. Inevitably, the suffragettes themselves resisted attempts to identify them through photographs and finger-printing. Initially, prison officers resorted to strong-arm tactics. One woman, Evelyn Manesta, was held in an arm-lock while her photograph was taken. The image of the prison warder behind her was later erased from the picture, but the doctored image was scarcely satisfactory as Manesta had kept her eyes shut. More subterfuge was required, so the Home Office enlisted a photographic firm whose employees hid inside a prison van and, using a new-fangled telephoto lens, took surreptitious photos of the women while they were in the exercise yard.[25]

The Cat and Mouse Act brought little credit to the Liberal administration. It was further shaken by the prospect that the Conservative Party would outmanoeuvre it on the suffrage issue, and that this, combined with the NUWSS alliance with Labour, could cause the Liberals serious problems in a forthcoming election. However, suppression was arguably working, even as the militant action continued. March 1914 saw another famous act of suffragette vandalism when Mary Richardson slashed Velázquez's *Rokeby Venus* in the National Gallery. This was not a unique instance: other suffragettes attacked paintings, especially female nudes as examples of the male objectification of women. However, Richardson claimed her gesture was designed to bring attention to

Emmeline Pankhurst's hunger strike – in itself an admission that the publicity value of that particular kind of militancy was on the wane.

The WSPU was now increasingly isolated. It had rebuffed approaches from the NUWSS for a renewed alliance, persisted with its militant tactics, and now, along with the Pethick-Lawrences, Sylvia Pankhurst had been forced out of the Union. Since 1912, Sylvia had devoted more and more of her time to her own East London Federation. This was already an organisation quite distinct from the WSPU. It advocated universal adult suffrage, had a working-class membership, did not sponsor arson, did not espouse anti-male attitudes, welcomed both male and female members and was both sympathetic to and cooperative with the local Labour movement. Sylvia still practised militancy, training her followers in martial arts and advising them to come armed to meetings, but she was publicly committed to more causes than simply women's suffrage.

It was her attendance at a meeting on 1 November 1913 organised by George Lansbury's socialist Herald League to protest against the lockout of Dublin workers and the imprisonment of the Irish trade union leader James Larkin that led her into direct conflict with Christabel. The elder sister used the pages of the *Suffragette* to distance the WSPU from any idea of support for the Herald League, and privately wrote to Sylvia, telling her that 'conflicting views and divided counsels inside the WSPU there cannot be'.[26] (This despite the fact that the Herald League had provided protection for WSPU 'mice', like the ex-boxer 'Kosher' Hunt, who guarded Sylvia Pankhurst, to prevent their rearrest.[27]) Following a meeting between Sylvia and Christabel in Paris in January 1914, the East London Federation formally separated from the WSPU.

With the Pankhurst family split, the Pethick-Lawrences ostracised and membership dwindling, the WSPU was in danger of going underground, transforming completely from a campaigning organisation into something like a tiny cell of arsonists and bombers. On 21 May 1914, Mrs Pankhurst was arrested for the last time, as a crowd of two hundred women rushed Buckingham Palace. But by this point militancy was a political dead-end. The comparisons that the suffragette movement as a whole frequently made between itself and the Ulster Unionists and previous British radical movements were apposite. In both of the latter cases the use of force had carried the very real threat of general insurrection. Though well supported financially, the WSPU on its own could not intimidate governments in the same way. Moreover, whereas the loyalists in Ulster had been willing to use lethal force, the WSPU, though it became less scrupulous about the risks to the public of militant action, never consciously aimed to cause death or serious injury. In this sense, it is inappropriate to describe its members as 'terrorists', as some historians have. They aimed largely at inconveniencing rather than incapacitating the public.

The decline of the WSPU, though, should not be equated with the decline of the women's suffrage movement as a whole. Indeed, under the leadership of the NUWSS it was in a stronger position than ever before, thanks to that organisation's astute alliance with the Labour Party. On the eve of war its activities had left the Liberal government so worried for its electoral survival that Lloyd George had approached Sylvia Pankhurst about reviving the idea of tacking a women's suffrage amendment on to a male suffrage bill.[28] In Sylvia's narrative history, this olive branch was presented as recognition of her own importance to the suffrage cause. In fact, Lloyd George's offer was far more the product of the campaigning work of the NUWSS than of the militancy of the WSPU. Rather than militancy bringing women the vote, it was the First World War that rescued the leading militants, Christabel and Emmeline Pankhurst, from the political wilderness.

As the threat of conflict grew ever greater, Christabel's writing took on an increasingly apocalyptic tone, a foreshadowing of her later spiritualist beliefs: 'This great war, whether it comes now, or by some miracle is deferred till later, is Nature's vengeance – is God's vengeance upon the people who held women in subjection.'[29] A week later, with war formally declared, Mrs Pankhurst announced that the militant campaign was over. She and Christabel now threw themselves enthusiastically into supporting the war effort. Their new, jingoistic rhetoric shocked some former supporters. The suffragist H. M. Swanwick, born in Munich, had been an admirer of Mrs Pankhurst,

> until a melancholy night in 1915, when the ghost of the woman she had been talked unbelievable nonsense about Germans at a Queen's Hall [London] meeting. There was a man there, I remember, who maintained that the stewards at Liberal meetings between 1906 and 1914 had been 'Huns'. 'You will remember', he roared, 'with what brutality these stewards treated the women?' Then, after a dramatic pause, he leant forward and snarled, 'It was not for nothing that they spoke with a foreign accent and in a guttural tongue.' Mrs Pankhurst nodded approval. I was so startled by this absurdity that I let out a shout of laughter. But the audience turned on me with a shocked 'Hush!' I had brawled in church. Nothing was, at that time, too fantastic to be believed against Germans.[30]

Ironically, this anti-German rhetoric overlooked the fact that one of the leading suffragette activists before the war, 'Kitty Marion', was born Katherina Schafer in Dortmund, Westphalia.[31]

The WSPU eagerly worked to recruit men for the war effort and women to help manufacture munitions. On 17 July 1915, Lloyd George and Churchill reviewed a two-mile procession of thirty thousand women, some of whom carried banners with such oxymoronic inscriptions as 'Shells made by a wife may save a husband's life'. On 15 October, in the clearest sign yet of the WSPU's commitment to the war effort, the *Suffragette* was rechristened

Britannia. Through the pages of *Britannia*, Christabel would return to the pathological themes of *The Great Scourge*, denouncing pacifism as a 'disease', urging the annihilation of the German nation and labelling wartime strike action as the work of either 'Bolsheviks' or the Kaiser's agents.[32] The Pankhursts and their supporters showed that they had lost none of their militant spirit, taking the patriotic cause right into the heart of pacifist, socialist 'Red Clydeside'. When workers interrupted an anti-strike rally in Glasgow by singing the 'Red Flag', Pankhurst supporters

> [leapt] down from their places, and like a troop of lancers, went clean through the pacifists. It was a wild, weird scene . . . There was one lady who was a regular master of fistcuffs [she was trained in ju-jitsu]. One big beefy-looking shirker tried to punch her, but she ducked and his arm went nowhere and the lady's fist just got the place it was meant to, and he collapsed at her feet, gobbling and groaning.[33]

The WSPU's unqualified enthusiasm for the war was not matched by the other suffrage societies. The NUWSS's conference resolution in its support was modified by some members who secured the inclusion of a phrase calling for 'the substitution for force . . . of a real European partnership based on the recognition of equal rights and established and enforced by a common will'.[34] A number of NUWSS members joined a new anti-war group, the Union of Democratic Control, which included radical Liberals such as Brailsford, ILP figures such as MacDonald and former WSPU activists such as Pethick-Lawrence. Until 1915, the NUWSS maintained unity by taking an active part in relief work only. Over £150,000 was raised to support medical units.

However, when the patriotic Millicent Fawcett that year refused to permit the NUWSS to participate in an anti-war conference at The Hague, large numbers of pacifist members left the Union. Sylvia Pankhurst's East London Federation likewise maintained its pacifist, socialist stance. Indeed, she publicly attacked *Britannia* for whipping up anti-German feeling, citing an attack on a German bakery in Hoxton as an example of the violence this rhetoric provoked against innocent immigrant communities.[35] In the East End, she worked tirelessly to combat poverty and deprivation, opening milk distribution centres, four mother-and-baby clinics and a 'cost-price restaurant' which in 1915 served seventy thousand two-penny meals. She was increasingly influenced by Marxism, chaning the name of her paper, the *Women's Dreadnought*, to the *Workers' Dreadnought*. It carried articles by the Scottish communist John McLean and even pieces by Christabel's old university nemesis Walter Newbold, and it was through these Marxist contacts that she encountered an Italian anarchist-socialist, Silvio Corio, with whom she would later have a child.

The pacifist stance of some former suffragettes and suffragists was largely outweighed by the patriotic contribution of women to the war effort. The numbers working in the munitions industry rose from 83,000 in July 1914 to 947,000 by the end of the war. Whether this work raised women's position in society is debatable. Sylvia Pankhurst characterised munitions work as 'sweated labour', and the wages paid to the women in these factories, only two-thirds of men's, lent some truth to the accusation. However, in two important ways war work did contribute to the advancement of women's suffrage.

First, the patriotic stance of the leadership of both the WSPU and the NUWSS allowed the Liberal Party to draw a line under militant activity. On 7 May 1916, replying to a letter from Mrs Fawcett on the issue of male suffrage and the insertion in any forthcoming bill of a clause relating to women, Asquith assured her: 'You may be certain that the considerations set out in your letter will be fully and impartially weighed, without any pre-judgement from the controversies of the past.'[36] Second, far from representing the abandonment of suffrage agitation, the war work of both the WSPU and the NUWSS contributed to a redefinition of citizenship during the First World War. Instead of emphasising that, as human beings, men and women were due the same political rights, many advocates of women's suffrage now suggested that citizenship was dependent on service and sacrifice. Just as male soldiers who had been prepared to give their lives for their country deserved the vote, so too did women doctors, nurses and munitions workers. Individuals, male or female, who were not prepared to defend the nation, such as conscientious objectors or striking workers, should be denied the right to vote.[37] This new rhetoric nonetheless employed some of the old tactics of militancy: old WSPU activists were at the forefront when it came to handing out white feathers to men who refused to enlist.[38]

The establishment of a coalition government during the war had also brought in more pro-suffrage ministers, including Robert Cecil and Arthur Henderson. But Asquith suggested in August 1916 that the issue of the franchise was too controversial to be broached during wartime, a statement that met with an uncharacteristically muted response from the WSPU. However, the resignation of Asquith on 5 December over the conduct of the war, and his replacement by Lloyd George, opened the way for a quicker resolution of the issue. Further good news for the suffrage campaign followed, with the resignation from the Conference on Electoral Reform a week later of the two leading opponents of votes for women, Sir Frederick Banbury and Lord Salisbury. When the conference reported its conclusions the following January, it announced that as well as male suffrage on residency qualification, some form of women's suffrage would be confirmed.

In supporting the report, Lloyd George reiterated that women's war work made them deserving candidates for the vote. On 19 June 1917, the clause in favour of women's suffrage was passed by 385 votes to 55, the bill finally passing the Lords on 10 January 1918 and receiving the royal assent on 6 February. Women over thirty were enfranchised if they were householders, wives of householders or university graduates, or if they occupied property with a rental value of more than £5 a year. In accordance with the notion that the vote was a reward for war service, male conscientious objectors were disenfranchised.[39] Under the terms of the 1918 Representation of the People Act, thirteen million men now had the vote, along with eight and a half million women – the first time any women had been enfranchised since 1832.

In the final analysis, militancy had played little part in securing women the vote. Taken at face value, neither had women's war work: as a number of women's organisations pointed out at the time, the 1918 act left most working-class women without a vote. The perception that triumph for the movement for women's suffrage had come not with a bang but a whimper was neatly expressed by the feminist writer Vera Brittain:

> With an incongruous irony seldom equalled in the history of revolutions, the spectacular pageant of the woman's movement, vital and colourful in adventure, with initiative, with sacrificial emotion, crept to its quiet, unadvertised triumph in the deepest night of wartime depression.[40]

In her account of the suffragette movement, Sylvia Pankhurst wrote that the 1918 act dispelled 'the mirage of a society regenerated by enfranchised womanhood as by a magic wand'.[41] It was a slight both at her sister Christabel's expectation of an imminent feminine millennium and at the more long-standing British radical belief that the vote could be an elixir for all social and economic evils. Many historians have concurred with this pessimistic assessment of the impact of enfranchisement on the status of women. By the early 1920s, most women had lost the jobs they had had during the war, jobs that in any case had largely been traditionally female and of relatively low status. Conservative critics attacked the morality of young single women in postwar Britain. Sylvia Pankhurst herself was not immune to vilifying so-called 'flappers'. In an article commissioned to commemorate the twenty-first anniversary of Emily Wilding Davison's death, she complained: 'Amongst crowds of young women, the emancipation of today, displays itself mainly in cigarettes and shorts . . . and other absurdities of dress and deportment, which betoken the slave woman's sex appeal rather than the free woman's intelligent companionship.'[42]

Such a pessimistic analysis, though, overlooks both the achievements of the suffrage movement and its remarkable vitality after the war. The equalisation of suffrage in 1928 was not a political inevitability, but the product of further hard campaigning by former suffragettes and suffragists. A July 1926 demonstration and meeting at Hyde Park in support of universal suffrage showed the continuing solidarity within the suffrage movement, with a procession that included Millicent Fawcett, Charlotte Despard, Flora Drummond, Annie Besant, Mrs Pankhurst and Margaret Ashton. Militancy did not return, but this was a tactical decision, not a moral judgement on the past. As Eleanor Rathbone put it: 'We acquired by experience a certain flair which told us when a charge of dynamite would come in useful and when it was better to rely on the methods of a skilled engineer.'[43]

If women remained under-represented in Parliament (the first woman elected to the Commons in 1918, Countess Markievicz, as a Sinn Fein member, did not take her seat), they were clearly making ground in other fields. By 1925, fourteen thousand had been enrolled on degree and diploma programmes, there were half a million women clerical workers, thirteen hundred qualified women doctors, and, for the first time, women were allowed to sit exams for the highest administrative class of the civil service. By 1927, there were even 142 women police officers, a role which had its origins in the operation of volunteer women police units raised by the WSPU to protect women workers during the First World War.

Mrs Pankhurst died on 14 June 1928. As her daughter Christabel noted,

The House of Lords passed the final measure of Votes for Women in the hour her body, which had suffered so much for that cause, was laid in the grave. She, who had come to them in their need, had stayed with the women as long as they still might need her, and she went away.[44]

Emmeline Pankhurst is now revered as the leading figure in the history of British women's political emancipation. She emerged as twenty-seventh in the BBC's 2002 poll of 'Great Britons', between Queen Elizabeth II and Guy Fawkes. In contrast, vitally important figures such as Millicent Fawcett are scarcely known beyond academic circles. We now closely associate the struggle for the vote with militant action, but this is to misunderstand both militancy and the wider suffrage movement. Militancy has, quite rightly, been seen by a number of historians as eventually counterproductive. From 1905 to 1908, WSPU militancy undoubtedly helped revive a movement that had struggled to be taken as anything more than the intellectual hobby-horse of bored middle-class women. After this point, militancy largely frustrated the cause of women's enfranchisement by making it virtually impossible for politicians to do a deal without appearing to sanction violence.

But reading militancy in this way is to miss what was truly revolutionary about it. As Emmeline Pethick-Lawrence said, 'Christabel cared less for the political vote itself than for the dignity of her sex, and she denounced the false dignity earned by submission and extolled the true dignity accorded by revolt. She never made any secret of the fact that to her the means were even more important than the end. Militancy to her meant the putting-off of the slave *spirit*.'[45]

Militancy was not simply the means to an end, then; it was an end in itself. Militant acts demonstrated the freedom of suffragettes from the bondage of a male-dominated world. They destroyed the objects they were supposed to idolise, rejected the masculine authority to which they were supposed to submit and affirmed in the most violent way possible that their bodies were their own and no one else's. If commemorating militancy as the essence of the suffrage struggle obscures the vital role of suffragists, this is understandable. Militancy not only helped achieve the 'bloodless revolution': it was the essence of that revolutionary spirit.

The Fight against Fascism

Nothing more than a wishy-washy Reformist Government
which, when all the big issues that really matter came
to be decided, would be swept along in the wake of a
capitalist policy.

Sylvia Pankhurst on the Labour Party in 1918[1]

For the Labour Party, as for the Women's Social and Political
Union and the National Union of Women's Suffrage Societies,
the First World War represented a watershed. Keir Hardie had
attempted to develop Labour into an internationalist, socialist
party opposed to imperialism and war. Yet, despite the grotesque
human carnage at the Somme and at Passchendaele, as hundreds
of thousands of men died under the relentless bark of machine
guns or drowned neck-deep in the grim mire of no-man's land,
anti-war sentiment never reached revolutionary proportions in
Britain as it had done in Russia. This was largely due to the fact
that fighting a 'total war' required the mass involvement of the
British people, both men and women. There were tangible benefits for many British workers. While strike action was forbidden by
agreement between the government and the TUC, that agreement
had also provided union leaders with new access to the political
executive, a relationship that would develop into a very powerful

connection over the next half-century. Even left-wing opponents of the war such as Ramsay MacDonald were forced to concede that the conflict had achieved far more social reform than had individual radical and trade union campaigns over the course of a century. With the creation of Lloyd George's three-party wartime coalition in December 1916, the Labour Party was brought into government. Social reformers such as William Beveridge and Seebohm Rowntree and even socialists like Beatrice Webb were involved in policy-making discussions. Public education was improved and the school leaving age raised to fourteen by H. A. L. Fisher's act of 1918. The way was opened up for subsidised local authority housing, and, with the creation of the new Ministry of Health, for the coordination of health services.

If the historical reports of the death of the Liberal Party after 1918 are greatly exaggerated, it was nonetheless Labour and the Conservatives who were the main beneficiaries of peace. Whereas the in-fighting between Asquith and Lloyd George during the war had weakened the Liberal Party, Labour emerged strengthened by the experience of the war years. Union membership had almost doubled and the anti-war stance of some of the party's left-wing members became increasingly attractive in the later, bloodiest stages of the conflict. Labour also gained most from the 1918 franchise reforms, which massively expanded the working-class electorate.

But electoral success brought its own problems. For much of the inter-war period Labour was caught between fighting off right-wing 'red scare' smears, which sought to link the Labour movement with communism, and attempting to present itself as a moderate, responsible party of government. These twin pressures tended to negate any move towards truly radical political solutions. Equally, the actual level of socialist intellectual commitment within the Labour movement was debatable, given that many members, including leading figures like Arthur Henderson, remained wedded to a radical-Liberal political philosophy. The political dominance of the left wing of the Labour Party was by and large a temporary aberration, restricted to periods of internal division such as the late 1970s and early 1980s. More importantly, thoroughgoing British socialist/communist parties proved resolutely unpopular and, in the case of the Communist Party of Great Britain, were really only sustained as a significant force by Soviet support. Arguably, this unpopularity stemmed not simply from the success of Conservative negative propaganda but also from the poor fit of organisations like the CPGB with well-established domestic political traditions.

The Labour Party constitution of 1918 is often felt to reflect the more confident socialist outlook of the party at this point, encapsulated in that great shibboleth of the Labour left, Clause IV. But Clause IV's promise 'to secure for the workers by hand or by brain the full fruits of their industry' arguably demonstrated the continued power of radical-Liberal traditions within the Labour Party, not the dominance of socialist ideology. As its author, the Fabian Sidney Webb, explained, its socialism was 'no more specific than a definite repudiation of the individualism that characterised all the political parties of the past generation and that still dominates the House of Commons'.[2] Harking back to an earlier trope of radical rhetoric, the language of Labour's new constitution was political, rather than sectional. It divided society not into economic classes, but into the 'idle' rich and the 'producers', a largely moral distinction.[3] In its reference to the 'workers by hand or by brain', it also reached out to white-collar workers and professionals. Even its famous commitment to common ownership was remarkably vague, or, perhaps more generously, flexible, and certainly not an endorsement of state socialism. Common ownership, as far as Webb was concerned, might include cooperatives and even partnership structures such as the John Lewis group, as well as nationalised industries under direct central government control.[4]

If this was 'wishy-washy' socialism, as Sylvia Pankhurst called it, it was also a well-tuned mission statement for a party that now aimed to tackle the Liberals head on in elections across the country, rather than ride upon its political coat-tails. It presented a party that was distinct enough from Liberalism without alienating either remaining radical Liberals within the party or the electorate. Significantly, Arthur Henderson, who had become party leader as a result of MacDonald's opposition to the war, barely mentioned socialism in his election speeches. Indeed, though Clause IV is often seen as representing the Labour Party's formal commitment to socialism, it was only in 1995, when Tony Blair successfully moved that the old Clause IV be replaced with a new text, that the constitution explicitly declared Labour to be a 'democratic social-ist party', precisely at the moment when 'New Labour' had ceased to resemble anything of the kind.

Though the Labour Party did not increase its number of MPs sig-nificantly at the 1918 election, in fact losing some leading figures such as Arthur Henderson, Philip Snowden and Ramsay MacDonald, its share of the vote rose to 22.2 per cent. It was start-ing to look like a realistic party of government, but this possibility, and the obstacles in its path, would now hang heavily over it for the next two decades. Lloyd George's coalition government came to an end on 19 October 1922 when it appeared that he had brought a war-weary nation to the brink of conflict once more, this time over the defence of the Greek position in Asia Minor and the protection of the Dardanelles from Turkey. In the subsequent elections, Labour supplanted the Liberals as the second-largest political party, and in January 1924, in coalition with the Liberals, the first Labour administration in British history was formed.

The government was not successful, however, and within nine months the new Prime Minister, Ramsay MacDonald, was forced to call a general election in the wake of the Liberals' refusal to back the lenient government line in the 'Campbell Case', concerning the prosecution of the editor of the communist *Workers' Weekly* for sedition, which MacDonald had seen as a political vote of con-fidence in his administration. The election was a disaster for

Labour: the party's results were badly affected by the publication of the so-called 'Zinoviev letter' in the *Daily Mail*. Purporting to have been sent by the Comintern to the CPGB, the letter advocated further pro-Soviet agitation within the British state, including in the armed forces, and ordered the proliferation of Leninist propaganda within the British Labour movement as a means to promote a rising of the proletariat. The letter was almost certainly a forgery, created by the Secret Intelligence Service (MI6) in order to smear Labour as a Trojan horse for Bolshevism and ensure a good electoral return for the Conservatives. MacDonald himself said that the publication of the letter left him feeling like a man 'sewn into a sack and thrown into the sea'. This shameful propaganda was successful in its ends, and the Conservatives emerged the majority party.

The relationship between the Labour Party and the Communist Party of Great Britain, founded in 1920, was fraught, not least because the CPGB, whatever the authenticity of the 'Zinoviev letter', was largely directed by Moscow and, until 1928, was intent on infiltrating the Labour movement. It was on Labour tickets that the communists Walter Newbold and Shapurji Saklavala, the Indian barrister, were elected in 1922. The CPGB could never pose a significant challenge to Labour's public support. However, it made up for its limited popular appeal with the hefty subsidies that it received from the Comintern, which in 1927 equalled two-thirds of the income of the much larger Labour Party.

This comparatively wealthy little party was able in 1931 to employ forty-one full-time staff, one for every 165 party members. Leading party workers earned as much as £5 a week, a considerable sum at a time of global economic depression and mass unemployment. Financial security underlined ideological commitment to ensure a relatively uncritical line towards the orders from the Comintern.[5] As the former CPGB member Eric Hobsbawm would later remark, 'We tell [the public] that we do not give the USSR "uncritical support", but when they ask us when we disagreed with its policy, all we can point to is Nina Ponomareva's hats.'[6]*

Aside from attempting to ally itself with the Labour Party, up to 1928 the CPGB also sought to develop, with some success, militant cadres within trade unions. Under the new Conservative administration of Stanley Baldwin, industrial relations, especially with the miners, which had already reached a low in the last years of the coalition government, deteriorated further. In April 1926, Baldwin refused to renew a subsidy to the mining industry; the following May, he broke off negotiations with the TUC delegation. The unions decided to call a general strike. From 3 to 12 May, Britain stood at a standstill. In the end, it was left to the TUC to call off the strike, though the miners continued to hold out for several bitter, fruitless months. The government had been preparing for such a manoeuvre for over nine months.

The belligerent Chancellor, Winston Churchill, took control of the TUC's newspaper, the *British Worker*, and order was maintained by hundreds of recently drafted special constables. The dispute ended with no guarantee secured from the government that the striking workers would be able to return to their jobs. For the miners, who had initiated the dispute, there was only a deterioration in their working conditions, as pit-owners imposed wage cuts and increased their working hours. The difficulty for the unions had already been demonstrated in 1921 with the strike of the 'triple alliance' of miners, railwaymen and dockers. As Lloyd George put it, the unions could paralyse the country with a general strike – 'We are at your mercy' – but for their action to be a success they would have to be prepared to take control of the government. Despite the efforts of the CPGB, true revolutionaries among the ranks of the TUC were hard to find. The union leaders were constitutionalists

* Ponomareva was a Soviet discus thrower who had been arrested for stealing hats from an Oxford Street store. In protest at her arrest, the Soviet team withdrew from the White City Games. The CPGB's *Daily Worker* newspaper broke with the Moscow line by describing the decision to withdraw as 'regrettable'.

and gradualists, like most of the Labour movement, and they could not contemplate overriding the usual channels of government.[7]

This was the fundamental problem, noted by the historian Henry Pelling, faced by the CPGB: it was 'a revolutionary party in a non-revolutionary situation'.[8] In the 1810s and 1840s, when the idea of a general strike had first been mooted, industrial action carried the scarcely concealed threat of insurrection. Now it represented no more than a temporary stop, which a well-prepared government could easily weather. Even so, despite this lack of militancy, with Labour having returned to power in May 1929, in the wake of the Wall Street Crash in October that year the government's initial concessions to the unions were followed by a much tougher line. With the majority of his Cabinet, MacDonald believed that the only solution to the crisis was to cut government spending and raise taxes in order to prop up the pound. The only significant voice of dissent within the administration came from the economist John Maynard Keynes, ostensibly a Liberal but in fact the prophet of the mixed economy and supply-side economics.

For MacDonald, however, it was vitally important that the still-young Labour Party present the face of a responsible party of government. Like so many Labour prime ministers after him, the quest for respectability led him further and further away from the party's roots. His government's policy led him into a direct confrontation with the unions, and it was a clash that MacDonald was determined to win, writing in August 1931: 'If we yield now to the TUC, we shall never be able to call our bodies or our souls or our intelligences our own.' The conflict led to a split within the Cabinet, Arthur Henderson and a significant minority of dissidents threatening their resignations should the spending cuts go ahead. On 23 August, MacDonald told King George V that every member of his Cabinet had resigned. Initially, MacDonald had intended to step down as well, but under pressure from Baldwin, Neville Chamberlain and the King himself he was persuaded to head up a 'national government' to deal with the economic crisis.

However, though this move briefly saw the pound rally, by late September the government was forced in any case to abandon the gold standard, as party in-fighting further weakened Britain's fragile economic confidence. MacDonald was forced to dissolve Parliament on 7 October and fresh elections were called.

The results proved a disaster for the Labour Party, whose fratricidal behaviour had witnessed a decline in their share of the popular vote – down by 1.5 million – and the lowest return of MPs for the party since 1918. For MacDonald, with a majority of five hundred, it was, however, a perverse kind of victory. By siding with the 'national government' rather than his old party, he had effectively become a prisoner to the whims of the Conservatives. The Tory line dominated economic policy and made no concessions to former advocates of free trade. MacDonald would continue as Prime Minister until 1935, but his influence, as well as his health, was rapidly failing. The attacks of old Labour colleagues cut him deeply: he was portrayed as a grasping social climber, satirised for his relationships with aristocratic women (namely, Lady Londonderry), and depicted as a man who had deliberately betrayed his party in order to gain the premiership. Afflicted by dimming sight and failing mental capacities, MacDonald sought solace in séances in which a medium called Grace Cooke claimed to put him in touch with his long-dead wife.

The rise of the far right threatened to make the internal squabbles between the Westminster parties an irrelevancy. By this stage, the threat of fascism had been brought home by the efforts of one of MacDonald's own former Cabinet colleagues, Oswald Mosley. Mosley had been expelled from the Labour Party in 1931 for forming his breakaway New Party that same year. The New Party had already shown signs of Mosley's future leanings in its preference for direct action over parliamentary politics, and its recruitment of 'enforcers' such as the boxer Kid Lewis to 'protect' its members from the efforts of Jewish and communist groups to expose the 'cloven hoof of fascism' that lay behind its agenda. Following a trip to Italy, during which he met Benito Mussolini, Mosley formed the British Union of Fascists in October 1932. The new movement found support from the press baron Lord Rothermere, whose paper, the *Daily Mail*, loudly proclaimed from its front page: 'Hurrah for the Blackshirts!' However, mainstream support for the BUF disintegrated after the violent end to the party's rally at Olympia on 7 June 1934, when stewards brutally ejected hecklers from the crowd.

Mosley himself was careful not to let his rhetoric stray too far into outright anti-Semitism, but he did nothing to suppress anti-Jewish action and rhetoric from his rank-and-file supporters. Matters culminated at the famous 'Battle of Cable Street' on 4 October 1936, when a legal march of BUF supporters, accompanied by a police escort to prevent disruption by anti-fascist groups, clashed with Jews, socialists and trade unionists, who had erected barricades to prevent them from coming through the East End. The anti-fascists succeeded in stalling the march and forced the BUF to disperse. The union between Jewish, socialist, Irish and communist groups that day formed powerful memories. One eyewitness, Professor Bill Fishman, who was fifteen at the time, recalled that he was moved to tears by the sight of 'bearded Jews and Irish Catholic dockers standing up to stop Mosley. I shall never forget that as long as I live, how working-class people could get together to oppose the evil of racism.'[9]

The 'Battle of Cable Street' is rightly celebrated as a victory against fascism, but nonetheless it sits, like the Jarrow 'Crusade' of the same month, rather uneasily within a history of the Labour movement. The actions of the two hundred unemployed men who marched from Wearside to London to petition the Prime Minister, Stanley Baldwin, for relief, were endorsed by neither the Labour Party nor the TUC. These organisations were concerned that the march might be affiliated with the communist-influenced National Unemployed Workers' Movement – indeed, the Jarrow men had called their action a 'crusade' in a bid to distance themselves from the NUWM. It was left to the MP for Jarrow and former communist 'Red' Ellen Wilkinson to raise the marchers' plight in the Commons. Despite her efforts, and the severity of economic conditions in Jarrow (unemployment ran to 72 per cent), the marchers returned with little more than their train fare back to the North East.

Similarly, not only did the Labour Party refuse to endorse the actions of anti-fascists at Cable Street, the party's leadership actively worked to suppress such militant activity. The local Labour MP for Whitechapel did support the Jewish petition for the BUF's march to be called off, but George Lansbury, the former party leader, would only go so far as to call for the march to be re-routed through 'less congested' areas. Those who chose to resist the march by force, he suggested, were only giving the BUF undue publicity. In the wake of the battle, the Labour conference (which had started on the eve of the march) condemned the actions of the fascists, the communists and Independent Labour Party activists. It did, though, also condemn the decision to let the march go ahead and called for new measures to prevent 'militarised politics'. The government put such measures into effect with the Public Order Act of the same year, which banned the wearing of uniforms in political demonstrations. However, the powers granted in the act were used more against anti-fascist groups than against Mosley's BUF.[16] This use of the act fulfilled the aims of the major Labour spokesman in favour of it, Herbert Morrison, then leader of the London County Council, who hoped it would be 'framed in such a way as to deal with Fascists or anybody else who wants to upset the constitutional liberties of this State by force or conspiracy, with the aid of money got from abroad'[17] – this last a clear dig at the CPGB as well as the BUF.

Labour's unease over the tactics deployed by the anti-fascists at Cable Street was linked to broader disquiet over the CPGB's leadership of the opposition to fascism in the 1930s. As Walter Citrine, the TUC General Secretary, argued,

The TUC stands for the principle of democracy against dictatorship, and it is not ready to make qualifications between the
dictatorship of the so-called proletariat, which is nothing more
than the dictatorship of a handful of Communists in Russia, and
the dictatorship of the Fascists. Let us be very careful to make clear
to the public at large that our principles are fundamentally different from those advanced by the Communist Party. They believe in
force and fighting on the streets, however they may disguise it.[12]

Though the CPGB had recently shifted from its policy of attacking the Labour Party to urging a 'united front' of Labour, the now
disaffiliated ILP and communists against the fascist threat, these
overtures were resisted. This resistance was not just the result of a
desire to oppose political extremism outside of the party. The
betrayal of 1931, with the establishment of a national government,
had led some within Labour itself to advocate more drastic measures. In 1933, Sir Stafford Cripps proposed that any newly elected
Labour government should immediately pass an Emergency
Powers Act and, if this were resisted by the Lords, meet the constitutional crisis head on and make the government 'temporarily
into a dictatorship'.[13] Statements like this, and Cripps's noisy disagreement with the party leadership over the 'united front', led to
his temporary ejection from the party. The Labour Party was also
ambivalent in its response to the fascist threat internationally,
initially favouring non-intervention in the Spanish Civil War, a
stance that allowed the CPGB to make considerable political capital from its role as a recruiting agent for International Brigades.[14]

By late 1937, though, largely through the efforts of Hugh
Dalton, the party's spokesman on foreign affairs, Labour had
shifted from semi-pacifism to opposition to appeasement and
support for rearmament. After Hitler's invasion of Poland, radical
journalists such as Frank Owen and the future Labour leader
Michael Foot lambasted the 'guilty men' who had supported
Chamberlain's policy of appeasement. Chamberlain resigned in

May 1940; Winston Churchill replaced him as Prime Minister; and Labour along with Liberals joined his government.

The conduct of Labour members of the War Cabinet massively enhanced the reputation of the party: Cripps jettisoned the image of left-wing maverick to become a highly effective minister in charge of aircraft production; Herbert Morrison evolved as a key figure on the home front; and Ernest Bevin, as Minister for Labour, managed the delicate balancing act of supplying the war effort while not only protecting but also enhancing workers' rights. However, although the War Cabinet projected a front of national unity, Churchill's premiership did not go uncriticised during the 1940s. Frank Owen, writing under the suitably radical pseudonym of 'Thomas Rainsboro', attacked the Prime Minister's failure to come to the aid of the Soviet Union following the German invasion of 1941, and repeatedly called for the opening of a second front to relieve the Russians.

The war effort transformed British society: as everyone pulled together, the nation was infused with a spirit of egalitarianism. The mood was reflected in the pioneering journalism of Tom Hopkinson and J. B. Priestley, feeding a conviction that, should peace come, this time the opportunity of creating a 'land fit for heroes' would not be squandered. The Beveridge Report of November 1942, with its promise of a 'cradle to grave' welfare system, made its dry, academic author an instant celebrity and popular figurehead. The white paper of 1944 underscored a government commitment to full employment, underpinned by a revolution in economic theory, which had seen the triumph of interventionist, Keynesian fiscal policy. What had seemed forward-thinking policies in the 1930s became necessities in the context of total war – industries were to be nationalised, inherited wealth was to be taxed, the medical profession was to become state-directed and publicly funded. A mood of popular radicalism could be detected in the country at large, with electoral successes for the Christian Socialist Common Wealth Party and widespread public enthusiasm for the Red Army and its heroic defeat of the Germans at Stalingrad.

Even Winston Churchill's revered status as war leader could do nothing to halt the tide of popular opinion moving towards the left. The election of 1945 saw a landslide unprecedented since the great Liberal victory of 1906, with Labour winning 394 seats to the Conservatives' 210. The quiet, clerkish, hitherto Deputy Prime Minister Clement Attlee was installed in 10 Downing Street as the head of a government with one of the largest popular mandates ever. The moment when Labour finally took power with a decisive majority was at once exhilarating and bewildering. The measures taken during the 1940s had all, by and large, been the product of the necessities of war. Now, with peace, an uncertain future presented itself to Britain's new governors. As one new minister, James Griffiths, put it, 'After this – what?'

The achievements of the Attlee government are without doubt the most celebrated in the history of the Labour Party. Here, it is often claimed, was a socialist administration that radically transformed British society through the creation of a welfare state and the nationalisation of key industries. The problem, though, was that these achievements were only partly those of Labour figures, and also, by 1945, they were not that radical. The Keynesian interventionist approach adopted towards the economy was now neither innovative nor, indeed, distinctly socialist: elements of it could be seen in Roosevelt's 'New Deal', in Lloyd George's later political works, even in the policies advocated by the New Party and the BUF. The key architect of the new system of social security, William Beveridge, was politically a Liberal and briefly stood in the Commons as MP for Berwick-upon-Tweed until he lost his seat in 1945 to a Conservative. And it was a Conservative politician, 'Rab' Butler, who was responsible for the formulation of the 1944 Education Act that laid the framework for a comprehensive system of education available to all.

Attlee's administration certainly scored many key victories, most notably Aneurin Bevan's successful creation of the National Health Service in 1946 in the face of fierce opposition from the British Medical Council, as well as the establishment in the same year of a national insurance system along the lines developed by Beveridge. However, these were achieved only by making significant concessions at various points. Public schools thrived, despite the advent of free state secondary education, as they reaped the financial rewards from their dubious status as charitable institutions. Bevan had to permit the medical profession to continue private practice and allow 'pay beds' within nationalised hospitals. The provision of public housing was limited by pressure from the building industry and from those who argued for a 'property-owning democracy'. These compromises would eventually lead Bevan and two other ministerial colleagues to resign in April 1951, over the imposition of NHS charges for dentures and spectacles.

Even the most apparently socialist element of government policy between 1945 and 1950, nationalisation, was less controversial than it seemed. In some cases, particularly that of coal, these were industries long earmarked for public control; in others, there was little resistance, as the government effectively took on loss-making enterprises. When Attlee's government stood for re-election in 1950, it was noticeably unambitious about rolling out the policy: only sugar, cement and water were listed as industries suitable to be taken under public control.[15] As the journalist Anthony Howard later remarked, 'Far from introducing a "social revolution" the overwhelming Labour victory of 1945 brought about the greatest restoration of traditional social values since 1660.'[16] By the start of the 1950s the Attlee administration had, in some ways, profoundly changed the nation. The creation of the NHS had helped cut infant mortality by half and the 'white plague' of tuberculosis had been virtually wiped out.[17] In other ways, however, the differences were almost imperceptible: the old terraced slums remained, their smoky coal fires providing the sole source of heat, and with communal lavatories still the norm for half of the nation's population.[18]

Gradually, though, postwar austerity gave way to growing affluence, supported by the safety-net of the welfare state, rising wages, negligible unemployment and easier consumer credit. In such a period of plenty, radical political solutions appeared unnecessary. Overall, the ideological ground between the two parties perceptibly narrowed during the 1950s and 1960s. In 1950 a group of nine Conservative MPs, including the future Prime Minister Edward Heath, produced the pamphlet *One Nation*, in which they committed themselves to the principle of full employment, describing it as the 'first responsibility of government'. The Labour Party lost the 1951 general election to the Conservatives, but neither Churchill, in his second term as Prime Minister, nor his successors, Eden, Macmillan and Douglas-Home, attempted to reverse the social policy of the first postwar administration. Keynesian economic policy continued to dominate government thinking, the unions retained their powers of collective bargaining and the welfare state was further entrenched.

Outside the political mainstream, more radical groups were faltering. The CPGB, by 1951, had committed itself to taking a parliamentary, reformist route towards a socialist Britain. British communism, always a numerically far smaller force than its Italian or French equivalents, was badly hit by the revelations of Khrushchev's secret speech to the Twentieth Congress of the Communist Party of the Soviet Union in which he denounced Stalin, and more cataclysmically by the actions of Warsaw Pact tanks and troops against Hungarian and Polish protesters in 1956. Peter Fryer covered the events for the *Daily Worker*, but saw that his dispatches were being doctored by the central party leadership. Their actions led Fryer and many other British communists to leave the party. By the 1960s the CPGB would, ironically, be represented in Parliament in the Upper House only, when Wogan Philips, a life-long member of the party, inherited his father's title as Lord Milford.

This political consensus built around Keynesian economics and the welfare state would remain relatively unchallenged until the 1970s. Even then, the resurgence of the left wing within Labour ranks, and the championing of figures such as Tony Benn by many constituency members, was more a reaction to present circumstances than the resurfacing of a suppressed strain of long-term thought within the party. From this point of view, the policy review initiated by Labour after its third successive election defeat to the Conservatives in 1987 represented an opportunity to return to the party's radical-Liberal roots. Recent far-left impositions such as withdrawal from the Common Market, unilateral nuclear disarmament and further nationalisation were swiftly jettisoned.[19] Rather than heralding the arrival of 'New Labour', the party's increasing emphasis in the 1990s on moral values, individual responsibility and 'social justice' rather than social planning really represented the revival of 'very old Labour'.

The achievements of the Labour Party have frequently been located in the British 'radical tradition'. In a sense, this represents no more than the continual process of agglomeration and re-invention that the tradition has undergone since the medieval period. It is like an old, familiar standard: the tune remains largely the same, but different players add flourishes of their own. The appropriation by Labour and the TUC of Cable Street and the Jarrow Crusade may represent a few bum notes. Equally, the new coda of the establishment of a welfare state might not be as radical or socialist as it might at first seem. If many Liberals and even some Conservatives could welcome the welfare state, equally, most leading Labour figures accepted the goodness of the constitution bequeathed by radical Liberalism and, if more indirectly, through the efforts of popular radicals including the Chartists. Voices such as that of Stafford Cripps in 1933, urging even a temporary Labour 'dictatorship', were swiftly marginalised.

This was more than an attempt to dodge 'red scare' tactics. In 1934, in the wake of the violent BUF rally at Olympia, Attlee told the Commons:

Whatever differences we may have with hon. Members in other parts of the House, I believe we all value our English political institutions. We feel in this House something that makes us all members one of another in the building up of the structure of Government, in which for so many years we have avoided these violent outbursts. We have managed to carry on and to make transformations in our society without rupturing friendly personal relations, without dividing house from house, without dividing our whole social life as it is divided in some continental countries by a political line. We believe that that tradition is worth preserving and that it is essential to preserve it.[20]

Despite the horror and barbarism of what subsequently unfolded in Europe, it is rarely asked whether the anti-fascists who used violence to combat the BUF pursued the right tactics. Certainly, their actions punctured the confidence of Mosley's Blackshirts, but the BUF was never a well-supported party and by the time of the 'Battle of Cable Street', its membership was already in decline. In fact, it was the broad support for the British constitution and parliamentary democracy, even during periods of acute economic depression and social distress, that made the country such a poor recruiting ground for either communists or fascists. The danger, though, was that the widespread acceptance of this constitutional tradition could, in turn, lead to a dangerous complacency about the security of British democracy.

EPILOGUE

I never thought I would be in the House of Commons on
the day Magna Carta was repealed.

Tony Benn, June, 2008[1]

On 18 June 2008, the Shadow Home Secretary David Davis
formally resigned as an MP in protest at the government's
narrow victory over the counter-terrorism bill and, specifically, the
extension of the limit for detention without charge from twenty-
eight to forty-two days. In his resignation speech, Davis alluded to
the upcoming anniversary of Magna Carta, 'a document that guarantees the fundamental element of British freedom, habeas corpus.
The right not to be imprisoned by the state without charge or
reason.'[2] Although, through his resignation, it was he who
attracted most press attention, other Conservative politicians,
including Sir John Major and Bill Cash, expressed their disgust at
the government's apparent assault on ancient British freedoms.[3]

The opponents of forty-two-day detention were a rather motley
crew, including old left-wingers such as Tony Benn, Conservatives
such as Davis and celebrities such as Sir Bob Geldof.[4] The invoca-
tion of Magna Carta may have been inaccurate: one columnist,
Simon Heffer, noted that Habeas Corpus was actually codified in
law in 1679, not 1215.[5] It may also have signified a misrepresentation

of the debate itself: Davis had already conceded that twenty-eight days' imprisonment without charge might be justified, surely itself a significant breach of 'ancient liberties'. Yet, the controversy sparked by his resignation revealed the enduring power of the belief that Magna Carta is a talisman of British liberty. It was a belief that could unite a civil liberties campaigner, Shami Chakrabarti of Liberty, with an old Eurosceptic MP, Bill Cash, if not necessarily inspire the voters of Haltemprice and Howden. (Though Davis won the by-election with 72 per cent of the vote, he had no significant opponents and the voter turnout was half that of the 2005 general election.[6])

The campaign over forty-two-day detention does not mark the first time in recent years that Britain's radical tradition has attracted some odd political bedfellows. In an article published in September 2006 promoting his part-memoir, part-musing on national identity, *The Progressive Patriot*, the left-wing singer-songwriter Billy Bragg wrote that reading about Britain's 'tradition of dissent' had taught him that

> the freedom I enjoyed had had to be fought for, from the Peasants' Revolt to the Diggers & the Levellers, to the Chartists and the Suffragettes. For the first time I heard of Tom Paine and the Tolpuddle Martyrs, of *The Ragged Trousered Philanthropists* and the Battle of Cable Street. I began to appreciate how the Labour land-slide of 1945 had shaped my life through the establishing of the Welfare State.[7]

Bragg's book was prompted by the election of a British National Party councillor in his home borough of Barking. It contributed to a long tradition of works by (mainly English) left-wing writers, politicians and performers who sought to 'reclaim the flag' from the far right. The irony, however, was that not only had the BNP appropriated the flag, but their election manifesto had co-opted Bragg's cherished 'tradition of dissent'. The 2005 BNP manifesto, entitled *Rebuilding British Democracy*, described the country as 'the birthplace of modern democracy' and claimed:

> From Magna Carta to the Peasants' Revolt, through the Levellers, the Chartists, the early Labour movement and the suffragettes, we have defied the executioner, the rack, and the prison door to wrest liberty of conscience, speech, action, and political association from monarchs, barons and bosses, and from popes, priests and censors.[8]

The fact that both Bragg and the BNP could see themselves as inheritors of the same 'radical tradition' is a reminder of that tradition's malleability. For Bragg, it was inevitably hitched to the Labour movement. Yet there was much, historically, of the radical tradition that could appeal to Conservatives, too. The 'state socialism' that formed one strand of the Labour Party's ideological heritage, though a relatively minor one, arguably sat less well with most British radical movements than did the historical Liberal/modern Conservative emphasis on low taxation, individualism and self-reliance. Thomas Paine may have wanted to redistribute taxation to fund pensions and education, but he was generally in favour of reducing the burden of taxes. Through most of the eighteenth, nineteenth and early twentieth centuries, radical thinkers such as Paine distinguished between the 'idle' and the 'deserving' rich, though the identity of these fat-cats shifted over time from aristocratic landlords to plutocratic capitalists. Few radical movements were genuinely intent on social 'levelling', and even those figures who did advocate land reform, such as Thomas Spence or Feargus O'Connor, largely did so with the dream of creating a Britain of self-sufficient, independent smallholders. The urge remained at root individualist, or at best localist, rather than collectivist. This historical preference for a smaller rather than a bigger role for the state was scarcely surprising, given that for most of British history the main business of government was to wage war, to raise funds to pay for it and to recruit men to fight it. The impact of war taxation and conscription was felt hardest by the poor. Until even the second half of the twentieth century, local communities, rather than central government, were seen as the best engine for social and economic reform.

As the debate over forty-two-day detention demonstrated, there was also a powerful, if ambiguous, strain of British radicalism that venerated the nation's law as the embodiment of its liberties. One of the most distinctive features of late medieval English society was its remarkable litigiousness, and resort to the courts remained a key way of both publicising and defending radical causes. Figures such as John Lilburne, John Wilkes and William Hone largely owed their prominence in the radical pantheon to their appearances before the bench. There was an important element of radical thinking that saw the law as it presently operated in Britain as largely a tool of the ruling classes, evident in the writing of Gerrard Winstanley, the Levellers, William Godwin and later the militant suffragettes. Even so, many of these same figures continued to believe that there was a historic set of freedoms, usually located in a misty Anglo-Saxon Utopia, which, if recovered, would gift people their full rights and liberties.

The veneration of British law – which generally meant English common law – points to one other feature of this 'radical tradition' that appeals to Conservatives, and even leaves it open to manipulation by the far right: its predominantly patriotic outlook. This became especially pronounced after 1815, as British radicals strove to dissociate themselves from loyalist accusations of treachery, given weight by the pro-French rhetoric of radicals such as Paine. However, even during the height of British revolutionary Francophilia, Paine's associates in the London Corresponding Society had continued to base their arguments on English legal precedents – the 1689 Bill of Rights, for example – and framed their language in terms of what the historian James Epstein has accurately described as the British 'constitutionalist idiom'.[9] The Levellers too, while talking of natural human rights, invoked the language of the 'freeborn Englishman', liberty as the birthright of a particular nation.

This yoking together of freedom and Britishness has continued, through the writing of George Orwell in *The Lion and the Unicorn*, to the present day, with Gordon Brown's calls for a new sense of national identity constructed around British values of 'liberty, tolerance and fair play'. The BNP would certainly struggle to live up to the second of those values. It is hard to see how British radical movements such as the Chartists, which included prominent black members and supported the abolition of the slave trade, or the suffragettes, who included leading anticolonialists such as Sylvia Pankhurst, can fit into the BNP's bleached-white vision of Britain. Yet, in the radical tradition's appropriation by the far right, we can nonetheless see some of the dangers in claiming universal values such as tolerance, fairness and liberty as peculiarly British.

The debate over forty-two-day detention presents us with a problem, but also an opportunity. The problem rests in the persistent belief that our rights are defended by ancient charters of liberties such as Magna Carta and that such rights are under threat from laws such as the Counter-Terrorism Act. In fact, as we have seen, though portions of the Great Charter continue to have the force of law, they do not prevent people from being either forcibly detained or exiled against their will. The Counter-Terrorism Act represents not so much an assault on British freedom, but rather the very limited nature of British liberty itself. At the root of this weakness lies the untrammelled power of Parliament. As Judith Mather, a British political scientist who conducted a survey of European representative institutions in 2000, concluded:

> If democracy requires the existence of popular rights, the British constitution provides for none. Parliament may make provision for freedom of expression, for regular elections, for freedom of the individual from arbitrary or unnecessary interference. Parliament

may legislate to increase equality in any or all of its manifestations. However, Parliament need do none of these things and it has the ultimate authority within the Constitution to abolish popular rights, and to rewrite the constitutional documents that have hitherto enshrined them.[10]

Most recently, the British Parliament's ability to ignore the will of the people has been amply demonstrated by the Commons' vote in support of the invasion of Iraq, despite massive public demonstrations against the war.

Unfortunately, one other legacy of the patriotic element of the British 'radical tradition' has been the tendency to dismiss 'foreign' perspectives or ideas. Indeed, it might be said that the British emphasis on freedom as emerging organically from the steady progress of time tends by its very nature to be inimical to ideas full stop. There is a touch of this ideological jingoism in David Cameron's recent call for a new British 'bill of rights', which would replace strange importations into our native law such as the 1998 Human Rights Act – according to Cameron, 'practically an invitation to terrorists to come to Britain'.[11] Yet, opportunistic as Cameron's idea was, some body of specially protected British constitutional law, incorporating the rights of the citizen, is surely necessary if further assaults by the government on civil liberties are to be prevented. The cross-party opposition to forty-two-day detention has provided an opportunity for non-partisan discussion of what such a statement of rights should contain. One recent, astonishingly radical, product of this debate has been the draft bill of rights produced by the Commons Committee on Human Rights. Dispensing with the pessimistic and authoritarian language of 'duties', 'values' and 'responsibilities' favoured by the Brown government, the draft bill of rights incorporates not only classical civil liberties – freedom of expression, association and conscience – but key social and economic rights such as free healthcare, free education and a decent standard of living.[12]

History can play a vital role in informing and inspiring this discussion of our rights and liberties. The 2006 *Guardian* competition to find Britain's most overlooked moment of radical history offered a valuable reminder that, as a nation, we can call upon a rich democratic heritage. It has rightly emphasised the importance of place and community in sustaining the memory of that tradition, a tradition that is so much more than the stuff of history books. But such celebrations of our democratic heritage can be counterproductive if all they do is encourage backward-looking complacency, and we should remember that radical groups have attempted, sometimes successfully, to change the world they inhabit. As Patrick Wright has noted, it seems rather perverse to recall such dynamic movements by freezing them 'as fond figures in the historical memory'.[13]

Instead, this book has emphasised the many ways in which radical movements have succeeded. We owe many of the political rights we now enjoy to the actions of these groups and individuals. It is important to remember their achievements, as all too often the history of progressive movements in this country is unfairly depicted as a string of heroic failures. Yet, right as it is to celebrate the victories of the British 'radical tradition', we do need to acknowledge its failures too. 'Freedom' did not, with apologies to Tennyson, 'slowly broaden down / From precedent to precedent'. It moved in fits and starts, with many a backward step taken. As we have seen, the intense radical ferment of the 1640s and 1650s was largely forgotten until the late nineteenth century. The exercise of voting rights diminished over the course of the eighteenth century and the early nineteenth. Even with the passage of the 1832 Reform Act, alterations in the franchise and, most of all, population growth meant that fewer men as a proportion of the population now exercised the vote than did in the age of Queen Anne (5.2 as opposed to 4.7 per cent), and women for the first time had been formally disenfranchised.[14]

These failures and setbacks remind us that, especially given our antiquated constitutional and electoral system, our fragile freedoms need to be jealously guarded if they are not to be encroached upon. The recent debate over counter-terrorism laws and the supposed threat to our 'Magna Carta rights' offers a reminder that we should be sure we are venerating the substance of liberty and not merely its symbols. The radical journalist Thomas Wooler approached the nub of the problem in the first issue of his periodical, the *Black Dwarf*, back in January 1817:

> States must either proceed, or retrograde. While we contented ourselves with boasting of our advance, we have been silently, but rapidly falling back . . . The people ought to have remembered that they were the guardians of the constitution. Instead of that the simpletons expected protection from the constitution; which is in fact nothing but the recorded merits of our ancestors. The country has boasted of being free, because Magna Charta was enacted; when the least share of penetration would have taught us, that Magna Charta was only enacted because our ancestors were *determined to be* free. Our ancestors, with swords in their hands, and the tyrant John on his knees before them, would have been just as free, whether they had insisted upon the signature of Magna Charta, or not. Their freedom was in their power, and their will.[15]

Our freedom lies in our power. Pessimists may point to demonstrations against the war in Iraq as evidence of modern government's capacity to ignore the will of the people. However, the millions who marched against that illegal war also remind us of the readiness of the British people once again, in the words of Shelley, to rise 'like lions after slumber'. This is the lesson of Britain's radical history: the struggle for our freedom goes on.

NOTES

Abbreviations

CWTP   P. S. Foner, ed., *The Complete Writings of Thomas Paine* (2 vols, New York, 1969)
ODNB   *Oxford Dictionary of National Biography*
TMEWC   E. P. Thompson, *The Making of the English Working Class* (rev. edn, London, 1968)

INTRODUCTION

1 H. E. Marshall, *Our Island Story: A History of Britain for Boys and Girls from the Romans to Queen Victoria* (Civitas reprint, Bath, 2005), p. 68.

2 My account of the cakes myth here is based on ibid., pp. 67–8.

3 For the origins of the story see A. P. Smyth, *King Alfred the Great* (Oxford, 1995), ch. 13.

4 Quoted in D. Horspool, *Why Alfred Burned the Cakes: A King and his Eleven-Hundred-Year Afterlife* (London, 2006), pp. 148–9; see also S. Keynes, 'The cult of King Alfred', *Anglo-Saxon England*, 28 (1999), 225–357.

5 Quoted in P. Readman, 'The place of the past in English culture, c. 1890–1914', *Past and Present*, 186 (2005), 147–201, at 182.

6 Horspool, *Why Alfred Burned the Cakes*, p. 194.

7 Marshall, *Our Island Story*, p. 73.

8 Ibid., p. 71.

9 See John Clare, 'Any questions? This week, making history', *Daily Telegraph*, 15 June 2005.

10 A. Roberts, 'Parenting: death, poison, treachery – the best bedtime read', *The Times*, 3 July 2005.

11 T. Hunt, 'Conscription of the past', *Guardian*, 11 June 2005.

12 A. Fraser, 'Great stories that will bring the past to life for a new generation', *Daily Telegraph*, 23 June 2006.

13 Marshall, *Our Island Story*, p. 72.

14 Ibid., p. 73.

15 Ibid., p. 157.

16 Ibid., p. 87.

17 For the 'Norman yoke' see C. Hill, 'The Norman yoke', in his *Puritanism and Revolution* (London, 1958), ch. 3; and M. Chibnall, *The Debate on the Norman Conquest* (Manchester, 1999).

18 Marshall, *Our Island Story*, pp. 167–8.

19 Ibid., p. 227.

20 Ibid., ch. 78.

21 R. Mitchell, 'H. E. Marshall', in H. C. G. Matthew and B. Harrison, eds, *ODNB*.

22 Marshall, *Our Island Story*, p. 15.

23 Mitchell, 'Marshall', *ODNB*.

24 Marshall, *Our Island Story*, p. 364.

25 H. E. Marshall, *The Story of Oliver Cromwell* (London, 1907), p. vi.

26 M. Sawer, 'Pacemakers for the World?', in her, ed., *Elections: Full, Free and Fair* (Annandale, NSW, 2001), ch. 1.

27 For Don see S. Merrifield, 'Don, Charles Jardine (1820–1866)', *Australian Dictionary of Biography* (Melbourne, 1972).

28 Quoted in P. A. Pickering, 'A Wider Field in a New Country: Chartism in Colonial Australia', in Sawer, ed., *Elections: Full, Free and Fair*, ch. 2, p. 34.

29 Ibid., p. 39.

30 Quoted in P. A. Pickering, '"The hearts of millions": Chartism and popular monarchism in the 1840s', *History*, 88 (2003), 227–48, at 238.

31 Ibid., 232; see also R. G. Hall, 'Creating a People's History: Political Identity and History in Chartism, 1832–1848', in O. Ashton, R. Fyson and S. Roberts, eds, *The Chartist Legacy* (Woodbridge, 1999), ch. 10, esp. p. 237.

32 Ibid., p. 232.

33 G. Brown, 'The golden thread that runs through our history', *Guardian*, 8 July 2004.

34 *OED*.

35 Nathaniel Bacon, *An historical and political discourse of the laws and government of England* (1689 edn), p. 175; see the similar use of 'radical' made by Sir Robert Filmer in his 'The Anarchy of a limited or Mixed Monarchy', published in *The Freeholder's Grand Inquest* (1679 edn), pp. 281–2.

36 See C. Condren, *The Language of Politics in Seventeenth-Century England* (Basingstoke, 1994), ch. 5.

37 Quoted in G. Burgess and M. Festenstein, eds, *English Radicalism, 1550–1850* (Cambridge, 2007), p. 4.

38 C. Hill, 'From Lollards to Levellers', in M. Cornforth, ed., *Rebels and Their Causes: Essays in Honour of A. L. Morton* (London, 1978), ch. 3.

39 I owe the athletic metaphor to Burgess's Introduction in Burgess and Festenstein, eds, *English Radicalism*.

40 G. E. Aylmer, 'Collective mentalities in mid-seventeenth century England: III varieties of radicalism', *Transactions of the Royal Historical Society*, 5th

series, 38 (1988), 1–25; for another important but slightly more elaborate working definition see J. C. Davis, 'Radicalism in a traditional society: the evaluation of radical thought in the English Commonwealth 1649–1660', *History of Political Thought*, 3 (1982), 193–213.

41 See E. Hobsbawm and T. Ranger, eds, *The Invention of Tradition* (Cambridge, 1983).

42 Nora's original term was *lieu de mémoire*, 'memory place', P. Nora, *Realms of Memory: Rethinking the French Past* (3 vols, New York, 1996–8).

PART ONE: A TALISMAN OF LIBERTY

1 David Redden, vice-chairman of Sotheby's, New York, quoted in J. Barron, 'Magna Carta is going on the auction block', *New York Times*, 25 September 2007.

2 A. Pallister, *Magna Carta: The Heritage of Liberty* (Oxford, 1971), p. 1.

CHAPTER 1

1 V. H. Galbraith, 'Penrose Memorial Lecture: Runnymede revisited', *Proceedings of the American Philosophical Society*, 110 (1966), 307–317, at 310.

2 A similar characterisation was offered by John Arden, who described King John in the notes on his play as 'corpulent, short, with dark hair turning to grey and going bald, well-trimmed beard, a grinning wolfish mouth full of bad teeth'. J. Arden, *Left-Handed Liberty: A Play about Magna Carta* (London, 1965), p. v.

3 For these wars, see F. McLynn's *Lionheart and Lackland: King Richard, King John and the Wars of Conquest* (London, 2006), esp. pp. 404–10.

4 Quoted in D. Danziger and J. Gillingham, *1215: The Year of Magna Carta* (London, 2003), p. 267.

5 See W. Morris, *Signs of Change: Seven Lectures Delivered on Various Occasions* (London, 1888), pp. 65–6.

6 My narrative of the events surrounding Magna Carta is based on Danziger and Gillingham, *1215*.

7 Quoted in J. Gillingham, 'Historians without Hindsight: Coggeshall, Diceto and Howden on the Early Years of John's Reign', in S. D. Church, ed., *King John: New Interpretations* (Woodbridge, 1999), ch. 1, p. 1.

8 Pallister, *Magna Carta*, p. 3

9 On this see Sir J. C. Holt, *Magna Carta* (2nd edn, Cambridge, 1992), p. 9.

10 Ibid., p. 10.

11 M. Ashley, *Magna Carta in the Seventeenth Century* (Charlottesville, 1965), p. 4.

12 Ibid., p. 1.

13 Holt, *Magna Carta*, p. 5.

14 Sir Ivor Jennings, *Magna Carta and Its Influence on the World Today* (London, 1965), pp. 9–11.

15 Sir Herbert Butterfield, *Magna Carta in the Historiography of the Sixteenth and Seventeenth Centuries* (Reading, 1968), pp. 7–9.

16 Holt, *Magna Carta*, pp. 10–11.

17 Ashley, *Magna Carta*, p. 31.

18 See R. B. Seaberg, 'The Norman Conquest and the feudal law: the Levellers and the argument from continuity', *Historical Journal*, 24 (1981), 791–806.

19 Pallister, *Magna Carta*, p. 18.

20 Ibid., p. 15.

21 Ibid., p. 17.

22 Ibid., p. 41.

23 Ibid., p. 47.

24 Ibid., p. 55.

25 Ibid., p. 60.

26 Ibid., p. 64.

27 Ibid., p. 57.

28 Ibid., p. 77.

29 Ibid., p. 69; see also M. Thale, ed., *Selections from the Papers of the London Corresponding Society 1792–1799* (Cambridge, 1983), p. 106.

30 Pallister, *Magna Carta*, p. 74.

31 Morris, *Signs of Change*, p. 64.

32 'Runnymede issue still before the world: archbishop on the lesson of Magna Carta', *The Times*, 11 June 1965.

33 'Freedom society protests', *The Times*, 11 June 1965.

34 *750th Anniversary of Magna Carta 15th June 1215–1965* (London, 1965).

35 Jennings, *Magna Carta*, pp. 36–8.

36 'An English hillside . . . for ever America', *Daily Mirror*, 15 May 1965; 'Kennedy family coming for memorial inauguration', *The Times*, 8 May 1965; 'The Queen inaugurates Kennedy memorial – three acres of America in Runnymede', *The Times*, 15 May 1965; Lord Denning, 'Runnymede, fount of English liberty', *The Times*, 9 June 1965.

37 A. O'Hagan, 'Magna Carta means nothing to the Scots', *Daily Telegraph*, 31 May 2006.

38 L. Colley, *Britons: Forging the Nation, 1707–1837* (London, 1992).

39 Jennings, *Magna Carta*, p. 23.

40 Quoted in L. Blom-Cooper, 'The role of the judge in modern society', *Political Quarterly*, 57 (1986), 144–55, at 144.

41 Quoted in J. Pilger, *Freedom Next Time* (London, 2006), p. 38.

42 Ibid., pp. 20–1.

43 On the case of the Chagos Islanders see R. Gifford, 'The Chagos Islands – the land where human rights hardly ever happen', *Law, Social Justice and Global Development*, 1 (2004), http://elj.warwick.ac.uk/global/issue/2004-1/gifford.html; Pilger, *Freedom Next Time*, ch. 1; S. Bangaroo, 'A short analysis of the exile of an indigenous population from beginning to end', *Hertfordshire Law Journal*, 3 (2005), 3–7; 'Foreign Office challenges Chagos Island [sic] ruling', *Guardian*, 5 February 2007.

44 P. Oborne, 'Magna Carta 2007 – an updated version to protect us from an overweening state', *Daily Mail*, 27 September 2007.

45 Hoffmann is quoted in the full judgement of the 2000 case of the Chagos Islanders vs Government, http://www.hmcourts-service.gov.uk/judgments-files/j501/queen_v_fco.htm.

46 R. Hilton, *Bond Men Made Free* (London, 1973), p. 231.

PART TWO: WHEN ADAM DELVED AND EVE SPAN

CHAPTER 2

1 Quoted in Hilton, *Bond Men Made Free*, pp. 11–12

2 For these revolts see ibid., ch. 2; C. Wickham, *Framing the Early Middle Ages* (Oxford, 2005), ch. 9.

3 Channel 4 Television used the title for its series of documentaries on the period.

4 R. S. Dobson, ed., *The Peasants' Revolt* (London, 1970), p. 60.

5 Ibid., pp. 62–3.

6 Ibid., p. 61.

7 http://www.fordham.edu/halsall/seth/statute-labourers.html, accessed on 20 September 2007.

8 F. E. Baldwin, 'Sumptuary legislation and personal regulation in England', *Johns Hopkins University Studies in Historical and Political Science*, 44 (1926), 44–6; see also Alan Hunt, 'The governance of consumption: sumptuary laws and shifting forms of regulation', *Economy and Society*, 25 (1996), 410–27; Alan Hunt, *The Governance of the Consuming Passions: A History of Sumptuary Law* (Basingstoke, 1996).

9 J. Whittle, 'Peasant Politics and Class Consciousness: The Norfolk Rebellions of 1381 and 1549 Compared', in C. Wickham, ed., *Rodney Hilton's Middle Ages*, *Past and Present*, Supplement 2 (2007), 233–47, at 239.

10 A. Dunn, *The Peasants' Revolt: England's Failed Revolution of 1381* (2nd edn, Stroud, 2004), p. 26.

11 Parts of this law remain in force, although elements were excised in 1948; http://www.statutelaw.gov.uk/content.aspx?LegType=All+Primary&PageNumber=107&NavFrom=2&parentActiveTextDocId=1517690&ActiveTextDocId=1517690&filesize=9654, accessed on 20 September 2007.

12 Dunn, *Peasants' Revolt*, pp. 72–3.

13 Dobson, ed., *Peasants' Revolt*, p. 132.

14 Dunn, *Peasants' Revolt*, pp. 83–4.

15 Dobson, ed., *Peasants' Revolt*, p. 133.

16 Hilton, *Bond Men Made Free*, pp. 141–2.

17 See on this A. Musson, *Medieval Law in Context: The Growth of Legal Consciousness from Magna Carta to the Peasants' Revolt* (Manchester, 2001), pp. 243–4; M. Aston, 'Corpus Christi and Corpus Regni: heresy and the Peasants' Revolt', *Past and Present*, 143 (1994), 3–47.

18 A. Prescott, 'Wat Tyler', *ODNB*.

19 A. Prescott, 'John Ball', *ODNB*.
20 S. Justice, *Writing and Rebellion: England in 1381* (London, 1994), ch. 2.
21 Quoted in Hilton, *Bond Men Made Free*, p. 222.
22 Quoted in Dunn, *Peasants' Revolt*, pp. 81–2.
23 Ibid., p. 103.
24 Ibid., p. 105.
25 Ibid., pp. 107–9.
26 Quoted in Dobson, ed., *Peasants' Revolt*, p. 184.
27 Ibid., p. 172
28 Dunn, *Peasants' Revolt*, p. 125.
29 Ibid., p. 174.
30 See on this Musson, *Medieval Law in Context*, pp. 250–2.
31 Dunn, *Peasants' Revolt*, p. 133.
32 Dobson, ed., *Peasants' Revolt*, p. 246.
33 Ibid., p. 258.
34 Ibid., p. 260.
35 Ibid., p. 261.
36 G. Harriss, *Shaping the Nation: England, 1360–1461* (Oxford, 1998), p. 234.
37 P. B. Munsche, *Gentlemen and Poachers: The English Game Laws 1671–1831* (Cambridge, 1981), p. 11.
38 Quoted in Harriss, *Shaping the Nation*, p. 254.

CHAPTER 3

1 I. M. W. Harvey, *Jack Cade's Rebellion of 1450* (Oxford, 1991), p. 26.
2 R. A. Griffiths, *The Reign of King Henry VI* (2nd edn, Stroud, 1998), p. 139.
3 Ibid., p. 140.
4 Harvey, *Cade's Rebellion*, pp. 29–30. See also M. E. Aston, 'Lollardy and sedition, 1381–1431', *Past and Present*, 17 (1960), 1–44.
5 M. Mate, 'The economic and social roots of medieval popular rebellion: Sussex in 1450 to 1451', *Economic History Review*, 45 (1992), 661–76, at 672.
6 M. Bohna, 'Armed force and civic legitimacy in Jack Cade's revolt, 1450', *English Historical Review*, 118 (2003), 563–82, at 578.
7 Harvey, *Cade's Rebellion*, p. 88.
8 For a modernised text of the complaint see http://en.wikisource.org/wiki/The_Complaint_of_the_Poor_Commons_of_Kent, accessed on 7 October 2007.
9 I. M. W. Harvey, 'Was There Popular Politics in Fifteenth-Century England?', in R. H. Britnell and A. J. Pollard, eds, *The McFarlane Legacy: Studies in Late Medieval Politics and Society* (Stroud, 1995), pp. 155–74, at p. 164.
10 Bohna, 'Armed force and civic legitimacy', 575.

11 Mate, 'Economic and social roots of medieval popular rebellion', 674

12 Ibid., 664.

13 Harvey, 'Popular politics', pp. 167–68.

CHAPTER 4

1 A. Wood, *The 1549 Rebellions and the Making of Early Modern England* (Cambridge, 2007), pp. 262–3.

2 A good summary is offered in S. Hindle, *The State and Social Change, c. 1550–1640* (Basingstoke, 2000), pp. 44–8.

3 See A. C. Jones, '"Commotion Time": The English Rising of 1549' (unpublished Warwick University Ph.D. thesis, 2003), p. 33 and ch. 1 passim. Attacks on game occurred elsewhere in 1549: see ibid., pp. 113–14.

4 C. E. Moreton, 'The Walsingham conspiracy of 1537', *Historical Research*, 63 (1990), 29–43

5 Norwich Cathedral Ledger Book, NRO, DCN 47/1, f. 71.

6 Norfolk Record Office, COL/9/117, f. 1.

7 On the identity of the leader of the 'Commonwealth of Kent', see J. D. Alsop, 'Latimer, the "Commonwealth of Kent" and the 1549 rebellions', *Historical Journal*, 28 (1985), 379–83.

8 See Jones, '"Commotion Time"', p. 167.

9 D. MacCullough, 'Kett's rebellion in context', *Past and Present*, 84 (1981), 36–59, at 39.

10 Wood, *1549 Rebellions*, pp. 62–3.

11 B. L. Beer, 'The Commoyson in Norfolk, 1549: a narrative of popular rebellion in sixteenth-century England', *Journal of Medieval and Renaissance Studies*, 6 (1976), 80–99, at 87.

12 NRO COL/9/117, f. 2v.

14 MacCullough, 'Kett's rebellion in context', 46.

15 Ibid., 45–6.

16 A. Neville, *Norfolke Furies*, trans. R. Wood (London, 1623), sig. I1v; and see Beer, 'Commoyson in Norfolk', 94; the incident is recounted in A. Wood, 'Kett's Rebellion', in C. Rawcliffe and R. Wilson, eds, *Medieval Norwich* (London, 2004), pp. 282–4.

17 Neville, *Norfolke Furies*, sig. I4r.

18 Ibid., sig. K4r.

19 Wood, *1549 Rebellions*, p. 71.

20 Ibid., p. 72.

21 R. B. Manning, 'The rebellions of 1549 in England', *Sixteenth-Century Journal*, 10 (1979), 93–99, at 98.

22 Quoted in D. K. Baker, 'Topical Utopias: radicalising humanism in sixteenth-century England', *Studies in English Literature*, 36 (1996), 1–30, at 28n.

23 Ibid., passim.

24 Quoted in A. Wood, *Riot, Rebellion and Popular Politics in Early Modern England* (Basingstoke, 2002), pp. 70–1.

25 Jones, "'Commotion Time'", p. 176; Somerset paid Latimer £4 for his assistance in pacifying the Kent and Sussex rebels.

26 M. Bush, 'Debate: Protector Somerset and the 1549 rebellions: a postrevision questioned', *English Historical Review*, 115 (2000), 103–12, at 109.

27 The novelty of Somerset's policies is clearly delineated by Ethan Shagan, "'Popularity" and the 1549 rebellions revisited', *English Historical Review*, 115 (2000), 121–33.

28 Jones, "'Commotion Time'", p. 161.

29 Quoted in Wood, *Riot, Rebellion and Popular Politics*, pp. 73–4.

30 Hindle, *State and Social Change*, p. 47.

31 J. Walter, A "rising of the people"? The Oxfordshire rising of 1596', *Past and Present*, 107 (1985), 90–143.

32 See J. Walter, 'Robert Kett', *ODNB*.

33 G. Kett, *The Pedigree of Kett of Wymondham, co. Norfolk. AD 1180–1913* (Cambridge, 1913), Preface.

34 Quoted in Wood, *1549 Rebellions*, p. 261.

35 See Justice, *Writing and Rebellion*, ch. 5; Wood, *1549 Rebellions*, ch. 6.

36 See, for example, A. L. Morton's Communist Party of Great Britain pamphlet, *When the People Arose: The Peasants' Revolt of 1381* (London, 1981).

37 See the work of M. L. Bush, summarised in 'The Risings of the Commons in England, 1381–1549', in J. Denton, ed., *Orders and Hierarchies in Late Medieval and Renaissance Europe* (Manchester, 1999), ch. 7; in a broader context see P. Zagorin, *Rebels and Rulers, 1500–1600*, vol. 1, *Society, States and Early Modern Revolution: Agrarian and Urban Rebellions* (Cambridge, 1982), chs 3, 7.

38 For example, G. Fourqin, *The Anatomy of Popular Rebellion in the Middle Ages* (Amsterdam, 1978), p. 25; A. D. Wall, *Power and Protest in England, 1525–1640* (London, 2000).

39 Justice, *Writing and Rebellion*, p. 45. In a broader European context see S. K. Cohn, 'Popular Insurrection and the Black Death: A Comparative View', in C. Wickham, ed., *Rodney Hilton's Middle Ages: Past and Present*, Supplement 2 (2007), 188–204, at 203–4; S. K. Cohn, *Lust for Liberty: The Politics of Social Revolt in Medieval Europe: 1200–1425, Italy, France and Flanders* (Cambridge, Mass., 2006).

40 A. Fletcher and D. MacCullough, *Tudor Rebellions* (5th edn, Harlow, 2004), p. 13.

PART THREE: THE POOREST HE . . . THE GREATEST HE

1 Quoted in Burgess and Festenstein, eds, *English Radicalism*, p. 4.

2 Tony Benn, 'The Levellers' legacy', extracts from speech given at the second 'Levellers' Day' in 1976, at http://www.channel4.com/history/microsites/H/history/a-b/benn.html.

CHAPTER 5

1 The same source claimed that Den or Denne was in fact the 'Emissary' of the Grandees: J. Wood, *The Levellers falsely so-called* (1649), p. 8.

2 *The Declaration of the Prince of Wales to the Commissioners of Scotland . . . also The Declaration and Speeches of Cornet Thompson and the rest of the Levellers* (1649), p. 3.

3 T. Vallance, 'Celebrating England's radical history', newstatesman.com, 23 May 2007; see also J. Blundell, 'The invention of a radical tradition: the case of the Levellers and "The Business at Burford"', paper presented at the British Marxist Historians and the Making of Social Movements conference, Edgehill College, 2002.

4 B. Manning, *The Far Left in the English Revolution* (London, 1999), pp. 105–6. But the executed mutineers were certainly claimed by the Leveller movement as 'martyrs': J. White, *The Levellers (fals'y so called) Vindicated* (1649); and their opponents also thought they had suppressed a 'Leveller' mutiny: see Folger Shakespeare Library, Washington DC, MS X. d. 483 (38), 'Sir H Waller at his retourne to London fro leveling ye levellers May 29th 1649'.

5 For Godwin see W. Godwin, *History of the Commonwealth of England from its Commencement, to the Restoration of Charles the Second*, with an introduction by John Morrow (8 vols, Bristol, 2003), i, p. 5.

6 B. Worden, 'The Levellers in History and Memory c. 1660–1960', in M. Mendle, ed., *The Putney Debates of 1647* (Cambridge, 2001), pp. 256–82.

7 The work of Colin Davis is very important here; J. C. Davis, 'Religion and the struggle for freedom in the English Revolution', *Historical Journal*, 35 (1992), 507–31; J. C. Davis, 'The Levellers and Christianity', in B. Manning, ed., *Politics, Religion and the English Civil War* (London, 1973), pp. 225–50.

8 For these connections see the manuscript cipher key discovered by S. Barber, *A Revolutionary Rogue: Henry Marten and the English Republic* (Stroud, 2000), p. 30. Much of the new research on the Levellers is detailed in P. Baker and E. Vernon, eds, *Foundations of Freedom: The Agreements of the People, the Levellers and the Constitutional Crisis of the English Revolution* (London, forthcoming).

9 J. Morrill, B. Manning and D. Underdown, 'What was the English Revolution?', *History Today*, 34 (1984), reprinted in P. Gaunt, ed., *The English Civil War: The Essential Readings* (Oxford, 2001), ch. 1, at p. 19.

10 G. Burgess, 'Radicalism and the English Revolution', in Burgess and Festenstein, *English Radicalism*, p. 69.

11 For the Family of Love see C. W. Marsh, *The Family of Love in English Society 1550–1630* (Cambridge, 1993); on antinomianism in pre-civil-war England see D. R. Como, *Blown by the Spirit: Puritanism and the Emergence of an Antinomian Underground in Pre-Civil War England* (Stanford, 2004).

12   On Denison see P. Lake, *The Boxmaker's Revenge: 'Orthodoxy', 'Heterodoxy' and the Politics of the Parish in Early Stuart London* (Manchester, 2001).

13   N. McDowell, *The English Radical Imagination: Culture, Religion and Revolution, 1630–1660* (Oxford, 2003), p. 4.

14   See D. Como, 'Secret printing, the crisis of 1640, and the origins of civil war radicalism', *Past and Present*, 196 (2007), 37–82, at 69 for the evidence.

15   A. Cromartie, *The Constitutionalist Revolution: An Essay on the History of England, 1450–1642* (Cambridge, 2006), p. 263.

16   Quoted in C. Russell, 'John Hampden', *ODNB*.

17   For Popery see P. Lake, 'Anti-Popery, the Structure of a Prejudice', in R. Cust and A. Hughes, *Conflict in Early Stuart England: Studies in Religion and Politics, 1603–42* (Basingstoke, 1989), ch. 3.

18   This is the position developed in J. S. A. Adamson, *The Noble Revolt: The Overthrow of Charles I* (London, 2007).

19   In A. Sharp, ed., *The English Levellers* (Cambridge, 1998), pp. 38–9.

20   Quoted in Cromartie, *Constitutionalist Revolution*, p. 33.

21   Sharp, *English Levellers*, p. 39.

22   Wood, *Riot, Rebellion and Popular Politics*, p. 130.

23   A. J. Hopper, *'Black Tom': Sir Thomas Fairfax and the English Revolution* (Manchester, 2007), p. 38.

24   On this see D. Cressy, *England on Edge: Crisis and Revolution, 1640–1642* (Oxford, 2006), p. 426.

25   Quoted in K. Lindley, *The English Civil War and Revolution: A Sourcebook* (London, 1998), pp. 89–90.

26   Ibid., p. 73.

27   R. J. Acheson, *Radical Puritans in England, 1550–1660* (London, 1990), p. 96.

28   See A. Hughes, *Gangraena and the Struggle for the English Revolution* (Oxford, 2004), p. 37.

29   Ibid., p. 88.

30   Ibid., pp. 88–9.

31   Quoted in J. S. Morrill, *Cheshire 1603–1660: County Government during the 'English Revolution'* (Oxford, 1974), p. 50.

32   Quoted in Cressy, *England on Edge*, p. 247; J. P. Kenyon, *The Stuart Constitution* (Cambridge, 1986), p. 20.

33   [John Milton,] *Of Reformation* (1641), in R. Fletcher, ed., *Prose Works* (Harvard, 1835), pp. 11, 13.

34   Milton's commonplace book revealed early support for popular rebellion: J. Scott, *Commonwealth Principles: Republican Writing of the English Revolution* (Cambridge, 2004), p. 114.

35   Quoted in Lindley, *Civil War and Revolution*, pp. 83–4.

36   J. Peacey, 'Popularity and the Politician: An MP and his Public, 1640–1644', paper delivered at University of Liverpool, 30 March 2007.

37   Cressy, *England on Edge*, p. 218.

38 P. Gregg, *Free-born John: The Biography of John Lilburne* (London, 1986), p. 89.

39 Cressy, *England on Edge*, pp. 392–3.

CHAPTER 6

1 The best account of the experience and impact of the fighting is Charles Carlton's *Going to the Wars: The Experience of the British Civil Wars, 1638–51* (London, 1994).

2 Quoted in Sharp, *English Levellers*, p. 122.

3 For the army preachers see A. Lawrence, *Parliamentary Army Chaplains, 1642–1651* (Woodbridge, 1990).

4 James Holstun brilliantly explores the various meanings of this encounter in *Ehud's Dagger: Class Struggle in the English Revolution* (London, 2000), ch. 1.

5 Sharp, *English Levellers*, p. 120.

6 See W. Walwyn, *Toleration Justified* (1646), in Sharp, ed., *English Levellers*, p. 11.

7 [R. Overton,] *The Arraignement of Mr Persecution* ('Europe', 1645), p. 11; elsewhere, Overton does employ the more familiar tolerationist argument that, by persecuting, the civil magistrate usurps Christ's jurisdiction by presuming to judge those who reject him before the last day, p. 16. However, this is in the midst of mainly secular arguments for tolerance.

8 Walwyn, *Toleration Justified*, in Sharp, ed., *English Levellers*, p. 20.

9 Ibid., p. 20.

10 Ibid., pp. 22–3.

11 See McDowell, *English Radical Imagination*, p. 3.

12 My discussion of Edwards's work is here based on the work of Hughes, *Gangraena and the Struggle*, esp. ch. 4.

13 Sharp, *English Levellers*, p. 161.

14 D. Farr, *Henry Ireton and the English Revolution* (Woodbridge, 2006), pp. 86–9.

15 W. Lamont, 'Puritanism, Liberty and the Putney Debates', in Mendle, ed., *Putney Debates*, ch. 12, pp. 243–5.

16 Sharp, *English Levellers*, p. 103.

17 Ibid., p. 116.

18 Ibid., p. 112.

19 Rainborowe's famous words look very similar to J. Lilburne, *The charters of London, or the second part of London's liberty in chaines discovered* (1646), p. 4.

20 Sharp, *English Levellers*, pp. 93–4.

21 [Edward Sexby?,] *The Case of the armie truly stated* (1647), p. 15. For the authorship of this document see J. S. Morrill and P. Baker, 'The Case of the Armie Truly Re-Stated', in Mendle, ed., *Putney Debates*, pp. 103–24.

22 Sharp, *English Levellers*, p. 112.

23 See Burgess, 'Radicalism and the English Revolution', in Burgess and Feisenstein, eds, *English Radicalism*, p. 70.

24 See Johannes Dillinger's important article, 'Comparing communities: local representation and territorial states in early modern Europe and New England', *German Historical Institute Bulletin*, 27 (2000), reproduced at http://www.ghi-dc.org/publications/ghipubs/ bu/027/b27dillingerframe.html.

25 On this see Farr, *Ireton*, pp. 112, 153.

26 Hopper, *'Black Tom'*, p. 99.

27 Quoted in A. Woolrych, *Britain in Revolution 1625–1660* (Oxford, 2002), p. 397.

28 Lindley, *Civil War and Revolution*, p. 167.

29 Cromwell to Robert Jenner and John Ashe, MPs, 20 November 1648, in Thomas Carlyle, *The Letters and Speeches of Oliver Cromwell*, ed. S. C. Lomas (3 vols, London, 1904), i, 387.

30 Woolrych, *Britain in Revolution*, p. 424.

31 Quoted in A. Sharp, 'John Lilburne', *ODNB*.

32 *The Humble Representation of the Committee, Gentry, Ministry, And other well-affected Persons in the County of Leicester* (London, 17 March 1648[9]), p. 11. An MS version of the Officers' Agreement in the British Library, Egerton MS 1048 ff. 91–2, carries the small marginal note 'The forme of ye subscription for the Officers of ye Army', indicating that copies were being prepared of this version for signing before it was abruptly abandoned.

CHAPTER 7

1 For Winstanley's biography see J. Gurney, *Brave Community: The Digger Movement in the English Revolution* (Manchester, 2007), ch. 3.

2 See A. Hessayon, 'William Everard', *ODNB*.

3 *Truth Lifting up Its Head above Scandals* (1648), in G. Winstanley, *The Works of Gerrard Winstanley*, ed. G. H. Sabine (New York, 1945), p. 104.

4 Ibid., p. 113; see also p. 107.

5 This already takes on a political hue: 'Lands and Kingdoms are most commonly governed more by the wisdome of the flesh, than of the spirit'. Ibid., p. 129; see also p. 137.

6 Ibid., p. 124.

7 Ibid., p. 124.

8 C. Hill, ed., *Winstanley: The Law of Freedom and Other Writings* (Harmondsworth, 1973), p. 18.

9 Agricultural improvement allied to millenarian expectation was not unique to Winstanley: see T. Leng, *Benjamin Worsley (1618–1677): Trade, Interest and the Spirit in Revolutionary England* (Woodbridge, 2008), pp. 25–6, 62 and chs 5–6 passim; see also Gurney, *Brave Community*, pp. 137–8.

10 Winstanley, *Works*, p. 190.

11 Ibid., pp. 182–3.

12 Winstanley, *Works*, p. 255. On the use of the Covenant by radicals see my *Revolutionary England and the National Covenant* (Woodbridge, 2005), ch. 7.

13 Winstanley, *Works*, p. 259.

14 Ibid., p. 260.

15 Ibid., p. 262.

16 Ibid., p. 266.

17 *Light Shining in Buckingham-shire* (1648), p. 3.

18 *More Light Shining in Buckingham-shire* (1649), p. 4.

19 For the status of the Diggers see Gurney, *Brave Community*, pp. 128–37. For the mistaken presentation of the Diggers as landless 'peasants' see D. Purkiss, *The English Civil War: A People's History* (London, 2006), p. 524.

20 For this aspect of enclosure riots and other forms of popular protest see K. Wrightson, *English Society 1850–1680* (2nd edn, London, 2003), pp. 181–90.

21 Some of the hostility may have originated less from disputes over land use than from long-standing conflicts, as between the family of one of the Diggers, Henry Bickerstaffe, and his neighbour William Starr, which had spilled over into violent confrontation. See Gurney, *Brave Community*, pp. 155–7.

22 Ibid., p. 124.

23 Quoted in Wood, *Riot, Rebellion and Popular Politics*, p. 159.

24 Winstanley, *Works*, p. 353.

25 Ibid., p. 373.

26 Quoted in Gurney, *Brave Community*, p. 211.

27 See A. Hessayon, 'Gold Tried in the Fire': *Theaurau John Tany and the English Revolution* (Basingstoke, 2007), pp. 197–8.

28 See J. C. Davis, *Utopia and the Ideal Society* (Cambridge, 1983), ch. 7.

29 Winstanley, *Works*, p. 523, the 'hell of prisons, whips and gallows'. For the laws (which included whipping as a punishment) see ibid., pp. 591–600. This did go back on Winstanley's prohibition of capital punishment in *The New Law of Righteousness* (1649), in Winstanley, *Works*, p. 192.

30 K. Kesselring, *Mercy and Authority in the Tudor State* (Cambridge, 2003), pp. 28–9. Kesselring also notes some similarities between the system of punishment employed by Winstanley and the short-lived 1547 vagrancy laws which sentenced offenders to branding and two years as private slaves. Ibid., p. 39.

31 Winstanley, *Works*, p. 534.

32 Gurney, *Brave Community*, p. 183. For Winstanley's answers to charges of 'Ranterism' see *A Vindication of those whose Endeavors is only to make the Earth a Common Treasury, Called Diggers* (1650), in Winstanley, *Works*, pp. 397–403.

33 Ibid., p. 459.

34 Quoted in J. C. Davis, *Fear, Myth and History: The Ranters and the Historians* (Cambridge, 1986), p. 159.

35 Ibid., p. 163.

36 Ibid.

37 Ibid., p. 186.

38 See A. Hessayon, 'Mary Adams', *ODNB*.

39 Milton, quoted in J. Coffey, 'A Ticklish Business: Defining Heresy and Orthodoxy in the Puritan Revolution', in D. Loewenstein and J. Marshall, eds, *Heresy, Literature, and Politics in Early Modern English Culture* (Cambridge, 2006), ch. 5.

40 This is the main thrust of Davis, *Fear, Myth and History*; a similar conclusion is drawn about the impact of the Quakers by Barry Reay, *The Quakers and the English Revolution* (London, 1985).

41 T. L. Underwood, ed., *The Acts of the Witnesses: The Autobiography of Lodowick Muggleton and Other Early Muggletonian Writings* (Oxford, 1999), pp. 58, 60–1. Reeve was the effective leader of the sect and the group only became known as the 'Muggletonians' after his death in 1658.

42 Quoted in Davis, *Fear, Myth and History*, p. 63.

43 Ibid., p. 147.

44 These similarities are picked up on by Gurney, *Brave Community*, pp. 180–3.

45 Davis, *Fear, Myth and History*, p. 149.

46 Ibid., p. 54.

47 W. R. D. Jones, *Thomas Rainborowe (c. 1610–1648): Civil War Seaman, Siegemaster and Radical* (Woodbridge, 2005), p. 123.

48 See P. Linebaugh and M. Rediker, *The Many-Headed Hydra: Sailors, Slaves, Commoners, and the Hidden History of the Revolutionary Atlantic* (London, 2000), pp. 132–4, the cases of Marcellus Rivers and Oxenbridge Foyle, sold into slavery for their part in gun-running for the Royalists. On the rhetoric of slavery in the civil war see Q. Skinner, 'Classical Liberty and the Coming of the English Civil War', in M. Van Gelderen and Q. Skinner, eds, *Republicanism: A Shared European Heritage*, vol. 2, *The Values of Republicanism in Early Modern Europe* (Cambridge, 2002), ch. 1.

49 Gregg, *Free-born John*, pp. 343–4.

50 Ruth E. Mayers, *1659: The Crisis of the Commonwealth* (Woodbridge, 2004).

51 See L. Knoppers, '"This so horrid spectacle": "Samson Agonistes" and the execution of the Regicides', *English Literary Renaissance*, 20 (1990), 487–504, at 487.

52 Scott, *Commonwealth Principles*, p. 321.

53 Rumbold's quarters were not displayed in Scotland but transported to England and hung outside his residence at Rye House, where the plot to assassinate Charles II had allegedly been hatched in 1683. For Jefferson's use of Rumbold see Douglass Adair, 'Rumbold's dying speech, 1685, and Jefferson's last words on democracy, 1826', *William and Mary Quarterly*, 9 (1952), 521–31.

54 Godwin, *History of the Commonwealth*, p. xxix. The radical printer, publisher and antiquarian William Hone was an exception to this general tendency by Georgian radicals to neglect the Levellers: see M. Wood, *Radical Satire and Print Culture: 1790–1822* (Oxford, 1994), pp. 121–31, and this volume, pp. 315–17, 351.

55 B. Disraeli, *Sybil*, ed. T. Braun (London, 1980), p. 40.

56 C. L. R. James, 'Cromwell and the Levellers', *Fourth International*, 10, no. 5 (1949), pp. 143–8, reproduced at http://www.marxists.org/ archive/james-clr/works/1949/05/english-revolution.htm, accessed on 22 January 2008.

57 An exhaustive discussion of the referencing of civil-war radicals, from the late seventeenth century onwards, is given in A. Hessayon, 'Fabricating radical traditions', http://www.cromohs.unifi.it/seminari/hessayon2_radical.html.

58 Sharp, *English Levellers*, p. 152.

PART FOUR: THE AGE OF PAINE

1 P. S. Foner, ed., *The Complete Writings of Thomas Paine* (2 vols, New York, 1969), i, 341–2, 344. Henceforth, Foner, ed., *CWTP*.

2 Quoted in C. Emsley, *Britain and the French Revolution* (Harlow, 2000), p. 85.

CHAPTER 8

1 D. Hay and N. Rogers, *Eighteenth-Century English Society* (Oxford, 1997), pp. 56–63.

2 Quoted in J. Sainsbury, *John Wilkes: The Lives of a Libertine* (Bodmin, 2006), p. 57; see also, for Chevalier D'Éon, pp. 113–14. A. Clark, *Scandal: The Sexual Politics of the British Constitution* (Princeton, 2004), ch. 2, esp. pp. 44–5 where Clark suggests that rumours of an affair between Wilkes and d'Éon were intended to throw back in his face Wilkes's own accusations of sodomy made against the Georgian court. Wilkes also initiated the novel device of sending every one of his voters a thank-you card in a bid to retain their loyalty in future elections; see A. H. Cash, *John Wilkes: The Scandalous Father of Civil Liberty* (Yale, 2006), p. 58.

3 Sainsbury, *Wilkes*, p. 121.

4 For Wilkes's exploitation of his privileges as an MP see ibid., p. 215.

5 P. Langford, *A Polite and Commercial People: England, 1727–1783* (2nd edn, Oxford, 1998), pp. 712, 716.

6 G. Rudé, *Wilkes and Liberty: A Social Study* (2nd edn, London, 1983), ch. 5, for the voting figures. Wilkes succeeded in repeatedly securing an overwhelming majority of the vote, even though his supporters faced a massive government campaign of propaganda and intimidation.

7 On this aspect of radical language in the mid-eighteenth century see G. Newman, *The Rise of English Nationalism* (New York, 1987).

8 E. Foner, *Tom Paine and Revolutionary America* (2nd edn, Oxford, 2005), p. 3.

9 C. Brent, 'Thirty-something: Thomas Paine at Bull House in Lewes – six formative years' (forthcoming Sussex Archaeological Society article); G. Hindmarsh, *Thomas Paine: The Case of the King of England and His Officers of Excise* (privately printed, 1998). My thanks to Paul Myles for sending me a copy of Colin Brent's important article.

10 See East Sussex Record Office, NU1/3/4–5. There is also a letter from Ollive witnessed by Paine in NU1 3/3, and a report of the lawyer Thomas Erskine's attack on Paine's *Age of Reason* in SAS/A740. Erskine, as we shall see, successfully defended a number of radicals in the 1790s, but he was also a devout Christian who found Paine's work repugnant.

11 Foner, ed., *CWTP*, i, 235, 496.

12 Although he did argue for the improvement of excise officers' pay in *The Rights of Man Part the Second* (1792), Foner, ed., *CWTP*, i, 411.

13 Ibid., ii, 8–9.

14 Ibid., ii, 11. Though he disowned this pamphlet, Paine returned to the issue of the pay of excise officers in his most famous work, *Rights of Man*. Ibid., i, 441.

15 On this see C. Wagner, 'Loyalist propaganda and the scandalous life of Tom Paine: "Hypocritical Monster!"', *British Journal for Eighteenth-Century Studies*, 28 (2005), 97–115.

16 Foner, ed., *CWTP*, ii, 1130.

17 See ibid., i, 258.

18 Ibid., i, 57–8.

19 Quoted in J. Keane, *Tom Paine: A Political Life* (London, 2003), p. 100.

20 Foner, ed., *CWTP*, ii, 18.

21 Ibid., ii, 19.

22 Ibid., i, 25.

23 Ibid., ii, 1160–5; Foner, *Paine*, p. 78.

24 See T. Loughran, 'Disseminating *Common Sense*: Thomas Paine and the problem of the early national bestseller', *American Literature*, 78 (2006), 1–28.

25 Foner, ed., *CWTP*, i, 13. See here Keane's masterful discussion, *Paine*, 116–17.

26 Foner, ed., *CWTP*, i, 28.

27 Ibid., i, 3.

28 Ibid., i, 3–4.

29 Ibid., i, 7–8.

30 Ibid., i, 27.

31 Ibid., i, 19.

32 Ibid., i, 37.

33 Quoted in H. T. Dickinson, 'Charles Wyvill', *ODNB*.

34 For their influence and for an accessible, cheap edition of the letters, see D. L. Jacobson, ed., *The English Libertarian Heritage* (repr. San Francisco, 1994), esp. pp. xlviii–lx. See also A. Goodwin, *The Friends of Liberty: The English Democratic Movement in the Age of the French Revolution* (London, 1979), pp. 33–8.

35 On this see the introduction to my *The Glorious Revolution: 1688 and Britain's Fight for Liberty* (London, 2006).

36 Quoted in Keane, *Paine*, p. 141.

37 Foner, ed., *CWTP*, i, 50. In another letter Paine suggested that the allegiances of Americans should be tested by an oath renouncing all allegiance to the George III. Ibid., i, 99–100.

38 Ibid., i, 191.

39 Goodwin, *Friends of Liberty*, pp. 86–7. For Price, see P. Buck, 'People who counted: political arithmetic in the eighteenth century', *Isis*, 73 (1982), 28–45; D. O. Thomas, *The Honest Mind: The Thought and Work of Richard Price* (Oxford, 1977).

40 Quoted in C. Franklin, *Mary Wollstonecraft: A Literary Life* (Basingstoke, 2004), pp. 85–6.

41 Ibid., p. 87. For a good discussion of Price's sermon see T. W. Davis, 'The influence of Richard Price on the Burke–Paine debate', *Proceedings of the Consortium on Revolutionary Europe 1750–1850* (1990), 800–6.

42 Quoted in Franklin, *Wollstonecraft*, p. 88.

43 Ibid., p. 89.

44 Quoted in P. Langford, 'Edmund Burke', *ODNB*.

45 Quoted in Vallance, *Glorious Revolution*, p. 10.

46 On this see Colley, *Britons*, pp. 232–3.

47 For an excellent summary of Burke's position see Emsley's *Britain and the French Revolution*, p. 11.

48 See F. O'Gorman, *British Conservatism: Conservative Thought from Burke to Thatcher* (London, 1986).

49 C. Bewley and D. Bewley, *Gentleman Radical: A Life of John Horne Tooke, 1736–1812* (London, 1998), p. 96.

50 Ibid., pp. 53, 120.

51 Franklin, *Wollstonecraft*, p. 96.

52 Ibid., p. 97.

53 J. Todd, *Mary Wollstonecraft: A Revolutionary Life* (London, 2000), p. 168.

54 Franklin, *Wollstonecraft*, p. 98.

CHAPTER 9

1 Franklin, *Wollstonecraft*, p. 100.

2 Foner, ed., *CWTP*, ii, 481.

3 For the grotto, see *Marsden Rock: or, the story of Peter Allan and Marsden Marine Grotto* (Sunderland, 1848); J. P. Robson, *Summer Excursions in the North of England; including A Trip to Warkworth; A Ramble to Marsden Rocks; Picnicings at Finchale Priory, A Week at Gilsland* (Newcastle, 1851). The legal case over the rent appears to have brought Allan to an early death in 1849: see *Newcastle Courant*, 14 September 1849.

4 Quoted in Goodwin, *Friends of Liberty*, p. 95.

5 Foner, ed., *CWTP*, i, 250.

6   Ibid., i, 252.

7   Ibid., i, 260; see also i, 419n.

8   Ibid., i, 382–3.

9   Ibid., i, 279.

10 Ibid., i, 280, 382.

11 Ibid., i, 260.

12 Ibid., i, 256.

13 Ibid., i, 266.

14 Ibid., i, 291.

15 Note also that the earlier English meaning of tolerance was the enduring of evil or suffering.

16 Foner, ed., *CWTP*, i, 281.

17 Ibid., i, 289.

18 Ibid., i, 326.

19 Ibid., i, 280–1.

20 Emsley, *Britain and the French Revolution*, pp. 12, 29.

21 D. Vincent, ed., *Testaments of Radicalism: Memoirs of Working-Class Politicians 1790–1885* (London, 1977), p. 45.

22 Quoted in M. T. Davis, 'London Corresponding Society', *ODNB*.

23 Quoted in Goodwin, *Friends of Liberty*, p. 168.

24 Thale, ed., *Selections*, pp. 18, 76.

25 Ibid., p. 106.

26 See Goodwin, *Friends of Liberty*, p. 175.

27 Ibid., pp. 164–7.

28 Foner, ed., *CWTP*, i, 355.

29 Ibid., i, 365.

30 Ibid., i, 366.

31 Ibid., i, 374.

32 Ibid., i, 359.

33 Ibid., i, 358–61.

34 Thale, ed., *Selections*, p. 256.

35 Foner, ed., *CWTP*, i, 404.

36 Ibid., i, 410–11. The interrelationship between success in the brewing industry and landed wealth is demonstrated by the rise of the Whitbread dynasty in the eighteenth and early nineteenth centuries: see D. Rapp, 'Social mobility in the eighteenth century: the Whitbreads of Bedfordshire, 1720–1815', *Economic History Review*, 27 (1974), 380–94.

37 Foner, ed., *CWTP*, i, 434.

38 Ibid., i, 428–9. Paine was referring here to the frequent disputes between parishes over paying the costs of paupers' burials. See for legal discussions of the issue of removal orders, pauper deaths and the costs incurred M. Nolan, *A Treatise of the Laws for Relief and Settlement of the Poor* (4th edn, 3 vols, London, 1852), ii, 488.

39 Foner, ed., *CWTP*, i. 431.

40 Ibid., i, 430.

41 Thale, ed., *Selections*, p. 253.

42 See M. McCormack, *The Independent Man: Citizenship and Gender Politics in Georgian England* (Manchester, 2005), pp. 132–3, for the irony that Wollstonecraft's ideal female citizen was defined by the virtues of 'manly independence'.

43 M. Wollstonecraft, *A Vindication of the Rights of Woman*, ed. C. Ward (Dover Thrift edn, New York, 1996), p. 15.

44 Ibid., p. 151.

45 Ibid., pp. 7, 78. One of those on Wollstonecraft's shortlist of admirable women was not even female. 'Madame d'Éon' was the same Chevalier d'Éon rumoured to have had a sexual relationship with John Wilkes. To be fair to Wollstonecraft, though, d'Éon's sex was only discovered following an autopsy in 1810.

46 Ibid., p. 9. A similar concern for fashion and beauty deterred women (again, wealthy women) from breast-feeding their children – once more, Wollstonecraft felt, to the detriment of proper child-rearing: p. 147.

47 Ibid., pp. 60–1.

48 Ibid., p. 178.

49 Ibid., pp. 177–8.

50 Quoted in Taylor, 'Wollstonecraft', *ODNB*.

51 Todd, *Wollstonecraft*, p. 185. Although More almost certainly did read the work and respond critically to it when she came to produce her own highly successful works on women's education.

52 W. Godwin, *An Enquiry Concerning Political Justice*, ed. M. Philp and A. Gee (London, 1993), p. 357. Henceforth, Godwin, *Enquiry*, ed. Philp and Gee.

53 Quoted in P. Marshall, *William Godwin* (London, 1984), p. 1.

54 Emsley, *Britain and the French Revolution*, p. 17.

55 Godwin, *Enquiry*, ed. Philp and Gee, p. 7.

56 W. Godwin, *An Enquiry Concerning Political Justice, and its Influence on General Virtue and Happiness* (Woodstock reprint, Oxford, 1992), p. viii. Henceforth Godwin, *Political Justice*.

57 Godwin, *Enquiry*, ed. Philp and Gee, p. 212.

58 Ibid., pp. 230–1.

59 Ibid., p. 238.

60 Ibid., p. 53. Very similar sentiments are expressed later in Godwin, *Political Justice*, p. 426.

61 Ibid., p. 438.

62 See M. Philp, 'William Godwin', *ODNB*.

63 Marshall, *Godwin*, pp. 123–4.

64 Godwin, *Enquiry*, ed. Philp and Gee, p. 453.

65 Ibid., p. 454.

66 Ibid., p. 50.

67 Quoted in Marshall, *Godwin*, p. 2.

68 Ibid., p. 49.
69 Godwin, *Enquiry*, ed. Philp and Gee, p. 456. Malthus himself later moved closer to arguing that 'moral restraint' might offer a means of averting catastrophe.
70 Marshall, *Godwin*, pp. 22–3.
71 Emsley, *Britain and the French Revolution*, p. 33 See also T. C. F. Stunt, 'Richard Brothers', *ODNB*. Blake's debt to the radical 'fringe' of Protestantism was at the core of E. P. Thompson's *Witness against the Beast* (London, 1993), but he almost certainly exaggerated Blake's connections with the Swedenborgians.
72 Marshall, *Godwin*, p. 112.
73 Ibid., p. 117.
74 Ibid., p. 118.
75 Ibid.
76 Godwin, *Political Justice*, p. 3.
77 Quoted in Marshall, *Godwin*, pp. 141–2.

CHAPTER 10

1   R. E. Schofield. *The Enlightened Joseph Priestley: A Study of His Life and Work from 1773 to 1804* (Pennsylvania, 2004), pp. 284–9.
2   Quoted in F. W. Gibbs, *Joseph Priestley* (London, 1965), p. 204. See also Emsley, *Britain and the French Revolution*, pp. 40–1.
3   W. Hutton, *The Life of William Hutton*, Introduction by Carl Chinn (Studley, 1998), p. 105.
4   Emsley, *Britain and the French Revolution*, pp. 18, 42.
5   F. O'Gorman, 'The Paine burnings of 1792–3', *Past and Present*, 193 (2006), 111–55, at 139–40.
6   Ibid., 145.
7   Quoted in Emsley, *Britain and French Revolution*, p. 95.
8   This point is forcefully made by O'Gorman, 'Paine burnings', 155.
9   Emsley, *Britain and the French Revolution*, p. 18.
10 G. Claeys, 'Republicanism versus commercial society: Paine, Burke, and the French Revolution debate', *Proceedings of the Consortium on Revolutionary Europe 1750–1850* (1989), 3–24.
11 *Buff, or a Dissertation on Nakedness* (1792), p. 9.
12 Ibid., pp. 10–11.
13 Claeys, 'Republicanism', p. 15.
14 Todd, *Wollstonecraft*, p. 185
15 Susan Pederson, 'Hannah More meets Simple Simon: tracts, chapbooks, and popular culture in late eighteenth-century England', *Journal of British Studies*, 25 (1986), 84–113.
16 Emsley, *Britain and the French Revolution*, p. 69. Wilberforce supported the Combination Acts and the suspensions of Habeas Corpus.
17 Godwin, *Enquiry*, ed. Philp and Gee, p. 466.

18 Thale, ed., *Selections*, p. 106.

19 Bewley and Bewley, *Gentleman Radical*, p. 161.

20 M. T. Davis, 'John Horne Tooke', *ODNB*.

21 Ibid.

22 Emsley, *Britain and the French Revolution*, p. 34.

23 For good discussions of the novel see E. F. Knapp, 'William Godwin's *Caleb Williams* and the origins of revolution', *Proceedings of the Consortium on Revolutionary Europe 1750–1850* (1989), 189–200; G. Kelly, *The English Jacobin Novel, 1780–1805* (Oxford, 1976).

24 W. Godwin, *Caleb Williams, or Things as They Are* (4th edn, London, 1831), p. xx.

25 Ibid., pp. 211–12.

26 Godwin, *Enquiry*, ed. Philp and Gee, p. 403.

27 Though Godwin disagreed with Howard's suggested remedy of solitary confinement as the answer to the evils of prison. Ibid., p. 404.

28 Godwin, *Caleb Williams*, p. 249.

29 Ibid., p. 281.

30 Ibid., p. 430. On the original ending of the novel see Kelly, *English Jacobin Novel*, pp. 184–5.

31 Godwin, *Caleb Williams*, p. 452.

32 Quoted in Emsley, *Britain and the French Revolution*, p. 37.

33 Godwin singled out the Black Act as an example of legal tyranny in *Caleb Williams*, pp. 101–2. The classic study of the act remains E. P. Thompson, *Whigs and Hunters: The Origins of the Black Act* (London, 1975). For alternative perspectives see E. Cruikshanks and H. Erskine-Hill, 'The Waltham Black Act and Jacobitism', *Journal of British Studies*, 24 (1985), 358–65.

34 This point is well made by Kesselring, *Mercy and Authority*, p. 3/; C. Emsley, *Crime and Society in England, 1750–1900* (3rd edn, Harlow, 2005), pp. 256–63, gives a good summary of the controversy between historians.

35 Emsley, *Crime*, p. 256, summarising the arguments of V. Gattrel, *The Hanging Tree: Execution and the English People, 1770–1868* (Oxford, 1994).

36 Quoted in D. Hay *et al.*, *Albion's Fatal Tree* (Harmondsworth, 1977), p. 37.

37 Godwin, *Enquiry*, ed. Philp and Gee, p. 420.

38 Quoted in Emsley, *Crime*, 291n. For a contemporary example of a death sentence for a trivial crime against property, see the case of Sophia Jones, convicted of shoplifting a roll of muslin on 24 April 1790: http://www.hri-online.ac.uk/oldbailey/html_units/1790s/t17900424-4.html, accessed on 4 August 2008.

39 Vincent, ed., *Testaments of Radicalism*, p. 75n.

40 Goodwin, *Friends of Liberty*, p. 372.

41 On this see J. Barrell, *Imagining the King's Death: Figurative Treason, Fantasies of Regicide, 1793–1796* (Oxford, 2000).

42 In Emsley, *Britain and the French Revolution*, p. 105.

43 Ibid., pp. 103–4.

44 For contrasting opinions on the Despard conspiracy see M. Elliott, 'The Despard conspiracy reconsidered', *Past and Present*, 75 (1977), 46–61; R. Wells, *Insurrection: The British Experience, 1795–1803* (Gloucester, 1983).

45 C. Nelson, *Thomas Paine: Enlightenment, Reason, and the Birth of Modern Nations* (London, 2006), p. 306.

46 See ibid., ch. 12; P. Collins, *The Trouble with Tom: The Strange Afterlife and Times of Thomas Paine* (London, 2006), pp. 53–83.

47 Franklin, *Wollstonecraft*, p. 173.

48 Ibid., p. 175.

49 Ibid., p. 176.

50 Ibid., p. 196.

51 Clark, *Scandal*, pp. 137–40.

52 http://www.thomaspainefriends.org/stprocs.htm, accessed on 4 March 2008. H. J. Kaye's *Tom Paine and the Promise of America* (New York, 2005), an attempt to reclaim Paine for the left in the USA, shows how far Paine has been assimilated into the canon of conservative heroes.

PART FIVE: THE MASK OF ANARCHY

1 Quoted in M. L. Bush, *The Casualties of Peterloo* (Lancaster, 2005), p. 27.

CHAPTER 11

1 See F. O'Gorman, *Voters, Patrons and Parties: The Unreformed Electoral System of Hanoverian England 1734–1832* (Oxford, 1989), p. 179.

2 For the Middlesex election see J. Ann Hone, *For the Cause of Truth: Radicalism in London 1796–1821* (Oxford, 1982), pp. 133–46.

3 On the rather uneasy relationship between Whiggery and popular radicals see L. G. Mitchell, 'The Whigs, the people and reform', *Proceedings of the British Academy*, 100 (1999), 25–41; B. Hilton, *A Mad, Bad and Dangerous People? England 1783–1846* (Oxford, 2006), pp. 49–50. On radical uses of history see R. Poole, 'French Revolution or Peasants' Revolt? The Rebellions of 1817 and the Rise of the Mass Platform', paper delivered on Chartism Day, June 2007, Sheffield, pp. 7–8. I thank Robert Poole for giving me a pre-publication copy of his paper.

4 G. D. H. Cole and R. Postgate, *The British Common People, 1746–1946* (London, 1961), p. 182.

5 Hone, *Radicalism in London*, p. 161.

6 For Hunt see J. Belchem, *'Orator' Hunt: Henry Hunt and English Working-Class Radicalism* (Oxford, 1985).

7 On this shift in Cartwright's tactics see R. Eckersley, 'Of radical design: John Cartwright and the redesign of the reform campaign c. 1800–1811', *History*, 89 (2004), 560–80, at 567.

8 Hone, *Radicalism in London*, p. 166.

9 Ibid., p. 176.

10 N. C. Miller, 'John Cartwright and radical parliamentary reform, 1808–1819', *English Historical Review*, 83, no. 329 (1968), 705–28, at 714.

11 M. Baer, 'Burdett, Sir Francis', *ODNB*.

12 Hone, *Radicalism in London*, p. 188.

13 Eckersley, 'Of radical design', 579.

14 Miller, 'Cartwright and radical parliamentary reform', 715.

15 Eckersley, 'Of radical design', 577.

16 J. R. Dinwiddy, *From Luddism to the First Reform Bill: Reform in England 1810–1832* (Oxford, 1986), pp. 5–6.

17 Hone, *Radicalism in London*, pp. 195–6.

18 Ibid., pp. 197–200.

19 Ibid., p. 203.

20 Ibid., p. 207.

21 On the formation of these clubs, once attributed solely to Cartwright, see N. C. Miller, 'Major John Cartwright and the founding of the Hampden Club', *Historical Journal*, 17 (1974), 615–19.

22 O. Smith, *The Politics of Language, 1791–1819* (Oxford, 1984), p. 34, and see pp. 30–4 for petitioning in general.

23 House of Commons Information Office, 'Public Petitions', at http://www.parliament.uk/documents/upload/p07.pdf, accessed on 9 May 2008.

24 E. P. Thompson, *The Making of the English Working Class* (rev. edn, London, 1968), p. 595. Hereafter *TMEWC*.

25 Cole and Postgate, *British Common People*, pp. 174, 189.

26 Dinwiddy, *From Luddism to the First Reform Bill*, p. 25.

27 Thompson, *TMEWC*, p. 666.

28 Miller, 'Cartwright and radical parliamentary reform', 719.

29 Thompson, *TMEWC*, p. 667.

30 Ibid., p. 668.

CHAPTER 12

1 K. Binfield, ed., *Writings of the Luddites* (London, 2004), p. 94.

2 Quoted in Thompson, *TMEWC*, p. 623.

3 K. Navickas, 'The search for "General Ludd": the mythology of Luddism', *Social History*, 30 (2005), 281–95, at 292. Bellingham's grudge against the government was personal, not political. He viewed the authorities as culpable for failing to act in his favour when imprisoned for debt in the Russian port of Archangel

4 Binfield, *Writings of the Luddites*, p. 28.

5 Ibid., p. xiv; B. Bailey, *The Luddite Rebellion* (Stroud, 1998), pp. x–xi, suggests an alternative origin for the term in the name of the ancient British king Ludd.

6 See for example Bailey, *Luddite Rebellion*, passim, for an account that

largely dismisses the political aspects to machine-breaking. Thompson, *TMEWC*, pp. 647–8 is scathing in his attack on the lack of attention given to the Luddites in 'New Liberal' and Fabian accounts of the 'rise of Labour'.

7   Binfield, *Writings of the Luddites*, pp. 14–15.

8   J. Horn, 'Understanding crowd action: machine breaking in England and France, 1789–1817', *Proceedings of the Western Society for French History*, 31 (2003), 138–52, at 150.

9   Binfield, *Writings of the Luddites*, p. 15

10   Bailey, *Luddite Rebellion*, p. 35.

11   Binfield, *Writings of the Luddites*, pp. 22–3.

12   Ibid., p. 130.

13   Navickas, 'The search for "General Ludd"', 285

14   M. Taylor, 'Ned Ludd', *ODNB*.

15   Navickas, 'The search for "General Ludd"', 287.

16   Binfield, *Writings of the Luddites*, p. 23.

17   Ibid., p. 45.

18   Thompson, *TMEWC*, pp. 652–9; J. Belchem, 'Brandreth, Jeremiah', *ODNB*, suggests that the insurrectionist Brandreth's silence at his trial was a result of his unwillingness to uncover the radical underground that supported the 1817 Pentrich rising and linked 'Luddism' to out-and-out revolutionary movements.

19   Thompson, *TMEWC*, p. 597.

20   Quoted in Cole and Postgate, *British Common People*, p. 186. 'Jeffreys' was a reference to James II's Lord Chancellor, infamous for his role in the 'Bloody Assizes' which followed Monmouth's rebellion.

21   M. Kelsall, 'Byron's Politics', in D. Bone, ed., *The Cambridge Companion to Byron* (Cambridge, 2004), ch. 3, pp. 47–9.

22   Cole and Postgate, *British Common People*, pp. 188–9.

23   Horn, 'Understanding crowd action', 151.

24   Thompson, *TMEWC*, p. 614. At Booth's funeral the minister, Jonathan Saville, was stoned by mourners for delivering a service in which he called Booth an 'infidel'. Ibid., p. 641.

25   Ibid., p. 659.

26   Stockport weavers in June 1819 presented parliamentary reform as their last resort: 'The fate of their . . . petitions and memorials to Parliament is so well known as not to require description. By those [from] whom the weavers sought protection they have been rewarded with punishment.' Quoted in Dinwiddy, *From Luddism to the First Reform Bill*, p. 27.

27   On this 'ultra-radical' subculture see Iain Macalman, 'Ultra-radicalism and convivial debating clubs in London, 1795–1838', *English Historical Review*, 102 (1987), 309–33; for Hunt and the Spenceans, see Belchem, *'Orator' Hunt*, pp. 54–8.

28   See Macalman, 'Ultra-radicalism', 325.

29 Quoted in Hone, *Radicalism in London,* p. 263.

30 Ibid., p. 262.

31 Quoted in Thompson, *TMEWC,* p. 661; Belchem, *'Orator' Hunt,* p. 61.

32 Thompson, *TMEWC,* p. 685. See also Belchem, *'Orator' Hunt,* p. 60.

33 Belchem, *'Orator Hunt'*, p. 62.

34 Hone, *Radicalism in London,* p. 264.

35 Belchem, *'Orator' Hunt,* p. 70.

36 Quoted in Hone, *Radicalism in London,* p. 266.

37 J. Stevens, *England's Last Revolution, Pentrich 1817* (Stoke, 1977), p. 16.

38 Miller, 'Cartwright and radical parliamentary reform', 724.

39 S. Bamford, *Passages in the Life of a Radical* (Oxford, 1984), p. 31. On radical petitions to the monarchy see S. Poole, *The Politics of Regicide in England, 1760–1850* (Manchester, 2000), ch. 2.

40 J. A. Epstein, *Radical Expression: Political Language, Ritual and Symbol in England, 1790–1850* (Oxford, 1994), p. 15

41 Poole, 'French Revolution or Peasants' Revolt?', p. 6. See also for these connections I. Prothero, *Artisans and Politics in Early Nineteenth-Century London* (Folkestone, 1979), ch. 6.

42 Quoted in Epstein, *Radical Expression,* p. 16. Brougham's flirtation with reform was almost completely opportunistic. He once described the members of the LCS as ignorant savages 'fit only for being tools'.

43 See B. Wilson, *The Laughter of Triumph: William Hone and the Fight for the Free Press* (London, 2005), p. 196. Wilson, though, as Jason McElligott demonstrates in 'William Hone, Print Culture, and the Nature of Radicalism', overestimates both Hone's and Wooler's political moderation.

44 Thompson, *TMEWC,* pp. 792–3.

45 J. McElligott, 'William Hone', p. 12. I thank Jason McElligott for letting me see a pre-publication copy of his paper.

46 Quoted in Epstein, *Radical Expression,* p. 53.

47 Quoted in A. J. Bunting, 'The Pentrich Rising of 1817', unpublished dissertation, p. 14, reproduced at www.pentrich.org.uk/documents/a.j.bunting.pentrich.pdf, accessed on 14 May 2008.

CHAPTER 13

1 Bunting, 'The Pentrich Rising', p. 29.

2 Ibid., p. 17. See also Poole, 'French Revolution or Peasants' Revolt', p. 6.

3 Quoted in Stevens, *Pentrich,* p. 17; see also Bamford, *Passages,* pp. 64–8.

4 Stevens, *Pentrich,* p. 18.

5 Ibid., p. 60.

6 Ibid., p. 66.

7 Belchem, *'Orator' Hunt,* pp. 76–7.

8 Hone, *Radicalism in London,* pp. 274–5, notes that metropolitan radicals generally ignored the plight of the Pentrich men until the role of Oliver was fully revealed.

9   Quoted in Bunting, 'Pentrich', p. 21.
10 Shelley's address is at http://www.pentrich.org.uk/html/an.address2. html, accessed on 14 May 2008.
11 The argument of Thompson, *TMEWC*, p. 735.
12 Miller, 'Cartwright and radical parliamentary reform', 727; R. Poole, 'The march to Peterloo: politics and festivity in late Georgian England', *Past and Present*, 192 (2006), 109–55, at 115; Belchem, *'Orator' Hunt*, pp. 60, 99–102.
13 On this see Poole, 'March to Peterloo', passim.
14 Ibid., 147–8. Quoting Bamford, *Passages*, p. 132. The term 'military array' was used in the treason trial of Hunt, Bamford and the other leading Peterloo protesters. Ibid., p. 189.
15 Bamford, *Passages*, pp. 141–2; for narratives of the day see R. Poole, '"By Law and the Sword": Peterloo revisited', *History*, 94 (2006), 254–76; J. Marlow, 'The day of Peterloo', *Manchester Region History Review*, 3 (1989), 3–8.
16 M. L. Bush, 'The women at Peterloo: the impact of female reform on the Manchester meeting of August 16 1819', *History*, 89 (2004), 209–32, at 212.
17 Ibid., 214, 217. A. Clark, *The Struggle for the Breeches: Gender and the Making of the British Working Class* (Berkeley, 1995), p. 159, notes that women's friendly societies came under increasing surveillance during the 1810s.
18 Bush, 'Women at Peterloo', 215. Bush implausibly suggests that women did not speak at public meetings because their voices were too weak to be heard above such large crowds. Ibid., 218.
19 Bamford, *Passages*, pp. 143–5.
20 Bush, *Casualties of Peterloo*, p. 94; the casualty lists inspected by Bush give this child as only being injured; E. and R. Frow, *Radical Salford* (Manchester, 1984), p. 8, give it as being killed.
21 Bamford, *Passages*, p. 152.
22 Bush, *Casualties of Peterloo*, p. 96. The *Observer* reported that she was so badly beaten that when she appeared in the dock to answer the charges against her she looked pale, emaciated and almost fainting for weakness in consequence of the wounds which she had received at the meeting and her subsequent solitary confinement. Ibid., p. 97.
23 See *Manchester Times*, 14 August 1830, reprinted at http://www.spartacus. schoolnet.co.uk/PRhunt.htm.
24 Marlow, 'The day of Peterloo'; Bush, *Casualties of Peterloo*, p. 134.
25 Bamford, *Passages*, p. 153.
26 Bush, *Casualties of Peterloo*, p. 2.
27 Ibid., p. 44.
28 Ibid., p. 126.
29 Ibid., p. 12.
30 See the cases of Margaret Downs and William Evans, in ibid., pp. 90, 92.
31 Ibid., p. 139; see also Bamford, *Passages*, p. 164.

32 Bush, *Casualties of Peterloo*, p. 31.

33 Ibid., p. 93.

34 Ibid., pp. 103–4.

35 Ibid., p. 105.

36 Clark, *Struggle for the Breeches*, p. 161.

37 Epstein, *Radical Expression*, p. 189.

38 A. J. Cross, '"What a world we make the oppressor and the oppressed": George Cruickshank, Percy Shelley and the gendering of revolution in 1819', *English Literary History*, 71 (2004), 167–204, at 186.

39 For this image see D. Donald, 'The power of print: graphic images of Peterloo', *Manchester Region History Review*, 3 (1989), 21–9.

40 Clark, *Struggle for the Breeches*, p. 156.

41 Cross, 'Cruickshank', p. 168.

42 Quoted in Bush, 'Women at Peterloo', 222.

43 Ibid., 174–5; Bamford, *Passages*, p. 154.

44 Epstein, *Radical Expression*, p. 96.

45 M. Levene, Introduction to M. Levene and P. Roberts, eds, *The Massacre in History* (Oxford, 1999), p. 9.

46 Thompson, *TMEWC*, p. 754. There is also the possibility that some of the violence was motivated by sectarian hatred. The yeomanry had connections with the British Grand Orange Lodge (based in Manchester). Thompson believed that there was little involvement in Peterloo of the Manchester Irish, but Bush's research shows that ninety-seven of the casualties claimed Irish descent: Bush, *Casualties of Peterloo*, p. 29. See also D. MacRaild, *Faith, Fraternity and Fighting: The Orange Order and Irish Migrants* (Liverpool, 2005), p. 39.

47 Bush, *Casualties of Peterloo*, p. 138.

48 Thompson, *TMEWC*, pp. 751, 768.

49 Ibid., p. 81.

50 Ibid., pp. 53–4.

51 Ibid., pp. 55–6.

52 Ibid., p. 157.

53 On Hunt's 'sufferings' in gaol see M. C. Finn, 'Henry Hunt's *Peep into Prison*: the radical discontinuities of imprisonment for debt', in Burgess and Festenstein, *English Radicalism*, pp. 190–217, at pp. 201–2. These pleasures were eventually removed from Hunt as a result of investigations by the former prison taskmaster Daniel Lake, who alleged, among other things, that the gaoler's wife, Mrs Bridle, had been offering sexual favours to the prisoners.

54 Here I cannot agree with Belchem's assessment that the 'authorities were quite confounded by the nature of the radical challenge'. 'Peterloo' was quite easily accommodated into dominant narratives of the unruliness of the people. Belchem, *'Orator' Hunt*, p. 109.

55 'Manchester Aug. 26th', *The Times*, 28 August 1819.

56 J. Wroe, *Part One: The Peter Loo Massacre!* (Manchester, 1819), p. 9.

57 Quoted in M. Wainwright, 'Battle for the memory of Peterloo', *Guardian*, 13 August 2007.

58 'Salford sessions – libel, Manchester Jan 27 1820', *The Times*, 29 January 1820.

59 Figure quoted in R. Holmes, *Shelley: The Pursuit* (rev. edn, London, 1994), p. 540.

60 National Archives, MPI 1/134, http://www.nationalarchives.gov.uk/ human-rights/1815-1848/doc-peterloo-image.htm, accessed on 14 May 2008.

61 Quoted in Cross, 'Cruikshank', 187.

62 W. Keach, 'The Political Poet', in T. Morton, ed., *Cambridge Companion to Shelley* (Cambridge, 2006), ch. 7, at p. 131.

63 Introduction, in ibid., p. 1.

64 For these references see McElligott, 'William Hone', pp. 6–9.

65 Dinwiddy, *From Luddism to the First Reform Bill*, p. 34.

CHAPTER 14

1 Bush, 'Women at Peterloo', p. 223.

2 'High Treason: Preston, Dec. 4', *The Times*, 7 December 1819.

3 D. Johnson, *Regency Revolution: The Case of Arthur Thistlewood* (Salisbury, 1974), p. 109.

4 Quoted in Thompson, *TMEWC*, pp. 73–4.

5 See M. Chase, 'Cato Street Conspirators', *ODNB*; Johnson, *Regency Revolution*, for the Cato Street Conspiracy.

6 P. Berreford Ellis, 'John Baird', *ODNB*.

7 Thompson, *TMEWC*, p. 775–6.

8 Dinwiddy, *From Luddism to the First Reform Bill*, p. 38.

9 Clark, *Struggle for the Breeches*, p. 171.

10 Clark, *Scandal*, pp. 106–7

11 Ibid., p. 196.

12 Quoted in Epstein, *Radical Expression*, p. 119.

13 Dinwiddy, *From Luddism to the First Reform Bill*, p. 8.

14 Quoted in P. Schofield, 'Jeremy Bentham, the French Revolution and Political Radicalism', in F. Rosen, ed., *Jeremy Bentham* (Farnham, 2007), ch. 22, at p. 544.

15 F. Rosen, 'Jeremy Bentham's Radicalism', in Burgess and Festenstein, eds, *English Radicalism*, ch. 9, pp. 230–2.

16 J. R. Dinwiddy, 'Bentham's Transition to Political Radicalism, 1809–1810', in his *Radicalism and Reform in Britain, 1780–1850* (London, 1992), ch. 15, p. 288.

17 Dinwiddy, *From Luddism to the First Reform Bill*, p. 33.

18 Rosen, 'Bentham's Radicalism', p. 228.

19 Dinwiddy, *From Luddism to the First Reform Bill*, p. 17.

20 Ibid., p. 18.

21 Ibid., p. 14.

22 Ibid., p. 28.

23 Thompson, *TMEWC*, p. 567.

24 Hone, *Radicalism in London*, pp. 320–1.

25 Hilton, *Mad, Bad and Dangerous People?*, p. 574.

26 Ibid., p. 576.

27 Cole and Postgate, *British Common People*, p. 240.

28 Dinwiddy, *From Luddism to the First Reform Act*, p. 59.

29 Dinwiddy, 'Bentham's Transition', pp. 286–7.

30 See D. Hirst, *The Representatives of the People? Voters and Voting in England under the Early Stuarts* (Cambridge, 1975), p. 105. But, as Mark Kishlansky points out, the right to vote and the actual exercising of that vote were two different things: *Parliamentary Selection: Social and Political Choice in Early Modern England* (Cambridge, 1986).

31 The point is well made in Hilton, *Mad, Bad and Dangerous People?*, pp. 422–3. For categorical evidence that the Great Reform Act 'diminished the penetration of the electorate down the social scale', see O'Gorman, *Voters, Patrons and Parties*, p. 217.

32 Although O'Gorman notes that labourers voted two to one against Hunt at the 1830 election: ibid., p. 221.

33 T. Morton, 'Receptions', in T. Morton, ed., *Cambridge Companion to Shelley* (Cambridge, 2006), ch. 2, at p. 40.

34 Quoted in S. Schofield, *Short Stories about Failsworth Folk* (Blackpool, 1905), pp. 40–1. Another old Chartist, Ben Wilson, also began his political autobiography with Peterloo: see Vincent, ed., *Testaments of Radicalism*, p. 195. In Britain, the memory of Peterloo continues to be commemorated, thanks in large part to the efforts of the Peterloo Memorial Campaign: see D. Ward, 'New plaque tells truth of Peterloo killings 188 years on', *Guardian*, 27 December 2007.

PART SIX: A KNIFE-AND-FORK QUESTION

1 Quoted in D. Thompson, *The Chartists: Popular Politics in the Industrial Revolution* (Aldershot, 1986), p. 146.

CHAPTER 15

1 Quoted in P. Jones, 'The Tolpuddle Martyrs Museum and related sites', *Labour History Review*, 67 (2002), 221–8, at 225.

2 On the legal aspects of the case see J. Marlow, *The Tolpuddle Martyrs* (London, 1971), chs 5–7. This line of attack was used in other cases to hobble early trade associations: see J. V. Orth, *Combination and Conspiracy: A Legal History of Trade Unionism, 1721–1906* (Oxford, 1991), pp. 113–14. On the importance of oaths and other ritual aspects to early trade unions, see M. Chase, *Early Trade Unionism: Fraternity, Skill and the Politics of Labour* (Aldershot, 2000), pp. 167–70.

3 Marlow, *Tolpuddle Martyrs*, p. 115.

4 Chase, *Early Trade Unionism*, pp. 162–6.

5 For their conditions see Marlow, *Tolpuddle Martyrs*, chs 10–11.

6 Ibid., p. 272.

7 Quoted in J. Epstein, *The Lion of Freedom: Feargus O'Connor and the Chartist Movement, 1832–1842* (London, 1982), p. 18.

8 On the links between Loveless and Chartism see R. Wells, 'Southern Chartism', in J. Rule and R. Wells, *Crime, Protest and Popular Politics in Southern England 1740–1850* (London, 1997), ch. 7, at p. 129; C. V. J. Griffiths, 'Tolpuddle Martyrs', *ODNB*.

9 Epstein, *Lion of Freedom*, pp. 90–1.

10 Quoted in M. Chase, *Chartism: A New History* (Manchester, 2007), p. 21.

11 Hay and Rogers, *Eighteenth-Century English Society*, p. 9.

12 G. Claeys, ed., *The Chartist Movement in Britain 1838–1850* (6 vols, London, 2001), i, p. xx.

13 F. Engels, *The Condition of the Working Class in England*, trans. and ed. W. O. Henderson and W. H. Chaloner (Stanford, 1958), p. 312.

14 Quoted in Chase, *Chartism*, p. 22.

15 E. Royle, *Chartism* (3rd edn, Harlow, 1996), p. 97; Vincent, ed., *Testaments of Radicalism*, p. 187.

16 On the debate over the 'economic' or 'political' nature of Chartism see G. Stedman Jones, 'Rethinking Chartism', in his *Languages of Class: Studies in English Working-Class History 1832–1982* (Cambridge, 1983), ch. 3.

17 On the full powers given by the coercion bill and the English reaction to it see Thompson, *Chartists*, p. 19.

18 D. Slack, ed., *Lives of Victorian Political Figure*, II: vol. 4, *James Bronterre O'Brien* (London, 2007), p. xii. See for O'Brien's interest in land reform, prefiguring the Land Plan by over a decade, A. Plummer, *Bronterre: A Political Biography of Bronterre O'Brien 1804–1864* (London, 1971), p. 36.

19 Though Slack suggests that Bronterre's increasingly 'difficult' behaviour was the result of mental illness, not heavy drinking: see Slack, *O'Brien*, pp. xxxv–xxxvii.

20 See the reproduction in Claeys, *Chartist Movement*, i, p. 120. For a discussion of the People's Charter which goes beyond the Six Points see M. Taylor, 'The Six Points: Chartism and the Reform of Parliament', in O. Ashton, R. Fyson and S. Roberts, *The Chartist Legacy* (Woodbridge, 1999), ch. 1.

21 Epstein, *Lion of Freedom*, p. 23.

22 M. Chase, 'London Working Men's Association', *ODNB*.

23 Thompson, *Chartists*, p. 120.

24 Ibid., pp. 57–8.

25 P. A. Pickering, '"And Your Petitioners &c.": Chartist petitioning in popular politics 1838–48', *English Historical Review*, 116 (2001), 368–88, at 378. Thompson, *Chartists*, p. 60, questions the worth of petitioning in binding together Chartist groups. However, she arguably employs too restrictive a definition of who was a Chartist. Chartism was a mass movement, but not

a mass membership movement. In this respect, as in others, it was like a modern political party.

26 Pickering, 'Chartist petitioning', 379.

27 Ibid., 378.

CHAPTER 16

1 Stephens, 'The Political Pulpit', no. 6, delivered at Shepherdess Fields, Islington, London, 12 May 1839, in Claeys, *Chartist Movement*, i, p. 264.

2 Thompson, *Chartists*, p. 67.

3 For these rumours, see D. J. V. Jones, *The Last Rising: The Newport Insurrection of 1839* (Oxford, 1985), p. 94.

4 Chase, *Chartism*, p. 113.

5 Ibid., p. 116.

6 Jones, *Last Rising*, p. 198.

7 See for example Stephens, 'The Political Pulpit', no. 12, sermon delivered at Ashton-under-Lyne, 9 June 1839, which employed King Alfred, Henry of Bracton, Queen Elizabeth I, Algernon Sidney and William Blackstone (on the Bill of Rights), in Claeys, *Chartist Movement*, i, pp. 340–1.

8 Ibid., ii, p. 13.

9 See Eckersley, 'Of radical design', p. 572.

10 See Thompson, *Chartists*, p. 67: 'The question was much more one of tactics than one of fundamental principle.' This is half right. Public attitudes towards the right of resistance shifted according to circumstances, but the point is that the right of resistance had been an accepted part of one British political ideology, Whiggery, for well over a century.

11 *The Northern Star*, III, 142, 1 August 1840, reproduced at http://ncse-viewpoint.cch.kcl.ac.uk/Repository/NSS/1840/08/01/101-NSS-1840-08-01-PG0 01.PDF#OLV0_Page_0001, accessed on 18 June 2008. See also M. Chase, 'National Charter Association of Great Britain', *ODNB*.

12 Quoted in Thompson, *Chartists*, p. 131. For women and Chartism generally see ibid., ch. 7.

13 Stephens, 'The Political Pulpit', no. 2, in Claeys, *Chartist Movement*, i, p. 214.

14 Thompson, *Chartists*, p. 137.

15 Engels, *Condition of the Working Class*, p. 259.

16 K. Marx, 'The Chartist movement', *New York Tribune*, 25 August 1852, reproduced at http://gerald-massey.org.uk/jones/b_marx.htm, accessed on 20 June 2008. For other comments from Marx lauding the Chartists see Chase, *Chartism*, p. 289.

17 Ibid., p. 250.

18 See for example Tom Nairn, *The Enchanted Glass: Britain and Its Monarchy* (2nd edn, London, 1994), pp. 205, 327.

19 Quoted in Pickering, 'Popular monarchism', 243.

20 R. Carlile, *An Address to that Portion of the People of Great Britain and*

Ireland calling themselves Reformers (1839), in Claeys, *Chartist Movement*, ii, 136.

21 Engels, *Condition of the Working Class*, p. 259. Of course, the anti-democratic Bagehot thought that this 'sham' was actually a good thing, as it served to distract the disgruntled working classes from the true source of their misery.

22 Pickering 'Popular monarchism', 242.

23 Quoted in Chase, *Chartism*, p. 241.

24 Ibid., p. 168.

25 Claeys, *Chartist Movement*, i, p. 244.

26 Chase, *Chartism*, p. 171.

27 Ibid., p. 172.

28 Ibid., p. 174.

29 Ibid., p. 197.

30 Ibid., p. 183.

31 See Marx, 'The Chartist movement'.

32 Chase, *Chartism*, p. 202.

33 Claeys, *Chartist Movement*, i, p. 135.

34 Chase, *Chartism*, p. 206.

35 Ibid., p. 214.

36 Quoted in Chase, 'National Charter Association of Great Britain', *ODNB*.

37 Chase, *Chartism*, p. 223.

38 Ibid., p. 224.

39 Ibid., p. 214.

40 Ibid., p. 241.

CHAPTER 17

1   See R. Moran, 'Daniel McNaughtan', *ODNB*.

2   Chase, *Chartism*, p. 209.

3   Ibid., p. 248.

4   Ibid., pp. 250–1.

5   Ibid., p. 249.

6   Ibid., p. 253.

7   Quoted in J. Bronstein, 'The homestead and the garden plot: cultural pressures on land reform in nineteenth-century Britain and the USA', *European Legacy*, 6 (2001), 159–75, at 168.

8   Chase, *Chartism*, p. 260.

9   Ibid., pp. 260–1.

10 Ibid., p. 284.

11 Quoted in S. Roberts, 'Feargus O'Connor in the House of Commons, 1847–1852', in Ashton *et al.*, eds, *The Chartist Legacy*, ch. 5, at p. 105.

12 Chase, *Chartism*, p. 294.

13 Ibid., p. 295.

14 For a detailed breakdown of the figures see D. Goodway, *London Chartism, 1838–1848* (Cambridge, 1982), pp. 136–40.

15 Quoted in Claeys, *Chartist Movement*, i, p. xxxii.

16 Chase, *Chartism*, p. 302.

17 Quoted in Royle, *Chartism*, p. 45.

18 Quoted in Vincent, ed., *Testaments of Radicalism*, p. 202.

19 P. Fryer, 'William Cuffay', *ODNB*.

20 Pickering, 'A Wider Field', p. 43; Chase, *Chartism*, p. 311.

21 In Claeys, *Chartist Movement*, i, p. xxxii.

22 P. A. Pickering, 'The Chartist Rites of Passage: Commemorating Feargus O'Connor', in P. A. Pickering and A. Tyrrell, eds, *Contested Sites: Commemoration, Memorial and Popular Politics in Nineteenth-Century Britain* (Basingstoke, 2004), ch. 5, pp. 116–17. The statue is currently in a rather neglected state: see http://pmsa.cch.kcl.ac.uk/NM/ SB0077.htm, accessed on 11 June 2008.

23 Chase, *Chartism*, p. 328.

24 Quoted in Bronstein, 'Homestead and the garden plot', 168.

25 Ibid., 171.

26 Royle, *Chartism*, p. 49.

27 Ibid., p. 50.

28 Ibid., p. 86.

29 B. Brierley, *Home Memories and out of Work* (Bramhall, 2002), p. 23.

30 Vincent, ed., *Testaments of Radicalism*, p. 141.

31 Ibid., p. 211.

32 G. Monbiot, 'These objects of contempt are now our best chance of feeding the world', *Guardian*, 10 June 2008.

33 For the commemoration of Tolpuddle see C. V. J. Griffiths, 'Remembering Tolpuddle: rural history and commemoration in the inter-war labour movement', *History Workshop Journal*, 44 (1997), 145–70; Jones, 'Tolpuddle Martyrs Museum'.

34 J. Lawrence, 'Popular socialism and the socialist revival in Britain', *Journal of British Studies*, 31 (1992), 163–82, at 172, for the influence of Chartism on the early Labour Party.

35 P. Wright, *On Living in an Old Country: The National Past in Contemporary Britain* (London, 1986), p. 56.

36 M. Chase, '"Wholesome object lessons": the Chartist Land Plan in retrospect', *English Historical Review*, 118 (2003), 59–85, at 85.

37 I thank Malcolm Chase for this point.

38 www.chartists.net.

PART SEVEN: THE BLOODLESS REVOLUTION

1 Annie Kenney, *Memories of a Militant* (London, 1924), p. xx.

CHAPTER 18

1 Quoted in P. Foot, *The Vote: How It Was Won, How It Was Undermined* (London, 2005), p. 148.

2 J. Rendall, 'The Citizenship of Women and the Reform Act of 1867', in C. Hall, K. McClelland and J. Rendall, eds, *Defining the Victorian Nation: Class, Race, Gender and the British Reform Act of 1867* (Cambridge, 2000), ch. 3, p. 135.

3 Ibid., p. 136; for the figures see K. T. Hoppen, *The Mid-Victorian Generation 1846–1886* (Oxford, 1998), p. 253. The relatively small increase in the county franchise reflected, along with the redistribution of pocket boroughs to counties rather than large Liberal-voting cities, Disraeli's cunning skewing of the act to favour Tory voters.

4 J. Purvis, *Emmeline Pankhurst: A Biography* (London, 2002).

5 M. Phillips, *The Ascent of Woman: A History of the Suffragette Movement and the Ideas behind It* (London, 2003), p. 242. Phillips's approach was neatly lampooned by June Purvis in her review 'Man-hating lesbian precursors of the Nazis and their struggle for higher morality', *Times Higher Education Supplement*, 10 October 2003.

6 See Martin Pugh's *The Pankhursts* (London, 2001). Pugh's work came in for heavy criticism: J. Purvis, 'Pugh's book is full of errors', *Times Higher Education Supplement*, 22 January 2002; H. Swain, 'The Pankhursts – politics and passion', *Times Higher Education Supplement*, 25 January 2002; J. Liddington, 'Pankhursts and provocations', *Times Higher Education Supplement*, 31 January 2003.

7 An exception is Pugh's *Pankhursts*.

8 On the centenary see J. Liddington, 'Era of commemoration: celebrating the suffrage centenary', *History Workshop Journal*, 59 (2005), 195–218.

9 E. Pankhurst, 'Why We Are Militant', in J. Marcus, ed., *Suffrage and the Pankhursts* (London, 1987), p. 154.

10 S. S. Horton, 'British Freewomen: National Identity, Constitutionalism and Languages of Race in Early Suffragist Histories', in E. J. Yeo, ed., *Radical Femininity: Women's Self-Representation in the Public Sphere* (Manchester, 1998), ch. 6; J. Rendall, 'Citizenship, Culture and Civilisation: The Languages of British Suffragists, 1866–1874', in C. Daley and M. Nolan, eds, *Suffrage and beyond: International Feminist Perspectives* (Auckland, 1994), pp. 127–50; L. E. N. Mayhall, 'Defining militancy: radical protest, the constitutional idiom, and women's suffrage in Britain, 1908–1909', *Journal of British Studies*, 39 (2000), 340–71; E. S. Pankhurst, *The Suffragette Movement: An Intimate Account of Persons and Ideals* (London, 1931), p. 30.

11 H. Mitchell, *The Hard Way Up: The Autobiography of Hannah Mitchell, Suffragette and Rebel*, ed. G. Mitchell (London, 1968), p. 132.

12 Pugh, *Pankhursts*, p. 1.

13 J. Purvis, 'Emmeline Pankhurst', *ODNB*; A. Rosen, *Rise Up, Women! The Militant Campaign of the Women's Social and Political Union 1903–1914* (Aldershot, 1974), p. 8.

14 Ibid., p. 3.

15 J. Liddington and J. Norris, *One Hand Tied Behind Us: The Rise of the Women's Suffrage Movement* (2nd edn, London, 2000), p. 23.

16 Hoppen, *Mid-Victorian Generation*, p. 318.

17 S. S. Holton, *Feminism and Democracy: Women's Suffrage and Reform Politics in Britain, 1900–1918* (Cambridge, 1986), p. 10.

18 Rosen, *Rise Up, Women!*, pp. 4–5.

19 Hoppen, *Mid-Victorian Generation*, pp. 330–1.

20 On the connections see Rendall, 'Citizenship of Women'.

21 Rosen, *Rise Up, Women!*, p. 6.

22 A. Dingsdale, 'Kensington Society', *ODNB*.

23 On the richness of suffrage propaganda see L. Tickner, *The Spectacle of Women: Imagery of the Suffrage Campaign* (Chicago, 1988).

24 See M. L. Bush's comments regarding the militant tone of women's banners at Peterloo: Bush, 'Women at Peterloo', 220–3.

25 M. Taylor, 'John Bright', *ODNB*.

26 Rosen, *Rise Up, Women!*, p. 8.

27 E. S. Pankhurst, *Suffrage Movement*, p. 39; see also Rendall, 'Citizenship of Women', p. 138

28 However, a limited number of propertied women left on the electoral roll were able to exercise the vote after 1867: ibid., p. 149.

29 E. S. Pankhurst, *Suffrage Movement*, p. 11.

30 Quoted in Pugh, *Pankhursts*, p. 21.

31 Quoted in Rosen, *Rise Up, Women!*, p. 16n.

32 J. R. Walkowitz, 'Josephine Elizabeth Butler', *ODNB*.

33 J. Harris, 'J.S. Mill', *ODNB*.

34 L. Bland, *Banishing the Beast: English Feminism and Sexual Morality, 1885–1914* (London, 1995), ch. 3.

35 Rosen, *Rise Up, Women!*, p. 10.

36 Ibid., p. 11n.

37 E. S. Pankhurst, *Suffragette Movement*, pp. 83–4.

38 Quoted in A. Taylor, 'Annie Besant', *ODNB*.

39 Quoted in Rosen, *Rise Up, Women!*, p. 17.

40 Mitchell, *Hard Way Up*, p. 116.

41 On Morris's conversion see F. MacCarthy, *William Morris: A Life for Our Time* (London, 1994), ch. 14; E. P. Thompson, *William Morris: Romantic to Revolutionary* (London, 1955), ch. 7.

42 E. S. Pankhurst, *Suffragette Movement*, p. 111.

43 Quoted in Pugh, *Pankhursts*, p. 63.

44 Quoted in Holton, *Feminism and Democracy*, p. 58.

45 A. A. McBriar, *Fabian Socialism and English Politics 1884–1918* (Cambridge, 1966), p. 26. Though Pugh notes that the leading Fabian, Beatrice Webb, actually signed an anti-suffrage petition in 1889: *Pankhursts*, p. 63.

46 See E. Hobsbawm, 'The Fabians Reconsidered', in his *Labouring Men: Studies in the History of Labour* (London, 1986), ch. 14, at p. 268.

47 Holton, *Feminism and Democracy*, p. 56.

48 Ibid., p. 55.

49 Mitchell, *Hard Way Up*, p. 96.

50 Ibid., p. 149.

51 Quoted in Liddington and Norris, *One Hand Tied Behind Us*, pp. 28–9.

52 Ibid., pp. 34–5.

53 Ibid., p. 96.

54 Holton, *Feminism and Democracy*, p. 57.

55 Mitchell, *Hard Way Up*, p. 131.

56 C. Pankhurst, *Unshackled: The Story of How We Won the Vote*, ed. Ld Pethick-Lawrence (London, 1987), p. 43.

57 Quoted in McBriar, *Fabian Socialism*, p. 78.

58 Ibid., p. 81.

59 A. Wright, 'British socialists and the British constitution', *Parliamentary History*, 43 (1990), 322–40, at 324.

60 Ibid., passim.

61 For 'Bloody Sunday' see Thompson, *William Morris*, pp. 482–503.

62 Quoted in ibid., p. 490.

63 Quoted in MacCarthy, *William Morris*, p. 573.

CHAPTER 19

1 Motto of the Women's Social and Political Union.

2 Kenney, *Memories of a Militant*, p. 27.

3 Quoted in Rosen, *Rise Up, Women!*, p. 28.

4 Quoted in Liddington and Norris, *One Hand Tied Behind Us*, p. 174.

5 K. Hunt, 'Rethinking the early years of the WSPU', *Bulletin of the Marx Memorial Library*, 139 (2004), 7–23.

6 L. P. Hume, *The National Union of Women's Suffrage Societies, 1897–1914* (London, 1982), p. 55.

7 See George Dangerfield's classic *The Strange Death of Liberal England* (London, 1997), pp. 147–8. Of Annie Kenney: 'it was very like the story of Cinderella, with Mrs Pankhurst for fairy godmother, and for Prince Charming?'

8 E. S. Pankhurst, *Suffragette Movement*, pp. 185–6.

9 Ibid., p. 200.

10 Quoted in Hume, *National Union*, p. 17.

11 Quoted in Rosen, *Rise Up, Women!*, p. 38.

12 Ibid., p. 41.

13 This point is made by S. S. Holton in 'WSPU', *ODNB*.

14 E. S. Pankhurst, *Suffragette Movement*, p. 214; for Newbold see *ODNB*.

15 Pugh, *Pankhursts*, pp. 118–19.

16 E. S. Pankhurst, *Suffragette Movement*, p. 217.

17 Pugh, *Pankhursts*, p. 142.

18 Kenney, *Memories of a Militant*, p. 71.

19 Rosen, *Rise Up, Women!*, p. 66.

20 Ibid., p. 70.

21 Quoted in Holton, *Feminism and Democracy*, p. 55.

22 Ibid., p. 37.

23 Rosen, *Rise Up, Women!*, p. 74.

24 E. Pethick-Lawrence, *My Part in a Changing World* (London, 1938), Preface.

25 Quoted in Rosen, *Rise Up, Women!*, pp. 76–7.

26 Ibid., p. 77.

27 J. Dodge and S. Forward, 'Miss Agnes Resbury (1858–1943): the memoirs of a warder at Holloway', *Women's History Review*, 15 (2006), 783–80, at 786.

28 Quoted in Rosen, *Rise Up, Women!*, p. 77.

29 See Hume, *National Union*, pp. 28–32.

30 Rosen, *Rise Up, Women!*, p. 83.

31 Ibid., p. 97.

32 Quoted in E. S. Pankhurst, *Suffragette Movement*, p. 285.

33 Quoted in Rosen, *Rise Up, Women!*, p. 105.

34 C. Pankhurst, *Unshackled*, p. 95.

35 Mitchell, *Hard Way Up*, pp. 152–3.

36 E. Pethick-Lawrence, *My Part in a Changing World*, p. 161.

37 Pugh, *Pankhursts*, p. 178.

38 Ibid., p. 183.

39 On the important constitutionalist grounding of Christabel's argument see Mayhall, 'Defining militancy', 354–5.

40 Pugh, *Pankhursts*, p. 184.

41 Rosen, *Rise Up, Women!*, p. 113

CHAPTER 20

1 The *Daily News* on the WSPU's move towards hunger-striking, quoted in E. S. Pankhurst, *Suffragette Movement*, p. 312.

2 Rosen, *Rise Up, Women!*, p. 118.

3 See L. E. N. Mayhall, *The Militant Suffrage Movement: Citizenship and Resistance in Britain, 1860–1930* (Oxford, 2003), p. 3.

4 Christabel stated that the hunger strike was 'entirely [Dunlop's] own initiative': C. Pankhurst, *Unshackled*, p. 133

5 C. J. Bearman, 'An army without discipline? Suffragette militancy and the budget crisis of 1909', *Historical Journal*, 50 (2007), 861–89, at 878.

6 Rosen, *Rise Up, Women!*, pp. 122–3.

7 Bearman, 'An army without discipline?', 873.

8 Ibid., 871–2.

9   Quoted in K. O. Morgan, 'David Lloyd George', *ODNB*.

10 Rosen, *Rise Up, Women!*, p. 123.

11 Bearman, 'An army without discipline?', 881.

12 J. F. Geddes, 'Culpable complicity: the medical profession and the forcible feeding of suffragettes, 1909–1914', *Women's History Review*, 17 (2008), 79–94, at 82.

13 Ibid., 85, notes that some medical officers suggested beginning forcible feeding on the day that food was refused.

14 Rosen, *Rise Up, Women!*, pp. 123–4.

15 E. Crawford, 'Police, prisons and prisoners: the view from the Home Office', *Women's History Review*, 14 (2005), 487–506, at 501.

16 E. S. Pankhurst, *Suffragette Movement*, p. 327.

17 C. Pankhurst, *Unshackled*, p. 145.

18 Geddes, 'Culpable complicity', 85–7.

19 Rosen, *Rise Up, Women!*, p. 127.

20 For what really happened at the Bermondsey by-election, see the discussion in Mayhall, 'Defining militancy', 365–6.

21 Quoted in Mayhall, *Militant Suffrage Movement*, p. 105.

22 Quoted in Liddington and Norris, *One Hand Tied Behind Us*, p. 210; attributed to Esther Roper in G. R. Searle, *A New England? Peace and War 1886–1918* (Oxford, 2004), p. 458.

23 F. W. Pethick-Lawrence, *Fate Has Been Kind* (London, 1940), p. 96.

24 Rosen, *Rise Up, Women!*, p. 131.

25 Ibid., p. 140.

26 Ibid., p. 150.

27 Ibid.

28 A point well made in Crawford, 'Police, prisons and prisoners', 493.

29 Rosen, *Rise Up, Women!*, p. 155.

30 Ibid., p. 160.

31 Quoted in Holton, *Feminism and Democracy*, p. 80.

32 See Holton, 'NUWSS', *ODNB*; Pugh, *Pankhursts*, p. 152.

33 Searle, *A New England?*, p. 465.

34 Holton, *Feminism and Democracy*, p. 94.

CHAPTER 21

1   Rosen, *Rise Up, Women!*, pp. 176–7.

2   For Craggs see E. Crawford, *The Women's Suffrage Movement: A Reference Guide* (Basingstoke, 1999), pp. 146–7

3   Rosen, *Rise Up, Women!*, p. 160.

4   Ibid., p. 189.

5   C. J. Bearman, 'An examination of suffragette violence', *English Historical Review*, 120 (2005), 365–97, at 367.

6   I. Kramnick and B. Sheerman, *Harold Laski: A Life on the Left* (London, 1993), pp. 66–9.

7   Bearman, 'Suffragette violence', 393 estimates that there were between twenty and thirty-five incidents during this period in which human life was at risk.

8   Rosen, *Rise Up, Women!*, pp. 199–200.

9   E. S. Pankhurst, *Suffragette Movement*, p. 468.

10 Rosen, *Rise Up, Women!*, p. 211.

11 Holton, *Feminism and Democracy*, pp. 119–20.

12 Ibid., p. 100.

13 Quoted in Rosen, *Rise Up, Women!*, p. 197.

14 Reproduced in Marcus, ed., *Suffrage and the Punkhursts*, pp. 197–241.

15 Ibid., p. 195. See for context Rosen, *Rise Up, Women!*, pp. 205–6; Bland, Banishing the Beast, p. 244.

16 Quoted in Mayhall, *Militant Suffrage Movement*, p. 94.

17 Marcus, ed., *Suffrage and the Pankhursts*, p. 204.

18 Ibid., p. 209.

19 Quoted in Mayhall, *Militant Suffrage Movement*, p. 95.

20 E. S. Pankhurst, *Suffragette Movement*, p. 522.

21 For Kitchener see Marcus, ed., *Suffrage and the Pankhursts*, p. 200; Pugh, *Pankhursts*, p. 301.

22 Bearman, 'Suffragette violence', 392.

23 Rosen, *Rise Up, Women!*, p. 216.

24 Geddes, 'Culpable complicity', 87. Sylvia Pankhurst was certain that suffragettes were being administered 'chemical coshes' in prison: *Suffragette Movement*, pp. 557–62.

25 Liddington, 'Era of commemoration', 205.

26 Rosen, *Rise Up, Women!*, p. 221.

27 Holton, *Feminism and Democracy*, p. 128.

28 Ibid., pp. 125–6.

29 Rosen, *Rise Up, Women!*, pp. 146–7.

30 Ibid., pp. 151–2.

31 Bearman, 'Suffragette violence', 387.

32 A. K. Smith, 'The Pankhursts and the war: suffrage magazines and First World War propaganda', *Women's History Review*, 12 (2003), 103–118, at 109, 113.

33 Quoted in N. F. Gullace, *The Blood of Our Sons': Men, Women and the Renegotiation of British Citizenship during the Great War* (Basingstoke, 2002), p. 135.

34 Holton, *Feminism and Democracy*, p. 135.

35 Smith, 'Pankhursts and the war', 111.

36 Rosen, *Rise Up, Women!*, p. 257.

37 On this see Gullace, *The Blood of Our Sons*, esp. pts II and III.

38 Ibid., p. 96.

39 Ibid., p. 171.

40 Quoted in Searle, *A New England?*, p. 792.

41 E. S. Pankhurst, *Suffragette Movement*, p. 608.

42 Mayhall, *Militant Suffrage Movement*, p. 141.

43 C. Law, *Suffrage and Power: The Women's Movement 1918–1928* (London, 1997), p. 227.

44 C. Pankhurst, *Unshackled*, p. 299.

45 E. Pethick-Lawrence, *My Part in a Changing World*, pp. 150–1.

CHAPTER 22

1 Quoted in Pugh, *Pankhursts*, p. 340.

2 K. Coates, *Common Ownership: Clause IV and the Labour Party* (Nottingham, 1995), ch. 2, at p. 9.

3 Ibid., p. 8.

4 On the debt owed in Clause IV to an earlier radical-Liberal tradition see A. J. Reid and H. Pelling, *A Short History of the Labour Party* (12th edn, Basingstoke, 2005), p. 38.

5 J. McIlroy and A. Campbell, '"Nina Ponomareva's Hats": the new revisionism, the Communist International, and the Communist Party of Great Britain, 1920–1930', *Labour/Le Travail*, 49 (2002), 147–87

6 Quoted in H. Pelling, *The British Communist Party: A Historical Profile* (London, 1975), pp. 185–6.

7 See Reid and Pelling, *Short History of the Labour Party*, p. 53.

8 Pelling, *British Communist Party*, p. 182.

9 A. Gillan, 'Day the East End said "No pasaran" [They shall not pass] to Blackshirts', *Guardian*, 30 September 2006.

10 See R. Thurlow, 'The straw that broke the camel's back: public order, civil liberties and the Battle of Cable Street', *Jewish Culture and History*, 1 (1998), 74–94; Cole and Postgate, *British Common People*, pp. 610–11.

11 Quoted in N. Newman, 'Dictatorship versus democracy: Labour's struggles against British Fascism', *History Workshop Journal*, 5 (1978), 67–88, at 72.

12 Ibid., 70.

13 Quoted in Wright, 'British socialists and the British constitution', 328.

14 Reid and Pelling, *Short History of the Labour Party*, p. 71.

15 Ibid., p. 89.

16 M. Sissons and P. French, eds, *The Age of Austerity 1945–51* (Harmondsworth, 1963), p. 19. My thanks to Dominic Sandbrook for this reference.

17 D. Sandbrook, *Never Had It So Good: A History of Britain from Suez to the Beatles* (London, 2005), p. 55.

18 Ibid., ch. 3.

19 A point made in A. J. Reid, *United We Stand: A History of Britain's Trade Unions* (London, 2005), p. 415.

20 Newman, 'Dictatorship versus democracy', 71.

EPILOGUE

1 Quoted in P. Vallely, 'So will the revolution start in Haltemprice and Howden?', *Independent*, 14 June 2008.

2 Text of the speech as in *Guardian*, 13 June 2008.

3 H. Porter, 'The future of democracy hangs on the 42 day debate', *Observer*, 8 June 2008; M. White, 'The Magna Carta question', *Guardian*, 11 June 2008.

4 B. Geldof, 'Don't let "Brave New Britain" remove our fundamental rights', *Telegraph*, 10 July 2008.

5 S. Heffer, 'Is our liberty or the PM's authority more important?', *Telegraph*, 11 June 2008.

6 http://www.ukpolitical.info/By-election_turnout.htm. The 34 per cent turnout was better than predicted, and sits about mid-range for by-elections between 1997 and the present. Not a disaster, but not a massive endorsement of Davis's civil liberties agenda either.

7 *The Times*, 30 September, 2006. B. Bragg, *The Progressive Patriot: A Search for Belonging* (London, 2006), esp. chs 6 and 10.

8 Campaign literature for the 2005 general election detailed at http://www.webarchive.org.uk/col/c8100.html. The BNP is noticeably reticent about putting its campaign literature online.

9 J. Epstein, 'The constitutional idiom: radical reasoning, rhetoric and action in early nineteenth-century England', *Journal of Social History*, 23 (1990), 553–74.

10 Quoted in Reid, *United We Stand*, p. 393.

11 'Tory Bill of Rights bid slammed', *BBC News*, 26 June 2006, http://news.bbc.co.uk/1/hi/uk_politics/5115912.stm

12 G. Aitchison, 'A new bill of rights for Britain?', Opendemocracy.net, 12 August 2008, http://www.opendemocracy.net/blog/ourkingdom-theme/guy-aitchison/2008/08/12/parliaments-proposals-on-a-new-bill-of-rights#comment-474045; T. Vallance, 'A bill of rights for Britain?', Newstatesman.com, 24 September 2008.

13 Wright, *On Living in an Old Country*, p. 140.

14 Contrast the revised figures offered by O'Gorman, *Voters, Patrons and Parties*, p. 179, with those employed by Barry Coward, *The Stuart Age: England 1603–1714* (3rd edn, Harlow, 2003), p. 349.

15 *The Black Dwarf*, no. 1, 29 January 1817.

SELECT BIBLIOGRAPHY

References to newspapers, magazines and websites have been omitted for reasons of space. All works dated before 1800 were published in London unless otherwise stated.

PRIMARY SOURCES

Manuscripts

British Library, Egerton MS 1048 ff. 91–2

East Sussex Record Office, NU1/3/4–5; NU13/3; SAS/A740

Folger Shakespeare Library, Washington DC, MS X. d. 483 (38), 'Sir H Waller at his retourne to London fro leveling ye levellers May 29th 1649'

National Archives, Kew, MPI 1/134

Norfolk Record Office: Norfolk Cathedral Ledger Book, DCN 47/1 f.71; COL/9/117 f. 71; COL/9/117 f. 2v

Printed Books, Edited Collections

Arden, J., *Left-handed Liberty: A Play about Magna Carta* (London, 1965)

Bacon, N., *An historical and political discourse of the laws and government of England* (1689 edn)

Bamford, S., *Passages in the Life of a Radical* (Oxford, 1984)

Beer, B. L., 'The Commoyson in Norfolk, 1549: a narrative of popular rebellion in sixteenth-century England', *Journal of Medieval and Renaissance Studies*, 6 (1976), 80–99

Binfield, K., ed., *Writings of the Luddites* (London, 2004)

Brierley, B., *Home Memories and Out of Work* (Bramhall, 2002)

Buff, or a Dissertation on Nakedness (1792)

Carlyle, T., *The Letters and Speeches of Oliver Cromwell*, ed. S. C. Lomas (3 vols, London, 1904)

Claeys, G., ed., *The Chartist Movement in Britain 1838–1850* (6 vols, London, 2001)

The Declaration of the Prince of Wales to the Commissioners of Scotland . . . also The Declaration and Speeches of Cornet Thompson and the rest of the Levellers (1649)

Disraeli, B., *Sybil*, ed. T. Braun (London, 1980)

Dobson, R. S., ed., *The Peasants' Revolt* (London, 1970)

Dodge, J., and Forward, S., eds, 'Miss Agnes Resbury (1858–1943): the memoirs of a warder at Holloway', *Women's History Review*, 15 (2006), 783–80

Engels, F., *The Condition of the Working Class in England*, trans. and ed. W. O. Henderson and W. H. Chaloner (Stanford, 1958)

Eyre, W., *The Serious Representation of Col. William Eyre* (1649)

Filmer, Sir Robert, 'The Anarchy of a limited or Mixed Monarchy', in *The Freeholder's Grand Inquest* (1679 edn)

Foner, P. S., ed., *The Complete Writings of Thomas Paine* (2 vols, New York, 1969)

Godwin, W., *An Enquiry Concerning Political Justice*, ed. M. Philp and A. Gee (London, Pickering & Chatto, 1993)

_____, *An Enquiry Concerning Political Justice, and its Influence on General Virtue and Happiness* (vol. 1, London, 1793) (Oxford, Woodstock repr., 1992)

_____, *Caleb Williams, or Things as They Are* (4th edn, London, 1831)

_____, *History of the Commonwealth of England from its Commencement, to the Restoration of Charles the Second*, ed. J. Morrow (Bristol, 2003)

The Humble Representation of the Committee, Gentry, Ministry, And other well affected Persons in the County of Leicester (London, 1648[9])

Hutton, W., *The Life of William Hutton*, Introduction by Carl Chinn (Studley, 1998)

Jacobson, D. L., ed., *The English Libertarian Heritage* (repr. San Francisco, 1994)

Kenney, Annie, *Memories of a Militant* (1924)

Kenyon, J. P., *The Stuart Constitution* (Cambridge, 1986)

Light Shining in Buckingham-shire (1648)

Lilburne, J., *The charters of London, or the second part of London's liberty in chaines discovered* (1646)

Lindley, K., *The English Civil War and Revolution: A Sourcebook* (London, 1998)

Marcus, J., ed., *Suffrage and the Pankhursts* (London, 1987)

Marsden Rock: or, the story of Peter Allan and Marsden Marine Grotto (Sunderland, 1848)

[Milton, J.,] *Of Reformation* (1641), in *Prose Works*, ed. R. Fletcher (Harvard, 1835)

Mitchell, H., *The Hard Way Up: The Autobiography of Hannah Mitchell, Suffragette and Rebel*, ed. G. Mitchell (London, 1968)

More Light Shining in Buckingham-shire (1649)

Morris, W., *Signs of Change: Seven Lectures Delivered on Various Occasions* (London, 1888)

Neville, A., *Norfolke Furies*, trans. R. Wood (London, 1623)

Nolan, M., *A Treatise of the Laws for Relief and Settlement of the Poor* (4th edn, 3 vols, London, 1852)

[Overton, R.,] *The Arraignement of Mr Persecution* ('Europe' [London], 1645)

Pankhurst, C., *Unshackled: The Story of How We Won the Vote*, ed. Ld Pethick-Lawrence (London, 1987)

Pankhurst, E. S., *The Suffragette Movement: An Intimate Account of Persons and Ideals* (London, 1931)

Pethick-Lawrence, E., *My Part in a Changing World* (London, 1938)

Pethick-Lawrence, F. W., *Fate Has Been Kind* (London, 1940)

Robson, J. P., *Summer Excursions in the North of England; including A Trip to Warkworth; A Ramble to Marsden Rocks; Picnicings at Finchale Priory; A Week at Gilsland* (Newcastle, 1851)

Schofield, S., *Short Stories about Failsworth Folk* (Blackpool, 1905)

[Sexby, E.,] *The Case of the armie truly stated* (1647)

Sharp, A., ed., *The English Levellers* (Cambridge, 1998)

Slack, D., ed., *Lives of Victorian Political Figures, II: vol. 4, James Bronterre O'Brien* (London, 2007)

Thale, M., ed., *Selections from the Papers of the London Corresponding Society 1792–1799* (Cambridge, 1983)

Underwood, T. L., ed., *The Acts of the Witnesses: The Autobiography of Lodowick Muggleton and Other Early Muggletonian Writings* (Oxford, 1999)

Vincent D., ed., *Testaments of Radicalism: Memoirs of Working-Class Politicians 1790–1885* (London, 1977)

White, J., *The Levellers (falsl'y so called) Vindicated* (1649)

Winstanley, G., *The Works of Gerrard Winstanley*, ed. G. H. Sabine (New York, 1945)

———, *The Law of Freedom and Other Writings*, ed. C. Hill (Harmondsworth, 1973)

Wollstonecraft, M., *A Vindication of the Rights of Woman*, ed. C. Ward (New York, 1996)

Wood, J., *The Levellers falsely so-called* (1649)

Wroe, J., *Part One: The Peter Loo Massacre!* (Manchester, 1819)

SECONDARY SOURCES

ARTICLES

Adair, D., 'Rumbold's dying speech, 1685, and Jefferson's last words on democracy, 1826', *William and Mary Quarterly*, 9 (1952), 521–31.

Alsop, J. D., 'Latimer, the "Commonwealth of Kent" and the 1549 rebellions', *Historical Journal*, 28 (1985), 379–83.

Aston, M. E., 'Lollardy and sedition, 1381–1431', *Past and Present*, 17 (1960), 1–44

———, 'Corpus Christi and Corpus Regni: heresy and the Peasants' Revolt', *Past and Present*, 143 (1994), 3–47

Aylmer, G. E., 'Collective mentalities in mid-seventeenth-century England: III Varieties of Radicalism', *Transactions of the Royal Historical Society*, 5th series, 38 (1988), 1–25

Baker, D. K., 'Topical Utopias: radicalising humanism in sixteenth-century England', *Studies in English Literature*, 36 (1996), 1–30

Baldwin, F. E., 'Sumptuary legislation and personal regulation in England', *Johns Hopkins University Studies in Historical and Political Science*, 44 (1926), 44–6

Bangaroo, S., 'A short analysis of the exile of an indigenous population from beginning to end', *Hertfordshire Law Journal*, 3 (2005), 3–7

Bearman, C. J., 'An examination of suffragette violence', *English Historical Review*, 120 (2005), 365–97

_____, 'An army without discipline? Suffragette militancy and the budget crisis of 1909', *Historical Journal*, 50 (2007), 861–89

Blom-Cooper, L., 'The role of the judge in modern society', *Political Quarterly*, 57 (1986), 144–55

Bohna, M., 'Armed force and civic legitimacy in Jack Cade's revolt, 1450', *English Historical Review*, 118 (2003), 563–82

Bronstein, J., 'The homestead and the garden plot: cultural pressures on land reform in nineteenth-century Britain and the USA', *The European Legacy*, 6 (2001), 159–75

Buck, P., 'People who counted: political arithmetic in the eighteenth century', *Isis*, 73 (1982), 28–45

Bush, M. L., 'Debate: Protector Somerset and the 1549 rebellions: a post revision questioned', *English Historical Review*, 115 (2000), 103–12

_____, 'The women at Peterloo: the impact of female reform on the Manchester meeting of August 16 1819', *History*, 89 (2004), 209–32

Chase, M., '"Wholesome Object Lessons": the Chartist Land Plan in retrospect', *English Historical Review*, 118 (2003), 59–85

Claeys, G., 'Republicanism versus commercial society: Paine, Burke, and the French Revolution debate', *Proceedings of the Consortium on Revolutionary Europe 1750–1850* (1989), 3–24

Como, D., 'Secret printing, the crisis of 1640, and the origins of civil war radicalism', *Past and Present*, 196 (2007), 37–82

Crawford, E., 'Police, prisons and prisoners: the view from the Home Office', *Women's History Review*, 14 (2005), 487–506

Cross, A. J., '"What a world we make the oppressor and the oppressed": George Cruikshank, Percy Shelley and the gendering of revolution in 1819', *English Literary History*, 71 (2004), 167–204

Cruikshanks, E., and Erskine Hill, H., 'The Waltham Black Act and Jacobitism', *Journal of British Studies*, 24 (1985), 358–65

Davis, J. C., 'Radicalism in a traditional society: the evaluation of radical thought in the English Commonwealth 1649–1660', *History of Political Thought*, 3 (1982), 193–213

_____, 'Religion and the struggle for freedom in the English Revolution', *Historical Journal*, 35 (1992), 507–31

Davis, T. W., 'The influence of Richard Price on the Burke–Paine debate', *Proceedings of the Consortium on Revolutionary Europe 1750–1850* (1990), 800–6

Dillinger, J., 'Comparing communities: local representation and territorial states in early modern Europe and New England', *German Historical Institute Bulletin*, 27 (2000)

Eckersley, R., 'Of radical design: John Cartwright and the redesign of the reform campaign, c. 1800–1811', *History*, 89 (2004), 560–80

Elliott, M., 'The Despard conspiracy reconsidered', *Past and Present*, 75 (1977), 46–61

Epstein, J., 'The constitutional idiom: radical reasoning, rhetoric and action in early-nineteenth-century England', *Journal of Social History*, 23 (1990), 553–74

Galbraith, V. H., 'Penrose Memorial Lecture: Runnymede revisited', *Proceedings of the American Philosophical Society*, 110 (1966), 307–17

Geddes, J. F., 'Culpable complicity: the medical profession and the forcible feeding of suffragettes, 1909–1914', *Women's History Review*, 17 (2008), 79–94

Gifford, R., 'The Chagos Islands – the land where human rights hardly ever happen', *Law, Social Justice and Global Development* [electronic law journal], 1 (2004)

Glover, S. D., 'The Putney Debates: popular versus elite republicanism', *Past and Present*, 164 (1999), 47–80

Griffiths, C. V. J., 'Remembering Tolpuddle: rural history and commemoration in the inter-war Labour movement', *History Workshop Journal*, 44 (1997), 145–70

Horn, J., 'Understanding crowd action: machine breaking in England and France, 1789–1817', *Proceedings of the Western Society for French History*, 31 (2003), 138–52

Hunt, A., 'The governance of consumption: sumptuary laws and shifting forms of regulation', *Economy and Society*, 25 (1996), 410–27

Hunt, K., 'Rethinking the early years of the WSPU', *Bulletin of the Marx Memorial Library*, 139 (2004), 7–23

Jones, P., 'The Tolpuddle Martyrs Museum and related sites', *Labour History Review*, 67 (2002), 221–8

Keynes, S., 'The cult of King Alfred', *Anglo-Saxon England*, 28 (1999), 225–357

Knapp, E. F., 'William Godwin's *Caleb Williams* and the origins of revolution', *Proceedings of the Consortium on Revolutionary Europe 1750–1850* (1989), 189–200

Knoppers, L, '"This so horrid spectacle": "Samson Agonistes" and the execution of the regicides', *English Literary Renaissance*, 20 (1990), 487–504

Lawrence, J., 'Popular socialism and the socialist revival in Britain', *Journal of British Studies*, 31 (1992), 163–82

Liddington, J., 'Era of commemoration: celebrating the suffrage centenary', *History Workshop Journal*, 59 (2005), 195–218

Loughran, T., 'Disseminating *Common Sense*: Thomas Paine and the problem of the early national bestseller', *American Literature*, 78 (2006), 1–28

Macalman, I., 'Ultra-radicalism and convivial debating clubs in London, 1795–1838', *English Historical Review*, 102 (1987), 309–33

MacCullough, D., 'Kett's rebellion in context', *Past and Present*, 84 (1981), 36–59

Manning, R. B., 'The rebellions of 1549 in England', *Sixteenth-Century Journal*, 10 (1979) 93–9

Marlow, J., 'The day of Peterloo', *Manchester Region History Review*, 3 (1989), 3–8

Mate, M., 'The economic and social roots of medieval popular rebellion: Sussex in 1450 to 1451', *Economic History Review*, 45 (1992), 661–76

Mayhall, L. E. N., 'Defining militancy: radical protest, the constitutional idiom, and women's Suffrage in Britain, 1908–1909', *Journal of British Studies*, 39 (2000), 340–71

McIlroy, J., and Campbell, A., '" Nina Ponomareva's hats": the new revisionism, the Communist International, and the Communist Party of Great Britain, 1920–1930', *Labour/Le Travail*, 49 (2002), 147–87

Miller, N. C., 'John Cartwright and radical parliamentary reform, 1808–1819', *English Historical Review*, 83 (1968), 705–28

_____, 'Major John Cartwright and the founding of the Hampden Club', *Historical Journal*, 17 (1974), 615–19

Mitchell, L. G., 'The Whigs, the people and reform', *Proceedings of the British Academy*, 100 (1999), 25–41

Moreton, C. E., 'The Walsingham conspiracy of 1537', *Historical Research*, 63 (1990), 29–43

Morrill, J., Manning B., and Underdown, D., 'What was the English Revolution?', *History Today*, 34 (1984), reprinted in P. Gaunt, ed., *The English Civil War: The Essential Readings* (Oxford, 2001), ch. 1

Navickas, K., 'The search for "General Ludd": the mythology of Luddism', *Social History*, 30 (2005), 281–95

Newman, N., 'Dictatorship versus democracy: Labour's struggles against British Fascism', *History Workshop Journal*, 5 (1978), 67–88

O'Gorman, F., 'The Paine burnings of 1792–3', *Past and Present*, 193 (2006), 111–55

Pederson, S., 'Hannah More meets Simple Simon: tracts, chapbooks, and popular culture in late eighteenth-century England', *Journal of British Studies*, 25 (1986), 84–113

Pickering, P. A., '"And Your Petitioners &c.": Chartist petitioning in popular politics 1838–48', *English Historical Review* 116 (2001), 368–88

_____, '"The Hearts of Millions": Chartism and popular monarchism in the 1840s', *History*, 88 (2003), 227–48

Poole, R., '"By Law and the Sword": Peterloo revisited', *History*, 94 (2006), 254–76

_____, 'The march to Peterloo: politics and festivity in late Georgian England', *Past and Present*, 192 (2006), 109–55

Rapp, D., 'Social mobility in the eighteenth century: the Whitbreads of Bedfordshire, 1720–1815', *Economic History Review*, 27 (1974), 380–94

Readman, P., 'The place of the past in English culture, c. 1890–1914', *Past and Present*, 186 (2005), 147–201

Seaberg, R. B., 'The Norman Conquest and the feudal law: the Levellers and the argument from continuity', *Historical Journal*, 24 (1981), 791–806

Shagan, E., '"Popularity" and the 1549 rebellions revisited', *English Historical Review*, 115 (2000), 121–33

Smith, A. K., 'The Pankhursts and the war: suffrage magazines and First World War propaganda', *Women's History Review*, 12 (2003), 103–18

Thurlow, R., 'The straw that broke the camel's back: public order, civil liberties and the Battle of Cable Street', *Jewish Culture and History*, 1 (1998), 74–94

Wagner, C., 'Loyalist propaganda and the scandalous life of Tom Paine: "Hypocritical Monster!"', *British Journal for Eighteenth Century Studies*, 28 (2005), 97–115

Walter, J., 'A "rising of the people"? The Oxfordshire rising of 1596', *Past and Present*, 107 (1985), 90–143

Wright, A., 'British socialists and the British constitution', *Parliamentary History*, 43 (1990), 322–40

BOOKS

Acheson, R. J., *Radical Puritans in England, 1550–1660* (London, 1990)

Adamson, J. S. A., *The Noble Revolt: The Overthrow of Charles I* (London, 2007)

Ashley, M., *Magna Carta in the Seventeenth Century* (Charlottesville, 1965)

Ashton, O., Fyson, R., and Roberts, S., eds, *The Chartist Legacy* (Woodbridge, 1999)

Bailey, B., *The Luddite Rebellion* (Stroud, 1998)

Barber, S., *A Revolutionary Rogue: Henry Marten and the English Republic* (Stroud, 2000)

Barrell, J., *Imagining the King's Death: Figurative Treason, Fantasies of Regicide, 1793–1796* (Oxford, 2000)

Belchem, J., *'Orator' Hunt: Henry Hunt and English Working-Class Radicalism* (Oxford, 1985)

Bewley, C., and Bewley, D., *Gentleman Radical: A Life of John Horne Tooke, 1736–1812* (London, 1998)

Bland, L., *Banishing the Beast: English Feminism and Sexual Morality, 1885–1914* (London, 1995)

Bragg, B., *The Progressive Patriot: A Search for Belonging* (London, 2006)

Burgess G., and Festenstein, M., eds, *English Radicalism, 1550–1850* (Cambridge, 2007)

Bush, M. L., *The Casualties of Peterloo* (Lancaster, 2005)

Butterfield, Sir H., *Magna Carta in the Historiography of the Sixteenth and Seventeenth Centuries* (Reading, 1968)

Carlton, C., *Going to the Wars: The Experience of the British Civil Wars, 1638–51* (London, 1994)

Cash, A. H., *John Wilkes: The Scandalous Father of Civil Liberty* (Yale, 2006)

Chase, M., *Early Trade Unionism: Fraternity, Skill and the Politics of Labour* (Aldershot, 2000)

_____, *Chartism: A New History* (Manchester, 2007)

Chibnall, M., *The Debate on the Norman Conquest* (Manchester, 1999)

Clark, A., *The Struggle for the Breeches: Gender and the Making of the British Working Class* (Berkeley, 1995)

_____, *Scandal: The Sexual Politics of the British Constitution* (Princeton, 2004)

Coates, K., *Common Ownership: Clause IV and the Labour Party* (Nottingham, 1995)

Cohn, S. K., *Lust for Liberty: The Politics of Social Revolt in Medieval Europe: 1200–1425, Italy, France and Flanders* (Cambridge, Mass., 2006)

Cole, G. D. H., and Postgate, R., *The British Common People, 1746–1946* (London, 1961)

Colley, L., *Britons: Forging the Nation, 1707–1837* (London, 1992)

Collins, P., *The Trouble with Tom: The Strange Afterlife and Times of Thomas Paine* (London, 2006)

Como, D. R., *Blown by the Spirit: Puritanism and the Emergence of an Antinomian Underground in pre-Civil War England* (Stanford, 2004)

Condren, C., *The Language of Politics in Seventeenth-Century England* (Basingstoke, 1994)

Coward, B., *The Stuart Age: England 1603–1714* (3rd edn, Harlow, 2003)

Crawford, E., *The Women's Suffrage Movement: A Reference Guide* (Basingstoke, 1999)

Cressy, D., *England on Edge: Crisis and Revolution, 1640–1642* (Oxford, 2006)

Cromartie, A., *The Constitutionalist Revolution: An Essay on the History of England, 1450–1642* (Cambridge, 2006)

Dangerfield, G., *The Strange Death of Liberal England* (London, 1997)

Danziger, D., and Gillingham, J., *1215: The Year of Magna Carta* (London, 2003)

Davis, J. C., *Utopia and the Ideal Society* (Cambridge, 1983)

_____, *Fear, Myth and History: The Ranters and the Historians* (Cambridge, 1986)

Dinwiddy, J. R., *From Luddism to the First Reform Bill. Reform in England 1810–1832* (Oxford, 1986)

Dunn, A., *The Peasants' Revolt: England's Failed Revolution of 1381* (2nd edn, Stroud, 2004)

Emsley, C., *Britain and the French Revolution* (Harlow, 2000)

_____, *Crime and Society in England, 1750–1900* (3rd edn, Harlow, 2005)

Epstein, J. A., *The Lion of Freedom: Feargus O'Connor and the Chartist Movement, 1832–1842* (London, 1982)

_____, *Radical Expression: Political Language, Ritual and Symbol in England, 1790–1850* (Oxford, 1994)

Farr, D., *Henry Ireton and the English Revolution* (Woodbridge, 2006)

Fletcher, A., and MacCullough, D., *Tudor Rebellions* (5th edn, Harlow, 2004)

Foner, E., *Tom Paine and Revolutionary America* (2nd edn, Oxford, 2005)

Foot, P., *The Vote: How It Was Won, How It Was Undermined* (London, 2005)

Fourqin, G., *The Anatomy of Popular Rebellion in the Middle Ages* (Amsterdam, 1978)

Franklin, C., *Mary Wollstonecraft: A Literary Life* (Basingstoke, 2004)

Frow, E., and Frow, R., *Radical Salford* (Manchester, 1984)

Gattrel, V., *The Hanging Tree: Execution and the English People, 1770–1868* (Oxford, 1994)

Gibbs, F. W., *Joseph Priestley* (London, 1965)

Goodway, D., *London Chartism, 1838–1848* (Cambridge, 1982)

Goodwin, A., *The Friends of Liberty: The English Democratic Movement in the Age of the French Revolution* (London, 1979)

Gregg, P., *Free-born John: The Biography of John Lilburne* (London, 1986)

Griffiths, R. A., *The Reign of King Henry VI* (2nd edn, Stroud, 1998)

Gullace, N. F., *'The Blood of Our Sons': Men, Women and the Renegotiation of British Citizenship during the Great War* (Basingstoke, 2002)

Gurney, J., *Brave Community: The Digger Movement in the English Revolution* (Manchester, 2007)

Harriss, G., *Shaping the Nation: England, 1360–1461* (Oxford, 1998)

Harvey, I. M. W., *Jack Cade's Rebellion of 1450* (Oxford, 1991)

Hay, D., *et al.*, *Albion's Fatal Tree* (Harmondsworth, 1977)

Hay, D., and Rogers, N., *Eighteenth-Century English Society: Shuttles and Swords* (Oxford, 1997)

Hessayon, A., *'Gold Tried in the Fire': Theaurau John Tany and the English Revolution* (Basingstoke, 2007)

Hill, C., *Puritanism and Revolution* (London, 1958)

_____, *The World Turned Upside Down* (London, 1972)

Hilton, B., *A Mad, Bad and Dangerous People? England 1783–1846* (Oxford, 2006)

Hilton, R., *Bond Men Made Free* (London, 1973)

Hindle, S., *The State and Social Change, c. 1550–1640* (Basingstoke, 2000)

Hindmarsh, G., *Thomas Paine: The Case of the King of England and His Officers of Excise* (privately printed, 1998)

Hirst, D., *The Representatives of the People? Voters and Voting in England under the Early Stuarts* (Cambridge, 1975)

Hobsbawm, E., and Ranger, T., eds, *The Invention of Tradition* (Cambridge, 1983)

Holmes, R., *Shelley: The Pursuit* (rev. edn, London, 1994)

Holstun, J., *Ehud's Dagger: Class Struggle in the English Revolution* (London, 2000)

Holt, Sir J. C., *Magna Carta* (2nd edn, Cambridge, 1992)

Holton, S. S., *Feminism and Democracy: Women's Suffrage and Reform Politics in Britain, 1900–1918* (Cambridge, 1986)

Hone, J. A., *For the Cause of Truth: Radicalism in London 1796–1821* (Oxford, 1982)

Hoppen, K. T., *The Mid-Victorian Generation, 1846–1886* (Oxford, 1998)

Hopper, A. J., *'Black Tom': Sir Thomas Fairfax and the English Revolution* (Manchester, 2007)

Horspool, D., *Why Alfred Burned the Cakes: A King and his Eleven-Hundred-Year Afterlife* (London, 2006)

Hughes, A., *Gangraena and the Struggle for the English Revolution* (Oxford, 2004)

Hume, L. P., *The National Union of Women's Suffrage Societies, 1897–1914* (London, 1982)

Hunt, A., *The Governance of the Consuming Passions: A History of Sumptuary Law* (Basingstoke, 1996)

Jennings, Sir I., *Magna Carta and Its Influence on the World Today* (London, 1965)

Johnson, D., *Regency Revolution: The Case of Arthur Thistlewood* (Salisbury, 1974)

Jones, D. J. V., *The Last Rising: The Newport Insurrection of 1839* (Oxford, 1985)

Jones, W. R. D., *Thomas Rainborowe (c. 1610–1648): Civil War Seaman, Siegemaster and Radical* (Woodbridge, 2005)

Justice, S., *Writing and Rebellion: England in 1381* (London, 1994)

Kaye, H. J., *Tom Paine and the Promise of America* (New York, 2005)

Keane, J., *Tom Paine: A Political Life* (London, 2003)

Kelly, G., *The English Jacobin Novel, 1780–1805* (Oxford, 1976)

Kesselring, K., *Mercy and Authority in the Tudor State* (Cambridge, 2003)

Kett, G., *The Pedigree of Kett of Wymondham, co. Norfolk. AD 1180–1913* (Cambridge, 1913)

Kishlansky, M., *Parliamentary Selection: Social and Political Choice in Early Modern England* (Cambridge, 1986)

Kramnick, I., and Sheerman, B., *Harold Laski: A Life on the Left* (London, 1993)

Lake, P., *The Boxmaker's Revenge: 'Orthodoxy', 'Heterodoxy' and the Politics of the Parish in Early Stuart London* (Manchester, 2001)

Langford, P., *A Polite and Commercial People: England 1727–83* (2nd edn, Oxford, 1998)

Law, C., *Suffrage and Power: The Women's Movement 1918–1928* (London, 1997)

Lawrence, A., *Parliamentary Army Chaplains, 1642–1651* (Woodbridge, 1990)

Leng, T., *Benjamin Worsley (1618–1677): Trade, Interest and the Spirit in Revolutionary England* (Woodbridge, 2008)

Levene, M., and Roberts, P., eds, *The Massacre in History* (Oxford, 1999)

Liddington, J., and Norris, J., *One Hand Tied Behind Us: The Rise of the Women's Suffrage Movement* (2nd edn, London, 2000)

Linebaugh, P., and Rediker, M., *The Many-Headed Hydra: Sailors, Slaves, Commoners, and the Hidden History of the Revolutionary Atlantic* (London, 2000)

McBriar, A. A., *Fabian Socialism and English Politics 1884–1918* (Cambridge, 1966)

MacCarthy, F., *William Morris: A Life for Our Time* (London, 1994)

McCormack, M., *The Independent Man: Citizenship and Gender Politics in Georgian England* (Manchester, 2005)

McDowell, N., *The English Radical Imagination: Culture, Religion and Revolution 1630–1660* (Oxford, 2003)

McLynn, F., *Lionheart and Lackland: King Richard, King John and the Wars of Conquest* (London, 2006)

MacRaild, D., *Faith, Fraternity and Fighting: The Orange Order and Irish Migrants* (Liverpool, 2005)

Manning, B., *The Far Left in the English Revolution* (London, 1999)

Marlow, J., *The Tolpuddle Martyrs* (London, 1971)

Marsh, C. W., *The Family of Love in English Society 1550–1630* (Cambridge, 1993)

Marshall, H. E., *The Story of Oliver Cromwell* (London, 1907)

_____, *Our Island Story: A History of Britain for Boys and Girls from the Romans to Queen Victoria* (Civitas edn, Bath, 2005)

Marshall, P., *William Godwin* (London, 1984)

Martin, R., *The Lancashire Giant: David Shackleton, Labour Leader and Civil Servant* (Liverpool, 2000)

Mayers, R. E., *1659: The Crisis of the Commonwealth* (Woodbridge, 2004)

Mayhall, L. E. N., *The Militant Suffrage Movement: Citizenship and Resistance in Britain, 1860–1930* (Oxford, 2003)

Mendle, M., ed., *The Putney Debates of 1647* (Cambridge, 2001)

Morrill, J. S., *Cheshire 1603–1660: County Government during the 'English Revolution'* (Oxford, 1974)

Morton, A. L., *When the People Arose: The Peasants' Revolt of 1381* (London, 1981)

Morton, T., ed., *The Cambridge Companion to Shelley* (Cambridge, 2006)

Munsche, P. B., *Gentlemen and Poachers: The English Game Laws 1671–1831* (Cambridge, 1981)

Musson, A., *Medieval Law in Context: The Growth of Legal Consciousness from Magna Carta to the Peasants' Revolt* (Manchester, 2001)

Nairn, T., *The Enchanted Glass: Britain and Its Monarchy* (2nd edn, London, 1994)

Nelson, C., *Thomas Paine: Enlightenment, Revolution, and the Birth of Modern Nations* (London, 2006)

Newman, G., *The Rise of English Nationalism* (New York, 1987)

Nora, P., *Realms of Memory: Rethinking the French Past* (3 vols, New York, 1996–8)

O'Gorman, F., *British Conservatism: Conservative Thought from Burke to Thatcher* (London, 1986)

_____, *Voters, Patrons and Parties: The Unreformed Electoral System of Hanoverian England 1734–1832* (Oxford, 1989)

Oman, Sir C., *The Great Revolt of 1381* (Oxford, 1906)

Orth, J. V., *Combination and Conspiracy: A Legal History of Trade Unionism, 1721–1906* (Oxford, 1991)

Pallister, A., *Magna Carta: The Heritage of Liberty* (Oxford, 1971)

Pelling, H., *The British Communist Party: A Historical Profile* (London, 1975)

Phillips, M., *The Ascent of Woman: A History of the Suffragette Movement and the Ideas behind It* (London, 2003)

Pilger, J., *Freedom Next Time* (London, 2006)

Plummer, A., *Bronterre: A Political Biography of Bronterre O'Brien 1804–1864* (London, 1971)

Poole, S., *The Politics of Regicide in England, 1760–1850* (Manchester, 2000)

Prothero, I., *Artisans and Politics in Early Nineteenth-Century London* (Folkestone, 1979)

Pugh, M., *The Pankhursts* (London, 2001)

Purkiss, D., *The English Civil War: A People's History* (London, 2006)

Purvis, J., *Emmeline Pankhurst: A Biography* (London, 2002)

Reay, B., and McGregor, J. F., eds, *Radical Religion in the English Revolution* (Oxford, 1984)

_____, *The Quakers and the English Revolution* (London, 1985)

Reid, A. J., and Pelling, H., *A Short History of the Labour Party* (12th edn, Basingstoke, 2005)

_____, *United We Stand: A History of Britain's Trade Unions* (London, 2005)

Rosen, A., *Rise Up, Women! The Militant Campaign of the Women's Social and Political Union 1903–1914* (Aldershot, 1974)

Royle, E., *Chartism* (3rd edn, Harlow, 1996)

Rudé, G., *Wilkes and Liberty: A Social Study* (2nd edn, London, 1983)

Sainsbury, J., *John Wilkes: The Lives of a Libertine* (Bodmin, 2006)

Sawer, M., ed., *Elections: Full, Free and Fair* (Annandale, NSW, 2001)

Schofield, R. E., *The Enlightened Joseph Priestley: A Study of His Life and Work from 1773 to 1804* (Pennsylvania, 2004)

Scott, J., *Commonwealth Principles: Republican Writing of the English Revolution* (Cambridge, 2004)

Searle, G. R., *A New England? Peace and War 1886–1918* (Oxford, 2004)

Sissons, M., and French, P., eds, *The Age of Austerity 1945–51* (Harmondsworth, 1963)

Smith, N., *Perfection Proclaimed: Language and Literature in English Radical Religion, 1640–1660* (Oxford, 1989)

Smith, O., *The Politics of Language, 1791–1819* (Oxford, 1984)

Smyth, A. P., *King Alfred the Great* (Oxford, 1995)

Stevens, J., *England's Last Revolution, Pentrich 1817* (Stoke, 1977)

Thomas, D. O., *The Honest Mind: The Thought and Work of Richard Price* (Oxford, 1977)

Thompson, D., *The Chartists: Popular Politics in the Industrial Revolution* (Aldershot, 1986)

Thompson, E. P., *William Morris: Romantic to Revolutionary* (London, 1955)

_____, *The Making of the English Working Class* (rev. edn, London, 1968)

_____, *Whigs and Hunters: The Origins of the Black Act* (London, 1975)

_____, *Witness against the Beast* (London, 1993)

Tickner, L., *The Spectacle of Women: Imagery of the Suffrage Campaign* (Chicago, 1988)

Todd, J., *Mary Wollstonecraft: A Revolutionary Life* (London, 2000)

Vallance, E., *Revolutionary England and the National Covenant* (Woodbridge, 2005)

_____, *The Glorious Revolution: 1688 and Britain's Fight for Liberty* (London, 2006)

Wall, A. D., *Power and Protest in England, 1525–1640* (London, 2000)

Wells, R., *Insurrection: The British Experience, 1795–1803* (Gloucester, 1983)

Wickham, C., *Framing the Early Middle Ages* (Oxford, 2005)

_____, ed., *Rodney Hilton's Middle Ages, Past and Present*, supplement 2 (2007)

Wilson, B., *The Laughter of Triumph: William Hone and the Fight for the Free Press* (London, 2005)

Wood, A., *Riot, Rebellion and Popular Politics in Early Modern England* (Basingstoke, 2002)

_____, *The 1549 Rebellions and the Making of Early Modern England* (Cambridge, 2007)

Wood, M., *Radical Satire and Print Culture: 1790–1822* (Oxford, 1994)

Woodhouse, A. S. P., ed., *Puritanism and Liberty: Being the Army Debates (1647–9) from the Clarke Manuscripts with Supplementary Documents* (London, 1938)

Woolrych, A., *Britain in Revolution 1625–1660* (Oxford, 2002)

Wright, P., *On Living in an Old Country: The National Past in Contemporary Britain* (London, 1986)

Wrightson, K., *English Society 1850–1680* (2nd edn, London, 2003)

Zagorin, P., *Rebels and Rulers, 1500–1600*, vol. I, *Society, States and Early Modern Revolution: Agrarian and Urban Rebellions* (Cambridge, 1982)

CHAPTERS IN BOOKS

Bush, M. L., 'The Risings of the Commons in England, 1381–1549', in J. Denton, ed., *Orders and Hierarchies in Late Medieval and Renaissance Europe* (Manchester, 1999), ch. 7

Coffey, J., 'A Ticklish Business: Defining Heresy and Orthodoxy in the Puritan Revolution', in D. Lowenstein and J. Marshall, eds, *Heresy, Literature, and Politics in Early Modern English Culture* (Cambridge, 2006), ch. 5

Davis, J. C., 'The Levellers and Christianity', in B. Manning, ed., *Politics, Religion and the English Civil War* (London, 1973), pp. 225–50

Dinwiddy, J. R., 'Bentham's Transition to Political Radicalism, 1809–1810', in his *Radicalism and Reform in Britain, 1780–1850* (London, 1992), ch. 15

Gillingham, J., 'Historians without Hindsight: Coggeshall, Diceto and Howden on the Early Years of John's Reign', in S. D. Church, ed., *King John: New Interpretations* (Woodbridge, 1999)

Harvey, I. M. W., 'Was There Popular Politics in Fifteenth-Century England?', in R. H. Britnell and A. J. Pollard, eds, *The McFarlane Legacy: Studies in Late Medieval Politics and Society* (Stroud, 1995), pp. 155–74

Hessayon, A., 'Fabricating Radical Traditions', in M. Caricchio and G. Tarantino, eds, *Cromohs Virtual Seminars. Recent Historiographical Trends of the British Studies (17th–18th Centuries)*, 2006–7, 1–6

Hill, C., 'From Lollards to Levellers', in M. Cornforth, ed., *Rebels and Their Causes: Essays in Honour of A. L. Morton* (London, 1978), ch. 3

———, 'Censorship and English Literature', in *The Collected Essays of Christopher Hill* (Brighton, 1985), i, pp. 32–71

Hobsbawm, E., 'The Fabians Reconsidered', in his *Labouring Men: Studies in the History of Labour* (London, 1986), ch. 14

Horton, S. S., 'British Freewomen: National Identity, Constitutionalism and Languages of Race in Early Suffragist Histories', in E. J. Yeo, ed., *Radical Femininity: Women's Self-Representation in the Public Sphere* (Manchester, 1998)

Kelsall, M., 'Byron's politics', in D. Bone, ed., *The Cambridge Companion to Byron* (Cambridge, 2004), pp. 47–9

Lake, P., 'Anti-Popery, the Structure of a Prejudice' in R. Cust and A. Hughes, eds, *Conflict in Early Stuart England: Studies in Religion and Politics, 1603–42* (Basingstoke, 1989), ch. 3

McWilliam, R., 'Radicalism and Popular Culture: The Tichborne Case and the Politics of "Fair Play", 1867–1886', in E. Biagini and A. J. Reid, eds, *Currents of Radicalism: Popular Politics and Party Politics in Britain, 1850–1914* (Cambridge, 1991), ch. 3

Pickering, P. A., 'The Chartist Rites of Passage: Commemorating Feargus O'Connor', in P. A. Pickering and A. Tyrrell, eds, *Contested Sites: Commemoration, Memorial and Popular Politics in Nineteenth-Century Britain* (Basingstoke, 2004), ch. 5

Rendall, J., 'Citizenship, Culture and Civilisation: The Languages of British Suffragists, 1866–1874', in C. Daley and M. Nolan, eds, *Suffrage and Beyond: International Feminist Perspectives* (Auckland, 1994), pp. 127–50

———, 'The Citizenship of Women and the Reform Act of 1867', in C. Hall, K. McClelland and J. Rendall, eds, *Defining the Victorian Nation: Class, Race, Gender and the British Reform Act of 1867* (Cambridge, 2000)

Schofield, P., 'Jeremy Bentham, the French Revolution and Political Radicalism', in F. Rosen, ed., *Jeremy Bentham* (Farnham, 2007), ch. 22

Skinner, Q., 'Classical Liberty and the Coming of the English Civil War', in M. Van Gelderen and Q. Skinner, eds, *Republicanism: A Shared European Heritage*, vol. 2, *The Values of Republicanism in Early Modern Europe* (Cambridge, 2002), ch. 1

Stedman Jones, G., 'Rethinking Chartism', in his *Languages of Class: Studies in English Working-Class History 1832–1982* (Cambridge, 1983), ch. 3

Wells, R., 'Southern Chartism', in J. Rule and R. Wells, *Crime, Protest and Popular Politics in Southern England 1740–1850* (London, 1997), ch. 7

Wood, A., 'Kett's rebellion', in C. Rawcliffe and R. Wilson, eds, *Medieval Norwich* (London, 2004)

UNPUBLISHED PAPERS AND THESES

Blundell, J., 'The Invention of a Radical Tradition: The Case of the Levellers and "The Business at Burford"', paper presented at the British Marxist Historians and the Making of Social Movements conference, Edgehill College, 2002

Brent, C., 'Thirty-something: Thomas Paine at Bull House in Lewes – Six Formative Years', forthcoming article, Sussex Archaeological Society

Bunting, A. J., 'The Pentrich Rising of 1817', unpublished dissertation

Jones, A. C., '"Commotion Time": The English Rising of 1549, unpublished Ph.D. thesis, Warwick University, 2003

McElligott, J., 'William Hone, Print Culture, and the Nature of Radicalism', chapter in A. Hessayon, ed., *Rediscovering Radicalism in the British Isles and Ireland* (forthcoming)

Peacey, J., 'Popularity and the Politician: An MP and His Public, 1640–1644', paper presented at University of Liverpool, 30 March 2007

Poole, R., 'French Revolution or Peasants' Revolt? The Rebellions of 1817 and the Rise of the Mass Platform', paper presented at Sheffield, Chartism Day, June 2007

ACKNOWLEDGEMENTS

This book would not have happened without my editor, Richard Beswick, at Little, Brown. The book was Richard's brainchild and I am very grateful to him for thinking that I might be able to turn a great idea into a decent book. Richard is an ideal editor: hands off most of the time, but ready to offer guidance and advice whenever you need it. He was ably assisted at Little, Brown by his colleagues Zoë Gullen, Stephen Guise and Rowan Cope. At A. M. Heath, my agent Bill Hamilton and his assistant Corinne Chabert helped seal the deal. This book has also taken me a very long way out of my historical comfort zone, seventeenth-century Britain. I am consequently heavily indebted to a number of my fellow historians – Mike Braddick, Malcolm Chase, Steve Hindle, Matt Houlbrook, Matthew McCormack, Robert Poole, Andy Wood – who looked over the chapters and gave me the benefit of their considerable expertise. I've also benefited from the generosity of scholars in sharing their work with me. Owen Ashton, Phil Baker, Jason McElligott, Tom Leng and Elliot Vernon all provided me with access to unpublished research. Paul Myles brought the important research of Colin Brent and the late George Hindmarsh on Thomas Paine to my attention. Marios Costambeys and Dominic Sandbrook dug up some helpful references for me. All of the above has been a welcome reminder that academia still manages, despite everything, to be a place where information and ideas can be freely shared.

Sue Wingrove and Dave Musgrove at *BBC History Magazine* and Ben Davies at the *New Statesman* kindly let me inflict my work on their unsuspecting readerships. The book has a blog (www.edwardvallance.wordpress.com) and I am also very grateful to my readers and fellow bloggers for their comments and suggestions: tips of the hat go to Scott Pack, Nick at Mercurius Politicus, Gavin at Investigations of a Dog, Chris at Virtual Stoa, Ralph E. Luker at Cliopatria, Sharon Howard at Early Modern Notes and Chris Dillow at Stumbling and Mumbling. Simon Hooper bigged up my David Davis obsession on the *New Statesman*'s website. A few others helped and may not have realised it: Nick Harvey asked me when he was slightly less than sober what I thought the most radical moment in British history was (a fair enough question, but one that had failed to occur to me until that very point). Martin O'Neill and Alex Barber both suggested that my original title sounded rather unsavoury. On their suggestion, it was dropped.

I am also grateful for having such a supportive employer. The University of Liverpool gave me a year's sabbatical to write and research the book. Less tangible but no less important support came from my Liverpool colleagues, especially two very understanding heads of department, Michael Hughes and Brigitte Resl. This book could not have been written, either, without the help of the staff of the Sydney Jones Library, Liverpool, the Bodleian Library, Oxford, the Norfolk Record Office, the Folger Shakespeare Library, the East Sussex Record Office and, most of all, my home from home, the rare books room of the British Library.

However, my greatest debt is to my wife, Linnie. To paraphrase Benjamin Disraeli, she is my 'sternest critic, but the perfect wife!' Linnie has given up her weekends when she could have been doing something much more interesting instead, to edit and proofread the entire manuscript. The book has been massively improved as a result of her suggestions. Much more than this, Linnie has given me the strength and support to carry this project through to the end: she has bucked me up when I have been feeling low and kept me sane when I was stressed to the eyeballs. My only complaint is that I don't know how I can fully repay such a debt. A book dedication certainly seems inadequate.

INDEX

THE GLORIOUS REVOLUTION

Edward Vallance

'A brisk, taut and lucid account . . . with the pace of a thriller'
Independent

In the summer of 1688, seven English peers wrote to
William of Orange requesting his assistance in overturning their
monarch, James II. On 5 November William had landed with a
massive invasion force and within six weeks James had fled the
country, fearing for his safety. Three months later William and
his English wife Mary, James's Protestant daughter, were
crowned joint monarchs, accepting the Declaration of Rights
that affirmed Parliament's ancient rights and liberties.

In this highly readable narrative of the period,
acclaimed historian Edward Vallance counters the claim
made by generations of Whig historians that this was a bloodless
revolution – a victory for progress. Civil war was avoided by the
narrowest of margins and the conflict was characterised
instead by warfare and bloody massacre.

ABACUS
978-0-349-11733-1

RUBICON

Tom Holland

'Narrative history at its best . . . it really held me, in fact, obsessed me' Ian McEwan, Book of the Year, *Guardian*

'I owe a debt of gratitude to Tom Holland not just for reminding me of the great figures who bestrode the Roman world – Pompey and Crassus, Cato, Cicero and Caesar – but for explaining what it was that made Rome the greatest superpower the world has known, why it lasted so long and what caused its eventual fall' Christopher Matthew, *Daily Mail*

'The bloodstained drama of the last decades of the Roman republic is told afresh with tremendous wit, narrative verve and insight' *Independent on Sunday*

ABACUS
978-0-349-11563 4

PERSIAN FIRE

Tom Holland

'Thrilling . . . masterly . . . gripping'
Independent on Sunday

It was 2,500 years ago that East and West first went to war. In the early 5th Century BC, a global superpower was determined to bring truth and order to what it regarded as two terrorist states. The superpower was Persia, whose kings had founded the first world empire, incomparably rich in ambitions, gold and men. The terrorist states were Athens and Sparta, eccentric cities in a poor and mountainous backwater: Greece. The story of how their citizens took on the most powerful man on the planet, and defeated him is as heart-stopping as any episode in history.

'Holland has a rare eye for detail, drama and the telling of anecdote. His account of the Battle of Thermopylae is surely the most exciting in print. A book as spirited and engaging as *Persian Fire* deserves to last . . . It has turned the stuff of public-school translation exercises into vibrant, bloodthirsty popular history, told with a rich sense of irony and irresistible narrative timing' Dominic Sandbrook, *Daily Telegraph*

ABACUS
978-0-349-11717-1

MILLENNIUM
Tom Holland

'A blaze of colour lights up the Dark Ages'
Independent

In 900 AD, few would have guessed that the splintering
kingdoms of Europe were candidates for future greatness.
Hemmed in by implacable enemies and an ocean, there were
many who feared that they were nearing the time when the
Antichrist would appear, heralding the world's end.

Instead there emerged a new civilisation. It was the age of
Otto the Great and William the Conqueror, of Viking sea-kings,
of hermits, monks and serfs. It witnessed the spread of castles,
the invention of knighthood, and the founding of a papal
monarchy. It was a momentous achievement: for this was
nothing less than the founding of the modern West.

'An exhilarating sweep across European history
either side of the year 1000; riveting'
Allan Massie, Books of the Year, *Spectator*

ABACUS
978-0-349-11972-4

ENDGAME 1945

David Stafford

'A harrowing masterpiece of modern history' *Sunday Express*

In this remarkable account of the end of the Second World War,
David Stafford looks behind the headlines of history and
uncovers the stories of those, soldier and civilian alike,
who had lived through the war and now must endure the daily
horrors and hardships of its aftermath. *Endgame 1945* is an
unforgettable panorama of the defeat of Fascism, of ordinary
men and women and extraordinary valour, and
of Europe in every way tested to its limits.
It is the final chapter of war.

'Stafford has assembled a remarkable gallery of human stories –
heroic, tragic, squalid, moving'
Max Hastings, *Daily Mail*

'Intimate and compelling . . . What a rollercoaster of dramatic
highs and lows' James Delingpole, *Mail on Sunday*

ABACUS
978-0-349-11912-0

BLOODY FOREIGNERS
Robert Winder

'Supremely readable'
The Times

'Our aristocracy was created by a Frenchman, William the
Conqueror, who also created our medieval architecture, our
greatest artistic glory. Our royal family is German, our language
a bizarre confection of Latin, Saxon and, latterly, Indian and
American. Our shops and banks were created by Jews. We did
not stand alone against Hitler, the empire stood beside us. And
our food is, of course, anything but British . . . Winder has a
thousand stories to tell and he tells them well. Topical,
formidable and engaging . . . A tremendous read'
Sunday Times

'Enlightened and illuminating. Winder goes a long way towards
defining what we are as a nation'
Independent

ABACUS
978-0-349-11566-5

Now you can order superb titles directly from Abacus

☐ The Glorious Revolution	Edward Vallance	£9.99
☐ Rubicon	Tom Holland	£10.99
☐ Persian Fire	Tom Holland	£9.99
☐ Millennium	Tom Holland	£9.99
☐ Bloody Foreigners	Robert Winder	£10.99
☐ Endgame	David Stafford	£10.99

The prices shown above are correct at time of going to press. However, the publishers reserve the right to increase prices on covers from those previously advertised, without further notice.

────────────── ⟨ABACUS⟩ ──────────────

Please allow for postage and packing: **Free UK delivery.**
Europe: add 25% of retail price; Rest of World: 45% of retail price.

To order any of the above or any other Abacus titles, please call our credit card orderline or fill in this coupon and send/fax it to:

Abacus, PO Box 121, Kettering, Northants NN14 4ZQ
Fax: 01832 733076   Tel: 01832 737526
Email: aspenhouse@FSBDial.co.uk

☐ I enclose a UK bank cheque made payable to Abacus for £ . .
☐ Please charge £ . . . . to my Visa/Delta/Maestro

☐☐☐☐☐☐☐☐☐☐☐☐☐☐☐☐☐☐

Expiry Date ☐☐☐☐   Maestro Issue No. ☐☐

NAME (BLOCK LETTERS please) . . . .
ADDRESS . . . .
. . . .
. . . .
Postcode . . . . Telephone . . . .
Signature . . . .

Please allow 28 days for delivery within the UK. Offer subject to price and availability.